LUTHER:
LECTURES ON ROMANS

THE LIBRARY OF CHRISTIAN CLASSICS

ICHTHUS EDITION

LUTHER:

LECTURES ON ROMANS

Newly Translated and Edited by

WILHELM PAUCK, D. Theol.

Charles A. Briggs Graduate Professor of Church History
Union Theological Seminary, New York City

Philadelphia

THE WESTMINSTER PRESS

Published simultaneously in the United States of America and in Great Britain by The Westminster Press, Philadelphia, and the S. C. M. Press, Ltd., London.

Library of Congress Catalog Card No. 61–13626

9 8 7 6 5 4 3 2 1

Printed in the United States of America

GENERAL EDITORS' PREFACE

The Christian Church possesses in its literature an abundant and incomparable treasure. But it is an inheritance that must be reclaimed by each generation. THE LIBRARY OF CHRISTIAN CLASSICS is designed to present in the English language, and in twenty-six volumes of convenient size, a selection of the most indispensable Christian treatises written prior to the end of the sixteenth century.

The practice of giving circulation to writings selected for superior worth or special interest was adopted at the beginning of Christian history. The canonical Scriptures were themselves a selection from a much wider literature. In the patristic era there began to appear a class of works of compilation (often designed for ready reference in controversy) of the opinions of well-reputed predecessors, and in the Middle Ages many such works were produced. These medieval anthologies actually preserve some noteworthy materials from works otherwise lost.

In modern times, with the increasing inability even of those trained in universities and theological colleges to read Latin and Greek texts with ease and familiarity, the translation of selected portions of earlier Christian literature into modern languages has become more necessary than ever; while the wide range of distinguished books written in vernaculars such as English makes selection there also needful. The efforts that have been made to meet this need are too numerous to be noted here, but none of these collections serves the purpose of the reader who desires a library of representative treatises spanning the Christian centuries as a whole. Most of them embrace only the age of the church

fathers, and some of them have long been out of print. A fresh
translation of a work already translated may shed much new light
upon its meaning. This is true even of Bible translations despite
the work of many experts through the centuries. In some instances
old translations have been adopted in this series, but wherever
necessary or desirable, new ones have been made. Notes have been
supplied where these were needed to explain the author's meaning. The introductions provided for the several treatises and
extracts will, we believe, furnish welcome guidance.

JOHN BAILLIE
JOHN T. McNEILL
HENRY P. VAN DUSEN

CONTENTS

PREFACE

This translation is based on the critical edition of Luther's *Römerbriefvorlesung* by Johannes Ficker, published as Vol. 56 of the so-called Weimar Edition of Luther's Works (Weimar: Böhlau, 1938). (In referring to this edition, I follow the general custom with respect to the use of abbreviations. For example, *WA* 56, 45, 15 means Weimar Edition, Vol. 56, page 45, line 15.)

Luther's commentary consists of two parts: the *Gloss* and the *Scholia*. I have translated the latter (*WA* 56, 155–528) in their entirety. It would not be practical to translate also all the interlinear and marginal glosses (*WA* 56, 1–154). However, I have translated all glosses to which Luther himself refers in the Scholia. Moreover, all glosses that contain important interpretations or have assumed a special importance in modern Luther research are included in this translation. (They appear in the footnotes at the appropriate places.) In order to give a representative sample of Luther's method of Biblical interpretation, I have translated *all* the glosses on Rom. 8:18–30.

In the Scholia, Luther does not comment on every part of Paul's letter. He singles out certain terms and passages in order to discuss them sometimes closely, sometimes generally. However, he does not lose sight of the context in which these terms and phrases stand. In order to enable the reader to see Luther's comments in relation to the entire Pauline letter, I quote the whole passage of the letter to which the part belongs that Luther discusses. This part is set in boldface type.

Ficker attempts to identify all Luther's references to the Bible and to general and theological literature, historical events, proverbs, etc. I have, of course, derived great benefit from his prodi-

gious labors. My explanatory notes are mostly an echo and a re-
flection of Ficker's comments. In order to enable interested readers
quickly to find the more explicit explanations that Ficker offers
in his edition, I frequently refer to specific notes of his (e.g., Ficker,
p. —, n. —).

Ficker also tries to identify all Luther's Biblical references,
whether they were explicit or not. I follow him in this, but I do
not indicate in each case whether Luther himself identified the
quotation or not. Readers of this translation should be aware of
the fact that Luther's original lecture notes do not contain all the
specific identifications of quotations from the Bible that are included in this translation.

They should also be mindful of the fact that Luther used the
Vulgate. In order to reproduce the true character of Luther's
exegesis, it is necessary in this translation to approximate as
closely as possible the words and the mannerisms of the Vulgate,
especially where Biblical quotations are involved. I rely, therefore, on the Douay and Rheims edition of the translation of the
Latin Vulgate (Baltimore: Murphy, 1899), but not slavishly so.
I think that I can say that my renderings of Luther's quotations
from the Bible pretty accurately reflect his usage. (In the numbering and naming of the Biblical books, I follow, not the Roman,
but the Protestant tradition. Where necessary, particularly in
connection with the book of The Psalms, I make the required
adaptations. At the time of his lectures on Romans, Luther, of
course, still followed the Roman tradition.)

The most significant part of Ficker's work as editor of these
lectures was that he endeavored to show the sources on which
Luther depended. Following Ficker for the most part but not entirely, I indicate these sources in the footnotes. (A list of the works
appears in the Bibliography.) The works of the fathers and of
the Scholastics are quoted in the conventional way so that the
section referred to by Luther can readily be identified in any edition or translation. In certain cases—i.e., when commentaries are
referred to—it is not necessary to identify the sources. These references can be found in connection with the exegesis of the Biblical
passage that is under discussion. Thus, references identified by the
name of the author only (e.g., Lyra or Faber) or by the title of a
work only (e.g., *Glossa ordinaria*) are to the Biblical passage under
discussion in the respective commentaries.

Occasionally I direct the reader's attention to the treatment of
a particular part of Luther's lectures in a modern work of Luther
interpretation, but I do this only because, in my judgment, this
discussion is especially enlightening. A full list of all books, essays,

and articles dealing with Luther's lectures on Romans is given at the end of this book.

There is a German translation of these lectures by Eduard Ellwein. The first edition appeared in 1927. The presently available fourth edition was published as a supplement to the so-called Munich edition of Luther's works. (Martin Luther, *Ausgewählte Werke*, ed. by H. H. Borcherdt and Georg Merz. Ergänzungsreihe, Vol. II. München: Kaiser, 1957.) I have carefully compared this translation with mine and I have greatly benefited from this comparison.

There exists also an English translation of Luther's lectures, its author John Theodore Mueller, professor in Concordia Theological Seminary, St. Louis, Missouri. (It was published in 1954 by Zondervan in Grand Rapids, Michigan.) Mueller himself calls his work a "digest" of Luther's lectures. He translates most of the marginal gloss but omits the major part of the Scholia; moreover, he does not indicate what parts of Luther's work he chooses to include or to exclude. He depends heavily on Ellwein, and significant sections of his translation are not entirely true to the original.

A few of the recent English or American works dealing with Luther contain translations of key passages of Luther's commentary. Among these, that of Prof. E. G. Rupp, now of Manchester University, deserves special mention (*The Righteousness of God: Luther Studies*. London and New York, 1953). I have gratefully adopted some of his phrasings.

W.P.

General Introduction

ONE OF THE MOST THOROUGH OF LUTHER'S MODERN interpreters, Karl Holl, a scholar who was not readily given to exaggeration, regarded Luther's exposition of the letter to the Romans as a work of genius, "an achievement that remains unsurpassed even today."[1] This judgment appears to be supported by the fact that in recent Luther research the lectures on Romans are treated as one of the most important works of the Reformer.

Yet these lectures were published for the first time only in 1908.[2] Until then, they had been unknown to the readers of Luther's works and the students of his thought. But as soon as they became generally available, they were treated as the chief source of the knowledge of Luther's theological development. And, indeed, they show that the basic ideas of the Protestant Reformation were formed in Luther's mind before he began his career as a reformer.

They also furnish clear and impressive proof that the man who, two years later, on October 31, 1517, was to publish the "Ninety-five Theses on the Power of Indulgences" and who thus chanced to begin the Reformation, was spiritually and theologically mature and resourceful (he was then thirty-four years old). One can understand why the author of these lectures could not be forced, by the mere assertion of authority, to recant his views and why it was impossible to silence him by the conventional means of dealing with a heretic. Whoever would oppose him in order to refute him would have to meet him on the ground of that understanding

---

[1] Karl Holl, *Luthers Bedeutung für den Fortschrift der Auslegungskunst (Gesammelte Aufsätze*, Vol. I: *Luther* [2d ed., Tübingen, 1923], p. 550).
[2] Johannes Ficker, *Luthers Vorlesung über den Römerbrief* 1515/1516 (Leipzig, ed. 1908).

of the gospel which he had slowly achieved by conscientious study and spiritual struggle.

This evidence of the direction of Luther's thought and of the power of his mind is all the more impressive because he wrote the documents that contain it for his own personal use and not for publication. He that reads them now encounters Luther as he got ready to teach an academic course on Paul's letter to the Romans. To be sure, he himself seems to have attributed considerable significance to this work of his, for his own manuscript (which has come down to us) is written with great care. The major part of it appears to be the final clean copy which Luther himself prepared from notes that he had put on loose slips of paper (called by him *schedae* or *schedulae*). It was this carefully prepared manuscript which he used in the classroom.

According to the custom of the times, he *dictated* to his students the substance of what he wanted them to know. Some of the notes that the students took down in Luther's course on the letter to the Romans are still in existence. Prof. Johannes Ficker, who discovered and first published Luther's lectures and finally edited them with admirable care in the Weimar Edition of Luther's Works, succeeded in locating several sets of them. Not all of them are complete, and not all of them represent the notes that were directly taken down in the classroom (a few are copies of such notes), but altogether they give a vivid picture of Luther's teaching. They show how carefully he dictated (he repeated difficult words or pronounced them syllable by syllable) and how he spoke (his pronunciation was that of a Saxon and as such he tended to pronounce *b* as if it were *p*, and *g* as if it were *k*, etc., just as the Saxons do today).

A comparison of the students' books with his own lecture notes shows how he used his manuscript: he dictated its philological parts almost verbatim, but he greatly abbreviated the theological exposition he had written out; he left unmentioned most of those sections which, from our modern point of view, are the most interesting and important ones, namely, those where he sharply criticizes the church and its theological teachers and administrative leaders, and especially those where he struggles for the understanding of the gospel and for the clarity of his own thought about it.

I. THE HISTORY OF THE MANUSCRIPT

On October 19, 1512, Luther became a doctor of theology in the University of Wittenberg. This promotion enabled him to assume the chair of Biblical theology hitherto occupied by Johann von

Staupitz, the General-Vicar of the German (Observant) Congregation of the Augustinian Friars, his own superior and special friend. Teaching was not new to him. In accordance with the rules of medieval universities, he had been an instructor of sorts ever since he had obtained the degree of M.A. in 1505; particularly since he had become a student of theology, he had taught, in 1508, the basic course in Aristotle in the University of Wittenberg to which he was then temporarily assigned, and, in 1509, he had been responsible in his own University of Erfurt for the introductory course in theology, based on Peter Lombard's *Four Books of Sentences*. But now, after his definitive transfer from Erfurt to Wittenberg and on becoming a full member of the theological faculty, he could choose the Biblical courses he wanted to teach.

He decided to begin with The Psalms. They kept him busy for two years, from the beginning of the summer semester of 1513 until the end of the winter semester of 1515. Two of Luther's own manuscripts of these lectures have come down to us. They were found in the latter part of the nineteenth century and published as Vols. 3 and 4 of the Weimar Edition in 1885.[3] They show that Luther followed the methods of interpretation customary in medieval schools, but they also reveal a mind of solid scholarship capable of deep penetration and gifted with creative originality. Luther had the printer Johann Grunenberg, who had a shop in the Augustinian monastery of Wittenberg, print the text of The Psalms in such a way that there was left a large space between the lines and also a wide margin on each page so that interlinear and marginal glosses could readily be inserted. In preparing his lectures, Luther entered these two types of glosses in his own copy of the text. In the classroom, he then dictated them to the students to each of whom he had furnished a printed copy of the Biblical text like his own. We should note that this still highly limited use of the art of printing was something novel, and it was perhaps because he was conscious of this that Luther had the printer use Roman type which was preferred by the Humanists.

When he was finished with The Psalms, Luther turned to the letter to the Romans. He followed the same method he had employed in interpreting The Psalms. Grunenberg again had to print the text in such a way that the glosses could readily be inserted. It seems that, probably on the advice of Luther, he followed the Vulgate according to the Basel Edition of 1509, printed

---

[3] This publication was premature, as later studies revealed. It has now been found necessary to re-edit these lectures. This work is now in progress.

by Froben, and that he corrected this version of the text here and there on the basis of the treatment of the Pauline letters by Faber Stapulensis, the French Humanist, in his commentary of 1512–1515. Luther then wrote out his own interlinear and marginal glosses on the twenty-eight leaves of Grunenberg's printed text (each page had fourteen lines) and, on one hundred and twenty-three separate sheets of paper, he prepared his own extended commentary. As the student notes show, he used most of his glosses in the classroom, but only selected parts of the scholia.

We know that Luther met these classes of his twice a week, Mondays and Fridays, at 6 A.M. He needed three semesters for the course on Romans: the summer semester of 1515, the winter semester of 1515–1516, and the summer semester of 1516. In other words, he began at Easter of 1515 and was done in early September of 1516.

Careful attention to the marks Luther inserted in his manuscript and a close analysis of the students' manner of writing their notes make it possible to tell (from the ink marks and the *ductus* of the hands of the writers) when the individual lectures were begun and ended. Thus Ficker concludes[4] that Luther's course on Romans consisted of ninety class hours, and that he dealt with Rom. 1:1 to 3:4 during the first semester; during the second semester with chs. 3:5 to 8:39; and during the third semester with chs. 9:1 to 16:27.

Luther remained a professor of Biblical theology until the end of his life and, throughout his career, his academic lectures were devoted to Biblical exegesis. He next took up the letter to the Galatians[5] (winter semester, 1516–1517) and then he turned to The Letter to the Hebrews (summer semester, 1517, and winter semester, 1517–1518) in order then to deal once more with The Psalms. He published a commentary on The Psalms in 1519–1520 (it contains the exegesis of only twenty-two psalms), which was based on his lectures, and he also published a commentary on the letter to the Galatians (1519)[6] in the preparation of which he made use of his earlier lecture notes.[7] In his later teaching, he dealt repeatedly with certain individual psalms and he published his interpretations of many of them. Moreover, he lectured once more on the letter to the Galatians in 1531.[8] But he never again

---

[4] Cf. *WA* 56, p. XXIX.
[5] *WA* 57 (Gal.).   [6] *WA* 2, 451–618.
[7] A student's notebook of Luther's lectures on this letter has survived. It came to light only in 1877 in the catalog of an antiquarian bookseller. It was finally published by Prof. Hans von Schubert in 1916. A final edition was prepared by K. A. Meissinger for the Weimar edition (Vol. 57, Gal.).
[8] *WA* 40, I, 1–688; 40, II, 1–184.

took up the letter to the Romans. The reason probably was that, soon after becoming a professor in the University of Wittenberg (1518), Philip Melanchthon established the tradition of lecturing on this book of Scripture. It seems not improbable that he made use of Luther's lecture notes. These appear to have circulated also among others of Luther's friends, followers, and colleagues.

As far as we know, Luther himself made no mention of his Romans manuscript in later years, either in his correspondence or in his table talk. But he must have preserved it carefully, for, after his death, it came into the possession of his heirs. They seem to have treasured it highly. During the last decade of the sixteenth century, it was still in the hands of his son, Dr. Paul Luther, a physician in the service of the elector of Saxony. In a letter of 1592, addressed to Anna, Electress of Saxony, he mentions that he was thinking of arranging for a German translation of his father's early lectures.[9] One must assume that it was this Paul Luther who, in 1582, had the manuscript bound in very stately fashion (the rich leather covers were decorated with the coat of arms of the elector August of Saxony and his wife, Anna). At about this time the volume was seen by a certain Johann Wiegand, the author of a work on Schwenkfeld (*De Schwenckfeldismo*, 1587). In the dedicatory letter that served as a preface, he mentioned that he had handled and examined Luther's first works (he called them *initia Lutheri*). "I have held his own autographs in my hands," he said, "and looked at them with admiration." ("*Autographa enim ipsius in mea manu habui atque inspexi et miratus sum.*")[10]

This testimony was known to Veit von Seckendorf, the first Protestant historian of the Lutheran Reformation. He had access to the archives of the Saxon princes and he relied on original documents for his history, but he found no traces of these early manuscripts and presumed them lost. He did not know—he *could* not know—that, probably in 1594, the sons of Paul Luther had sold all the handwritten and printed writings of their grandfather that they had in their possession to Joachim Frederick, Margrave of Brandenburg.

In this way, Luther's Romans manuscript came to be deposited in the library that later was known as the Royal Library of Berlin and, since 1918, as the Prussian State Library. The guardians of this collection never made a secret of the fact that this Luther manuscript was among their holdings (nor did they make an extra mention of it as if they regarded it as an unusual treasure), and

[9] The whole story of the strange fortune of Luther's manuscript is told by Ficker in the introductions to his two editions of it.
[10] Cf. Ficker (ed. 1908), p. IX.

nobody apparently showed any special interest in it. It was listed in the oldest printed catalogue of the library (1668). When, in 1846, the library put up a special exhibit of Luther items by way of observing the three-hundredth anniversary of Luther's death, the manuscript was prominently displayed.

Afterward, it was placed in a showcase in the large entrance hall leading to the public reading room of the library. Although it was properly identified as an early Luther manuscript, it did not come to the notice of anyone able to recognize its importance. The author of the catalogue of the Latin manuscripts in the Royal Library in Berlin, the librarian Valentin Rose, who, of course, listed Luther's work, frequently expressed surprise at the fact that no scholar ever came to examine it. He did not know that at the same time he published his catalogue (1905) an extensive search for this very piece of writing was going on because, a few years earlier, a copy of it had been found in the Vatican Library.

As detailed studies revealed, this copy was the work of Johann Aurifaber, one of Luther's several faithful *famuli*, to whose industry in taking notes we owe much of our knowledge of the "older" Luther, particularly through part of the table talk. It appears that, at about 1560–1570, Aurifaber was engaged by Ulrich Fugger to make copies of certain ones of Luther's manuscripts, including the lectures on Romans. Ulrich Fugger (+1584), the great-grandson of Jacob Fugger (+1469), the founder of the famous banking house, and the great-nephew of Jacob Fugger the Rich (+1525), who made his firm a European power, was a collector of rare books and manuscripts. A Protestant, he desired to include in his collection also originals of Luther's writings. When he found that he could not acquire these, he engaged Aurifaber to furnish him copies of such of Luther's works as existed only in the form of manuscripts. In his will, he left his library to the elector Palatine. He himself saw to it that it was deposited in the Church of the Holy Spirit in Heidelberg.

At the end of the second stage of the Thirty Years' War, the so-called "Palatinate War," the Upper Palatinate came into the possession of Maximilian I, Duke of Bavaria (1623). It was shortly after the conquest of Heidelberg by General Tilly (on September 16, 1622) that Maximilian, an ardent partisan of the Roman Church, gave the Fugger Library (then and thereafter known as *Bibliotheca Palatina*), which with its 3,527 manuscripts was the finest and most valuable library in Germany, to Pope Gregory XV as a token of his loyalty and esteem. The pontiff accepted the extraordinary gift and had the treasures transported across the

Alps to Rome and ordered them to be incorporated in the Vatican Library.

At the end of the nineteenth century, Pope Leo XIII made the Vatican Library freely accessible to researchers and scholars. This was one of the reasons why, in 1899, Johannes Ficker, then a professor of church history in the University of Strassburg, a specialist in the history of handwriting and handwritten texts, asked a friend and former student of his, Dr. Hermann Vopel, who happened to be in Rome, to search in the Vatican Library for certain exegetical works of Melanchthon. Dr. Vopel found catalogue listings of manuscripts not only of Melanchthon but also of other Reformers, including Luther.

On closer examination, one of these pieces turned out to be Aurifaber's copy of Luther's lecture manuscript on the letter to the Romans. Other remarkable items were found: for example, a copy of a student's notes of Luther's lectures on The Letter to the Hebrews. Dr. Vopel, Prof. Johannes Ficker, and the latter's brother, Gerhard, also a professor of church history then at Kiel, made a copy of the great find.

Prof. Johannes Ficker at that time began an extensive search for Luther's original manuscript, but he was able to locate only several students' notebooks containing Luther's classroom dictation. The Royal Library in Berlin replied negatively to a questionnaire he sent to all libraries that could be presumed to house Luther manuscripts.

In the meantime, the significance of a fuller knowledge of these early works of Luther's was demonstrated by the publication (in 1904) of the work *Luther und Luthertum in der ersten Entwicklung, quellenmässig dargestellt,* by Heinrich Denifle, a very learned but extremely anti-Protestant Roman Catholic historian, a member of the Dominican order. He had made extensive use of the Vatican manuscript of Luther's lectures on Romans, chiefly in order to demonstrate that Luther was not so well trained in theology as in his, Denifle's, opinion he ought to have been. In the course of the heated debate that this work provoked, it became clear that a detailed examination of Luther's theological development, especially in connection with later Scholasticism, was urgently necessary for a proper understanding of the beginnings of the Reformation. Thus the need of publishing Luther's early exegetical lectures assumed major importance.

In 1905, the existence of Luther's original manuscript in the Berlin library was brought to the attention of Prof. Nikolaus Müller. He was a professor of church history who in his capacity as director of the Melanchthon House in Bretten had come into possession of the text of the lectures on Galatians that Luther had delivered in 1516. Although he had so far not contributed anything to the investigation of the *initia Lutheri*, he claimed the right of publishing the Romans manuscript as his prerogative. It was only under considerable difficulty and with much embarrassment that Professor Ficker gained access to the piece of writing for which he had diligently searched for such a long time. But now he was enabled to collate the two available texts and, in 1908, he finally published what he called a provisional version of the lectures. Only in 1938 was he able to bring out the definitive edition which, as we stated earlier, was published as Vol. 56 of the Weimar Edition of Luther's Works.

II. LUTHER'S EXEGESIS OF THE LETTER TO THE ROMANS IN THE LIGHT OF THE HERMENEUTICAL WORK OF HIS ANCIENT AND MEDIEVAL PREDECESSORS

One cannot read a single part of Luther's lectures without being made aware of his dependence upon the methods and traditions of medieval exegesis. Yet he was no mere traditionalist. He was as little interested in merely preserving what others who had gone before him had done as he was concerned to break up what they had achieved. He wanted to understand the Scripture as thoroughly and adequately as possible. That is why he used all means available to him in order to accomplish a full and true interpretation: he employed the methods of traditional Biblical exegesis as well as most recent Biblical research. He relied upon Scholasticism and, at the same time, he made thorough use of the philology of the Humanists. In the end, he overcame both Scholasticism and Humanism because, in the last resort, he depended for the understanding of the Scripture upon the insights of his own deeply penetrating mind and upon the judgments of his conscience. Thus he was to inaugurate an entirely new phase in the history of exegesis in general and of Biblical exegesis in particular.

In the lectures on Romans, all these aspects of his work as an expositor become visible. He appears to conform to the standards of medieval exegesis, not only in the way in which he arranges his exposition, but also with respect to the textbooks on which he relies; yet, at the same time, he eagerly employs the most modern exegetical helps of his era, e.g., Reuchlin's Hebrew Dictionary, Faber's Biblical commentaries, and especially Erasmus' edition of the Greek New Testament and his "Annotations." Indeed, he combines the purposes of Scholastic exegesis (in so far as it aimed at establishing the spiritual meaning of the Scripture) with those of the Humanists (in so far as they endeavored to make the authors of the Biblical books speak for themselves). But he accomplished this "combining," not by means of an external synthesis, but through a profound spiritual effort that engaged all his inner powers. The lectures on Romans prove that, because of this, Luther was on the way to a new understanding of the Bible and, in connection therewith, to a fresh hearing of the gospel, long before his clash with the authorities of the Roman Church caused him to become the leader of the Reformation.

The most characteristic device of the medieval exegetes was the "gloss." They based the interpretation of texts on the exposition of individual words and terms—with the result that they tended to lose sight of the meaning of larger passages and of the connection between them. They often got stuck in details as, even today, is characteristic of many Biblical exegetes.

It was customary to make two glosses, an interlinear and a marginal one. The *interlinear gloss* was a paraphrase of the text stressing the specific meaning of the different words, the logical connection between them, and the interrelation of the several parts of a sentence. The *marginal gloss* (which represented the oldest part of the tradition of exegetical scholarship, for it was already widely practiced among the Greeks) consisted of brief interpretations of small units of the text that were written on the page margins. Generally, they were excerpts from established and recognized exegetical works to which amplifying or other explanatory remarks were added by the individual exegetes.

Then there was also the *scholion, or scholium,* which differed from the gloss in so far as it was an exposition of those parts of the text which in the opinion of the exegete required an extensive interpretation. Nevertheless, it resembled the gloss in so far as it, too, was an exposition of small parts of the text rather than of an entire coherent passage. The medieval Biblical exegetes often filled their scholia with what we would call nowadays practical exegesis, but they also used them for controversies and arguments with opponents and others with whom they differed.

But all this describes merely the form of medieval exegetical work and does not touch on what was really distinctive of it. The most telling feature of the learning of the Scholastics was that they orientated their thinking and reasoning to *auctoritas* and *auctoritates,* namely, the authority of the canonical Scriptures, of the creeds and the canons, of the councils and other ecclesiastical judicatories, of the fathers, of tradition. In exegetical work, this orientation manifested itself in the fact that, before proceeding to advance their own interpretations, the Schoolmen quoted and exploited certain basic works that not only constituted authority in themselves but also represented collections of the opinions and judgments of traditional authorities.

The basic marginal gloss on which most later ones were built was that of Walafrid Strabo (+849), a scholar of the school of Alcuin. He attempted to give a universal commentary on the Scripture by interpreting it word for word, or rather sentence by sentence, in the light of more or less relevant extracts from the works of the fathers, i.e., Ambrose, Augustine, Gregory the Great, Origen, Chrysostom, Jerome, Isidore of Seville, Cassiodorus, Alcuin, Bede, and Rabanus Maurus. This work was known as *Glossa ordinaria,* and it was regarded as *auctoritas* speaking for the Scripture itself *(lingua ipsa Scripturae).*[11]

The *Glossa ordinaria* was commonly copied and later printed together with the *Glossa interlinearis* of Anselm of Laon (+1117). This was a translation of the words and terms of the Bible into their inner meaning, or what Anselm regarded as such, an interpretation of the individual phrases of the Biblical texts not in terms of philology but for the purpose and in the manner of spiritual edification.

Luther was steeped in this tradition. His early commentaries consist of interlinear and marginal glosses and of scholia. Moreover, in his comments on every passage, he refers outspokenly or by implication to the *Glossa ordinaria* and the *Glossa interlinearis.*

In his first exegetical lecture course, the *Dictata super Psalterium,* he was still very closely bound to this established manner of interpretation. Later on, he gradually freed himself from it. Indeed, from 1519 on, he abandoned it altogether. In the lectures on Romans, he exhibits a use of it that we may regard as characteristic of his way of doing intellectual work: under his hands, the interlinear gloss often becomes a very succinct restatement of the words and ideas of the apostle. For he explains the individual passages of the letter by illuminating them through reference to its other parts. Moreover, he formulates his explanatory comments and paraphrases so as to exclude meanings that the apostle could not have had in mind when he wrote the letter.

As far as Luther's marginal glosses are concerned, they are no longer mere collectanea from the writings of the fathers, but brief incisive comments on selected short passages or individual terms or phrases. He combines them with quotations from the Scripture or with critical or commendatory remarks on the writings of certain ones of the fathers (chiefly Jerome, whom he makes the butt of many criticisms, and especially Augustine, on whom

[11] Peter Lombard, IV *Sent., d.* 4 (PL 113, 17).

he generally bestows high praise) or with references to the interpretations of recent scholars (mainly Faber Stapulensis and Erasmus).

His scholia, finally, are short or lengthy essays, sometimes of a philological-grammatical character but mostly dealing with theological ideas or with monastic or ecclesiastical practices. We should also note that his language and manner of speaking, though obviously representative of academic convention and conforming to the ways of the classroom, are often highly impassioned and personal, certainly in what he writes in his own notebook, though hardly at all in what he dictates to his students on the basis of these notes.

All this, however, does not give a complete picture of Luther's entanglement in tradition. The Scholastic interpretation of the Bible was even more complex than we have indicated so far. For, according to the Pauline saying of II Cor. 3:6: "The letter kills, but the spirit gives life," the Scripture was believed to require not only a literal exposition but also a spiritual one. In dependence upon the hermeneutical practices of the ancient Greeks, who had found it difficult, for example, to take Homer literally and therefore devised an allegorical interpretation of his poems, the exegetes of the ancient church, and particularly Origen, as Luther never failed to remember, had laid down rules that enabled one to read the books of the Bible both in the literal, i.e., historical, and in the spiritual, i.e., allegorical, sense.

In the course of time, the allegorical meaning was further defined, and consequently the spiritual interpretation of Scripture had to be achieved by several hermeneutical steps. Thomas Aquinas defined the matter very well. He wrote:[12] "God is the author of Holy Scripture. He has given a meaning not only to the words but also the things they signify, so that the things signified in turn signify something else. First of all, the words signify things, which is the historical sense; but secondly, the things signify other things, and we get the spiritual sense. The latter is of three sorts: The Old Law is allegorically interpreted in the New Law, but the interpretation of matters affecting Christ and our obligation is tropological, and that which deals with the eternal glory is the anagogical or celestial sense." These four senses constituted "rules by which," as Guibert de Nogent (+1124) put it in a book on the construction of sermons,[13] "every page of Scripture turns as on so

[12] *Summa Theol.*, I, q. 1, a. 10.
[13] *Quo Ordine Sermo Fieri Debet* (PL 156, 25 f.), as quoted by John T. McNeill in his article on "The History of Interpretation" in *The Interpreter's Bible*, Vol. I (Abingdon Press, 1950), p. 121.

many wheels: *History* speaks of things done; *allegory* understands one thing by another; *tropology* is a moral way of speaking; and *anagoge* is the spiritual understanding by which we are led to things above." Luther quotes the following verse which expresses the same idea, and which students of the later Middle Ages had to memorize in school:[14]

4 senses of scripture

> *"Littera gesta docet; quid credas allegoria;*
> *Moralis quid agas; sed quid speres anagoge."*

("The letter lets you know what happened, and allegory what you must believe; the moral sense what you must do, and anagoge what you may hope for.") In his lectures on Galatians where he cites this verse, he illustrates the meaning of this so-called quadriga by reference first to Jerusalem and then to Ishmael and Isaac. Literally, Jerusalem means the "Jewish city"; allegorically, the church; tropologically or morally, the human soul; and anagogically, heaven. Similarly, Ishmael and Isaac must be understood literally as the two sons of Abraham; allegorically, as the two Testaments, or the synagogue and the church, or law and grace; tropologically, as the flesh and the spirit; and anagogically, as hell and heaven.[15]

In his excellent Luther Studies entitled *The Righteousness of God*, E. G. Rupp suggests[16] that this was "a more adequate framework than might at first sight be supposed." And then he goes on to say: "The literal prophetic sense laid the foundation of devotion and interpretation in the mighty acts of God in his Son Jesus Christ, that historical revelation . . . which is the center of the Christian proclamation. . . . The tropological sense . . . links what God has done 'for us' with his saving activity 'in us.' This interpretation is saved from the perils of atomism and mysticism . . . by the allegorical interpretation which insists . . . that all religious experience is ecclesiastical experience, that God addresses man within the solidarity of creation, of humanity, and of the people of God. Finally, not less necessary, the anagogical interpretation insists that all problems and solutions are broken and partial in time, since they relate to *homo viator* and point to strangers and pilgrims beyond the horizon."

Rupp himself says that "this is to dress up medieval exegesis in the jargon of modern ecumenical theology." Though the framework that suggests this is undoubtedly there, the actual exegetical

---

[14] *WA* 57 (Gal.), 95, 24. Cf. *WA* 2, 550, 21.
[15] *WA* 57 (Gal.), 96, 1.
[16] E. G. Rupp, *The Righteousness of God*, p. 134.

practice in medieval schools did not conform to such a full view of man in relation to God and the church. In most cases, the interpretation was artificial and stilted. Fortunately, the imagination of individual interpreters was not given as much free play as one might suspect. The formalism and conventionalism of medieval thought caused this exegetical method, which in its basic conception left room for a great diversity of interpretations, to remain confined to certain established patterns and themes. But even under these conditions, the discussion of the meaning of a Biblical passage often dealt with matters not mentioned at all in the text. Many parts of Luther's lectures on Romans show how he, too, was steeped in these ways and to what an extent he was bound to them simply because he used the exegetical method of the schools.

But, nevertheless, his concern for an adequate interpretation of the Scripture was so earnest that, even though his exegetical principles and his Biblical thinking were decisively shaped by the fourfold method, he found himself inwardly pressed to attempt going beyond it. Indeed, we know that he finally freed himself from it. He came to regard the allegorical method in particular as a way of distorting the Scripture. For this reason, he was later bitterly critical of Origen, for he considered him, not unjustly, as the father of the allegorical exegesis of the Bible.

In this connection, he learned to appreciate the work of Nicholas of Lyra (+1340), a Franciscan and a doctor of the Sorbonne in Paris. Lyra was the author of a Biblical commentary which, as he conceived of it, should serve as a supplement to the glosses of Walafrid Strabo and Anselm of Laon: the *Postillae perpetuae in Vetus et Novum Testamentum.*[17] As a converted Jew, Lyra had not much use for the "spiritual" interpretation, especially in view of the fact that he knew Hebrew and therefore was able to benefit from Jewish commentaries on the Old Testament, i.e., mainly from the exegetical work of Rabbi Solomon Rashi (+1105). He therefore stressed the importance of the literal or historical interpretation, and he tried to tone down the theological exegesis inspired by the spiritual allegorical methods. It was on account of

[17] In the Bibles published by John Froben of Basel in six-folio volumes (in 1498 and in 1509), the interlinear gloss of Anselm was printed on top of the text of the Vulgate. The *Glossa ordinaria* was placed on the left margin of the page and the *Postil* of Nicholas of Lyra on the right margin. On the lower margin of the page, there appeared the corrections added to Lyra's *Postil* by Paul of Burgos and by Matthias Döring. This publication thus was a veritable mine of information. We know that the young professor M. Luther used it thoroughly.

this that Luther, when he was older, grew fond of Lyra, all the more so because, at the beginning of his career as an exegete, he had almost detested him.

In order to be fair, however, we should recognize that the Scholastic exegetes regarded the *sensus literalis* or *historicus* as the basis of all interpretation. For example, it served them as the norm of the *sensus spiritualis* in so far as they did not regard it permissible to give a passage a spiritual meaning that was not clearly indicated in or by another part of Scripture. Thomas Aquinas stated this rule in the following words:[18] *"Nihil sub spirituali sensu continetur fide necessarium quod Scriptura per literalem sensum alicubi manifeste non tradet."* ("Nothing can be subsumed under the spiritual sense as necessary for the faith which the Scripture does not somewhere plainly hand down through its literal meaning.") What was unusual in the work of Lyra was that he strongly stressed the *sensus literalis historicus.*

In criticizing him for this, the young Luther was dependent on the views of the famous French Humanist Faber Stapulensis (+1536). In the *Dictata super Psalterium,* Faber served as one of his chief authorities. Also the lectures on Romans show how greatly Luther was indebted to him. Faber's two chief exegetical works, the text-critical exposition of the Psalter (*Quincuplex Psalterium, Gallicum, Romanum, Hebraicum, vetus conciliatum,* Paris, 1509) and the commentary on the Pauline letters (*Sancti Pauli Epistolae XIV,* Paris, 1512; 2d ed., 1515) served as his chief references. It is apparent that he had Faber's volumes before him as he prepared his own lecture notes.

He learned from the Frenchman an exegetical principle that was to become most important for him. In order to avoid both an unspiritual literal-historical exegesis and an ungrammatical allegorical-spiritual one, Faber proposed that the interpreter of the Bible must search for the literal sense that its author, the Holy Spirit, intended it to have. He therefore distinguished between two literal senses or meanings of the Biblical text, the historical-literal meaning and the prophetic-literal meaning. He regarded the former as improper because he judged it to be the product of human imagination (*humani sensu fictus*), but the latter appeared to him as eminently proper because he believed it to be inspired by the Holy Spirit (*divino spiritu infusus*). He therefore attempted to interpret the Bible in a literal-grammatical way but on the assumption that it must have a prophetic-spiritual meaning or a literal sense that is in agreement with the Holy Spirit or to which

[18] *Summa Theol.,* I, q. 1, a. 10.

the Holy Spirit leads the exegete (*sensus literae qui cum spiritu concordat et quem spiritus sanctus monstrat*).[19]

Thus he believed himself to be qualified for exegetical work that would avoid the historicism of a Lyra as well as the hermeneutical fancifulness of the allegorists. Yet by endeavoring, on the one hand, to establish an accurate grammatical understanding of the Hebrew and Greek texts of the Bible, he thought to do justice to Lyra's concern for a literal-historical interpretation; and by demonstrating, on the other hand, the spiritual meaning of the Biblical writings by interpreting them in their entirety in terms of the spiritual situation out of which they were written or to which they were addressed, he believed that he was carrying out the true intention of the allegorists which they themselves, however, in his opinion failed to live up to. He achieved this spiritual exegesis by a Christocentric interpretation that was determined by the ideas and attitudes of Neoplatonic mystics from Dionysius Areopagitica and the Victorines down to Nicholas of Cusa and Marsilio Ficino.

In his lectures on The Psalms, Luther was so strongly under the influence of these ideas that Faber's mentality was reflected not only in his thoughts but also in his vocabulary. Following Faber, he made abundant use of the contrast between spirit and letter (he had not yet felt the impact of Augustine's treatise *On the Spirit and the Letter*), and he interpreted it in terms of a comprehensive dualism between things spiritual and carnal; invisible and visible; hidden and manifest; inner and outer; divine and human; heavenly and earthly; eternal and temporal; future and present; full of truth and filled with vanity.

One can notice the same tendency also in the lectures on Romans. However, it is there not so predominant as in the earlier work. The Christocentric emphasis, however, is as strong as before. Indeed, at the very beginning of his exposition, Luther declares in a marginal gloss on Paul's appeal to "the gospel of God which he had promised before, by the prophets, in the Holy Scriptures" (Rom. 1:1–2): "There is opened up here a broad approach to the understanding of Holy Scripture: we must understand it in its entirety with respect to Christ [*tota de Christo sit intelligenda*], especially where it is prophetic. Now it is in fact prophetic throughout, though not according to the superficial literal meaning of the text" (Gl. 5, 9 ff.).

In his comment on Rom. 10:6, where Paul interprets the question of Moses, "Who shall ascend into heaven?" (Deut. 30:12) by

(handwritten margin note: *Faber*)

---

[19] See his preface to the *Psalterium Quincuplex*. Cf. Hahn, in *Zeitschr. f. syst. Theol.*, XII (1934), p. 166. Also Auguste Renaudet, *Préréforme et Humanisme à Paris (1494–1517)*; 2d ed. Paris, 1953, pp. 515 ff., 622 ff.

the parenthetical remark, "That is, to bring Christ down," Luther expresses the same idea. He says: "Moses writes these words in Deut., ch. 30, and he does not have in mind the meaning they have here, but his abundant spiritual insight enables the apostle to bring out their inner significance. It is as if he wanted to give us an impressive proof of the fact that the whole Scripture, if one contemplates it inwardly, deals everywhere with Christ, even though, in so far as it is a sign and a shadow, it may outwardly sound differently. This is why he says: 'Christ is the end of the law' (Rom. 10:4); in other words: every word of the Bible points to Christ. That this is really so, he proves by showing that this word here, which seems to have nothing whatever to do with Christ, nevertheless signifies Christ."[20]

It was in connection with this Christocentrism that Luther developed the exegetical method that, though it reflected a profound influence of others upon him, was the product of his own insight and the result of his inner struggle for a true understanding of the gospel. Faber believed that the interpretation of the Scripture according to the *sensus literalis propheticus* superseded the Scholastic exegesis in terms of the fourfold meaning of the Bible and he therefore abandoned the traditional method. But Luther handled the whole hermeneutical issue in a much more complicated fashion.

He made the literal-prophetic, i.e., Christocentric, meaning the basis of the fourfold meaning.[21] In other words, he combined Faber's method with that of the Scholastics. And not only that: he also eagerly made use of the philological-grammatical approach to literature and particularly to the Bible which the Humanists had opened up. This is why, next to the works of Faber, he studied with great care also those of Reuchlin and, as soon as they became available to him, Erasmus' contributions to Biblical exegesis. However, much as he admired it, he found himself as deeply dissatisfied with Erasmus' scholarship and that of men like him as he was with that of Jerome. In his judgment, the writings of Augustine, and not only the theological but also the exegetical ones, were much more helpful for a proper understanding of the Scripture.[22]

The upshot of all this was that he developed a spiritual exegesis in which he essentially combined the quadriga with Faber's method in such a way that the literal-prophetic understanding of

---

[20] *WA* 56, 414, 13.

[21] Cf. on all of this the illuminating article by Gerhard Ebeling in *Z.Th.K.* XXXVIII (1951), pp. 175 ff., on *Die Anfänge von Luthers Hermeneutik* (particularly pp. 220 ff.).

[22] Cf. Luther's letters of 1516.

the Scripture became connected and interpenetrated with a reading of the text in terms of the tropological or moral sense.

This method gradually assumed a more and more definite character for Luther as he was engaged with the exposition of the Psalter. In the lectures on the letter to the Romans, he proved himself to be already a master of it, although he showed himself still somewhat uncertain in its use—due to the syncretistic influence of the several sources from which he had derived it. We may say that the essence he extracted from these sources was a comparatively simple rule, namely, that the Bible must be understood to speak *literaliter spiritualiter* (in terms of its spiritual-literal meaning) only of Christ and at the same time *tropologice* (in terms of the moral sense) of the believer in Christ. In other words, what is true of Christ is true also of his disciples; as God is and acts in Christ, so he is and acts also in those who believe in Christ. Indeed, in reading the Scripture aright, the Christian comes to know that God is and remains the same in everything he does—yesterday (*literaliter*), today (*tropologice*), and forever (*anagogice*).[23]

One can readily understand that The Psalms could be interpreted to speak literally of Christ and tropologically of the life of the Christian. Hence, it was while he was working on his lectures on The Psalms that the tropological method of interpreting the Scripture became for Luther more and more the *sensus primarius Scripturae*,[24] always on the assumption, we should note, that the Bible is taken to be the work of God and as such as the work of the Holy Spirit speaking of Christ. Luther therefore always correlated the tropological interpretation of the Scripture in terms of which he saw God's word in action in every act of faith with the literal-Christological interpretation according to which he read the Bible as the witness to God's revelation in Christ.

He said:[25] "*Opera Dei sunt verba eius . . . idem est facere et dicere Dei*" ("God's works are his words . . . his doing is identical with his speaking"). Such a view of God required a "causative interpretation" of the Biblical statements about him.[26] He therefore thought, for example, that the Biblical phrase "God's way" referred to the way in which God causes us to walk,[27] and that by calling God holy, it means to say that he is holy in so far as he

---

[23] E. Vogelsang, *Die Anfänge von Luthers Christologie* (Berlin, 1933), p. 63.
[24] *WA* 3, 531, 33. Cf. Holl, *op. cit.*, p. 546; also E. Hirsch, "*Initium theologiae Lutheri*" (in *Luther-Studien*, Vol. II, p. 30).
[25] *WA* 3, 154, 7.
[26] Cf. Ebeling, *op. cit.*, pp. 228 f.
[27] *WA* 3, 529, 33.

causes men to be holy, i.e., in so far as he sanctifies them.[28] According to the prophetic-literal meaning of the Scripture, Christ is the righteousness of God (*iustitia Dei*), but, tropologically understood, it is faith in Christ (*fides Christi*) which is this righteousness.[29]

This was the insight which Luther regarded as the key to the understanding of the Scripture. It enabled him to understand "the righteousness of God that is revealed in the gospel from faith to faith" (Rom. 1:17). We must note that it was an *exegetical* insight.

The "righteousness of God," therefore, became a major theme of his Biblical exegesis. This is made especially clear in the lectures on Romans. The topic of discourse to which Luther returns again and again in this work is this: God alone is righteous; before him, man is a sinner and nothing but a sinner, especially so, if in view of his attainments, including the moral and religious ones, he regards himself as righteous. This self-righteousness, which is presumptuousness and pride, makes man a liar before his own true self and before God. For it prevents him from recognizing himself as he actually is as well as from giving God the glory. But he that listens to the voice and verdict of his conscience and acknowledges himself as a sinner before God and submits to his judgment finds that God sends grace through his justice, for he reveals himself as righteous in order to make man righteous: he kills in order to make alive; he breaks down man's pride and self-sufficiency in order to heal him forever; he condemns him in order to forgive him; he humiliates him in order to accept him in grace and in order to make him righteous.[30]

"The righteousness of God is that righteousness by which he makes us righteous just as the wisdom of God is that by which he makes us wise."[31]

III. LUTHER'S INTERPRETATION OF THE LETTER TO THE ROMANS IN THE LIGHT OF ANCIENT AND MEDIEVAL THEOLOGY

Luther gives a good summary of his basic understanding of Paul's letter in the following statement:[32] "In this letter, the apostle does not speak against those who obviously are sinners through and through but against those who in their own eyes are righteous

---

[28] *WA* 3, 465, 33.
[29] *WA* 3, 466, 26.
[30] Holl, *op. cit.*, pp. 188, 193 f.
[31] *WA* 56, 262, 21.
[32] *WA* 56, 33, 13.

and thus are confident that they will be saved by their works. It is these people he tries to lead to the realization that they must take the grace of God more seriously [*inducere ad magnificandam gratiam Dei*], but one cannot take it seriously unless one first acknowledges and takes seriously [*magnificatur*] the sin that is forgiven by it. This is why some were scandalized by this when they heard about it. They thought that the apostle was preaching that one must do evil in order to magnify the glory of God. But, as a matter of fact, our iniquity and falsehood 'abound to his glory' when, humbling ourselves by confessing them, we glorify God for the sake of his abundant grace as he forgives us our sins.

"But he would not be glorified in this way if we believed that we had no need of his grace but that we could stand before him sufficient to ourselves. He that acknowledges that he has many sins is, therefore, better than one who, like the Pharisee, acknowledges that he has much righteousness and no sin. For the former glorifies God's mercy, but the latter his own righteousness."

We must realize that for Luther himself this way of taking seriously (or as he liked to say, "magnifying") God's grace and man's sin constituted nothing else than the discovery of the gospel. It enabled him to understand his own vocation as a Christian and thus it fulfilled the quest that he had begun by becoming a monk. It also provided him with the sense of mission that he needed as a professor of Biblical theology. Indeed, he had the feeling that he had rediscovered the gospel for Christendom and the church, for he was sure that both the theologians and the churchmen of his time were bound to ways of thought and practice that were leading them away from Christ.

We do not mean to assert that, on achieving this basic understanding of the gospel, Luther also felt himself called to reform the church. To be sure, his lecture notes on the letter to the Romans amply show to what an extent his discovery of the gospel drove him to speak up against Scholastic theology, monastic religion, and ecclesiastical ceremonialism. His faith certainly caused him to call for changes in the teaching, order, and work of the church. However, this does not imply that his new religious-theological insight set him straightway on that road to reformation which he found himself compelled to travel later on. What is plain is that, from the beginning, his faith in the gospel, once it was free and clear and certain, led him to ask all he could reach that they should repent, i.e., change their minds, for he was persuaded that, as he wrote later in his book against Erasmus:[33] "The word of God wherever it comes, comes to change and renew the world."

[33] *WA* 18, 626, 25.

Only in this sense did the discovery he made as a Biblical theologian lead directly to the work he had to perform as a reformer of the church. At any rate, his new Biblical theology compelled him to advance fundamental criticisms against Roman Catholic beliefs and practices. In a decisive way, the Protestant Reformation was thus the result of his theology. However, we must qualify this statement by going on to say that, when Luther became involved in the conflict with the Roman Catholic authorities to the extent that he found it impossible to submit to them, his theological teachings came to be strongly determined by the moves and countermoves that, in the course of time, were to issue in his condemnation by the papacy and in the formation of nonpapal, Reformed, Evangelical churches.

There is a remarkable document written by Luther himself which has assumed special importance in this connection: his preface to the first volume of the Wittenberg Edition of his *Collected Latin Works* (1545). Therein Luther reviews the events that culminated not only in his rejection at Worms of the demand that he recant his views but also in the imposition of the ban upon him by church and empire. Luther engages himself in these reminiscenses in order to explain the background and purpose of the writings he published in the years 1517–1521, for these were the content of the first volume of his Collected Works. In this connection, he makes mention also of the Commentary on The Psalms (*Operationes in Psalmos*), which he had published in 1519–1520 in a fragmentary form, seeing that because of his controversy with his papal opponents he would be unable to complete it. His statement throws light also on the question: What importance did he himself attach to his lectures on Romans?

He writes:[34] "In that year (1519), I had meanwhile turned once more to the interpretation of The Psalms, relying on the fact that I was better schooled after I had dealt in the classroom with the letter of Saint Paul to the Romans and the Galatians and that to the Hebrews. I had been seized with a really extraordinary ardor to understand Paul in the letter to the Romans, but until then there stood in my way, not coldness of blood, but this one word, i.e., Rom. 1:17: 'The justice of God is revealed in it.' For I hated this word 'the justice of God' which by the use and usage of all the doctors I was taught to understand philosophically in terms of that so-called formal or active justice with which God is just and punishes the sinners and the unrighteous.

"For, however irreproachably I lived as a monk, I felt myself before God to be a sinner with a most unquiet conscience, nor

[34] *WA* 54, 179–187.

could I be confident that I had pleased him with my satisfaction. I did not love, nay, rather I hated, this righteous God who punished sinners, and if not with tacit blasphemy, certainly with huge murmurings I was angry with God, saying: 'As though it really were not enough that miserable sinners should be eternally damned with original sin and have all kinds of calamities laid upon them by the law of the Ten Commandments, God must go and add sorrow upon sorrow and even through the gospel itself bring his justice and wrath to bear!' I raged in this way with a wildly aroused and disturbed conscience, and yet I knocked importunately at Paul in this passage, thirsting more ardently to know what Paul meant.

"At last, God being merciful, as I thought about it day and night, I noticed the context of the words, namely, 'The justice of God is revealed in it; as it is written, the just shall live by faith.' Then and there, I began to understand the justice of God as that by which the righteous man lives by the gift of God, namely, by faith, and this sentence 'The justice of God is revealed in the gospel' to be that passive justice with which the merciful God justifies us by faith, as it is written: 'The just lives by faith.'

"This straightway made me feel as though reborn and as though I had entered through open gates into Paradise itself. From then on, the whole face of Scripture appeared different. I ran through the Scriptures then as memory served, and found that other words had the same meaning, for example: the work of God with which he makes us strong, the wisdom of God with which he makes us wise, the fortitude of God, the salvation of God, the glory of God.

"And now, much as I had hated the word 'justice of God' before, so much the more sweetly I extolled this word to myself now, so that this passage in Paul was to me a real gate to Paradise. Afterward, I read Augustine *On the Spirit and the Letter*, where unexpectedly I came upon the fact that I, too, interpreted the justice of God in a similar way: namely, as that with which God endues us when he justifies us. And although this was said still imperfectly, and he does not clearly explain about 'imputation,' it was gratifying to me that he should teach a justice of God by which we are justified.

"Having become better armed by these reflections, I began to interpret The Psalms a second time and my work would have resulted in a large commentary if I had not been compelled to put aside what I had begun to work on because, in the following year, I was called to appear at the Diet of Worms, which was convened by the emperor Charles V."

It seems obvious that in these comments which were meant to

serve as an introduction to the Commentary on The Psalms of
1519–1521, the only one of his early interpretations of Biblical
books that he published, Luther assigns to his work on the letter to
the Romans a special significance for his discovery of the gospel in
connection with his understanding of the Pauline doctrine of justification.

Indeed, what Luther says here is borne out by the evidence that
is furnished by his lectures on Romans. Any reader of this work
can plainly see that, when he wrote it, he was already in possession
of that understanding of the righteousness of God of which he says
in this Preface that it set him free. What is astonishing is that, inasmuch as the passage of Rom. 1:17 was of such signal importance
to him, he chose to give but a brief and rather cursory explanation
of it in his lectures. However, we should note that his comment
supports in every way that view of it which he mentions in his
autobiographical statement.

As a matter of fact, throughout his commentary on the letter to
the Romans, Luther appears to be in full possession of that understanding of justification which, at the end of his life, he hailed as
having opened to him not only the gospel but also the gates of
Paradise, i.e., the way to eternal salvation. Therefore, those interpreters of Luther are probably correct who assume that he a-
chieved the decisive insight _before_ he took up the letter to the
Romans. Luther himself gives support to their thesis, not only by
his remark (in the Preface) that _after_ his rediscovery he read
Augustine's _On the Spirit and the Letter_ (for, in the lectures on
Romans, he shows himself acquainted with this treatise), but also
by the whole manner of theologizing that he displays in the earlier
lectures on The Psalms.

It should not surprise anyone that in the _Dictata super Psalmos_
as well as in the lectures on Romans, Luther is speaking as a man
who still is feeling his way toward a theological position of his
own. This agrees with his own interpretation of himself as one
who _scribendo et docendo profecit_[35] (made progress while he wrote
and taught).

However, we can clearly recognize in these writings the thinker
who was to become the Reformer of the church and, as such, the
one who introduced a new Biblical theology into Christendom.

Here we must take notice of Luther's theological heritage. We
have already dealt with this subject (but only in part) in connection with the discussion of Luther's place in the history of exegesis.
Just as he developed his own _exegetical_ method by way of a critical
and creative dependence upon the Biblical interpreters of former

[35] _WA_ 54 (Clemen, IV, 428).

ages and of his own time, so he formed his own *theological* understanding of the Christian gospel by engaging in a searching conversation with other theologians, old and new.

His lectures on Romans clearly show that his theological outlook was determined, first of all, by the Bible, then by Augustine, and thereafter by the mystics, particularly Bernard of Clairvaux and Tauler but also by Dionysius the Areopagite, and then by the Scholastics from Peter Lombard and Duns Scotus to the nominalists, especially Ockham, Pierre d'Ailly, and Gabriel Biel. Moreover, he proves himself to be under the theological influence of the major exegetes on whom he relied—from Ambrose, Jerome, and Augustine down to Faber, Reuchlin, and Erasmus.

Futhermore, there is ample evidence that his monastic life and training shaped his basic theological attitudes and concerns. His mind was steeped in the liturgical tradition and discipline of the Augustinian order and his thinking about religion was formed and stimulated not only by his observation of himself and by his analysis of the heights and depths of his own religious life but also by his evaluation of the religious attitudes and practices of his fellow monks.

Moreover, his theological schooling and particularly his training as a teacher had left a deep mark upon his mind. This is made evident by his manner of reasoning (he thought about everything in terms of contrast) and by the way in which he refers to Aristotle and Peter Lombard (on both of whom he had taught courses in 1508 and 1509). However, his being at home in the writings of Aristotle, particularly the *Ethics,* did not prevent him from being critical of them, just as the fact that his theological outlook was determined by the nominalists (to such an extent that, as Melanchthon reports, he knew by heart long passages from d'Ailly and Biel's writings) did not restrain him from expressing sharp criticisms of them.

His writings and debates show clearly the source and norm of all his agreements with other writers and also of his disagreements with them. It was the Bible—the Bible read and pondered in the light of Paul's teaching. The following statement[36] of his expresses this very pointedly (and what Luther says in it can readily be applied to his exposition of the letter to the Romans): "What others have learned from Scholastic theology is their own affair. As for me, I know and confess that I learned there nothing but ignorance of sin, righteousness, baptism, and of the whole Christian life. I certainly did not learn there what the power of God is, and the work of God, the grace of God, the righteousness of God,

[36] *WA* 12, 414, 22 (cf. Holl, *op. cit.,* p. 28, n.2).

and what faith, hope, and love are. . . . Indeed, I lost Christ there, but now I have found him again in Paul."

Luther's knowledge of the Bible was extraordinary. He himself said[37] (in the Preface of 1545) that the diligent study of the Bible in which he had been engaged privately as well as publicly (i.e., as a teacher) had enabled him to learn almost all of it by heart. Karl Holl goes so far as to say that the knowledge of the Bible that was at Luther's command at the time when he worked on his first course on The Psalms is comparable only to that of the best Biblicists of antiquity, namely, Tertullian and Origen. Howsoever this may be, nobody is likely to deny that Luther's way of interpreting the letter to the Romans through other books of the Scripture constitutes a remarkable feat of exegesis. What is especially noteworthy in this is his reliance on The Psalms. He knew them intimately not only because monastic devotions and worship services were based on them but also because, from the beginning of his career, he had made a special study of them. In the lectures on Romans, we can observe how he tended to read the Psalter with the eyes of Paul and how he interpreted Paul through the piety of The Psalms. The themes, therefore, that he takes up again and again are God's dealing with man in righteousness and mercy and man's standing before God knowing himself as sinner or as one forgiven.

A characteristic feature of Luther's use of the Bible, which comes to the fore especially in the lectures on Romans, is that he frequently introduces special themes which certain Biblical passages suggested to him. These themes continued to govern his thinking throughout his life. We imagine that these passages struck his fancy perhaps because they state a truth through a contrast or because they sharply illuminate the condition of man. (Luther was a keen observer of the human scene. He was able to see in some single act of an individual something that impressed him as typical of all men. It was for this reason that he was fond of proverbs and that he liked to quote them.) Thus, for example, his thoughts frequently turned to I Sam. 2:6–7: "The Lord kills and makes alive; he brings down to hell and brings back again. The Lord makes poor and makes rich; he humbles and he exalts." As Luther read these words, they spoke of the crucified and risen Christ and of the Christian's dying and rising with Christ, and he therefore interpreted them in the following way: "It is God's nature first to destroy and to turn to nothing whatever is in us before he gives us his own."[38]

Another way in which he liked to describe God's dealing with

[37] *WA* 54 (Clemen, IV, 426).
[38] *WA* 56, 375, 18; 193, 10; 450, 19.

men was through the assertion that "God does a strange work in order to perform a work that is properly his own."[39] Also, this thought was derived from a Biblical passage, namely, Isa. 28:21: "For the Lord shall stand up as in the mountain of divisions; he shall be angry as in the valley which is in Gibeon, that he may do his work, his strange work; that he may perform his proper work —his work is strange to him."

That Luther could find major theological themes expressed in these and many other Biblical passages was a result of his close acquaintance with the books of the Bible. His mind was so filled with the Bible that Biblical words formed his thoughts and that he could not help expressing his own thoughts through Biblical words.

Thus it could happen that he turned Biblical phrases into statements of significant theological themes by taking them out of context. This explains, for example, why, in the lectures on Romans, he quotes several times[40] from S. of Sol. 8:6: "Love is strong as death, jealousy as hard as hell." These words are part of a sentence that, as it is rendered in the Vulgate, is almost unintelligible (at least to us): "Put me as a seal upon thy heart, as a seal upon thy arm, for love is strong as death, jealousy [*emulatio*] as hard as hell; the lamps thereof are fire and flames." We must assume that the phrase "Love is strong as death," etc., had fastened itself upon Luther's mind as he memorized the Bible and then suggested itself to him in all kinds of connections. We can make a similar observation with respect to many other Biblical sayings, for example, Lev. 26:36: "The sound of a rustling leaf shall terrify them." Luther quotes this only once in these lectures,[41] but later in his career it became for him a telling description of the terrified conscience.

We point to these examples in order to indicate how Luther's thinking was enlivened by the Bible. They seem to show that he was arbitrary in his way of using it. But it would be a great mistake to think that he was. The lectures on Romans prove with what thoroughness he pondered and interpreted the Biblical books and with how great an effort he endeavored to understand what the apostle had had in mind in every word and sentence he wrote. In order to accomplish such an exact understanding, Luther availed himself, as we have seen, of every exegetical tool accessible to him.

He used with great eagerness the commentaries of the Humanists. But much as he appreciated their philological and lexico-

[39] *WA* 56, 376, 8.
[40] *WA* 56, 359, 29; 388, 13; 491,1.
[41] *WA* 56, 410, 28.

et the
modern
scene—ie.
historical
critical
vs.
canonical
exegesis

graphic work, he regarded their theological exposition of the Bible as inadequate. In these lectures, he frequently quotes Faber and (beginning with the ninth chapter) Erasmus, but he scarcely ever proves himself to be dependent on them for theological ideas, certainly only slightly on Faber but not at all on Erasmus. In a letter to his friend Spalatin, written on October 16, 1516[42] (i.e., at the time when he had just completed the course on the letter to the Romans), he plainly states the reasons for his dissatisfaction with Erasmus: that he was incapable of grasping what Paul was thinking about. Luther complains that Erasmus applied to the observance of ceremonial laws what the apostle writes about the righteousness of works, or the righteousness of the law, or self-righteousness, and that he was unable to comprehend that Paul did not think as Aristotle did, especially about the relation between being and doing. Luther is sure that Paul did not teach as Aristotle did that men become righteous by doing righteous deeds, but he is persuaded that the basic assumption the apostle made was that by being or becoming righteous, men find themselves able to perform righteous acts. Luther also writes[43] that Erasmus did not understand what in Rom., ch. 5, Paul means by original sin, and he attributes this failure to the fact that Erasmus had apparently not read Augustine's anti-Pelagian writings and especially the treatise *On the Spirit and the Letter*. In this connection, Luther says: "In the exposition of Scripture, I put Jerome as far behind Augustine as Erasmus puts Augustine behind Jerome."

Luther
vs.
Erasmus

This judgment is certainly borne out by the lecture notes on the letter to the Romans. Luther there refers directly to Jerome twelve times but to Augustine more often than one hundred times, indeed, more often than to any other author. Moreover, Augustine is frequently quoted at considerable length. Luther shows himself acquainted with almost the whole body of Augustine's work (though it is surprising that he does not use *On Predestination* and *On the Gift of Perseverance*), but in these lectures he depends particularly on the anti-Pelagian writings. He naturally cites most frequently Augustine's *Exposition of Certain Themes of the Letter to the Romans (Expositio quarundam propositionum ex ep. ad Romanos)*, the books *Against Julian* and, particularly, *On the Spirit and the Letter* (he quotes this work twenty-seven times, apparently from memory). The references Luther makes to Cyprian and Chrysostom are taken from Augustine. Melanchthon, therefore, was certainly correct when he said of Luther:[44] "He frequently

Luther
+
Augustine

[42] *WA, Br* 1, 70, 4.
[43] *Ibid.*, 70, 17.
[44] Otto Scheel, *Dok.*, 2d ed., Nr. 532, pp. 199, 40.

read all the writings of Augustine and had them firmly in mind."

When Luther began his lectures on the letter to the Romans, he had just become acquainted with certain of the anti-Pelagian writings of Augustine, and especially with *On the Spirit and the Letter*.[44a] Augustine was authoritative for him because of his Paulinism. Luther regarded him as the one church father who had understood the apostle correctly and who therefore interpreted the gospel in terms of what he had learned from Paul. However, in order to understand Luther properly, we must note that he held Augustine in such high esteem not only because he enabled him to comprehend Paul but chiefly because Luther judged that Augustine was a true Paulinist. In other words, Luther himself was primarily a Paulinist and only secondarily an Augustinian. He felt that Augustine was his ally in his fight against the Pelagian tendencies of Scholasticism, but he did not hesitate to go against him if he was sure that Augustine, too, did not do full justice to the gospel, as, for example, in his teaching on love.

Indeed, we may say that although Luther generally agreed with Augustine over against the Scholastics in so far as they did not seem to him to take full account of human perversity and evil, he nevertheless felt that Augustine did not reach the profundity of Paul's understanding of the situation of men before God.[45]

Over against the Scholastic-Aristotelian teaching (i.e., that of the Occamists, and especially that of Gabriel Biel) that sin consists of single acts of wrongdoing, he understood sin (as Augustine did) as the basic proneness toward evil that determines man's whole being in such a way that every single sin must be seen as a manifestation of sinful human nature, i.e., of original sin. Luther and Augustine apparently also agree in interpreting the nature of sin as pride (*superbia*). Both say that pride is the cause of man's disobedience of God's commandments. But here we must observe that although Augustine only rarely advances this pointed interpretation, and then generally in order to identify sin with evil desiring or coveting (*concupiscentia*), which manifest themselves in lust or in the longing for earthly happiness, Luther consistently defines sin as defiance and self-righteousness, i.e., as that presumptuousness which is inspired by man's tendency to seek himself in everything.[46]

The same difference is apparent also in the conception of sal-

---

[44a] In 1518, Luther published an edition of Augustine's *De spiritu et litera*. In the Introduction he praises Augustine as the best source of Christian learning next to the Bible. Cf. Ficker (ed. 1908), p. LXXVIII.

[45] Cf. Hamel II, 1 ff.

[46] *Ibid.*, II, 14 f.

vation: Luther criticized the Scholastics for believing that original sin and actual sins are canceled and annulled by sacramental grace; for he was of the conviction that sin is forgiven by God, in the sense that God does not count it, and that, in so far as it is forgiven, it is not annulled; rather, it remains, except in so far as the grace of forgiveness of which man will continue to be in need commences a healing that will be completed after death and there-fore can be apprehended in this life only by hope. Augustine oc-cupied a position between the Scholastics and Luther. He was of the persuasion that although the guilt and punishment of sin are forgiven, concupiscence remains not as sin but as the spur that can induce new sin. In regard to this last point, Luther found it im-possible to go along with Augustine. In his judgment, concupi-scence was basically selfishness and hence sin itself, and not only the spur to sinning or the material of sin.

Luther could not help viewing man, i.e., the Christian man, as simultaneously sinful and righteous, a sinner in fact and a right-eous man in hope, i.e., as a repentant sinner or as a forgiven sinner.

This bold doctrine of the Christian as *simul peccator ac iustus* cannot be found in Augustine's writings. He could go only so far as to say that the Christian is "partly" (*partim*) righteous and "partly" sinful.[47]

To be sure, we must not exaggerate Luther's uniqueness. In-deed, we must be ready to admit that also in this teaching, which reflects so characteristically his interpretation of the nature of the Christian life, he was under the *influence* of Augustine. This is most obvious in the assertion, which in the lectures on Romans he makes again and again, that man, though actually a sinner, is nevertheless righteous because God, the good Samaritan, has promised him health and has already begun to heal him, or be-cause God accepts him inasmuch as he has proved himself before Him. Nevertheless, the basic teaching that Luther here advanced was a doctrine of his own. Its substance was this: the Christian is sinful and righteous at the same time because he has the right-eousness of Christ—Christ's righteousness "covers" him and is "imputed" to him. He is forgiven "because of Christ" (*"propter Christum"*) and he has a "foreign" righteousness that comes to him from without.

For example, Luther writes:[48] "*The saints know that there is sin in them but that it is covered and not counted because of Christ [propter Christum], and . . . they . . . give testimony of*

[47] *WA* 56, 269 ff.; 349 ff.; 441 ff.
[48] *WA* 56, 280, 2.

the fact that *all their good is outside of them in Christ who is nevertheless in them through faith. . . .* We are his Kingdom, and the beauty that is in us is not ours but his, and he covers our hideousness with it." And in interpreting the passage, "I myself with the mind serve the law of God, but with the flesh the law of sin" (Rom. 7:25), he writes:[49] "Notice that it is one and the same man who serves both the law of God and the law of sin, that he is at the same time righteous and one who sins. . . . Notice, then, what I stated before: The saints are at the same time sinners while they are righteous; *they are righteous because they believe in Christ whose righteousness covers them and is imputed to them,* but they are sinners because they do not fulfill the law and are not without concupiscence. They are like sick people in the care of a physician: they are really sick but healthy only in hope and in so far as they begin to be better, or rather, are being healed; i.e., they will become healthy. Nothing could be so harmful to them as the presumption that they were in fact healthy, for it would cause a bad relapse."

Passages of this sort prove to what an extent Luther's doctrine of justification was distinctly his own. It was different from Augustine on account of the emphasis, on the one hand, on the weight of human sin, which remains even though the sinner is forgiven, and, on the other hand, on the wonder of divine righteousness, which imputes to the sinner the righteousness of Christ. Nevertheless, Luther cites Augustine at great length and with approval in the context of these very sentences which state points that cannot be found in Augustine's writings. When in his thinking on Paul's teaching he was in fact led to go beyond Augustine, he felt himself largely in agreement with him.

And when he was aware that he *was* in fundamental disagreement with Augustine, he plainly hesitated to say so directly. This is all the more remarkable because ordinarily he expressed himself forcefully and even vehemently when he differed with others about important doctrines.

This can be illustrated in connection with his discussion on the commandment of love in the lectures on Romans. Here he sharply differed from Augustine. For he rejected the notion that there is an order of love (*caritas ordinata*) in which self-love has a rightful place. He also knew that the Scholastics were following Augustine's authority in so far as they based their entire interpretation of love on this notion of "ordered love." He discusses the whole issue in the following manner: He cites Gregory the Great in support of his own view that Christian love (*caritas*) is never self-

[49] *WA* 56, 347, 2.

love and then goes on to say:[50] "But Gregory's statement and also
our own appear to be in conflict with a certain well-known definition of the different ways of loving and their order. For, referring
to Blessed Augustine, also, the Master of the Sentences adduces
the following definition: 'We must first love God and then our
soul, after that the soul of the neighbor, and finally our body.'
Ordered love, therefore, begins with itself. In answer to this, we
say: As long as we persist in not properly understanding the nature of love, we shall fail to realize love. For as long as we are
the ones who lay the first claim to any good, we are in no way concerned for our neighbor." Then he proceeds to assert, in sharp
opposition to the Augustinian tradition, that self-love can in no
way be the pattern of the love of the neighbor. But he introduces
his lengthy exposition with the following cautious words in which
Augustine is not specifically mentioned: "With due respect for the
judgment of others and with reverence for the fathers, I must state
what is on my mind, and speaking up like a fool, I say: It does
not seem to me to be a solid understanding of the commandment
'Thou shalt love thy neighbor' if one interprets it in terms of the
notion that, inasmuch as the commandment itself says 'as thyself,'
the one who loves is the model according to which he loves his
neighbor."

The point at issue here is the one on which Luther's whole interpretation of the letter to the Romans hinges, namely, that man's
tendency to seek himself in everything because he is bent in upon
himself, even in his moral and religious life, must first be recognized in all its seriousness in order that the gospel of Christ and
the liberty it bestows on men can be understood. Because he was
convinced that the Scholastics had failed to see this inasmuch as
they did not sufficiently "magnify" sin and falsely attributed to
man potentialities of religious attainment (e.g., the achievement
of the love of God by his natural powers), thereby distorting the
gospel, Luther severely criticized them. In his lectures, he frequently takes them to task in strongest terms for their failure,
even to the point of insulting them, but he excepts Augustine from
such criticism. This is astonishing, for he appears not to have been
fully aware of the close connection between the Augustinian teaching and the main tenets of Scholastic theology.

In his opinion, Augustine was *the* Scriptural theologian who as
such had the right comprehension of the nature of sin and grace.
The Scholastic theologians lacked this understanding, so he was
sure, and he attributed this failure of theirs to the fact that they
were under the influence of Aristotle.

[50] *WA* 56, 517, 3.

This evaluation of Augustine, on the one hand, and of the Scholastics, on the other hand, is most clearly reflected in Luther's exposition of Rom. 4:7 (which is a quotation from Ps. 32): "Blessed are they whose iniquities are forgiven and whose sins are covered." Here he presents in detail his doctrine of the Christian man as *simul iustus ac peccator* and then he goes on to say:[51] "If this is so, then I must say either that I have never understood the matter or that the Scholastic theologians did not deal adequately with sin and grace. For they imagine that original sin is entirely taken away just like actual sin. . . . The ancient holy fathers Augustine and Ambrose, however, dealt with these issues quite differently, namely, according to the method of Scripture. But the Scholastics follow the method of Aristotle in his *Ethics,* and he bases sinfulness and righteousness and likewise the extent of their actualization on what a person does. But Blessed Augustine said most plainly that 'in baptism sin [concupiscence] is forgiven, not in the sense that it is no longer there, but in the sense that it is not counted as sin.'"

Then Luther refers to his own struggle for salvation and his difficulty in understanding himself as a sinner in view of the teaching that as a recipient of grace through the sacrament of penance he was free from sin. "I did not know," he goes on to say,[52] "that though forgiveness is indeed real, sin is not taken away except in hope. . . , so that it is only not reckoned as sin." And then he continues as follows:[53] "For this reason it is sheer madness to say that man can love God above everything by his own powers" (as Ockham, Pierre d'Ailly, Gabriel Biel, and others had affirmed) "and live up to the commandment according to the substance of the deed but, because he is not in grace, not according to the intention of him who gave it. O you fools! You pig-theologians! So then grace would not have been necessary, except for the sake of a new exaction over and above the law! For if we can fulfill the law by our own powers, as they say, grace is not necessary for the fulfillment of the law but only for the fulfillment of a divinely imposed exaction that goes beyond the law. Who can tolerate such sacrilegious opinions!"

Luther then declares that according to the Bible and experience the law cannot be fulfilled, because, on account of concupiscence, man is unable to love God except if grace enables him to do so, and he concludes[54] that the Scholastic theologians "did not know the nature of sin and forgiveness." This judgment seems to him to

---

[51] *WA* 56, 273, 3.
[52] *WA* 56, 274, 8.
[53] *WA* 56, 274, 11.
[54] *WA* 56, 275, 17.

be confirmed by the fact that these same theologians could be so optimistic about the moral and religious potentialities of man because of their doctrine of the synteresis according to which man is naturally, though only slightly, "inclined toward the good."[55] But in contrast to this view, "all the saints," he writes,[56] "acknowledged themselves as sinners, as the books of Augustine show. Our theologians, however, have failed to consider the nature of sins and have concentrated their attention upon good works . . . and so they cause people to become proud in thinking that they are already righteous by having outwardly done good works." This certainly is nothing else than to establish righteousness by means of works "and to fail to recognize that the Christian life consists of the righteousness of faith, i.e., of the confidence that we are freed from our sins not by our 'own powers but by the action of God' who causes our sin to be 'covered by Christ as he dwells in us.' "[57]

Then Luther returns once more to the theme of the Scholastic conception of law and grace and quoting Pierre d'Ailly (yet without mentioning his name), he declares:[58] "To say that 'God has obliged us to have grace and therefore to what is impossible' is an inept and foolish way of speaking. I excuse the most blessed God. He is innocent of this deception. He has not done this. He has not obliged us to have grace, but he has obliged us to fulfill the law in order to give us grace when, humiliated, we ask for it. But these men make grace into something that . . . is hateful. For what does it mean to say: God has obliged us to have grace and does not want to accept the fulfillment of the law according to the substance of the deed, if it is not also fulfilled according to the intention of the lawgiver? It can mean only this: We could, we could fulfill the law without grace. But it is not enough that God has burdened us with the law; he imposes still another burden upon us and demands that we should possess his grace! What pride! What ignorance of God! What ignorance of the law!"

A further examination of this leads Luther to a discussion of the Scholastic teaching on the fulfillment of the law "according to the substance of the deed" through "an action that is done for the sake of God from the heart and in such a way that an act of the will is naturally elicited [*naturaliter voluntatis actu elicito*]."[59] Luther denies this vigorously and asserts that man is unable to keep the law; and then he goes on to affirm man's justification by

55 *WA* 56, 275, 20.
56 *WA* 56, 276, 5.
57 *WA* 56, 278, 2.
58 *WA* 56, 278, 25.
59 *WA* 56, 279, 15.

the imputation of Christ's righteousness to him. Thereupon he takes up once more the idea of "the elicited act of the will":[60] "Many yield to indolence and security because they rely on a word that Blessed Augustine is supposed to have said: 'Wanting to be righteous is a large part of righteousness'" (Augustine did say something like this in one of his letters[61] which Luther quotes several times). "So they [i.e., the Occamists, especially d'Ailly and Biel] identify this 'wanting to' with a very tiny 'elicited act of the will,' which, moreover, soon falls apart."

The conclusion to which Luther comes is this (and we must not fail to notice that by interpreting Augustine's sentence in such a way that he can agree with it, he gives it a Pauline meaning):[62] "Now it is true that wanting to be righteous is not only a large part of righteousness but all the righteousness we can have in this life. Yet this 'wanting to be' is not that willing of which we have just been speaking, but it is what the apostle has in mind when he says: 'To will is present with me but to accomplish I find not.' Our whole present life is a time wherein we want righteousness but never accomplish it; this can happen only in the life to come. 'To will,' therefore, means to demonstrate with all our powers, efforts, prayers, actions, passions, that we long for righteousness but do not yet have possession of what we shall be. Read Blessed Augustine, who has written about this very fittingly and adequately [locupletissime] in many books, especially in the Second Book Against Julian, where he quotes Saint Ambrose, Hilary, Cyprian, Chrysostom, Basil, Nazianzen, Irenaeus, Retitius, and Olympus."[63]

Luther regarded Augustine as his ally against the Scholastics and did not notice that they, too, were Augustinian in a fashion. He appealed to the anti-Pelagian writings. But the Scholastics, who also considered Augustine as *the* church father, stressed those of his ideas which were in line with Neoplatonic humanism according to which man is able to ascend to God and which reflected his churchmanship and his confidence in the healing powers of the sacraments.

Luther understood Augustine's saying that 'wanting to be righteous is a large part of righteousness' as if it referred to a longing that can never be fulfilled in this life, but the Scholastics

[margin: Luther vs. Scholastics]

---

[60] WA 56, 280, 10.
[61] Augustine, Ep. 127, 5.
[62] WA 56, 280, 14.
[63] In his letter to Spalatin of Oct. 16, 1516, Luther lists Augustine's anti-Pelagian writings and then he names the same theologians he enumerates here, remarking that Erasmus should make it a point to read all these authors in order that he thus might achieve a better understanding of Paul and of Augustine.

interpreted it to mean that in so far as men want to be righteous they also have the power to become so. Luther read Augustine in the light of Paul's understanding of the gospel and he depended chiefly on Augustine's teachings in his fight against the Pelagianism of the Scholastics, and he believed himself to be of one mind with him when he castigated them for their failure to understand the difference between the law and the gospel.

Now it is very important that we identify the Scholastic theologians against whom Luther inveighs so forcefully in these lectures. Following the practice of the medieval schools, he only rarely names the authors with whom he agrees or whom he opposes. He is content to refer to "the Scholastic theologians," "the metaphysical theologians," "the subtle doctors," "the recent doctors," or "our theologians," etc. He quotes directly only two medieval theologians: Bernard of Clairvaux and Peter Lombard. Toward both, but particularly the former, he felt himself favorably disposed because he regarded their teaching as Scriptural and Augustinian. To Bernard he felt attached not only on account of his mysticism but also because of his teaching on the *personal* faith in the forgiveness of sins.[63a]

None of the so-called High Scholastics is specifically named by him except Duns Scotus, but it is only once that Luther refers to him and then in connection with a sarcastic reference to the notion of the "virtual intention" ("*intentio virtualis*") of which Luther was sharply critical. There is no direct or indirect reference to Thomas Aquinas,[64] unless one regards an allusion to "the Thomists, and Scotists, and other schools [*sectae*]" as such. The context within which this reference occurs is this: Luther criticizes[65] the monks who by imitating the saints, or their fathers and founders, succeed only in aping them in an unspiritual way. And then he goes on to say: "The Thomists, Scotists, and other schools display the same kind of poor judgment in the manner by which they uphold the writings and sayings of their founders, for they disdain it to inquire for the spirit behind them; they even extinguish this spirit by the excessive zeal with which they venerate these men."

In writing this, Luther was probably thinking also of his own school, that of the Occamists. They are the ones he has chiefly in mind when he assails the Scholastics. The opinions against which he argues are mainly those of Pierre d'Ailly and Gabriel Biel, but

<hr/>

[63a] *WA* 56, 369, 28.

[64] Ficker (ed. 1908, p. LIII) assumes that Luther follows closely the outline of Paul's letter, which Thomas Aquinas prepared in connection with his commentary.

[65] *WA* 56, 335, 26.

also those of Ockham and Duns Scotus (as our notes show), not to mention his own teachers at Erfurt, Jodocus Trutvetter, Bartholomew Arnoldi of Usingen, John von Paltz, and John Nathin.

We are here face to face with the remarkable fact that, in condemning Scholasticism, Luther opposed the theologians to whose school he himself belonged and among and from whom he had received his training. In manner and method of theological argument, he remained an Occamist all his life. In these lectures, the "modernist" orientation of his mind is most apparent in his general view of God and the world, in his psychological conceptions,[66] and especially in his interest in the proper understanding of terms and words, and in the interpretation of them according to their etymological meaning. However, in view of the fact that he radically broke with Scholasticism in general and with Occamism in particular when he rediscovered the gospel in connection with his fresh understanding of the Pauline doctrine of justification, we must not be surprised if we find that Occamism influenced him negatively rather than positively. In other words, in directing his criticism of Scholastic theology chiefly against certain tenets that were characteristic of the teachings of his own theological masters, he let his thinking be determined and colored by themes and emphases characteristic of Occamism.

The lectures on Romans show plainly that what he was opposed to in Scholasticism was, first of all, the interpretation of the Christian gospel through the philosophy of Aristotle, whose metaphysics he regarded as "fallacious" ("*fallax*")[67] and whose ethics he believed to be "the worst enemy of grace."[67a]

Luther expresses this criticism of philosophy in an impressive way in connection with his comment on Rom. 8:19: "The expectation of the creature waits for the revelation of the sons of God." He writes in part:[68] "The apostle philosophizes and thinks about the things of the world in another way than do the philosophers and metaphysicians, and he understands them differently from the way they do. . . . He does not speak of the 'essence' of the creature, and of the way it 'operates,' or of its 'action' or 'inaction,' and 'motion,' but, using a new and strange theological word, he speaks of 'the expectation of the creature.' . . . But alas, how deeply and painfully we are caught up in categories and quiddi-

---

[66] I.e., he distinguishes basically between *intellectus* and *affectus*. Melanchthon (CR 6, 159) reports concerning Luther's Ockhamism: "*Huius acumen anteferebat Thomae et Scoto. Diligenter et Gersonem legerat.*"

[67] *WA* 56, 349, 23.

[67a] *WA* 1, 226, 10: "*Tota fere Aristotelis Ethica pessima est gratiae inimica.*"

[68] *WA* 56, 371, 2.

ties, and how many foolish opinions befog us in metaphysics!
When shall we learn to see that we are wasting much precious
time with such useless studies. . . !

"Indeed, I believe that I owe this duty to the Lord of crying out
against philosophy and turning men to Holy Scripture. . . . I have
been in the grind of these studies for, lo, these many years and am
worn out by it and, on the basis of long experience, I have come
to be persuaded that it is a vain study, doomed to perdition. . . .
It is high time that we be transferred from these other studies and
learn Jesus Christ and 'him crucified.' "[69]

Another objection of Luther's to Scholasticism is closely connected with this rejection of philosophy: he was persuaded that
the Scholastics agreed with the opinion of Aristotle expressed in
the *Nichomachean Ethics*, namely, that "we become righteous by
performing righteous actions."[70] In opposition to this, Luther advanced the thesis that he states several times in this commentary
(and which, as a matter of fact, he maintained throughout his
career) that "we are not made righteous by doing righteous deeds,
but that in so far as we are righteous we perform righteous acts."[71]
Indeed, in these lectures on Romans, he introduces this view for
the first time in connection with the brief comment on Rom. 1:17.
Quoting Augustine over against Aristotle and pointing his remarks at the Scholastics, he there sharply distinguishes the "righteousness of men" (in terms of which they are righteous in themselves and before their fellow men) from the "righteousness of
God" (by which, through faith in the gospel, they are made
righteous). In other words, he maintains that men are always in
need of being made righteous, for, in themselves, they are unrighteous even if they think that they are righteous.

It is this view of man's predicament and salvation which in
these lectures on Romans, Luther presents to his readers almost
to the point of tiring them.

As we have already pointed out, it was mainly about the con-

---

[69] It seems that Luther never found philosophy attractive. He wrote to his
friend John Braun, a priest at Eisenach, on March 17, 1509, when he was
a lecturer in philosophy at the University of Wittenberg: "My studies are
very severe, especially philosophy, which from the first I would gladly have
exchanged for theology; I mean that theology which searches out the meat
of the nut and the kernel of the grain and the marrow of the bones." (*WA,
Br* 1, 17, 4; cf. P. Smith, *Luther's Correspondence* [Philadelphia, 1913], I,
24.)

[70] *Eth. Nicom.*, II, 1 (Penguin ed., tr. by J. A. K. Thompson), p. 56. This
point is not so prominent in Aristotle's *Ethics* as Luther makes it appear in
his criticisms.

[71] *WA* 56, 255, 19. Cf. *WA* 1, 226: *"Non 'efficimur iusti iusta operando' sed
iusti facti operamur iusta."*

ception of human nature that he found himself in disagreement with the Occamists. In a letter to his intimate friend John Lang (who taught Greek and exegesis in Wittenberg, from 1511 until 1516, and who, in 1518, was to become Luther's successor as District Vicar of the Saxon Augustinians) Luther wrote at the beginning of October, 1516, just after he had completed his Romans lectures:[72] "I know what Gabriel Biel says, and it is all very good, except when he deals with grace, love, hope, faith, and virtue. To what an extent he there Pelagianizes together with his Scotus, I can now not explain by letter."[73] These words show that Luther regarded Biel and Scotus (and, of course, Ockham too) as Pelagians; he believed that they held a view of human nature that was irreconcilable with the Biblical conception of salvation. Two notions in particular aroused his ire, as his frequent, often passionately bitter, discussions of them in the Romans commentary indicate: (1) The teaching that man is able to love God above everything by his natural powers, apart from grace; and (2) the teaching that under grace, i.e., by virtue of the infused habitus of grace, man is enabled to perform works of righteousness and earn merits thereby.

Luther was certain that in each case not only man's need of justification but also the actuality of his justification through God's grace in Christ was being denied. Hence his angry characterization of the Occamists as *Sautheologen*, i.e., theologians who made a mess of interpreting the Christian gospel; and hence also his frequent impatient criticisms of the *"iustitiarii"* ("justiciars," i.e., persons who pretend to have achieved justice or righteousness in themselves and who, therefore, are "moralists" and "meritmongers" because they handle morality or righteousness in the same way in which lawyers are wont to deal with justice).

These basic points in the teachings of the Scholastics implied doctrines that also aroused Luther's opposition. There was, first of all, the distinction between the fulfillment of God's law according to the substance of the deed (*quoad substantiam facti*) and that according to the intention of God, the lawgiver (*ad intentionem precipientis*). This doctrine, which can be found in the writings of Duns Scotus and particularly in those of Ockham and

---

[72] *WA, Br* 1, 66, 3: *"Cum Scoto suo, quantum pelagizet Gabriel."*
[73] These remarks show that Luther himself was aware to what an extent he was indebted to Gabriel Biel. And this is not surprising, for, as we have already mentioned, he knew large parts of Biel's writings by heart (according to Melanchthon). Nevertheless, he was sure that Biel had misunderstood the main tenets of the Christian faith. Cf. Paul Vignaux, *Philosophy in the Middle Ages* (Meridian Books, Inc., 1959), p. 213.

Biel,[74] implied that man is able by his own powers to accomplish a true love of God but in such a way that he does not earn eternal life thereby, because for this, supernatural grace is necessary. Luther rejected this co-ordination of nature and grace because he felt that grace was understood therein as if it were a new "exaction" or requirement of God in addition to the law. Moreover, all this appeared to him as theological teaching of a Pelagian sort. In the lectures on Romans he takes no account of the fact that Ockham (who taught, indeed, that man can perform good works apart from grace) tried to avoid Pelagianism by advancing the radical view that no human work can be meritorious, i.e., earn eternal life, by virtue of the fact that a man performs it, no matter whether he does so under grace or apart from it, but only by virtue of God's freely accepting it (*est in libera acceptatio divina*).[75]

To be sure, one can observe a certain kinship between Ockham and Luther in so far as both insisted that man becomes acceptable to God, not by his own merit or action, but only by God's.[75a] However, Luther was never able, as Ockham was, to stress divine as well as human freedom. Nor could he follow Ockham in separating morality from religion. He affirmed with great vigor that God demands the fulfillment of his law, and he held on to this conviction precisely in the teaching that it is not human virtue but divine mercy that is the condition of the fulfillment of the law. He understood the gospel to say that God accepts the sinner by mercifully justifying him, i.e., by making him righteous through forgiveness. It is therefore not surprising that he did deal specifically with Ockham's teaching on the divine *acceptatio:* He directed the fifty-sixth thesis of his *Disputation Against Scholastic Theology* expressly against Ockham. It reads: "God cannot accept man apart from justifying grace."[76]

---

[74] Cf. Duns Scotus, III *Sent.*, d. 27, q. un., n. 13; Ockham, III *Sent.*, q. 8B; Biel, II *Sent.*, d. 28K. See Holl's discussion in *Ges. Aufs.* I, 171 ff., also that by Iserloh, in *Gnade und Eucharistie*, pp. 129 f.

[75] Cf. Ockham, I *Sent.*, d. 17, q. 2E: "*Dico primo quod actus meritorius nec etiam actus charitatis excedit totam facultatem naturae humanae, quia omnis actus charitatis quem secundum communem cursum habemus in via et eiusdem rationis cum actu ex puris naturalibus possibilis et ita illa actus non excedit facultatem naturae nostrae. Verum illum actum esse meritorium non est in potestati naturae humanae . . . sed est in libera dei acceptatione.*"

[75a] Cf. Luther's gloss on Rom. 4:3–4, where he says that the words "counted to him unto righteousness" of Gen. 15:6, which Paul quotes ("Abraham believed, and it was counted to him," etc.), express only God's free acceptance ("*solam gratuitam Dei acceptationem*") and not the merit of the believer (*WA* 56, 41, 23).

[76] *WA* 1, 227: "*Non potest deus acceptare hominem sine gratia justificante.*" (*Contra Occam.*)

It was in line with the rejection of this doctrine of Occamist theology that he also found untenable the teaching that by acting according to his natural moral sense (*facere quod in se est*) man can earn merits before God (*meritum de congruo*), and that once he is in possession of grace (through the sacrament), he is able to "elicit" from his soul acts of loving God or to produce the "good intention" of doing good works. This teaching concerning man's ability of doing good (*facere quod in se est*) as well as that concerning man's sacramentally conditioned potentiality for good works (the doctrines about the *actus eliciti* and the *bonae intentiones*) aroused his ire, as his repeated arguments in the exposition of the letter to the Romans show, because, in his judgment those who advanced these teachings did not take seriously, on the one hand, man's sin, i.e., his inability of doing the good, and on the other hand, God's sovereignty, i.e., the all-sufficiency of his freely given mercy and grace.

If we ask what motivated Luther to advance the criticisms against Scholastic theology, we must answer (on the basis of his statements in this commentary) that he regarded the piety which underlay this theology as an irreligious affectation of religion (to use Calvin's phrase),[76a] because it was marked, he felt, by a concern for eternal happiness reflecting man's love of God for his own sake and not for God's sake. Luther calls this way of loving God through which men seek eternal bliss *amor concupiscentiae*, i.e., a covetous or selfish love.

He writes, for example, in connection with Paul's statement (Rom. 9:3), "I wish that I myself were anathema for my brethren's sake": "we should note that these words must appear strange and even foolish to those who regard themselves as holy and who love God with a covetous love, i.e., for the sake of their own salvation and eternal rest and for the purpose of avoiding hell; in other words: not for God's sake but for their own sake. These are the ones who babble that ordered love (*caritas ordinata*) begins with self-love and that everyone must first desire his own salvation and then also his neighbor's in the same way as he yearns for his own. . . . But, as a matter of fact, to be blessed means to seek in everything God's will and God's glory and to want nothing for oneself neither here nor in the life to come."[77]

[76a] Cf. John Calvin, *Institutes of the Christian Religion*, II. viii. 5: "*irreligiosa religionis affectatio.*"

[77] *WA* 56, 390, 23. The "babblers" Luther here has in mind appear to be Duns Scotus (III *Sent.*, d. 29, q. *un.*) and Gabriel Biel (III *Sent.*, d. 29, q. *un.*, a. 2). Cf. also his comment on Rom. 5:5 (*WA* 56, 307, 28): "To love God for the sake of his gifts and for the sake of one's advantage is to love

This last sentence states Luther's fundamental religious and
mysticism theological principle. We do not fully understand it unless we
realize that it was in part inspired by mysticism. We, therefore,
find ourselves directed to still another source on which Luther relied in preparing his lectures. We must not fail to observe that he
here depends on Dionysius the Areopagite (whom he later came
to detest), especially in so far as he insists that man can think of
God only *via negationis* and that he can reach him only through a
rapture that takes him out of himself. But we must notice especially how strongly he is here under the influence of John Tauler.
(In his lectures, he mentions him specifically only once,[78] but then,
to be sure, with high praise.)

What the mystics (among whom we should mention also the
author of the *German Theology* and particularly Staupitz to
whom, according to his own confession, Luther owed much)
meant to him is very well stated in a letter he addressed on March
31, 1518, to Staupitz in which he defends himself against certain
charges that he had condemned rosaries and good works generally;
it is a letter that also reflects enlighteningly a significant aspect of
Luther's attitude toward Scholasticism. He says:[79] "Now what
I have done is that I follow the theology of Tauler and of that
book[80] which you recently gave to Christian Düring to print; I
teach that men should trust in nothing save in Jesus only, and not
in their own prayers, or merits, or works, for we shall not be saved
by our own exertions but by the mercies of God (Rom. 9:16). . . .

"My adversaries excite hatred against me from the Scholastic
doctors, because I prefer the fathers and the Bible to them; . . . I
read the Scholastics with judgment, not as they do, with closed
eyes. . . . I neither reject all that they say nor approve all. . . . If
Duns Scotus, Gabriel Biel, and others like them had the right to
dissent from Aquinas, and if in turn the Thomists have the right
to contradict everybody so that there are as many schools among
the Schoolmen as there are heads, or as hairs on each head, why
should they not allow men the same right against them as they
use against each other?"

Luther, therefore, knew that Scholasticism did not represent a

---

him with a very cheap love, i.e., to love him selfishly [*concupiscentia eum
diligere*]." Then Luther adds, characteristically, "This means to use God
and not to enjoy him." The words and the notion are Augustine's.
Augustine is thus invoked against the Scholastics. Luther does not seem to
have observed that his criticism would fit Augustine too.
[78] *WA* 56, 378, 13.
[79] *WA, Br* 1, 160, 8 (Smith, *Corr.* I, 78). To Staupitz, March 31, 1518.
[80] Probably the complete *German Theology*, which Johann Grunenberg
printed in Wittenberg.

united theological front, but also then the Roman Church through the papacy and the hierarchy tended to impose a uniformitarian authoritarianism upon the thinking of its members, as he must have realized when he wrote this letter. Yet he believed in debate—of the kind that the medieval scholars taught and practiced. Indeed, throughout his life, he employed the method of "disputation"; it enabled him to develop his own agreement and disagreement with the position of others. In virtue of his scholastic training and from personal inclination, he was a dialectical thinker who said yes as well as no to the teachings of others.

Just as the rejection of certain parts of the doctrines of the Occamists, therefore, did not prevent him from approving other parts of it, so his hearty approval of Tauler did not mean that he accepted all of Tauler's views. Indeed, as we who belong to a later generation easily recognize, Luther was no mystic in his own right, even though he was profoundly influenced by the medieval mystical theologians. He learned from them resignation and an understanding of humility that was more personal than that induced by monastic discipline. Moreover, they taught him (i.e., Bernard, Hugh of St. Victor, Pseudo-Dionysius, Gerson, and especially Tauler) the language and speech of religious devotion. He felt for a long time that he owed to Tauler something that was decisive for his whole religion. "I learned more from Tauler alone than from all the other Scholastics," he wrote to John Eck on Jan. 7, 1519;[81] and, almost two years earlier, he had urged his friend Spalatin, who was then enthusiastic about Humanism, to read Tauler's sermons, which he himself had studied with much care and profit. "With all your powers," he admonished him,[82] "lay hold of the book of Tauler's sermons. . . . From this book you will see how the learning of our age is iron—or rather, earthen—be it Greek, Latin, or Hebrew, compared to this learning of true piety."

What Luther had in mind here was probably the renunciation of all self-righteousness, for this was the "learning" which he himself endeavored to communicate to his students as he lectured to them on the letter to the Romans. What he understood the "learning of true piety" to be, he describes very well in a letter to his one-time *contubernalis*, i.e., monastic companion, George Spenlein, written on April 8, 1516, i.e., at a time when he was still occupied with the letter to the Romans. Indeed, he expresses the basic idea of his lectures as he writes:[83] "Now I would like to know

[81] *WA, Br* 1, 296, 24 (Smith, *Corr.* I, 147). To John Eck, Jan. 7, 1519.
[82] *WA, Br* 1, 96, 21 (Smith, *Corr.* I, 56). To Spalatin, ca. May 6, 1517.
[83] *WA, Br* 1, 35, 15 (Smith, *Corr.* I, 34). To George Spenlein, April 8, 1516.
  Cf. a similar statement in *WA* 56, 204, 14.

whether your soul, tired of her own righteousness, would learn to breathe and confide in the righteousness of Christ. For nowadays the presumption besets many, especially those who with all their powers try to be righteous and good. They do not know the right-eousness of God, which is most bountifully and freely given us in Christ, and so they seek to do good in and by themselves until such a time as they feel confident that they can stand before God adorned with their own virtues and merits, but this cannot pos-sibly be done. You yourself were of this opinion, or rather error, and so was I, and even now I fight against this error and have not yet conquered it.

"Therefore, my dear brother, learn Christ and him crucified, learn to pray to him, despairing of yourself, saying: 'Thou, Lord Jesus, art my righteousness, but I am thy sin; thou hast taken on thyself what thou wast not, and hast given to me what I was not.' Beware of ever aspiring to such purity that you do not want to seem to yourself, or to be, a sinner. For Christ dwells only in sinners.

"It was for this that he came down from heaven, where he dwelt in the righteous, that he might dwell also in sinners. Think about this love of his and you will see how beautifully it will comfort and sustain you. For if it is only by our own efforts and strivings that we can achieve a quiet conscience, what did he die for? You will therefore find peace only in him, in faith despairing in your-self and your own works [per fiducialem desperationem tui et operum tuorum]; and thus you will learn that as he took you up and made your sins his own, he made his righteousness yours."

"The learning of true piety"—this is a term which describes the mystic's way of life, but it also characterizes the work of a monk. Now it is Luther, the monk, that we must think of as we follow his exposition of the theology of the apostle Paul. Again and again, we see him directing his thought to the practice of religion—ac-cording to the fashion of a religiosus, a monk. Indeed, we are made vividly aware of the fact that a monk is talking to monks in these lectures: we find Luther discussing with his hearers the mission and the trials of the monastic life; we notice that he weaves phrases from the liturgy and the breviary of the Augustinians into his ex-position; and we realize as we hear him quoting the Psalter, the prayer book of the monks, how all his thinking is shaped by the piety of The Psalms understood in terms of Christian doctrine and worship. But the most decisive evidence of the influence of the monastic life and discipline upon his thought are his repeated de-scriptions and analyses of the several ways of religious devotion and his many characterizations of the practitioners of this devotion. He appears to have been a sharp observer of his fellow monks as well as of himself. Otherwise, he would not be able to speak so realistically of the whole scale of religious vices, from self-satisfied pride to anguished despair, or of the broad range of the virtues of the religious, extending from abject humility to a triumphant sense of liberty. What makes so many of his interpretations of the religious life so touching and so moving is that often he evidently speaks out of his own experience about his spiritual failures and victories.

But we have still not mentioned that part of his thought which represents the plainest echo of his monastic experience, namely, that which is obviously a reverberation of the conflict of the Augustinian convent at Erfurt with the leadership of the order about the projected union of the German congregation of the so-called observant cloisters with the so-called conventual or "lax" convents (1509–1511). The Erfurters were Observants; they insisted upon a strict enforcement of the rule and refused to make common cause with those who did not. Luther probably shared their view concerning the policy the order should pursue; otherwise, he would not have been sent to Rome as *socius itinerarius* of the brother who was instructed to lay the views of the Observants before the highest superiors of the Augustinian order. But when this mission had ended in failure, he urged his fellows to yield freely and obediently to those of higher authority (who, by the way, soon thereafter abandoned their plan of union). It may well be that, at the behest of Staupitz, he was then definitely transferred from Erfurt to Wittenberg in order to be extricated from a difficult situation in relation to his fellow monks, but we have no solid information about this.

It may also be that his own religious development was decisively affected by the whole dispute, but we have no certain knowledge about this either. However, many passages in the lecture notes on The Psalms and on the letter to the Romans deal outspokenly with this monastic conflict and with the religious attitudes that were disclosed by many who were involved in it. Luther speaks here on behalf of obedience to the superiors and in opposition to all forms of nonconformity. Again and again he demands that Christians should submit to their superiors (*prelati*). He condemns the *monii* (individualists) who apparently insisted, to the point of fanaticism, on having their way according to their own lights (*singularitates*).[84]

Their religious zeal and their puritanical concern for strict

[84] The most searching discussion of Luther's relation to the Observants is that of Holl (*op. cit.*, pp. 199 ff.).

moral standards remind him of the religion of Baal which, he says,[85] "represented a dreadful righteousness and a superstitious religion" ("*monstrum iustitiae et pietatis superstitiosae*"). And then he continues: "Both have prevailed widely until today. They are to be found among the Jews, the heretics, and the nonconformists, i.e., those conceited individualists who worship the true God according to their own mind. In their exceedingly foolish zeal and eccentric religiousness [*nimia pietate*], they are worse than all the godless: for the sake of God, they are enemies of God; because of the fear of God, they despise him; for the sake of religion, they become ungodly; for the sake of peace, they disturb the peace; because of love and saintliness, they become jealous and profane; and because of humility, they are proud."

It is not difficult to imagine that, in the course of all these discussions and debates about the standards of the monastic life, Luther's personal inner struggle for "a merciful God" was pushed to the point of decision and resolution. His own share in these conversations perhaps brought about in his mind that understanding of the Christian gospel which, in his own judgment, constituted a rediscovery of the gospel, giving him that sense of authority as an interpreter of God's word from which he spoke henceforth. However, we have no documents in which this is recorded and we cannot therefore further pursue this point. But this much we know from ample and reliable sources: Luther himself attributed to his training and experience as a monk a decisive significance (both positive and negative in character) for his becoming a believer in Christ and a Christian man.

Also in connection with this aspect of his thought, we are thus led to observe that Luther found himself compelled to criticize and oppose that with which he himself was deeply at one. He was a faithful and devout monk, but he transcended monasticism by the thoroughness and relentlessness of his examination of what God requires of men. Likewise, he was a loyal son of the Roman Catholic Church (and in many respects, this commentary is an impressive example of his Roman Catholic churchmanship), but he could not be a submissive respecter of the authority of the leaders of the church in so far as he found them faulty if their acts were measured by the standard of the Bible and faith in Christ (*fides Christi*). Even in these lectures, he inveighs with ruthless honesty and from a sense of prophetic mission against the corruption of the faith in highest places, including the Curia at Rome.

We have seen that he dealt similarly with Occamist theology: from a thorough knowledge of it that only a follower and partisan

[85] *WA* 56, 430, 6.

could command, he examined its religious adequacy—or rather, its Biblical-Christian adequacy—and he found it wanting. Likewise, despite his deep attachment to Augustine, whom he considered his greatest theological ally, he found himself driven to go beyond him at a decisive point, a point decisive for Augustine and for himself: Augustine's religion somehow remained grounded in and pointed to self-fulfillment, but Luther's religion was a free trusting in God's _gift_ of forgiveness and therefore a reliance upon a "foreign righteousness" that entailed an utter self-surrender and a becoming dependent on resources that no man can ever call his own.

It was this religion which forced Luther to reject any form of self-righteousness as a lie and self-deception, and to search with inflexible honesty for truthfulness in the presence of God who can never lie. The two sources of this religion were Jesus Christ (according to the witness of the Bible interpreted in terms of the teachings of the apostle Paul) and his conscience (i.e., his knowledge of himself before God[86] at the deepest level of his being).

This is Luther as he speaks from these lecture notes—linked by many strains of thought to a great variety of teachings and traditions but at the same time transcending them all in virtue of the sovereignty of his faith in Christ alone.

IV. THE SIGNIFICANCE OF LUTHER'S LECTURES

We have dealt all along with the significance of these lectures. We shall not attempt to sum up the several remarks we have made, nor shall we try to give now a résumé and evaluation of the whole work (for this would far exceed the limits of an introduction). We shall confine ourselves to a few concluding observations that may be found helpful to anyone who wishes properly to understand this work.

The reader of these lectures must never lose sight of the fact that he follows the thinking of Luther, a professor of Biblical theology in the early sixteenth century, as he prepared himself for the classroom sessions with his students (most of whom were Augustinian monks) in the recently founded University of Wittenberg.

One of these students has left us a vivid picture of Luther at his lectures: "He was a man of middle stature, with a voice which combined sharpness and softness: it was soft in tone; sharp in the

---

[86] See Luther's remark at the very end of his commentary, where he identifies conscience with man's standing before God (_"coram Deo"_): "Our conscience either puts us to shame or robes us with honor before God." Cf. Hirsch, _op. cit._, Vol. I, 140.

enunciation of syllables, words, and sentences. He spoke neither too quickly nor too slowly, but at an even pace, without hesitation and very clearly, and in such fitting order that each part flowed naturally out of what went before. He did not expound each part in long labyrinths of words, but first the individual words, then the sentences, so that one could see how the content of the exposition arose and flowed out of the text itself. . . . For this is how he took it from a book of essential matter which he had himself prepared, so that he had his lecture material always ready to hand— conclusions, digressions, moral philosophy, and also antithesis; and so his lectures never contained anything that was not pithy or relevant. And, to say something about the spirit of the man: if even the fiercest enemies of the gospel had been among his hearers, they would have confessed from the force of what they heard that they had witnessed, not a man, but a spirit, for he could not teach such amazing things from himself, but only from the influence of some good or evil spirit."[87]

That Luther's lectures on the letter to the Romans made a deep impression on his students is attested by the fact that the notebooks of several of them, apparently much used, have come down to us. Students generally keep only those of their notebooks which they cherish and to which they attribute some value! And only those notebooks survive several generations which, from the outset, had the reputation of being important!

There is nothing in these students' notes that cannot be found in Luther's own text. The difference between the two sets is that what Luther dictated and spoke in the classroom was clear and succinct, whereas what he had written down in preparing himself for the course was frequently groping, long-winded, and circumstantial. This applies only to the scholia; the glossae were transmitted to the class exactly as he had prepared them. It is astonishing to see how much of the material of his own notebook he left out in his classroom teaching. Passages in which he discloses his own deepest thoughts or in which he attacks either the Scholastics or the secular and ecclesiastical powers for their failure to live up to the gospel are not directly reflected in the students' notes.

We must therefore read his lectures with the thought that, in following his exposition, we observe him as he endeavors to understand the words and arguments of the apostle Paul in order to be able to interpret them to his students. In other words: this book contains Luther's ideas as he formulated them in the study in getting ready for his responsibility as a teacher. It is a book that is

[87] Cf. H. Boehmer—H. Bornkamm, *Der junge Luther* (Hamburg, 1939), p. 367, as translated by Gordon Rupp in *Luther's Progress to the Diet of Worms, 1521* (Wilcox and Follett, 1951), p. 44.

not addressed to any audience. It was written in the knowledge that only parts of it would be communicated to students in a classroom, and the author knew as he wrote it that he would not publish it in the form it assumed as he worked on it under the pressures of the teaching routine and within the limits of the academic timetable. Yet as he wrote, he thought of the students whom he soon would have to instruct. And so he would sometimes write out a direct appeal to them and address them directly. It is noteworthy that these direct appeals and admonitions do not appear in the notebooks of the students. He does not seem actually to have delivered them as he thought he would when he planned what he was going to say.

If we want to assess the significance of this book, we can therefore not reckon with that factor which is generally regarded as highly important for the evaluation of a publication, namely, the immediate influence it exercises upon the public of its readers. This book had no reading public until it was published nearly four hundred years after it was written! Then, to be sure, it had a profound effect. Indeed, it became the springhead and focus of a Luther renaissance in Protestant thought and life. Through it Luther became again a living influence. This fact points to the main reason why this book is so significant: it is a telling document of Luther's development.

The content and method of this book show why, by 1516, Luther was the leader of the reform of the theological curriculum at Wittenberg: Biblical theology was substituted for philosophical theology, Paul for Aristotle, Biblical exegesis for the interpretation of Peter Lombard's *Books of Sentences*. Here was a man whose searching studies of the Bible had made him see that Scholastic theology had become barren, and who was so bold as to introduce changes. His words and ideas carried persuasion, for he won the support not only of his students but also of his colleagues. He had a sense of mission. Without it he could not have accomplished what he did. But he believed that he was merely doing his duty. Though he rejoiced in the response he received and the success he obtained and though he believed in the necessity of a general reform of theological studies and of ecclesiastical practices, he did not entertain the ambition of playing the role of a reformer on the stage of world history.

It is true, he demanded not only a reform of theological studies but also one of the church and religion, but he advanced these demands only in connection with his office as a theological doctor and teacher and not in connection with any aspiration toward the role of a prophet.

In his interpretation of the first two thirds of Paul's letter, he criticizes mainly Scholasticism. He calls for the abandonment of the philosophical (i.e., Aristotelian) approach to theology. In the last third, in connection with the exposition of the Pauline ethic, he attacks all kinds of evil practices of the church, including those perpetrated in highest places, and he calls for a basic reform of Christian piety. "It is foolish and preposterous," he writes,[88] "today and at any time, to identify the Christian religion outwardly with this ostentatious display that . . . is being practiced in the observance of distinctions between feast days, foods, habits, and places, while in the meantime God's commandments and faith and love are utterly disregarded." Or, referring to the commandment of loving the neighbor, he says:[89] "It is strange, indeed, that there is not more concern for such an important teaching of so great an apostle, a teaching which is manifestly that of the Holy Spirit. Instead, we occupy ourselves with matters that are trifling by comparison: we build churches; we expand ecclesiastical property; we accumulate money; we provide the church with more and more ornaments and vessels of gold and silver; we install organs and other ostentatious pieces of display. We practice all our piety in activities of this kind and are not one whit concerned about what the apostle here commands. And I have not even mentioned the monstrous display of pride, ostentation, greed, extravagance, and ambition that is connected with these enterprises!"

There is a direct line between statements of this kind and the *Theses on the Power of Indulgences* which, as things were to turn out, started an open conflict between Luther and the Roman Church, and consequently inaugurated the Protestant Reformation. Luther was consistently of the conviction that right teaching would produce the necessary changes in the church. Thus he could write, early in 1518 (when the opposition against him was just beginning to raise its head) to his former teacher in Erfurt, Jodocus Trutvetter, who was greatly disturbed about the debate that was going on about the source and norm of Christian truth:[90] "I simply believe that it is impossible to reform the church unless the canon law, the Decretals, Scholastic theology, philosophy, and logic as they are now taught are thoroughly rooted out, and other studies put in their stead. With respect to this opinion, I proceed in such a way that I daily ask the Lord as far as now may be that the pure study of the Bible and the fathers may be restored. You think I am no logician; perhaps I am not, but I know that I fear no one's logic when I defend this opinion."

[88] *WA* 56, 496, 4.
[89] *WA* 56, 452, 2.
[90] *WA, Br* 1, 170, 33.

It is in this same vein that he wrote his commentary on the letter to the Romans. Its importance, therefore, consists in this, that it shows Luther on the road to the Reformation—at a time when, as these lectures also clearly demonstrate, he was bound with all the fibers of his soul to the Roman Catholic Church, hating nothing so much as heresy and arbitrary defiance of clerical authority.

But a weightier explanation of the significance of these lectures is this: they prove that Luther became a reformer not because he felt that he was one in the long succession of those who had called and were calling for a renewal of the church. There is scarcely any evidence in his early writings that he was interested in the reforming movements and programs connected with the names of Wycliffe, Hus, Savonarola, the *devotio moderna,* or Erasmus. He became a reformer because his basic understanding of the Christian gospel led him to oppose teachings and practices that he found irreconcilable with it and not because he identified himself or sympathized with any advocates of reform.

What his basic understanding of the gospel was and how he achieved clarity about it—this is what is impressively and movingly displayed in these lectures on the letter to the Romans, more so than in any other of his writings. And this understanding of the gospel was unique, in the sense that nobody else among his contemporaries attained and explained it in quite the same way as he did, namely, by way of a marvelous concentration upon the Pauline and Augustinian teachings on justification and through a creative interpretation of the whole Bible in terms of these teachings, an interpretation that was at the same time quickened by what he underwent in his own struggle for salvation and in his direct experience of the wrath and the love of God. How this understanding assumed a definite personal form of thought—in the setting of the complexities of medieval Biblical exegesis, the arguments and disputations of Scholastic theology, and the piety and asceticism of the cloister—this is all forcefully displayed in these exegetical lectures.

There are few commentaries that are marked by as pronounced a personal character as this one. From almost every page Luther speaks personally to his would-be hearers and readers, not in the sense that he speaks about himself, but in the sense that he shows how he personally obtains the understanding of Paul's teaching. This book, therefore, is unusual because it is personal in several respects: (1) It vividly shows how its author endeavors to comprehend the meaning of Paul's letter to the Romans not merely through his philological and theological intellect but at the depth of his personal being. (2) It presents an interpretation of the letter in which there is presupposed with respect to everything that is asserted the personal involvement of the reader. (3) It documents the personal growth of the commentator: at the end of his lectures, Luther speaks much more freely, more boldly, and with greater certainty than at the beginning. We who know what role Luther was to play in the course of his career cannot help sensing that he speaks from these lecture notes as a man of destiny.

"If God gives his promise," he writes in the gloss on Rom. 4:17,[91] "and there is none who believes him as he gives it, then certainly God's promise will not amount to anything and it cannot be fulfilled, for inasmuch as there is none to receive it, it cannot be a promise to anyone. Therefore, faith must be there to ratify the promise, and the promise needs the faith on the part of him to whom it is given."

This notion was the nerve center of Luther's religion. And this commentary, written when he was still a monk and a faithful member of the Papal Church, explains more powerfully and persuasively than any writing of his composed later as a Reformer and as the leader of Lutheranism what he took God's promise and man's faith to be: the justification of the sinner through the gift of Christ's righteousness as it is received with humility and the surrender of self, God's righteousness triumphant over all human self-righteousness. For "the purpose of every word of Scripture and of God's every action is to effect the change by which every man becomes spiritually a sinner, and this change must take place in our self-awareness and self-esteem."[92]

---

[91] WA 56, 46, 13.
[92] WA 56, 233, 5: "Sed dicendum, Quis modus iste sit, quo hominem spiritualiter fieri oportet peccatorem. Est enim non naturalis. Quia sic non fit, Sed est omnis homo peccator. Sed tota Vis huius mutationis latet in sensu seu estimatione ac reputatione nostra. Hunc enim mutare intendit omnis sermo Scripturae et omnis operatio Dei."

LECTURES ON ROMANS

ROMANS, CHAPTER ONE

Paul, a servant of Jesus Christ. (Rom. 1:1.)
The sum and substance of this letter is: to pull down, to pluck up, and to destroy all wisdom and righteousness of the flesh (i.e., of whatever importance they may be in the sight of men and even in our own eyes), no matter how heartily and sincerely they may be practiced, and to implant,[1] establish, and make large the reality of sin (however unconscious we may be of its existence). Hence, Blessed Augustine says in the seventh chapter of his book *On the Spirit and the Letter:*[2] The apostle Paul "contends with the proud and arrogant and with those who are presumptuous on account of their works," etc.; "moreover, in the letter to the Romans, this theme is almost his sole concern and he discusses it so persistently and with such complexity as to weary the reader's attention, yet it is a useful and wholesome wearying." There have always been some among the Jews and the Gentiles who believed it to be sufficient if they possessed virtue and knowledge, not of the kind that is outwardly put on but that which is inward and comes from the heart. This was also the opinion of many philosophers. The best and sincerest among them, only a few of whom except Socrates are well known, practiced this morality not in order to impress other people or to seek their own glory but adhered to it from a true feeling of virtue and wisdom—and yet they could not refrain from being inwardly pleased with themselves and to praise themselves in their heart as righteous and good men. Of such, the apostle says: "Professing themselves to be wise, they became fools," etc. (Rom. 1:22).
But here just the opposite shall be taught. For in the church we

[1] Or: affirm.
[2] Augustine, *De spir. et lit.,* 7, 12.

must not merely see to it that our righteousness and wisdom, which are not worth anything, are neither upheld by our own sense of glory nor extolled by the good opinion of others, but rather, we must take pains that they are destroyed and plucked up from our own complacent inner feeling (even though, according to the Gospel [Matt. 5:15], "the lamp that is lit is not to be put under the bushel but on the stand so that it shines unto all that are in the house" and "the city set on a hill cannot be hid" [Matt. 5:14]). (For when we ourselves despise them, it will be easy for us not to care for the judgment and praise of others.)

As Christ says through the prophet Jeremiah: "to pluck up and to break down and to destroy and to overthrow" (Jer. 1:10), namely, everything that is in us (i.e., all that pleases us because it comes from ourselves and belongs to us) and "to build and to plant," namely, everything that is outside us and in Christ.

This is also the meaning of Daniel's figure of speech concerning the stone which "smote the image" (Dan. 2:34).[3]

For God does not want to save us by our own but by an extraneous righteousness which does not originate in ourselves but comes to us from beyond ourselves, which does not arise on our earth but comes from heaven. Therefore, we must come to know this righteousness which is utterly external and foreign to us. That is why our own personal righteousness must be uprooted[4]—according to Ps. 45 (where we read): "Forget also thine own people and thy father's house" (Ps. 45:10)—just as also Abraham was told to leave his own country. And in the Song of Solomon we read: "Come from Lebanon, my bride, and thou shalt be crowned" (S. of Sol. 4:8). Also, the exodus of the people Israel has for a long time been interpreted to signify the transition from vice to virtue. But one should, rather, interpret it as the way from virtue to the grace of Christ, because virtues are often the greater and worse faults the less they are regarded as such and the more powerfully they subject to themselves all human affections beyond all other goods. So also the right side of Jordan was more fearful than the left one.[5]

But now Christ wants all our feeling to be so bare that, on the one hand, we are not afraid to be cast into confusion on account of our faults, nor delight in praise and vain joy on account of our virtue, yet, on the other hand, we do not glory before men in that

---

[3] Nicholas of Lyra interpreted this passage with reference to Christ, the cornerstone.

[4] "*Igitur omnino externa et aliena iustitia oportet erudiri. Quare primum oportet propriam et domesticam evelli.*"

[5] Cf. Josh. 3:16 and Ps. 114:1–3: "When Israel went out of Egypt, the house of Jacob from a barbarous people, Judah was made his sanctuary, Israel his dominion. The sea saw and fled; Jordan was turned back." Cf. Lyra's comment on this passage.

external righteousness which, coming from Christ, is in us, nor suffer defeat because of those sufferings and evils which befall us for his sake.[6]

Moreover, a true Christian must be so completely stripped of all that he calls his own that neither honor nor dishonor can affect him, because he knows that whatever honor is done to him is done to Christ, whose righteousness and gifts shine in him, and that whatever ignominy is inflicted upon him is inflicted on him as well as on Christ. But, apart from special grace, much practice is required in order that one may reach this perfection. For even if by his native and spiritual gifts a man is wise, righteous, and good in the sight of men, he is not so regarded by God, especially if he himself considers himself as such. Therefore we must keep ourselves humble in all these respects, as if we were still bare, and look for the naked mercy of God that he may reckon us righteous and wise.[7] This, God will do if one has been humble and has not anticipated the divine action by justifying himself and by entertaining too high an opinion of himself—as we read in I Cor. 4:3-5: "I judge not mine own self, but he that judges me is the Lord; wherefore judge nothing before the time," etc.

Certainly there are many who, like the Jews and the heretics, for God's sake disregard and willingly give up all goods at their left hand,[8] namely, the temporal ones; but there are few who for the sake of obtaining Christ's righteousness regard as nothing the goods at their right hand, namely, spiritual goods and righteous works. Certainly the Jews and the heretics are unable to do this. And yet, without this, no one can be saved. For we all hope and wish our own achievements to be accepted by God and rewarded by him. But it remains forever true: "It is not of him that wills, nor of him that runs, but of God that has mercy" (Rom. 9:16).

But in order to come to the letter: I do not believe[9] that its recipients, in view of the fact that the apostle calls them saints

---

6 This sentence seems to be inspired by the piety of the mystics who influenced the young Luther, i.e., Bernard of Clairvaux, Tauler, and Staupitz.

7 Luther's exegesis of the letter to the Romans is determined by the emphasis upon humility as its main theme. This was the dominating note also of his interpretation of the psalms. (Cf. WA 3, 575, 25: "humilitas tota iustita.") Correspondingly, he regarded superbia (pride) as the root of all sin. In this respect, he put special stress upon a theme that was part and parcel of medieval theology. (Cf. Peter Lombard, II Sent., d. 42, c. 7: "Superbia radix cuncti mali, et initium omnis peccati.")

8 Luther liked this figure of speech (at or of the right hand, at or of the left hand). It was derived from the Bible and was used in traditional exegesis, esp. by Augustine.

9 This remark may be directed against Nicholas of Lyra, who believed that the letter was written for the purpose of recalling the Roman Christians from an error of faith.

who are called and beloved of God, were of such a sort that it was necessary for the apostle to mediate between them in their strife and then come to the conclusion that they were all sinners; for if they were Christians, they knew this by their faith. Rather, I think that he took the opportunity of writing to the believers in Rome in order to make available to them a great apostle's witness to their faith and teaching as they struggled with the Jews and Gentiles of Rome who persisted in unbelief and gloried in the flesh over against the humble wisdom of the believers, for these believers had then no choice but to live among them and thus to become involved in contradictions in all they heard and spoke. In this sense he writes in the fifth chapter of Second Corinthians: "We are not again commending ourselves unto you, but speak as giving you occasion of glorying on our behalf, that you may have wherewith to answer them that glory in appearance and not in heart" (II Cor. 5:12).

It is the duty of a prudent minister of God to hold his ministry in honor and to see to it that it is respected by those who are in his charge.

Moreover, it is the duty of a faithful minister not to exceed his powers and not to abuse his office in pride but, rather, to administer it for the benefit of his subjects.

He must be a "prudent and faithful servant" (cf. Matt. 24:45). If he is not prudent, he will become useless, unfit, and unworthy of respect. Persons who in unwise humility practice familiarity with nearly everybody and place themselves on one level with those put in their charge cannot but lose the true authority of leadership, and their familiarity breeds contempt. How gravely they sin! For what belongs to God and is put into their stewardship, and what they should cause to be honored, they permit to be despised! If he is not faithful, he turns into a tyrant who wants to terrify by his power. Instead of seeking to make their high position useful to others, such people want to be feared. Yet according to the apostle, the power of their office is given to them not to destroy but to edify.

If we are to specify these two faults, we say that they are: softness and austerity. Of the first we read in Zech. 11:17: "Woe to the worthless shepherd that leaves the flock!" And of the second, Ezekiel says (Ezek. 34:4): "With force and with rigor have you ruled over them." These are the two main faults from which all the faults of clergymen arise. And no wonder! For softness is rooted in concupiscence, and austerity in irascibility. These are the source of all evil, as we well know. Therefore, it is very perilous to assume an office unless these two beasts have been slain, for they will do the more harm the more power to do harm is available.

In the prologue or preamble of his letter, the apostle presents himself as a most effective example of one who opposes these two monsters. For, in the first place, in order not to be despised by those in his charge as unfit and soft, he magnifies his ministry by endowing it with high honor. In the second place, in order not to be regarded as a willful tyrant, he assures himself of the affection of his subjects by expressing his good will toward them. By a mixture of fear and love he thus prepares them most effectively for the reception of the gospel and the grace of God.

Following the example of the apostle, every clergyman in the church (like an animal that parts the hoof and is clean)[10] should first of all clearly distinguish between himself and his office, i.e., between "the form of God" and "the form of a servant,"[11] and, regarding himself always as the lowliest of all, perform his office in between fear and love entirely for the welfare and advantage of his subjects. Moreover, he must know that because every office is given only for the welfare of the subjects, he must be willing to give it up if he finds that he cannot administer it to the furtherance of the benefit of his subjects or that he blocks it by his person. Certainly, this is the whole sin of a clergyman: that he deprives his ministry of its fruit by one or both of these faults; he will be strictly held responsible for his failure.

Hence, the apostle says: "a servant of Jesus Christ." In this word, there is majesty as well as humility: there is humility in it in so far as he does not consider himself lord and creator according to the manner of proud tyrants who use their power in such a way that they appear to think of nothing else but their own power as if they had produced it and as if they had not received it from someone else. Therefore, they do not find joy in the fruit of power but merely enjoy power itself.

There is majesty in it in so far as he is glad to serve such a Lord. For if it is perilous not to honor and welcome a servant of the emperor, what will happen to those who do not honor and welcome the servants of God? The phrase "a servant of Jesus Christ" is therefore a great and terrible word. I believe that "servant" is here a term used for an office and a dignity; it does not refer to Paul's own service and homage of God, i.e., I believe that the apostle

---

[10] Cf. Lev. 11:3 ff. and Deut. 14:6 ff. These passages were subjected to an allegorical interpretation (e.g., by Lyra). The distinction (made in the Jewish law) between animals that "part the hoof and chew the cud" (and are therefore clean) and animals that "chew the cud but do not part the hoof" (and are therefore unclean) was applied to the difference between the Old and New Testaments. The Jews were regarded as unclean, because they believed in the law (i.e., "chew the cud") and because they do not accept the dogma of the Trinity (i.e., "do not part the hoof").

[11] Cf. Phil. 2:6–7.

does not wish to call attention to his own personal works by which he serves God privately, because this would exemplify arrogance. For who can be so bold as to say with finality: I am a servant of God! in view of the fact that he cannot know whether he has done all that God requires of him? So he says of himself in I Cor. 4:3: "I do not judge mine own self." For it belongs to God alone to judge and decide whether one is a servant or an enemy. So he calls himself emphatically a servant because he wants to confess that he has received his office over others from God, as if he were to say: I preach the gospel and teach the church; I baptize and do other works which are God's alone. And I do not do all this as a lord who is set over you but as a servant who is commissioned to minister to you. So I am a servant in your behalf, and my "service" does not refer to anything else but my duties toward you. Its ultimate concern is God.

This is not the case in that "service" which all of us are equally expected to render to God. To put it briefly: according to the moral and *tropological* sense, everyone is a *servant of God* by and for himself, but, according to the *allegorical* sense, a certain someone is a *servant of God* for others and over others and for the sake of others. The latter, therefore, signifies a sublime dignity, and the former, a complete form of submission and humility. Moreover, concerning the one, one can be certain and can glory in it, but not so with respect to the other. Likewise, the one benefits others and serves them, but by the other one everyone gains benefits only for himself. The one is the special gift of some, but the other must be common to all. The one must perform definite and clearly delineated tasks, while the other must do whatever it can. The one can be there without grace, but the other cannot be there except by grace. The one has more worth, but the other is more wholesome. The one is manifested to men in glory, but the other is sufficiently known not even to oneself, as has been stated above.

Called an apostle (Rom. 1:1), i.e., in order to put it more clearly, called to be an apostle or to the apostolate.

By this term he more definitely specifies the nature of his service and his ministry. For many are servants and ministers of Jesus Christ but not all are apostles. But all apostles are also servants, i.e., ministers, i.e., such as perform the work of the Lord toward and in others as his representatives.

With the first word ("called"), he strikes down three kinds of men who are not called to offices of honor. *First,* the pseudo apostles, who at that time could be found everywhere and whom the devil sowed like tares among the wheat,[12] sending them from

[12] Cf. Matt. 13:25.

the north like the boiling caldron of Jeremiah.[13] *Secondly,* those
who assume an office because of ambition. They may not be false
apostles or false servants, inasmuch as they teach what is right and
true and lead others in a catholic way, yet because they are not
called to this office, they are indicted by this word "called." They
may not be "thieves and robbers"[14] like the false apostles, but still
they are mercenaries who seek their own advantage and not the
cause of Jesus Christ; they show concern for their sheep only in
so far as they expect to reap a profit of honor, gold, or pleasure.
Today a significant number of these is to be found in the church.
To be sure, the Scripture does not indict and condemn them in
the same way as it does the false prophets and the false apostles
(i.e., the heretics and schismatics and the unbelievers) of whom it
is written[15] that they run although they are not sent and speak
without being authorized to do so, and seek after lying (Ps. 4:2),
etc. Yet God finds them wanting, because it is not from free love
but from grasping cupidity that they assume and seek honor for
themselves. *Thirdly,* similar to these are those who force themselves upon their charges or let themselves be forced upon them.
These are worse than those of the second group but not so bad as
those who belong to the first one. But because the holy offices are
so sublime, no danger in this world and the next is more to be
feared; indeed, there is no greater danger than to assume such an
office without a call of God. But, alas, many are today completely
insensitive to all this and do not give it the slightest thought. How
will they be spared if not even those are secure whom God has
called! Judas, the apostle, came to ruin;[16] Saul fell;[17] and David,
the chosen one, fell[18]—and yet they were sublimely called and
anointed! Woe, then, to these wretched ones here.

By the second word ("apostle"), he heightens the dignity of his
office and induces all the greater reverence for it upon the part of
his charges and hearers. For if one must receive every servant of
God with reverence and love (as one who performs God's work in
us), how much more so an apostle! He is the supreme messenger
and the highest angel of the Lord of Lords, i.e., of Jesus Christ.

Indeed, among the many benefits with which God has richly
provided us, we must acknowledge with praise and deepest gratitude also this, that out of his abundant kindness he has given men
such power, lest we should be too much frightened and our sal-

---

13 Cf. Jer. 1:13.
14 Cf. John 10:1.
15 Cf. Jer. 23:21: "I did not send prophets, yet they ran; I did not speak to
them, yet they prophesied."
16 Cf. Luke 22:3.
17 Cf. I Sam. 15:1 ff.
18 Cf. II Sam. 11:2 ff.

vation and the work of God in us should be impeded by too great
a dread if he were to perform his work in us either himself or by
angels. But like a very kindly physician concerned for our infirmity, he has chosen men like ourselves, beings who are familiar
to us and whom we do not need to fear at all, in order that thus
his work in us might prosper and proceed most fruitfully under
the absence of that fear and terror which, in olden times, the
prophets had to suffer when they had to receive the word either
from God or from an angel. Even Moses could not bear this fright.
Because the word had not yet been made flesh,[19] we were not yet
able to comprehend it because of its sublimity and our weakness.
But now it is within our reach and it has become flesh and it is
being transmitted to us by men of flesh and blood. But for that
reason it is not less to be feared and loved. For it is the same word
as before, even if it is no longer terrifying but inspires love. But
the time will come when it will be all the more terrifying to those
who do not want to revere and love it.

Separated unto the gospel of God. (Rom. 1:1.)
This can be understood in a twofold way:
First, according to what is written in Acts 13:2: "The Holy
Spirit said, Separate me Barnabas and Saul for the work whereunto
I have called them." Then the meaning would be this: only he is
placed in the apostolate to the Gentiles, while Peter and the other
apostles are assigned to the ministry of the circumcision and the
Jews. In this way he defines his ministry more fully: he is not only
a "servant" and not only an "apostle of God" but he is also "set
apart" from others, in order by himself alone to be sent to the
Gentiles.
Secondly, according to the word of Gal. 1:15: "But when it was
the good pleasure of God, who separated me even from my
mother's womb, and called me through his grace to reveal his Son
in me, that I might preach him among the Gentiles." Then the
meaning is this: in preference to other Jews he was ordained by
God even from his mother's womb to become an apostle to the
Gentiles. This is prefigured by Jeremiah, who was told: "Before
you came forth out of the womb I sanctified you; I have appointed
you a prophet unto the nations" (Jer. 1:5). This, only Paul has
truly fulfilled. For in the Scriptures the words "sanctify," "separate," and "set apart" signify almost one and the same thing.
It sounds less pretentious and more modest that he calls himself
"set apart" rather than "sanctified," because he does not want to
speak arrogantly of himself.

[19] Cf. John 1:14.

For what is consecrated by God as holy is set apart and separated and thus sanctified, namely, separated, from any association with unholy things.

That is why "I have sanctified you" is the same as to say, "I have set you apart from all profane things." And it is the holy will of God that, in terms of the allegorical interpretation, you set yourselves apart from evil men and, in terms of the moral interpretation, from sins.

Therefore, to say "separated unto the gospel of God" is the same as to say: Relieved from all other tasks, I am dedicated, introduced, and consecrated to this single office to teach the gospel, as a priest is set apart and separated in order to offer the sacrifice. This meaning is more acceptable than the one I mentioned first.

In short, with this word he rebukes those who, though they are set apart to the ministry of God and are therefore in the business of the Lord, are yet involved in other and secular undertakings as if they were of the world. Indeed, the apostle directs our attention to the fact that he is not set apart for any kind of work but solely for the gospel; he says: My chief work is to spread the gospel, as in I Cor. 1:17: "Christ sent me not to baptize but to preach the gospel"; the other apostles may be set apart for other kinds of work, but I am set apart for the gospel.

Which he promised afore. (Rom. 1:2.)

This he says in order that one should not think that the strongest and most telling proof of the truth of the gospel, namely, that its coming is testified to by the Law and the Prophets, is the fruit of our merits and the invention of human wisdom. For the gospel proclaims what according to prophecy it should proclaim. This proves that before it became what it is, it was foreordained in God's counsel to be what it has become. Thus the glory of this teaching belongs to God alone and not to us and our merits and achievements. Before we came into being, it was ordained—as it says itself: "I was set up from everlasting and of old" (i.e., in the form of the law), "before the earth was" (i.e., the church) which was made through me [scil., wisdom] (Prov. 8:23). It is the gospel, the wisdom and power of God, which has established the church and does all that wisdom says of itself in its own praise. So it is written in Amos 3:7: "Surely the Lord God will do nothing except he reveal his secret unto his servants the prophets." And so also in Isa. 48:5 f.: "I have declared it to you from of old" (i.e., in the old law): "before it came to pass I showed it to you, lest you should say, Mine idol" (i.e., the imagination of my wisdom) "has done them and my molten image has commanded them.

You have heard it" (at the time of the Law and the Prophets); "behold all this" (namely, now in the time of grace), etc.

Through his prophets in the Holy Scriptures. (Rom. 1:2.)

He says this in order to indicate the difference of the gospel from the promise given before the times, about which Titus (Titus 1:2) says: "which God, who cannot lie, promised before times eternal." For this promise is the foreordination from eternity of all things to come. But the promise through the prophets happens in time and in human words. It is a wonderful sign of God's condescension that, over and above his eternal promise, he gives this pledge in human words, and not only in oral but also in written ones. All this is done in order that, as the promise is fulfilled, they will serve as the evidence that he had planned it so, so that one may recognize that Christianity[20] did not originate by accident or in the fate of the stars[21] (as many empty-headed people presume), but that it became what it was to be by the certain counsel and premeditated ordination of God. And, for another reason, he rightly adds: "in the Holy Scriptures." For if he had merely said: "through his prophets," the calumny would be possible that he was adducing the dead who, together with their words, no longer exist. But now he refers and points to their writings which are available to this day.

Concerning his Son, who was made to him of the seed of David according to the flesh, who was predestinated the Son of God in power according to the spirit of sanctification by the resurrection of Jesus Christ from the dead. (Rom. 1:3–4.)

As far as I know, this passage has not been adequately and correctly interpreted by anyone. The ancients were blocked by an inadequate interpretation of it, and the moderns because they lacked the Spirit. Nevertheless, making use of the work of others, we are so bold as to test our intellect at it, avoiding any infringement of the spirit of true piety. It seems to me that what the apostle means to say is as follows: The substance, or the object, or (as some say[21a]) the subject of the gospel is Jesus Christ, the Son of

---

[20] Luther writes: *"religio Christi."* In Luther's time, the term *religio* had a twofold significance: (1) It meant the monastic life. A monk was called *religiosus.* (2) In accordance with Cicero's usage (e.g., *De inventione* II, 110), it meant the "service of God." This was also Augustine's understanding of the term (cf. *De civ. Dei,* X, 3: *"Religio . . . nihil aliud est quam cultus divinus"*).

[21] This reference to astrology may have been inspired by the criticisms of Gerson and Pico della Mirandola.

[21a] Nicholas of Lyra.

God, born of the seed of David according to the flesh and now established in power as the King and Lord of all and this according to the Holy Spirit who raised him from the dead. Here the Greek text[22] is most helpful; it reads as follows: "*Concerning his Son, made of the seed of David, who was selected or designated, declared, ordained to be the Son of God in power according to the spirit of sanctification by the resurrection from the dead, even Jesus Christ our Lord.*" Now as to the details: The gospel deals with "his Son," not with the Son of God as such, but with the incarnate One who was born of the seed of David. This means that he emptied himself and became weak. He who was before all, and who made all, now has himself a beginning and was made. Yet the gospel speaks not only of the humility of the Son of God by which he emptied himself but, rather, of the glory and power which after his humiliation he received from God in his humanity; in other words: as the Son of God by his humbling and emptying himself was made the son of David in the weakness of the flesh, so by contrast the son of David, who is weak according to the flesh, is now in turn established and declared to be the Son of God in all power and glory; and, as according to the form of God, he emptied himself into the nothingness of the flesh by being born into the world, so, according to the form of a servant, he fulfilled himself unto the fullness of God by ascending into heaven.

Note how very appropriately the apostle chooses his words: he does not say: "who was the Son of God in power," in the same way in which he says: "who was made according to the flesh." For from the very moment of Christ's conception it was correct to say, in view of the union of the two natures: This Son is the son of David and this man is the Son of God. The first is true because his divinity is emptied and hidden in the flesh. The second is true because his humanity is fulfilled and translated into divinity. And though he was not born as the Son of God but as a human son, he was nevertheless always the Son and is even now the Son of God. But men did not recognize his designation and appointment as the Son of God. Though he was endowed with power over all and was indeed the Son of God, he did not yet exercise it and was not acknowledged as the Son of God. This happened only through the spirit of sanctification. For the Spirit was not yet given because Jesus was not yet glorified. "He shall glorify me" (John 16:14), he

---

[22] Luther used the Pauline commentary of Faber Stapulensis (*Epistolae Pauli Apostoli.* Paris, 1512; 2d ed., 1515). Faber attempted a new translation from Greek into Latin. However, Luther relied chiefly on Laurentius Valla (*Annotationes in latinam Novi Testamenti interpretationem,* edited by Erasmus; Paris, 1505).

said. Through the apostles, the Holy Spirit designated and declared him to be the Son of God with power over all, to whom everything should be subject because God the Father had made him Lord and Christ.[23]

This is what is meant by the phrase "who was predestined to be the Son of God," i.e., this man, the son of David according to the flesh, is declared to be the Son of God in power, namely, set over all things, because he was the son of David in weakness subject to all—and all this "according to the spirit of sanctification." To him, the glorification of Christ must be attributed, as was stated before.

But the Holy Spirit did this only after the resurrection of Christ. Therefore, the apostle adds: "by the resurrection from the dead." For the Holy Spirit was given only after Christ had risen.

It is therefore obvious that "predestined" is a poor translation, in view of the fact that the Greek text reads "*oristhentos*," i.e., "designated," in the sense of "designation" and "determination." So also in the schools, *orismos* means the "designation," "delineation," and "determination" of something that is declared, manifested, and indicated as something to be held and believed. For a "designation" is an indication that "denotes" something. So then, this passage must be understood as follows: In the gospel, Christ is by the Holy Spirit declared and manifested to be the Son of God in power over all things. Before the resurrection this was not revealed and manifested but was, rather, hidden in the flesh of Christ.

And when the passage reads: "the spirit of sanctification" rather than the "Holy Spirit," this does not matter much, for it is the same Spirit who in terms of his effect is called either holy or sanctifying.

Furthermore, when the text says: "in power," it must be understood to speak of the power over all things according to the prophetic word in Ps. 8:6 and Heb. 1:2: "Whom he appointed heir over all things."

We conclude then: the gospel deals with his Son who was born out of the seed of David, and is now manifested as the Son of God with power over all things through the Holy Spirit that was given from the resurrection from the dead, even Jesus Christ our Lord. So you see that the gospel is the message about Christ the Son of God, who was first humbled and then glorified through the Holy Spirit.

To be sure, this genitive: "of Jesus Christ, our Lord"[24] is am-

---

[23] Cf. Acts 2:36.
[24] Cf. Valla. Lyra and Faber argue for the ablative.

biguous. It can be taken as either a genitive or an ablative, because the meaning of the Greek text cannot be definitely determined. If it is a genitive, it must be connected with the word "resurrection" so as to read: "by the resurrection of our Lord Jesus Christ from the dead." If it is an ablative, it must be connected with the phrase: "concerning his Son, who was born," etc.

And when our translation[25] reads: "of the dead," its meaning is obscure even though this does not make much difference. Therefore, we think it is better to translate according to the meaning rather than literally, i.e., " from the dead."

COROLLARY[26]

"The gospel" is not only what Matthew, Mark, Luke, and John have written. This is made plain enough in this passage. For it states specifically that the gospel is the word of the Son of God, who became flesh, suffered, and was glorified.

Therefore, it makes no difference whether Matthew or Thomas wrote it down and taught it and in what words and in what language: the gospel of God is the same. It does not matter how many books and authors teach it, for what they all teach is one and the same thing. When, therefore, the apostle says of a certain brother: "whose praise is in the gospel through all the churches,"[27] this is not necessarily to be understood to refer to the Gospel of Luke[28] but, rather, to the fact that it was his praise and distinction that he could teach the gospel, i.e., the word of God. So also Apollos and others had similar praise because they knew how to preach Christ well and richly.

Also the passage which says: "according to my gospel" (Rom. 2:16) does not need to be interpreted with reference to the Gospel of Luke, as if Luke had written down what Paul preached or as if what the former had written down the latter had preached. But he says "my" gospel because he himself preached the word of God "concerning his Son," as the passage we are dealing with puts it.

For I am not ashamed of the gospel. **For it is the power of God** *unto salvation to everyone that believes, to the Jew first and to the* Greek. (Rom. 1:16.)

It is to be noted that in this passage *"virtus"* is to be understood as "potency" or "power," or as *"Muglickeit,"*[29] which means

---

[25] The Vulgate.

[26] *Corollarium* (garland), an appendix, stating a conclusion implied in a foregoing exposition.

[27] Cf. II Cor. 8:18.

[28] So Faber, in his Commentary.   [29] = *Möglichkeit.*

"possibility." And "power of God" does not mean that power by which he is powerful in himself but that power by which he makes powerful and strong. As we speak of "God's gift," "God's creature," "God's concern," so we also speak of "God's power" (i.e., the potency which comes from God). So we read in Acts 4:23: "and with great power gave the apostles their witness of the resurrection of the Lord Jesus Christ," and in Acts 1:8: "And ye shall receive power when the Holy Spirit is come upon you," and in the last chapter of Luke (ch. 24:49): "until you be clothed with power from on high," and in Luke 1:35: "The power of the Most High shall overshadow you."

It is to be noted, secondly, that the "power of God" is here distinguished from the power of men. For this latter power is the potency from which man derives his strength and health according to the flesh and by which he is enabled to do what is of the flesh. But God has completely annulled this power by the cross of Christ in order to give his own power by which the spirit is strengthened and saved and by which one is enabled to do what is of the spirit (Ps. 60:11 f.): "Vain is the salvation of man; through God we shall do mightily"; and Ps. 33:16 f.: "The king is not saved by much power; nor shall the giant be saved by his own great strength; a horse is a vain thing for safety; neither shall he be saved by the abundance of his strength." This, then, is the meaning of the phrase "The gospel is the power of God": The gospel is the power of the spirit or the riches, arms, ornaments, and every good of this Spirit (all that it is able to do) and this comes from God. In the same way, we commonly understand riches, arms, gold, silver, kingdoms, and other things of this sort to mean the power of men by means of which they are enabled to perform their deeds and without which they can do nothing. But as I have said before, all these things must be entirely destroyed, or at least the yearning for them; otherwise, the power of God will not be in us. For the rich and powerful do not receive the gospel and therefore neither do they receive the power of God, as it is written: "The poor have good tidings preached unto them" (Luke 7:22). "But," as we read in Ps. 49:6, "they trust in their own strength and glory in the multitude of their riches."

Therefore it is to be noted, in the third place, that whosoever does not really believe is to this day not only "ashamed" of the gospel but also sets himself over against it, at least in his own thought and action. This is because one that finds pleasure and enjoyment in the things of the flesh and the world can necessarily not find taste and pleasure in the things of the Spirit and of God: so not only is he ashamed to bring the gospel to others but he refuses to have it brought to himself. For he hates the light and loves darkness; therefore he cannot bear to be told the truth of salvation.

Moreover, "to be ashamed of the gospel" is the fault of a clergyman who lacks courage; but to set himself against it and to refuse to hear it is the fault of a layman who has become foolish. This becomes apparent when a preacher lets himself be intimidated by the power or favor or number of his listeners and does not utter the necessary truth, and when an insensitive man in the pew despises the lowliness and humbleness of the word. Then it becomes to him foolishness, as if it were something insane. "The natural man receives not the things of the Spirit of God; for they are foolishness to him, and he cannot know them." (I Cor. 2:14.) "The mind of the flesh is enmity against God; for it is not subject to the law of God, neither indeed can it be." (Rom. 8:7.)

We therefore come to the following conclusion: he who believes in the gospel must become weak and foolish before men, so that he may be strong and wise in the power and wisdom of God, as it is written in I Cor. 1:17, 25: "God chose the foolish things of the world that he might put to shame them that are wise. Because the foolishness of God is wiser than men, and the weakness of God is stronger than men." When you therefore observe that the power of God can readily be rejected, let this be a sign of the power of the flesh and the world. This is why all power, wisdom, and righteousness are hidden and buried and not apparent, in accordance with the image and likeness of Christ, who emptied himself in order to hide completely his power, wisdom, and goodness, disclosing only his weakness, foolishness, and harsh suffering. In a similar way, one who is powerful, wise, and at ease must have these goods as if he had them not. That is why the life of the princes of this world and of the lawyers is the most dangerous one, because they must maintain themselves by power and knowledge. For when these are not apparent and when they are hidden even to the slightest extent, they no longer count for anything. But when they are apparent, then "there is death in the pot" (II Kings 4:40), especially if one likes to parade them before men in order that they should be appreciated by them. For it is difficult to despise and hide from one's own esteem what everyone regards highly.

The righteousness of God is revealed. (Rom. 1:17.)

Human teachings reveal the righteousness of men, i.e., they teach who is righteous and how a man can be and become righteous before himself and his fellow men. But only the gospel reveals the righteousness of God (i.e., who is righteous and how a man can be

by faith alone

and become righteous before God) by that faith alone by which one believes the word of God.[30] "He that believes and is baptized shall be saved; but he that disbelieves shall be condemned." (Mark 16:16.) For the righteousness of God is the cause of salvation.[31] Here, too, *"the righteousness of God"* must not be understood as that righteousness by which he is righteous in himself, but as that

passive justice

righteousness by which we are made righteous (justified) by Him, and this happens through faith in the gospel. Therefore, Blessed Augustine writes in the sixteenth chapter of his book *On the Spirit and the Letter:*[32] "The righteousness of God is that righteousness which he imparts in order to make men righteous. Just as that is the Lord's salvation by which he saves us." He says the same thing in the ninth chapter of the same book. The righteousness of God must be distinguished from the righteousness of men which comes from works—as Aristotle in the third chapter of his *Ethics*[33] clearly indicates. According to him, righteousness follows upon and flows from actions. But, according to God, righteousness precedes works and works result from it. Similarly, no one can perform the works of a bishop or a priest unless he is first consecrated and sanctified to such an office; righteous works of men who are not yet righteous can thus be likened to the works of someone who performs the functions of a priest and bishop although he is far from being a priest; in other words, such works are foolish and done for sport and resemble the doings of circus entertainers.

We must note further that the phrase **from faith unto faith** (Rom. 1:17) is interpreted in various ways. Lyra wants to understand it as if it meant "from unformed faith to formed faith."[34] But this is meaningless, because no righteous man lives by an unformed faith. But Lyra says here both of these things, unless he wants to understand the unformed faith as the faith of beginners and the formed faith as that of the perfect. But unformed faith is, strictly speaking, no faith at all but, rather, the object to which faith is directed. At any rate, I do not think that it is possible for

[30] In his first Commentary on The Psalms, Luther remarked on Rom. 1:17–18: *"Haec est conclusio totius Epistolae S. Pauli ad Romanos"* (WA 3, 174, 14). It is significant that this remark was made in connection with an exposition of Ps. 31:2: "Deliver me in thy righteousness [*in iustitia libera me*]," for, as Luther, later on in his life, frequently said, it was the phrase "the righteousness of God" that had caused him deep spiritual trouble, especially in so far as it was to be understood in relation to the "good news" of the gospel.

[31] Cf. Heb. 5:9.

[32] Augustine, *De spir. et lit.*, 11, 18; 9, 15.

[33] Aristotle, *Eth. Nicom.*, III, 7; V, 9; V, 10. The Scholastics generally cited II, 1.

[34] *"Ex fide informi ad fidem formatam."*

anyone to believe by unformed faith—all that one can accomplish by it is to get an insight of what one must believe and thus to remain in suspense.

Others interpret the passage as follows: "from the faith of the fathers of the old law to the faith of the new law." This interpretation is passable, though one can readily refute it by the argument that the text "The righteous man lives by faith" cannot possibly mean that the righteous man lives by the faith of his ancestors. The fathers had the same faith as we; there is only one faith, though it may have been less clear to them, just as today the scholars have the same faith as the laymen, only more clearly.

The meaning of the passage appears, then, to be as follows: the righteousness of God is entirely from faith, yet growth does not make it more real but only gives it greater clarity—according to II Cor. 3:18: "We are transformed into the same image from glory to glory," etc., and Ps. 84:7: "They shall go from strength to strength." And just so also "from faith to faith," by always believing more and more strongly, so that he "who is righteous can be justified still" (Rev. 22:11) and so that no one should think that he has already apprehended[35] and thus ceases to grow, i.e., begins to backslide.[36]

Saint Augustine writes in the eleventh chapter of *On the Spirit and the Letter*:[37] "from the faith of those who confess it by word of mouth to the faith of those who prove it by their obedience." And Burgos offers this interpretation: "from the faith of the synagogue" (as the starting point) "to the faith of the church" (as the finishing point). But the apostle says that righteousness comes from faith; yet the heathen did not have a faith from which, in order to be justified, they could have been led to another one.

That which is known of God *is manifested in them.* (Rom. 1:19.)

This is a Greek form of speech which in our language is best rendered in abstract terms, as e.g., "the knowledge of God." So when we read in I Cor. 1:25: "The weakness of God is stronger than men, and the foolishness of God is wiser than men," this means that the weakness and foolishness of God are more powerful, stronger, and wiser than the strength or power and the wisdom of men. All this is said to be God's, not because it is in him, but because it is in us coming from him. The foolishness and weakness of God are the same as the life according to the gospel

---

35 Cf. Phil. 3:12.
36 *"Desinat proficere,"* i.e., *"incipiat deficere."*
37 Augustine, *De spir. et lit.,* 11, 18.

by which God makes us appear foolish and weak before men—and this is our outer being. But the wisdom and power of God are the life according to the gospel and the very rule of the Christian life, by which he makes and reputes us wise and strong before himself— and this according to our inner being. Thus there prevails here an alternate relationship: the foolishness and weakness of God before men are wisdom and power before God and, by contrast, the wisdom and power of the world are weakness, even death, before God, as will be explained below in ch. 6 of the letter before us.[38]

For the wrath of God is revealed *from heaven against all ungodliness and injustice of those men that detain the truth of God in injustice.* (Rom. 1:18.)

The apostle turns chiefly upon those who in this world have power and knowledge, because he knows that, when they are humbled, also their subjects and the common people will readily humble themselves. Moreover, in his opinion it was they who most strongly opposed the gospel and the word and the life of the cross and incited others to opposition against it. Therefore, he imputes guilt and sin seemingly to these alone and proclaims the wrath of God upon them.

For to no one the preaching of the cross appears so foolish as to the philosophers and the men of power, because it goes contrary to all they are and feel.

For the invisible things of him, **from the creation of the world,** *are clearly seen, being understood by the things that are made; his eternal power also and divinity: so that they are inexcusable.* (Rom. 1:20.)

Some[39] (and, unless I am mistaken, also the Master of the Sentences)[40] interpret as follows: "By the creature of the world," i.e., "the invisible things of God are seen." But this rendering can easily be refuted by reference to the Greek text which reads: "Since the creation of the world" or, as it is put in Matt. 25:34: "from the foundation of the world."

So we must say: "From the creation of the world" (i.e., from the beginning of the world, not merely from now on) it has always been so, that the invisible nature of God was seen and perceived in his works, as will become plain farther on.

The meaning therefore is this: Even if the wise of this world should be unable to perceive that the world is created, they could

---

[38] Cf. Rom. 6:8 ff.
[39] Lyra.
[40] Peter Lombard, I *Sent.*, d. 3. The Vulgate reads: *"A creatura."*

perceive the invisible things of God in the works of the created world if, namely, they were to regard these works that witness to God, as word and Scripture. "For seeing that in the wisdom of God the world through its wisdom knew not God, it was God's pleasure through the foolishness of the preaching to save them that believe." (I Cor. 1:21.) This interpretation seems to be contradicted by the fact that the text says that they knew God, but the difficulty is readily solved by what we read a little farther on: Even if they knew God, "they refused to have God in their knowledge," i.e., by their actions they gave themselves the appearance of not knowing him.

For the sake of a clearer understanding we must note that the apostle rebukes in these words not the Romans only, as many believe.[41] He addresses himself, not to certain persons, but to all people, including the Romans. This can be seen clearly in the words of the apostle below in ch. 3:9 of this letter: "We laid to the charge both of Jews and Greeks, that they are all under sin." He therefore excepts none, because he says "all." One must imagine that, while speaking, the apostle has the entire world before his eyes as if it were one whole body. The members of this body are different; individually they have therefore not done all the apostle charges them with, but altogether they have done all of it (some by committing one fault, and others by committing another), so that he can attribute all these faults to the whole body and not to the head alone. For there can be no doubt that neither all Romans nor all Gentiles were guilty of all of this. But because as non-Christians they were members of this body, they are rebuked one with another. Such is the usage of the Scripture according to the second and fourth rule of Scriptural interpretation, i.e., it passes from a part to the whole and, conversely, from the species to the genus.[42] In one breath it speaks in the same way about the good and the evil ones; it assails and even punishes the former together with the evil ones, and it bestows benefits and favors upon the latter together with the good ones. Everyone who addresses himself to the general community must necessarily observe this rule, though experience shows that not all its members are equally

---

41 Lyra.

42 In the second prologue to his *Postil*, Lyra set down four rules for the proper understanding of Scripture. The first deals with Jesus Christ and his church; the second, with the true body of Christ; the third, with the spirit and the letter (in one and the same literal word there is to be found a historical and a mystical meaning); the fourth, with the species and the genus, or with the part of a whole, i.e., with the transition from the one to the other and conversely. ("*Quarta regula est de specie et genere sive de parte a toto cum de uno transit ad aliud et e converso.*")

culpable or laudable. Nevertheless, he rebukes the Romans and the people of culture all the more severely and strongly because they are and were the leaders of the world by virtue of their political power and their knowledge. So, following the very order of Baptism, he begins with them as with the head and then gradually goes down to the others and finally includes all in the sentence: "being filled with all iniquity," etc.

Moral Rule:[43] The lesson he teaches here is that the preachers of the gospel must first of all rebuke the prominent leaders among the people, not, to be sure, in their own words produced from their own sick and perturbed minds, but in the words of the Gospel; i.e., they must show how and when they act and live counter to the gospel. To be sure, today the number of such workers is small. In a similar way, according to common belief, John the Baptist poured water upon our Lord from the head down,[44] not water that he himself had specially obtained for this purpose, but water from the Jordan. Take note of this mystery lest you tell the story of the gospel in terms of your own wild imagination.

So the letter of Paul is (as all preaching of the word of God must be) like a river that springs from Paradise and like the Nile that inundates all of Egypt. Yet such an inundation must start somewhere. So also the flood which the Lord releases through the apostle Paul covers the whole world and all peoples, but it makes its entry from the heads and leaders of this world and gradually overflows all others. This must be carefully noted. Otherwise, if we follow Lyra and those who agree with him, it will be very difficult to understand the letter, as there will then be no connection between what follows and what precedes, in view of the fact that he sees in the first chapter only the Romans criticized (which opinion also his Prologue supports) and yet what follows must be understood with respect to all nations, indeed the whole mass of the lost human race.[45] For it is the purpose of the apostle to demonstrate Christ as the savior of all men and not only of the Romans or of the Jews at Rome, though, to be sure, he shows him primarily to them—but then together with them also to others.

Because that which is known of God is manifested in them. **For**

[43] The rule that can be derived from the "moral" or "tropological" interpretation of Scripture. Nicholas of Lyra offered the following definition: "When a Scripture passage is read in terms of what it signifies about what we must do, then this is the moral meaning." (Cf. Ficker, p. 175, n. 9.)

[44] The reference is to popular pictures, esp. in the form of Bible illustrations (e.g., in the *Biblia pauperum*).

[45] *"Universa massa perditionis"* (Augustine, *De gratia et pecc. orig.*, 2, 29, 34).

God has manifested it unto them. *For the invisible things of him, from the creation of the world are clearly seen, being understood by the things that are made, his eternal power also and divinity: so that they are inexcusable.* (Rom. 1:19, 20.)

With this he gives to understand that also the natural goods are to be ascribed to God as the giver. The sentence which follows shows plainly that it is the natural knowledge of God which is here dealt with: it says how he has manifested himself to them by the fact that **the invisible things of him are clearly seen from the creation of the world** (i.e., are knowable in a natural way from their effects). This means that, from the creation of the world, it has always been the case that the "invisible things of him are clearly seen," and this is said in order that nobody may cavil and say that only in our time it was possible to know God. For it has been possible to know him from the beginning of the world and at all times, and it is possible now.

But in order that the apostle may be more clearly understood in his arguments, I shall try my hand at explaining what I think he means, in the hope that my readers will either support or criticize me.

That, as we read here, the knowledge of God was open to all men, and especially to idolaters, so that they are without excuses when it is proved to them that they had known the invisible things of God, namely, his very divinity and eternity and power, can plainly be demonstrated by the fact that all who made idols for themselves worshiped them and called them gods or God, believing that God was immortal (i.e., eternal) and also capable and able to help, thereby giving clear evidence that they had the knowledge of God in their hearts. For how could they call a picture or some other created thing God, or believe that created things resembled him, if they had no knowledge of God and what pertains to him? How could they attribute such qualities to a stone or to that which they thought the stone represented if they did not believe God to be entitled to them? Now when they held that the divine (which, to be sure, they divide into many gods) is something invisible and that he who has divinity is invisible, immortal, powerful, wise, and gracious to those who call upon him, I say, when they hold this so definitely that they profess it also by their actions, namely, by the invocation, worship, and adoration of those in whom they believe divinity to reside, it follows most certainly that they were endowed with a knowledge or notion of the divine nature. And without a doubt, they have it because God gave it to them, as our text says. Their error was that in their worship they did not take the Godhead for what it is in itself, but changed it by fitting it to their own needs and desires. Everyone wanted the Godhead to be in him whom he happened to like, and thus they turned the truth of God into a lie.

They knew, therefore, that it is the nature of divinity or of God to be powerful, invisible, righteous, immortal, and good, and thus they knew the invisible things of God and his eternal power and divinity. This "major" of the "practical syllogism,"[46] this basic theological "insight of the conscience," is in every mind and can never be obscured. But in the "minor" (of the practical syllogism) they erred when they made the statement: This one here, i.e., Jupiter or someone else whom this idol represents, is of this sort, etc. Here lay the beginning of the error that led to idolatry: everyone wanted to subsume the Godhead under his own interest. If they had therefore remained in this awareness of God, saying: "This we know: whosoever this god or this godhead may be, whose nature it is to be immortal and powerful and able to fulfill the prayers of those who call upon him, we will worship and adore him and we will neither call him Jupiter nor say that he resembles this or that but we shall worship him in his very nature whosoever he is (for exist he must),"[47] they would without a doubt have been saved, although they did not acknowledge him as the creator of heaven and earth nor recognize any particular part of his handiwork. This, then, is what is meant by the sentence: "That which is known of God is manifest in them."

But where and how is it manifest? Answer: "The invisible things of God are clearly seen, being understood by the things that are made." One can observe how men and beasts and even things help and further one another according to their greater power and endowment, and how that which is superior and of greater worth either raises or puts down that which is its inferior. In the same way, there must be that in the universe which is sublimer than everything else, which is higher than all and helps all. For men measure God in terms of the benefits they receive from him.

---

[46] According to later medieval Scholasticism (Gerson, Biel, Trutvetter, etc.), the "practical" syllogism (which was distinguished from the "speculative" syllogism) consisted of the following three parts: major premise, *syntheresis;* minor premise, *ratio (iudicium);* conclusion, *conscientia.* Synteresis, originally a misreading of the Greek *Syneidēsis* (conscience), was defined as a "natural inclination" of the soul toward the good, an inextinguishable spark (*scintilla*) of reason, an inborn *habitus. Conscientia* (conscience) was understood in relation to specific actions. It was therefore defined as changeable, either accusing or excusing. Cf. Ficker, p. 177, n. 14; Ellwein, p. 484, n. 25; and for the whole history of the doctrine of conscience down to Luther: E. Hirsch, *op. cit.,* Vol. I (an important, illuminating treatise).

[47] *"Necesse est esse."*

Hence, as we read in Pliny,[48] in ancient times people deified their benefactors in order thus to express their gratitude to them.

Because that, when they knew God, they have not glorified him as God, *or given thanks; but became vain in their thoughts, and their foolish heart was darkened. For professing themselves to be wise, they became fools. And they changed the glory of the incorruptible God into the likeness of the image of a corruptible man, and of birds, and of four-footed beasts, and of creeping things.* (Rom. 1:21–23.)

If they did not "**glorify** him as God" ("*ut Deum*") or as if he were God (*sicut Deum*), did they then glorify something else than God? He obviously seems to indicate this, and what follows has the same meaning: **and changed the glory,** etc. (Rom. 1:23), i.e., they did not worship him as God but as if he were the likeness of an image, and thus they did not worship God but a figment of their own making. This interpretation I readily accept. The Children of Israel, too, were rebuked for having worshiped Baal and calves, and yet they obviously intended to worship the true God in these symbols and idols, and this they were forbidden to do.

How many there are even today who worship him not as if he were God but as if he were as they themselves imagine him for themselves! Look at the odd practices of superstition and see how utterly vain they are! If you disregard what you ought to do and worship God by a work of your own choosing, and believe at the same time that God is one who concerns himself for you and your affairs as if he were another than the one who has manifested himself to you by his commandments—does this not mean exchanging the glory of God for a likeness of the imagination and your own fancy? So, as we can everywhere observe, also today many have fallen victim to a selfish and reprehensible way of thinking.

One can also say simply: "They did not glorify him as God,"[49] which means they did not glorify God as it would have been proper for them to glorify him and to give him thanks. The word "not" then emphasizes the failure to glorify God. If the word "not" negates the adverb "as," then, in accordance with our first interpretation, the act of glorifying is affirmed while the manner by which it is performed is denied. The context allows both interpretations.

Now, take note of the order of the stages of perdition. *The first is ingratitude* or the failure to be grateful. Thus, Lucifer before the Fall was ungrateful to his Creator. It is the result of self-com-

[48] Pliny, *Nat. hist.*, II, 7 (5), 19.
[49] Lyra.

placency: forgetting the giver, one delights in accepting gifts as if one had not received them. *The second is vanity:* one feeds on one's own self and all that is created and enjoys that which lets itself be used, and so one becomes necessarily vain "in his own thoughts," i.e., in all one's plans, efforts, and undertakings. For whatever one looks for and seeks is altogether vain, because one seeks only himself, i.e., his own glory, delight, and advantage. *The third is deluded blindness:* deprived of the truth and immersed in vanity, one necessarily becomes blind in one's whole feeling and thinking because one is blocked in upon himself. Thus confined to darkness, what else can one undertake but what one who blindly wanders about looks for in his ignorance? For a blind man easily falls into error; indeed, in a way, he is always in error. Therefore *the fourth is to be in error toward God,* and this is the worst because it leads to idolatry. To have come this far means to have come to the abyss. For to one who has lost God, nothing is left but to be exposed to every kind of turpitude that the devil invents. The result is that deluge of evils and bloodshed of which the apostle speaks below.

By the same stages, people even today come to commit spiritual idolatry of a more subtle kind, and it is quite frequent: they worship God not as he is but as they imagine and desire him to be. Ingratitude, namely, and the love of vanity (i.e., the sense of self-importance and of self-righteousness or, as one says, of "good intentions")[50] delude people terribly, so that they become incorrigible, unable to believe anything else but that they behave splendidly and are pleasing to God. Thus, they make themselves a gracious God, though this does not correspond to reality. And so they worship the product of their own imagination more truly than the true God himself, who they believe resembles this product of their fancy. Here now "they change him into the likeness of their own imagination" (Rom. 1:23), which exists only in their corruptible minds that know only carnal desires. See, then, how great an evil ingratitude is: it produces a love of vanity, and this results in blindness, and blindness in idolatry, and idolatry brings about a whole whirlpool of vices.[51]

[50] As his frequent treatment of this theme in these lectures shows, Luther was greatly preoccupied with the theological-psychological notion of "good intention" (*bona intentio*), especially in so far as later medieval piety and theology prescribed that in order to be acceptable in God's sight (*coram Deo*), man must give evidence of a "good" or "pious" intention. Cf. Gabriel Biel, II *Sent.,* d. 40, q. un., n. 2. Ficker (p. 179, n. 14) quotes a passage from the Meissen Breviary: "We must earn the intention of good will [*intentionem bonae voluntatis debemus mereri*]."

[51] "*Gurges vitiorum,*" a term that, according to Ficker (p. 179, n. 22), was part of the apocalyptic terminology of the late Middle Ages.

Gratitude

Gratitude, however, keeps the love for God and thus holds the heart directed toward him. Because it is thereby also illumined, it worships, once it is illumined, only the true God, and to this worship there soon attaches itself the whole chorus of virtues.[52]

Wherefore God gave them up to the lusts of their own hearts. (Rom. 1:24.)

This "giving up" is not so much a permission as a commission, a command, of God. This is plainly shown in the last chapter of the first book of Kings (I Kings 22:22 f.), where the Lord says to the lying spirit that he should entice Ahab, the King of Israel: "Thou shalt entice him, and shalt prevail also; go forth and do so." Then follows the word of the prophet addressed to the same king: "Now, therefore, behold, the Lord has put a lying spirit in the mouth of all thy prophets." So also David said of him who cursed him (II Sam. 16:10): "Because the Lord has said unto him, Curse David, . . . let him alone, and let him curse; for the Lord has bidden him." In the same way the Lord orders also the devil or the flesh to tempt and overwhelm a man who deserves before God that this should happen to him because of his impiety.

If someone objects and says: God forbids evil, therefore he does not give anyone up to evil, i.e., he does not awaken evil in order that it may dominate and triumph, nor does he command that this should happen, we answer: This is true when he acts in his goodness; but when he punishes in his severity, he causes the wrongdoers all the more to sin against his commandments in order then to punish them all the more.

If we correlate both ideas, we come to the following conclusion: from the viewpoint of the man who is "given up," this "giving up" appears to happen by the permission of God because he withdraws his help from him and deserts him. Then the devil, who is always prepared to expect something of this sort, quickly takes over from God the power of command, or he thinks at least that he has thereby taken it over. In this sense, it happens because God so orders. For it is not correct to say that God orders man to do evil—no, one must rather say that he deserts him so that he cannot resist the devil, who now goes into action by the command and will of God. We may twist and turn the matter as much as we want: we must assert that it is God's will that a man be overwhelmed by sin; moreover, he wills this by his good pleasure in so far as he lets him be overcome by that which he [God] hates most, causing him to become enslaved to that which He intends to pun-

[52] One is reminded of medieval paintings and sculptures depicting a chorus of virtues.

ish most. For this is the greatest severity: to deliver someone into
the hands of him whom he hates most.

It does not follow from this that God wills sin, even though it is
done by his will; but what follows is that he does not will it at all
and that he hates it. For he lets it be done by his will in order that
a man be subjected to what he hates most so that this man may
know what a terrible judgment hangs over him; and so God by
his will lets that become a fact which he hates most only for the
purpose of punishing him, for there is nothing more base than
sin. Therefore, in order to let a man who is already covered with
shame become subject to sin, He lets that be done which he consistently forbids. Therefore, God lets sin be done, not for sin's
sake, but for the sake of penalty and punishment. Just as a man
who sins does not will to sin for the sake of sinning (for he would
rather that there were no sin) but for the sake of a good which he
pursues, so also God wills sin, not for the sake of sin (for he, too,
would rather that it were not and he hates all that is sin), but for
the sake of punishment and the ill that is contained in it so that
he may have regard for the punishment rather than the sin.

This, to be sure, God alone may will. For he is not bound not
to will that there be sin, although by his nature he necessarily
can neither will nor love it, but he can will and love it, not in so
far as it is sin, but in so far as it is punishment. Just so, a father
hates to see his son dirtied and stained, yet when the son commits
a grave offense, he elects to stain him not in order thereby to please
himself but in order to soil the son. Those, therefore, who want to
infer from this that God loves and wills evil think in much too
simple terms, but still more simple-minded are those who deny
that God wills evil only in order that they be not forced to the
conclusion that he allows sins to happen.

Therefore, God measures justly when he elects what is evil in
sin for the purpose of punishing man, for thereby he elects what
is good in sin. For punishment consists (not, as Lyra thinks, in
sinning itself *per accidens,* but) in the vileness of sin. For it is
something painful to be or have been subject to a vile sin. The
apostle clearly indicates this when he says: "Wherefore God gave
them up to sin, that their bodies should be dishonored among
themselves" (Rom. 1:24). For no other punishment is so ignomini-
ous as that which one receives when one is cast into sin. For it is
more shameful to be cast into a vile sin than to bear any kind of
penalty. Hence, it is not correct to say, as Lyra does, that because
God withholds his grace and thus makes sin possible, sin is *per accidens* also the penalty for sin. No, no! Sin, or rather the shame
which is connected with sin, is in itself the penalty. The fact that

grace is withheld is not the punishment. God intends it to be so; he despises sin, to be sure, yet because he cannot bring about shame except in connection with sin, he wills that a man commit sin in order that this shame should overwhelm him. If it were at all possible that such ignominy could become a fact without sin, God would bring this about and he would prohibit sin. But this cannot be.

COROLLARY

It is true that God wills evil and sin;[53] it is equally true that he understands what evil is and what sinning is. This astounds some authors[54] and leads them to assert that the whole Scripture says that he does not will evil and that he hates evildoers. Hence, there must be a contradiction here.

Answer: That he wills evil must be understood in a twofold way (i.e., that he brings it forth from his own will in the same way in which man wills evil—this is impossible with God). He wills evil in a different way—in view of the fact that it remains outside him and that someone else, be it a man or a demon, does it. This is true. For if he did not will it, it would not be done.[55] And conversely: He does not will the good because, while he wills that we all should be bound to his commandments, he yet does not will that all obey them. Therefore, all these statements are true: God wills evil; God wills the good; God does not will evil; God does not will the good. But here they raise the objection[56] that where there is guilt, there must be free will. But for a profounder theology[57] this objection amounts to nothing. To be sure, we are dealing here with the most subtle mysteries of theology, which can be treated only in the circle of experts but not in the presence of simple and inexperienced minds. Because they are able to take only milk but not this very strong wine, they may be plunged into blasphemous thoughts.

For how these two statements can be reconciled and by what criterion they are correct, namely, that God wants to bind me and all other men to himself and yet gives his grace only to whom he wills to give it, and, moreover, that he does not will to give it to all but reserves it for himself to elect some among them—this, I say,

---

[53] Ockham, I Sent., d. 47, q. un.
[54] Cf. Peter Lombard, I Sent., d. 46, 4 ff.; Gabriel Biel, II Sent., d. 37, concl. 1, 2 and II Sent., d. 22, q. 1.
[55] Peter Lombard, I Sent., d. 47, 3.
[56] Gabriel Biel, II Sent., d. 30, q. 1.
[57] Ficker (p. 182, n. 10) calls attention to a similar judgment of Luther's, expressed in his lectures on The Psalms: "disputatio profundissimi theologi Pauli" (WA 3, 31, 15) and "profunda theologia" (WA 3, 283, 18).

True!

we shall see only in the future. Now we can only believe that this is just, because faith is the conviction of things unseen.[58] Nevertheless it is true that God never wills any sin for the sake of sin itself. One must, rather, say that according to his will and pleasure he does not justify some in order through them to display an all the greater glory in the elect. And so when he wills sins, he wills them for the sake of something else, namely, for the sake of his glory and for the sake of the elect. This is made clear farther down,[59] where it is said that God incited and hardened Pharaoh in order to show his power in him, and again in the passage that says: "I will have mercy on whom I have mercy," etc.[60] In the same way, it is by the fall of the Jews that salvation is given to the Gentiles. In order to show his mercy more clearly to the Gentiles, he caused them to fall. For how could they possibly be evil and do evil if he did not permit it? Indeed, he does this not against his will, but he permits it by his own will. And he wills it in order that the good may shine all the more brightly in contrast to evil.

At this point they cry out in protest and say:[61] So, then, one is innocently condemned because he is bound to the commandments and yet is unable to keep them, or one is obliged to do what is impossible. To this the apostle replies: "Nay, but, O man, who art thou that repliest against God?" (Rom. 9:20). For if your argument is valid, it follows that preaching, prayer, exhortation, yea, even the dying of Christ, are not necessary. But God did not predestine the elect to salvation in this way but through all these means.[62] But more of this later.

The lesson to be learned from this text is, then, that when a man yields to such passions, this signifies that, having turned away from God, he has worshiped an idol or changed the truth of God into a lie. For "those who have refused to have God in their knowledge" (Rom. 1:28) can be recognized by the fact that "God" lets them fall into all kinds of vices. And if such portents abound also today, this signifies that much idolatry is being practiced, and of a spiritual kind, of course. *It is very bad* to change the glory of God into the likeness of an image; this is the sin of blindness and ignorance or of a mistaken heart. But *it is worse* still not merely to be mistaken but from a perverted mind to worship such things and to adore something created.

---

[58] Cf. Heb. 11:1.
[59] Cf. Rom. 9:17.
[60] Cf. Rom. 9:15; Ex. 33:19.
[61] Cf. Pierre d'Ailly, *Quaestiones super IV libros Sent., Principium in I Sent., G, quinta propos; I Sent., q.* 14R. Gabriel Biel, II *Sent., d.* 28, *concl.* 2.
[62] Cf. Rom. 8:29, 33–34.

By comparison, *it is less bad* "not to have God in one's knowledge." Accordingly, the apostle makes a threefold distinction among those who are given up: a first group is given up to uncleanness (Rom. 1:24 f.); a second one, to unnatural lust (Rom. 1:28 f.); a third one, to "those things which are not fitting" (Rom. 1:28 f.) or not right. The case of the third group is not too surprising. For where there is no concern for "having the knowledge of God," there the fear of God is necessarily lacking, there men are prone to fall into all kinds of sin. But with respect to the first and second groups, the question arises why exactly this kind of penalty is imposed upon them for this kind of guilt. Answer: Just as one attributes to those who go to see and worship God the highest purity, namely, that of the heart—for this is what they must have if they want to know and worship God—so it is only right, by way of contrast, that those who do not have or refuse to have God in their knowledge should be plunged into the deepest and worst kind of uncleanness, because they are not only unclean of heart (which is the effect of idolatry) but also unclean of body, because those who refuse to be pure of heart cannot be pure of body. For the quality of the soul's relation to God determines the quality of the body's relation to the soul: if one is unclean, then so is the other, and if one is clean, then so is also the other (purity is matched by purity, and impurity by impurity). If they have not glorified God either inwardly or outwardly but, rather, transferred his glory to something else, namely, to an idol, and this out of the fullness of their shameful hearts, it is only right that they should heap shame upon their own bodies and upon one another's (for those who do not give honor to God must dishonor themselves as well as one another). So they receive shame instead of glory for either sin: for having thought God to be like themselves and for having changed him into their own likeness, they must receive the disgrace of uncleanness; and for having transferred their worship from God to something else, they must receive the shame of mutually disgracing their outer bodies. What is more just than that those who turn away from the glory of God should be dishonored, not only in their hearts (and this is idolatry) but also in their bodies?

It is to be noted, however, that, in the opinion of the apostle, not all idol worshipers have done these terrible things but only many among them, as has often been stated. Some did this and others that, but everything together fell at one sweep under God's punishment. There were doubtless many (as, for example, some Roman consuls) who were not subject to such enormous vices, for a great number of them are famous for having been men of admirable propriety and virtuousness though they were idolaters.

Nor must one think that he wants these three ways of "being given up," which he enumerates, to be understood as if they represented the actions of different persons. But it could happen that some were given up to all three, others to one, still others to two—according to the judgment of God. It is the purpose of the apostle to show that all were sinners and that all were in need of the grace of Christ. Even if they all individually did not commit all these crimes, yet, because every individual among them was an idolater, they were at least in God's sight the associates and equals of those who were given up to that terrible penalty.

It seems that the first part of the second chapter of this letter turns against these same people, as if they had set themselves up as judges over the others despite the fact that they had committed crimes similar to theirs, though, to be sure, not all of them.

Unto uncleanness, that their bodies should be dishonored among themselves. (Rom. 1:24.)

The apostle identifies this kind of dishonor as uncleanness and effeminacy. In I Cor. 6:9 f., he says: "Be not deceived: neither fornicators, nor adulterers, nor the effeminate, nor abusers of themselves with men, etc., shall inherit the Kingdom of God." And in Eph. 5:3: "All uncleanness or covetousness, let it not even be named among you, as becomes saints." And in II Cor. 12:21: "They have not repented of the uncleanness and fornication and lasciviousness which they committed." He calls it also a contumely and a disgrace. For as the glory of the body (at least in this connection) lies in chastity, continence, and, at least, its proper use, so its disgrace consists in its unnatural abuse. Just as a golden vessel is ennobled when it is used as a container of a noble wine, and disgraced when it is used as a container of excrement and filth, so our body (in this respect) is ordained to an honorable marriage and to chastity which is still more honorable. But it is most disgraced and humiliated, not by adultery and unchastity, but by being polluted by an even worse turpitude.

Now "uncleanness," or effeminacy, is every intentional and individual pollution that can be effected in various ways, as by the passionate incitement of lascivious thoughts or by the rubbing of the hands or by the petting of another's body, especially that of a woman, or by obscene movements, etc. I call this kind of uncleanness "intentional" in order to except that pollution which may happen during the night, or even the day, and during waking hours but, as many experience it, is involuntary because it is not brought about intentionally. I call it "individual" because when it happens in sexual intercourse with a person of the same or the other sex it is called by a different name.

Rule: I hardly believe that a young person is chaste if he has no spark of devotion to God in his heart but goes about freely without a concern for God. As he must live either by the flesh or the spirit, either his flesh or his spirit must become inflamed. And there is no better victory over the ardor of the body than the flight and aversion from it by means of devout prayer. For when the spirit is filled with fervor, the body soon cools off and becomes cold, and conversely.

And worshiped and served the creature rather than the Creator. (Rom. 1:25.)

The second cause for "being given up" is this actual idolatry, just as its first cause was the idolatry of thought in which God was identified with pictures. The penalty for this is all the heavier because the guilt of it is graver. For the disgrace which is passed to another man is all the greater because one disgraces one's body not only at one's own, but at another's, body. Hence, also, the guilt is greater, for the aberration of idolatry and of an empty knowledge of God is now seated not merely in the mind but in deed and action, thus becoming an example and a stumbling block that leads others into temptation. When, within the limits of their reverence for his holy name, they disgrace God in their thoughts by conceiving of him in a fashion that is more than unworthy of him, it is only right that all this should fall back upon their heads, and that they should think and correspondingly act in a way that is unworthy of their humanity.

But, alas, even today a great many people think of God in a way that is unworthy of him; in bold and daring arguments they define God to be such and such, and not one among them grants God so much honor as to elevate God's all-excelling majesty above his own judgment and comprehension. Instead, they raise their own thinking to such a level that it is no more difficult and terrifying for them to pass judgment on God than it is for a simple cobbler to appraise his leather. In their presumptuousness they dare assert that God's nature, his righteousness, and his mercy are what they think they ought to be, as if they were filled and, indeed, drunk with the spirit that searches the deep things of God,[63] which in fact they completely lack. Of this sort are the heretics, the Jews, the folk of spiritual pride, and all who are outside God's grace. For no one can think rightly about God unless the Spirit of God is in him.

[63] Cf. I Cor. 2:10.

Apart from him, he will speak and judge wrongly about whatever may come under his judgment—God's righteousness or mercy, himself or others. For the Spirit of God must give testimony to our spirit.[64]

The third way of "being given up" (which, compared to the others, is less disgraceful) is the failure to know God: **They refused to have God in their knowledge** (Rom. 1:28). On account of this guilt they are given up to various vices, i.e., there are various and many vices to which or to some of which God has given them up and, if not to all of them, then to some of them. For not all of them are implicated in murder or in all the other vices. And God does not punish and give them all up in the same way, although they all have sinned somehow in the same way. If you ask why this is so, we answer: God wants it so according to his hidden judgment and because he wants all presumptuous talk to be stopped in view of the fact that one man, though a sinner, does at the same time something good, while another does nothing of the kind or, in case he does, does less of it. Nobody has the right to define the rule by which God punishes sins or rewards the good. Accordingly, therefore, when he lets men fall into sin, he nevertheless has mercy on the one and forgives him, while he hardens another and condemns him. Similarly, he lets people live a good life and yet he reproves and rejects the one and accepts and crowns another.

"Being filled with **unrighteousness"** (Rom. 1:29); for so reads the Greek text, and not "with iniquity."[65] In the Holy Scriptures the following distinction is made between unrighteousness and impurity (if one compares the translation[66] with the Hebrew text): unrighteousness is the sin of unbelief or the absence of that righteousness which comes from faith, for, as we read in Rom. 1:17; Mark 16: 16, and in many other passages, righteous is he who believes and unrighteous he who does not believe. A man who does not believe is disobedient, and a man who does not obey is unrighteous. For the very character of disobedience is unrighteousness and sin, according to a word of Ambrose, who says:[67] "Sin is disobedience of the divine commandments."

"Iniquity," however, is the name for the sin of self-righteousness, which men choose for themselves out of a foolish zeal for piety. Thus it is said in Matt. 7:23: "Depart from me, all you that

---

[64] Cf. Rom. 8:16.
[65] The Vulgate reads *"iniquitate."* Faber translates the Greek *"adikia"* by *"iniustitia."*
[66] I.e., the Vulgate.
[67] Ambrose, *De paradiso*, 8, 39.

work iniquity," precisely with reference to the mighty works they claim to have done in the name of Christ. We can therefore make the following simple definition: iniquity consists in this, that you fail to live up to what you are bound to do, and do instead what seems right to you, while uprightness, by contrast, consists in this, that you do what you ought to do, regardless of what seems right to you. Lawyers, of course, define the same terms differently. Iniquity is then to be taken as a relative or comparative term, specifically in comparison with true righteousness, on the one hand, and self-righteousness, on the other.

Malice (Rom. 1:29) is that perverse tendency in man to do evil despite the good he has received, indeed, the tendency to use for evil purposes all the goods he has received from God or man. Goodness, by contrast, is the tendency in man to do the good even though his effort is hindered and checked by some wrong done to him; it makes evil serve for good. Yet, in contrast to worldly goodness, a man is not good in the spiritual sense of goodness if he does the good only as long as he prospers and no one opposes him. In German, the accurate meaning of *bonus* is *fromm* and of *malus*, *böse*. This is the sense also of the saying of Matt. 7:18: "A good tree cannot bring forth evil fruit, neither can an evil tree bring forth good fruit." This is said against the foolish people who shift their own guilt upon others and say: "It would not be difficult for me to be good if I could live among good people or could get rid of the bad ones that trouble me."

In similar contrast stand the terms: benignity and malignity. Benignity is a friendly readiness to live together with others; it is kindness, i.e., the tendency of mind to do good to others and to be indulgent toward them. It is of two kinds: there is the perfect, or Christian, benignity, which remains the same in the face of gratitude or ingratitude; and there is human, or worldly, imperfect benignity, which remains constant only as long as it finds a response but ceases when it encounters ingratitude or some evil. "You shall be perfect as your father in heaven is perfect" (Matt. 5:48), and "You shall be the sons of the Most High, for he is kind toward the unthankful and evil" (Luke 6:35). Malignity, by contrast, is the perverse and harsh tendency to do ill to others and to be vindictive toward them. It, too, is of two kinds: there is that malignity which is the opposite of that heroic and catholic or Christian kindness: from a perverseness of the heart it inflicts injury upon the grateful and the good, not only upon the evil (and it does not make a halt even before benefactors). This is brutal unkindness. The other sort of malignity is the opposite of human and imperfect benignity: it seeks to harm others and to do them ill but it makes a halt before benefactors. In this light we can understand the saying of the apostle in Gal. 5:22: "The fruit of the spirit is goodness and kindness."

Wickedness (Rom. 1:29) is that mental perverseness which causes one to avoid intentionally an opportunity to help his fellow man and to protect him from evil. In this sense Blessed Augustine seems to interpret it in his book *On Order*,[68] for he states there that the word *"nequitia"* (which translated means "wickedness") is derived from *nequire* (to be unable), so that one (who has *nequitia*) is unable to do good, namely, from maliciousness. Others behave in this way out of envy or from sheer insolence.

Dissolute (Rom. 1:31) are those who are coarse in their speech, action, and dress, live in dissolute license, and do as they please.

A whisperer (Rom. 1:29) differs from a **detractor** (Rom. 1:30) in this, that a detractor tries to undermine another's reputation, while the whisperer sows discord by secretly suggesting this to the one and that to the other. Every whisperer is double-tongued, but a detractor is not (Ecclus. 28:15).

[68] A similar interpretation is to be found in Augustine, *De beata vita,* 8, but nowhere in *De ordine.*

ROMANS, CHAPTER TWO

Wherefore you are without excuse, O man, whosoever you are, etc. (Rom. 2:1.)

The exegesis of this text is threefold: First, one can understand it with respect to those who hold the public office of judges and who by authority of their office condemn and punish men from whom they themselves do not differ in, or as to their capability to commit, crimes. Some, therefore, want to turn this word of the apostle upon the Romans, in so far as they were the ones who exercised the right to judge all malefactors throughout the earth though they themselves were entangled in the crime of idolatry and other vices, as if the apostle reproved them for proudly exercising the power of judgment without being concerned in fear and sorrow about the extent of their own sins.

But the apostle has already made it sufficiently clear that he does not have only the Romans in mind. Hence, this comment is not convincing, chiefly because it is forced. Granted that the text of the apostle is to be understood as criticizing those who are established in positions of power and that it can be applied practically in the manner of declamation that is customary in the churches, it can be much more emphatically directed against those who in our time hold positions of power, who turn with raging anger upon their fellow men and pass severe judgments upon their subjects while they themselves go unpunished for having committed not lesser but much worse crimes. It is they to whom the apostle addresses himself in order to awaken them from their profound blindness. Or is it not a fact that the secular as well as the spiritual lords[1] are guilty of pride, dissoluteness, adul-

[1] With respect to these accusations, Ficker (p. 189, n. 8) calls attention to Berthold Pürstinger, *Onus ecclesiae*, 1524. This book contains a description

37

tery, and still worse sorts of thievery, and that they disregard God and men and cause unjust wars, i.e., commit multiple murder! And yet they punish their people for these same crimes with utmost severity. But because they do not find their judge among men, they do not care about what will happen to them. Yet they will not "escape the judgment of God," as the apostle says here. But let me speak more clearly and suggest how one should preach about this matter on the basis of the words of the apostle:

By what authority do princes and secular rulers help themselves to all game and fowl, so that no one but they can go on the hunt? By what right? If an ordinary man would do such a thing, he would rightly be called a thief, a robber, and a crook, because he would take from the community something not belonging to him. But when the rulers do something of this sort, they cannot be thieves because they are the rulers. Should one then say in the manner of Demodocus[2] that, though princes and rulers are no robbers, they nevertheless act like thieves and thugs? The vice of Nimrod, "the first mighty and strong hunter before the Lord,"[3] is so deeply ingrained in them that they cannot rule without oppression and without being strong, i.e., violent hunters, which means: they seize whatever they want. In the same sense, Blessed Augustine says in *The City of God*:[4] "What else are the great kingdoms but great robberies?" In the same place he tells this story: "When Alexander the Great asked a pirate who had been taken prisoner how he dared to infest the safety of the sea, he got from him the very frank and insolent reply: 'And how do you venture to make the whole earth unsafe? When I do this with a small boat, they call me a robber, but when you do it with a large fleet, they call you an emperor.' " If, therefore, one wants to direct this word of the apostle against these thieves, one must apply it to them by saying: They hang the thieves and behead the robbers, and thus the big thieves sit in judgment over the little ones.

And do you reckon this, O man, who judge those who do such things, and do the same, that you shall escape the judgment of God? (Rom. 2:3.)

Similar to this is their habit of exploiting the people by imposing unnecessary taxes, or by changing or devaluing the coin, yet they sentence their subjects to severe punishment for illegal

---

of the religious and ecclesiastical conditions of the sixteenth century. The author believes that they are signs of the imminent end of the world.

[2] Cf. Demodocus about the Milesians in Aristotle, *Eth. Nicom.*, VII, 8.

[3] Cf. Gen. 10:8.

[4] Augustine, *De civ. Dei*, IV, 4.

profit or avarice. This is nothing else than stealing what belongs to others. Indeed, how can one say that such fellows are no thieves when one sees that they are the recipients of regular taxes and other payments to which they are entitled and yet do not fulfill their duty toward the people by giving them protection, furthering their welfare, and administering justice, and that it is their sole interest to lord it over the people, to gather wealth, and to make a pretentious show with all they have acquired?

Even the children in the street can know that the spiritual princes, being almost totally blinded, commit the same, if not worse, crimes: luxury, ambition, pomp, envy, avarice, gluttony, and an utter neglect of religion do not seem to faze them. They are filled to the brim with all this. Any restriction of their privileges and income and a reduction of their pensions which, as it may sometimes happen, their subjects cannot prevent, they regard worthy of the harshest judgments and penalties. What, in your opinion, I ask you, would God—no, not God but an Orestes[5] or someone even crazier than he—make of it if he saw an ambitious, greedy, extravagant bishop annoying his people by fulminating the ban against them on account of a mere half florin! Will he not judge him to be an Orestes twice, nay, seven times over, and will he not say to him: "And do you reckon this, O man, who judge those who do such things, and do the same, that you shall escape the judgment of God?" But today all such things are so common that one does not attach any significance to them on account of their frequency. How awfully does God chastize us today in his anger that he wants us to live with such trials, letting us experience such an unfortunate desolation of the holy church, for it is worse than any devastation or ruin that could be inflicted upon it by its enemies!

In the second place, the text has those in mind who judge others privately in their thoughts and also by word of mouth when they scold them, and yet are like them in all respects. We cannot but call it impudent when a conceited man criticizes another who is also conceited, when a squanderer blames another for wastefulness, and when a miser cuts someone else down for avarice. Although this impudence is so obvious that even fools consider it ridiculous and stupid, a great many are so deluded that they have become afflicted with this disease: more or less conceited people criticize each other for being proud; great and small misers jump upon

---

[5] The "insane Orestes" is referred to by Lang in the preface of his edition of two letters of Jerome together with Filelfo's comparison of Jerome and Augustine. (The preface is dated *IV. Id. Jan.* 1515. Cf. Ficker, p. 190, n. 21.)

other misers, and so forth. To such people our text certainly applies: "Do you reckon this, O man, who judge," etc. For they should judge themselves instead of condemning others who are exactly as they are. Therefore they convict themselves. "Judge not, that you be not judged" (Matt. 7:1), i.e., that you do not bring judgment upon yourselves while you put it upon others. However, we are blind toward our own failings but have sharp eyes for the faults of others.

The text deals, *thirdly,* with those who regard themselves as holy. As I have said before, people of this sort are themselves caught in another sin than that which they condemn, and so they assume themselves to be righteous for the sole reason that they do not act entirely in the same way as others do—just as if it were not a fact that they, too, are unrighteous because they do at least part of what others do! They emphasize the good they do to such an extent that they are incapable of seeing their faults. It is of these people that the apostle speaks most particularly—and it is difficult to teach them and to set them right because they cannot be called impudent when they condemn sins of which, or at least of some of which, they themselves are free, and yet do not know that they, too, are unrighteous or do not notice that they, too, commit the sins they condemn. We can put the matter more adequately in the words of Blessed Augustine in the eighth chapter of *On the Spirit and the Letter:*[6] "They do the works of the law according to the letter without the spirit, i.e., for fear of punishment and not out of love for righteousness. According to their real intention, they would like to act differently if they could do so without being punished, although their will would become guilty. What do works that are done outwardly profit a man if his will is sinful before God, though humanly speaking his actions may appear righteous?" They therefore do that which they condemn, i.e., in their mind they do what others do in fact, and they themselves would do it too if it were permitted. Now this is the ugliness of the synagogue and the cause of its repudiation. In this weakness we are all equal to one another; none must therefore judge another, lest he himself be judged.

It is these people, then, that the apostle tries to bring to true self-knowledge by teaching them that no man who is not a Christian should be placed outside the rank of sinners, no matter how good he is and no matter how severely he condemns sinners. He will always be one of them, even if he does not see it that way; and he always does what he condemns, even if he does not believe that he does.

The apostle then calls attention to the three good gifts which

[6] Cf. Augustine, *De spir. et lit.,* 8, 13.

God offers to sinners, namely, goodness, forbearance, and long-suffering, or rather the riches, i.e., the multitude and magnitude of his goodness, forbearance, and long-suffering (Rom. 2:4).

By the riches of his goodness he means the abundance of physical as well as spiritual benefits, as, for example, the goods of body and soul we enjoy, the use and service we derive from everything that is created, the protection we receive from the angels, etc. By the riches of his patience (i.e., his forbearance and tolerance; for this is the meaning of the Greek word and of the phrase in Rom. 3:25: *"in sustentione Dei"* [in the forbearance of God]) he means his immense forbearance of their ingratitude for all his gifts and of their evil-doing toward him in the multitude and magnitude of their vices, by which, as far as they can, they insult God, who deals kindly with them, and repay him with evil. They mar his glory and desecrate his name (i.e., they do not sanctify it) and they profane and blaspheme all that relates to God.[7]

By the riches of his long-suffering, he means the very long delay of punishment for such ingratitude and evil-doing and his expectation of a change for the better on their part, as if he really hoped that they would become better. But the more patiently God waits, the more severely will he judge if he must wait in vain. Hence, there follows (in the next verse) the word: **You treasure up wrath for yourself.** The apostle does not say: "You will deserve wrath," but "You treasure up," i.e., you will deservedly come to feel God's fully heaped up anger. As Valerius Maximus, who was a heathen, to be sure, put it: "Divine anger balances the slowness of punishment by the severity of judgment."[8]

From this text one can learn what a hardened heart is. It is a heart which despises God's goodness, patience, and long-suffering; a heart which receives much good and does much evil and never proposes to change itself. This attitude is shown by two kinds of people: some display it because they are motivated by lust and physical desire; others because they cling to their own opinion and wisdom, stubbornly maintaining their own holiness in the manner of Jews, heretics, schismatics, and individualists.[9] This is why Blessed Bernard writes in the first chapter of *On Considera-tion*:[10] "That heart is hardened which cannot be softened by good gifts, nor frightened by threats, nor corrected by blows, nor moved by promises," etc.

People of the second type are more hardened and more im-

---

[7] Cf. Rom. 2:23–24.
[8] Valerius Maximus, *Memorab.*, I, 1, 3.
[9] *"Singularitatis amatores."* Ellwein translates *Sonderlinge.* Perhaps *Eigen-brötler* would be best.
[10] Cf. Bernard of Clairvaux. *De consideratione,* I, 2.

penitent because of the complacency with which they consider themselves wise and holy, not knowing that they are doubly foolish and wicked. "Have you seen a man wise in his own conceit? There is more hope of a fool than of him." (Prov. 26:12.)

Not knowing that the goodness of God leads you to repentance? (Rom. 2:4.)

There is so much blindness in a sinner that he misuses what is given to him for his good, thus causing his own ruin. On the other hand, there is so much light in a righteous and religious man that he uses for his good what is given to him for ill. Hence, the godless man does not know that the goodness of God leads him to repentance, but the righteous man understands that the severity of God also works toward his salvation. For he breaks down and heals, "he kills and makes alive."[11]

In the day of wrath and revelation of the righteous judgment of God. (Rom. 2:5.)

The Last Day is called the day of wrath and the day of mercy; the day of tribulation and peace; the day of confusion and glory. For then the godless will be punished and confounded, but the God-fearing will be rewarded and glorified. Just so one calls also that spiritual day which prevails through the light of faith in the heart of believers a day of wrath and grace, a day of salvation and perdition. See Ps. 110:5: "The Lord at thy right hand has broken kings in the day of his wrath," i.e., in the day and time of grace which is now; and Zeph. 1:14 ff.: "The voice of the Day of the Lord is bitter, the mighty man" (i.e., the powerful and proud man) "will there meet with tribulation. That day is a day of wrath, a day of trouble and distress, a day of calamity and misery, a day of darkness and gloominess, a day of clouds and whirlwinds, a day of the trumpet and alarm," etc.

By patience in well-doing. (Rom. 2:7.)

So necessary is patience that no work can be good if it lacks patience. Yet the world is so perverse, and the devil such a crook, that he cannot let any good work be done without attaching himself to it. But yet in his marvelous good pleasure it is by this that God tests the good work that pleases him.

Let us therefore observe the following rule: When, in doing the good, we do not suffer persecution, hatred, and evil or adversity, we must fear that our work does not yet please God. For

[11] This idea, suggested by I Sam. 2:6, constitutes one of the major themes in Luther's theological thinking. He gives frequent expression to it in all his writings, beginning with his lectures on The Psalms and on this letter.

then it has not yet been tested by patience, nor has God approved it because he has not yet tested it. For he approves only what he has first tested.

But when persecution quickly follows our work, let us rejoice and be confident that it is pleasing to God and even believe that it comes from him. For all that comes from God must be crucified in the world (and so long as it is not led to the cross, i.e., the readiness to endure shame, it cannot be recognized as coming from God). Even his only-begotten Son was not exempted from this but was placed before us as an example for this. "Blessed, therefore, are they that are persecuted for righteousness' sake." (Matt. 5:10.) "Rejoice and be exceeding glad, for great is your reward," etc. (Matt. 5:12.)

COROLLARY

Those who are impatient, and complain of the suffering they have to bear while doing the good, thereby show that their doing the good is not from God but that it is, rather, an assumption of human righteousness by which man does the good for his own sake, because he seeks to be honored and respected thereby, and because he resents it to be slandered, defamed, and hated on account of it. So it is made plainly evident that he did not do the good from love and humility alone for God's sake, but for his own sake, and in order to enhance his reputation (out of hidden pride and self-love). One who acts from love and humility toward God says, when he is praised because of this: I did not begin it for thy sake, dear applause; therefore I shall also not complete it for thy sake. And when he is rebuked, he says: I did not begin it for thy sake, you scold, and for thy sake I shall not let it go. And, protected at his right and left, he happily pursues what he has begun in the love of God.

This is why it is said in James 1:4: "Let patience have its perfect work," i.e., though any virtue may produce a good work, only patience will bring forth the perfect good, namely, something that is not beset by any vice nor begun in the love of praise of self nor left undone for fear of blame, but completed and brought to an end in the love of God. "For you have need of patience, that, having done the will of God, you may receive the promise." (Heb. 10:36.)

COROLLARY

The heathen word of Cicero:[12] "Virtue increases when it is applauded" is rightly denied and rejected in the church of God.

---

[12] In this form, the saying is quoted by Lyra in connection with his comments on Heb. 6:10, but he does not attribute it to Cicero. As a matter of fact, Cicero too criticized the idea.

For the apostle says just the opposite: "Virtue is made perfect through weakness," i.e., good works are made perfect through suffering. "For when I am made weak, then I am made strong." (II Cor. 12:10.) Human virtue, therefore, increases when it is applauded, because it wants to be praised; Christian virtue, however, grows when it is scolded and subjected to suffering; and it is reduced to nothing when it is applauded, according to Ps. 53:5: "For God has scattered the bones" (virtues) "of those who please men; they have been confounded because God has rejected them." Now if human virtue increases when it is praised, what happens when it is scolded? Does it decrease? Yes, certainly, because it turns into fury and desperation. Finally, even those whom the apostle here calls "factious" on account of their lack of patience have done good. But because they did not know patience and wanted to be praised by others, they came to disbelieve the truth and were reduced to their own wisdom in terms of which they regarded as good what in fact is evil; in other words, they came to think that "to be righteous" is the same as "to be in honor acceptable to oneself and other men."

Glory and honor (Rom. 2:7) (i.e., glorious honor).
"Glory" (so says Blessed Augustine with reference to John, ch. 16[13]) "is, in the definition of the most famous ancient Latin authors, the fame that steadily accompanies a man"—or, as he writes in *The City of God*, Chapter 12[14]: "It is the judgment of men in so far as they think well of other men." In the same sense the Holy Scriptures often speak of glory and glorification[15] and correspondingly of "being glorified and being transfigured." Honor, however, is, according to Aristotle,[16] the reverence shown to a man in recognition of his virtue or the reverence one shows to a man by word, deed, or sign in recognition of his virtues.

Honor and glory are thus plainly different from each other: glory is something that goes out from one person to others, while honor goes from others toward or into a person. Glory flows outward and leaves for the outside, but honor flows inward and makes an entrance. The one, therefore, is realized by going out, and the other, by entering in.

Wrath and indignation. (Rom. 2:8.)
I take this to mean the wrath of indignation or wrath of anger which God sends upon body and soul: it is the wrath of his sever-

---

[13] Augustine, *Tract. CV in Joann., c.* 17.
[14] Augustine, *De civ. Dei*, V, 12.
[15] *"Claritas et clarificatio."* Cf. John 12:16, 23.
[16] Probably according to *Eth. Nicom.*, IV, 5.

ity. It is to be noted, by the way, that he is angry also with the righteous; as they themselves say: "He has been angry and he has shown us mercy" (Ps. 60:1), and again: "In wrath remember mercy" (Hab. 3:2). This is the wrath of goodness and the rod of the father. The psalmist prays thus (Ps. 6:1): "O God, rebuke me not in thy anger," which means: Thou must rebuke me, for such is thy wrath, but do not do this to me in anger but in mercy, so that thou destroyest only the old man but savest the new one.

Tribulation and anguish. (Rom. 2:9.)

These words must be understood as an exposition of the phrase: "wrath and indignation." I take it to mean that they belong together and mean the same. The tribulation which is here meant is not any kind of tribulation but that which is connected with anxiety, i.e., it is the tribulation from which there is no way out and in which there is no hope of an end—it is a tribulation without consolation. To be sure, also the saints are troubled, but in their very tribulation they are consoled, as we read in Ps. 4:1: "Thou hast set me at large when I was in distress," and in II Cor. 1:4: "who comfortest us in all our afflictions." This kind of comfort flows from hope and faith in God. But the godless in distress are filled with anxiety through despair, for they have no hope or faith in anything, because in their godlessness they do not believe that they can ever be set free. As joy, therefore, is some kind of largeness of heart also in tribulation, so anxiety is the sense of being narrowed in and constricted in tribulation.

Occasionally, God lets even his own fall into this double distress, for we read in Ps. 116:3: "I found trouble and sorrow," i.e., "anxiety," as the Hebrew text has it,[17] but the godless are forever caught in it. The apostle suggests this by saying *"upon every soul"* (Rom. 2:9), not merely upon the body as is the case with the elect.

For whosoever have sinned without the law **shall perish without the law;** *and whosoever have sinned in the law, shall be judged by the law.* (Rom. 2:12.)

The "law" must be understood here (i.e., in the whole chapter) as the whole law of Moses where the Ten Commandments and the love of God and the neighbor are taught. How can it then be that they shall perish without this law and that they have sinned without it, for without it there is neither sin nor merit and therefore also neither punishment nor reward?

[17] The Vulgate has *"tribulatio"* ("trouble"), but Jerome *(Liber psalmorum . . . , ad loc.)* has *"angustia"* ("anxiety"). Cf. Faber Stapulensis, *Quincuplex Psalterium, ad loc.*

Answer: The apostle means to say that they will perish "without the law" of the written tradition, though they knew it perhaps in another way, as he says farther on: "in that they show the work of the law written in their hearts." Or "without the law" can mean "without the co-operation of the law" in the sense that the law did not occasion sin. For a law that does not exist cannot occasion sin. And it is clear that the Gentiles did not know of a revealed law. To be sure, they did not receive the rites and ceremonies of the law of Moses and they had no tradition concerning it. Therefore, they were under no obligation to it and they could not fall into sin by disobeying it, as was the case with the Jews who had accepted it, entered through it into a covenant with God, and received in it the promise of Christ. But, nevertheless, they did receive a spiritual law, and, according to the "moral" interpretation of the Scriptures, the rites and ceremonies of the Mosaic law signified this (quite apart from the fact that they symbolize Christ). This law is impressed upon all, Jews as well as Gentiles; and all are therefore bound to obey it. In this sense our Lord says in Matt. 7:12: "All things therefore whatsoever you would that men should do to you, do you also unto them; for this is the law and the prophets." The whole law handed down to us is, therefore, nothing else than this natural law which everyone knows and on account of which no one is without excuse.

This, then, is obviously what the apostle has in mind: "They shall perish without having received the law" or, in other words, as they did not become sinners, like the Jews, by not observing the law they had received, and as they will therefore not perish on account of their failure to observe this law, the cause of their perdition is something else, namely, the fact that they knew this very law which, to be sure, they did not receive in the way of the Jews but in a different way, and that they did not observe it. The very fact that they received the law will bring the Jews to judgment, as Saint Stephen announces to them in Acts 7:53: "You have received the law and kept it not."

"They shall perish without law" means then: It is not the law that was handed down and received that condemns them, and they will therefore perish without this sort of law, but not without any law at all, but by one which is the same though it was not handed down to them in writing and contained and represented therein.

Here the question may be raised whether Gentiles who, though living outside Christ, nevertheless fulfill the law according to their conscience in a natural way, can be saved, in view of the fact that original sin is not taken away without Christ and no law fulfilled without grace (even though one may substantially have fulfilled it in fact[18]) and that salvation is by Christ alone. To be sure, the apostle seems here to assert that some have done or do the things of the law by their natural ability. But it is suspicious that he does not say that they fulfill the law but that they observe some and certain parts of the law. For he says "the things of the law," i.e., part of the law and not the whole law, and so they all are still under the sway of sin because of all that they have not done, as he says later on in the third chapter of this letter.

If one understands the apostle to say that they do fulfill all the things of the law, the question must, it seems, be answered in the affirmative. And if someone objects to this answer by reference to Christ, original sin, and grace, one must reply to him with the statement that whosoever fulfills the law is in Christ and obtains grace by virtue of the fact that he has prepared himself for it to the limit of his ability. For God could forgive them original sin (even if they did not know or confess it) on account of some humble action directed toward God and the highest being they knew. Moreover, neither they nor the Jews were in any way bound to the gospel and the Christ who was specifically made known by it.

Or one can say that, by the special prevenience of God's mercy, all people of this kind received as much light and grace as they needed for their salvation, as (for example) Job, Naaman, Jethro,[19] etc. The first answer, according to which they have not done all things of the law, does not seem satisfactory to me, in view of the fact that the apostle says farther on (Rom. 2:27): "And shall not that which by nature is uncircumcision, if it fulfill the law, judge you," etc. This means that uncircumcision, namely, the Gentile, fulfills the law. In the same connection (Rom. 2:26) he says: "If the uncircumcision keeps the ordinances of the law, shall not his uncircumcision be reckoned for circumcision?" They have therefore fulfilled the law. But what they lacked (and for this lack their invincible ignorance is a valid excuse) God in his forbearance certainly supplied in order that it might be made perfect by the Christ to come—not different from what he did to the circumcised children who were killed for his sake[20] and not different from what he does today to our children.

For there is no respect of persons with God. (Rom. 2:11.)
This he says, first, in criticism of the pride of the Jews, who extolled themselves because it was they who had received the law and who boasted of being its bearers and disciples. Therefore, they

---

18 *"Etiamsi substantiam facti habeant."*
19 Cf. Job 42:10; II Kings 5:1 ff.; Ex. 18:1 ff.
20 Cf. Matt. 2:16.

resented it that, with respect to the good, the Gentiles were put on the same level with them and they on the same level with the Gentiles, with respect to evil, when the apostle said: "to the Jew first and also to the Greek" (Rom. 2:9), and again: "to every man . . . , to the Jew first, and also to the Greek" (Rom. 2:10). But they wanted God to act in such a way that he would attribute good only to the Jews and evil only to the Gentiles, just as if all descendants of Abraham were *eo ipso* equal to Abraham in their merits.

Thus the Jews always incline to make God a respecter of persons. It is this foolishness of theirs which the heretics and all the spiritually proud imitate when they presume that just as they have elected themselves before others because of their sanctity and wisdom, and are pleased with themselves in preference to others, so also God will elect them and have pleasure in them. They do not know that, on the contrary, God elects and favors only a soul that despises itself and considers itself worthy only to be rejected in the house of God, that chooses to prefer others to itself and to take pleasure in them. In exactly the same way, he proceeds to pierce also the pride of the Gentiles when they puff themselves up with the excuse that because they did not know the law, they do not deserve his anger. To this he replies: No! for "they shall perish without the law," just as they observe their own law. And this is a law which is inborn and indigenous to them, not given; a law which was there before they came into being and is therefore no mere tradition; a law which is alive and not merely written down.

When we do to another what we want done to ourselves (and we want for ourselves only something good, glorious, and great), we must first of all make an offering to God of our own will, judgment, and glory, and of all the things of God which we have arrogated to ourselves in league with Lucifer, and then, in order that they too may be our superiors, we must make the same offering to our fellow men, whom we generally try to outstrip. Only then we have fulfilled the whole law of humility toward God as well as toward men, i.e., the whole righteousness of perfection. Indeed, the entire Scripture teaches nothing else than humility: we must be subject not only to God but also to every creature. But we want all and everything to be subject to us and we want this out of a perverse tendency of our mind. However wrong our will may be, we say that we want to do to others what we would expect them to do to us. And lo and behold! Precisely this is quite right and of the highest perfection. For what could be more concise and more useful than this small teaching? But how rarely is it

understood in all its comprehensiveness! Also, our Lord stated it
as briefly as possible when he gave men only this rule: "All things
whatsoever that you would that men should do to you, do you
also unto them" (Matt. 7:12). So then, when you extol yourself
above the sinner, above the unlearned and the common man, ex-
pecting them to take this kind of treatment from you—you must
take the same treatment from them unless you dare deny that the
sinful and unlearned and common people are human.

For whosoever have sinned without the law *shall perish without
the law.* (Rom. 2:12.)

One must take care that the phrase "without the law" is not
combined with the words "have sinned" and "shall perish"; one
must, rather, understand the passage in this way: as many as have
sinned without the law, i.e., without the law's help in making sin
possible, without its furnishing the occasion for sin. In the same
way the phrase "they shall perish without the law" means: without
the law's giving testimony against them and pronouncing sentence
upon them, because it is not that kind of law but another kind.
For every law occasions sin unless, under the influence of grace,
feeling, mind, and will are bent toward the law. For the will always tends to go in a direction opposite to that in which it should
go and it would rather do something else if it could, even though
it does outwardly what the law commands. Indeed, when it is
brought under the rule of the law, it is stimulated in the direction
of sin rather than helped against it.

Blessed Augustine says in the fourth chapter of *On the Spirit
and the Letter:*[21] "I do not know why it is that what one desires
becomes more agreeable when it is forbidden." Or as the poet[22]
says: "We yearn for what is forbidden and always desire what is
denied to us. Thus a dam is a threat to the waters that it controls."
"What one may have is worthless, what one may not have gives
the more edge to one's desires." "That which pursues me, from it
I fly; that which flies, I ever pursue." In line with this, Blessed
Augustine says aptly in the eighth chapter of *On the Spirit and the
Letter:*[23] "A man who fulfilled the law without being helped by
the spirit of grace did so from fear rather than from love of
righteousness. Hence, before God there was not in his will what
before men was apparent in the deed," (and, conversely, what
was not apparent in the deed was, nevertheless, before God in the

[21] Augustine, *De spir. et lit., c.* 4.
[22] Ovid, *Amores,* III, 4, 17, 18: *"Sic interdictis imminet aeger aquis."* But
Luther has *agger* (dam) for *aeger.*
[23] Augustine, *De spir. et lit.,* 8, 13.

will) "and he was regarded as guilty, because God knew that he would commit evil (if he could do so without incurring punishment)." Of this kind were the Jews, as the Gospel plainly shows in Matt. 5:20 when it says: "Except your righteousness shall exceed the righteousness of the scribes and Pharisees," etc. For they said that being angry with one's brother was no sin, but to kill him was, etc. That is why it is written in Ps. 1:2: "*But his delight is in the law of the Lord,*" but God gives this only by grace through the *Holy Spirit.* Otherwise, sin is offered new occasions by the law and kills thereby (and even if great deeds are done, the will lies dead), as it is said in I Cor. 15:56 f.: "The power of sin is death, but the sting of death is sin: but thanks be to God, who gives us the victory through our Lord Jesus Christ."

But the doers of the law shall be justified. (Rom. 2:13.)

In the twenty-sixth chapter of *On the Spirit and the Letter*,[24] Augustine explains this passage in two ways: First, "the doers of the law shall be justified" in the sense that by justification they become or are made to be what they had not been prior to justification, namely, doers. Secondly, (and this is better): "They will be justified" in the sense that they will be considered and declared righteous,[25] as it has been stated in the Gloss.[26] This is plainly the sense of the context. "For not the hearers of the law are righteous before God," and if you ask: Who else can be righteous before God except the hearers? you must be given the answer: Only the doers will be righteous, i.e., justified and regarded as righteous. In this sense it is written in Ps. 143:2: "For in thy sight no man living is righteous," and below in this letter, ch. 3:20: "By the works of the law no flesh shall be justified in his sight," and in Luke 10:29: "And he desired to justify himself" (i.e., to declare, to establish that he was righteous, and to put all sin away from himself as if he did not know who was his neighbor whom he was commanded to love), and in many other places in a similar way.

When the Gentiles who have not the law **do by nature the things of the law.** (Rom. 2:14.)

---

[24] Augustine, *De spir. et lit.,* 26, 45.

[25] "*Iusti habebuntur et deputabuntur.*" (Cf. Augustine, *De spir. et lit.,* 26, 45.)

[26] *WA* 56, 22, 24 ff.: "For 'to be righteous before God' is the same as 'to be justified before God.' For it is not because he is righteous that he is so regarded by God, but because God regards him so, he is righteous, as it is stated below in ch. 4. But no one is regarded as righteous unless he fulfills the law. Yet none fulfills it unless he believes in Christ. And so the apostle points to the conclusion that, outside Christ, none is righteous and none fulfills the law."

This, too, Augustine understands in a double way (as above in Chapter 26):[27] First, he takes these Gentiles to be the believers among the Gentiles who were justified by the grace of Christ and whom the apostle wants to contrast with the unbelievers and with the Jews who presumptuously rely on the law and its righteousness. On the basis of this he interprets "by nature" (i.e., by that nature which was corrupted by sin and restored by the grace of Christ through the Holy Spirit) as follows:[28] "Grace is not negated by nature but, rather, nature is restored by grace." He himself is inclined toward this understanding of the passage. Secondly, he says that it can also be understood with respect to those who, although they lead an ungodly life and do not worship God truly and rightly, nevertheless do some good, so that they deserve to be regarded as people who do and understand the law.

Their "excusing thoughts" must, therefore, be understood as "thoughts" by which they excuse themselves in order to obtain a milder punishment. For just as certain venial sins which in this life are unavoidable do not exclude a righteous man from the life eternal, so few good works which will hardly be lacking even in the life of a very bad man cannot secure eternal salvation for a godless man. But this view conflicts with the statement that they do by nature the things of the law; and the doers of the law are righteous. It seems, therefore, that the apostle does not speak of this kind of ungodly men. But also not of the first-mentioned ones, namely, those who believe in Christ. For this exposition of "by nature" is forced, and I cannot see for what reason the apostle should have chosen to use this particular word unless he wanted to conceal from his reader what he really meant, especially in view of the fact that elsewhere he does not speak in this way. Therefore, I think that he really has in mind those who stand in between the godless Gentiles and the believing ones, people who by some good action toward God, according to the measure of their natural ability, earned grace which then directed them farther—not as if grace were given to them in recognition of such a merit, because then it would not have been grace, but because they thus prepared themselves for receiving it as a free gift.

This interpretation will prove tenable if one grants that the passage must be understood with reference to particulars when it says: "They did the things of the law" (i.e., some of them) "by nature." Then the text is quite plain and the second interpretation of Blessed Augustine is most adequate. In that case the apostle refers to these Gentiles for the reason that they observed the law as little as the Jews did. Even though they have done some of the

[27] Augustine, *De spir. et lit.*, 26, 46.
[28] *Ibid.*, 27, 47.

good works of the law, hoping that because of this they will not have to suffer a heavy punishment on the Day of Judgment, they nevertheless are still found to be in need of the grace and mercy of Christ, just as it was of no advantage to the Jews that they had observed the law externally. Both, therefore, are under the sway of sin, regardless of the good they have done: the Jews with respect to the inner man, (on account of their observance only of the letter of the law) and the Gentiles with respect to something twofold, namely, that they fulfilled the law only in part and then not wholeheartedly. I gladly accept this interpretation in view of the fact that the whole argument of this chapter (as the apostle himself says farther on in ch. 3:9 of the letter before us: "We have charged both Jews and Gentiles that they are all under sin") is nothing else than the demonstration that all, and this means both Jews and Gentiles, are sinners in need of the grace of God.

How can one combine with this interpretation a proper understanding of the saying of the apostle that the work of the law is written in their hearts (Rom. 2:15), especially in view of the fact that even the prophet[29] says that it would be given at a future time only to a believing people, that God would write his law not on tables of stone but on their hearts? Now it seems to me (without wanting to prejudice a better opinion) that it is one thing to say "that the work of the law is written in their hearts" and another that "the law is written in their hearts." For the apostle did not intend to say here (even if he could have done so on the basis of knowledge) that they had the law written in their hearts, but he wanted to say only "the work of the law."

I believe, therefore, that "the law is written in their hearts" means the same as "love is shed abroad in their hearts through the Holy Spirit" (Rom. 5:5). This love is the law of Christ and the fulfillment of the law of Moses or, rather, it is a law without law, without measure, without end, without limit, but extended above and beyond everything the law prescribes or can prescribe. But "the work of the law is written in their hearts" means that the knowledge of the law is written in them, i.e., the law written in letters concerning what must be done but not grace which enables one to do this. Hence, those who have had only the work of the law written in their hearts must necessarily have remained confined until now in the letter that kills.

They show that the work of the law is written in their hearts. (Rom. 2:15.)

How do they show it? First of all, and before others, by the fact that they do the things of the law. Secondly, and this now before

[29] Cf. Ezek. 11:19; II Cor. 3:3.

themselves and before all on the Day of Judgment, by the fact that their conscience gives them testimony about themselves. How does it do so? By giving good testimony about good deeds (and this happens by the thoughts that accuse or excuse[30] them) and by giving bad testimony about evil deeds (and this happens by the thoughts that accuse them and fill their conscience with remorse). This proves that the law was not unknown to them but that they had a knowledge of good and evil, for their remorse shows them that they have done evil. For they would not feel remorse unless they recognized the evil they have done.

As they thus judge themselves before themselves in their conscience that gives testimony about themselves and by "the thoughts that accuse and excuse," so God will judge them by the evidence furnished by the same witnesses. Nor do they see themselves in the light of other people's opinions about them and their praise or rebuke but in the light of their innermost considerations of themselves which are so deeply inward that the soul cannot flee or escape from them nor silence them as it can silence the opinions and words of men.

So also God will judge all men according to their inner thoughts, and he will disclose our most secret thoughts of ourselves in such a way that there will be no deeper inwardness or secrecy to flee to. But our thoughts will lie naked and open before all as if God were to say: Behold, I do not judge you but assent to your own judgment about yourself and confirm it, and as you cannot judge differently about yourself, neither can I. According to the witness of your thoughts and of your conscience, you therefore deserve either heaven or hell. As it is said: "For by thy words thou shalt be justified, and by thy words thou shalt be condemned." (Matt. 12:37.) And if by words, then how much more by thoughts, which are witnesses much more secret and reliable!

And their thoughts one with another accusing or else excusing them. (Rom. 2:15.)

From our conscience we have surely only accusing thoughts, because before God our works are nothing (unless he himself works in us through his grace). It is true that it is easy for us to excuse ourselves before ourselves, because we are easily pleased with ourselves. But what good is this to us except it proves to us absolutely that we know the law? For such complacent thoughts testify for us that we have done the good or avoided evil. But this does not yet mean that we have satisfied God or really fulfilled the law.

[30] Cf. Rom. 2:12.

Wherefrom, then, shall we take the thoughts that excuse us? Only from Christ and in Christ. For when his own heart reproaches a Christian and accuses him by testifying against him that he has done evil, he presently turns away from it and turns to Christ and says: He made satisfaction, he is righteous, he is my defense, he died for me, he made righteousness to be mine, and made my sin his own. And if he made my sin his own, then I have it no longer, and I am free. And if he made his righteousness mine, then I am righteous in the same righteousness as he. But my sin cannot swallow him up but it is swallowed up in the infinite abyss of his righteousness, for he is God himself to whom be praise forever and ever. Thus, "God is greater than our heart." (I John 3:20.) As our defender he is greater than our accuser, and infinitely so. God is our defender, the heart our accuser! Is this the proportion? Yes, yes, indeed, so it is![31] "Who shall lay anything to the charge of God's elect?" No one! Why? Because "it is God that justifies." "Who is he that condemns?" No one! Why? Because "it is Jesus Christ" (who is also God) "that died, yea, rather, that was raised from the dead," etc. "If God is for us, then who can be against us?"[32]

You that teach another, do you not teach yourself? (Rom. 2:21.)
How can one teach without knowing something beforehand and without having been taught? For a teacher must know and first be taught in what he teaches others. Now the apostle indicates here clearly that he is speaking of spiritual teaching and learnedness in the law, and he points out that those who teach others in it according to the letter have themselves not learned it correctly. In other words, the works of the law must be done by a willing and pure heart. Thus, because the nobler and better part of man, which is also more agreeable to God (namely, the heart and will), is not engaged in doing the works of the law, they do not fulfill it at all, at least not in God's sight, however much they engage the meaner part, namely, the body, against its natural inclinations in the observance of the law. And so he goes on to say emphatically: **You who preach that a man should not steal, you steal, and you who say a man should not commit adultery, you commit adultery** (Rom. 2:21 f.). And so also: You who say a man should not kill, you kill, as the fact that Christ was killed plainly shows, etc.

This is what our Lord means when he says in Matt. 23:2 f.: "The scribes and the Pharisees sit on Moses' seat: all things, there-

---

[31] *WA* 56, 204, 25: *"Sic, Sic, etiam Sic!"*
[32] Cf. Rom. 8: 31 ff.

fore, whatsoever they say to you, these do and observe: but do not according to their works; for they say, and do not." How can we understand this to be true in view of the fact that outwardly they appeared to other men as righteous? Our Lord himself confirmed this in the same chapter, which he certainly would not have done if they had not accomplished works of righteousness. That one should not act according to the standard of their works, which appear to be good works, can mean only that one must not imitate them by observing the law, as if this sufficed, only according to the letter and in order to be seen by men and without having one's heart in it (which means in fact: observing it with an unwilling heart). So "they say" (i.e., they do teach the law, to be sure, and recite it correctly, and for this they are not rebuked, just as the apostle does here not criticize those that teach the law to others) but "do not." They can keep the law they teach only if they do so with a joyful and pure will, i.e., with a heart that is circumcised of all lusts and desires, so that they do or do not keep the law merely by observing it outwardly but do or do not keep it with all their heart and will. In other words, they must be pure and free from evil works, in the sense that they must be free from all inner cupidity and not perfect only in outward acts; and they must be ready to do good works, in the sense that they do them with a willing mind and not from physical necessity. So they teach, it is true, the right and whole law but they do not keep it and they do not fulfill it. They do not keep it inwardly and they do not fulfill it outwardly.

It follows from this, that "they bind heavy burdens and grievous to be borne, and lay them on men's shoulders; but with a finger of their own they will not move them" (Matt. 23:4). These burdens are the commandments of the law which, as the apostle said before, they should keep. But if one understands them literally, they become heavy and grievous to be borne, for then they kill and do not make alive. For in so far as they teach that the law must be fulfilled at least by an outward deed, regardless of whether it is being kept in the heart, and fail to show where or how this fulfillment of the law can be accomplished, they confront those they teach with something impossible. For one can never fulfill these commandments if one does not fulfill them inwardly in the heart. But "they themselves do not move" these commandments "with their finger," i.e., they do not try, even in the slightest way, to deal with them inwardly, but confine themselves solely to the outward deed. And thus they become vainglorious, as can be seen from the saying: "But all their works they do to be seen of men" (Matt. 23:5). Note that our Lord says here that they do the works of the law, yet he stated just before that they do not move a finger in order to accomplish this. But there is no contradiction here, because they do the works outwardly and with a desire for vainglory, but inwardly they do not move them with a finger. It is these works of theirs which, as he said before, we should not imitate, although he here admits that they are good, but they are not really good.

All this makes it obvious that the "to do" of this passage and the "to commit adultery," "to steal," "to kill" of this chapter we are discussing, refer to the attitudes of the inner man, for in the sight of God anyone who desires to do anything of this sort is regarded as one who has in fact done it, as it is said farther on in ch. 7:16, 18 of this letter: "But what I would not, that I do, but the will to do that which is good is not in me."

Hence, they themselves do not understand these words, nor do they believe that they are men of such a kind. For example, according to Acts 5:28, they said (believing that it was not they that had killed Christ because they had not killed him with their own hands): "You intend to bring this man's blood upon us," and, according to Acts 7:52, when Saint Stephen reproached them in the same way with the words: "You are the murderers of this righteous man," etc., "they gnashed at him with their teeth" (Acts 7:54). This is why, in Prov. 30:20, they are called "an adulterous woman" (the synagogue which is iniquitous of heart and righteous only physically)[33] "who eats" (i.e., has devoured Christ by killing him) "and wipes her mouth" (i.e., exculpating herself from her sins) "and says: I have done no wickedness."

In view of the fact, therefore, that (as I have already said) they do not understand the words of the apostle or believe that they are such men as preach that one must not steal yet steal, the apostle goes on to say (and he still speaks in the spiritual sense and of a spiritual doing): **Circumcision indeed profits** (Rom. 2:25) and, still more clearly farther on (Rom. 2:28): "For he is not a Jew who is outwardly circumcised; neither is that circumcision which is outward in the flesh," etc., and again: **who are with the letter and circumcision a transgressor of the law** (Rom: 2:27). "With the letter," he says, because you are a thief in the spiritual sense, though not according to the letter. He emphasizes, namely, the word "letter," because he wants to indicate that he is speaking in the spiritual sense, in order that they might understand what they should have known, etc.

Now someone will object and say: This circumcision of the heart can be brought about only by grace. For as I have already

[33] Luther here follows Lyra.

said, human nature is inclined toward evil and without strength toward the good; it despises rather than loves the law which enjoins the good and prohibits evil, and, therefore, it has no immediate liking for the law, but resents it. And so, unless helped from above, it continues to be held in evil longing contrary to the law and it is filled with selfish lusts, even though, from the compulsion of the fear of punishment or under the leading of the love for temporal satisfactions, it may perform good works. It is not the voice of human nature or of the old Adam which says: "Thy law do I love, but I hate them that are of a double mind" (Ps. 119:113), or: "How sweet are thy words unto my taste, yea, sweeter than honey to my mouth!" (Ps. 119:103) or: "More to be desired are they than gold, yea, than much fine gold, sweeter also than honey and the droppings of the honeycomb" (Ps. 19:10). This is the voice of the new and spiritual man, for the psalmist goes on to say: "Moreover thy servant has loved them and keeps them." Now if grace brings this about, why do the apostle and even our Lord himself accuse and reprove the Jews?

I answer: It is the one concern of the apostle and his Lord to humble the proud and to make them acknowledge this fact; to teach them that they are in need of grace and to destroy their own righteousness so that humbled they ask for Christ, confess that they are sinners and thus obtain the grace of salvation. It is this same conclusion which the apostle explains farther on in this letter in ch. 11:32: "For God has shut up all unto disobedience, that he might have mercy upon all."

But they did not want to hear and accept this, and when they heard this voice (according to Ps. 95:7–8) "they hardened their heart." Therefore, "they have not known the ways of the Lord and shall not enter into his rest." (Ps. 95:10 f.) This "they have not known" means "they did not want to know" in the same sense in which we say "they did not do it" and take this to mean "they did not do what they should." They are, then, not excused but rather accused by the fact that they did not know because they should have known and did not, as it says in Rom. 10:16: "But all do not obey the gospel," which means they do not want to obey, although they should.

You that abhor idols commit sacrilege. (Rom. 2:22.)
A sacrilege is a robbery and theft of the holy.[34] The Jews committed it in a twofold way: first, by withdrawing their heart and mind from the truth and the spirit and by relying instead upon

---

[34] Reuchlin, *Vocabularius breviloquus* (Strassburg, 1504): *"Sacrilegium committitur auferendo sacrum de sacro."*

their own understanding; second, and this is much more relevant to
the discussion, in the following way: They took the letters and the
words of Scripture, which is not only holy but the Holy of Holies,
and distorted them by giving them a false meaning, and thus they
cast and carved them into a spiritual idol, as it says in Ezek. 16:17:
"You took your fair jewels of my gold and of my silver, which I
had given you, and made for yourself images of men," etc. It is,
then, a sacrilege that Jerusalem took gold and silver (i.e., it ar-
bitrarily singled out certain words of Scripture) but worse still
is the idolatry that it fashioned them into idols and pictures, i.e.,
dead and static, i.e., obstinately maintained, conceptions, which it
placed in the temple of its heart. According to the letter, it abominates idols, but according to the spirit, they not only worship them
but even fashion them for themselves. "Of their silver and their
gold have they made idols to themselves that they might perish"
(Hos. 8:4), and "Gilead is a city of workers of idols" (Hos. 6:8),
i.e., of a false and deceitful teaching. But, in the eyes of the apostle,
sacrilege is worse than idolatry, because to invent something erro-
neous is not so great a sin as to put a false meaning on Scriptures,
i.e., to disregard the holy. The simplest interpretation of the text
would, therefore, be one that parallels that of the preceding verse,
so that the meaning of the apostle would be the following: you
commit a sacrilege, if not by what you actually do then by what
you want and yearn to do.

If, then, the uncircumcised keep the ordinance of the law, *shall
not this uncircumcision be reckoned for circumcision?* (Rom.
2:26.)

He speaks here of the uncircumcised, who believe in Christ, and
he contrasts them with the Jews, who take pride in their own
righteousness. Otherwise (i.e., if they do not believe in Christ),
they could not keep the ordinances of the law. This is also proved
by the fact that farther on, in order to explain, as it were, why
the uncircumcised will condemn the Jew, he makes a distinction,
namely, when he says: "For he is not a Jew who is one outwardly,"
etc. (Rom. 2:25). If "he who is a Jew outwardly" is judged by
someone uncircumcised, it cannot be that the uncircumcised one
is the one who is outwardly a Jew, but he is one who is a Jew in
concealment,[35] namely, by his faith in Christ, for otherwise he
could not judge the Jew.

For he is not a Jew who is one outwardly. (Rom. 2:28.)

We must construe this as follows: not one who is outwardly a

35 WA 56, 208, 17: *"in abscondito."*

Jew is a real Jew, and not that which is outwardly circumcision is the real circumcision, but one who is a Jew in concealment is a real Jew and the circumcision of the heart is the real circumcision, in the spirit and not in the letter. He explains here what he had said earlier (Rom. 2:25): "Thy circumcision is become uncircumcision," i.e., outward circumcision is not circumcision before God.

Whose praise is not of men, but of God. (Rom. 2:29.)

This is the same as what our Lord says in Matt. 23:5 about the moralists:[36] "They do all their works in order to be seen by men."

Outer righteousness is praised by men and reproved by God; inner righteousness, however, is praised by God and reproved and persecuted by men. Moreover, this righteousness seems foolish and even unrighteous to men as the other one is foolish before God; indeed, it is a double unrighteousness.

This, then, is the lesson: one who has not yet evaded the commendation of men, or suffered calumny, reproof, and persecution for his actions, has not yet attained to perfect righteousness. About this see the exposition given above of the word: "by patience in well-doing" (Rom. 2:7). see p. 42

[36] *"Iustitiariis,"* commonly translated "workmongers."

ROMANS, CHAPTER THREE

What advantage, then, has the Jew? Or what is the profit of circumcision? (Rom. 3:1.)

Because he has condemned the Jews according to the flesh and the circumcision which is done to the body, it may seem that he regards circumcision as useless and that he wants to affirm that its observance amounts to nothing. But this is not so. Therefore, he shows in this chapter what it was good for—and what Judaism did positively represent.

(1) The chief significance of circumcision was that **the words of God were believed** (Rom. 3:2), i.e., circumcision was of value because in it one believed in the promises of God, trusting that they would be fulfilled. This is the advantage of the Jew over the Gentiles. For, to them, God did not give any promise, but it was from pure mercy that, when the time was fulfilled, he regarded them as worthy to be put on the same level with the Jews. But toward the Jews he was not only merciful but also truthful, because he really actualized the mercy he had promised to them. That is why these two, mercy and truth, are so often conjoined with one another in the Scriptures. So, for example, farther on in ch. 15:8 f, of this letter: "For I say that Christ has been made a minister of the circumcision for the truth of God, that he might confirm the promises given unto the fathers, and that the Gentiles might glorify God for his mercy," etc.

One should note that the apostle does not say: "The words of God were believed by them," but, as the phrase goes in Greek:[1] "The words of God were believed in." He does not say specifically by whom, for against a statement to this effect the objection could easily be raised, which he refutes in what follows, namely, that

[1] This is how Faber translates in his Commentary.

they are not believed in by all. This, then, is the meaning of the text: the chief value of the circumcision, not only for itself, but for the whole world, was that in it the words of God were believed in, i.e., that in it some were found who believed the words of God and that thus the promise of God's grace and mercy was received, in which now also the Gentiles share.

For if they had not been believed there, they would not have been believed anywhere, and thus the promises of mercy would have found no response. So, in any case, circumcision was useful for the future righteousness, even though it did not make anyone righteous. Then the apostle turns to reply to the objection that the words of God were here not believed in because not all believed them, and that, therefore, the Jew had no advantage and that there was no profit in circumcision.

His reply is this: "For what if some were without faith? Shall their want of faith make of none effect the faithfulness of God?" (Rom. 3:3), i.e., because the words of God have found faith there, his promise certainly remains in effect; indeed, God has now bound himself and, because he is truthful, one may expect to see the fulfillment of his promise. And if his promise remains in effect because of their faith, the unfaith of some cannot make the faithfulness and truthfulness of God of none effect. The circumcision has, therefore, been wonderfully useful, for through it the promise of God was begun and established. One may, therefore, most certainly expect it to be fulfilled, because God is truthful.

So also our Lord says (John 4:22): "Salvation is from the Jews," even though the Jews themselves may not be saved, for in his promises God is more concerned for his own truthfulness for the sake of the faith of a few than for the multitude of unbelievers because of whom, one might think, he might render his promise invalid. For God does not lie but is truthful.

(2) One can understand the text also in the sense that it refers to the words of the Gospel, namely, that it was necessary that the word should first be spoken to the Jews (Acts 13:46) because of the promises of God. And then it went forth from the Jews also to the Gentiles. The circumcision was, therefore, very useful indeed because it was deemed worthy to receive the law of the gospel of which, later on, also the Gentiles became partakers. This, then, was the "advantage of the Jews" that the Gentiles received the sayings of God from them and that they did not receive them from the Gentiles.

But the first interpretation is the better one. For if the text is interpreted in the sense that the apostle speaks here of the words of the Gospel, then he must be understood to say that it is the advantage of the Jews not only that they have the words but also that they were the first to have the gifts of grace since, indeed, the apostles as the leaders and the highest and noblest part of the church came from them.

The passage has, then, the following meaning: The advantage of the Jews or the circumcision is not undone by the fact that a few did not believe. It is sufficient that some did believe, and it was through their faith that the promise was fulfilled and received. And so theirs is the advantage that they had the words of God before the Gentiles had them. In this sense it is said farther on in the letter in ch. 9:6: "It is not as though the word of God," i.e., the promise, "has come to nought," for the reason, namely, that many did not believe. Because of the fact that many did not believe, it may seem that God cast off his people and did not fulfill his promise. In this case, then, his words were not believed in and therefore the Jew has no advantage over the Gentile.

But the fact is that their "unbelief did not make the faithfulness of God" of none effect, i.e., it will not be the cause on account of which one would have to say that God is not truthful, for "he did not cast off his people which he foreknew" (Rom. 11:2). For not all those are his people who belong to his people by the flesh, but those who belong to it by the promise. We must, therefore, construe the interpretation of the passage as follows:

What advantage, then, has the Jew and what is the profit of circumcision? Much every way.

First of all (chiefly or mainly) **that they were entrusted with the words of God** (Rom. 3:2), i.e., that they were deemed worthy to receive the promises that are contained in the law, which is something that was not granted to the Gentiles. This is why the apostle says farther on in ch. 15:8 f. of this letter: that God has revealed Christ to the Jews because he is truthful and to the Gentiles because he is merciful. For he promised him not to the Gentiles but to the Jews, and among them his words were received in faith.

You may now object and say: If God gave his promise to the circumcision or if his words found faith in its midst, then he should have granted it his promise in such a way that all who belong to the circumcision could obtain it; otherwise, it might seem that he does not keep his promise and that he therefore is neither faithful nor truthful (indeed, it does seem that he did not make a promise to them, for, because he is truthful, he would keep it once he has made it, and that therefore the Jew has no advantage and that the words of God found no faith),[2] and, indeed, the opposite has happened, for not only has the circum-

[2] This parenthetical remark is written on the margin of the MS.

cision not obtained the fulfillment of the promise but it has instead been given to others, namely, to the Gentiles; and the majority of the circumcision did not obtain it.

To this objection the apostle replies: **For what if some were without faith?** (Rom. 3:3) (i.e., if they did not obtain faith and the promise), for only those are guilty who did not want to receive the fulfillment of the promise. This need not hinder anyone from believing that God is truthful. God did not give his promise, and his words did not find faith in the circumcision in such a way that, regardless of whether they want it or not, they must necessarily obtain the fulfillment of the promise. For then the truthfulness and faithfulness of God could be realized only if he were to grant the fulfillment of his promise to those who resist it as well as to those who do not want it. But this is absurd. For then the truthfulness and faithfulness of God would depend upon the human will, as if God were truthful only if men believe in him and are ready to accept his gifts. Therefore, we must say that "their want of faith shall not make of none effect the faithfulness of God," i.e., because some of the circumcision refused to receive what God promised to those who belong to the circumcision, one must not reproach him by saying that he is not truthful. It is enough that he did fulfill his promise to the circumcision, i.e., to some, not to all, namely, the elect. For God cannot lie. Hence, the apostle concludes: **For God is truthful.** (Rom. 3:4.)

You may persist in objecting and say: Whatever the case may be, the fact remains that he gave his promise to the Jews or to the circumcision and not to the Gentiles. If he, therefore, is truthful, he should have given it to all of them; and if he foresaw that he would not fulfill his promise to them on account of their unbelief, why did he give it to the circumcision at all? The answer to this is given farther on in chs. 9 and 11 of the letter. Here he touches the matter only briefly in order not to get too far afield from his topic. What he does say is that the promise was not made to all the children of Abraham, but only to the elect and those children of God who were to be adopted from the circumcision.

He is. (Rom. 3:4.)

The Greek text reads: "God shall be truthful" or "Let God be truthful."[3] These words give expression not so much to the truthfulness of God as to a confession of the truthfulness of God. What they mean is this: It is right that all should confess and admit that

---

[3] *WA* 56, 212: *"Graecus habet: 'Esto' sive 'Sit autem Deus verax.'"* Faber remarks on *"Esto": "per imperativum dicendum est."* Erasmus translates *"ginesthō"* by *"sit"* (in his *Annotationes,* he adds *"sive fiat"*).

God is truthful. One should, therefore, let him be so and regard him as truthful and believe him to be faithful in all his words, however much others disbelieve him. That the word is to be taken as an imperative is proved by the authority of the passage which the apostle quotes: "That thou mayest be justified," etc. (Rom. 3:4), i.e., let it be so, let all confess it, let it be made plain to all that thou art righteous and truthful in all thy words, regardless of how much the unbelievers will oppose and judge thee "in thy words," i.e., condemn thee (Rom. 3:4).

There is a difference between saying simply that God "is justified" and saying, "God is justified in his words" or works; the same difference prevails between God "is judged" and he "is judged in his words"; between God "is victorious" and he is "victorious in his words." For God as he is in himself can be justified by none, because he is justice itself, nor can he be judged, because he himself is eternal law and judgment and truth. So he is also in himself victorious over all, and it is not necessary to wish and pray that he be victorious. Thus we pray that his will be done (Matt. 6:10), although we know that it cannot be impeded.

Now, God is justified in his words when his word is reputed and received by us as just and truthful and this is done by faith in his word. And he is judged in his words when his word is reputed as false and deceitful and this is done by unbelief and "pride in the imagination of our heart" (Luke 1:51), as the Holy Virgin says. For our human wisdom does not only refuse to believe and obey the words of God, it also thinks that they are not words of God; it even believes itself to have the words of God and presumes to have truth. Such is the foolishness of the Jews and heretics and all stiff-necked men. And he is victorious in his words when his word prevails against all who try to oppose it—as it has happened with the gospel, which always is and has been triumphant. For the truth is all-victorious. He is, therefore, justified in those who in humility yield to his leading and believe in it. But he triumphs over those who disbelieve and judge him and contradict him. He is a sign "set for the resurrection" of the former and "for the fall" (Luke 2:34) of the latter, a "sign which is spoken against," i.e., they judge him, but in vain. In the same way we pray that his will be done, i.e., that his word and his every work, be it good or ill, may readily and freely be received by us.

COROLLARY

The fulfillment of this his will is, therefore, rather the fulfillment of our will according to the prayer that we might will what God wills. For what God wills is something difficult and hard—

something that far exceeds our will. In the same way, God is justified in his words when we are justified. And his being judged or condemned is really our being judged and condemned, according to the saying: "He that disbelieves shall be condemned" (Mark 16:16).

This, then, is the meaning of the passage: Must one say that God is not truthful because some do not believe, i.e., because they judge him in his words and are bent to make him a liar but regard themselves as bearers of the truth? No. We must, rather, say that he is all the more truthful and they all the more untruthful, for truth is all the more triumphant when it is impugned and it manifests its superiority all the more when it is held down. It is its nature that it marches forward when it encounters resistance; a symbol of this is the exodus of Israel and the drowning of Pharaoh. Hence, the apostle says: God is indeed truthful and man a liar, because it is written that it shall be so, namely: "That thou mayest be justified," etc., i.e., that thou wilt be found true when all will be proved to be liars, either when thou makest them righteous or when thou dost triumph over them, when, namely, thou justifiest those who worship thee and believe, and triumph over those who judge thee and disbelieve. Hereby is rendered invalid the objection of anyone who says: Apparently that circumcision was of no use and it profited them nothing that the words of God were entrusted to them, because most of them—and as what a liar he appears to them—have taken no advantage of it. From this, one concludes by implication that God did not keep what he promised, because the majority of the circumcision did not accept his promise. Or it follows from this that those are wrong who say that God did not keep his promise and that, therefore, either they or God are liars.

To this conclusion, which is fair enough, the apostle answers: "For what if some were without faith?" i.e., circumcision was useless because they did not believe, for God has nevertheless fulfilled his promises to the circumcision. Nor has God's faithfulness[4] been rendered vain because of them, but, rather, they themselves are hereby proved to be liars, for God is truthful but man is a liar. This is proved by the fact that he triumphs over their judgment about him. **Shall their want of faith make of none effect the faithfulness of God?** (Rom. 3:3), i.e., does it follow from the fact that they have not perceived the promise that it is not perceived at all, so that the Jews have no advantage over the Gentiles? For if it were the case that they were not preferred or did not have the words of God entrusted to them because most of them

4 *"Fides Dei."*

did not believe, it would follow, indeed, that God lied when he
gave his promise to this people. But this conclusion is absurd and
false. For (according to the clearer treatment of this problem
farther on in chs. 9 to 11 of the letter) not those who are children
after the flesh "are Abraham's seed" (Rom. 9:7). Indeed, those who
did not believe are liars, and not God, for he has given his promise
and kept it, not, to be sure, in all, but still in all children of the
promise.

That thou mayest be justified. (Rom. 3:4.)

This word of Scripture must here not be understood in terms
of the meaning and context it has in its own place, namely, in
Ps. 51:6, but solely in so far as it is cited in order to confirm the
statement that God is truthful in his words. For then it is put in
another connection. To be sure, the apostle, too, does not fail to
observe this, for quite incidentally he argues on the basis of the
same text according to the meaning it has in the psalm, by saying:
"But if our unrighteousness," etc. (Rom. 3:5). For there it is
stated that God is justified by the confession of our sin. Even
though he is righteous and truthful in himself, he is not so in us
unless we confess and say: "Against thee, thee only, have I sinned"
(Ps. 51:4). Then he is acknowledged as the only righteous one.
And so he is made righteous also in us.

But if our unrighteousness *commend the righteousness of God,*
what shall we say? **(Rom. 3:5.)**

Some say that God's righteousness is proved by our unrighteousness when he punishes it, because then it becomes apparent that
he is righteous in that he does not let the unrighteous go unpunished. This opinion is correct.[5] But it has nothing to do with the
topic the apostle treats in this context, for he does not here speak
of the righteousness of God by virtue of which he is righteous in
himself. Indeed, he denies that the righteousness of God is proved
by our unrighteousness; if he affirms this, he does so only in accordance with the meaning of the word of the psalm: "Against
thee, thee only, have I sinned," etc. And the psalm does not say
that it is our sin that justifies God but, rather, that it is the confession and acknowledgment of sin that humbles him who proudly
regards himself as righteous, trusts in his own righteousness and
thereby deprives God of his righteousness. To him alone belongs
righteousness—and also power and wisdom and all that is good.

For he who humbly puts all righteousness away from himself
and confesses himself a sinner before God thus glorifies God who

[5] In opposition to Faber.

alone is righteous. Therefore, not our unrighteousness, which God hates evermore as the enemy of his glory, but the acknowledgment and confession of our unrighteousness give him glory and praise because they show how needful to salvation his righteousness is.

Others, however, say that our unrighteousness incidentally commends God's righteousness, just as opposites placed next to each other shine all the more brightly—like colors and shadows in a picture.[6] But the apostle absolutely denies that our unrighteousness can in any way set off God's righteousness. Only carnal men can find such a meaning in the words of the psalm. This is made plain by the fact that when the apostle quotes the saying of the psalm "that thou mayest be justified," he draws conclusions from it, not with respect to God's righteousness, but to his truth.

He, therefore, does not speak here of the righteousness by virtue of which he is righteous in himself but of that by virtue of which he, being righteous, makes us righteous, and he alone is righteous with respect to us. Our unrighteousness, if it really has become our own (i.e., if it is acknowledged and confessed), greatly sets off his divine righteousness, for it makes us humble; it makes us throw ourselves down before God and causes us to ask for his righteousness. And when we have received it, we glorify, laud, and love God as the giver. Conversely, our righteousness reproves God's righteousness; indeed, it suspends it and denies it and declares it to be a falsehood and a lie—and this happens whenever we resist the words of God, saying that we do not need his righteousness and believe that our own is sufficient. One must, therefore, speak as follows: "Against thee, thee only, have I sinned, that thou mayest be justified"[7] (Ps. 51:4) (i.e., that thou mayest be proclaimed with praise and glory as the only righteous one who justifiest us "in thy words," i.e., as thou hast promised and testified).

For if the truth of God *has more abounded through my lie, unto his glory, why am I also yet judged as a sinner?* (Rom. 3:7.)

This means: If, then, we are to think that the truth of God abounded unto his glory through my lie and his righteousness through my unrighteousness (this is to speak after the manner of men [Rom. 3:5], and so those did indeed think who said: "Let

---

[6] Quoted by Nicholas of Lyra (ad Rom. 5:2; 7:15) from Aegidius Romanus, I *Sent.*, d. 46, q.2. Aegidius refers to Aristotle, *Elench.*, 15.

[7] Cf. Ps. 50:6. Luther here repeats literally his interpretation in the lectures on The Psalms. (Cf. *WA* 3, 284, 25.)

us do evil that good may come"[8]), how can God then punish the
world and condemn me as a sinner? Should he not, rather, give me
a crown instead, especially in view of the fact that his righteousness, truth, and glory thus increase more and more and that
thereby his own purpose is fulfilled? And thus we do his will by
committing evil.

By raising the matter in the form of a question, the apostle
clearly forbids us to interpret it in this way. It is not to be understood according to the literal meaning of the text, or after the
manner of men, but, as has been stated before, with reference to
righteousness and unrighteousness. The righteousness of God is
not set off because I act unrighteously but, rather, because I acknowledge that I have acted unrighteously and cease to do so in
order to embrace the righteousness of God or that which comes
from God, for all my righteousness is unrighteousness before him.
Wherefore I do not boast but am covered with shame before God.
And thus he alone is glorified in the righteousness by which he
justifies me, because he alone is justified (i.e., acknowledged as
righteous).

It is the same with truth: the truth of God is not glorified because I am caught in lies but because I acknowledge that I am a
liar and cease to be one, and embrace the truth which comes from
God in order to be rendered truthful by it and not by anything I
have of myself. Thus, all self-adulation will cease, and only God
will be glorified in me, because he alone has given me truth and
made me truthful—inasmuch as all truth of my own is mendacious before him.

Now what is said here about truthfulness and falsehood and
about righteousness and unrighteousness is applicable to all the
other perfections and their opposites—power and weakness, wisdom and foolishness, innocence and sin, etc. For about all of them
God and we conceited men, especially the Jews, are engaged in a
continuous harsh controversy, whereas God in his mercy desires
by his truth, righteousness, wisdom, power, and purity to make
one and all—who are lying, unrighteous, foolish, weak sinners—
truthful, righteous, wise, strong, and pure in order to free them
from lying, unrighteousness, foolishness, weakness, and sin, to the
end that his truth, righteousness, wisdom, power, and purity be
glorified and acclaimed by them and in them. Yet in their pride
they resent this as if by their own power and initiative they were
actually truthful, righteous, wise, strong, and pure. So they speak
up against God, set themselves up as judges over him, and try

[8] Luther writes by mistake: *"faciamus bonum,"* but the Vulgate reads: *"faciamus mala ut veniant bona."*

their best to make him appear mendacious, unrighteous, foolish, weak, and sinful. And all this because they want to establish their truthfulness, righteousness, wisdom, power, and purity, not wishing to be regarded as lying, unrighteous, foolish, weak sinners. Therefore, either God or they must be caught in falsehood and be unrighteous, weak, etc.

This is as if (to quote the story of Persius[9]) a physician, intent on curing a patient, came upon a man who denies that he is sick and calls the doctor a fool who is much sicker than he because he presumes to promise health to a healthy man. This resistance makes it impossible for the physician to prove the effectiveness of his medical art. But he would succeed if this sick man, admitting that he is sick, would submit to the cure and say: I am indeed sick and you will be acclaimed as a healthy man, i.e., when you have restored my health.

So it is also with the godless and the proud. When, in God's sight, they are sick, they regard themselves as in the best of health. Therefore, they do not only reject God as the physician but they regard him also as a foolish liar sicker than themselves because he presumes to heal them as if they were sick and not in the best of health. To be sure, thereby they do not censure God as he is in himself in his essence (because no creature and not even any malice can do this), but in his words. This is why the psalmist adds appropriately: "That thou mightest be justified in thy words." For the words which God lets go forth to men are regarded as foolish, mendacious, and meaningless, as if they were not God's. However, he has arranged to heal them by his speaking. Yet they refuse to admit that they are ill and, considering him as foolish and as sicker than themselves, resist and contradict him, set themselves up as judges over him and condemn him. But in vain. For God's words affirm themselves when they are judged in this way, or, rather, God affirms himself over against men in these his words when they set themselves up as judges over him by rejecting them. By this, their rejection of them, they obviously regard him as foolishly ignorant and weak, and yet they profess to love nothing but wisdom, power, and truth—as if they could say: How can he be wise who says that we are stupid? Must he himself not, rather, be stupid, because it is a fact that we keep ourselves to wisdom and follow it. And so it is with everything else. Can he (namely, God or his word) be truthful, righteous, strong, etc., when he censures us for being mendacious, unrighteous, and weak, while we keep ourselves to the ways of truth, righteousness, and virtue? He himself must be what he accuses us of being, for he does not share our

[9] Cf. Persius, *Sat.* III, 90 ff. *Satyrarum opus* (Venice, 1499).

knowledge of where the good is to be found. In exactly the same way, so the Gospel tells us, they said of Christ: "We know that this man is a sinner" (John 9:24). And again: "This man is not of God." (John 9:16.) The same is said in Ps. 4:6: "Many there are that say, Who will show us any good?" i.e., We know what is good; anyone who presumes to teach us something else must be in error; he cannot show us the good. So also John 9:40: "Are we also blind? Jesus said unto them: If you were blind, you would have no sin: but now you say, We see. Your sin remaineth."

We conclude, therefore, that God cannot become wise, righteous, truthful, strong, good, etc., in his words unless we believe him and, yielding to him, confess that we are foolish, unrighteous, liars, weak, evil. Therefore, humility and faith are needed. This is what these words point out and affirm. We must become inwardly nothing, emptied of everything, and, completely rid of ourselves, say with the prophet: "Against thee, thee only, have I sinned, that thou mayest be justified in thy words." To thee I am foolish and weak, in order that thou be wise and strong in thy words. Every created being teaches us this: "They that are whole have no need of a physician" (Matt. 9:12); "Only the lost sheep are sought" (Luke 15:4), and "Only the captives are set free" (Luke 4:18); only the poor will be filled with riches, only the weak strengthened, only the humble exalted; only what is empty is filled, and only what is unbuilt is put together. Do not also the philosophers[10] say: A matter cannot be formed unless it was first formless or unless the previous form has been done away with; and the "possible intellect" cannot obtain a form unless the ground of its essence is bare of all form and like a *tabula rasa?*[11]

Inasmuch as every created being gives such testimony, it cannot happen that one who is full of his own righteousness can be filled with the righteousness of God. He fills only those who hunger and thirst. Whoever, therefore, is satiated with his own truth and wisdom is incapable of comprehending the truth and wisdom of God, for they can be received only in emptiness and a vacuum. Let us, therefore, say to God: Oh, that we might willingly be emptied that we might be filled with thee; Oh, that I may willingly be weak

---

[10] Cf. Aristotle, *Physics, I, c.* 5–7. See the fuller discussion by Ficker (p. 128, n. 22).

[11] The picture of the *tabula rasa* is used by Aegidius Romanus (II *Sent., d.* 28, q. 1, a. 1) on the basis of Aristotle, *De anima*, III, 4. See also Thomas Aquinas, *Summa Theol.*, I, q. 79, a. 2. The Scholastics distinguished between *intellectus possibilis* and *intellectus agens*. In so far as the "possible intellect" apart from the "active intellect" has only the "possibility" to know anything, a man about to accomplish knowledge may be compared to a writing slate on which as yet nothing is written.

that thy strength may dwell in me; gladly a sinner that thou mayest be justified in me, gladly a fool that thou mayest be my wisdom, gladly unrighteous that thou mayest be my righteousness!

This is what is meant by the saying: "Against thee, thee only, have I sinned, that thou mayest be justified in thy words."

By way of a summary, we may say that *God is justified in three ways:*

First, when he punishes the unrighteous, for then he shows himself as righteous and his righteousness is manifestly acclaimed by the punishment of our unrighteousness. But this is only slight evidence, because also the godless punish the godless.

Secondly, in an indirect and relative way as in the case of opposites which, when they are placed next to each other, are more enhanced in their individual character than when each stands by itself. In the same way, God's righteousness is the more beautiful, the more detestable our unrighteousness is.

But, in this passage, the apostle does not have this in mind, for this comparison applies to God's internal and formal righteousness.

Thirdly, when he justifies the godless and infuses his grace or when one believes that he is righteous in his words. For by such believing he justifies, i.e., he reputes as righteous. This is why this righteousness is called the righteousness of faith or of God.

This is similar to the way by which a good craftsman proves himself a master. First, when he criticizes the inexperienced and rebukes them for their mistakes. Secondly, when, in comparison with them, he appears to have greater skill than they. Thirdly, when he transmits the perfection of his craft to others who did not have it before. And this is true proof of mastership. For to criticize others and thus to give evidence of one's skill does not mean that one is a good craftsman, but to cause others to become skillful like oneself, this is evidence that one is a master craftsman. In the same way, God is righteous in the sense that he causes us to be righteous and thus he proves himself a master.[12] But just as the unskilled do not want to be taught, the proud do not want to be justified.

God is proved righteous and truthful[13] in a threefold way:

First, when he punishes and condemns one who is unrighteous, mendacious, and foolish, etc.; for then he proves himself righteous, truthful, etc. Thus his righteousness, truthfulness, etc., are wonderfully set off and made manifest by our unrighteousness and falsehood. But this is but slight evidence; for also a liar often pun-

---

[12] *"Artifex,"* an artist; a master of any art. Luther frequently speaks of God as a master artist. In so doing, he was in line with Scholastic tradition.
[13] *"Deus iustificatur, verificatur."*

ishes and rebukes another who is a liar, and one who is unrighteous does the same to another who is unrighteous, and yet they
are, because of this, not immediately hailed as wholly truthful and
righteous.

Secondly, by way of comparison,[14] just as opposites when placed
next to each other become more apparent than when they stand
by themselves, so his righteousness is all the more admirable in
comparison with our detestable unrighteousness. But the apostle
does not speak here of these two modes, for they would apply
to God's internal and formal righteousness, but of this he does
not speak here.

Thirdly, by way of his working upon us,[15] i.e., when we cannot
become righteous by our own power and approach him that he
should make us righteous as we confess that we cannot overcome
our sin. He does this when we believe his words; for by such
believing he justifies us, i.e., he reputes us as righteous. This is
what we call the righteousness of faith and the righteousness which
God works in us.

COROLLARY

The apostle is not by any means saying here that "our unrighteousness commends the righteousness of God" (Rom. 3:5). Indeed,
he denies this, because it is not true. But he raises the question in
the name of some who believe that this is implied in the words of
the psalm. But this is not so. For neither the psalmist nor the
apostle meant to say that our sin justifies or commends God, for
not our sin does this, but our acknowledgment and confession that
we are sinners. Hence, it says (in Ps. 51:3): "For I know my iniquity," etc., and then there follows: and thus, "To thee only have
I sinned" (i.e., I know that before thee only I am a sinner).

For such an acknowledgment causes one to yearn for the righteousness of God, and such a confession makes one commend it.
For when I acknowledge that I cannot be righteous before God
because it is written: "In thy sight no man living shall be justified"
(Ps. 143:2), and similarly in many other places where God says
that we are in sins, then I begin to ask him for righteousness. Thus,
my acknowledgment of my sins has brought it about that God
was justified in me (i.e., that I believed in him and that he thus
justified me). This confession, then, commends and glorifies him
as the one who alone is righteous and makes us righteous. But he
is in no way commended wherever there is no confession and acknowledgment of sin and wherever it is the case that one does not

---

[14] "Relative."
[15] "Effective."

yearn for his righteousness because one is pleased and satisfied with one's own.

It is as in the case of a good craftsman: he can recommend himself in three ways. First, when he exposes and unsettles those who do not understand anything of his craft. But this is a meager and haughty recommendation. Secondly, when in comparison with others (even though he does not criticize them) he gives evidence of greater experience. Thirdly, when he transmits the mastery of his craft to others who ask him for it because they would not be able to achieve it by themselves. The first way of behavior often conceals pride and conceit, the second way, envy and arrogance, but the third is truly that of benevolence and humaneness. In the same way, God is righteous by making us righteous, and worthy of praise because he makes us similar to himself.

Yet, just as that craftsman cannot transmit his skill to any who do not trust him or who think of themselves as sufficiently skilled, and just as he cannot expect that they will praise and commend him for his dexterity and mastery unless they first acknowledge themselves as unskilled and believe him when he tells them that they are unskilled (even though their pride will not let them believe it), so the wicked do not believe that they are wicked and in no way acknowledge themselves as such. So, in short, they do not let God be justified in them and proved truthful, and thus they do not let him be commended and glorified.

Brief Summary

What advantage, then, has the Jew? (Rom. 3:1) (namely, he who is a Jew outwardly and according to the letter, for if he is not regarded as a Jew, he is in all respects like the Gentiles and has no advantage). **Or what is the profit of circumcision?** (Rom. 3:1) (namely, that which is in the flesh according to the letter, for if it is not regarded as circumcision, as was stated in the preceding chapter of this letter, must it, then, not be without profit?). **Much** (Rom. 3:2) (it is of advantage and of much profit). **In every way.** (Rom. 3:2.) This is either a way to assert something as in the form of a vow or it expresses the ways by which circumcision can be of profit as he enumerates them below in ch. 9:4 f. of the letter where he says: "to whom belongs the adoption, and the giving of the law, and the glory, and the covenant, and the service of God, and the promises; whose are the fathers," etc. **Chiefly** (i.e., in so far as I now choose to emphasize) **because unto them were committed the words of God.** (Rom. 3:2.) For this and other things the Gentiles did not have in the same way, according to Ps. 147:20: "He has not dealt so with other nations." For this and other things were the advantage only of the Jews before the Gentiles, also of those who were Jews only outwardly and according to the letter.

"Committed" means "received in faith." "Words" are what, below in ch. 9, he calls promises. The apostle does not say *"unto them,"*[16] but we can let the word stand and relate it either to "Jew" or "circumcision" in the first verse. In this sense, he says below in ch. 15:8 that "Christ was minister of the circumcision but not of the Gentiles, for the truth of God," scil., because God so promised it to them (the Jews) and not to the Gentiles.

For what, if some did not believe? (Rom. 3:3.) This "did believe" must be taken in an absolute, unqualified sense, in difference from the phrase "were committed," for one must not by implication understand it with reference to "words." For, in fact, all have received the words and promises of God and are still waiting for the promised coming of Christ. In other words: they do believe, but they are not faithful believers in Christ. This, then, is the meaning of the text: What does it matter?[17] What can we do about it? Is it not too bad just for them? Certainly not for God or for us. For it is clear that neither God's truth nor our faith are made without effect by their unbelief.

Shall their unbelief make the faith of God without effect? (Rom. 3:3) (i.e., the truthfulness and faithfulness of God). He says all this only because one could object to his statement that the promises are committed to the circumcision of the flesh and to the Jew who is outwardly a Jew, and ask: Why is it that no one who is a Jew outwardly, and according to the letter, received the promise? For if the promises that were given to the Jews according to the flesh and the letter (and it is in this respect that they have an advantage over the Gentiles) have not been kept, for none of them has received them and, indeed, they have not been fulfilled to this day, does it then not appear as if they had no promise at all or as if God had not kept it (for the Jew according to the flesh should have received the fulfillment of the promise because it was given to the Jew according to the flesh)?

The apostle meets this objection as follows: as if he were hammering on one nail with another, he says: So God's truth is without effect, his promise is empty, and his words are invalid. This is impossible and, therefore, also a conclusion of this sort. Nevertheless, the apostle does not settle the argument here but defers this to the

---

[16] Following Faber, Luther believed that the word *illis* should be stricken from the text of the Vulgate.

[17] Luther uses the German phrase: *"Was leit"* [liegt] *"daran?"*

ninth chapter. For there he shows how the fulfillment of the promise came to that Israel of the flesh which is the Israel of the promise and election as well as of the flesh, but never to that Israel which is Israel only according to the seed. Therefore, their unbelief cannot render the truth of God invalid. Thus he puts that objection aside for the time being. He simply rejects it, affirms over against it the truth of God and asserts that he always did fulfill his promises.

God forbid. (Rom. 3:4.) He calls the faith of God that promise which is now fulfilled in Christ according to the word of Ps. 85:11: "Truth is sprung out of the earth" (i.e., the promised Christ has come forth from the virgin). The meaning of the text, then, is this: God has now fulfilled his promises and has been proved truthful, but these people do not believe him and do not accept him. Shall it now be untrue, only because they do not believe, that God kept his promise, and must one say that the truth which now has been manifested is untrue? God forbid. If it were, the apostles, or rather God in them, would lie, because he himself witnesses to the fulfillment of his promises in Christ.

According to my understanding, "faith" here does not mean the faithfulness of God but rather "believing in God." This is the fulfillment of the promise, as is made plain in many passages of the Bible. For it is the righteousness that comes from faith which has been promised. Romans 1:17: "The just shall live by faith." (But there is no contradiction in this distinction. For precisely what according to the literal sense is regarded as the objective truth of faith must be understood according to the moral sense as faith in this truth.) The meaning, then, is perfectly plain: Shall we now give up our faith in God and follow them and deny the fulfillment of the promise rather than believe God when he says that he has fulfilled his promise? This question deserves only one answer: God forbid. We will not follow them but hold to the faith of God. **For God is true** (Rom. 3:4), and therefore he must be trusted. But **every man is a liar** (Rom. 3:4), and therefore he must not be trusted and followed. Or, as the Greek text has it: "Let God be true" (put your trust in God rather than in man, for he is a liar).

Thus he invalidates the objection that said: Israel of the flesh did not obtain the fulfillment of the promises that were given to it: therefore, they have not yet been fulfilled. Do they, then, speak the truth and God a falsehood? God forbid. They say: No, God: yes. This, then, is the reply to the objection: One must believe God, because he is truthful. **As it is written** that one must

Rom. 1:17

believe him (following the Greek text), for "to be justified" means "to believe" as it will be explained below. That thou mayest be justified in thy words and mayest overcome when thou art judged. (Rom. 3:4.) The apostle cites this word of Scripture in its plain meaning and not in a causal meaning, i.e., it must be understood in terms of "that" and not of "why,"[18] as if it read: You will be justified in your words and you will overcome when you are judged. It does not matter much that, farther on, he makes a digression and there deals with that causal sense of the saying. God, then, is justified in his words when one believes him in what he says in the gospel about the fulfillment of the promise and thus regards him as righteous and truthful. For his words are the word of the gospel. He is justified in them when one believes that he speaks the truth in them and that what is prophesied in this word of the psalmist will come to pass. Moreover, he will not only be justified by those who believe but he will also overcome when he is judged, i.e., when he is reproved by those others who deny that Christ has come and that the promises have been fulfilled. For they judge and condemn these words and do not regard them at all as right,[19] i.e., they do not believe that they are just and true. They even judge and condemn God in them, while the others regard him as righteous. But they do not prevail. He triumphs and maintains his victory, because however much they resist it, this faith of God, this "justification of God in his words" that is here spoken of (i.e., the trusting belief in his word), will persevere. For the justification of God and the trusting belief in God are one and the same.[20] He will prevail and remain; indeed, he gains ground and increases while the unbelievers decrease and perish.

"God is justified in his words" means that he is rendered just and true in his words or that his words are rendered just and true. And this comes to pass when one believes and accepts them and holds them true and just. The only resistance against this justification comes from the pride of the human heart through unbelief. For it does not regard the words of God as right but condemns and judges them. It does not believe them, because it does not regard them as true. And it does not regard them as true, because it regards as true only its own understanding, and this contradicts them. In this case, judging God in his words is the same as to reject him or his words and to render them untrue and unjust. And this comes to pass through the pride of unbelief and rebellion.

---

[18] WA 56, 225, 11: "Hanc authoritatem adducit apostolus secundum sensum, non secundum causam sensus, i.e., non ut causaliter, sed ut indicative intelligatur."
[19] "Nequaquam iustificant."
[20] WA 56, 226, 1: "Iustificatio Dei et credulitas in Deum idem est."

It is, then, obvious that this justification which is really a condemnation of God is extrinsic of God and his word; in fact, it happens in men. For intrinsically, God and his words are just and true. But they do not become so in us until our wisdom and knowledge yield to them and through faith make room for them and accept them. This is why Ps. 51:4 says: "Against thee have I sinned," i.e., I give up my righteousness and my understanding that resist and condemn thy words, and I confess that I am sinful and unrighteous and untruthful in order that thy words may dwell in me and be regarded as true and be and become true (in order that they may become in us what they are in themselves, for they are words that are justified in and for themselves).

COROLLARY

By this "justification of God" we are justified. And this passive justification of God by which he is declared righteous by us[21] is our active justification by God. For he reputes the faith as righteous that regards his words as righteous, according to what is said in the fourth chapter (Rom. 4:5) and in the first: "The just shall live by faith" (Rom. 1:17). And conversely: the passive condemnation of God by which he is condemned by the unbelievers is their own damnation. For he reputes as unrighteousness and damnation that unbelief by which they judge and condemn his words. This is in accordance with the Hebrew text which reads:[22] "Against thee have I sinned that thou mayest justify" (i.e., thou wilt bring about justification), "when thou speakest and thou wilt make clean when thou art judged." For he justifies (and triumphs) in his word when he makes us such as his word is, namely, righteous, true, wise, etc. And thus he changes us into his word, but not his word into us. And he makes us such as we believe his word to be, namely, righteous and true. For then certainly there is conformity between the word and the believer, i.e., in truth and righteousness. Therefore, when he is declared righteous, he makes righteous, and when he makes righteous, he is declared righteous. The same idea is therefore expressed by an active word in Hebrew and by a passive word form in our translation.[23]

But God will triumph, i.e., he will prevail and, in the end, he will prove as untruthful and false all who do not believe, i.e., those who have defiled him by their judgment, as it is made plain in the case of the Jews and as it will become still plainer in the

---

21 *"A nobis iustificatur."*

22 The Vulgate reads *"iustificeris"* ("thou mayest be justified"). The version to which Luther here appeals was proposed by Reuchlin (*Septem psalmi ponitentiales hebraici cum grammatica translacione latina,* 1512).

23 I.e., the Vulgate.

Last Judgment. For this reason, the Hebrew text reads: "Thou wilt make clean" (i.e., effect a cleansing) "when thou art judged," i.e., thou wilt make clean thy word and those who believe in it and thyself in them, and wilt prove this over against the lie which those unbelievers put upon it. And these thou wilt defile and prove them as filthy liars (and this means that their unbelief does not invalidate the faith of God).

faith /
trust

COROLLARY

The passive and active justification of God and faith or trust in him are one and the same. For when we acknowledge his words as righteous, he gives himself to us, and because of this gift, he recognizes us as righteous, i.e., he justifies us. And we do not justify his words, until we believe that they are righteous.

But if our unrighteousness commend the righteousness of God, *what shall we say?* (Rom. 3:5.)

This question has a twofold origin: it is occasioned by the quotation of the Bible passage from Ps. 51, and it arises naturally from the substance of the matter that is here dealt with. For because the psalm speaks causally (at least in our translation and in the Septuagint) when it says "that thou mayest be justified," it can give one the impression that it means to say that we committed sins in order that God might be justified and, therefore, that we must sin in order that God may be glorified. Moreover, the matter under discussion implies that God or his words cannot be regarded as just and become true unless we become untruthful and unrighteous over against them, and that thus he is made righteous by our sin.

the
Spirit

The problem is solved in the following way: the apostle speaks in the Spirit; he can therefore be understood only by those who are in the Spirit. The solution of Lyra—namely, that sin contributes accidentally to the commendation of God—can therefore not be maintained, for sin cannot possibly enhance the glory of God either by itself or by accident, especially if one keeps in mind the intrinsic truth of God or of his words.

However, "morally" or "tropologically," sin can be understood to enhance the truth of God by its being what it is, i.e., the trust by which we believe God that we are sinful, though we ourselves do not think or imagine that we are—this very faith establishes us as sinners and gives God the glory by accepting his words of grace and truth as fulfilling our needs. For who can be a recipient of grace and righteousness unless he confesses that he is a sinner?

COROLLARY

From what has been said it is plain that the phrase "that thou mayest be justified in thy words" means the same as "God is true but every man is a liar," and the sentence "and mayest overcome when thou art judged" means the same as "Shall their unbelief make the faith of God without effect?" The apostle, therefore, rightly puts in between both **as it is written** (Rom. 3:4), proving both by the Scriptures.

Likewise, in the same sense in which we can understand the statement that God and his words are justified when in faith we believe them to be true and righteous, though they are so in themselves also without our believing, we must take the sentence that we must become sinners and liars and fools and that all our righteousness, truth, wisdom, and virtue must perish. But this becomes a fact when we believe that we are sinners, liars, etc., and that our virtue and righteousness are absolutely nothing before God. And thus we become inwardly, inside ourselves, what we are outside ourselves, namely, before God, although inside ourselves we are not so, i.e., we do not believe that we are so. For as God, who alone is true and righteous and powerful in himself, wants to be such also outside himself, namely, in us, in order that he may thus be glorified (for this is the glory of any good that is in anyone that it must pour itself out beyond itself among others), so he wants also that man, who outside himself (i.e., before God) is wholly and without exception unrighteous and weak, become so also inside himself, i.e., that he confess and acknowledge himself to be as he actually is. By his outgoing, God thus causes us to enter into ourselves, and by making himself known, he causes us to know ourselves.[24] For if God did not first go out from himself in this way, seeking to prove himself in us as true, we should not be able to enter into ourselves and become unrighteous liars. For it would be impossible for man to know from his own self-knowledge that he is a liar before God unless God himself revealed it to him. "For who has known the mind of the Lord? and who has been his counselor?" (Rom. 11:34.) Otherwise, man would always believe himself to be truthful, righteous, and wise, especially because he is so in his own eyes and in the judgment of other men.

But now God has revealed to us what he thinks of us and what he judges us to be, namely, that we are all sinners. We must, therefore, yield to this, his revelation and his words, and believe them and thus acknowledge them as just and true in order in their light

---

[24] The terms *"intra se extra se"* and *"exire-introire"* are taken over from Tauler (*Sermones*, 1508).

to confess ourselves as sinners, which is something that we could not have known from ourselves. As the apostle says: "If any man among you seem to be wise in this world, let him become a fool that he may be wise." (I Cor. 3:18.) What he says here about foolishness applies to all other imperfections: one who wants to be righteous, truthful, and strong must become one who is sinful, mendacious, and weak.

This outgoing[25] is spiritual and not physical or natural. It is to effect nothing less than the destruction of our self-will,[26] which causes us to misjudge ourselves so badly. Thus, "He scattered the proud in the imagination of their heart." (Luke 1:51.) This is all the strength he has shown. It follows, then, that when we are told that we must become sinners, this is something entirely spiritual. Many, however, understood the apostle literally and in a carnal sense when he preached how a righteous man turns into a sinner. So he says in what follows.

The same theme runs through Psalm 51. It says: "For I know my transgressions" (Ps. 51:3), and then immediately thereafter: "Against thee have I sinned" (Ps. 51:4), i.e., before thee I acknowledge myself a sinner, however much I may be righteous before men. But thereby I do not escape the judgment that to thee I am a sinner in order that "thou mayest be justified," i.e., in order that I may be led to believe thy words so that I, too, may be justified. Farther on, the psalm speaks of "the uncertain and hidden parts of thy wisdom," i.e., of the fact that thou hast revealed to me that hidden wisdom which we never can have from ourselves, that before thee we are sinners.

Corollary: It is not a satisfactory exegesis of this "Before thee, thee only, have I sinned," etc., to say, as some do,[27] that David spoke in this way only because princes have only God above them to whom they can confess their sins and by whom they may expect to be punished. No, he speaks here for himself as a spiritual person, in the same way in which everyone else must do so, as, for example, in Ps. 32:6: "For this" (namely, because of the iniquity of his sin) "everyone that is holy shall pray to thee," i.e., whoever wants to be holy will confess himself to be sinful and unholy, and to those who say, "I will confess my transgression before thee; thou wilt forgive the wickedness of their sin" (Ps. 32:5). The same is said in I John 1:10 and 9: "If we say we have not sinned, we make God a liar" (and this is a double sin), "but if we confess our sins, he is faithful to forgive our sins." And again: "If we say that

---

[25] "Itio."
[26] "Sensum proprium" (Eigensinn).
[27] I.e., Lyra and the Glossa ordinaria, ad loc.

we have no sin, we deceive ourselves and the truth is not in us."
(I John 1:8.) Therefore, let us say with the prophet: "And my
mouth shall show forth thy praise" (Ps. 51:15), not ours; and again:
"My tongue shall sing aloud of thy righteousness" (Ps. 51:14), and
not of ours.

We have, then, given more than sufficient proof that God alone
is truthful and every man a liar. "Their unbelief," therefore, does
not need "to make the faith of God without effect." What does it
matter to our faith if they do not believe? We do not need to give
up our faith because of their unbelief, nor is God's truthfulness
undone by it, but the fact is that they are liars.

COROLLARY

Even if we recognize no sin in ourselves, we must yet believe
that we are sinners. This is why the apostle says: "I know nothing
against myself, yet am not hereby justified" (I Cor. 4:4). For as
through faith the righteousness of God lives in us, so through
faith also sin is alive in us, i.e., by faith alone we must believe that
we are sinners, for this is not obvious to us; indeed, quite often
we are not even conscious of it. Therefore, we must stand in the
judgment of God and believe him when he says that we are sinners,
for he cannot lie. And it must be so, although it is not evident, for
"faith is the evidence of things not seen" (Heb. 11:1) and rests
content with the words of God alone.

The Kingdom of Christ that has been prophesied will consist
of this very humility and judgment. For thus "he judges among the
nations" (Ps. 110:6). And "there are set thrones for judgment"
(Ps. 122:5), for we must continuously accuse, judge, and condemn
ourselves and confess ourselves as evil in order that God may be
justified in us. It is this same faith which speaks out of words like
these: "Clean thou me from hidden faults. Who can disclose his
errors?" (Ps. 19:12), and again: "Remember not the sins of my
ignorance" (Ps. 25:7).

Now, we must seriously ponder the idea that it is not enough to
confess with one's mouth that one is sinful, unrighteous, untruthful, or foolish. For what is easier to do than that, particularly if
you have peace of mind and are not upset?[28] No, when you have
said in so many words that you are a sinner, you must have the
same feeling about yourself in your heart and behave accordingly
in all you do and undertake. For this reason, it is exceedingly rare
that a man acknowledges himself to be a sinner. For how can he
acknowledge himself as a sinner if he cannot even tolerate a word
of criticism against himself or his actions or intentions, but im-

[28] "Extra tentationem."

mediately flares up in anger, refusing to admit that he ever even spoke an untruthful word but claiming always to have been truthful and well-meaning? So he regards it as mean of others to oppose him and to accuse him unjustly. When he is forced to endure this or that, he gets furious and wearies everyone around him with the complaint that he and he alone has been done an injustice. What a hypocrite he is! He did confess himself a sinner, but he does not want to do or bear anything that behooves a sinner to do but only what a righteous and holy man is entitled to!

Every one of us is thus quick to say: I am a most miserable sinner; but hardly anyone ever wants to be a real sinner. For what else is a sinner but one who deserves to be punished and upset in every way? But to admit in words that one is a sinner and to refuse to act like one means that one is a hypocrite and a liar. Only a righteous man is entitled to peace, joy, glory, honor, and every good. Therefore, if you deny that you are righteous, you must refuse to accept any of these. And if you admit that you are a sinner, you must be willing to take punishment, injury, and ignominy as if it were what you had coming to you and what you deserve. You must avoid those goods as something that belongs to someone else, indeed, only to the righteous. So, when you happen to be insulted or shamed or beaten or injured or blamed or if you fall sick and you say: "I do not deserve this—why must I bear this? I am done an injustice; I am innocent!" do you then not deny that you are a sinner and do you then not resist God while your own words convict you as a liar? As a matter of fact, by all this (as if by his word, for "he spake and it was done" [Ps. 33:9]), God proves and confirms that you are a sinner by letting you bear what a sinner deserves. And he cannot possibly err or lie. But you rise up in angry protest contradicting God and contending against him as if he had done something evil, foolish, and false. And so you resemble those who were spoken of earlier as "those who are contentious and do not believe the truth but believe unrighteousness" (Rom. 2:8). For you do not believe the truth (i.e., what God does against you when he lets all this befall you).

But if you say when something like this happens: Oh, yes, I deserve this; it serves me right; I readily admit that all this is just and right because I am, indeed, a sinner; certainly I have sinned against thee and what thou doest and sayest is justified, O God, truthful and righteous; thou art not mistaken with me and thou art not wrong, for I am indeed the sinner thou hast proved me to be by all this!—behold, this is to say: "Against thee, thee only, have I sinned and done what is evil in thy sight, that thou mayest be justified in thy words" (Ps. 51:4). And just so Dan. 3:31, 29:

"All thou hast done to us, O Lord, thou hast done rightly, for we have sinned against thee," etc.

It is just as if, when two men fight about something, one of them humbly gives in and says: I am ready to give in so that you can be right and true. I want to have been in error and in the wrong in order that you may be right in what you do and feel. Will the other not say: I have been wrong and you are right? And so they will be of one mind, whereas otherwise they would have remained in angry discord. Yes, yes, "be not wise in your own conceit" (Rom. 12:16).

This is why I have said how unusual and difficult it is to become a sinner and to speak this verse correctly and from the heart. For nobody is eager to be contradicted in what he thinks of himself, or reproved in what he does, or despised in what he plans to accomplish. Nevertheless, if one were willing to take it and say: Tell me what I must do, I shall be glad to do it; and if he would thus never take this side or that, how happy he would be! But the pride of our feeling and willing is much too deep-seated. Nobody is entirely free from this pest, especially if things go against us. *Pride*

Now we must say a word about the way in which man must become spiritually a sinner. For this is nothing natural. For, naturally, every man does not become a sinner—he is one. But all that is able to bring this change about lies concealed in our mind or self-regard and self-esteem. To change our mind is the purpose of every word of Scripture and every action of God. For in our mind are "the evil eye" (Matt. 20:15) and, humanly speaking, incorrigible pride. This is why the Holy Virgin says: "He has shown strength with his arm; he has scattered the proud in the imagination of their heart" (Luke 1:51), i.e., in their self-satisfied ways of thinking by which they set themselves over against God. Hence, this attitude of mind is called "the counsel of the godless" (Ps. 1:1) and "the golden calf" in the desert (Ex., ch. 32), mystically understood, and likewise, the idol of Baal and Moloch, etc., from which "the wicked shall not rise again in judgment" (Ps. 1:5). *... becoming a sinner.*

To become a sinner means, then, to destroy this obstinate way of thinking that lets us imagine that we live, speak, and think well, piously, and justly, and to take on another understanding of ourselves (which comes from God), according to which we believe in our heart that we are sinners who do, speak, and live evil, and are in the wrong, so that we must accuse, judge, condemn, and detest ourselves. "He that does these things shall not be moved forever." (Ps. 15:5.)

What we have said here, must, of course, be rightly understood: the disapproval of righteous, good, and holy works must not be interpreted in the sense that they are not to be done at all but with respect to the attitude of mind that causes us to esteem and regard them highly; in other words, we must not trust in them to such a degree and esteem and value them so highly as if, because of them, we were worthy before God to measure up to the requirements of righteousness. It is this display of vanity and this foolish estimation of ourselves that are to be rejected by what we have been saying.

good works

In other respects, we must perform good works with utmost eagerness and fervor to the end that through them, in a preparatory course as it were, we finally become fit and capable of obtaining the righteousness of God. Our good works, therefore, do not constitute righteousness but they are our prayer for righteousness. Thus, they do not represent our righteousness so long as we do not impute them to ourselves as such. By all this we must prepare the way of the Lord[29] who will come to us. But good works are not the way of the Lord. The way of the Lord is the righteousness of God in so far as the Lord alone, as he is present in us, effects it in us after they have been done.

Corollary

God is mutable to the highest degree.[30] This is obvious, because one can justify and judge him, according to Ps. 18, 26: "With the elect thou wilt be elect, and with the perverse thou wilt be perverted." For as everyone is in himself, so God is to him objectively.[31] If he is righteous, God is righteous; if he is pure, God is pure; if he is unjust, God is unjust, etc. So he will appear as unjust to

---

[29] Cf. Isa. 40:3; Matt. 3:3.

[30] In the interlinear gloss, Luther comments as follows on Rom. 1:23 (*WA* 56, 12 f., 13 ff.): Et mutaverunt *non Deum ipsum, quia incorruptibilis* gloriam incorruptibilis Dei, *i.e., gloriosam et incorruptibilem divinitatem* in similitudinem imaginis" ("*And changed* not God himself, who is incorruptible but *the glory of the incorruptible God,* i.e., his glorious and incorruptible divinity, *into an image*"). In the marginal gloss, he defines the nature of the change further: "'*Mutaverunt,*' sc. in seipsis (sc. per viciosam estimationem) *non in Deo, qui est immutabilis*" ("'They changed,' namely, in themselves [on account of their defective judgment] and not in God, who is immutable"). On the problem of the divine immutability, cf. Peter Lombard, I *Sent., d.* 8, *c.* 2; Gabriel Biel, I *Sent., d.* 8, *q.* 7.
  Luther's interpretation of justification here must be seen in relation to nominalist teaching. Cf. Gabriel Biel, I *Sent., d.* 17, *q.* 1, *c.* 2, *a.* 3, *dub.* 1. See Feckes, *Die Rechtfertigungslehre des Gabriel Biel* (Münster, 1925), p. 21.

[31] *WA* 56, 234, 3: "Qualis est enim unusquisque in seipso, talis est ei Deus in obiecto. Si iustus, iustus; si mundus, mundus; si iniquus, iniquus, etc. Unde et damnatis inaeternum iniquus videbitur, iustis vero iustus et sicut in seipso est. Verum haec mutatio extrinseca est."

those who are eternally damned, but to the righteous, as righteous, and so he is in himself. This change, however, is extrinsic. This is plainly implied in the word "Thou wilt be judged." For as God is judged only from the outside, on man's part, so he is also justified only from the outside. Hence, one can necessarily say only extrinsically of God: "That thou mayest be justified."

For if the truth of God has more abounded through my lie, unto his glory, why am I also yet judged a sinner? And not rather (as we are slandered and as some affirm that we say) let us do evil, that there may come good—whose damnation is just.[32] *What then? Do we excel them? No, not so.* **For we have charged** *both Jews and Greeks.* (Rom. 3:7–9.)

Even though the Jews excel in the advantages that have been named and that are enumerated in more detail below in the ninth chapter of this letter, they are on this account not better before God but stand under sin equally with the Gentiles. From this it then follows plainly that when the apostle spoke earlier of "the Gentiles who know by nature the things contained in the law" (Rom. 2:14), he intended to attribute to them only the particular righteousness of the law but not the universal one that is infinite, eternal, and wholly divine, and which only Christ gives to us. For as it is not enough to do the works of the law outwardly, so it is also not sufficient to do them inwardly except on the basis of the justification through Christ. If we, nevertheless, say of someone that he does the works of the law inwardly, we must be mindful that, as the Scripture says (Gen. 8:21), our heart and mind are always inclined toward evil and unwilling to do the good that

---

[32] Here is Luther's marginal gloss on Rom. 3:8 (*WA* 56, 33, 13 ff.): "This passage shows clearly that, in this letter, the apostle does not speak against those who obviously are sinners, through and through, but against those who in their own eyes are righteous and are confident that they will be saved by their works. It is these whom he tries to induce to take seriously the grace of God, but it cannot be taken seriously, unless one first acknowledges and takes seriously the sin which is forgiven by it. This is why some were scandalized by this when they heard about it. They thought that the apostle was preaching that one must do evil in order to take seriously the glory of God.

"Now, our iniquity and falsehood 'abound to his glory,' as, by humbling ourselves in confessing them, we glorify God for the sake of his abundant grace as he forgives us our sins. But he would not be glorified in this way, in case we should believe that we had no need of his grace but that we were standing before him sufficient to ourselves. One who acknowledges that he has many sins is, therefore, better than one who, like the Pharisee, acknowledges that he has much righteousness and no sin. For the former glorifies God's mercy, but the latter his own righteousness."

the law prescribes; and so, as we have sufficiently stated before, we actually do not do the good.

They are all under sin. (Rom. 3:9.)

This entire passage must be understood as being spoken in the Spirit, which means that it does not deal with men as they appear in their own eyes and before other men but as they are before God, where they are all under sin, both those who are obviously evil even in the sight of men and those who appear to be good to themselves as well as to other men.

This can be explained as follows: Those who are obviously evil sin both inwardly and outwardly and are without an appearance of righteousness even in their own judgment. But those who seem to themselves as well as to others outwardly good sin in the inward man. Even though they do good works outwardly, they do them either because they fear punishment or because they love riches or glory or some other created good, but not because they want to do them gladly; so the outer man, it is true, applies himself diligently to good works, but the inner man is filled to overflowing with opposite lusts and desires. For if this kind of man could do so with impunity and if he knew that he could not obtain either glory or peace of mind by his actions, he would rather let the good go and do evil just like those others. What, then, is the difference before God between one who does evil and another who wants to do evil but does not do so only because he is restrained by fear or enticed by the love of some temporal good?

A man who regards this outward righteousness as sufficient and opposes those who teach an inward one; who defends himself against the criticism or does not recognize that he is meant by the criticism, not that he does not do anything good but that he does not act from an upright heart; who does not amend the inclination of his will toward desires that are opposite of what he does— such a man will be worse off than any other. For certainly his good works are doubly evil, first, because they are not done from good will and are therefore evil, and, secondly, because he affirms and defends them as good from a second, new kind of pride. As it says in Jer. 2:13: "My people have committed a double sin," etc.

We shall, therefore, always be under sin unless this inclination of our mind is healed by the grace of Christ, so that we do the works of the law freely and gladly and, acting neither from fear of punishment nor from self-love, seek nothing else than to please God and to do his will.

Hence, he says: **There is none righteous.** (Rom. 3:10.) Here, now, everyone must look out, keep his eyes open, and pay close attention. For the righteous man, whom the apostle here has in mind, is rare indeed. This is because we seldom analyze ourselves so profoundly that we recognize this weakness or, rather, this vicious pest of our will. This is why we humble ourselves so rarely and seldom seek the grace of God in a right way, for, as it says here, we lack understanding. For this disease is so subtle that even the most spiritual men cannot effectively deal with it. The truly righteous, therefore, implore God with groanings for his grace, not only because they see that they have an evil will and are thus sinful before God, but also because they see that they cannot possibly ever penetrate and confine the evil of their will. So they believe that they are permanently sinful as if the depth of their evil will were inexhaustible.[33] So they humble themselves and pray with weeping and groaning until they are healed and rendered whole, but this happens only in death.

This is, then, why we are always in sin. "We fail in many things." (James 3:2.) And "if we say that we have no sin, we deceive ourselves." (I John 1:8.) Who, for example, does the good and avoids evil from such a mind that he would persist in thus doing and not doing even without a commandment or prohibition? I believe that if we really analyze our heart, nobody, unless he is absolutely perfect, will find himself to be this sort of man, but if he could, he would leave much good undone and do evil. This is what it means to be in sin before God, whom we should serve freely from that attitude of mind that I have described. So then, "there is not a righteous man on earth that does good and sins not." (Eccl. 7:20.) Hence, the righteous always confess themselves as sinners (Ps. 32:6): "For this shall everyone that is holy pray to thee in a seasonable time."

Yes, who knows or can know, though he imagines that he means to do good and not evil, whether this is really so, since only God will judge this and we ourselves cannot possibly act as judges in this case, according to the words of the apostle in I Cor. 4:7: "Who makes thee to differ" and, again, "Judge nothing before the time," etc. (I Cor. 4:5). If some really imagine that they have such an attitude of mind, they make a dangerous presumption, in connection with which most are very cunningly deceived: confident that they are already in possession of divine grace, they fail to search the secrets of their heart; then they grow more indifferent from day to day and, in the end, they literally perish. If they would inquire whether they are moved to do good and avoid evil by fear of punishment or love of glory, by shame, inclination, or some

[33] *"Velut voluntatis malae infinita sit profunditas."*

other desire, they would doubtless discover that they are moved
by motivations of the sort that we have just spoken of, and not
by the will of God alone, or, at least, that they do not know
whether it is by the will of God that they do the right. As soon as
they would find (as they inevitably must) that this is so, they surely
would be scared, especially since we tend to anticipate, not something better, but the bad, because from ourselves we are naturally
evil, and they would humble themselves, constantly seek the grace
of God with wailing and groaning, and thus they would make
steady progress. For when we are told to hope, we are certainly
not told so in order that we might hope to have done what we
should, but that the merciful God who alone can see into the
innermost depth of our being (beyond the surface of which we cannot penetrate) will not impute our deeds as sin to us so long as we
confess to him. As Job says: "Although I should be simple, even
this my soul shall be ignorant of" (Job 9:21), and again: "I feared
all my works," etc. (Job 9:28), because he could not know whether
he had acted out of the duplicity of his heart or whether he had
sought his possessions from a completely hidden cupidity.

In view of this, it is an expression of pride and every kind of sin
that Seneca says: "Even if I knew that men would never be aware
of it and that the gods would not notice it, I should never commit a sin."[34]

For, *first*, man cannot possibly have such a will from himself,
because he is always inclined toward evil to such an extent that
only the grace of God can arouse him to do good. A man who is
presumptuous enough to think himself capable of this has not yet
come to know himself. Now it is true, I grant, that one can do and
will some but not every good from such an attitude of mind, because we are not so thoroughly inclined toward evil that there is
not left to us a portion which is affected toward the good, as
is evident in the synteresis.[35]

Secondly, even if he says that he would not commit a sin, if he
knew that the gods would not notice it and men would not become aware of it, would he also be bold enough to say that he
would do the good even though he knew that neither the gods nor
men would care about it? If he says he would, he is as proud as he
is bold, because he could not avoid being self-satisfied in his own

---

[34] This saying cannot be found in Seneca's writings. But, according to Ficker
(p. 236, n. 32), it is quoted in a very similar form in a commentary (by
Limperger, published in Strassburg, 1490) on the Rule of the Augustinians (37) and is there attributed to Seneca. It is also to be found as a quotation from Seneca in Jodocus Windheim's "Penitential [*Beichtbüchlein*]
for the students of Erfurt" (Erfurt, 1515), *fol.* A 3b.

[35] "*Syntērēsis*" (cf. Chapter I, note 46).

boasting vainglory. This is because man cannot but seek his own
and love himself above everything. This is the sum and substance
of all his faults. For this reason, people like this seek themselves
even in the good they try to accomplish, i.e., they want to please
and applaud themselves.

There is none that is righteous (Rom. 3:10), because nobody is
willing of himself to fulfill the law of God, but all oppose the will
of God (at least in their heart), inasmuch as he is righteous "whose
will is in the law of the Lord" (Ps. 1:2).

And so also, **There is none that understands** (Rom. 3:11), because the wisdom of God is hidden and unknown to the world.
"And the word was made flesh" (John 1:14) and wisdom incarnate,
and thus it is hidden and comprehensible only to proper understanding just as Christ is knowable only by revelation. For this
reason, people who know only what they see and are knowledgeable only in what is visible (and of this sort are all men who are outside faith and who know nothing about God and the future life) do
not understand and know anything, i.e., instead of having understanding and wisdom, they are stupid and blind; and even though
they may be wise in their own eyes, they have become foolish.
Their wisdom consists of what is within the reach of human inquiry but not of the knowledge of things that are concealed.

There is none that seeks God. (Rom. 3:11.)
This is said both of those who are obviously not concerned about
God and of those who seek him or, rather, think they seek him,
for in fact they do not seek him as God wants to be sought and
found, namely, in humility through faith and not through one's
own wisdom in presumptuousness.

COROLLARY

As the sentence "There is none righteous" must be understood
with respect to two kinds of people, namely, those who digress
toward the left and others who digress toward the right, so also
this passage: "There is none that understands; there is none that
seeks God." For some, since they are not righteous, have no understanding and fail to seek God because they have no interest in doing so and simply let it go, while others are in the same predicament because they overreach and venture too much. They are
excessively righteous and understand and seek too much, so that
they are unteachable —or as the comic poet puts it: *"Faciunt ne*

intelligendo, ut nihil intelligunt"[36] ("They do nothing without understanding and therefore understand nothing"). And again: "*Summa iustitia saepe summa stultitia*"[37] ("The greatest justice is often the greatest foolishness") or rather injustice, namely, when one stubbornly insists upon it and refuses to yield to the opposite party. As the common proverb puts it: "*Weiss Leut narrn groblich*" ("The wise make the greatest fools").

It says here first: "There is none that understands," and then there follows: "There is none that seeks." For knowing precedes willing and doing; and "seeking" requires affection and the deed. But this follows upon understanding. Hence, the godless on the left have no understanding because in their vain desiring[38] they are blinded by what is immediately within their reach. And those on the right have no understanding because they are ensnared in the conceit of their own wisdom and righteousness. And thus they shut themselves out from the divine light.[39]

Over against these two types, a man can be called righteous in the true sense of the word if he has understanding and seeks God according to such understanding. For understanding without this seeking would be dead, just as faith without works is dead (James 2:17) and without power either to give life or to justify. By contrast, that man is unrighteous who neither understands nor seeks God. Hence, the apostle says first: "There is none righteous." And by way of an explanation of what it means not to be righteous he says: "He does not understand and does not seek God."

COROLLARY

The understanding of which the apostle here speaks is nothing else than faith itself or the knowledge[40] of things that cannot be seen but must be believed. Thus it is an understanding in concealment, for it is concerned with things that man cannot know by means of his own resources,[41] as we read in John 6:44: "No one comes to the Father but by me" and again: "No man can come to me, except my Father draw him" (John 14:6). And to Peter,

---

[36] Terence, *Andria* 17.

[37] Terence, *Heautontim.*, 796 ("*ius summum saepe summa malitia est*"). Cicero said, "*Summum ius summa iniuria.*"

[38] "*In vanitate concupiscentiae.*"

[39] "*Et sic sibiipsis sunt obex lucis divinae*" ("And so they are to themselves a bolt against the divine light"). "*Obicem ponere*" ("to put a bolt before") is a term used in the theology of the sacraments; it refers to mortal sin as a "bolt" that keeps out grace.

[40] "*Fides seu notitia.*" Cf. Gabriel Biel, III *Sent.*, d. 23, q. 2, a. 1, n. 1.

[41] *WA* 56, 239, 1: "*Est intellectus in abscondito, quia eorum, quae homo ex seipso nosse non potest.*"

Christ said: "Blessed art thou, Simon Bar-Jonah, for flesh and blood has not revealed it to thee, but my Father who is in heaven." (Matt. 16:17.) How can the godless at the left and people who are bound to the senses possibly know this, in view of the fact that they put so much value on what can be seen? And how can the others at the right, in view of the fact that they consider and ponder so much the insights of their own minds? They both shut themselves off from the light of this understanding and put a foreign obstacle in their way toward it.

Now the yearning or seeking for God is the very love of God which causes us to will and to love what the understanding gives us to know. For even if one has come to understand and to believe, he cannot, without the grace of God, love and willingly do what he believes and understands. Now, it is appropriate that our text says: "There is none that seeks." For as long as we live on this earth we cannot possess God but must seek him.[42] We must always seek him and search for him and ever keep seeking him, as it says in Ps. 105:4: "Seek his face evermore." "For thither did the tribes go up," etc. (Ps. 122:4.) Thus the way goes from strength to strength and from clarity to clarity toward the same goal. For not he that starts to seek but he that "perseveres" in seeking "to the end will be saved" (Matt. 10:22; 24:13), one who begins his seeking all over again, ever seeking again what he has found. For he that does not go forward in God's way goes backward.[43] And he that does not persist in seeking loses what he has found, for there is no standing still in the way of God. Or, as Saint Bernard says: "When we begin not to want to become better, we cease to be good."[44]

[margin: Bondage of the will]

COROLLARY

Though one may understand this psalm also with reference to the godless at the left, it speaks principally of those at the right. For the former rarely err so profoundly that "they say in their heart: There is no God" (Ps. 14:1). They know of God and his commandments, but it is through their whole way of life that they say: "There is no God." What they tell us about him is not true: therefore there is no truth and no God.

Now the latter, too, say this with words and deeds but chiefly

[42] WA 56, 239, 14: "Quia huius vitae status non habendo, sed quaerendo Deo peragitur."

[43] WA 56, 230, 20: "Qui enim non proficit in via Dei, deficit." In his comment on Ps. 118:18 (WA 4, 350, 15) Luther says: "Proficere est nihil aliud, nisi semper incipere. Et incipere sine proficere hoc ipsum est deficere" ("to go forward is nothing else than to start afresh again and again. And to begin without going forward, this means to accomplish nothing at all").

[44] Bernard of Clairvaux, Ep. 91.

with their heart, because they do not really know God but picture him to themselves as they like. Therefore, they do not hear what God says nor know about it, but they think and assert that they have the word of God and demand to be listened to. This is how they go wrong in their heart and so, when they hear the voice of God, they harden their hearts as if it were not God's voice and as if it were not God speaking. And this because the voice of God speaks against everything they produce from their own mind (which seems so right and wise and filled with the things of God), and so it is that they say from a zeal for God and out of the love of truth and because of their abundant awareness of the divine: "There is no God." They deny the truth and become fools precisely because they claim to know everything.

All proud and self-sufficient people are in this moral predicament, particularly in connection with concerns that relate to God and the salvation of the soul. God certainly speaks here, but he speaks in such a way that it does not become apparent to the proud what word he speaks through a particular person at a particular time and place. Unbelieving and at the same time foolish as they are, they therefore draw back from it or object and say, at least in their heart: "There is no God," for only a humble man can receive the word of God.

All have turned out of the way; they are become unprofitable together: *there is none that does good, there is not so much as one.* (Rom. 3:12.)

The "all" here refers to those children of men who are not yet children of God by faith, born "of water and the Spirit" (John 3:5). Some of these turn from the way to the left, namely, those who are enslaved to the riches, honors, pleasures, and powers of this world. But others turn to the right, namely, those who are concerned to maintain their own righteousness, virtue, and wisdom; disregarding the righteousness of God to which they should be obedient, they contend in their spiritual pride against the humbleness of truth. This is why the Scripture says in Prov. 4:27: "Decline not to the right hand nor to the left," namely, from the way that is on the right hand, because the text goes on: "For the Lord knows the ways that are on the right hand, but those are perverse which are on the left hand." In other words, to turn to the right from the right means to overdo in knowledge and moral righteousness.

The word "together"[45] is to be taken in a collective sense, as if the text read: All have become unprofitable, i.e., empty and vain

[45] *"Simul."*

in their worthless pursuits. People who seek the unprofitable deservedly become unprofitable themselves, and also empty, because
they are concerned only for vanities; as we call people rich who
have wealth, so they are unprofitable because they possess only
worthless things. For the nature of that which we love becomes our
own nature.[46] "If you love God," says Saint Augustine,[47] "you are
God; if you love the earth, you are earth." For love is a unifying
power[48] that turns into one the lover and his love.

love

One can also call them "unprofitable" in another respect, in so
far, namely, as they are unprofitable to God and to themselves.
But the first interpretation is better, because the apostle wants
to show that they became worthless by turning from the truth
and righteousness of God toward their own ways.

One can also understand this series of statements as a kind of
reiteration that leads up to a climax: to say "there is none righteous" is the same as to say: "All have turned away"; and to say:
"There is none that understands" is the same as to say: "They are
together become unprofitable"; and to say that "none seeks God"
is the same as to say: **There is none that does good.**

"To turn away" thus means to become unrighteous. And to become empty means to lose the truth in one's understanding and
reflect on vanity. In many places of the Bible emptiness is therefore ascribed to the understanding of such people. Moreover, "not
to do good" means "not to seek God." Though outwardly they do
the good, they do not do so sincerely and do not seek God thereby,
but what they have in mind is glory and gain or, at least, freedom
from punishment. And thus they do the good not actively but
(if I may say so) passively;[49] i.e., fear and desire force them to do
the good that they would not do voluntarily. But people who seek
God do the good gratuitously and joyfully and only for God's sake
and not in order to obtain some created good either spiritual or
corporeal. But this is not the work of nature but of the grace of
God.

grace

[46] *"Quia qualia diligimus, tales efficimur."*
[47] Augustine, *Tract. 2 in ep. ad Johannem* (PL 35, 1997): *"Talis est quisque,
qualis eius dilectio est. Terram diligis? terra eris. Deum diligis? quid dicam?
Deus eris?"* ("A man's love determines what kind of person he is. Do you
love the earth? Then you will be earth. Do you love God? Do I dare say that
you will be God?"). Augustine quotes Ps. 82:6: "I said, you are gods; and all
of you sons of the Most High." Tauler quotes this saying of Augustine's
(*Sermones*, ed. Vetter, 1910, 232, 4).
[48] This reminds one of Augustine, *De trin.*, VIII, 10, 14. But cf. Thomas
Aquinas, commenting on Dionysius Areopagita, *Divina nomina, c.* 4: *"Est
enim amor unitio secundum quod amans et amatum conveniunt in aliquo
uno."* Cf. Ficker, p. 241, n. 5.
[49] *"Ac per hoc nec faciunt, sed potius . . . faciuntur bonum."*

Their throat is an open sepulcher; *with their tongues they have dealt deceitfully. The venom of asps is under their lips.* (Rom. 3:13.)

In the next three verses, it is shown how these people do wrong also to others. As he has described in the preceding how they are evil and godless in themselves and this because of their own aversion to God, so he shows now how they do evil toward others by converting them toward themselves in order to avert them from God in the same way as they themselves are averted from him.

This applies, first of all, to those who listen to them and imitate them. In these people they perform something threefold.

First, they devour the dead. This is what is meant by the phrase "Their throat is an open sepulcher." Just as a sepulcher is the receptacle of the dead, namely, of those who have died without the hope of rising again in the way in which one may hope to rise again from sleep, "like the slain," as it says in the psalm, "sleeping in the sepulchers, whom thou rememberest no more: and they are cast off from thy hand" (Ps. 88:5): so their teaching and mouth or throat (i.e., the word that issues from their mouth and throat) is one swallowing down of those who have passed from faith to faithlessness, a gulping down of them which leaves no hope of return from the death of this faithlessness. Only a most singular demonstration of divine power, as our Lord has presented it in the case of Lazarus who had been in the tomb for four days, can possibly call them back before they descend into hell.

It says "open," because they devour and seduce many, for "their speech spreads like a cancer" (II Tim. 2:17), or, as it says farther on (in the psalm the apostle here quotes): "Do they not know who devours my people as they eat bread?" (Ps. 14:4), i.e., as one does not loath bread that one eats oftener and in greater quantities than other food, so they unceasingly eat their dead and their pupils and yet are never satiated, because "the mouth of the womb" (i.e., the hellish doctrine) "is never satisfied" (Prov. 30:16). Indeed, as bread passes into him who eats it, so these pass into the faithlessness of their teachers. However, this resemblance can also be turned into a difference: these same godless men devour also the righteous, but not like a piece of bread, since they cannot absorb them in their bodies like bread, yet as they swallow them whole and alive and are therefore unable to digest them, they either perish or are led to betterment by their victims.

Hence, heresy or godless teaching is nothing else than some plague or pestilence that infects and kills large numbers of people just as in the case of the plague that affects the body.

The psalmist says "throat" rather than "mouth" in order to

characterize the effectiveness and persuasiveness of their teaching. For they overpower and devour their victims as one swallows something down one's throat, but not as one eats it in the mouth from where one can spit it out again. Their teaching is effective in the sense that it is presented in an alluring and attractive manner, as the apostle says: they are "teachers for whom the ears itch" (II Tim. 4:3). It is comparable to the throat that has no teeth like the mouth, for the mouth bites food with the teeth, but the throat swallows it down easily without chewing.

This leads to something else: because such teachers do not bite, they do not chew and grind, i.e., they do not criticize and down their pupils; they do not lead them to repentance and do not pull them down and break them up. But being what they are, they swallow them down whole in their faithlessness as it says in Lam. 2:14: "Your prophets have not opened your eyes to your sins that would induce you to repentance." To reprove and chasten a sinner with words, means to bite him with one's teeth until he becomes very small and soft (i.e., humble and meek). But to flatter him, to extenuate his sins, and to grant him many liberties, means to gulp him down one's throat, i.e., to leave him whole and big and strong, i.e., proud and hardened against repentance and unable to take any treatment. Hence, the bride in The Song of Solomon is said to have "teeth like a flock of sheep that are shorn" (S. of Sol. 4:2), i.e., words of rebuke taken from the Scripture without the intent to accuse anyone by them.

Also, here he goes on as if he wanted to explain with the following two phrases what he had in mind by saying, "Their throat is an open sepulcher," or how it can be that they devour their followers. And so,

Secondly, they teach **deceitfully.** The reason why their throat is an open sepulcher and why they devour ever so many is that they teach deceitfully. The reason why they devour and why their throat is an open sepulcher is that it surreptitiously infuses poison. And by this means they kill men and deaden them, but by the other means (easy teaching) they make many insensitive. For blandishment and sly persuasion first lure and attract the masses, and when they are attracted, then the poison kills them.

Hence, this is a very appropriately phrased sentence: "Their throat" (this means that they deaden with cunning and deceit) is an "open" (this suggests many, the mass) "sepulcher" (this refers to those they deaden). It all hangs together. "To deal with the tongue" means "to teach," "to admonish and to exhort," in short to use it in order to approach someone else. To teach "deceitfully" means to offer a pleasant and prurient teaching as if it were holy, saving, and divine, so that people who let themselves be deceived thereby believe they hear God speaking to them, because what is spoken appears to them as good, true, and from God. The pleasing and ingratiating impression which such speaking makes upon the listener is pointedly emphasized by the phrase "with their tongues," which parallels the expression "with the throat." For the tongue is soft, has no bones, and licks softly. Just so every word they speak only coddles the heart of people as they are satisfied with themselves in their wisdom and righteousness in all they say or do. As it says in Isa. 30:10: "Speak unto us pleasant things; behold not for us things that are right," i.e., do not say anything that goes against our grain. This, yes, indeed, this is the reason why they abhor the word of the cross (by which their self-conceit should have been mortified and torn to pieces as by teeth), and instead they want to hear something flattering. O horrible word! they say. So then: this deceitfulness makes the mass ready with expectancy and once made ready, the poison deadens them. And the sepulcher is wide open, etc. Hence:

Thirdly: They destroy the people who listen to their teaching, because **poison of asps is under their lips.** Precisely this flattering and agreeable teaching not only fails to quicken those who believe it, but it destroys them. Indeed, it destroys them utterly. For there is no cure for the poison of the asp. The asp is, namely, a species of the African snake whose sting, according to Aristotle,[50] is deadly. Just so there is no cure for a faithless and heretical people. But these utterly wretched folk do not even recognize this poison that deals death to their souls. This is why the text says "under their lips," i.e., death lurks underneath all that appears to them in what they are taught outwardly as life and truth. So then, because the poison of the asp is deadly and leaves one without any hope for recovery, the text speaks rightly of a "sepulcher." Now it is because truth and righteousness are given an outwardly alluring appearance that the sepulcher is open and the poison deadly and hopeless. It is characteristic of us that we all love truth and righteousness. Hence, we cling to truth when it has an attractive appearance, but we despise it when it appears to be unattractive— as it always does, as we can see in Christ who "had no form or comeliness" (Isa. 53:2). So it is the case with every truth that goes counter to our thinking.

Whose mouth is full of cursing *and bitterness, their feet swift to shed blood.* (Rom. 3:14–15.)

Notice, first, that here where they are up against those who refuse to follow them they are spoken of as having a mouth. Here

[50] Aristotle, *Hist. animal.*, VIII, 29.

the text does not say "throat" or "tongue," but "mouth" and, as it is implied in what follows, a mouth full of teeth at that.

Hence, we ask, secondly: How do they react to those who refuse to follow them but instead oppose them and try to teach them what is good and right, in order to turn them away from that threat of death of which we have just spoken? Now notice how they repay them! Again they do three things:

First: their "mouth is full of cursing." This is well said, because their cursing is not transferred to the ones they curse but stays with themselves. They do harm only to themselves, according to what is said with respect to Christ: "Cursed be everyone that curses thee"[51] (Gen. 27:29). Or, as it says in another psalm: "God will break their teeth in their mouth" (Ps. 58:7), and not in the wound or the body of someone else. He lets them bite, but in such a way that they do not harm anyone; hence, he breaks their teeth in their mouth. To be sure, they do not lack teeth or curses, but these are only in their own mouth which, as the text says, is "full" of them. The "cursing," of which it speaks, means striking someone openly with insults, imprecations, and blasphemies and wishing him ill. This is the way of all who feel that they are being contradicted in their set way of thinking (which to them appears to be true and just) and who are therefore ready to defend the truth, as it were, and to offer service to God (John 16:2) with greatest zeal which, however, is not "according to knowledge" (Rom. 10:2). They behave in this way not sluggishly but, as I have said, with great zeal. Hence, the text says "their mouth is full," i.e., they curse excessively.

Second: Their mouth is full of bitterness, i.e., full of the most invidious slanders. Now, it is envy that is the bitterness of the heart just as, by contrast, love is its sweetness. And from envy the proud and godless curse not only the righteous but slander one another with the bitterest words. Yet also this envy stays in their own mouth and does not harm those whom they envy. Hence, the text says: Though their mouth is full of bitterness, it does not make others outside itself bitter and evil.

Third: Their feet are swift to shed blood. This, too, is a graphic description. For evil teachers cannot always accomplish their purpose but they try to do all they can. For if they cannot overcome the messengers of truth with curses and slanders, they go so far as to take steps to do away with them by murder in order that their own way of thinking may not be undone. This is how the Jews (of whom the text here speaks, according to its literal meaning) acted, and with great tenacity, as the book of Acts shows. But also today every enemy of the truth acts in the same way in order to uphold

---

[51] Cf. also Num. 24:9.

his own doctrine, believing all the while that he has a good intention and acts from the love of God.

Destruction *and misery in their ways.* (Rom. 3:16.)
Here the text describes what befalls them.
First: "destruction"; i.e., they are crushed, cut to pieces, and laid low in body and soul, as one can see in the case of the Jews. "They are like the chaff which the wind drives away," according to Ps. 1:4, for, once great and powerful, they are being ground to bits until they are "trodden underfoot as the mire of the streets" (Micah 7:10). This physical destruction, which takes place in public, is accompanied by an even more miserable spiritual one. It is inflicted upon them by demons who tread upon them and "do not leave stone upon stone" (Matt. 24:2). As they are being reduced in their ways but try to maintain themselves in them, they become ever more hardened in their wickedness, just as, by contrast, people who walk in the ways of Christ constantly grow in spiritual stature. These experience a real growth, but these others are reduced by being pounded to bits.
Second: misery, i.e., misfortune. As Christ prospers in all he does, so they, by contrast, have no good fortune in their undertakings. This is plainly manifest in the Jews. Though they make progress in their faithlessness, they are in other ways weighed down with very many reverses.

The way of peace they have not known. (Rom. 3:17.)
Why have they not known it? Because, inasmuch as it is peace in the Spirit, it is concealed and hidden in much tribulation. For who can believe that it is the way of peace when he sees how Christians are exposed to suffering with loss of property and their good name, honor, and life, so that, throughout their life, they do not count peace their own, but suffering and the cross. (But those others try to attain a carnal peace by their way of righteousness— and therefore they lose both peace and righteousness.) But under these tribulations there is concealed a peace that no one knows unless he experiences it in faith. But the people of whom the psalmist here speaks did not want to believe and they abhorred the experience of faith. "Great peace have" only "they that love thy law, and to them" that love it "there is no stumbling block." (Ps. 119:165.) Hence, only they who hate it will have occasion to stumble.

Now the cause of all the evils that have here been mentioned is pride, because it renders men utterly incapable of receiving the good. The fear of God is all-humiliating, to be sure, but humility makes one capable of receiving every good. The reason why these folk here do not obtain anything good is that they are proud, and they are proud because they do not fear God. And the reason why they do not fear God is that in their presumptuousness they are sure that he must approve of their ways and actions, because they regard him as just and right according to their own standards. But they are unmindful of the possibility that, when God judges, he will find nothing that is righteous and nothing that is pure. For the judgment of God is a judgment of an infinitely fine exactness. One can do nothing so finely and accurately that in his presence it may not be found coarse, and nothing is so righteous that before him it may not be unrighteous; nothing so true that it may not be untruthful; nothing so pure and holy that before him it may not be defiled and profane. Yet in case they are mindful of this, they claim for themselves a "respect of persons with God" (Rom. 2:11), to the effect that he will not judge and condemn their kind of truth and righteousness, i.e., that by a singular favor he will regard them as pure in their impurity.

But if they feared God, they would know that only Christ and his truth and righteousness cannot fall under God's judgment, inasmuch as all this is infinite. Praise and glory be to God forever who has given us all this in him and with him so that we may be righteous and true through him and thus escape the judgment. But with respect to all that is ours (and we can never be certain whether it ever belongs to us), we must always be in fear before God.

Nevertheless, they imagine that they have "the fear of God" (Rom. 3:18) to the fullest extent. For what virtue do the proud not arrogate to themselves? Just as they regard themselves as righteous God-seekers, so they believe they have also the fear of God and everything else the apostle asserts they have not; and, in their presumptuousness, they fancy themselves to be far, far removed from all that he ascribes to them. We must, therefore, in faith believe that what the Spirit says in this psalm is true and that none is righteous before God, for no one who is righteous in his own eyes will produce such a belief from himself. And so we must always consider that all this applies to us and that it can truly be said of every one of us that he is unrighteous and without the fear of God. And as we thus humble ourselves and confess to God that we are wicked and foolish,[52] we may become worthy to be justified by him.

---

[52] *Inphrynitus.* In Reuchlin's *Vocabularius breviloquus* this word appears as *"infrunitus."* It is defined to mean *"non fronitus,"* i.e., *"stultus"* ("stupid"), *"insipiens"* ("foolish"), *"indiscretus"* ("imprudent"), *"sine freno rationis"* ("without reason's bridle").

Now we know that whatsoever things the law speaks, it speaks to them that are in the law; that every mouth may be stopped, and all the world **may be made subject to God.** *Because by the works of the law no flesh shall be justified before him.* (Rom. 3:19–20.)

This "to be made subject" must be taken to mean "to be a debtor," "to be obligated or bound to pay a debt" so that the meaning of the text, as was stated in the gloss,[53] is this: the law declares all men to be unrighteous in order that, in view of this declaration, they may acknowledge themselves to be unrighteous and that they cease to consider themselves boastingly as righteous, keep silent about it, and confess themselves guilty before God's righteousness. Psalm 37:7: "Be subject to the Lord and pray to him" or as the Hebrew text has it: "Be silent before the Lord," etc. Isaiah 41:1: "Let the islands keep silence before me and the peoples change their strength," i.e., let them keep their mouth shut and be quiet, so that they cease boasting that they are righteous before me. Psalm 65:1: "A hymn becomes thee, O God in Zion," or, according to the Hebrew version:[54] "Silence be praise to thee, O God in Zion," i.e., we owe it to thee to keep silent about our righteousness, and precisely this is to sing the praises of thy righteousness. One may add in thought the conjunction "and": Silence and praise to thee, O God, etc. But the meaning is more clearly brought out without an express conjunction: this is to give God the honor and glory that we become silent and stop praising ourselves as if we amounted to anything.

Here the question arises: How can one be justified without the works of the law and how can it be that one cannot be justified by the works of the law (Rom. 3:20), inasmuch as James, citing the example of Abraham and Rahab, says plainly that "faith without works is dead" (James 2:26) and "that a man is justified by works" (James 2:24). Likewise, in Gal. 5:6, Paul himself speaks of "faith that works by love," and, in the second chapter of this

---

[53] *WA* 56, 35, 12 ff.: "*Now we know* and we do not need merely to believe, because it is certain *that whatsover things the law speaks,* in so far as it either promises the good or threatens evil, *it speaks to them that are in the law;* hence also this psalm speaks to and about the Jews. For concerning the Gentiles, they had no doubt that they were sinners, but concerning themselves they had great doubts whether they were sinners, indeed, they did not believe that they were: for the law was given to them *that every mouth* that proudly boasts before others of its own wisdom and righteousness *may be stopped and that all the world may be made subject to God,* to be obligated to him as a debtor or sinner, although, in his own eyes, he is nothing of the sort, inasmuch as just before he regarded himself as equal to God."

[54] Cf. Faber's *Quincuplex Psalterium.*

letter, he says that "the doers of the law shall be justified" (Rom. 2:13).

To this we reply: As the apostle distinguishes between the law and faith, or the letter and grace, so he distinguishes also between the works that result from them. He calls those deeds works of the law which one does apart from faith and grace and which the law impels either by the fear of punishment or by the alluring promise of temporal rewards. But works of faith he calls deeds which are done in the spirit of liberty and only from the love of God. These can be done only by people who have been justified by faith. The works of the law, however, do not contribute anything to the justification of anyone; indeed, they are a great hindrance because they keep one from seeing himself as unrighteous and in need of justification.

Consider this parable: Suppose a layman enacts outwardly all the official functions of a priest and celebrates mass, confirms, pronounces absolution, administers the sacraments, dedicates altars, churches, vestments, vessels, etc. His actions certainly resemble in all respects those of a real priest and perhaps they are more fittingly and adequately performed than real ones. But because he is not consecrated and ordained and sanctified, he enacts inwardly nothing, but he merely puts on a play and deceives himself and his friends. So it is with righteous, good, and holy works that are done outside of or before justification. For just as that layman does not become a priest by his actions, though it is possible for him to become a priest entirely without them, namely, by ordination, so he that is righteous by the law is not made righteous by these works of the law but without them by something else, namely, by faith in Christ.[55] By this faith he is justified and, as it were, ordained a righteous man for the performance of works of righteousness as a layman is ordained a priest in order to perform the acts of a priest. Now, it may happen that a man who is righteous by the law and the letter may do finer and more splendid works than a man who is righteous by faith. Nevertheless, he is not really righteous, but is all the more hindered thereby from obtaining righteousness and the works of grace.

Here is another comparison: A monkey can imitate human actions beautifully but he is not a man because of this. Were he to become a man, this would happen without a doubt not by virtue of the actions by which he emulated man but by virtue of a completely different action, namely, God's. But made a man, he certainly would perform human actions in the right way.

When, therefore, Saint James and the apostle say that one is

55 *"Per fidem Christi."*

justified by works, they argue against the false understanding of
those who think that faith without works is sufficient: and, as a
matter of fact, the apostle does not say that faith justifies without
its own works (for then it would not be faith, since, according to
the philosophers,[56] "a working or an action is the proof that there
is a form"), but what he does say is that faith justifies without the
works of the law.

Therefore, justification does not need the works of the law,
but it needs a living faith that produces its own works. (Compare
Gal. 5:6.)

But if justification is by faith with its own works but without
the works of the law, why are the heretics then regarded as being
outside justification, in view of the fact that they not only believe
but from such a faith do great works and almost greater ones than
other believers do? Yes, and all the proud spiritual folk in the
church who can point to so many great works that certainly proceed from faith—are they, too, unrighteous? Does it not seem,
then, that something else than faith in Christ with its works is
necessary for justification?

The answer is given briefly in the following word of James:
"Whosoever stumbles in one point is become guilty of all" (James
2:10). For faith consists of something indivisible:[57] it is either a
whole faith and believes all there is to believe, or it is no faith at
all if it does not believe one part of what there is to believe. This
is why our Lord likens it to one single pearl and one single mustard seed, etc. (cf. Matt. 13:45 f., 31 f.). (For Christ is not divided;
therefore, one either denies him in his totality when one denies
him with respect to one point or one affirms him in his totality.
But one cannot at the same time deny and confess him now in this,
and then in that, word.)

The heretics, however, always select from what must be believed
one or several points against which, out of their conceit, they state
their own understanding as if they were wiser than all other believers. And thus they believe nothing of what must be believed
and perish without faith and obedience to God despite their great
works that so closely resemble the real ones. Theirs is the fate of
the Jews, who also believe much of what the church, too, believes
as true. But against one point, namely, Christ, they put what their

---

[56] In his discussion of the Aristotelian concepts of form and matter, Trutvetter (*Summa in totam physicen*, I, *c.* 1) quotes the following saying as pro-
verbial: "*Operatio arguit formam sicut transmutatio materiam*" ("An action
is the evidence of form, just as change is the evidence of matter").
[57] "*Fides enim consistit in indivisibili.*"

own pride suggests that they think; therefore they perish in their faithlessness.

The case is not different with anyone else who conceitedly sticks to his own ideas as he withstands the precept or the counsel of a true teacher of salvation. In so far as he does not believe him, it must be said also of him that he believes nothing; his whole faith collapses because of the obstinacy with which he persists in one notion. Therefore, we must always be ready to surrender our own point of view so that we do not stumble on this rock of offense (cf. Rom. 9:32; Isa. 8:14), i.e., the truth which in humility stands over against us and is contrary to what we think it ought to be. We are so presumptuous as to believe that only what we think is the truth, and we want to hear and see as truth only what we agree with and approve. But this cannot be.

The works, therefore, of all these folk are works of the law and not of faith and grace; indeed, they are contrary to faith and contend against it. For this reason, justification can happen only without such works; indeed, it must happen without them, and, to use the words of the apostle, "they must be counted as dung because of Christ" (Phil. 3:8).

COROLLARY

It is always safer to listen to what goes counter to our judgment than to listen to opinions that approve and applaud what we think, and that agree with us.

Yes, unless a man learns to listen freely to what goes against him and is glad to have his own opinion rejected and criticized, and, on the other hand, unless he is apprehensive and sorry or at least suspicious when his word, opinion, and action are approved, praised, and sustained, he can certainly not be saved. For nothing proves more truly that one's opinion, word, or action are from God than when they are criticized or reproved. Everything that comes from God is, as one can see in Christ, rejected by man as are stones by the builders.[58]

But if it is not from God, it is much safer, indeed it is necessary that it be rejected, lest one persevere in it and perish. This is why even the godless king Ahab gives testimony to the effect that he hated the prophet Micah for no other reason than that he always prophesied him evil. (I Kings 22:8 ff.) For the same reason, King Jehoiakim cut the sayings of Jeremiah to pieces and burned them. (Jer. 36:23.) And all the Jews persecuted the prophets because they proclaimed evil to them and the opposite of what was agree-

58 Cf. Ps. 118:22; Matt. 21:42; Acts 4:11; I Peter 2:7.

able to their thinking. Instead, they should have received this humbly, with the acknowledgment of their guilt before God. On the contrary, they said: "Peace, peace!" (Jer. 6:14; 14:13; 23:17) "we are God's people; he will do no evil to us and will not punish us; we shall not see disaster because we are righteous." And so they never heard the voice of the Lord, indeed, they always opposed it. This is why the Lord says: "Woe unto you, when all men speak well of you, for in the same manner did their forefathers to the false prophets" (Luke 6:26). To be maligned, then, scolded, and accused is the way of security; but to be blessed, praised, and approved is the way of danger and perdition. The right thing to do is to keep waiting for the blessing and praise of the Lord; "his," not man's, "blessing is upon his people," as it says in Ps. 3:8.

But now the righteousness of God without the law is manifested, being witnessed by the law and the prophets; even **the righteousness of God which is by faith** *in Jesus Christ unto all and upon all that believe.* (Rom. 3:21–22.)

Doctrine: *Inasmuch as the faith in Christ by which we are justified consists in this, that one believe not only in Christ (or in the person of Christ) but in all that belongs to Christ, the proud and the heretics deceive themselves in the conviction it pleases them to hold that they believe in Christ while they refuse to believe in what belongs to him.*

They surely divide Christ when they say that it is one thing to believe in Christ and another thing to believe in what belongs to him, but, as a matter of fact, "Christ is not divided" (I Cor. 1:13), as the apostle says; and we have stated above that likewise faith in Christ is indivisible. Therefore, Christ and what belongs to Christ are one and the same.

Now, the heretics confess and boast that they believe in Christ according to what the gospels say of him, i.e., that he was born, suffered, died, etc.; but they do not believe in what belongs to him. And what is this? The church, of course; and every word that proceeds from the mouth of a superior of the church or of a good and holy man, is Christ's word, according to his saying: "He that hears you, hears me" (Luke 10:16). People, therefore, who withdraw themselves from their superiors and who do not want to hear what they say but want to follow their own ideas—how can they, I ask, believe in Christ? Or do they believe in his birth and suffering but not in one who teaches this? "Is Christ, then, divided" (I Cor. 1:13), because, on the one hand, they believe in him, and, on the other hand, they deny him? No, this cannot be!

Even by what they believe they deny the whole Christ, because one cannot deny and confess him at the same time. (The Master of the Sentences[59] says: "It is one thing to believe that God is, and it is another to believe him, and still another to believe in him." This applies also to faith in Christ. For to believe in Christ means to direct oneself to him with one's whole heart and to order everything with respect to him.)

This is why our Lord says in Matt. 4:4: "Man does not live by bread alone but by every word that proceeds out of the mouth of God." What is the mouth of God? The priest's mouth and the prelate's. Malachi 2:7: "They shall seek the law at the priest's mouth, because he is the angel of the Lord of hosts." And to Jeremiah, God says: "Thou shalt be my mouth." (Jer. 15:19.)

But why the phrase "by every word"? Because by disbelieving one single word you no longer live by the word of God. For the whole Christ is in every word, and he is wholly in all single words. When, therefore, one denies in one word him who is in all words, one denies him in his totality. (Thus he is enclosed on two sides.) Just so, if you kill one single Christian, sparing all others, you kill the whole Christ. So it is with everything else. If you deny Christ in one single host, you have thereby denied him in all.

If this is so, we must undergo an immense humiliation. For inasmuch as we cannot know whether we live by every word of God or deny none (in view of the fact that we hear many such words spoken to us by the superior, many by the brethren, many in the gospel and in the writings of the apostles, and many by God inwardly in ourselves), we can never know whether we are justified or whether we believe. For this reason, we should estimate our works as if they were works of the law and should humbly be willing to be sinners who desire to be justified only by his mercy. Even though we are certain that we believe in Christ, we are not certain that we believe in all his words. Hence, also, "the believing in him" is uncertain.

For the same reason, it is the one complaint of the prophets that the voice of the Lord is not heard by his people. But a man who with fear and trembling has made humble confession will receive the grace of justification and forgiveness, even though he may perhaps have done something from a hidden unbelief of which he was not aware. In this sense Job was afraid of all his works. (Job 9:28.) And the apostle "was not conscious to himself of anything" but he did not think himself "thereby justified" (I Cor. 4:4). For this reason, we must leave righteousness to Christ only and only with him works of grace and of the Spirit.

[59] Peter Lombard, III *Sent., d.* 23, 4.

But we ourselves shall always be found to do works of the law; we shall always be unrighteous, always sinners, in accordance with the saying of Ps. 32:6: "For this shall everyone that is holy pray to thee."

But a proud man who is not acquainted with this kind of humility and has no understanding of the fine distinctions that faith makes,[60] but who thinks that he is a believer and that he completely believes all there is to believe—he is unable to hear the voice of the Lord. Instead, he strives against it as if it were false because it goes counter to his thinking, which he believes to be right.

If you now raise the question: If the "No" is given so much weight that when one denies Christ in one respect one denies him in all, why is, then, the "Yes" not also so weighty that when one affirms him in one respect one affirms him in all?—it must be answered as follows: The good is perfect and simple. Hence, it is canceled by one single denial of it, but it is not validated by one single affirmation of it unless this is a straightforward "Yes" qualified by no negation whatever. For two opposites cannot prevail with respect to one and the same subject. And God wants to have everything pure and unblemished. But a denial is a blemish that defiles a confession, etc.

COROLLARY

In the prophetic books, the term "voice" means unconditionally "the voice of the Lord" in the sense that we must receive, believe, and acknowledge every spoken word, regardless of who speaks it, as if it were spoken by God himself, humbly submitting our own mind to it. Thus and in no other way we shall be justified. But "who can understand sins" and perceive them everywhere? Therefore, "from my secret ones, cleanse me, O Lord." (Ps.19:12 f.)

For through the law comes the knowledge of sin. (Rom. 3:20.)

This knowledge of sin through the law comes about in two ways: first, by mental insight,[61] as, for example, farther on in the seventh chapter of the letter: "I had not known concupiscence except the law said: Thou shalt not covet" (Rom. 7:7).

Secondly, by experience,[62] namely, by the work of the law or by our attempt to fulfill the law. For, in this connection, the law becomes an opportunity for sin in so far as the human will, which is inclined to evil, is directed by the law toward the good and thus

---

[60] *"Fidei subtilitatem."*
[61] *"Speculative."*
[62] *"Experimentaliter."*

becomes disinclined toward the good and detests it because it hates to be drawn away from what it loves, and, as the Scripture says, it loves evil (Gen. 8:21). But, nevertheless, by doing what the law compels him to do against his will, man is made to see how deeply sin and evil are rooted in him. He would never have understood this if he did not have the law and if he had not tried to fulfill it.

The apostle mentions this thought here only briefly because he plans to deal with it more fully farther on in chs. 5 and 7 (Rom. 5:12 ff.; 7:7 ff.); here he merely wanted to make the point, in reply to an objection, that, because the works of the law do not justify, the law is not useless.

So then, whenever something is prescribed or forbidden to us and we notice how unwilling we are to comply, we should thereby recognize that we do not love good but evil. And precisely thus we should come to know ourselves as evil and sinful, for a sinner is one who does not want to fulfill the law which prescribes the good and prohibits evil. For if we were righteous and good, we should readily assent to the law and take delight in it, just as now we take delight in our sins and evil desires. As the Scripture says: "Oh, how I love thy law!" (Ps. 119:97), and "His delight is in the law of the Lord," etc. (Ps. 1:2). So it is that the law makes us conscious of the sin that is in us, i.e., of our ill will that inclines toward evil and shrinks back from the good. And how useful this knowledge is! For a man who sees this feels humbled and implores God that he straighten and heal this will. But a man who does not see this does not ask, and because he does not ask, he does not receive and therefore is also not justified, for he does not know his sin. And so it makes no difference whether one says that through the law comes the knowledge of "sin" or that it makes us conscious that "we are sinners." For it makes us know that we are sinners and that there is sin in us, that we are evil and that there is evil in us.

COROLLARY

It is not the works one does in <u>preparation</u> *of the justification one hopes to attain that are called the works of the law, but those which, as such, one regards as sufficient for righteousness and salvation.*

A man who, by his actions, makes himself ready for the grace of justification is in some way already righteous. For we know that the will to be righteous is a large part of righteousness.[63] Other-

---

[63] In the lectures, according to the notes taken by his students, Luther appears to have said (*WA* 57, 158, 18): *"Velle esse iustum sit magna pars iusti-tiae, secundum beatum Augustinum"* (Ep. 127).

wise, the utterances and fervent prayers in which all the prophets called for Christ would have been pointless, and the lamentations of the penitent of all ages ineffective. (Then, too, Christ and John the Baptist would have taught in vain: "Do penance, for the Kingdom of God is at hand" [Matt. 3:2]). Yes, if all the righteous performed good works only in order to become more and more righteous,[64] none of them would be righteous. Their works are good, not when they put their trust in them, but when they do them in preparation for justification, confident that they will be made righteous through it alone.[65]

People who act in this way are not under the law, because they long for grace and detest the fact that they are sinners.

("Works of the law" and "fulfillment of the law" are not the same. Only grace is the fulfillment of the law, but not works. It is right that the apostle speaks of the "works of the law" and not of the "will of the law." For they do not will what the law wills even though they do what the law commands. But the law wills and needs a certain will in order to be fulfilled.)

Others do good works from the belief that they are thereby fulfilling the law and thus are righteous, but they do not long for grace and do not acknowledge and detest themselves as sinners, because they are sure that their actions conform to the law. (They are not disposed to seek righteousness, because they are boastfully confident that they have already attained it.) They are unaware of the fact that they observe the law, not from the love of God, but either with no will or rather a hostile will or, to say the least, from a love and cupidity for earthly goods. And so they remain self-content; it does not occur to them to do the works of the law in order thus to obtain the grace by which they might do the law willingly. Indeed, neither the good works that precede justification nor those that follow from it make a man righteous—how much less the works of the law! Those that precede it do not because they only prepare a person for justification, and those that follow from it do not because they presuppose that justification has already been accomplished. For we are not made righteous by doing righteous deeds but we do righteous deeds in so far as we are righteous. Therefore, grace alone makes righteous.[66]

Even the righteousness of God, **by faith in Jesus Christ,** *unto all and upon all them that believe in him, for there is no distinction.* (Rom. 3:22.)

[64] *"Ut iustificentur magis ac magis."*
[65] *"In qua sola confidunt iustitiam suam futuram."*
[66] *WA* 56, 255, 18: *"Non enim iusta operando iusti efficimur, sed iusti essendo iusta operamur. Ergo sola gratia iustificat."*

This is a useful additional remark directed to the protest of the proud in case they might say: We concede that we are unrighteous in and from ourselves and we are aware of the fact that we incline toward evil and inwardly hate the law. Therefore, we do believe that only God can justify us. But we ourselves want to obtain this righteousness by prayer and suffering and by confession; however, we do not want Christ; God can give us his righteousness without Christ.

The answer to this is as follows: This is impossible. Because Christ is also God. Righteousness is given only through faith in Jesus Christ. So it has been determined, so it pleases God, and so it will be. Who can resist his will? Therefore, it is only evidence of an exaggerated pride if one does not want to be justified by Christ.

Here also those people of whom I have spoken above should take notice, they who believe in Christ but not in his word, who do not listen to their superior but choose to rely on their own ideas. Instead of trusting a clergyman or a good man, i.e., Christ who speaks through them, they trust in themselves, thinking in their presumptuousness that they can be justified by their own works without such an obedience and faith in God. But this cannot be because over against them there stands what is said in the sentence:[67] "The righteousness of God, by faith in Jesus Christ." This leads us to the following corollary:

The phrase "without the law" must be understood as referring to the law together with its works, and, correspondingly, the phrase "faith in Christ" must be understood to mean faith in Christ and in the word of anyone through whom he speaks.

Just as "without the law" means "without the co-operation of

---

[67] Luther's marginal gloss on Rom. 3:11 reads as follows (*WA* 56, 36, 11 ff.): "Blessed Augustine writes in the ninth chapter of *On the Spirit and the Letter* (9, 15): 'The apostle speaks of the "righteousness of God," not the "righteousness of man" or the "righteousness of one's own will," but the "righteousness of God," not that by which God is righteous but that with which he covers man when he justifies the ungodly. Just as one speaks of "Christ-faith" and means by it not the faith by which Christ believes but the faith by which he is believed in, so one speaks of the righteousness of God and means not that righteousness by which God is righteous. Both are ours. But they are called God's and Christ's righteousness and faith, because they are given to us by his bounty.' He says the same in Book 11 [*ibid.*, 11, 18]. And in the same place he says [*ibid.*, 9, 15]: 'How can it be witnessed to by the law, if it is manifested without the law? Because it is a righteousness without the law. God imparts it to the believer by the spirit of grace without the help of the law, i.e., without being helped by the law. For by the law he shows man his weakness, so that by faith he may flee to mercy in order to be healed. It is said also of his wisdom that it carries the law and mercy on its tongue (Prov. 31:26), namely, the law by which he renders the proud guilty and mercy by which he justifies the humbled.'"

the law and works of the law," so faith in Christ means faith in
him wherever and through whomever he may speak. We must,
therefore, try to avoid being so definitely set in our own thinking
that at some time we become perhaps unable to believe in Christ
because we do not realize when, where, and through whom he
speaks to us. And it is almost always the case that he speaks through
someone at a certain time and in a way contrary to what we think
should be the person, time, and manner of his speaking to us. As
he said himself: "The Spirit blows where it lists, and thou hearest
the voice thereof but knowest not whence it comes and whither it
goes." (John 3:8.) For he is with us and in us but always in a
manner of appearance that is strange to us, not in the form of glory
but in humility and meekness, so that one thinks that it is not he
and yet it is really he. This is why the Holy Spirit enjoins:
"Hearken, O daughter, and see and incline thine ear" (Ps. 45:11),
i.e., you must at all times and places be ready to listen and keep
listening; you must do nothing else than listen with humility in
order that you may be taught, as it says in Ps. 2:10: "And now,
O kings, understand, receive instruction."

But now **without the law the justice of God is made manifest,**
being witnessed by the law and the prophets. (Rom. 3:21.)
    As, for example, in Hab. 2:4: "The just shall live by faith"; in
Hos. 2:20: "I will espouse thee to me in faith"; and in Jer. 31:31–
33: "I will make a new convenant with the house of Judah. I will
write my laws in their heart," etc. Likewise, in Genesis we find the
example of Abraham (Gen. 15:6) and others who were justified
by faith.
    Blessed Augustine writes in the thirteenth chapter of *On the
Spirit and the Letter:* "What the law of works commands by
threatening, the law of faith accomplishes by faith. The one says:
"Thou shalt not covet," and the other says: "When I knew that
I could not otherwise be continent except God gave it, I went to
the Lord and besought him," etc. (Wisd. of Sol. 8:21). And accordingly the Lord says by the law of works: Do what I command.
But by the law of faith we say to God with humble prayer: Give
what thou commandest. Now the law commands in order to advise
what faith should do (i.e., must do), or, in other words, that the
person commanded, if unable as yet to obey, should know what it
is he must ask." And, in Chapter 19, he writes: "The law was
given in order that grace might be sought. Grace was given that
the law might be fulfilled. That the law was not fulfilled was not
the fault of the law but of the wisdom of the flesh. And this fault
had to be pointed out by the law before it could be remedied by

grace. Romans 8:3 f.: "For what the law could not do in that it was weak through the flesh, God, sending his own Son in the likeness of sinful flesh and for sin, condemned sin in the flesh; that the justification of the law might be fulfilled in us who walk not after the flesh." John 1:17: "For the law was given through Moses; grace and truth came through Jesus Christ."

But who now will enable us to detect all the wiles by which the messenger of Satan (II Cor. 12:7) tries to deceive us? We all pray: Give what thou commandest, and yet we do not obtain what we pray for. We all believe and accordingly speak and make confession and act, yet we are not all justified.

Some who are still rather crude, he deceives in the following way: They do not realize how weak their will is and how prone toward evil, nor have they sufficiently analyzed themselves to know how unwillingly they observe the law of God and how little they love it. It is only from slavish fear that they believe and act accordingly, yet they think nevertheless that they do enough and regard themselves as righteous before God because they believe and do good works. Nor do they show any eagerness to do them gladly and with loving good will, and it does not occur to them that they need the grace of God for this. Depending only upon their own powers, they busily do good works but they are bored and morose in doing them. Instead, they should turn to God with fervent prayers asking him that he lift this boredom from them and endow their will with gladness and by his grace take away its proneness toward evil. Ah, but this can be had only through earnest prayer, readiness to learn, eager action, and much self-castigation; then, finally, that old way will be uprooted and the will renewed. For grace cannot be had unless one works on oneself in this way.[68] But the people I am talking about do not do anything of this sort: they are inattentive and gradually become tepid, stupid, arid, and hardened until, having lost their faith, they can no longer endure it all, and, full of desires of the worst kind, they become "unfit for every good work" (Titus 1:16).

But others who are more sensitive, he deceives by a more intricate method. He makes them do good works with joy and gladness in order, under this cover, to hide their weakness from them, so that they believe they have grace and, in a manner so subtle that one can hardly notice it, come to regard themselves as better than others and take pride in themselves, until, in the end, they affect eccentric and superstitious ways of a kind that one finds among heretics and fanatics who claim to speak in the name of

[68] *WA* 56, 257, 30: "*Non enim dabitur gratia sine ista agricultura suiipsius*" (*agricultura* = husbandry; cf. I Cor. 3:9).

truth and righteousness and display a "zeal that lacks knowledge" (Rom. 10:2). Then they turn into rebels: pretending to obey and fear God, they disobey and disregard God's spokesmen, i.e., Christ's vicars and messengers.

If, in the light of this, we examine ourselves carefully, we shall always find within ourselves at least some remnants of the flesh, by virtue of which, preoccupied with ourselves, we resist the good and incline toward evil. For if such remnants of sin were not in us and we could seek God with a pure heart, then what is human in us would certainly soon be dissolved and our souls would fly to God.[69] But the fact that it does not take wings is a sign that it is still caught in the body[70] until set free by the grace of God, and this can be expected to happen only in death. In the meantime, we can do nothing else than join the apostle in sighing: "Who shall deliver me from the death of this body?" (Rom. 7:24).[71] We must always be apprehensive that we do not sufficiently keep it down. Therefore, we must ever pray and see to it that grace and the spirit increase but that the body of sin decreases and is undone and that the old Adam in us declines. For God has not yet justified us, i.e., he has not yet made us perfectly righteous and our righteousness complete, but he has begun to perfect it,[72] so that, according to James 1:18, "we might be some beginning of his creature." An illustration of this is the man who was brought half-dead to the inn; after his wounds were bound, he was not yet whole, but he was taken in, in order to be cured (Luke 10:34 f.).

If we but pay attention, it is easy to see the perversity of our will in relation to the body, how we love what is bad for us and avoid what is good for us, in so far as, for example, we are disposed toward sensual lust, avarice, gluttony, pride, and honor but shrink back from chastity, generosity, sobriety, humility, and shame. It is easy, I say, to sense how we seek and love ourselves in all this, how we are bent in and curved in upon ourselves, if not in what we do, then at least in what we are disposed to do.

It is very difficult, however, to see whether we seek ourselves also in the things that belong to the realm of the spirit (i.e., in knowledge, righteousness, chastity, godliness). Inasmuch as the

---

[69] The notion that the soul will fly to God (on having received the remission of all sins) was popular at Luther's time. It is often expressed in penitentials and in books on dying. (Cf. Ficker, p. 258, n. 13.)

[70] *"Signum est, quod visco aliquo carnis adhuc haeret"* ("It is a sign that it still hangs on some birdlime of the flesh").

[71] This is how Luther quotes the passage. The Vulgate reads: "from the body of this death."

[72] *WA* 56, 258, 19 f.: *"Non enim iustificavit nos, i.e., perfecit et absoluit iustos ac iustitiam, sed incepit, ut perficiat."*

love of spiritual values is honorable and good, it very often becomes an end in itself, so that these values are not placed in relation to God and referred to him. And so we pursue them not because they are pleasing to God but because they give us delight
and inward satisfaction, and also because we thereby earn the
plaudits of men; in other words: we pursue them not for God's
sake but for our own. But this turns out to be a temptation. For
if we are criticized because we cultivate these values or if God
takes away our liking for them and our delight in them, we
quickly drop them or we pay back our critics in kind and strike
back at them.

COROLLARY

By such presumptuousness and pride even the works of grace
can be changed into works of the law and the righteousness of God
into the righteousness of man. This happens when, having done
good works in grace, people become satisfied with them, stop where
they are and do not care to go on with them, as if they had already
fully obtained righteousness, whereas, as a matter of fact, they
should go forward on the basis of these good works as though they
were but a preparation. Indeed, all righteous works that are done
in grace are a preparatory stage in the progress of justification, in
accordance with the saying "Let him who is righteous be justified
still" (Rev. 22:11). With the apostle, who stretches forward to the
things that are before (Phil. 3:13), "they will go from strength to
strength" (Ps. 84:7) and "from glory to glory" (II Cor. 3:18).
Therefore, no saint regards and confesses himself to be righteous,
but he always asks and waits to be justified, and because of this
he is reputed as righteous by God who has regard for the humble
(Luke 1:48).

In this sense, Christ is the King of the Jews, i.e., of those who
confess[73] that they are always beset by sin and who yet seek to be
justified and detest their sins. Hence, "God is wonderful in his
saints" (Ps. 68:35), because he regards as righteous those who
acknowledge and bewail themselves as sinners, but condemns those
who think that they are righteous.

This is what is said in Ps. 32:5 f.: "I said I will confess against
myself my unrighteousness, and thou hast forgiven the wickedness
of my sin. For this shall everyone that is holy (i.e., righteous,

---

[73] The *Glossa ordinaria* comments as follows on Luke 23:38: "Jesus is the
ruler [*imperator*] of believers and confessors. As such he is the King of the
Jews." This must be understood in the light of the fact that, on the basis
of Gen. 29:35, one commonly took Judah to mean "one who confesses or
praises [*confitens*]" and the Jews (*Judaei*), therefore, as "confessors."

justified) pray to thee." Is it not something wonderful that a righteous man prays for his sins! Just so it is said in Ecclesiaticus of the
righteous man: "He will make supplication for his sins" (Ecclus.
39:7) and in prayer he will confess his sins to the Lord. I will confess "against myself," he says; this is, as I have explained, what it
means for a righteous man to recognize himself a sinner and for
all that to hate his sin, just as, by contrast, the ungodly one recognizes his righteousness and is pleased with himself about it. In
this sense it says in Ps. 51:3: "For I know my transgression and"
(I not only know) "my sin" but "it is ever before me." I confess,
therefore, "that against thee only I have sinned and done that
which is evil in thy sight that thou mayest justify in thy word,"
i.e., because I acknowledge and hate my sin, thou forgivest and
justifiest me, because thou alone shalt be justified.

We are, therefore, saved only in so far as we, who are beset by
sin and live in sin, bewail the fact that we are beset by sin and
fervently pray to God for redemption, according to the word of
John: "If we say that we have no sin, we deceive ourselves and
the truth is not in us. If we confess our sins, he is faithful and
righteous to forgive us our sins and to cleanse us from all unrighteousness" (I John 1:8 f.).

Consequently, yes, indeed: consequently "the sacrifice to God
is a broken spirit; a broken and contrite heart, O God, thou wilt
not despise" (Ps. 51:17). "For there is no man on earth that sins
not," says Solomon in his prayer. (I Kings 8:46.) And Moses says
in Ex. 34:7: "before whom no one is innocent by himself." And
again, Ecclesiastes: "There is not a righteous man upon earth that
does good and sins not." (Eccl. 7:20.) And again: "Who can glory
in himself that he has a clean heart?" (Prov. 20:9.) And so "there
is none righteous; they all have gone out of the way." (Ps. 14:3;
Rom. 3:10,12.)

Hence, we pray: "Forgive us our debts" (Matt. 6:12).

And where do these sins and debts come from? From the fact
that no one fulfills the law except Christ. For no man living is
justified before God, because his heart is always too weak to do
the good and inclined toward evil. He does not love righteousness
without loving in some way also iniquity. But Christ "loves righteousness and hates iniquity" (Ps. 45:7). As the apostle explains
farther on in Rom. 7:25: "So then we serve with the flesh the law
of sin but with the mind the law of God." And so we are partly and
not wholly righteous. Hence, we have sin and debt. Therefore,
whenever we pray that righteousness be perfected in us and our
sin taken away, we ask at the same time for the end of this life.
For in this life the proneness toward evil is not perfectly healed

(just as, to speak figuratively, the Children of Israel were unable to drive out the Jebusites).[74] This is the reason why the prayer "Hallowed be thy name" (Matt. 6:9) (and this happens when our nature is hallowed from evils and sins) is immediately followed by the petition: "Thy Kingdom come" (Matt. 6:10), which is as much as to say that it will be fully hallowed only in thy Kingdom. But also this Kingdom will come only through tribulations. This is why there then follows the petition: "Thy will be done" (Matt. 6:10), as Christ prayed in the Garden at the time of his tribulation (Matt. 26:39 ff.).

Who, then, can pride himself over against someone else and claim to be better than he? Especially in view of the fact that he is always capable of doing exactly the same as the other does and, indeed, that he does secretly in his heart before God what the other does openly before men. And so we must never despise anyone who sins but must generously bear with him as a companion in a common misery. We must help one another just as two people caught in the same swamp assist each other. Thus we must "bear one another's burdens and fulfill the law of Christ" (Gal. 6:2). But if we despise the other, we shall both perish in the same swamp.

For all have sinned and **do need the glory of God.** *Being justified freely by his grace through the redemption that is in Christ Jesus, whom God has proposed to be a propitiation, through faith in his blood, to the showing of his righteousness, for the remission of former sins, through the forbearance of God, for the showing of his righteousness in this time; that he himself may be righteous and the justifier of him who is of the faith of Jesus Christ.* (Rom. 3:23–26.)

"Glory" must here be taken to mean "glorying" and "need" must be understood as referring to persons in the sense that they are empty or in lack of something, so that the meaning of the passage is this: They have no righteousness of which they could glory before God, as it says in I Cor. 1:29: "that no flesh should glory before God," and as above: "Thou gloriest in God," and as below in ch. 5:11 of this letter: "We glory in God through Jesus Christ." "They do need the glory of God" means therefore: "They have nothing about which they could glory in God or about God," as in Ps. 3:3: "But thou, O Lord, art the lifter up of my head and my glory," i.e., my glorying. So also below: "If Abraham was justified by works, he has whereof to glory, but not before God." (Rom. 4:2.) In the same way they have whereof to glory before

[74] Cf. Josh. 15:63.

NB again, how Luther draws on whole Bible.

men about their righteousness. The term "glory of God" is used in the same way as the terms "righteousness, wisdom, power of God," namely, in the sense that they are given to us by God so that we can glory about them before him and in him and with respect to him.

The Master of the Sentences and others[75] construe and interpret the phrase [to the showing of his righteousness] **for the remission of former sins, through the forbearance of God** (Rom. 3:25) to mean: God shows his righteousness, i.e., truth, for the remission of the sins of the people of the past (i.e., the fathers of the old law), whose sins he has forgiven "through forbearance," i.e., because of the satisfaction of Christ that was to come. By forgiving the sins he forbore them, and he let the satisfaction follow upon forgiveness; but in our case the satisfaction of Christ came first. And so the text of the apostle must be put more clearly in this way: to declare his righteousness by forgiving or in forgiving through divine forbearance the sins of those that have gone before. For the sins of all, those that have gone before as well as those that are to come, are forgiven by Christ alone.

But it makes a better sentence if we read it to mean: By forgiving the sins that we have done in the past, God shows himself as the justifier of all. Then the forgiveness of sins proves him as the one who is righteous and who has the power to justify. As it was said above: "that thou mayest be justified in thy words" (Rom. 3:4), an idea which he promptly repeats here by saying: **that he himself may be righteous and the justifier** (Rom. 3:26).

Now he says "of *former* sins" in order to indicate that God does not forgive all sins, lest someone might say: If, then, all sins are taken away by Christ, let us do what we want; nobody can sin any more" (as the people say who surrender their spirit "to the occasion of the flesh" [Gal. 5:13] and "make liberty a cloak for malice" [I Peter 2:16]). For grace and kindness are not given in order that we may sin and act as we please, as the apostle explains below where he says that we are not under the law and asks: "What then? Shall we sin because we are not under the law?" (Rom. 6:15). And he answers: God does not forgive in such a way that he imputes to no one anything as sin, no matter what he does, or that he cancels the law, but in such a way that he does not punish the sins of the past which he has borne in patience in order that he may justify; he is not kind to us in order that we may freely sin.

Then, too, the text shows clearly that the apostle calls God righteous because he justifies or makes righteous, as we have stated

[75] Cf. Peter Lombard, *Coll. in Ep. ad Rom.;* also *Gl. ord.* and Lyra.

before. And so it is plainly evident, and this is supported by the apostle as he explains his own words, that "the righteousness of God" is that righteousness by which he makes us righteous, just as the wisdom of God is that by which he makes us wise.

By the phrase "of the past" the apostle therefore put himself in opposition to a foolish and carnal interpretation of his words to this effect: God has fulfilled the law; he no longer imputes sin; he no longer wants to regard as sin what he has so regarded before. Therefore, we can safely sin, for what once was sin is such no longer.

"To establish the law" (Rom. 3:31) must be understood in two ways, namely, intrinsically and extrinsically. The law is intrinsically and formally established, when the tenor and the words of the law are invoked in order to indicate and signify what may or may not be done. By contrast, the law is "made of no effect" when it is canceled and abrogated so that it is no longer in force and it is permissible to act against it. It is in connection with this interpretation that carnal persons may think that the apostle makes the law invalid by his statement that we are justified by the law but that "the righteousness of God is manifested and given without the law."

On the other hand, the law is established and confirmed extrinsically, and in an exemplary way, when its prescriptions and prohibitions are complied with. This is what is meant in Jer. 35:14: "The words of Jonadab, that he commanded his sons, have prevailed, because they have obeyed the commandment of their father." Notice that "the words prevail" means "to obey them." And, farther on, Jeremiah says: "The sons of Jonadab have constantly kept the commandment of their father, but his people has not obeyed me" (Jer. 35:16), i.e., they have not kept and established my commandment but have destroyed it instead. So also, Ps. 10:3: "They have destroyed what thou hast made." And Ps. 119:126: "It is time, O Lord, to do; they have broken up thy law." Habakkuk 1:4: "Therefore the law is torn in pieces, and judgment comes not to the end." Jeremiah 31:32: "The covenant which they made void," namely, by not obeying it.

So then, the law is destroyed extrinsically when what it prescribes or prohibits is not complied with. Something of this sort the apostle has in mind when he says: "Do we then destroy the law through faith? God forbid. But we establish the law" (Rom. 3:31), i.e., we declare it fulfilled and confirmed by faith. But you would rather destroy it because you do not fulfill it, and even teach that it does not need to be fulfilled in view of the fact that you declare that the works of the law suffice, without faith. (Rom. 8:3:

"What the law could not do, in that it was weak through the flesh.")

As it says in Ps. 18:36: "Thou hast enlarged my steps under me, and my feet have not weakened," i.e., the example of my way of life is made more effective when there are many who imitate it. As we say in a common expression: This or that craft or this or that party is strong and healthy when there are many who adopt it. But when it has no members, it becomes weak and ineffective.

So then, the law is established in itself and in us—in itself, in so far as it is promulgated, in us, in so far as we fulfill it by word and deed. But nobody does this apart from faith. Whenever, therefore, we lack the grace through faith in Christ, we make God's covenant void.

Where is, then, thy boasting? It is excluded. **By what law? Of works? No, but by the law of faith.** *For we account a man to be justified by faith, without the works of the law.* (Rom. 3:27 f.)

The law of works necessarily puffs up and induces glorying, for a man who is righteous and who has kept the law without a doubt has something about which he can boast and be proud. Now the Jews believe that they have attained this status because they do outwardly what the law orders or prohibits. Therefore, they do not humble themselves and do not detest themselves as sinners. They do not seek to be justified and they do not fervently long for righteousness, because they are confident that they already possess it.

Here we must take notice of what we stated before by quoting Augustine, namely, that "the law of works says: Do what I command, but the law of faith: Give what thou commandest."[76] Therefore, the people of the law gives this reply to the law and to God as he speaks in the law: I have done what thou hast commanded; what thou hast ordered is accomplished. But the people of faith says: I cannot do it and I have not done it, but give thou what thou commandest. I did not do it, but I want to do it. And because I cannot do it, I pray and ask thee to give me the power that will enable me to do it. Thus that people becomes proud and boastful, but this one humble and contemptible in its own eyes. And so the true difference between the two peoples is this, that the one says: I have accomplished, and the other: I seek to accomplish; the one: Command what thou wilt and I shall do it, the other: Give what thou commandest so that I may do it. The one rests confident in an accomplished righteousness, the other longs for one that is still to be obtained.

In view of this, the whole life of the new people, the believing

[76] Augustine, *De spir. et lit.,* 13, 22.

people, the spiritual people, is this: with the sigh of the heart, the cry of the deed, and the toil of the body to ask, seek, and pray only for justification, ever and ever again until the hour of death; never to stand still and never to rest in accomplishment; not to regard any works as if they had ended the search for righteousness, but to wait for this end as if it dwelt somewhere ever beyond one's reach; and to know that as long as one lives, he will have his being in sins. So then, by saying that we are justified without the works of the law (Rom. 3:28), the apostle does not speak of works that one does in order to seek justification. For these are no longer works of the law but of grace and faith, because the person who does them does not believe that he is justified by them but he desires to be justified, and he does not think that he has fulfilled the law by them but he seeks to fulfill it.

What the apostle means by works of the law are works in which the persons who do them trust as if they are justified by doing them, and thus are righteous on account of their works. They therefore do not do them in order to seek righteousness but in order to glory in having obtained it. For this reason, they stand still as soon as they have done their works, as if the law were already entirely fulfilled and as if they had no need of further justification. This is without a doubt the height of pride and boastfulness. Moreover, it is not true that the works of the law can fulfill the law, inasmuch as the law is spiritual and needs a heart and a will that we cannot possibly have from ourselves, as we have stated again and again. For this reason, they live up to the law outwardly but not inwardly.[77]

So the people of faith spends its whole life in search of justification. And this is how it gives utterance to its quest: "Draw me, we will run after thee" (S. of Sol. 1:4). "In my bed I sought him; I sought him and found him not" (S. of Sol. 3:1); "I called him, and he did not answer me" (S. of Sol. 5:6); i.e., I never believed that I had attained, but I continually seek. This is why its utterance is at last called the voice of a turtledove (cf. S. of Sol. 2:12), because it sighs so longingly. And "blessed are they that hunger for righteousness." (Matt. 5:6.)

Psalm 34:10: "They that seek the Lord shall not be deprived of any good." Psalm 14:3: "There is none that seek after God," i.e., because they claim to have found him. Psalm 105:4: "Seek his face evermore," i.e., do not think that you have already found him. Psalm 105:45: "That they might seek his justifications." Isaiah 21:12: "If you seek, seek"; Isa. 65:1: "They have sought me that before asked not for me."

The same voice resounds through almost every verse of the

[77] WA 56, 264, 34: *"Idcirco opera legis faciunt, sed non voluntates legis."*

whole octonary psalm: "O that my ways may be directed to keep
thy justifications" (Ps. 119:5). "I will seek thy justifications." (Ps.
119:145.) "With my whole heart have I sought after thee; let me
not stray." (Ps. 119:10.)

So also the apostle does not think that he has already attained,
but in seeking he stretches forward to the things that are before,
and when he finds, he forgets the things that are behind. (Phil.
3:13.) Now a man who seeks thus within and without is certainly
already righteous before God by the very fact that he asks to be
justified and does not think that he is already righteous. He does
not confess himself to be a sinner, because he wants to be redeemed
and justified, ever saying: "Forgive us our debts"; "hallowed be
thy name" (Matt. 6:12,9).

But what does it mean that Isa. 65:1 says: "They have found me
that sought me not; I appeared openly to them that asked not
for me" (Rom. 10:20)? Shall one then not seek him but wait until
he lets himself be found by chance? This passage must be understood, first of all, as opposing the foolish quest of those who seek
God by a way of their own choosing and not by the one in which
God wants to be sought and found.

And it must be understood, secondly, with respect to the fact
that the righteousness of God is offered to us apart from our
merits and works while we are occupied with the search for
many other things than the righteousness of God. For who ever
sought or would ever have sought the Word incarnate if he had
not revealed himself? He was therefore found and not sought.
But once found, he wants to be still further sought for and again
and again to be found. We find him when we are converted to him
from our sins and we seek him as we persevere in this conversion.

There is, then, a difference between sinners and sinners. There
are some sinners who confess that they have sinned but do not
long to be justified; instead, they give up hope and go on sinning
so that, when they die, they despair and, while they live, they are
enslaved to the world. There are other sinners who confess that
they sin and have sinned, but they are sorry for this, hate themselves for it, long to be justified, and under groaning constantly
pray to God for righteousness. This is the people of God: it constantly brings the judgment of the cross to bear upon itself.

In the same way, there is a difference between the righteous.
Some are sure that they are righteous; they have no longing to be
justified but wait for a reward and crown. Others are sure that
they are not righteous; they fear the judgment and long to be
justified.

That we are sinners, therefore, does no harm so long as with all
our strength we seek to be justified.

For this reason, the devil, that artist of a thousand tricks,[78]
pursues us with an amazing craftiness. Some he leads astray by
getting them involved in manifest sins. Others, again, who regard
themselves as righteous, he causes to stand still, so that they become lukewarm and give up all longing for betterment (in accordance with what the book of Revelation says in ch. 3:14 about
the angel of Laodicea). Still others he seduces to fanaticism and
ascetic sectarianism, so that, believing themselves to be holier
than others and, as it were, experts in righteousness, they get
busy in their good works with a feverish zeal that is everything
else but lukewarm, and set themselves apart from others while in
their pride they despise them and look down upon them. Still
others he urges on to the foolish enterprise of trying to become
pure and sinless saints. As long as they feel that they are sinful
and that evil may unexpectedly overcome them, he keeps them in
terror before the judgment, and fatigues their conscience almost
to the point of despair. He senses what each individual's bent is
and tries to tempt him accordingly. But because these people
strive so fervently for righteousness, it is not easy to persuade them
to try the opposite. So he deals with them in the following way:
First he helps them in their project—with the result that they are
much too quick in their attempt to get rid of all concupiscence.
Then, when they find that they cannot accomplish their purpose,
he makes them sad, dejected, despondent, desperate, and utterly
upset in their conscience.

So there is nothing left to us but to remain in sins and, setting
our hope on the mercy of God, to pray fervently that we may be
freed from them. We are like a convalescent: if he is in too much
of a hurry to get well, he runs the chance of suffering a serious
relapse; therefore, he must let himself be cured little by little and
he must bear it for a while that he is feeble. It is enough that our
sin displeases us, even though it does not entirely disappear.
Christ bears all sins, if only they displease us, for then they are no
longer our sins but his, and his righteousness is ours in turn.

---

[78] "*Mille artifex*" (*Tausendkünstler*).

What shall we say, then, that Abraham has found, who is our father according to the flesh? For if Abraham were justified by works, he has whereof to glory, but not before God. For what says the Scripture? **Abraham believed God,** *and it was reckoned to him unto righteousness.* (Rom. 4:1-3.)

This "Abraham believed" must be understood in an absolute and general sense and not only with reference to the passage of Gen. 15:6, which the apostle here quotes. What is meant is this: Abraham was a man who, at all times, was ready to believe God; he was always a believer. This is shown by the fact that, according to chs. 12 (Gen. 12:1 ff.) and 13 (Gen. 13:1 ff.), it was in this way that he believed God, as he called him and commanded him to leave his own country and to go into a strange land. Also, there it was therefore "reckoned to him unto righteousness." Likewise, according to Gen. 22:1 ff., he believed God as he commanded him to sacrifice his son Isaac—and so also in other passages. He did all this out of faith—so the apostle intimates clearly in Heb. 11:8-10.

And so our text here follows without any conjunctive clause upon the preceding one, so that one should understand what follows as pertaining not only to the preceding passage in particular but, without any qualification, to every evidence of Abraham's faith. The text reads: "So shall your seed be" (Gen. 15:5), and then there follows immediately without any conjunctive clause: "And Abraham believed God" (Gen. 15:6). It does not say: "And Abraham believed God this," but it says simply that he believed. So then: "Abraham believed God" means that he regarded God as truthful; and "to believe God" is as much as to say "to believe him at all times and places." Now all this needed to be said, lest some fool should charge the apostle with trickery for his reasoning on faith as such on the basis of Abraham's example, and, also, lest someone should raise the objection that, prior to this particular passage, the Scripture speaks of Abraham's having found favor with God and that there it does not say anything to the effect that "Abraham believed God" and that "it was reckoned to him unto righteousness."

Now to him that works, the reward is not reckoned according to grace, but according to debt. But to him that works not, yet believes in him that justifies the ungodly, his faith is reckoned to righteousness, according to the purpose of the grace of God. **As David also terms the blessedness of a man, to whom God reckons righteousness without works. (Rom. 4:4–6.)**

One must construe this passage as follows: **His faith is reckoned for righteousness even as David terms (i.e., asserts) the blessedness of a man (i.e., that man is blessed, and that only that man has blessedness) unto whom God imputes righteousness without works.** And this "without works" must be understood, as we have stated before, to refer to works by the performance of which one thinks he has obtained righteousness, as if one were righteous by virtue of such works or as if God regarded and accepted him as righteous because he did them. But this is not true, because God does not accept a person on account of his works, but the works on account of the person, and the person before the works. As it is written: "And the Lord had respect" (first) "to Abel" and (afterward) "to his offerings." (Gen. 4:4.)

This shows that it is not so much works, as such, as the interpretation and foolish estimation one applies to them that are disapproved. For the righteous, too, do the same works as the unrighteous, but not from the same inner attitude. In other words: the righteous do them in order to seek and obtain righteousness thereby, the ungodly, on the other hand, in order to demonstrate their righteousness by them as if they had already obtained it. The former are dissatisfied with the works they have done and seek the justification of their heart and hope that it may be healed from wrong desires, but the latter are unconcerned for their inner attitudes and are content with the works they have done outwardly. Thus, they are simulators and hypocrites, i.e., outwardly they are like the righteous, but they lack inward righteousness. As it says in Job 39:13: "The wing of the ostrich is like the wings of the heron and the hawk," i.e., but it cannot fly and seek its prey like the heron and the hawk. So they decide for themselves that they are righteous. The others proclaim the teaching: A man who has done this or that is righteous, but these say: A man to whom God does not impute his sin is righteous. The others know how much and what a man must do in order to be righteous, but these do not know when they are righteous, because they are righteous only by God's reckoning them as such; but nobody knows his reckoning; one must ask and hope for it. The former know precisely when they are no longer sinners. But the latter know that they are always sinners.

If the passage that follows: "Blessed are they whose iniquities are forgiven and whose sins are covered" (Rom. 4:7), is to be rightly understood, we must therefore keep the following theses in mind:

(1) *The saints are intrinsically always sinners, therefore they are always extrinsically justified; but the hypocrites are intrinsically always righteous, therefore they are extrinsically always sinners.*

"Intrinsically" means as we are in ourselves, in our own eyes, in our own estimation, and "extrinsically," how we are before God and in his reckoning. Hence, we are extrinsically righteous in so far as we are righteous not in and from ourselves and not by virtue of our works but only by God's regarding us so. For his reckoning is not dependent upon us and does not lie in our power. Therefore, our righteousness, too, is not of our own making and it does not lie in our power. As Hosea says: "Destruction is your own, O Israel; your help is only in me" (Hos. 13:9), i.e., inside of you there is nothing but perdition, but your salvation is outside you. And Ps. 121:2: "My help comes from the Lord," i.e., not from me. So we are intrinsically sinners according to the law of correlation.[1] For if we are righteous only by virtue of the fact that God reckons us so, then we cannot be righteous by virtue of our life and work. For this reason we are intrinsically and from ourselves always ungodly. As it says in Ps. 51:3: "My sin is ever before me," i.e., I am always aware of the fact that I am a sinner. "Before thee have I sinned" (I am a sinner), "therefore thou wilt justify me in thy word," etc.

By contrast, the hypocrites who are intrinsically righteous are, according to what is implied in being reciprocally related, extrinsically (i.e., in the reckoning of God) unrighteous, as it says in Ps. 95:10: "I said: These always err in heart"; they turn all the words of Scripture upside down, as, for example, this one: "My sin is ever before me," for they say: My righteousness is ever before me (i.e., I am always aware of it) and blessed are they who work righteousness, etc. Before thee, so they say (I have not sinned, but) I

---

[1] *"Per naturam relativorum."* The *relativum* (being in relation) must be understood in terms of the Aristotelian doctrine of categories (*praedicamenta*). Cf. Ficker, 269, n. 8, 13.

work righteousness; indeed, before themselves they work right-eousness.

(2) *"God is wonderful in his saints"* (Ps. 68:35); *to him they are at the same time righteous and unrighteous. And God is wonderful in the hypocrites; they are to him at the same time unrighteous and righteous.*

For inasmuch as the saints are always aware of their sin and im-plore God for the merciful gift of his righteousness, they are for this very reason also always reckoned righteous by God. There-fore, they are before themselves and in truth unrighteous, but be-fore God they are righteous because he reckons them so on account of this confession of their sin; they are sinners in fact, but by vir-tue of the reckoning of the merciful God they are righteous; they are knowingly righteous and knowingly unrighteous, sinners in fact but righteous in hope.

And this is what is meant by what it says here: "Blessed are they whose iniquities are forgiven and whose sins are covered" (Ps. 32:1). Hence, there follows this: "I said I will confess against my-self my unrighteousness" (i.e., I am always aware of my sin, so that I can confess it to thee) and therefore "thou hast forgiven the wickedness of my sin" (Ps. 32:5), not only to me but to all. Hence, there follows: "For this let everyone that is holy pray to thee." (Ps. 32:6.) Notice here that everyone who is godly is a sinner who prays for himself. So a righteous man is basically one who accuses himself. And again: "The righteous man will make supplication for his faults" (Ecclus. 39:7) and once more in Ps. 38:18: "For I will declare my iniquity, and I will be sorry for my sin." It is the mercy of God, then, which is wonderful in its great sweetness: he takes us at the same time for sinners and nonsinners. Sin remains and simultaneously does not remain in us. (This psalm must there-fore be interpreted in the light of its heading.)[2] On the other hand, his wrath is wonderful in its severity, for he takes the un-godly at the same time for unrighteous and righteous. He does take their sin away and at the same time he does not.

COROLLARY

The apostle deals here not only with sins as they are committed in deed, word, and thought but also with the "tinder"[3] of sin

---

[2] "A Psalm of David, to bring to remembrance." Faber Stapulensis interprets this as follows *(Quincuplex Psalterium, ad loc.)*: "The prophet in spirit in-troduces Christ the Lord as the one who, in our stead, confesses our sins as his to God the Father."

[3] The Scholastics called concupiscence *(concupiscentia)* *"fomes peccati"* (the "tinder," or "fuel," of sin). This Corollary is recorded in the notes of Luther's students as follows *(WA* 57, 164, 21 to 165, 13): "He does not speak

which he defines in ch. 7 of this letter by the words "not I, but
the sin which dwells in me" (Rom. 7:20). He also calls it there
"the passions of sins" (Rom. 7:5), i.e., the sinful desires, feelings,
and inclinations which he says bring forth fruits unto death.
Therefore, actual sin (as the theologians call it) is, strictly speaking, the work and fruit of sin, and sin itself is that passion (tinder)
and concupiscence, or that inclination toward evil and resistance
against the good which is meant in the statement, "I had not
known that concupiscence is sin" (Rom. 7:7). (These passions
"work" in our members to bring forth fruit and are, therefore,
not themselves the work; but they are working to bring forth
fruit; they themselves are not the fruit.

Conversely, we may say: As the righteousness that comes to us
from God is that turning toward the good and that turning away
from evil which grace gives to us inwardly, and as good works are
not righteousness itself but rather its fruit, so sin is the turning
away from the good and the turning toward evil, and the works of
sin are the fruit of sin, as will be seen more clearly below in chs. 7
and 8.

It is with respect to sin in this sense that we must understand all
the aforementioned texts, namely: "Blessed are they whose iniquities are forgiven" and "I said, I will confess against myself my
unrighteousness to the Lord, and for this let everyone that is
holy pray unto thee," (Ps. 32:1, 5–6) and "For I know my transgressions, and my sin is ever before me," and "Against thee have
I sinned" (Ps. 51:3–4), etc. This is the evil which, inasmuch as it
is the reality of sin, God in his mercy forgives by his nonreckoning
to those who acknowledge and confess and hate it and ask to be

---

so much of the sins of deed, word, and thought as of the sin of the tinder.
Hence he says below in chapter 7: 'Not I, but the sin that dwells within me.'
There he calls it 'the passions of sins' (i.e., the desires, inclinations, etc.)
which, he says, 'bring forth fruit unto death.' Therefore, actual sin, as the
theologians call it, is not sin but rather the work and the fruit of sin. Now,
it is this sin which, in the gospel, our Lord calls a 'bad tree' (Matt. 7:17;
12:33), according to Blessed Augustine against Julian (Contra Jul. V, 21).
Therefore, as righteousness is the very inclination toward evil, so evil works
are the fruits of sins. It is as with a sick man who believes his physician when
he gives him the most certain assurance that he will get well. Hoping for
the promised recovery, he obeys the physician's orders and abstains from all
that is prohibited to him and waits for the fulfillment of the physician's
promise. This man is at once sick and healthy, sick in fact but healthy in
the hope for the promised health. In the same way, our Samaritan Christ
took the man who was half dead in order to cure him by promising him the
most perfect well-being in the life to come. Therefore, also, this man was
righteous and sinful at the same time, a sinner in fact but a righteous man
by virtue of his faith in the promise and of his hope that it would be kept."

healed from it. Thus it comes about that "when we say we have no *I John 1:8* sin, we are liars" (I John 1:8). And it is a mistake to think that this evil can be healed by good works, because experience shows that *Total Depravity* in every good we do there remains that concupiscence toward evil, *+* and nobody is free from it, not even an infant a day old. *Original Sin*

But it is by the mercy of God that this evil, though it remains, is not reckoned to those who fervently call upon him to set them free. With caution and circumspection, they will readily do good works because they eagerly long to be justified. So then, we are sinners before ourselves and yet in the reckoning of God we are righteous through faith. And we practice this faith in him who *good works* sets us free in so far as, while we wait till he takes our sin away, we meanwhile see constantly to it that it does not get the upper hand but is held in check. *sick man*

It is as with a sick man who believes his physician as he assures him that he will most certainly get well. In the meantime, he obeys his orders in the hope of recovery and abstains from whatever is forbidden to him, lest he slow up the promised cure and get worse again, until finally the physician accomplishes what he has so confidently predicted. Can one say that this sick man is healthy? No; but he is at the same time both sick and healthy. He is actually sick, but he is healthy by virtue of the sure prediction of the physician whom he believes. For he reckons him already healthy because he is certain that he can cure him, indeed, because he has begun to cure him and does not reckon him his sickness as death. In the same way, Christ, our good Samaritan, brought the man who was half dead, his patient, to an inn and took care of him (Luke 10:30 ff.) and commenced to heal him, having first promised to him that he would give him absolutely perfect health unto eternal life.[4] He does not reckon him his sin, i.e, his sinful desires, for death, but in the meantime, i.e., holding up to him the hope *hope* that he will get well, he forbids him to do or not to do anything that might impede his recovery and make his sin, i.e., his concupiscence, worse. Now can we say that he is perfectly righteous? No; but he is at the same time both a sinner and righteous, a sinner in fact but righteous by virtue of the reckoning and the certain promise of God that he will redeem him from sin in order, in the end, to make him perfectly whole and sound. And, therefore, he is perfectly whole in hope, while he is in fact a sinner, but he has already begun to be actually righteous, and he always seeks to become more so, always knowing himself to be unrighteous. (But if now this patient should like his feebleness so much that he

---

[4] Luther builds on the moral (or tropological) exegesis of Luke 10:31 ff. in the *Gl. ord.* and in Lyra.

does not want to be entirely cured, will he then not die? Yes, he will! And so it is with people who follow their desires in the world. Or when someone imagines that he is not sick but healthy and spurns the physician, he is of this sort. This is wanting to be justified and to be whole by one's own works.)

anti-Scholastics

If this is so, then I must say either that I have never understood the matter or that the Scholastic theologians did not deal adequately with sin and grace.[5] For they imagine that original sin, just like actual sin, is entirely taken away, as if sins were something that could be moved in the flick of an eyelash, as darkness

pro-Augustine

is by light.[6] The ancient holy fathers Augustine and Ambrose, however, dealt with these issues quite differently, namely, according to the method of Scripture. But the Scholastics follow the method of Aristotle in his *Ethics*, and he bases sinfulness and righteousness and likewise the extent of their actualization on what a person does.[7] But Blessed Augustine said most plainly that "in baptism sin (concupiscence) is forgiven, not in the sense that it is no longer there, but in the sense that it is not counted as sin."[8] And Saint Ambrose says: "I am always in sin, therefore I always commune."[9]

Fool that I was, I could not understand, in the light of this, in what way I should regard myself as a sinner like others and in what way I should not put myself ahead of anyone, inasmuch as I had contritely made confession of my sins, for I thought that thereby they had been taken away and made of no effect, also inwardly. But if I should regard myself as a sinner like them on account of my past sins[10] which, they say, must always be remembered (and here they speak the truth but not emphatically enough), then, I thought, they are really not forgiven, though God has promised to forgive them to such as confess them. Thus

Luther's struggle

I fought with myself, because I did not know that though forgiveness is indeed real, sin is not taken away except in hope, i.e.,

[5] Duns Scotus, IV *Sent.*, d. 1, q. 6, n. 7 and 8; d. 14, q. 1, n. 17–19. Gabriel Biel, IV *Sent.*, d. 4, q. 1, a. 2, concl. 1–3.
[6] Cf. Lyra, *ad loc.*
[7] Aristotle, *Eth. Nicom.*, III, 7; IV, 9; V, 10. The Scholastics generally quote II, 1.
[8] Augustine, *De nupt. et concup.*, I, 25, 28. Luther quotes this passage frequently, probably because it defined the forgiveness of sins as the nonimputation of sins. Augustine did not give a consistent interpretation of forgiveness (*remissio peccatorum*), and this had important influences upon the thinking of the Scholastics. For example, Gabriel Biel (IV *Sent.*, d. 14, q. 1, a. 1, n. 2G) speaks of *remitti seu deleri peccatum*, while Ockham (IV *Sent.*, q. 8 and 9) uses *deleri* and *remitti* indiscriminately. Cf. Ficker, p. 273, n. 4.
[9] Ambrose, *De sacramentis*, IV, 6, 28.
[10] Cf. Gabriel Biel, IV *Sent.*, d. 4, q. 1, n. 3; d. 14, q. 1, a. 1, n. 2.

that it is in the process of being taken away by the gift of grace
which starts this removal, so that it is only not reckoned as sin.

For this reason it is sheer madness to say that man can love God
above everything by his own powers[11] and live up to the commandment in terms of the substance of the deed but not in terms
of the intention of Him who gave it,[12] because he does not do so
in the state of grace. O you fools, you pig-theologians![13] So, then,
grace was not necessary except in connection with a new exaction
over and above the law! For if we can fulfill the law by our own
powers, as they say, grace is not necessary for the fulfillment of
the law but only for the fulfillment of a divinely imposed exaction that goes beyond the law. Who can tolerate such sacrilegious
opinions! Does not the apostle say that "the law works wrath"
(Rom. 4:15) and "that it was weak through the flesh" (Rom. 8:3)
and that it can absolutely not be fulfilled without grace?

Even their own experience could have made them aware of the
utter stupidity of this opinion and caused them to be ashamed of
themselves and to repent. For willy-nilly they must sense the
wrong desires in their own selves. Therefore, I say now: Hui! Go
to work, please! Be men! Try with all your powers to eliminate
these covetings that are in you! Give proof of what you say,
namely, that it is possible to love God "with all one's strength"
(Luke 10:27) naturally, in short, without grace! If you have no
sinful desires, we will believe you. But if you live in and with
them, you no longer fulfill the law. Does not the law say: "You
shall not covet" (Ex. 20:17) but "you shall love God" (Deut. 6:5)?
Can, then, one who covets and loves something else also love God?
Yet this concupiscence is always in us; therefore, the love of God
is never in us, except in so far as grace has given us a beginning of
it. We have the love of God only in so far as the rest of concupiscence, which still must be cured and by virtue of which we do not
yet "love God with our whole heart" (Luke 10:27), is by mercy
not reckoned as sin. We shall love God only at the end, when it
will all be taken away and the perfect love of God will be given
to those who believe and who with perseverance always yearn for
it and seek it.

These monstrous views were made possible by the fact that the

---

[11] Duns Scotus, III *Sent.*, d. 27, q. *un.*, n. 13, 15, 21. Pierre d'Ailly, I *Sent.*,
q. 2, a. 2F. Gabriel Biel, II *Sent.*, d. 28, *passim*; III *Sent.*, d. 27, a. 3, dub.
2; IV *Sent.*, d. 14, q. 1, a. 2, concl. 2.

[12] Aegidius Romanus, II *Sent.*, d. 28; Pierre d'Ailly, I *Sent.*, q. 2, a. 2M;
Gerson, *De vita spirituali*, lect. 1; Gabriel Biel, II *Sent.*, d. 28, a. 1, n. 4;
a. 2, concl. 3; III *Sent.*, d. 27, q. *un.*, a. 3, dub. 2, propos. 5. Cf. Ockham,
III *Quodlib*, q. 14.

[13] "*O stulti, O Sawtheologen.*"

Scholastic theologians did not know the nature of sin and for-giveness. For they reduced sin as well as righteousness to some very minute motion of the soul. They said, namely, that when the will is subject to synteresis, it is , only slightly to be sure, "inclined toward the good."[14] And this tiny motion toward God (of which man is naturally capable) they imagine to be an act of loving God above everything! And now look at man as he actually is, and see how his whole person is full of these sinful desires (and how that little motion has no effect at all). But, according to the law, he should be bare and empty in order to be wholly subject to God. Therefore, Isaiah laughs at them and says: "Do good or evil, if you can!" (Isa. 41:23).

So then, this life is a life of cure from sin; it is not a life of sinlessness, as if the cure were finished and health had been re-covered. The church is an inn and an infirmary for the sick and for convalescents. Heaven, however, is the palace where the whole and the righteous live. As Blessed Peter says: "The Lord will make a new heaven and a new earth, wherein dwells righteous-ness." (II Peter 3:13.) Yet here on earth righteousness does not yet dwell, but by healing sins it meanwhile prepares for itself a dwelling place.

All the saints had this understanding of sin, as David prophesied in Ps. 32.[15] And they all confessed themselves to be sinners, as the books of Blessed Augustine show. Our theologians, however, have neglected to consider the nature of sin and have concentrated their attention upon good works; they have been concerned to teach only how good works might be made secure, but not how with fervent prayers one must humbly seek the grace that heals and how one must acknowledge himself a sinner. And so they inevitably bring it about that people become proud, thinking that they are already righteous by having done good works outwardly, unconcerned as they are to make war on their evil desires by un-ceasing prayer and devotion to the Lord. This is also the reason why there is, in the church today, such frequent relapse after confessions. The people do not know that they must still be justi-fied, but they are confident that they are already justified; thus they come to ruin by their own sense of security, and the devil does not need to raise a finger. This certainly is nothing else than to establish righteousness by means of works. And even if they im-plore the grace of God, they do not do so rightly but only in order to get rid of the work of sin. But true Christians have the spirit of

---

[14] Duns Scotus, II Sent., d. 39, q. 2, n. 5. Gabriel Biel, II Sent., d. 39, q. un., a. 2, concl. 1.
[15] It is Ps. 32 which Paul quotes in the fourth chapter of his letter.

Christ and act rightly, even if they do not understand what we have just said; they act before they come to understand why they behave as they do; indeed, they obtain more understanding from life than from doctrine.

There remains one more point that is raised against what we have said so far, an objection against our assertion that the righteousness of God is imputed to believers without works. We read in the legends of many saints (so runs the argument) that some of their works or prayers were accepted by God and commended to others as an example; therefore, they were justified by their works. I answer: This is a nice argument; for on the one hand, it puts forth a great error, and on the other hand, it can help to clarify the right understanding of what we have said so far.

The error lies with those who presumptuously proceed to imitate all these works that were accepted by God, and thus want to be regarded as righteous because they claim to do the same as the saints to whom their works were reckoned unto righteousness. But this means to pervert the example of the saints and not at all to imitate them, for it is an attempt to accomplish a righteousness of works. For the saints, to whom these works were counted for righteousness, certainly did not do them in order to be regarded as righteous; indeed, they did not know whether God would behold them. But they did what they could in humble faith, always with the prayer that their works might be acceptable to God according to his mercy. And so they were first reckoned as righteous on account of the yearning of their faith, and only afterward also their works were accepted and approved. But foolish perverter that you are, you commence with the works that were accepted and you leave aside the inner yearning by which you, too, could first be reckoned as righteous just as they were. You want to be regarded as righteous by your works alone; you want to have "respect" directed "to the offering" rather than to "Abel" (Gen. 4:4), but this cannot be. And this madness rages today everywhere in the pulpits of preachers who are supposed to proclaim the word of God!

EXPOSITION OF THE VERSES OF THE PSALM (PS. 32)

The Hebrew text uses here three different terms for sin. According to Reuchlin,[16] it reads as follows: *"Blessed is the man who is being lightened of his crime, who is being covered to his sin. Blessed is the man to whom the Lord will not count his iniquity"* (Ps. 32:1–2). The first term: "crime," which is variously interpreted and in Hebrew is called *"pésha‘,"* I should understand as designat-

---

16 Reuchlin, in his exposition of the Penitential Psalms.

ing the work of sin. The second one: "sin," which is called *"ḥāṭā̆'"* and practically everywhere interpreted as sin, I take to refer to the root-sin in us or to concupiscence for evil. The third one: "iniquity," which is called *"'āwāh"* and is everywhere interpreted as iniquity, I should interpret to mean hypocrisy, if this were not made impossible by "Wash me thoroughly from my iniquity and cleanse me from my sin" (Ps. 51:2). Here the two terms appear to have the same meaning: a man is "iniquitous" when he turns away from the good, and he is a "sinner" when he turns toward evil; on the one hand, he is defiled by an omission and, on the other hand, by a commission, if, indeed, it is "iniquitous" to esteem God less than a creature, and "evil" or "a sin" to adhere to a creature. "Here" one is unable to find the good, and "there" it is iniquitously placed last.

So then, it says first: "Blessed is the man who is being lightened of his crime," i.e., who by grace is made free from the burden of his crime, namely, the actual sin he has committed. But this is not enough, unless he is at the same time "covered to his sin," i.e., unless the root-evil in him is not imputed to him as sin. His sin is covered when, though it is there, it cannot be seen—and what cannot be seen can also not be counted. That he is lightened or, rather, made light—this means that he is freed from his sin not by his own powers but by the action of God, while in himself he remains passive.[17] For it does not say: Blessed is the man who lightens himself, i.e., by his own powers, but: who is lightened.

Now, sin is covered by Christ when he dwells in us, as Ruth said allegorically to Boaz: "Spread your coat over your handmaiden, for you are a kinsman" (Ruth 3:9). "And she took off the coat and laid down at his feet" (Ruth 3:7), i.e., the soul lies down at the humanity of Christ and is covered by his righteousness. Likewise Ezek. 16:8: "I spread my garment over you and covered your nakedness." And Ps. 63:7: "Under the cover of thy wings I will rejoice." Likewise, Ps. 45:9: "The daughters of kings have delighted thee in thy glory," i.e., in thy adornment, when they are honored by thee and thou in them. And "with your comeliness and your beauty set out," etc. (Ps. 45:8), and thus the evil work is put away and the remainder of sin, i.e., of the "tinder," is not counted until it is healed.

Then follows, thirdly, that he is already an ungodly man who is justified; he is a sinner, to be sure, but not ungodly. A man is called ungodly if he is not a worshiper of God and turns away from him instead and does not fear and honor him. But a man who is justified and "whose sins are covered" is already turned toward

[17] *"Sed per Deum active et in se passive liberatur."*

him and is godly; he worships God and seeks him in hope and fear. And because of this, God regards him as devout and righteous. As it says in this same psalm: "Thou hast forgiven the ungodliness of my sin" (Ps. 32:5). What is here called "ungodliness" is above called "sin." For it is one and the same thing to say: "Thou hast forgiven the ungodliness" or "The Lord will not count as sin." The meaning, therefore, is this: It is not sufficient that we ourselves consider us godly, for it is the Lord's to accept us as such, and he accepts only those "whose transgressions are forgiven and whose sins are covered." For to them he does not impute their ungodliness but rather their godliness. For inwardly "there will be no guile" in them (Ps. 32:2), as it must necessarily be in the case of those who reckon to themselves no ungodliness and whose sins are not covered by God and whose transgressions are not forgiven.

COROLLARY

To say: "God has obliged us to have grace and therefore to what is impossible"[18] is an inept and foolish way of speaking. I excuse the most blessed God. He is innocent of this deception. He has not done this. He has not obliged us to have grace, but he has obliged us to fulfill the law, in order to give us his grace when, humiliated, we ask for it. But these men make grace into something that causes indignation and they imagine what is hateful. For what does it mean to say: God has obliged us to have grace, and he does not want to accept the fulfillment of the law according to the substance of the deed if it is not also fulfilled according to the intention of the lawgiver?[19] Is this not the same as to say: Look, can we, then, fulfill the law without grace? Is it not enough that he has burdened us with the law, without adding his demand that we should have grace, as a new exaction? What arrogance! What ignorance of sin! What ignorance of God! What ignorance of the law! Thus, when God offers grace to us miserable creatures because he sees that we cannot fulfill his law and so that we may now fulfill it by the power of grace, these people are not yet sufficiently humbled and they still do not know that the law cannot be fulfilled according to the substance of the deed as they themselves say. It may be, then, that they mean by "substance of the deed" an external action. But they do not do this at all; they have reference also to an internal action.

---

[18] Ficker (p. 278, n. 25) says that Luther thinks here especially of Pierre d'Ailly, I *Sent.*, q. 14, *propos.* 4R: "*Rationalis creatura potest obligari ad sibi impossibile. . . . Patet quia quelibet rationalis creatura tenetur habere gratiam.*" Cf. also the Scholastic definition of original sin as *carentia iustitiae originalis debitae*, e.g., in Gabriel Biel, II *Sent.*, d. 30, q. 1 and 2.

[19] Cf. Ockham, II *Sent.*, q. 26U; Pierre d'Ailly, I *Sent.*, q. 9S.

For they subsume under "substance of the deed" a work that is
done for the sake of God from the heart by an act of the will that
is naturally educed. Fools that they are, they do not notice that the
will, even if it could, would never do what the law prescribes. For
it resists the good and inclines toward evil. This they certainly
must know in their own experience, and yet they talk so irrever-
ently and sacrilegiously. For as long as it is reluctant toward the
law, it is turned away from it and thus does not fulfill it. Consequently, it needs grace to make it willing and cheerful toward the
law.

I was right, then, when I said that all our good is outside us; and
Christ is this good. As the apostle says: "He was made unto us wisdom from God and righteousness and sanctification and redemption." (I Cor. 1:30.) All these are in us only by faith and hope in
him. Therefore the church's entire praise in The Song of Solomon
belongs to Christ who dwells in it through faith just as all this
light of the earth does not come from the earth but from the sun
that shines upon it. So, in The Song of Solomon, the church often
confesses herself to be naked,[20] longing, so it is written, only for
the bridegroom and saying: "Draw me after thee, we will run in
the odor of thy ointments" (S. of Sol. 1:4). She always seeks, always
desires, and always praises the bridegroom. Thus she shows clearly
that she is inwardly empty and bare and that her fullness and
righteousness are outside her.

For if the confessions of the saints are to be understood only
with respect to their past sins and they show themselves pure in
the present, why, then, do they confess not only their past but also
their present sins? It is only because they know that there is sin
in them but that it is covered and not counted because of Christ,
and because they want to testify that all their good is outside
themselves in Christ who is nonetheless in them through faith.
Thus, in Psalm 45, the heart of the prophet "utters a good," i.e.,
sweet and consoling, "word" (Ps. 45:1). What is this word? "You
are beautiful above the sons of men" (Ps. 45:2), i.e., Christ alone
is beautiful and all children of men are ugly. Therefore, "with
your comeliness and your beauty set out, proceed prosperously
and reign." (Ps. 45:4.) We are his Kingdom, but the beauty in us
is not ours but his, and with it he covers our hideousness.

Hence, many yield to indolence and security, because they rely
on a word which Blessed Augustine is supposed to have said:
"wanting to be righteous is a large part of righteousness."[21] So
they identify this "wanting" with the smallest "elicited act of the

20 Cf. S. of Sol. 5:3; 7:12.
21 Cf. Augustine, Ep. 127, 5.

will,"[22] which, moreover, soon falls apart and leads to nothing, and they go on unconcerned, but, nevertheless, feel themselves very secure. Now, it is true that wanting to be righteous is not only a large part of righteousness but all the righteousness we can have in this life. But this "wanting" is not that of which we were just speaking but that which the apostle has in mind when he says: "To will is present with me, but to accomplish I find not" (Rom. 7:18). *Our whole present life is a time wherein we will righteousness but never accomplish it;* this happens only in the life to come. "To will," therefore, means to demonstrate with all our powers, efforts, prayers, works, sufferings, that we long for righteousness but that we do not yet have what shall be (I John 3:2). Read Blessed Augustine who has written about this very beautifully and extensively in many books, especially in the second book against Julian,[23] where he quotes Saint Ambrose, Hilary, Cyprian, Chrysostom, Basil, Nazianzen, Irenaeus, Retitius, and Olympus.

security / hypocrits

Now it is this security which is the mother of hypocrites and causes hypocrisy. The reason why God leaves us in the sin (of which we spoke), in the "tinder," in concupiscence, is that he wants to keep us in fear of him and in humility so that we may always keep running to his grace, always fearful that we may sin, i.e., always praying that he does not impute our sin to us and that he does not let it get dominion over us. Indeed, we fall into sin precisely by having no fear, for this evil in us (i.e., security) is by itself sin since, because of it, we do not love God above everything. It becomes a venial sin and is not counted as sin[24] only if we bemoan it and, deeply troubled, implore God that, in his mercy, he not condemn us because of it, nor impute it to us, and if we pray that he take it from us by his grace. Thus, we confess that we are sinners, and with our weeping, penitence, grieving, and tears we show that we are sinners also in our own eyes. As soon, namely, as such fear and uneasiness cease, the sense of security lays hold of us; and where security prevails, the divine decree of counting our sin to us is again in force, for God has decided that he will not impute sin to anyone who implores his mercy with fear and trembling. It is by this, his most merciful counsel, that God, whose name be blessed forever, forces us to tire of this life, to long for his mercy, to hate sin, to repent, etc.

[22] About the *actus voluntatis eliciti*, cf. Trutvetter, *Summa in totam physicen*, VIII, *Tract.* 1, *c.* 2; Ockham, II *Sent.*, q. 3P and Q; III *Quot lib.* q. 13–19; Gabriel Biel, II *Sent.*, d. 27, q. un.; III *Sent.*, d. 23, q. un.

[23] Augustine, *Contra Julianum*, II, 2, 4–10; I, 7, 32.

[24] On the opposite of this view, cf. Gabriel Biel, IV *Sent.*, d. 16, q. 5, a. 3, dub. 4: ("*Utrum . . . mortale peccatum possit fieri veniale*" "whether a mortal sin can become a venial one").

This is why, in the Holy Scriptures, hypocrites and people who regard themselves as holy are reproached for nothing so much as for this sense of security; it is considered as the source of the pride by which they give up the fear of God. Proverbs 1:29 f.: "Because they have hated instruction and received not the fear of the Lord, nor consented to my command," etc. Psalm 36:1:[24a] "There is no fear of God before their eyes." Hosea 10:3: "We fear not the Lord." This wretchedness results from the fact that people do not seek to drive out the internal sin, of which we have spoken, but give consideration only to the actual sin of deed, word, or thought. When they are rid of this kind of sin through confession, they go their way, feeling secure, and do not trouble themselves with the thought that, with a single sigh to God, they might cure also that internal sin, so that it is not imputed to them. As it says in Rev. 3:17: "Because you say, I am rich and have gotten riches, and know not that you are wretched and miserable, naked and poor." And the apostle says: "Purge out the old leaven, that you may be a new lump even as you are unleavened." (I Cor. 5:17.) But who among them sees that these two prevail at one and the same time, namely, that they are unleavened and yet that the old leaven must be purged out from them? This can be because the one is there in fact and the other is made up of hope and God's nonimputation because of the reverent humility of faith. They have the old leaven but they are grieved on account of it and invoke grace, and thereby they are unleavened by God's reckoning; he does not count the old leaven as sin, but he lets it remain so that it can be purged out. A man, therefore, who considers only his actual sin, and is anxious that it should be purged out, soon becomes presumptuous and secure because he knows that he can be cleansed by the sacrament and by confession, and so he walks about without fear and is no longer conscious of any sin.

Others, again, are too pusillanimous. They sin in a different way. They are in too great a hurry to have the old leaven purged out in order to obtain perfect health. They would like to root out entirely even the internal sin, but when they find this to be impossible because they fall from time to time, they become sad and dejected and lose hope. Inasmuch as grace does not co-operate with their excessive zeal, they try, therefore, to make themselves entirely pure by their own good works—and are most miserably dashed down. (These people do not have a sense of security, it is true, but they strive to obtain what those others have already achieved. Both, therefore, seek security and want to avoid the fear of God; the former are doing so in fact, and the latter wish to

24a Luther writes Ps. 14!

do so, and neither fears God.) They are too fearful, indeed foolishly so, because they think that they can please God only if they
are pure; and they believe that they are bound to displease him if
they are impure. This shows that they really do not know anything
of God's mercy. They should have implored it and then their impurity would not be imputed to them. And so, they too rely on
their own powers to their own greatest peril.

Those at the right, who have rid themselves of the fear of God,
sin through their sense of security, and those at the left, who have
given up the mercy of God, sin through their despair. These do
not know that this internal sin cannot possibly be taken away in
this life, but this is precisely what they want. The former, on their
part, do not know that it is to those who do not fear God that this
sin is imputed. Both, then, do not know this sin and do not properly attend to it. As I have said, they are concerned only about
actual sin, believing that it must be purged out so that one can
become pure. And if this does not happen, those at the left think
that they are lost. But the others at the right believe themselves
saved because they regard themselves as pure, while in fact, it is
impossible for anyone to be without any actual sin so long as that
radical and original sin remains.

This, therefore, is the royal road[25] and the way of peace in the
spirit: really to know and to hate sin and so to walk in the fear of
God, lest he count it and permit it to rule in us, and at the same
time to pray for his mercy that he free us from it and not impute
it to us. The fear of God cuts off the way at the right which leads

[25] The notion of the "royal road" (or *via media*), which Luther often referred to throughout his career, is derived from Num. 21:22: "[Israel sent
messengers to the king of the Amorites, saying:], 'Let me pass through thy
land: we will not go aside into the fields, or the vineyards; we will not
drink waters of the wells; we will go the King's Highway, till we have
passed thy borders.'" The *Gl ord.* interprets this in relation to Christ:
"*Hac via incedendum est et nusquam declinandum. . . . nec ad opera nec
ad sensus diabolicos volumus pacifice transire per mundum*" ("On this road
we must travel and we must not lose it. . . . Turning neither toward
works nor toward the devilish senses, we want peacefully to pass through
the world"). Bernard of Clairvaux often gave the admonition that Christians should keep to the middle: "*Tene medium. . . . Locus medius tutus
est. Medium sedes modi, et modus virtus*" ("Keep to the middle. . . . The
place in the middle is safe. The middle is the seat of moderation and moderation is a virtue") (*De consideratione*, II, 10). In connection with a discussion of the theological virtues, Biel says (III *Sent.*, d. 26, q. un., a. 3, dub. 5)
that "*spes mediare potest inter presumptionem et desperationem*" ("that
hope can hold the middle between presumption and despair"). On Luther's
thought, cf. Günther Jacob, *Das Bild vom "Weg in der Mitte" in der Theologie Luthers*, in H.-D. Wendland (ed.), *Kosmos und Ekklesia (Festschrift
für W. Stählin)* (Kassel, 1953), 84-92.

to security and vain self-satisfaction, and faith in the mercy of
God cuts off the way at the left which leads to despair of self and
despair of God.

In order at last to bring the discussion of the verses of the psalm
to a close, let us consider the three terms of which we have spoken
before,[26] namely: *"pésha',"* meaning "crimes"; "heinous deeds"
or "actual sins," "crooked actions," "transgressions"; *"ḥāṭā',"*
meaning "tinder of sin," "root-sin," "concupiscence," "sickness of
human nature"; *"'āwāh,"* meaning "unrighteousness" or "lack of
righteousness" or that one is not righteous before God even
though he does many good and righteous deeds. This unrighteousness is imputed to us on account of our crimes or our sin.
Unrighteousness, therefore, stands in relation to God's reckoning
just as righteousness does; it is a sin of omission and, as such, the
failure to worship and serve God. This is what the apostle has in
mind, when, in the third chapter of this letter, he quotes the saying
"There is none righteous" (Rom. 3:10); i.e., everyone has unrighteousness, and this having really means having nothing, or rather
that God does not regard one as righteous even though he does
good works, for good works do not establish righteousness in the
sight of God, just as they also do not annul unrighteousness. The
fourth term is the Hebrew word *"rāsha',"* meaning "ungodliness."
This is the vice of pride which becomes apparent when one denies
God's truth and righteousness, practices self-righteousness and
dogmatically asserts one's own wisdom. It makes people godless,
heretical, schismatic, eccentric, and individualistic or particularis-
tic.[27] Psalm 80:13 speaks of this in the words: "A singular wild
beast has devoured it."[28]

The meaning of the psalm is, then, as follows: Blessed is the
man (for the Hebrew text has the singular) who is lightened of his
crime, i.e., *pésha'* (i.e., who is forgiven for his evil deeds and
crimes, actual sins and crooked dealings, as they are produced by
the evil of the "tinder"), and whose sins are covered; or, as the
Hebrew text has it: to whom sin is covered or whose sin is covered,
namely, this very "tinder," by God's not reckoning it to him be-

---

[26] Here Luther relies on Reuchlin's *Septem psalmi poenitentiales.*

[27] Luther writes *"moniacos* [individualistic] . . . *sive monicos* [particularis-
tic]." These terms are derived from *monos* (i.e., *singularis*). The *Gl. ord.*
(quoting Augustine) and Lyra interpret *singularis* (cf. Ps. 80:13) as *superbus*
(proud). In his lectures on The Psalms, (*WA* 3, 172), Luther attributes the
vitium singularitatis to those "who reject obedience and the faith and establish their own righteousness" [*"qui reiecta obedientia et fide suam sta-
tuunt iustitiam"*]. Cf. Holl, *op. cit.,* pp. 198 ff.

[28] In his lectures on The Psalms, Luther interprets the "singular wild beast"
(*"singularis ferus"*) with reference to Antiochus, Herod, the Romans, and
the Turks.

cause of his humility and the yearning of his faith. God regards as righteous a man to whom these two evils are forgiven. Hence, the next line: "Blessed is the man to whom God will not impute iniquity." What our text[29] calls "sin" must more correctly be understood as "unrighteousness" in order to be consonant with the intention of the apostle who wants to prove from this word that righteousness is given without works by the reckoning of God; and this happens only by the nonimputation of unrighteousness.

Therefore, it is one and the same thing to say: to whom God reckons righteousness, and: to whom God does not impute sin, i.e., unrighteousness. But he will not forgive this unrighteousness to anyone, regardless of the many good works he may have done or do, unless his sin has first been covered (i.e., his root-sin, his original sin, the sin of his nature, which is covered by penitence, baptism, and a prayerful fear of God) and his iniquities, i.e., evil deeds or works, have been forgiven.

So there is an irksome confusion of these terms in this psalm, more so than in others. They should be read as follows: *"Blessed are they whose crimes are forgiven and whose sin is covered."* (Ps. 32:1.) *"Blessed is the man to whom God will not impute unrighteousness."* (V. 2.) And farther down, we read in the Hebrew text,[30] *"Because I have acknowledged my sin unto thee"* (v. 5), where our text[31] has "fault," though earlier the same word is rendered "sin." *"And my unrighteousness I have concealed."* (V. 5.) This is correctly and very well translated. For here the same word is used as above where it says: "God did not impute sin"; here the term "sin" is a poor translation of a word that means unrighteousness. And then: *"I said, I will confess my transgressions to the Lord"* (v. 5), where our text reads wrongly "my unrighteousness." As, in the second verse, the translator wrongly uses the plural "iniquities," so he uses here the wrong singular "unrighteousness." *"And thou forgivest* the ungodliness of my sin," i.e., *"the unrighteousness of my sin"* (v. 5). Here again he changes the word which, in the first verse, he had rendered "sin," and, in the fifth and here (as I have said, correctly), "unrighteousness." What is meant is: Thou hast not imputed to me the unrighteousness that is in me on account of that certain radical and deep sin. *"For this let everyone pray unto thee,"* etc. (v. 6), i.e., for the unrighteousness of his sin. For all will confess that in reality they are unrighteous before thee on account of this sin. Therefore, thou wilt forgive them and, by covering their sin, not impute unrighteousness to them.

And then: *"Many are the scourges of the sinner."* (V. 10.) Here

29 I.e., the Vulgate.
30 Following Reuchlin and Faber.
31 I.e., the Vulgate.

the translator should have said "the ungodly," i.e., one who justifies himself and despises God's righteousness by considering his unrighteousness as righteousness before God. And this is ungodliness and a double sin.

In the Hebrew text, these distinctions are consistently maintained, but in our translation every word stands for everything, and so there is plain confusion. So also in Psalm 51: *"According to the multitude of thy tender mercies, blot out my iniquity"* (v. 1) (i.e., "my transgressions"). *"Wash me thoroughly from my iniquity"* (instead of "unrighteousness") *"and cleanse me from my sin."* (V. 2.) *"For I know my iniquity"* (instead of "my evil deeds" or "transgressions") *"and my sin is ever before me."* (V. 3.) "Against thee only have I sinned," etc. (V. 4.) *"Behold I was conceived in iniquities"* (instead of "in unrighteousness") *"and in sin"* (i.e., "tinder") *"did my mother conceive me."* (V. 5.) *"Turn away thy face from my sins and blot out all my iniquities"* (v. 9) (instead of "all my unrighteousness").

Likewise: "I will teach the wicked" (instead of "transgressors") "thy ways and the ungodly" (instead of "sinners") "shall be converted to thee." (V. 13.)

Corollary

According to the Hebrew text, the verse: "Behold, I was conceived in iniquities," (i.e., in "unrighteousness" "and in sin my mother brought me forth" speaks specifically of original sin. For properly understood, the terms "unrighteousness" and "sin" must not be related to her who conceives and brings forth but to the one who is conceived and brought forth, so that what the text says, is this: Behold, when I was conceived, I was in unrighteousness before thee; I was not righteous because I lost righteousness through Adam and was thus conceived without it. For thou reckonest as unrighteous all that are conceived on account of the sin which is there transferred by the parents, even when they do not sin.

And "in sin," i.e., with the "tinder," concupiscence, "my mother brought me forth." For the mother does not sin when she gives birth, but the son who is born sins, i.e., is a sinner. He certainly does not confess the sin of someone else, but his own, not only in this verse but also in the preceding ones, wherever they speak of something that is "mine." But the reason why this verse speaks of "my" iniquities and "my"sin is that the sin in which he says he was conceived is common to all. And the sin belonging to all is now, he says, also become his. This is why he said first: "Wash me thoroughly from my iniquity," etc.

And another reason is this: this sin is his own and not his own.

This is why he did not say: conceived "in my iniquities," but "in iniquities," i.e., this inquity is there regardless of my involvement in it by deed or thought. I was conceived in it; I did not create it. It began to rule in me before I began to be; it and I were there at the same time.

For if this were only the sin of my parents, I could not possibly have been conceived in it, but they would have sinned before I was conceived. Therefore this iniquity and this sin were there and yet they were not mine; I was conceived in them without my consent. But now they have become mine. For now I know that I do evil and violate the law. The law prescribes: "You shall not covet" (Ex. 20:17), but if I do not observe the law, then it is I who sin and, indeed, it is I who covet. Therefore, sin is now also mine, i.e., it has my approval and my consent, for without grace I could not subdue it in me; and so, having acted in that "tinder" and concupiscence, I myself am now an actual, and not only an "original," sinner. This is why I said: "For I know my transgression," etc.

COROLLARY

The Scripture interprets "righteousness" and "unrighteousness" quite differently from the way the philosophers and jurists do. This is shown by the fact that they consider them as qualities of the soul.[32] But, in the Scripture, righteousness depends more on the reckoning of God than on the essence of the thing itself. For a person who possesses only the quality of righteousness does not have righteousness, for he is an unrighteous sinner through and through, but that person has righteousness whom God mercifully reckons as righteous because he confesses his unrighteousness and implores the divine righteousness; it is such a man that God wants to regard as righteous. Thus we are all born in iniquity; i.e., unrighteousness, and we die in it, but we are righteous, through faith in God's word, only as he mercifully regards us as righteous.

Let us now gather up the words of Scripture in which it is asserted that all men are sinners.

First: Moses in Gen. 8:21: "I will no more curse the earth for the sake of man. For the imagination and thought of man's heart are prone to evil from his youth."

Second: the same in Ex. 34:7: "O Lord God, who takest away iniquity and transgressions and sin, and no man of himself is innocent before thee," i.e., from the fact "that thou alone takest away sins" it follows "that none is righteous before thee," etc.

Third: Solomon in I Kings 8:46 and II Chron. 6:36: "For there is no man that sins not."

[32] Cf. Aristotle, Categor., 11.

Fourth: the same in Eccl. 7:20: "For there is no righteous man upon earth that does good and sins not."

Fifth: Job, and he speaks of it more fully than all the rest: in ch. 7:20 f. he says: "I have sinned, why dost thou not remove my sin," etc. And farther down in ch. 9:2: "Indeed, I know it is so, and that man cannot be justified compared with God." "Although I should have any just thing, I would not answer, but would make supplication to my judge." (Ch. 9:15.) In the same way he speaks throughout almost the whole book, though, in the twenty-seventh chapter, he adduces his own righteousness by saying: "My heart does not reprehend me in all my life" (ch. 27:6). But then, even the Lord himself commended him before Satan. (Ch. 1:8.)

Sixth: The Psalter: Ps. 32:6: "For this let everyone that is holy pray unto thee." Psalm 143:2: "For in thy sight, no man living shall be justified." And likewise: "And he will redeem Israel from all his iniquities." (Ps. 130:8.) And Ps. 72:14: "And he shall redeem their souls from usuries and iniquity." And there are many similar sayings.

Seventh: Isa. 64:6: "We are all become as one unclean and all our righteousness as a polluted garment."

Eighth: "I will chastize you in judgment that you do not seem innocent to yourself." (Jer. 30:11.)

From the New Testament:

Ninth: the apostle: "Jesus came to save sinners, of whom I am the chief." (I Tim. 1:15.) In Rom. 7:19, he says: "The evil which I will not, that I do," etc. And likewise: "I do not think that I have obtained." (Phil. 3:13.)

Tenth: James 3:2: "For in many things we all stumble."

Eleventh: I John 1:8: "If we say that we have no sin." Yet farther on, he says: "Who is born of God sins not" (I John 5:18).

Twelfth: Rev. 22:11: "He that is righteous, let him be justified still."

Hence, Blessed Augustine says in the twenty-ninth letter to Jerome:[33] "Love is the power by which one loves what is to be loved. In some it is stronger, in others weaker, in still others it is not at all; but to the fullest extent, so that it cannot be increased, it is in no one as long as man lives here on this earth. But as long as it can be made stronger, that in it which is less than it ought to be comes from a fault. Because of this fault 'there is not a righteous man on earth who does the good and does not sin' (I Kings 8:46). Because of this fault 'no man living will be justified in thy sight' (I John 1:8). Because of this fault 'we deceive ourselves and the truth is not in us when we say that we have no

[33] Augustine, *Ep.* 29 (*ad Hieron.*), 4, 15.

sin.' On account of this fault, it is necessary for us to say, even if we make much progress: 'Forgive us our debts' (Matt. 6:12), even if in baptism everything has been forgiven—all we have said, done, and thought." So far Augustine. The reasoning by which he here explains the necessity of baptism explains also the need of penitence and indulgences, indeed much more strongly so.

Thus it is obvious that no sin is venial according to its substance and nature, but there is also no merit. For even good works that are done over against the resistance of the "tinder" and sensuality are not done with such intensity and purity as the law requires, since they are not done with one's whole powers but only with the powers of the spirit that resist the powers of the flesh. For this reason, we sin even if we do good, unless God covers this imperfection through Christ and does not impute it to us because of our faith and the humble prayer that this imperfection be endured in Christ.

A man, then, who thinks that he must be regarded as righteous because of his works is very foolish, for measured in the judgment of God they are sins and are found to be such. As it says in Ps. 36:2: "For in his sight he has done deceitfully that his iniquity may be found unto hatred," i.e., before God and inside his spirit there was deceit and not the truth of righteousness, even when he shows his righteousness publicly. For he cannot be inwardly righteous without the mercy of God, because he is corrupted by the "tinder." And thus iniquity will be found in his righteousness, i.e., also his good works are unrighteous and sinful. This iniquity cannot be found in believers who humbly pray, because Christ helps them with the fullness of his purity and covers thereby this imperfection. Precisely this they ask and hope from him; the others, however, do not ask for it but presumptuously claim it for themselves.

COROLLARY

Pésha'. *"Evil-doing,"* iniquities, crimes, etc. They relate to actions that are evil in themselves and to sins.

Ḥāṭā'. *"Sin,"* understood as the "tinder" that inclines toward evil deeds and is their cause and thus the tree on which this kind of fruit grows.

'Āwāh. *"Iniquity,"* unrighteousness, those good works which are done over against the resistance of sin, especially if they are held to constitute righteousness. But they cannot be good works by virtue of the striving of him who runs, but by the indulgence of God who has mercy. Thus they are iniquities and unrighteousnesses and not righteous actions that conform to what is required.

Rāsha'. "Ungodliness." This is the basis of this very unrighteousness and this denial of sin; it manifests itself in this, that one
refuses to confess himself a sinner and declares his good works to
be righteousness and abominates only atrocities and crimes. The
result is that people of this sort are righteous in the judgment of
men but that, before God, they are unrighteous.

You ask: Why, then, is there so much preaching on the merits of
the saints? I answer: Their merits are not their own but they are
the merits of Christ in them. Because of him, God accepts their
works; otherwise, he would not accept them. For this reason, they
themselves never know whether they deserve or have merits, but
they do all their good works only because they want to obtain
mercy and escape the judgment. All the while, they pray for forgiveness rather than that they reach presumptuously for a crown.
Hence, "God is wonderful in his saints." (Ps. 68:35.) He keeps
them hidden in such a way that, in being saints, they appear to
themselves as common and profane. By the hope of mercy, "their
life is thus hid with Christ in God" (Col. 3:3). But by the fear of
judgment, their sin and death are manifest all about them and in
their own conscience. They always judge themselves in fear because they know that they cannot be righteous before God by their
own power. And so they fear the judgment of God in all their
doings, as Job says: "I was afraid of all my works, because I know
that thou wilt not spare him who fails" (Job 9:28). In order, then,
not to despair, they invoke God's mercy in Christ and thus they
are heard.

This is the wisdom which is hidden in a mystery (I Cor. 2:7);
this is the truth. For just as God and his counsel are unknown to
us, so also is our unrighteousness. For it totally depends on him
and his counsel. As it says in Ps. 51:6: "For, behold, thou hast
loved truth" (i.e., true righteousness in contrast to a figurative
and law-conforming one which depicts it as in a sign but is not
the truth). But how can I know this? "The uncertain and hidden
things of thy wisdom thou hast made manifest to me" (Ps. 51:6),
i.e., this I know that only an inner righteousness pleases thee and
that thou lovest it because it is the fullness of truth. I know it,
then, because thou hast given me wisdom that is in hiddenness in
order that I may know.

Consequently, because of the fact that we cannot fulfill the
commandment of God and thus are always deservedly unrighteous,
there is nothing left to us but that we ever fear the judgment and
pray for the remission of unrighteousness or, rather, for its nonimputation. As it says in Ps. 2:11: "Serve the Lord" (which can be

done only with gladness and with joy. But because this cannot be perfectly accomplished, therefore) "with fear"; serve him gladly with fear and "rejoice in him" (because of his mercy) "with trembling," on account of your sin that deserves to be condemned in judgment.

This blessedness, then, does it remain in the circumcision only, or in the uncircumcision also? For we say that unto Abraham faith was reputed to righteousness. How, then, was it reputed? When he was in circumcision, or in uncircumcision? Not in circumcision, but in uncircumcision. And he received the sign of circumcision, a seal of the righteousness of faith, which he had, being uncircumcised, that he might be the father of all them that believe, being uncircumcised, that unto them also it may be reputed to righteousness, and might be the father of circumcision; not to them only that are of the circumcision, but to them also that follow the steps of the faithful that is in the uncircumcision of our father Abraham. **For not through the law** *was the promise to Abraham, or to his seed, that he should be heir to the world, but through the righteousness of faith.* (Rom. 4:9–13.)

Again he shows that righteousness does not come from the law but from faith, according to what both bring forth and deserve. For they have deserved the opposite: the law, the wrath of God and the loss of the promise; faith, however, deserves grace and the fulfillment of the promise. In other words: if you do not believe the Scripture and the example it sets forth, believe at least your own experience. For by the law you have deserved the devastating wrath of God, but by faith, grace and the possession of the whole world. So also Abraham received the promise not through the law but through faith—as you do also who are his seed.

For the law works wrath. (Rom. 4:15.)

This is the outer effect of the law: it works wrath. That is to say: if it remains valid (as it needs must do if faith is lacking) and is not fulfilled, then those to whom it is given deserve God's wrath. Blessed Augustine writes in the nineteenth chapter of *On the Spirit and the Letter*:[34] "It was not by its own fault that the law was not fulfilled, but by the fault of the prudence of the flesh. This fault had to be pointed out by the law in order that it might be healed by grace." Consequently, it works wrath, i.e., if it is not fulfilled, it shows God's wrath to those who failed to take his wrath into account. Hence, not the law is evil, but those to whom

---

[34] Augustine, *De spir. et lit.,* 19, 34.

it is given. To them it works wrath as it works salvation to those
who believe, though, in this case, it is, strictly speaking, not the
law but grace which brings this about. *So then, if the fulfillment of*
the promise could come through the law which works wrath, the
promise would not be a promise but, rather, a threat. Thus the
promise would be abolished and with it faith too.

For if they who are of the seed be heirs, *faith is made void.*
(Rom. 4:14.)
Here the apostle shows that faith is made void in another way
than by the invalidation of the promise through the wrath of the
law, namely, through trust in the seed of the flesh. For if physical
descent would suffice to make us righteous and worthy of the
promise, faith would not be necessary. For if this were so, why,
then, was it that, by his faith, Abraham was justified and counted
worthy of the promises? Why was not he, too, justified because of
his physical descent? Then faith would be vain and vain also
everything that is written about it. People who can be justified by
their physical descent and by the law have no need of faith, as the
Jews in fact think. But just the opposite is the case: they are
damned through their trust in physical descent and the law.

For the promise that he should be the heir of the world, was
not *to Abraham or his seed* through the law (Rom. 4:13), i.e., by
the righteousness and the works of the law. The apostle does not
use the term "the righteousness of the law," but he says simply and
without qualification "the law," because it is actually not righteousness. Yet that he means "righteousness" when he says "law"
is shown by the contrast with which he continues: **by the right-**
eousness of faith, for it would have been sufficient if also here he
had said: "but by faith." But in view of the fact that the righteousness of the law is nothing, he rightly speaks only of "the law."
This passage confirms what he said earlier, namely, that Abraham
had the righteousness of faith before he was circumcised and that,
therefore, as it was promised to him, the Gentiles can follow him
in this faith as children follow their father. This promise certainly
was given to him on account of his faith and not through the law.
Having here connected the law and physical descent, he says of
both that they do not suffice for anyone to obtain the fulfillment
of the promise.
Hence, the two following sentences: **Faith is made void, and the**
promise made of none effect (Rom. 4:14), can be understood con-
junctively as well as separately. If they are understood conjunc-
tively, as referring to one another and implying one another (as we

have stated in the Gloss[35]), they mean the following: For the promise was not to Abraham either through the seed or through the law, etc., for if it were through physical descent or through the law, etc., faith and the promise would cease. But if one reads the sentence that faith would cease on account of a reliance on physical descent as if it implied the conclusion that, therefore, also the promise would cease on account of a reliance on the law, because "the law works wrath," one breaks up the text and makes it confusing. Read in the proper order, it must be understood as follows: The promise that they should be the heirs of the world was not given to Abraham and his seed by the law and by virtue of physical descent but by the righteousness of faith. For if they are heirs by virtue of the law and physical descent, faith is made void and the promise made of none effect. "For the law works wrath." But because "to be the seed" and "to have the law" is the same and because both refer to one and the same people, he uses now one and then the other form of expression.

But if one takes them separately, so that the first phrase is related to the preceding one and the second one to that which follows upon it, the meaning would be this: If seed and physical generation suffice to make a man righteous and worthy to inherit the world, it follows that faith is not necessary for justification and for the acquisition of such worthiness, for one who is righteous and worthy does not need to be made righteous and worthy. But this is apparently false, for precisely the opposite actually happens: It is spiritual generation that comes from faith which makes men righteous and worthy of the promise, and it suffices. But physical generation does not suffice at all; indeed, it is void; the believers are now the heirs, and the people of the seed are disinherited, as it says in Ps. 127:2 f.: "When he shall give sleep to his beloved, behold the inheritance of the Lord are children, the reward, the fruit of the womb," and in John 1:13: "Who were born not of blood, nor of the will of the flesh, nor of the will of

---

[35] Luther's interlinear gloss reads as follows (*WA* 56, 44, 11 ff.): "*For if those* [Abraham's] children, who are *of his seed,* only according to the flesh, of course, *be heirs,* possessors, namely, of the promise that is to be fulfilled, so that they possess the whole world, *faith is made void,* for then faith is made unnecessary, and it suffices that they are the children of his flesh. If they can become heirs by the seed (physical descent), what need is there of faith? *The promise is made of none effect,* i.e., it is abolished; it does not need to be fulfilled; and it is not fulfilled, and, therefore, it does not need to be believed."

The marginal gloss contains this comment on the last sentence (*WA* 56, 45, 15 f.): "For faith and the promise belong together [*quia fides et promissio sunt relativa*]; if the promise ceases, faith also ceases; and if the promise is taken away, faith too is taken away, and conversely."

men, but of God." And likewise in John 3:5: "You must be born
again from water and the spirit." And in Ps. 22:30 f.: "A seed
that serves him shall be declared to the Lord." And in Ps. 45:16:
"Instead of your fathers, sons are born to you," etc. Thus the
proposition is proved (that physical descent does not entitle anyone to inherit the world and that, instead, physical generation was
made void in order that the importance of a generation from
faith be established in opposition to those who seek to render
faith void in order to establish the importance of physical descent);
hence, it follows that the promise, too, would be made of none
effect by the law exactly as faith is by the reliance on physical
generation. For "the law works wrath," etc., as is shown by the
passage: **for where no law is,** there is no transgression; in other
words: it is the violation of the law which works wrath, but this
would not be so if there were no law.

The statement that the law works wrath must be understood
indirectly. For, strictly speaking, it is the violation of the law that
works wrath and renders the promise of none effect. But this
could not happen if there were no law. As long, namely, as the
law is without faith to fulfill it, it convicts all of sin and proves
them guilty and therefore unworthy of the promise, nay, rather,
worthy of God's wrath and destruction, and thus it turns the
promise into a threat. At any rate, it is the occasion that all this
can happen and befall man, i.e., that one knows that all this will
happen and come to pass, as the apostle says above: "By the law
comes the knowledge of sin" (Rom. 3:20). For whosoever has the
law without faith and grace certainly sees that he is a sinner who
is worthy of the wrath of God; therefore, the promise is made of
none effect to him.

*Therefore it is of faith, that according to grace the promise
might be firm to all the seed, not to that only which is of the law,
but to that also which is of the faith of Abraham, who is the father
of us all* (*as it is written:* **I have made you a father of many
nations**) *before God, whom he believed.* (Rom. 4:16–17.)

This "before God," etc., is not to be found in the Hebrew
Bible, but it can be elicited from the text if one considers rightly
in what respect Abraham was made a father of many nations. I
ask: Was he their father according to the flesh or according to the
spirit?

He cannot be the father of many nations according to the flesh,
because, again and again, there were people who did not descend
from him. But, nevertheless, he was given the promise that he
would be their father.

But if one objects and says that all nations will be destroyed so that only his descendants may rule the earth, he would be the father of only one nation and not of many.

Again, if all nations would be reduced to servitude, he would no longer be their father and the nations no longer his children but his slaves and he the lord of the nations; instead of fatherly care, there would prevail oppression and violence. And yet, the Jews blandly think that such a rule by oppression is promised to them and they wait for it in foolish hope. The only remaining conclusion to which we are driven is that he was given the promise to be their father "before God" and in his sight and in spirit.

If one objects again and says that he would then be their father by virtue of an office and in name only, just as Naaman, the Syrian, was called father by his servants (II Kings 5:13) and the princes of the peoples are called *patres patriae*, we reply and say that this would amount to a disparagement of the glory of the promise, because such a fatherhood is temporal and vicarious (and can fall to several and therefore not to Abraham alone, etc.); moreover, it is not perpetual, just as these official fathers are fathers only for the time of their reign.

But if the objector would persist in his impudence and say that he must be a father in the sense in which he is and was the father of the nations that descended from his second wife Keturah, then one must give the same reply as to the first objection and say that most nations had nothing to do with them and, indeed, were much more numerous than they. Because of these peoples, therefore, he would still not be a father of "many nations" but, rather, "of a few." And not even the Jews interpret the promise and await its fulfillment only with respect to these peoples. So, therefore, that inheritance is now actualized in Christ. He is the King and Lord of the nations. He has affirmed them for himself by a better victory than that by which the Jews long ago triumphed over the nation of Canaan. For he kills them spiritually with the sword of the word (Heb. 4:12) by making the ungodly godly and thus establishing his rule over them, even in their own land and possessions.

Who quickens the dead, *and calls those things that are not, as those that are.* (Rom. 4:17.)[36]

---

[36] The marginal gloss reads (*WA* 56, 46 f., 24 ff.): "These words are an incentive to faith. Abraham might have said: Behold, the inheritance that was promised to me can be given to me neither now while I live, nor after my death. For when I am dead and my children will obtain the inheritance, then it is not I but they who will have possession of it, although he gave

This may be historically true, but we must spiritually interpret it as a confirmation of the foregoing, i.e., the nations will be your children, and even though they are not yet, and are far from becoming, your children, nevertheless the Lord has power to raise them up and to call them so that they may become and be yours. As John the Baptist says in Luke 3:8: "Do not say: We have Abraham for our father, for God is able of these stones to raise up children unto Abraham." And so it strengthens the faith of Abraham and confirms the promise of God that he is told that he can become the father of many nations, if not by his own strength, then by the power of God, etc.

Who against hope believed in hope, that he might be made the *father of many nations, according to that which was said to him: So shall thy seed be. And he was not weak in faith; neither did he consider his own body now dead, whereas he was almost a hundred years old, nor the dead womb of Sara. In the promise also of God he staggered not by distrust, but was strengthened in faith, giving glory to God.* (Rom. 4:18–20.)

First of all, "hope" signifies something that is naturally hoped for. The hope that is here spoken of was not of this kind. But secondly, it signifies something that is supernaturally hoped for. In both cases, hope must be understood as what one hopes for but not as the power of hoping.

This suggests beautifully the difference between ordinary human hope and Christian hope. For human hope is not against hope but in accordance with what is hoped for, i.e., it is directed to what can readily become possible. For men do not hope where the opposite of what they hope for rises before their eyes, but where either something like it becomes evident or where there is a certainty that it will be realized. And so this hope is negative rather than positive, i.e., relying on what has begun to happen, one anticipates the realization of what one hopes for; then at length one hopes that nothing will prevent the realization of what one hopes for. Consequently, this hope wants to be certain and informed with respect to that which supports it, but with respect to what goes against it, it must remain uncertain.

By contrast, Christian hope is certain of what goes against it. For it knows that, as long as one hopes, what one hopes for must come about or cannot remain unrealized. For nobody can impede

---

the promise saying: 'to you and thy seed after you' [Gen. 17:7]. But if the inheritance is given to me while I live, then my whole seed will be able to possess it. And thus it always seems as if the promises of God contradicted one another and as if they were impossible for the wisdom of the flesh."

God. But with respect to its support, it is very uncertain, because it has no sure guarantee on which it can rely, but everything is deeply hidden and the opposite of what one hopes for stands before one's eyes. Hence, it is a positive rather than a negative hope.

In this passage, the apostle speaks in favor of both kinds: first, in so far as what supports hope is concerned, when he says that Abraham, not being weak in faith, **considered not his own body now dead,** when he was about a hundred years old, and secondly, as far as what denies hope is concerned, when he writes that **he staggered not at the promise of God through unbelief,**[37] most **fully knowing that whatsoever he has promised, he is also able to perform** (Rom. 4:21).[38] The positive militates against faith and hope because it can be seen, but the negative militates against them from within. The latter is the tendency of the heart to be so weak and inconstant as to be incapable of faith, while the former is represented by all that stands over against faith.

But was strengthened in faith, **giving glory to God.** (Rom. 4:20.)
What is implied in this is that, as the believer by his faith glorifies God, so, conversely, the unbeliever dishonors God by his lack of faith. First John 5:10: "He that believes not his Son has made God a liar, because he has not believed in the witness that God has borne concerning his Son." The believer thus makes God truthful and himself a liar. For he disbelieves his own mind as something false in order to believe the word of God as the truth, even though it goes utterly against all he thinks in his own mind. As it was said above in ch. 3:4 of this letter: "That thou mayest be justified in thy words," etc. "Let God be true and every man a

---

[37] In the marginal gloss, Luther comments as follows (*WA* 56, 48, 18 ff.): "There are two factors that make faith something arduous and difficult. First, it is the evidence 'of things not seen' [Heb. 11:1], indeed, of things that are opposite to what one sees, as if they could not possibly happen in view of the fact that all nature declares that they cannot be. When one has overcome this difficulty, a second and still greater one arises, namely, the anxious fear of the heart that God may change in his counsel and do something else. The first difficulty concerns the power of God and the second one his truth. Behind both his power and his truth, inwardly as well as outwardly, there is God's immutability."

[38] In the marginal gloss, Luther remarks on this passage (*WA* 56, 48, 25 ff.): "Num. 23:19: 'God is not man, that he should lie, nor as the son of man, that he should be changed. Has he said then, and will he not do it? Or has he spoken, and will he not fulfill?' But man oftentimes does not keep his word (because he does not have the power to live up to it but is changeable) even against his own will, for he cannot do what he promised when something that exceeds his power intervenes and prevents him from doing so. But this cannot happen in God."

liar," let him disbelieve in himself and believe God. Thus he will
become a liar and God will be made truthful. This is why Blessed
Augustine says[39] that one worships God by faith, hope, and love.
And, according to a saying that is often quoted,[40] one offends God
directly by the three vices of faithlessness, despair, and hatred.

*And therefore it was reputed to him for righteousness. Now it
is not written only for him that it was reputed to him for righteousness, but also for us, to whom it shall be reputed, if we believe in
him that raised up Jesus Christ, our Lord, from the dead,* **who
was delivered up** *for our sins and rose again for our justification.*
(Rom. 4:21–25.)

Christ's death is the death of sin, and his resurrection is the life
of righteousness. For by his death he has offered satisfaction for
our sins, and, by his resurrection, he has affirmed righteousness for
us. And so his death does not merely signify but it effects the remission of our sins as a most sufficient satisfaction. And his resurrection is not only the sign[41] of our righteousness, but, because it
effects it in us if we believe it, also its cause. (Heb. 5:9.) But about
this later.[42] All this the Scholastic theologians call one single
mutation: the expulsion of sin and the infusion of grace.[43]

[39] Augustine, *Enchiridion*, I, 3.
[40] One put "theological vices" over against the "theological virtues." Cf. Duns
Scotus, II *Sent.*, d. 43; G. Biel, II *Sent.*, d. 43, q. un.
[41] Lit., "sacrament."
[42] Cf. the exposition of Rom. 5:9 ff. and ch. 6:3 ff.
[43] Duns Scotus says expressly *"una mutatio realis"* (IV *Sent.*, d. 16, q. 2, n. b;
IV *Sent.*, d. 1, q. 6). Cf. also Ockham, IV *Sent.*, q. 3D and U ff.; Pierre
d'Ailly, IV *Sent.*, q. 3G.

ROMANS, CHAPTER FIVE[1]

Being justified therefore by faith, let us have peace with God, *through our Lord Jesus Christ.* (Rom. 5:1.)

This peace, of which all the prophets sing, is a spiritual peace. This is why he says: "*peace with God.*" It is prefigured in every peace which, in olden times, was given to the Children of Israel.

(It is nothing else than a quiet conscience and trust in God, just as, conversely, an unquiet conscience and mistrust in God mean spiritual disturbance. As Hosea says: "They sow the wind and shall reap the whirlwind" [Hos. 8:7]. For, according to Ps. 1:4, the penalty of a restless conscience is to be "like the chaff which the wind drives away.")

For this reason Christ is called Solomon[2] and the Prince of Peace. (Isa. 9:6.) Ephesians 2:14: "He is our peace, who has made both one." "And coming, he preached peace to you that were afar off, and peace to them that were nigh." (Eph. 2:17.) And John 16:33: "That in me you may have peace; in the world you have tribulation." Carnal peace is something else. It is spoken of in Matt. 10:34: "I am not come to send peace but the sword" (in contrast to carnal disturbance and temporal quietness). Hence, the word of Ps. 72:7: "In his days shall righteousness flourish and abundance of peace" must by no means be understood, as many think,[3] with reference to the temporal peace which prevailed under Augustus, but of this spiritual peace "with God."

[1] Note in Gloss (*WA* 56, 49, 17 ff.): "In this chapter, the apostle speaks with very great joy and gladness. In the entire Scripture, there is hardly a text that equals this chapter, at least not in expression. For it describes most clearly the nature and extent of God's grace and mercy toward us."

[2] Solomon, i.e., "*pacificus*" (cf. I Chron. 22:9: "He shall be called Peaceable").

[3] This exegesis is mentioned by Lyra, for example.

153

But it must be noted how the apostle bases the spiritual peace on righteousness. Therefore, he says first: "being justified by faith" and then only "we have peace." In the same way, "righteousness" precedes "peace" in the word of Ps. 85:10: "Righteousness and peace have kissed each other." So also in the passage: "In his days shall righteousness flourish, and abundance of peace." (Ps. 72:7.) It is due to the perversity of men that they seek peace first and then righteousness; consequently, they find no peace. In view of this, the words of the apostle suggest a fine contrast:

"A righteous man has peace with God but distress in the world because he lives in the spirit."

"An unrighteous man has peace with the world but distress and tribulation with God, because he lives in the flesh."

"But just as the Spirit is eternal, so the peace of the righteous and the tribulation of the unrighteous will be eternal."

"And just as the flesh is temporal, so the tribulation of the righteous and the peace of the unrighteous will be temporal."

Hence, Isa. 57:21 and 48:22: "There is no peace, says the Lord, to the wicked," spiritually, of course, for otherwise the wicked certainly have peace. Psalm 73:3: "Because I had a zeal on occasion of the wicked, seeing the prosperity of sinners." Psalm 28:3: "That speak peace with the neighbor, but evil" (i.e., not peace but disturbance and restlessness in relation to God) "is in their hearts."

By whom also we have access through faith *into this grace, wherein we stand, and glory in the hope of the glory of the sons of God.* (Rom. 5:2.)

Very instructively the apostle connects these two: "through Christ" and "through faith," just as he did before when he said: "Being justified by faith through our Lord Jesus Christ." The first is directed against the presumptuousness of those who believe that they can have access to God without Christ, as if it were sufficient for them to have believed. So they want to come to God by faith alone, not through Christ but past Christ, as if they no longer needed Christ after having received the grace of justification. So there are nowadays many who fashion from the works of faith works of the law and the letter, when, for example, after having received faith by baptism and penance, they want to become acceptable to God only in and with their own persons without Christ. But both are necessary: on the one hand, one must have faith and, on the other hand, one must, at the same time, always have Christ as the mediator in this kind of faith. Hence, it says in Ps. 91:1: "He that dwells in the secret place of the Most High shall abide under the shadow of God in heaven." Faith makes the dwelling, but Christ the shadow and secret place. And farther on in the same psalm it says: "He will cover you with his pinions and under his wings you shall hope." (Ps. 91:4.) And Mal. 4:2: "But unto you that fear my name shall the sun of righteousness arise with healing in its wings." And Ps. 31:3: "Be to me a God who protects and a house where I can take refuge," i.e., where I can abide. And again, Ps. 90:1: "Lord, thou hast been our dwelling place." It is these and similar words of Scripture the apostle explains here, together with many other symbolical words of the law.

In our own day, the hypocritical moralists[4] display a dreadful pride in imagining that they are saved and sufficiently righteous in themselves on account of the fact that they believe in Christ, but they do not want to acknowledge to themselves and others that they are unrighteous and foolish. What else is this than throwing away the protection of Christ and trying to approach God only from faith but not also through Christ? Yes, but then it is not really faith but only seems to be such—just as, at sundown, the rays and the light of the sun go down together. *But a wise man does not value light apart from the sun, but he wants to have light together with the sun.* These people, therefore, who approach God through faith, but not at the same time through Christ, actually go away from him.

Secondly, he turns against those who rely on too great a sense of security because of Christ and not because of faith, as if they could be saved through Christ without doing anything and without having to give any evidence of faith. They have too great a faith, nay, rather, none at all. For both must be in effect: "through faith" and "through Christ," so that we do and endeavor everything possible in faith in Christ. And yet we must recognize ourselves in all this as unprofitable servants, believing that only through Christ we are worthy of having access to God. *In all works of faith, our main concern must be to become worthy of Christ and to take refuge under the wings of his righteousness.* "Therefore, being justified by faith" and forgiven, we have access to God's grace and peace "but by our Lord Jesus Christ."

This affects also those who, following the mystical theology,[5] exert themselves in the inner darkness and, leaving aside all pictures of the suffering of Christ,[6] desire to hear and contemplate

(margin note: evidence of faith)

---

[4] Lit., *iuristae.*

[5] I.e., the "Mystical Theology" of Dionysius Areopagita. Some of the terms Luther uses are borrowed from this work. (Cf. *Myst. Theol.,* 1, 3.) Later in his life, Luther passed severe judgment on Dionysius. (Cf. *De capt. Bab., WA* 6, 562, 4.)

[6] Ficker states (p. 300, n. 28) that, on the title page of the volume of Tauler's Works which Luther used, there was a picture of Christ carrying the cross.

the uncreated Word itself without first having had the eyes of their heart justified and cleansed by the Word incarnate. For the heart must first be rendered pure by the incarnate Word, and only one who is thus purified can then in rapture ascend through the incarnate to the uncreated Word. But who can imagine his heart so clean that he can dare aspire to this, unless he is called, and, with the apostle Paul, carried away by God (II Cor. 12:2) and "taken up with Peter and James and John his brother" (Matt. 17:1). In short, this rapture cannot be called an "access."

And not only so; but we glory also in **tribulations,** *knowing that tribulation works patience.* (Rom. 5:3.)

This text shows clearly the distinction of a twofold wrath and of a twofold mercy of God and hence also that of a twofold tribulation. For there is a tribulation that comes from God's severity and another that comes from his kindness. That of his kindness works what is very good as in this case here, though it may accidentally result in something else. But this is due to the weakness of him upon whom tribulation is inflicted, in so far as he does not recognize its nature, power, and purpose, but judges and evaluates it only according to its outward appearance, i.e., wrongly, inasmuch as he should adore it as if it were the cross of Christ itself.

COROLLARY

(1) *Tribulation enlarges and enhances the nature and character of the person whom it befalls.* If a person who is carnal and weak, blinded, evil, irascible, proud, etc., is tried and tested, he becomes more carnal, weaker, more blinded, more evil, more irascible, and prouder, etc. But, conversely, a person who is spiritual, strong, wise, good, meek, and humble becomes more spiritual, stronger, wiser, better, meeker, and humbler, as it says in Ps. 4:1: "When I was in distress, thou hast enlarged me." But of the others it says in Matt. 7:27: "The floods came and the winds blew and smote upon that house, and it fell, and great was the fall thereof."

(2) *People who impute their anger or impatience to what injures or troubles them, talk foolishly. For tribulation does not make anyone impatient but it brings to light the impatience that was or is in him. Thus everybody can learn in tribulation what kind of man he really is, just as the glutton can when he itches, etc.*

(3) *People who outwardly bestow the highest reverence upon the holy relics of the cross and detest tribulations and adversities and run away from them are crude and puerile, indeed, they are hypocrites.* This is obvious, for, in Scripture, tribulations are expressly called the cross of Christ. First Corinthians 1:17: "lest the

cross of Christ should be made void." "He that does not take his
cross and follow after me." (Matt. 10:38.) And (Paul says) to the
Galatians: "Why am I still persecuted? Then is the scandal of the
cross made void." (Gal. 5:11.) And in Phil. 3:18: "I tell you weeping that they are the enemies of the cross of Christ." In the same
way, the theologians and leaders of the church of today can think
only of the Turks and the Jews when they have to identify these
"enemies of Christ." So it is done, for example, by the theologians
of Cologne in their argument with Reuchlin[7] and in the apostolic
bulls and in the jurists' commentaries on them.[8]

But it is they themselves who are in fact "the enemies of the
cross of Christ." For is it not true that only the friends of the cross
are its enemies, according to the word of Ps. 38:11: "My friends
and my neighbors are against me"? "And they that praised me did
swear against me." (Ps. 102:8.) For is there anyone who detests
tribulations and suffering more than the higher clergy and the
lawyers? Indeed, who is there that excels them in seeking after
riches, pleasures, leisure, honor, and glory?

(4) *Whosoever does not want to undergo tribulation can be sure
that he is not a Christian but a Turk and enemy of Christ.* For the
apostle speaks here of everyone when he says: **We glory in tribulations** (Rom. 5:3). Acts 14:21: "Through many tribulations we
must enter into the Kingdom of God." It says: "We must," not "it
so happens that" or "perhaps" or "we may." And I Peter 1:6:
"Now you must be for a little while made sorrowful in diverse
tribulations." He says: "You must," i.e., it cannot be done in any
other way.

But we should note the fact that there are two kinds of enemies
of the cross of Christ. Some use violence and others cunning.
Violent are those who want to make the cross of Christ ineffective
by force and who pounce upon it with all their strength; they seek
vengeance against anyone who offends them and they can and will
not rest until they have been vindicated. They fall into many ills
such as hatred, detractions, abuse, joy at the misfortune of their
fellow man, and sorrow over his good fortune.

Cunning are those who desert the cross by avoiding it. They do
not want to speak and do the truth to anyone, but they want to
please, coax, and flatter everyone and offend none, or, under cer-

---

[7] Cf. the preface of Arnold von Tungern to *Articuli sive propositiones de
iudaico favore nimis suspecto ex libello theutonico domini Ioannis Reuchlin* (1512): "*Perfidi canes inimici nominis Christi.*" Cf. also the title of Pfefferkorn's tract: *Sturm — wider die drulosen Juden, anfechter des leichnams
Christi und seiner glidmossen* (1514).
[8] Papal bulls against the Turks. Cf. Ficker (p. 301, n. 26).

tain circumstances, they withdraw to be by themselves (at least for this reason). It is these especially the apostle has in mind, when he says in Gal. 6:12: "As many as desire to please in the flesh, they compel you to be circumcised, only that they may not suffer the persecution of the cross of Christ."

We may note that this way of speaking in terms of an ascending scale or a gradation applies in reverse order to people who are not in this state of grace: tribulation works impatience, and impatience rejection, and rejection despair, and despair confounds eternally. And thus the hatred against God is poured out (i.e., the fact that it was poured out can be noted whenever this hatred becomes real) in their hearts by the evil spirit under whose sway they come, etc. For this reason, I say that a man who is impatient is not yet a Christian, at least before God, because by tribulation he was found to be rejected.

Inasmuch, therefore, as the Lord is called in many places Savior and Helper in need, a man who refuses to suffer as much as in him lies, deprives him of his proper titles and names. Thus he will not be a Jesus, i.e., a savior, to a man who does not want to be damned. He will not be God and creator for him, because he does not want to be that nothing out of which the Lord can create. He will not be his power, wisdom, and goodness, because he does not want to bear him in weakness, foolishness, and readiness to take punishment.

Knowing that tribulation works patience, and **patience trial.** (Rom. 5:3–4.)

The different kinds of impatience and its stages are known from the different degrees of anger which the Lord has indicated in Matt. 5:21 ff. in connection with his interpretation of the commandment "You shall not kill." For because impatience is the cause of anger, the effect of both is the same. But in case one separates impatience from anger, its different stages are intensive rather than extensive. For an impatient person is not patient in anything.

But here the apostle plainly suggests different stages of patience. Baptista Montanus[9] has quite adequately distinguished between them in the last chapter of the first book (of his work). To bear tribulation but unwillingly so and with the thought that one would rather not have to undergo such a trial is the lowest stage.

[9] Baptista Montanus, *De patientia,* I, 32. There was an edition of his works in Paris, 1513. This Carmelite poet was widely read, particularly in the circles of the Brethren of the Common Life.

Gladly and willingly to bear it but not to seek it is the next and ⎫ *patience*
middle stage. But to desire and seek, even to bring about, tribula- ⎬
tions as if they were a treasure—this is the highest stage of patience. ⎭
This is what is meant by the saying "We glory in tribulation"
and also that other one of Gal. 6:14: "We must glory in the cross
of our Lord Jesus Christ," etc.

And trial *hope*. (Rom. 5:4.)
"Trial" must here be understood in the sense that it is a good,
in so far, namely, as it is the goal one seeks to reach through
tribulation. For God does not accept anyone as righteous unless
he has first tried him, and he tries men precisely in the fire of
tribulation, as we read in Ps. 17:3: "Thou hast tried me by fire
and no wickedness was found in me." And in the word of the
Preacher: "He pleased God and was found perfect." (Cf. Ecclus.
44: 16–17.) And again, "Who was found to be without blemish."
(Ecclus. 31:8.) And so also in Ps. 11:5: "The Lord tries the righteous, but the wicked," etc. To such a trial one can come only
through patience. And this test takes place in order that everyone *cf Job*
may see his inner state of mind (i.e., in order that everyone may
come to know himself), whether he really loves God for God's
sake; but God knows this, of course, without an examination.
Hence, it says in Ps. 139:23–24: "Search me, O God, and know my
heart" (i.e., make it known to me too). "Try me and know my
thoughts and see whether there be any wickedness in me and lead *suffering as test*
me in the way everlasting." This beautifully expresses the reason
why God inflicts tribulations upon men: in order to test them,
i.e., in order through patience to give them the experience of
having stood the test. For *if God did not test us by tribulation, no
man could possibly be saved.*
This is so because, due to original sin, our nature is so curved
in upon itself at its deepest levels that it not only bends the best
gifts of God toward itself in order to enjoy them (as the moralists[9a]
and hypocrites make evident), nay, rather, "uses" God in order to
obtain them, but it does not even know that, in this wicked,
twisted, crooked way, it seeks everything, including God, only for
itself. As the prophet Jeremiah says in Jer. 17:9: "The heart of
man is crooked and inscrutable; who can know it?" i.e., it is so
curved in upon itself that no man, be he ever so holy, can know it
(apart from a testing experience). As it says in Ps. 19:12: "Who can
discern his errors? Clear thou me from my hidden faults!" And
Ps. 32:6: "For this let everyone that is godly pray unto thee at the

[9a] *"Iustitiarii"* ("workmongers").

proper time." The Scripture calls this fault by the very special name of " '*āwāh*," which means wickedness, crookedness, curvedness.[10] The Doctor of the Sentences[11] deals with it extensively in the first part of his first book in connection with a discussion of the difference between "enjoying" and "using" and between the love of friendship and selfish love.

So therefore, if what we have said is true, namely, that the wickedness that works impatience or, at least, causes us to be impatient is nothing else than this curvedness, which cannot but hate the cross because the cross mortifies everything we have, while our self tries to keep itself alive together with all that is part of it, then (we can understand) why God in his great goodness inflicts tribulation, trouble, and trial upon man soon after he has justified him and bestowed upon him the gifts of the Spirit: he wants to prevent his ungodly nature from rushing in upon them in order to enjoy them, because they are indeed lovely and most enjoyable; and he wants to save man from eternal perdition, for he would not know about this unless he were tried.

Thus man learns to love and worship God unconditionally, i.e., to worship him not for the sake of grace and its gifts but solely for his own sake. Thus "God scourges every son whom he receives." (Heb. 12:6.) If he did not do so, the son, carried away by the pleasantness of the new inheritance, would soon revel in the enjoyment of the gift of grace and offend the father more gravely than before. It is, therefore, in the best possible order that the apostle says "that tribulation works patience, and patience trial," i.e., that we should be proved by experience.

And hope confounds not. (Rom. 5:5.)
Without a test of the sort I have described, hope would confound, indeed, it would not be hope, but presumption, and even (and this would be worse still) the enjoyment of something created instead of the creator. Were a man to continue in this, he would be eternally confounded. Consequently, by testing and trying a man's patience, tribulation takes everything away from him and leaves him bare and naked; moreover, it does not let him find help and salvation in physical or spiritual merits, but it causes him to despair of everything created, to forsake all creatures and himself, and, outside himself and everything else, to seek help in

---

[10] "*Curvitas.*" This word was used by the Scholastics. Cf. Peter Lombard, II *Sent.*, d. 25, c. 6.

[11] Cf. Peter Lombard, I *Sent.*, d. 1, referring to Augustine, *De doctr. Christ.*, I, 4–6 ("A good man uses the world in order to enjoy God, but an evil man uses God in order to enjoy the world").

God alone and to sing the verse of the psalm: "But thou, O Lord, art a shield for me, and my glory" (Ps. 3:3). This is what it means to hope and to become hopeful through testing trials.

The experience of the ungodly is different from this. They are accustomed to trust in their own powers, and they are unwilling to bear tribulations quietly in order to be tested. And because they do not know what it means to hope unconditionally in God alone,[12] it is inevitable that when, in the last trial, all their goods and the mountains of their good works collapse, they themselves will be ruined forever. Then they shall say to the mountains: "Fall on us," etc. (Hos. 10:8; Luke 23:30). For their hope was no hope, but a crooked and presumptuous trust in their own works and their own righteousness.

But yet, one must know that tribulation is of two kinds.

The first kind is physical, and carnal people come to fall by it. When in connection with their concern for physical goods, they fail in property, health, or reputation, they draw away from God and, because of their impatience, fall into despair. Thus they surrender to the flesh and forsake God. The apostle says about them in Eph. 4:19: "Who despairing gave themselves up to uncleanness."

The other kind is the tribulation of conscience and the spirit, where self-righteousness and all the wisdom in which men put their trust are devoured and carried off. About them the Savior says, and this is to be understood in the mystical sense: "When a strong man fully armed guards his own court, his goods are in peace, but when a stronger than he shall come upon him and overcome him, he will take away from him his whole armor wherein he trusted, and will divide the spoils" (Luke 11:21 f.), i.e., he will strip a man who has fortified himself in his own moral accomplishments and teach him that he must achieve them for the common good and not in order to please himself.

Because the love of God *is shed abroad in our hearts.* (Rom. 5:5.)

This word must be understood as an explanation, or rather, as an instruction on the level of the spirit, why and how we can glory in tribulations; we are to learn that we cannot do this by relying on ourselves or our own power, but it is possible through love which is given by the Holy Spirit.

---

[12] *WA* 56, 306, 5: *"Quomodo in nudum Deum sperandum sit."* Throughout his career, Luther used the phrase *Deus nudus* ("The naked God" = God as he is in and by himself. Cf. the phrase in one of his earliest sermons: *"In nudum Deum confidere"* (*WA* 1, 85, 3).

It is, then, this "love of God" alone, this unqualified devotion to God,[13] which creates men of a right heart; it alone takes away iniquity; it alone extinguishes the enjoyment of self-righteousness. Because it loves only God in and for himself[14] and not what God gives, as the hypocritical moralists[15] think, it does not get exalted when physical and spiritual goods come flowing in. On the other hand, it is not broken up when they depart and physical and spiritual evils come in. "Knowledge puffs up" (I Cor. 8:1), and so does righteousness. But, conversely, want of knowledge makes humble, and so does sin. "But love bears everything" (I Cor. 13:7), even if one must glory in tribulation.

We must, therefore, take notice of the fact that it is called the *"love of God."* By it we love God alone. Here nothing can be seen and nothing can be experienced, either inwardly or outwardly, in which one can trust or which one can love or fear. But it is carried off, beyond everything that is, to God himself who is invisible, inexperienceable, incomprehensible, into the midst of inner darkness, not knowing what it loves but knowing what it does not love; it turns away from all that it has ever known and experienced, but it yearns for what it does not yet know and says: "I am sick from love" (S. of Sol. 2:5), i.e., what I have, I do not want, and what I do not want, I have. But this gift is utterly out of reach for those who want to see the evidences of their own righteousness and who are sad and desperate when they cannot see them but put their trust in them in so far as they can see them and then feel all the more secure. And thus they do not "glory in tribulation," and they are not tried, and so they also do not hope.

Now, this sublime power that is in us is not, so the apostle asserts, a product of our own, but it must be sought for from God. This is why it is **shed abroad** and in no way brought forth from us or originated by us. And this **by the Holy Spirit;** it is not acquired by moral effort and habit as the moral virtues are. **In our hearts,** i.e., deep down in the innermost parts of the heart and not on the surface of the heart in the way foam lies on water. Of this kind is the love of the hypocrites who imagine and pretend that they have love. But a trial brings to light the impatience and the pride that lie hidden deep within them.

Which is given to us, i.e., which we have not deserved; indeed, we deserve exactly the opposite. Now that this is so is proved by what follows in the text: It is really "given to us" and not merited. Also, Christ "died for the weak" (Rom. 5:6) and not at all for the strong and worthy. It is, therefore, called **charity** in difference from

---

[13] " 'Charitas Dei,' quae est purissima affectio in Deum."
[14] "Quia non nisi solum et purum Deum diligit."
[15] Lit., "hipocritae iustitiarii."

the very unfruitful and very low kind of love by which one loves a *charity* creature, for "charity" means to love something dearly and preciously or to esteem as precious what one loves. So also to esteem God above everything means to love him with a precious love, i.e., with charity. But to love him for the sake of his gifts or for the sake of advantage means to love him with a base kind of love, i.e., selfishly.[16] In other words, one uses God but does not enjoy him.[17]

Of God, it says, because thus one loves God alone and the neighbor for God's sake, i.e., because God wills it so, whose will one loves above everything.

We must also note that the dwelling place of love is only the heart, indeed, the innermost parts of the heart. This explains why there is a difference between the children and the slaves of God. For the children of God serve him gladly, voluntarily, and gratuitously, and not from fear of punishment or because of a desire for praise, but only because they want to do the will of God. But the slaves serve him under compulsion, from fear of punishment, and hence, involuntarily and sullenly, or from a desire for wages and hence, voluntarily, but in the way of hirelings, but never in order to do the will of God as such. (Especially in times of tribulation, the slave and hireling retreat, but the son perseveres, as it says in John 10:12: "But the hireling flees.") Therefore, God says to them in Mal. 1:10: "Who is there among you who shuts the doors and kindles fire on my altar gratuitously?" Then there follows this: "I have no pleasure in you, says the Lord of hosts," precisely in view of the fact that they are so presumptuous as to think that God must have pleasure in them. This is why, in the same place (Mal. 1:7-8), they reply to the saying of the Lord: "You offer polluted bread upon my altar," by asking as if they could not believe this: "Wherein have we polluted thee?"—in other words: We have done all thou hast commanded. And the Lord answers: "When you offer the blind for sacrifice, is this not evil? And when you offer the lame and sick, is this not evil?" This means: They worship God without love, but like hirelings, from the sinful desire for their own advantage; they are not like the bride (in The Song of Solomon) who has an eye only for the invisible God and is not concerned for herself or any other creature.[18]

And again we must note how the apostle connects the spring

---

[16] *"Concupiscentia."*

[17] Cf. Augustine, *De doctr. Christ.* V, 3-5, 22; Peter Lombard, I *Sent., d.* 1.

[18] Lit: "They do not have the one eye of the bride with which she sees only the invisible God, while she sees nothing of her own or of any other creature." The reference is to S. of Sol. 4:9, interpreted in the medieval manner in terms of Christ-mysticism: "Thou hast wounded my heart, my sister, my bride; thou hast wounded my heart with one of thine eyes and with one hair of thy neck." Cf. also Lyra and *Gl. ord.*

with the stream. He speaks of the "love that is . . . through the Holy Spirit which is given to us." For it is not sufficient to have the gift if the donor is not also present, just as Moses prayed (Ex. 33:15): "If thy presence go not with me, carry us not up hence." Just so, it is to love, and to it alone, that the apostle attributes the presence and, together with it at the same time, the gift of the Holy Spirit. For, as he says in I Cor. 12:7 ff., all other gifts are given by this Spirit, but not the Spirit himself. So he says here of love that it is not given unless first the Spirit himself is given which sheds it abroad in our hearts. But there he says: "But all these things are the works of one and the same Spirit." (I Cor. 12:11.) This is why he then goes on to say there: "But I show you a more excellent way" (I Cor. 12:31). Or, at all events, even if he is given in all gifts, he still does not shed love abroad in all.

For when we were as yet weak, **according to the time,** *Christ died for the ungodly. For scarce for a just man will one die; yet perhaps for a good man someone would dare to die. But God commends his love toward us; because when as yet we were sinners, Christ died for us; much more therefore, being now justified by his blood, shall we be saved from wrath through him. For if, when we were enemies, we were reconciled to God by the death of his Son, much more, being reconciled, shall we be saved by his life. And not only so; but also we glory in God, through our Lord Jesus Christ, by whom we have now received reconciliation.* (Rom. 5:6–11.)

Some[19] relate the phrase "according to the time" to the sentence that follows, so that the meaning of this phrase would be: When we were as yet weak, he died for the ungodly according to time, i.e., though he is immortal in eternity, he nevertheless died in time. He died because of his humanity that lived in time, but he lives forever because of his divinity that lives in eternity. Others read the phrase in this way: "He died according to the time when we were weak," i.e., he died at the time when we were not yet righteous and whole but weak and sick (so that the phrase "according to the time" must be understood with respect to that time when we were still weak). And this makes better sense, in view of the verse that follows later: **For if, while we were enemies, we were reconciled through the death of his Son** (Rom. 5:10). Others again relate the term to the preceding sentence, so that it means this: When we were weak according to time, even though before God we were already righteous in predestination. For, in God's predestination, all has already happened that, in the world of things, lies still in the future.

[19] Lyra.

As by one man sin *entered into the world, and death by sin; and so death passed upon all men in that all have sinned.* (Rom. 5:12.)

The apostle speaks here of original and not of actual sin. This statement can be proved in many ways and it must be taken as true in view of the fact that, *first,* he says "by one man." Hence, Blessed Augustine[20] says against the Pelagians in the first book of his work *On the Merits of Sins and Their Remission:* "If the apostle had wanted to recall that sin which entered the world not by propagation but by imitation, he would not call Adam but the devil its originator, and about him it is said in Wisd. of Sol. 2:24: 'They imitate him who are of his side.' In this sense also Adam imitated him and the devil became the originator of his sin. But here it says, 'by one man'—in the sense that all actual sins come and have come into the world through the devil, but original sin through one man." At the same place, Blessed Augustine says: "So, then, the apostle in making mention of that sin and death which passed from one to all by propagation, represents him as the originator from whom the propagation of the human race had its beginning." And he has other fitting passages.

(And Chrysostom[21] says on this passage: "It is apparent that not the sin that comes from a transgression of the law but that which comes from Adam's disobedience has contaminated everything.")

Second, he says: "by one." For actual sin comes into the world through many, because every individual brings his own sin with him.

Third, he says: "*enters* into the world." Now, no actual sin enters into the world, but everyone's sin is his own load, as it says in Ezek. 18:20: "Everyone must carry his own sin." Therefore, it does not enter into others but it remains in every individual. And that the term "world" does here not signify heaven and earth, but the human beings that are in the world, can be proved by reference to Rom. 3:6: "How shall God judge the world?" And to I John 5:19: "The whole world lies in the evil one." John 3:16: "For God so loved the world." And later: "if the world hates you" (John 15:18), and likewise: "I have chosen you not of this world" (John 15:19). This is because the physical world is insensitive and not capable of sin, so that sin and death do not enter it. For it neither dies nor sins; only man sins and dies. Consequently, that sin enters into the world means that the world becomes guilty and

[20] Augustine, *De peccat. merit. et remiss. et de bapt. parv.,* I, 9, 19.
[21] Chrysostom, *Hom. in ep., ad Rom.,* 10, as quoted by Augustine, *Contra Jul.,* I, 6, 27.

sinful through one man. As it says farther on: "for if by the trespass of one, many became sinners." (Rom. 5:12.)

Fourth: **and by sin death.** The death of the world (i.e., of all men) certainly is not the result of personal sin, inasmuch as people who have not sinned die too (as the next part of the passage shows). If, therefore, death is death through sin and would not be death without sin, sin must be in all. Consequently, it cannot be that personal sin is meant here. If it were, it would be false to say that death entered into the world through sin; then the apostle should have said instead: It came through the will of God.

Fifth: **So death passed upon all men.** But even if death enters in because of personal sin, it befalls only the person who has committed it, as the law says: "Fathers shall not be put to death for the children," etc. (Deut. 24:16).

Sixth: He says "sin," speaking in the singular of one only. If he wanted to be understood as speaking of actual sin, he would use the plural as he does farther on where he speaks "of many trespasses" (Rom. 5:16). There he obviously compares that one sin, of which he speaks in the singular, with the many others and concludes therefrom that the efficacy of grace is greater than that of sin.

Seventh: **in whom all have sinned.** And there is not another kind of personal sin "in which[22] all have sinned," but everyone sins in his own sin.

Eighth: **For until the law sin was in the world,** etc. (Rom. 5:13.) Actual sin was in the world also before Moses; men were charged with it just as men inflicted punishment because of it, but original sin was unknown until Moses revealed it in Gen. 3:16 ff.

Ninth: He says here: **They had not sinned after the similitude of Adam's transgression** (Rom. 5:14), i.e., by committing a similar sin by way of imitation, as Pelagius wanted this to be understood,[23] but all who commit this sin do so by actual sin.

Tenth: by this sin, **Adam is a figure of him who was to come,** and not by actual sin, else all men would be a figure of Christ; but now Adam alone is the figure of Christ because of the extension of his one sin to all.

As the apostle, in order to confound and break the obstinacy of future heretics whom he foresaw in spirit, continues to explain in what way Adam is a figure of Christ, he speaks from now on no longer only in the singular, lest some impudent joker might make nonsense out of it all and say: He regards the word "sin" as a

[22] *"In quo."*
[23] Cf. Augustine, *Op. imperf. contra Jul.,* II, 214.

collective term and uses it in the singular rather than the plural as the Scripture so frequently does. Hence, he says with emphasis: "by one that sinned," "by one to condemnation." Likewise, "through the offense of one," "by one man's disobedience." And he lays special stress upon the following comparison: "The judgment was by one to condemnation, but grace is of many offenses to justification." And, as Augustine says in Chapter 12 of the above-mentioned work,[24] "Also, judgment leads from many transgressions to condemnation." But inasmuch as he does not say this but rather "by one," it is readily obvious that he speaks of original sin. In the same way, he denies that many sinned except one when he says: "by the transgression of one," "through the transgression of one," "by one that sinned," etc. One can see, then, how both statements can be simultaneously true, that only one man sinned, that only one sin was committed, and that only one man was disobedient, and yet that because of him, many became disobedient sinners.

Original Sin ↓

What, then, is original sin?

First, according to the subtle definitions of the Scholastic theologians, it is the privation or lack of original righteousness.[25] They say that righteousness is only subjectively in the will and so, therefore, also its opposite, the lack of it. This conforms to what Aristotle says in the *Logic* and *Metaphysics* about the category of quality.[26]

Second, but according to the apostle and in accordance with an understanding that is marked by simplicity in Christ Jesus, it is not merely the privation of quality in the will, indeed, not merely the loss of light in the intellect or of strength in the memory, but, in a word, the loss of all uprightness and of the power of all our faculties of body and soul and of the whole inner and outer man. Over and beyond this, it is the proneness toward evil; the loathing

---

[24] Cf. Augustine, *De peccat. merit. et remiss.*, I, 12, 15.

[25] Cf. Ficker's full comment (p. 312, n. 2), also that of Ellwein (p. 494, n. 20). Ficker refers to Lyra's exegesis of Rom., ch. 5, and especially to the *Additio* III of Paul of Burgos: "*Peccatum originale licet habeat privationem originalis institiae, tamen non est pura privatio, sed est quidam habitus corruptus*" ("Original sin results, to be sure, in the privation of original righteousness, yet it is not a complete privation, but a certain corrupted disposition"). Burgos offers also this definition: "*Peccatum originale dicitur a doctoribus fomes peccati et peccati concupiscentia, quod sonat aliquid positivum*" ("The doctors call original sin the tinder of sin and the concupiscence of sin, and this means something positive"). Burgos refers to Peter Lombard, II *Sent.*, d. 30; Thomas Aquinas, *Summa Theol.*, II, 1, q. 82, a. 3; Duns Scotus, II *Sent.*, d. 30, q. 1, n. 2 (here the argumentation to which Luther refers).

[26] Aristotle, *Categor.*, 8. Cf. Ficker (p. 312, n. 5).

of the good; the disdain for light and wisdom but fondness for error and darkness; the avoidance and contempt of good works but an eagerness for doing evil. As it is written in Ps. 14:3: "They are all gone out of the way, they are together become unprofitable." And in Gen. 8:21: "The imagination and thought of man's heart are prone to evil." God hates and imputes not merely this lack (inasmuch as many forget their sin and are not aware of it) but this whole sinful cupidity that causes us to disobey the commandment "You shall not covet" (Ex. 20:17), as the apostle shows in a very clear analysis farther on in the seventh chapter of this letter. For it is this commandment that shows us our sin, as the apostle says: "I had not known that concupiscence is sin except the law had said: You shall not covet" (Rom. 7:7).

Accordingly, the ancient fathers[27] were correct when they taught that it is this original sin which is the "tinder"[28] of sin, the law of the flesh, the law of our members, the feebleness of nature, a tyrant, our original disease, etc. It is as with a sick man whose mortal illness is due to the fact that not merely one part of his body lost its health, but that his whole body is sick and that all his senses and powers are debilitated, so that, to cap it all, he is nauseated by what would be wholesome for him and consumed by the desire for what harms him. This sin is Hydra, that extremely stubborn monster with many heads with which we fight in the Lerna[29] of this life until death. Here is Cerberus,[30] that uncontrollable barker, and Antaeus,[31] who is insuperable when he is left on the earth.

I have found none that treats this theme of original sin so clearly as Gerard Groote[32] in his little tract *Blessed Is the Man;* he speaks there not like a thoughtless philosopher but like a sane theologian.

---

[27] Luther has Augustine in mind. This passage seems to be a quotation from Peter Lombard, II *Sent.*, d. 30, who there relies chiefly on Augustine.

[28] *"Fomes peccati."*

[29] Lerna, or Lerne, a swamp near Argos, which, according to the myth, was inhabited by the Lernaean Hydra, which Hercules slew.

[30] *"Latrator incompescibilis."* Cf. Vergil, *Aeneid,* 6, 417. Cerberus = the three-headed dog guarding the infernal regions at the gates of Tartarus.

[31] Antaeus was a powerful giant, ruler of Libya, who compelled all strangers coming into his country to wrestle with him. He was at last slain by Hercules, who, observing that each time Antaeus fell on the earth he gained new strength, held him aloft in the air and thus killed him.

[32] Luther does not mean Gerard Groote (who, as far as is known, wrote no such tract) but Gerard Zerbolt of Zütphen, whose *devotus tractatulus de spiritualibus ascensionibus* begins with the quotation of Ps. 84:5: "Blessed is the man whose help is from thee; in his heart he has disposed to ascend by steps." Cf. Ficker (p. 313, n. 14).

COROLLARY

If one thinks, therefore, that original sin is only the lack of righteousness in the will, this means that one encourages indecision[33] and dissolves the whole undertaking of penance. Indeed, one then plants pride and presumptuousness and uproots the fear of the Lord; one prescribes humility and invalidates the commandment of God and thus condemns it from beginning to end. At least this is the situation if one takes their teaching at its face value. Then too, it is easy for one to feel superior to another when he knows himself free from that sin in which he sees the other still involved.

This is also why many, who want to have a reason for humility, keep themselves busy by exaggerating their past sins, including those they might have committed, and they do the same also with respect to their present yet secret sins in order to practice humility by being on the lookout for them. In this way, you certainly can learn something. But look, there are also plainly visible present sins, and they do not let us entertain even the slightest feeling of superiority and complacency (as so frequently happens) when we see someone else being condemned. Now, the obvious reason for humility is the fact that sin remains in us but that "it has no dominion over us" (Rom. 6:14), because it is subject to the Spirit so that he may destroy what formerly reigned over him. When, therefore, someone despises another because he is a sinner, sin still has dominion over him, and doubly so. For inasmuch as he, too, is a sinner, he nevertheless compares himself with another as if he were righteous, and thus he becomes a liar and he does not sense that he is himself a sinner. This is a plain case of unrighteousness. He is forbidden to judge, and yet he judges. But no one is entitled to judge, unless he is superior or better. Consequently, he thinks himself better than the other by judging him, and thus he falls into sin, even though he has committed no other sin than that he has forgotten his own sinfulness and that he has taken it into his head that he is righteous.

A man, therefore, who knows that he has the sin in him that he should control certainly must be afraid that he may become enslaved to it and, even more, that he may judge somone. For one who judges knows what the Lord will say to him. How can you judge as if you were righteous, inasmuch as you are unrighteous? And if you ever were righteous, you have now defiled your righteousness, because you put your trust in it; you have become doubly unrighteous, because you not only set up your sin as righteousness but you also boast of it.

[33] Lit., *"Hoc est occasionem dare tepiditatis."*

Wherefore, as by one man sin **entered** *into the world.* (Rom. 5:12.)

The apostle uses this pointed expression in order to denote that original sin does not come *from* men but rather that it comes *to* them. But it is characteristic of actual sin that it comes forth from us, as the Lord says: "from the heart come forth evil thoughts" (Matt. 15:19). But original sin enters into men and they do not commit it but they endure it. As also Moses says in Ex. 32:24: "And this calf came out."

And so death passed upon all men **in that all have sinned.** (Rom. 5:12.)

It is uncertain in the Greek whether the term (which we translate "in that") is meant to be understood as masculine or neuter.[34] It seems, therefore, as if the apostle wanted it to be taken in both senses. Thus also Blessed Augustine interprets it in both senses in the tenth chapter of the work (we have just quoted.)[35] He says: " 'in that all have sinned.' It is certainly obvious that the personal sins, in which only those are involved as sinners who have committed them, are one thing, and that the one sin, in which all are involved as sinners in so far as all have been this one man, is another thing." From this work of Augustine's it seems to follow that original sin is the very first sin, namely, the transgression of Adam. For he interprets the phrase "they have sinned" in relation to an actual deed and not merely in relation to the transmission of a condition of guilt. He goes on to say: "But if this one man and not sin is meant, in the sense that in this one man all have sinned, what can be plainer than this plain statement?"

But the first interpretation suits better the context of the passage. For the apostle says farther on: "As by one man's transgression many were made sinners" (Rom. 5:19), and this is the same as to say: All have sinned in the sin of one.

Even so, one can still put forward the second interpretation, namely, by taking it to mean: While one sinned, all sinned. In this sense it says in Isa. 43:26 f.: "Tell if you have anything to justify yourself. Your father sinned first"; in other words: You cannot be justified, because you are a son of Adam who was the first to sin. Therefore you too are a sinner because you are the son of a sinner; a sinner cannot but beget a sinner like himself.

[34] Here Luther follows Faber, who understands *"in quo"* ("in that") in terms of the neuter gender, while Lyra decides for the masculine gender ("in whom").

[35] Augustine, *De peccat. merit. et remiss.*, I, 10, 11.

For until the law sin was in the world; *but sin was not imputed when the law was not.* (Rom. 5:13.)

Blessed Augustine explains this as follows in the tenth book:[36] "I.e., sin would not be taken away by the law, either natural or written. For no one could be justified by the works of the law." And at another place in the book of *Exposition of Certain Propositions,* etc., he says:[37] "The phrase 'until the law sin was in the world' must be taken to mean 'until grace came.' For he directs himself against those who think that sins can be taken away through the law. Instead, he states that sins were made manifest by the law but not taken away by it when he says: 'But sin was not imputed when there was no law.' He does not say: There was no sin, but: It was not counted. Nor was it taken away when the law was given, but since then it began to be counted, i.e., it began to be apparent. We must, therefore, not think that the phrase 'until the law' is to be understood as if there were no longer any sin under the law, but this 'until the law' is to be understood in the sense that he counts the whole time of the law until the law's end, which is Christ."

In this way, Blessed Augustine connects the phrase "until the law" with the statement "There was sin." But then one is forced to say as he does that there was sin not only until the law but much more under the law which entered in order that transgression might abound. But this forced interpretation of the phrase "until the law," which in any case indicates an end, is not necessary if one understands it in connection with the negation "It was not imputed." The meaning of the passage, then, would be this: Until the law sin (which, to be sure, was in the world always) was not imputed; in other words: it was not imputed or known until the law came; the law brought it forth—not in the sense that it called it into being, for it was there before, but in the sense that it called it to the attention of the mind so that it could be known. Or we may say: "Until the law sin was in the world," i.e., it was there in so far as it was in being, but going beyond the fact that it was there and remained there, it was acknowledged through the law. And so one must understand the phrase to mean, not that sin existed until the law and then ceased, but that through the law it obtained a knowledge of itself which it formerly had not had. Now, this meaning is clearly given in the words of the apostle "that sin was not counted when there was no law"; in other words: it was not taken away but counted through the law which it had preceded.

36 *Ibid.,* 10, 12.
37 Augustine, *Expositio quarundam propos. ex ep. ad Rom.,* 27–28.

But death reigned *from Adam unto Moses.* (Rom. 5:14.)

In other words: the penalty of sin, namely, death, was well known to all men through experience, but not the cause of death, namely, sin. Here again we must not understand the words to say that death reigned only until Moses, inasmuch as Moses, too, died and everyone will die until the end of the world; especially in the ungodly the reign of death will continue. "But it reigned unto Moses" means that, until Moses, one did not know why and for what reason death reigned. Blessed Augustine interprets this reign as follows (in the work we have quoted before):[38] "It prevails when the condition of sin has such dominion over men that it does not let them come to eternal life, which is true life, but brings upon them also a second death (which is eternal in punishment)."

Even over them that had not sinned after the likeness of Adam's transgressions. (Rom. 5:14.)

Blessed Augustine interprets this in the same work[39] as follows: over them that had not yet sinned from their own will in the same way as he did. Also Blessed Ambrose[40] understands it in this way. He relates the phrase "after the likeness" to the term "They had not sinned," because (he says) if the apostle had left the phrase "They had not sinned" undefined, he would have contradicted his own earlier statement "in that all have sinned." For how have all sinned and yet a few not, unless what happened was that while all sinned in Adam and in his sin, not all sinned after the likeness of Adam's sin or, rather, Adam's transgression. There is, namely, a slight difference between "sin" and "transgression," in so far as sin as a condition remains but a transgression as an act passes by. Consequently, all have sinned not by the same act but by involvement in the same condition; only Adam sinned both in terms of act and condition, in so far as he committed the first sin.

Faber Stapulensis,[41] however, understands the matter differently and he reconciles the contradiction between the phrases "in that all had sinned" and "over them that had not sinned" in a different way. But I doubt whether he does it well; indeed, I fear he does not. He says that the phrase "after the likeness" must be referred to the word "reigned"; and I am willing to grant this on account of John Chrysostom, who in expounding this passage says[42]: "How did [death] reign? After the likeness of the trans-

---

[38] Augustine, *De peccat. merit. et remiss.*, I, 11, 13.

[39] *Ibid.*, I, 9, 19.

[40] Ambrosiaster, *Comment. in ep. ad Rom., ad loc.*

[41] Faber in his Commentary, *ad loc.*

[42] Chrysostom, *Hom. 10 in ep. ad Rom.*, quoted by Augustine, *Contra Jul.*, I, 6, 27.

gression of Adam." On the basis of this, he thinks that the phrase "even over them that had not sinned" is put in parenthesis. Then the phrase "they have not sinned" must be understood in relation to personal sin and in a stricter sense than the earlier phrase "in that all have sinned." Just as the same teacher says of children:[43] "For this reason we baptize also the children, even though they have no sins," personal sins, of course, as Blessed Augustine amply proves, in the second book against Julian, by reference to the same author.

Who is a figure of him that was to come. (Rom. 5:14.)
According to Blessed Augustine[44] who quotes him, Chrysostom interprets this as follows: "After the likeness of the transgression of Adam 'who is a figure of him that was to come'; for this reason Adam is also a figure of Christ. But one asks, How is he a figure? Because, just as Adam became the cause of death to those who were born of him, even though they did not eat of the tree—that death which was brought about through the eating—so Christ became for the Christians, even though they have done nothing righteous, the provider of righteousness, and he bestowed it on us all through the cross." So then, the likeness of Adam's transgression is in us, because we must die, as if we had sinned in the same way as he. And the likeness of Christ's justification is in us, because we have life, as if we had done justice in the same way as he. Because of this likeness, therefore, Adam "is a figure of him who was to come," namely, of Christ who came after him. Indeed, in order to take away the likeness of Adam and to give us his, Christ "was made in the likeness of men" (Phil. 2:7) and was sent by the Father "in the likeness of sinful flesh" (Rom. 8:3). And so it is that "as in Adam all die, so also in Christ all shall be made alive" (I Cor. 15:22). For this same reason, I am inclined to agree with Chrysostom that the phrase "after the likeness" must be related to the word "reigned."

But not as the offense, so also is the free gift. (Rom. 5:15.)
Chrysostom[45] interprets this as follows: "If a Jew should ask you: How was the world saved by the power of the one Christ? you can answer him and say: How was the world damned by the one disobedient Adam? Nevertheless, grace and sin are not equal, and neither are death and life nor God and the devil." "For if sin

---

[43] As quoted by Augustine (from Ad neophyt. homil.), Contra Jul., I, 6, 22.
[44] Ibid., I, 6, 27.
[45] Chrysostom, Hom. 10 in ep. ad Rom., as quoted by Augustine, Contra Jul., I, 6, 27.

had power and the sin of one man at that, how should the grace of
God and the grace of one man not have more power? This seems
to be much more reasonable. For it does not appear to be very
reasonable to condemn one man for another. But that one man
should be saved for another seems to be much more fitting and
reasonable."

For if through the offense of one many died, much more **the
grace of God, and the gift, by the grace of one man,** *Jesus Christ,
has abounded to many.* (Rom. 5:15.)
The apostle connects grace and the gift of grace as if they differed from one another, but he does this in order to show clearly
the nature of him who was to come, as he said, namely, that as we
are justified by God and receive his grace, we do not receive this
grace by any merit of our own, but it is a gift the Father gave to
Christ in order that he should give it to men, according to the
word of Eph. 4:8: "Ascending on high, he led captivity captive;
he gave gifts to men." These gifts, then, are the gifts of the grace
of God which he received from the Father by his own merit and by
his own personal grace in order that he might give them to us, as
it says in Acts 2:33: "Having received of the Father the promise
of the Holy Spirit, he has poured forth this which you see and
hear."
The meaning of the phrase, then, is this: "The grace of God"
(by which he justifies us, or rather: which is in Christ as in its
origin just as the sin of man is in Adam) "and the gift" which
Christ pours out from the Father upon those who believe in him.
This gift is "by the grace of one man," i.e., it is due to his merit
and personal grace by which it pleased God to have him give us
this gift. The phrase: "by the grace of one man" must be understood with respect to the personal grace of Christ, in correspondence with the particular and personal sin of Adam; and "the gift"
is the righteousness which is given to us. So also original sin is (so
to say) the gift in the sin of the one man Adam. Now "the grace of
God" and "the gift" are one and the same, namely, the righteousness that is freely given to us by Christ. And he adds this grace because it is customary to give friends a gift. Yet this gift was given by
mercy also to enemies, and they were worthy to receive it only
because the mercy and grace of God made and counted them
worthy.

*And not as it was by one sin, so also is the gift. For judgment,
indeed, was by one unto condemnation, but grace is of many
offenses, unto justification. For if by one man's offense death*

reigned through one, much more they who receive abundance of grace, and of the gifts, and of righteousness, shall reign in life through one, Jesus Christ. Therefore as by the offense of one, unto all men to condemnation; so also by the righteousness of one, unto all men to justification of life. For as by the obedience of one man, many were made sinners; so also by the obedience of one, many shall be made righteous. **Now the law came in besides that sin might abound.** *And where sin abounded, grace did more abound. That as sin has reigned to death, so also grace might reign by justice unto life everlasting, through Jesus Christ our Lord.* (Rom. 5:15–21.)

This phrase, "it came in besides," is a very fitting one, i.e., sin entered and the law came in besides, i.e., after sin entered also the law came, and so sin was not taken away by the law. For "that it came in besides" signifies that sin remained, indeed, that it was increased. For sin entered and the law followed sin in order to excite it by prescribing what goes against it and by forbidding what it likes. Hence he says: *that sin* **might abound.** He speaks here not in a causal but in a consecutive sense, because the conjunction "that" points to the sequel and not to the final cause of the law. For the law did not come because of sin, though he says this too in Gal. 3:19: "What, then, is the law? It was added because of transgressions, till the seed should come to whom the promise had been made." But here he says that it came that sin might abound, i.e., because of sin.

This, then, is the meaning of the phrase: The transgression of the law made known that first sin; the law therefore came in because of the transgression, not in order that a transgression should occur, but because it followed necessarily upon the promulgation of the law in order that one should learn through this transgression of the law the sin of weakness, blindness, and evil desire. For it was not necessary to promulgate the law because of transgression, inasmuch as, also if this was not intended and the law was not promulgated on account of transgression, it had to happen necessarily that the law was violated, because without grace no one can overcome concupiscence and destroy the body of sin. So this affirmative sentence: "The law came in besides that sin might abound" does nothing else than point to this negative statement: the law did not give life and it did not take away sin, or: the law did not enter in order to take away sin or to quicken. Upon this there must necessarily follow the positive statement: therefore it came in order that sin might be increased. This is correct, and so this is what is meant: the law came, and, without its fault and without the intention of the lawgiver, it happened that its coming served to increase sin; that this occurred is due to concupiscence which could not fulfill the law.

This is why Blessed Augustine says in his book about *The Propositions of This Letter:*[46] "By this word he has indicated sufficiently that the Jews did not know for what purpose the law was given. For it was not given to quicken—grace alone quickens through faith—but in order to show by how many tight chains of sin people are bound who presume to fulfill the law by their own powers." This is a common way of speaking, and one can often hear it used. When, for example, a physician comes to a sick person to comfort him and finds that he cannot help him because there is no hope that he will improve, the patient can say: You came not to comfort me but to increase my despair. So also mankind did not obtain from the law the help and remedy it had so eagerly longed for (as all philosophers and all seekers after truth show), but an increase of its sickness. A symbol of this is the woman of the Gospel who had an issue of blood and spent all she had on physicians and always grew worse (Luke 8:43 ff.). Hence, we must pay very close attention to the apostle when he says: "The law came in besides," for this means that God did not promulgate the law "in order that sin might abound," but that this happened when the law entered.

sick person (margin note)

46 Augustine, *Propos. ex ep. ad Rom.,* 30.

ROMANS, CHAPTER SIX

What shall we say then? Shall we continue in sin that grace may abound? God forbid. How shall we that are dead to sin *live any longer therein?* (Rom. 6:1–2.)

Blessed Augustine comments on this passage:[1] "Beginning with this passage, the apostle describes exclusively a man who has been placed under grace, where in his mind he already serves the law of God even though in the flesh he may still serve the law of sin." Then he goes on to explain this double servitude under law and sin and says: "For he does not yield to the yearning of sin, however much his desires may still incite and summon him to consent to it, until also the body is revived and 'death is swallowed up in victory' (I Cor. 15:54). Hence, if we do not yield to perverse lusts, we are in grace and 'sin does not reign in our body' (Rom. 6:12). But he whom it still holds in its power is still under the law and not under grace, no matter how strongly he may resist sin."

These words make possible a clear understanding of what the apostle says. For all these propositions: (1) *to be dead to sin;* (2) *but to live unto God;* (3) *to serve the law of God with the mind and the law of sin with the flesh,* mean nothing else than this: not to yield to evil desires and to sin, even though sin continues in us. And this is the same as to say: (4) *Sin has no power and does not reign,* but (5) *righteousness reigns.* Hence, he says farther on in ch. 13:14: "Make no provisions for the flesh, to fulfill the lusts thereof," in other words: the yearnings of sin that are sin itself, namely, original sin and the rest of the paternal inheritance from Adam, continue, but do not obey them. And he says also: *"that the body of sin be done away"* (Rom. 6:6) which happens when the spirit does not yield but resists.

[1] Augustine, *Propos. ex ep. ad Rom.,* 35.

COROLLARY

We are in sin until the end of our lives. As Blessed Augustine puts it:[2] "Evil desires will trouble a man, until the body is revived and death is swallowed up in victory." So too, Gal. 5:17: "For the Spirit lusts against the flesh and the flesh against the Spirit, for these are contrary the one to the other; that you do not do the things that you would." And below in ch. 7:19 of this letter: "The good which I would, I do not, but the evil which I would not, that I do," etc. And also, James 4:1: "Whence come wars and whence come fightings among you? Come they not hence, even of your pleasures that war in your members?" And I Peter 2:11: "Abstain from fleshly lusts which war against the soul."

In this way, then, all apostles and saints confess that sin and concupiscence remain in us until the body is turned to ashes and a new one is raised up that is free from concupiscence and sin, as it says in the last chapter of II Peter (v. 13): "According to his promise, we look for new heavens and a new earth, wherein dwells righteousness," i.e., because sin dwells on this earth. So also the Lord says in Jer. 18:4 ff., that he will do (with us) as the potter who made of the broken vessel another. For the Lord hates the body of sin and gets ready to remake it into another one; therefore he also commands us to hate and destroy and mortify it and to pray for its end and "the coming of his Kingdom" (Matt. 6:10).

But so to hate the body of sin and so to resist it is not easy but exceedingly hard. This requires as many works of penance as one can possibly do, especially in view of the fact that they are a precaution against ease and idleness.

Know ye not that as many of us as were baptized into Jesus Christ were baptized into his death? (Rom. 6:3.)

Blessed Augustine writes in the third chapter of the fourth book *On the Trinity:*[2a] "For our double death the Savior expends his single death, and in order to effect a twofold resurrection for us in the sacrament and in his example, he has put before us his one resurrection. He was clothed in mortal flesh and only in it he died and only in it he rose again, and now only in it he joins together with us in something twofold, for in it he became a sacrament for the inner man and an example for the outer man. The following word is spoken with respect to the sacrament for the inner man: 'Knowing this, that our old man is crucified with him, that the body of sin might be destroyed' (Rom. 6:6). But to the example

[2] *Ibid.*

[2a] Augustine, *De trin.*, IV, 3.

the following word applies: 'Be not afraid of them that kill the body' (Matt. 10:28). To this he most strongly encouraged by this death of his those who belong to him."

That the resurrection of the body of the Lord pertains to the sacrament for the inner man is shown by the word of the apostle in Col. 3:1: "If you were raised together with Christ, seek the things that are above." Yet to the example the following word applies: "Not a hair on your head shall perish" (Luke 21:18), and also the fact that he showed his body to the disciples after the resurrection. So then, the apostle speaks in this passage about the death and the resurrection of Christ in so far as they are relevant to the sacrament but not in so far as they relate to the example.

Hence, we must note that there is a double death, namely, the natural or, better, temporal one and the eternal one. Temporal death is the separation of body and soul. But this death is a symbol and a parable; it is, in comparison with eternal death (which is spiritual), like a picture of death painted on a wall.[3] This is why the Scripture very frequently calls it sleep, rest, or slumber.

Also eternal death is twofold. One is a very great good. It is the death of sin and the death of death, by which the soul is freed and separated from sin and the body from corruption, and the soul is united by grace and glory with the living God. This is death in the strict and proper sense of the word (for in every other death some mixture of life remains, but not in this one, in which there is nothing but life itself: eternal life). It is only this death that the conditions of death fit absolutely and perfectly; whatever dies in it, and in it alone, vanishes entirely into everlasting nothingness, and nothing ever returns from it (indeed, it inflicts death also upon eternal death). Thus sin dies, and also the sinner when he is justified, for sin does not ever return, as the apostle says here: "Christ dies no more," etc. (Rom. 6:9). This is the principal theme of the Scripture. For God arranged to take away through Christ whatever the devil brought in through Adam. And the devil brought in sin and death. Therefore, God brought about the death of death and the sin of sin, the prison of prison and the captivity of captivity.[4] As he says through Hosea: "O death, I will be thy death; O hell, I will be thy bite." (Hos. 13:14.)[5] This is

---

[3] The reference is probably to the "dance of death," which, at Luther's time, was a frequent subject of the painters.

[4] Cf. Eph. 4:8.

[5] These ideas appear to have been suggested to Luther by the liturgies to the use of which he was accustomed among the Augustinians.

symbolically represented in the Old Testament by all the wars of the Children of Israel in which they killed the Gentiles.

The other death is eternal and a very great evil. It is the death of the damned. Here it is not sin and the sinner that die, while man is saved, but it is man that dies, while sin lives and remains forever. This is the "very evil death of the wicked" (Ps. 34:21). Now when the apostle speaks of the death of Christ as of a sacrament, he speaks of the second spiritual death, and thus his words can easily be understood.

I said: "the sin of sin." What does this mean? To commit the sin of sin means to act against the law of sin, to transgress the "law of the members" (Rom. 7:23) and to sin against the evil desires of the flesh; this is a very good kind of sin. Just as the defiance of death, and this is what life is, is the death of death, so righteousness is the sin of sin. Hence, the word of the Preacher: "Better is the iniquity of a man than a woman doing a good turn" (Ecclus. 42:14), i.e., it is better that the spirit transgresses the law of the flesh and acts in opposition to the flesh than that the flesh acts in accordance with its law. These are the works of the Lord in which he rejoices and in which he makes us rejoice, as it is written: "Let the Lord rejoice in his works" (Ps. 104:31), and below in ch. 8:3 of the letter before us: "For sin, he condemned sin."

The Spirit uses these negative statements, which are much sweeter than the affirmative ones, in order to express the eternity of the things he speaks of. For "death is killed" means that "death does not come again," and "captivity is held captive" means that "captivity will not return," and this cannot be expressed in affirmative statements. For one can think of a life without eternity. Thus it says also in the same psalm: "Our God is the God of salvation: and of the Lord, of the Lord are the issues of death" (Ps. 68:20) rather than the issues of life. For the entering into life can become, indeed it inevitably becomes, a going out from life, but "the going out from death" means to enter into a life that has no death. These are the "delights of Christ"[6] of which we read in Ps. 16:3: "To the saints that are in his land, he has made wonderful all my delights." And in Ps. 11:2: "Great are the works of the Lord, sought out according to all his delights."

For we are buried *together with him by baptism into death; that as Christ is risen from death by the glory of the Father, so we*

---

[6] In his lectures on The Psalms, Luther explains these "delights" as the "delights of Christ" (*"voluntates Christi"*). He writes: "The delights of Christ are the mortification and crucifixion of the flesh and the contempt of all that can be seen, etc." (*WA* 3, 104, 27 f.).

also may walk in newness of life. For if we have been planted to-
gether in the likeness of his death, we shall be also in the likeness
of his resurrection.[7] (Rom. 6:4–5.)

In a spiritual man, everything must become visible, as far as
men and even he himself are concerned, in the same way in which
Christ was manifest to the eyes of the Jews after he was dead and
buried. For he leads us, and we can only make response to him
from beginning to end.

First of all, when he was dead, Christ no longer sensed anything
of what was happening outside, even though he was still outside.
So it is also with the spiritual man; though with his senses he may
be aware of all things and involved in them, he is totally with-
drawn from them in his heart and dead to them. This is what
happens when a man thoroughly detests everything that belongs
to this life, nay, rather, when feeling distaste for the whole business
of this life, he endures it with joy and glories in the fact that he is
like a dead corpse and "the offscouring and the filth of this world"
(I Cor. 4:13), as the apostle says.

But we should note that it is not necessary that all be found in
this state of perfection as soon as they are baptized into this kind
of death. For they are baptized "into death," i.e., toward death; in
other words: they have taken only the first steps toward the attainment of this death as their goal. In fact, though they are baptized
to eternal life and the Kingdom of God, they do not right away
possess its fullness, but they have taken only the first steps toward
it—for baptism was ordained that it prepare us for this death and
through it give us life—therefore it is necessary that we comply
with what has been ordained for us.

There are three kinds of people in this order. First, there are
those who are unable to endure the cross and a mortification of
the kind we have described, and who are unwilling to die. They
belong with the robber who was crucified on the left of Christ,
for they blaspheme Christ, certainly in thought, but also by what
they do.[8] Others do endure the cross but with much feeling of
suffering and resistance and groaning, but yet they overcome all
this and finally die willingly. They find it hard to be despised and

---

[7] Luther's marginal gloss reads (*WA* 56, 58, 22): "This goes well together
with the word of John 12:24: 'Except a corn of wheat fall into the ground
and die, it abides alone. . . .' For he says 'likeness' in order that one should
not think that he speaks of a physical resurrection and death. In order to
indicate the nature of this 'being planted together,' there follows at the
same place the word: 'He that hates his life in this world shall keep it unto
life eternal.'"

[8] This exposition corresponds to the traditional exegesis. Cf. the *Gl. ord.* and
Lyra.

loathed by all. They belong with the robber at the right of the cross; indeed, Christ continues to carry them with grief and pain in his body. The third group, finally, consists of those who, as I have already said, go to this death with joy. Their prototype is Christ—Christ who died crying with a loud voice (Mark 15:37) like the bravest hero.[9]

Knowing this that **our old man** *is crucified with him.* (Rom. 6:6.)

Man, as the son of Adam, is "old," not by nature but because of a defect of his nature. For his nature is good, but its defect is evil. We use the phrase "old man," not merely with respect to the works of the flesh a man may perform, but chiefly with reference to the fact that he does the right, handles himself wisely, and keeps himself busy in all kinds of spiritual goods, yes, also with reference to the fact that he loves and worships God. It is the "old man" in him that makes him use God in all this so that he can enjoy his gifts. Only grace can correct the perversity of his abusive practice (which in the Scripture is called curvedness,[10] wickedness, and crookedness) and straighten him up. Ecclesiastes 1:15: "The crooked are hard to make straight." This is said not so much because of the stubbornness of crooked people but chiefly because of the defect that is in man by inheritance and because of the poison that is in him from the beginning of his days and infects the depth of his nature, so that, from his selfish disposition, he seeks even in God only himself and his own.[11] Psalm 72:14: "He shall redeem their souls from usuries and wickedness." In short, this wickedness is so bottomless that no one can know its depth, and in the Scriptures it is not it as such, but only the love of it, that is confuted by the mercy of God. Psalm 11:5: "He hates the soul of him who loves wickedness."[12] And Ps. 32:6: "For this," namely, wickedness, "let everyone that is godly pray unto thee," namely, because he

---

[9] Lit.: *"quos Christus cum valido clamore ut fortissimus Gygas moriens significavit."* (Gygas = giant. The giants [*Gigantes*] were the sons of Terra. They stormed the heavens but were killed by the lightning of Jupiter.)

Ficker (p. 324, n. 32) points out that the Missal of the Augustinian Hermits prescribed for the Ember Days the use (in the secret prayers) of Ps. 19:5: *"Exultavit ut gigas ad currendam viam"* (He has rejoiced as a giant to run the way").

[10] The term "curvedness" (*curvitas*) is not used in the Vulgate. About its significance, cf. Chapter V, note 10.

[11] *"Quo etiam in ipso Deo per amorem concupiscentiae querit homo, quae sua sunt."*

[12] Following Faber, Luther takes the psalm to read, *"Qui autem diligit iniquitatem, odit animan eius,"* instead of *suam* as the Vulgate has it ("He that loves iniquity hates his own soul").

hates it. All this is symbolized by the curvedness of that certain woman in the Gospel whom Satan held captive for eighteen years, as the Savior said (Luke 13:11).[13]

That the body of sin may be destroyed *to the end that we may serve sin no longer.* (Rom. 6:6.)

"To destroy" must here be taken spiritually. For if the apostle wanted to speak of corporeal destruction, it would not be necessary for the "old man" in us to be crucified for this. For he will be physically destroyed, whether or not we want it so, also in the case of those in whom the "old man" is not crucified. What is a necessity, therefore, cannot be a commandment or a counsel. It is for this reason, so Blessed Augustine remarks,[14] that the apostle, wanting to explain the nature of this destruction, goes on to say: "that we should no longer be in bondage to sin." This is an interpretation, says Blessed Augustine, of the sentence: "that the body of sin might be destroyed." To destroy the body of sin means, therefore, to break the desires of the flesh and of our old man by exertions of penitence and the cross, and so to decrease them from day to day and to put them to death. As the apostle says in Col. 3:5: "Put to death therefore your members which are upon the earth." In fact, in this same passage, he describes very clearly both the old and the new man.

It is to this destruction that several headings of the psalms refer: "That he shall not be destroyed" (Ps. 57:1; Ps. 58:1; Ps. 59:1). In Ps. 60:1, it says: "O God, thou that cast us off and hast destroyed us." And in Jer. 1:10: "to destroy, to break down, and to pluck up."

"The body of sin" must, therefore, not be understood as something mystical as many do[15] who imagine "the body of sin" to be the whole heap of our evil works, but it is the very body we carry around with us. It is called "the body of sin" because, in opposition to the spirit, it inclines toward sin. The seed of the devil is in it; hence, the Lord says to the serpent in Gen. 3:15: "I will put enmity between your seed and her seed." The seed of the woman is the word of God in the church,[16] because it inclines toward righteousness and the good. The seed of the devil is the very sin,

---

[13] Luke 13:11 ff.: "And behold, a woman that had a spirit of infirmity eighteen years; and she was bowed together, neither could she look upwards at all. And when Jesus saw her, he called her and said to her: 'Woman, thou art loosed from thy infirmity.' And he laid his hands upon her, and she immediately was made straight, and glorified God."

[14] Augustine, *Propos. ex ep. ad Rom.,* 32–34.

[15] The *Gl. ord.* and Lyra.

[16] The *Gl. ord.* interprets *"mulier"* by *"ecclesia."*

tinder, and concupiscence in the flesh. And this enmity goes on continuously, according to the word of the apostle in Gal. 5:17: "The flesh lusts against the spirit and the spirit against the flesh." The flesh has the seed of the devil and seeks to bring forth sin and sinful fruit, but the spirit has the seed of God and seeks to bring forth righteousness and its fruits. And so these two "are contrary the one to the other, that you may not do the things that you would." (Gal. 5:17.)

For he that is dead is justified from sin. Now, if we be dead with Christ, we believe that we shall also live with him, knowing that Christ being raised from the dead dies no more; death has no dominion over him. **For what has died to sin,** *died once; but what lives, lives unto God. So do you also reckon that you are dead to sin but alive unto God in Christ Jesus. (Rom. 6:7–11.)*[17]

[17] Here is Luther's gloss on Rom. 6:7-11 (first the interlinear and then the marginal gloss; the reference of the latter is indicated by numbers within parentheses): *"For he,* who actualizes this 'If we have been planted together,' etc., *is dead:* by a good spiritual death *he is made righteous from his sin,* i.e., he is risen in a spiritual resurrection. *Now if we be dead* by a spiritual death through baptism, in order to end sin *with Christ: we believe,* because this new life cannot be experienced but must be believed. For no one knows that he lives again or experiences that he is justified, but he believes and hopes *that we shall also live* in spirit and newness, now and forever, *with him. Knowing,* i.e., because we know *that Christ,* after he had died, *rising again from the dead,* to himself physically and to us sacramentally, *dies no more* (1): in eternity *death shall have no more dominion over him;* in other words: therefore it cannot have any dominion over you in spirit. *For in that he,* Christ, *died* physically, *he died once* (2) *to* sin, i.e., that sin should die, *but in that he lives, he lives* after the resurrection *to God* (3; 4) in righteousness and glory. *So do you also reckon,* i.e., feel, know, *that you are dead to sin,* I Peter 2:24: 'That we, having died to sins, might live to righteousness,' *but alive* in a spiritual life *to God in Christ Jesus,* by faith in Christ.

"(1) He does not say 'and will live,' but 'and dies no more,' because in the Scriptures negative statements are employed to signify and to emphasize all the more strongly that the eternal is meant. For example, 'That henceforth we should not serve sin "means" we shall be righteous forever.'

"(2) Heb. 9:12: 'By his own blood he entered once into the holies, having obtained eternal redemption.' And again (ch. 9:28): 'Christ was offered once to take away the sins of many.'

"(3)The Greek text reads (according to Faber): 'For what is dead to sin, has died to it once,' and this is much better. 'For what is alive, lives unto God.' *Quod* means 'whatever'; it must be taken as a pronoun and not as a conjunction. The passage speaks of the sacrament of the death of Christ; in other words: just as Christ, who died once, can never die again, so whosoever dies once spiritually to sin, dies never again, but will live in eternity.

"(4) This text shows that the translator has exercised the function not only of a translator but at the same time also that of an expositor. The

What he wants to say is that we must suffer this spiritual death only once. For one who dies in this way lives forever. Therefore we do not need to go back to sin in order to die to it once more. This interpretation opposes the Novatianists;[18] the nature of the spiritual life is such that once it has been laid hold of, it is necessarily eternal. For death does not put an end to it as it does to physical life; it is the beginning of eternal life. Hence, the saying of John's:[19] "Whosoever believes in me, shall never die," i.e., as long as he does not willingly turn away from this life in Christ, he cannot die. In time, the spiritual life is gradually so strengthened that a turning away from it will be utterly impossible, for no one endowed with the unshakable strength of the perfection of an eternal will would want to turn away from it.

As the ray of the sun is eternal because the sun is eternal, so the spiritual life is eternal because Christ is eternal. He is our life: through faith he flows into our life by the rays of his grace and remains in us.[20] For just as Christ is eternal, so also the grace that flows out from him is eternal by its very nature. And so, when a man sins again, the spiritual life in him does not die, but it is he who turns away from it that dies, while it remains in Christ forever. This is what the apostle means when he says here: "If we be dead with Christ, we believe that we shall also live with him." How shall we live with him? "Knowing," he says, "that Christ, being raised from the dead, dies no more," so also "what is dead to sin is dead to it once for all." He has Christ who dies no more, and so he, too, dies no more but lives with Christ forever. For this reason, we are baptized only once, affirming the life of Christ

(margin note: perseverance of the saints?)

(margin note: Baptized only once.)

---

translator cannot commit a greater fault than to transmit to others a meaning which does not lie in the text he has to translate but is his own. We must therefore disagree with Blessed Jerome,* who says in his book about Daniel that he could not translate what he had not first understood. This is nothing else than to want to understand and know everything and, to be sure, in so far as this suits his own modesty, Jerome may have spoken the truth."

* Cf. Jerome, _Contra Rufin._, II, 32: "I know how difficult it is to understand the prophets, and that no one can have a ready judgment about how they must be translated unless he has first understood what he has read." This passage (at the end of Jerome's prologue to Isaiah, just preceding the prologue to Daniel) is quoted by Lyra in his comments on Jerome's _De Daniele._

18 Luther may think of Ambrose, _De poenitentia_ (against the Novatianists), II, 9.
19 Luther thinks of John 6:40: "For this is the will of my Father, that everyone that beholds the Son, and believes in him, should have eternal life," but he actually quotes John 11:26.
20 A Roman Catholic sacramental conception!

thereby, though we may fall quite often and get up again. For the life of Christ can be recovered again and again, but one can begin it only once, just as a man who has never been rich can only once commence to become rich, although he can again and again lose and recover his wealth.

But what lives, lives unto God. (Rom. 6:10.)
Only what lives eternally and spiritually lives unto God, because God is eternal spirit. Only what is spiritual and eternal counts in his presence, but flesh and all that is temporal are nothing before him. Inasmuch as this life is eternal, a man who dies to his sin, needs to die only once, for upon such a death there can follow only a life that is eternal. There is no death in it, for otherwise it would not be eternal. Nor can a man who died once to sin die to it again, for upon this death there followed eternal righteousness which can never again fall into sin. Here we let follow the

Perseverance

Corollary

That the Novatianist heresy interpreted this text wrongly by assuming that it teaches that there is no hope for the lapsed to rise up again, because a man must die to sin once for all. But this "once for all" does not fix the limit and number of acts of penitence, but it sets off the eternity of grace (and excludes the possibility that there can be another kind of righteousness).[21] What is meant here is this: Whosoever has been baptized and done penance has thereby escaped from sin and acquired righteousness so that he does not need ever again to escape from another sin or acquire another righteousness. For this one and only righteousness suffices forever. This cannot at all be the case with any kind of human righteousness, for according to moral philosophy,[22] there remain always other virtues to be acquired once a man has acquired one.

However, what is here meant is not that when someone loses the righteousness he has once acquired, he cannot acquire it again. For Scripture contradicts this error; Prov. 24:16: "A righteous man falls seven times a day and rises up again." And our Lord said to Peter: "I say not unto thee, until seven times, but until seventy times seven" (Matt. 18:22).

Therefore, as I have said, this "once" does not state or rule out the number of alternations in righteousness, but it sets a limit to

---

[21] *"Et abnegat alietatem iustitiae."*
[22] Cf. the distinctions between the several virtues (following Aristotle) in the *Physics* of Trutvetter, II, *de habitibus animae;* Ockham, III *Sent., q.* 12, *a.* 2H ff.; Gabriel Biel, III *Sent., d.* 34, *q. un., a.* 1, *n.* 2 and 3.

diversity in righteousness, or, rather, it emphasizes the eternal
nature of righteousness: to the effect that it is not inconsistent
with its eternal nature that, in this life, one can repeatedly either
lose or find it again. Even Blessed Peter sinned after the sending
forth of the Holy Spirit by putting on the false show, of which we
read in Gal. 2:11 ff.; and this was certainly a mortal sin counter-
acting the gospel as well as the salvation of the soul, inasmuch as
the apostle says there expressly that he did not act in accordance
with the truth of the gospel.

*Let not sin therefore reign in your mortal body, so as to obey
the lusts thereof. Neither present your members as instruments of
iniquity unto sin, but present yourselves to God, as those that are
alive from the dead and your members as instruments of right-
ousness unto God. For sin shall have no dominion over you,* **for
you are not under the law, but under grace.** (Rom. 6:11–14.)

So then, sin has no dominion over those who are under the law.
This is sufficiently clear in the light of what we have said before in
interpreting ch. 3. A man who is without faith in Christ is always
in sin, even though he does good works. This is why we must note
that the apostle's way of speaking appears to those who do not
understand it as extraordinary and strange on account of its pronounced peculiarity. For they think that "to be under the law"
means "to have a law according to which one must live." But to
the apostle, "to be under the law" means "not to live up to the
law," to be a defendant before the law and its debtor and a transgressor, and this because the law rightly accuses and condemns
him, while he cannot satisfy it or rise above it. And so, while the
law has dominion over man, also sin has dominion over him, holding him captive. Hence, I Cor. 15:56: "The sting of death is sin,
and the power of sin is the law," i.e., sin is so powerful and has
dominion over us because the law has dominion over us.[23]

The sequence of thought, then, is this: Sin is the sting or power
of death by which death has power and dominion over us, just as
it says above in Rom. 5:12: "by sin death," etc. The law, however,
is the power or potency of sin through which sin continues and
has dominion over us.

From this dominion of law and sin one can be freed only by
Christ, as it says in the passage that follows the one just quoted:
"But thanks be to God who gives us the victory through our Lord

---

[23] Luther adds here " *'Virtus' hic, i.e., potentia dicitur"* (*virtus* here means
power) with reference to the Vulgate version of I Cor. 15:56: "*Virtus veri
peccati lex*" ("The power of sin is the law"). Luther frequently points to
this meaning of *virtus* in his lectures.

Jesus Christ!" (I Cor. 15:57). And our Lord himself says in John 8:36:[24] "If, therefore, the Son shall make you free, you shall be free indeed." And in John 16:33: "In the world you have tribulation, but be of good cheer; I have overcome the world." And in I John 5:4:[25] "This is the victory that has overcome the world, even your faith." "And who is he that overcomes the world but he that believes that Jesus Christ is the Son of God?" (I John 5:5.)[26] And so he says here that we can check the reign of sin because "we are not under the law but under grace." All this means "that the body of sin shall be destroyed" and that righteousness shall be gradually perfected.[27]

But thanks be to God that you were the servants of sin but have become obedient from the heart to that form of teaching **whereunto you have been delivered,**[28] *and being made free from sin, you have become servants of righteousness.* (Rom. 6:17–18.)

Though some want to understand this phrase by changing its parts,[29] so that it reads: "(You became obedient to that form of teaching) that was delivered to you," I believe that the Spirit speaking through the apostle spoke intentionally in the way of the text. For the wisdom of the flesh is hostile to the word of God, but the word of God is immutable and insuperable. Therefore, the wisdom of the flesh must undergo a change; it must give up its own form and take on the form of the word. This happens when by faith it yields and undoes itself and conforms itself to the word,[30] believing that the word is true and it itself untrue. "The Word became flesh" (John 1:14) and "took on the form of a servant" (Phil. 2:7), in order that the flesh should become word and man take on the form of the word; then, in terms of the third chapter of the letter before us, man will become as righteous, truthful, wise, good, meek, chaste as the word itself is whose form he takes on by faith.

[24] Luther writes: "in John 6."
[25] Luther writes: "I John 1."
[26] Here he notes: "ch. 4."
[27] *"Et perficiatur iustitia incepta."*
[28] In the marginal gloss, Luther says (*WA* 56, 62, 13 ff.): "I.e., from the form of error you are now delivered to the form of the gospel, because 'thy word, O Lord, shall remain forever' [Ps. 119:89]. For it is not the word that changes, but we are changed and yield to it. Isaiah 40:8: 'The grass withers, but the word of our God shall stand forever.' Matthew 5:25: 'Agree with your adversary,' in other words: give up your own likeness and put on the likeness of the word. For 'the Word became flesh' [John 1:14] in order that we should become the word ['*ut nos verbum efficiamur*']."
[29] *"Per hipallagen,"* according to Faber in his Commentary.
[30] *"Conformitas verbi."* Cf. Bernard of Clairvaux, *Sermones in Cantica.*

Hence, it is more meaningful to say, "whereunto you were delivered" than "which was delivered to you." For the teaching of the gospel is delivered also to the ungodly, although they do not deliver or conform themselves to it—and they are not delivered to it, because they do not truly and heartily believe it. Almost the same thought is expressed in this word to the Corinthians:[31] "Now that you have known (God) or, rather, are known by God"; and in exactly the same way, he could have said here too: which was delivered to you or, rather, "to which you were delivered" as it is characteristic of believers and saints. I refer you to ch. 7, below, in this letter where it is explained how we die to sin and the law rather than let the opposite happen.

For sin shall have no dominion over you. (Rom. 6:14.)

We must understand that this refers not only to the sinful desire for temporal goods and prosperity but also to our tendency to run away from temporal evils and adversities. For a man who has Christ through true faith does not desire any worldly goods (nor life itself), however much they may intrigue him; nor does he fear any evils and even death itself, however much they may frighten him. He stands firm on solid rock; he does not seek an easy life and does not mind getting hard knocks, not that he is not tempted to flee when fear overcomes him, or to yield to sinful desire when it entices him (for he is not insensitive to either lust or fear), but, in the end, he does not surrender, even though it costs him utmost exertion and pain just barely to resist and to come out on top, in accordance with the word of I Peter 4:18: "The righteous man is scarcely saved." In this trial and struggle, the righteous man always resembles more a loser than a victor, for the Lord lets him be tested and assailed to his utmost limits as gold is tested in a furnace. ("For he is not crowned except he contend lawfully." [II Tim. 2:5].)

COROLLARY

(1) He who fears death more than Christ and loves life more than Christ does not yet possess Christ through true faith. For sin has dominion over him, and he is under the law. We must understand this in the fullest sense in terms of his own teaching: John 12:25: "He that loves his life loses it." And elsewhere: "He that loves father and mother more than me is not worthy of me," and "He that does not take his cross and follow after me is not worthy of me" (Matt. 10:37–38). It is thus not easy to bring sin under control. Indeed, if God were not in us, "who is faithful and will not suffer

[31] Luther thinks of I Cor. 13:12, but actually quotes Gal. 4:9.

us to be tempted above that we are able" (I Cor. 10:13), we should certainly be drowned. However, he suffers unbelievers to be tempted, so that they fall, nay, rather, they have already fallen and are forever unable to stand, but he is faithful to those who by faith stand and call upon him.

(2) When sin does not succeed in getting dominion over the saints as it assails them, it is forced to serve them. "To them that love God all things work together for good." (Rom. 8:28.) As the apostle says: "But he will make with the temptation also the way of escape that you may endure it." (I Cor. 10:13.) Thus dissipation makes the soul chaster when it attacks it; pride makes it humbler; laziness, livelier; avarice, more generous; anger, more gentle; and gluttony, more abstinent. When the spiritual man gets involved in all this, there arises in him a greater and greater hatred against that which assails him. And thus his trial becomes very useful to him.

So then, sin rules in our mortal body if we yield to it, but it becomes a servant if we resist it, for it thoroughly arouses our hatred of iniquity and our love of righteousness. But in our future immortal body, it will neither have dominion, nor will it rule, nor will it be a servant. Let us recognize, then, how marvelous God's wisdom is! He furthers the good through evil and he perfects righteousness through sin, not only in us, but also in others. In the sins that others commit, he gives us cause to hate the sin against the neighbor and to give it up in order that we may practice love and piety toward him, and in order that, as far as we ourselves are concerned, we may yearn for righteousness and come to loathe unrighteousness—yet only if we call upon him from a pure and sincere faith.

Neither present your members **unto sin as instruments of iniquity.** (Rom. 6:13.)

The translation reads here "iniquity" instead of "unrighteousness more violently because he is in the law than he would if he determined by unbelief, just as, conversely, righteousness is the whole general way of life determined by faith; it is faith together with its works just as unrighteousness is unbelief together with its works, including the good and holy ones.

According to Blessed Augustine in his work *On the Spirit and the Letter*,[32] "sin" must here be understood, not as the work of sin, but as the law of sin or the law of the members, as concupiscence, "tinder," inclination toward evil, resistance against the

[32] Luther thinks perhaps of Augustine, *De nupt. et concup.*, I, 30 and 31. The argument here is directed against Lyra.

good. The apostle, therefore, wants to say that the members of the body must not be yielded to "sin," i.e., to concupiscence and the "tinder," so that, by such an obedience to sin, they become weapons of unbelief and so that believers are made into unbelievers, in so far as they do the works of unbelievers according to the desires of sin. But we must obey God, so that "our members may be instruments of righteousness," i.e., of a life of faith and faithfulness.

I speak a human thing, because of the infirmity *of your flesh. For as you have yielded your members to serve uncleanness and iniquity, unto iniquity; so now yield your members to serve unrighteousness, unto sanctification. For when you were the servants of sin, you were free men to righteousness. What fruit therefore had you then in those things, of which you are now ashamed? For the end of them is death. But now being made free from sin, and become servants of God, you have your fruit unto sanctification, and the end life everlasting. For the wages of sin is death. But the grace of God, life everlasting in Christ Jesus our Lord.* (Rom. 6:19–23.)

Above he spoke of the thorough mortification of concupiscence in such a way that he would not allow a concession to it even in marriage. But here he relaxes his demand, and he means to say this: If because of the infirmity of the flesh, one must yield at all to lust, this should happen at least apart from dishonor and uncleanness in a marriage that is sanctified by faith, inasmuch as even the heathen, people who are outside the faith, observe such cleanness in accordance with human custom. Thus the idea of this passage is, in brief form, the same that he develops more fully throughout the entire chapter in I Cor., ch. 7. There he says: "Because of fornication, let each man have his own wife" (v. 2), and, farther on, "that Satan tempt you not because of your incontinency" (v. 5). This is a human injunction, which is much less important than the counsel he offers saying: "Yet I would that all men were even as I myself," but not all are able to do this, therefore he continues: "but each man has his own gift from God, one after this manner, and another after that" (v. 7).

That also here he has been speaking of such a counsel and of the thorough mortification of the flesh he indicates when he says by way of reducing the strictness of the demand a little: "I speak a human thing," in other words: If you cannot be continent, behave at least chastely so that sin does not reign by the pollution and uncleanness of the flesh to the detriment of faith and righteousness and to the increase of unrighteousness.

To serve uncleanness. (Rom. 6:19.)

The apostle now turns around and does not hold to the antithesis, for he says first: (to serve) **"uncleanness and unrighteousness unto unrighteousness"** and then **"to serve righteousness unto sanctification,"** i.e., cleanness. (Hence, in the Old Testament, it often says "be holy," "sanctify yourselves" for "purify yourselves," "be clean from carnal pollution.")[33] For in his understanding, sanctification and cleanness are the same: they mean the chastity of the body, not any kind of chastity, but that which comes inwardly out of the spirit of faith that sanctifies. There is also a chastity of the heathen, but it is not a holy chastity or sanctification, because their soul is polluted. Hence, he says also here first: "Serve righteousness" and then: "unto sanctification." For the soul must first be made chaste by faith in order that the holy soul then can also make the body clean for the sake of God, for otherwise it would be an empty chastity. In the same way the Lord speaks to the hypocrites: "You hypocrites, cleanse first what is inside, that the outside may become clean also," in other words: If you have become clean inside, the body and everything outside will easily and spontaneously be clean. Consequently, if one serves righteousness, such service carries sanctification with it (Isa. 11:5): "And righteousness shall be the girdle of his waist and faith the girdle of his loins," in other words: He who believes and is righteous in spirit thereby easily overcomes and controls dissipation.

Conversely, one who serves uncleanness, i.e., dissipation and the pollution of the body, will become more and more unrighteous, because sin has taken hold of him and because, having given up his faith, he has become an unbeliever.

[33] Cf. Gen. 35:2; Isa. 52:11; Ezek. 36:25; Num. 11:18; Josh. 7:13.

ROMANS, CHAPTER SEVEN

Know you not, brethren (for I speak to them that know the law), **that the law has dominion over a man** *as long as he lives? For the woman that has a husband, while her husband lives, is bound to the law. But if her husband be dead, she is loosed from the law of her husband. Therefore, while her husband lives, she shall be called an adulteress if she be with another man; but if her husband be dead, she is delivered from the law of her husband, so that she is not an adulteress if she be with another man. (Rom. 7:1–3.)*

It is clear that the apostle speaks of the law, not from the metaphysical or moral point of view, but in a spiritual and theological sense, in accordance with the full discussion of this in the fourth chapter of the letter before us; in other words: he deals with the law with respect to the inner man and the will and not with respect to the outer man and his actions. Once one has seen what his characteristic basic propositions and principles are, one can easily understand everything else.

Here is the first of these propositions: The law brings about sin and the wrath of God. None, therefore, dies to the law unless he dies to sin, and whoever dies to sin, dies also to the law. Moreover, as soon as he is free from sin, he is also free from the law. And in so far as he is a slave of sin, he is also a slave of the law and thus the law will have dominion over him and rule over him as long as sin has dominion over him and reigns in him.

COROLLARY

The apostle's manner of argument is contrary to the metaphysical or moral method of reasoning. For the apostle makes it a point to say that it is man rather than sin that is taken away, so that sin continues as something that remains and man is cleansed from sin

193

rather than that the opposite is the case. In contrast to this, human self-understanding asserts that it is sin that is taken away and that it is man who remains and is cleansed. But the apostle's understanding is characteristic of him in the best sense and is perfectly in accord with God. For also the Scripture says in Ps. 81:6: "He removed his back from the burden." It does not say: He removed the burden from his back. (Similarly, it says in ch. 6:17 of this letter: "Whereunto you were delivered.") The exodus of Israel from Egypt is a parable of this: God did not take the Egyptians away from the Children of Israel, but he led Israel out of Egypt which remained behind. And in Ps. 21:12[1] it says: "In your remnants you shall prepare their face, for you shall make them turn their back." The Bible uses this way of speaking, because grace with its spiritual righteousness takes man and changes him and turns him away from sin even though it lets sin remain, so that while it makes the spirit righteous, it lets concupiscence remain in the flesh and in the midst of the sins of the world. (This way of speaking is a most effective device for use against the moralists.)[2]

Human righteousness, however, seeks first of all to remove and to change the sins and to keep man intact; this is why it is not righteousness but hypocrisy. Hence, as long as there is life in man and as long as he is not taken by renewing grace to be changed, no efforts of his can prevent him from being subject to sin and the law.

The first proposition, therefore, is this: "Sin comes through the law," as the apostle concludes farther on (Rom. 7:7). And thus the law is the law of sin, i.e., of the husband, and only he can die unto it who dies unto sin. But if a man has become dead to sin and is removed from it, then certainly sin is most effectively taken away from him and is dead to him. But when a man has not become dead to sin by being taken away from it, all efforts to get rid of sin and to become dead to it will fail.

It is then plain that, as the apostle understands it, sin is removed spiritually, i.e., the will to sin is mortified, but these others want this to be understood metaphysically when they say that the works of sin and sinful desires are removed as white paint is taken from a wall and heat from water.[3] This is why Samuel says in I Sam. 10:6: "And you shall be turned into another man." He does not say: Your sins shall be turned into something else, but: you shall first be changed and when you have turned into another man, also your actions will be entirely changed.

---

[1] Luther says Ps. 16 (Vg.).
[2] "Iustitiarios."
[3] Cf. Gabriel Biel, II Sent., d. 35, q. un., a. 1; n. 1B.

Hence, we can only marvel at the foolishness of the hypocrites who weaken themselves by their many efforts to change their works instead of humbling themselves enough to pray that their persons might be changed by grace. Ephesians 2:10: "For we are his workmanship, created in Christ Jesus in good works." He does not say that good works are created in us. And James 1:18: "that we might be some beginning of his creature."

So therefore, if we do not first die to sin, it will remain in us, so that it has dominion over us, and thereby also the law through which sin exercises its dominion over us. For a man who is not quickened in his will by the Spirit cannot but be a slave to sin, even though he does many good works; what, in Prov. 11:15, is said of people of his kind will befall him too: "The foolish shall be afflicted with pains."

People, therefore, who want to imitate the works of the saints and glory in their fathers and forefathers, as the monks do today, are extremely foolish because all they accomplish is to ape them.[4] Fools that they are, they do not look first for their spirit in order to become like them, but, unconcerned for the spirit, they do the same works they did.

The Thomists, Scotists, and other schools display the same kind of rash imprudence when they uphold the writings and sayings of their founders not only by disdaining to inquire for the spirit behind them but also by extinguishing it in their excessive zeal to venerate them. They believe it to be sufficient to keep only their words, regardless of the spirit. Just so also the Jews and all who are proud think that all they need to do is to understand the Holy Scriptures literally, but they care nothing about the spirit from which this understanding must proceed and about the method by which the spirit wants to be understood. Therefore, Isaiah says rightly in the eleventh chapter, not that "wisdom" but that "the spirit of wisdom shall rest upon him," etc. (Isa. 11:2). For only the Spirit understands the Scriptures rightly and in accordance with God. But in every other case, men do not understand them even though they think they understand them, "seeing, they see not and hearing, they hear not" (Isa. 6:9; Matt. 13:13). So it is also with these hypocrites: being saints, they are not saints; being righteous, they are not righteous; they do good but accomplish nothing good.

Man must therefore first of all pray for grace that, changed in spirit, he will want to and will do everything from a cheerful and ready heart, not from slavish fear or puerile cupidity, but from a

---

[4] "*Simianam fabulam agere,*" probably a translation of the German phrase *ein Affenspiel treiben,* which Luther liked to use.

free and manly attitude of mind. But only the Spirit can bring this about.

Therefore, my brethren, you also *are become dead to the law, by the body of Christ; that you may belong to another, who is risen again from the dead, that we may bring forth fruit unto God.*[5] (Rom. 7:4.)

Blessed Augustine says about this passage: "Three are here spoken of: the soul as if it were the woman, the passions of sins as if they were the husband, and the law as if it were the law of the husband." And "it is to be noted that the resemblance ceases where he says that the soul is not set free when the sins are dead just as it would be when the husband dies, but that the soul itself must die to sin and be set free from the law and married to another."[6] We have already stated why this must be done.

For when we were in the flesh, the passions of sins, which were through the law, did work in our members to bring forth fruit unto death. But now we are loosed from the law of death, wherein we were detained; so that we should serve in newness of spirit and not in the oldness of the letter. (Rom. 7:5–6.)

The apostle means by "letter" not merely those parts of Scripture that have a symbolical significance[7] and the teaching of the

---

[5] Luther writes in the marginal gloss (*WA* 56, 65, 14 ff.): "The apostle expresses in this chapter a wonderful and profound judgment. Lyra and others have interpreted it not only superficially but wrongly, with the one exception, as far as I can see, of Augustine. In the last resort, the apostle wants to show that there are two men in the believer, the old and the new; on the one hand, Adam, and, on the other hand, Christ. But we cannot know the old man in us, before the law is made known and proclaimed, for he is born, so to speak, when the law is proclaimed. And thus it is through the law that we are subject to the old man in us and to sin (i.e., we know by the law that we are subject to them) and thus sin had dominion over us through the law just as the husband over the woman. Without the law, it would have no dominion over us, i.e., we should not know that it had dominion over us. If, therefore, the old man in us is dead, we are dead also to the law, for it no longer makes us subject to sin but it has lost its power over us."

[6] Augustine, *Propos. ex ep. ad Rom.,* 36.

[7] Cf. Luther's marginal gloss (*WA* 56, 67, 18 ff.): "The term 'letter' must here not be taken to mean only the symbolic parts of Scripture, as Augustine shows in an extensive discussion in chapters 4 and 6 of *On the Spirit and the Letter.* Lyra is therefore mistaken in saying that Christ made the law of no effect in so far as it deals with judicial and ceremonial matters but not in so far as it deals with moral issues. As a matter of fact, the apostle speaks here obviously of the law in so far as it deals with moral issues, and as such it is the law of death and of the letter."

law, but, rather, every teaching that prescribes what constitutes the good life whether it is to be found in the Gospel or in Moses. For when one learns it and keeps it in one's memory and the Spirit of grace is not present, it is merely an empty letter and the soul's death. This is why Blessed Augustine writes in the fourth book of *On the Spirit and the Letter*:[8] "That teaching by which we receive the commandment that we live continently and rightly is the letter that kills, unless the Spirit is present that gives life. For the term 'letter' is not to be understood to mean that any figurative expression, whose natural meaning is absurd, is to be taken literally, but also and, indeed, chiefly, in the way which the apostle very clearly indicates when he says: 'I should have known that coveting is sin, except the law had said: You shall not covet.' Here nothing figurative is said." And farther down in the fourteenth chapter he says more extensively:[9] "When the apostle speaks of the law by which none can be made righteous, he wants to have it understood that by 'law' he means not merely those ordinances which were given to them as figures of the promise but also those works which enable everyone who does them to live righteously." "But he makes the point still more clearly when he says to the Corinthians: 'The letter kills, but the spirit gives life' (II Cor. 3:6), for he wants 'the letter' understood as the Decalogue itself as it is written on the Two Tables." And so forth.

COROLLARY

The so-called moral or, more correctly, spiritual interpretation of Scripture deals only with love and the disposition of the heart, with the love of righteousness and the hatred of unrighteousness, in other words: with whatever the Scripture teaches we must do or not do. We must understand that this doing or not doing must be freely accomplished by the love of God with all one's heart and not from a slavish fear of punishment or from a childish desire for advantage, and that this is impossible without the love that is shed abroad by the Holy Spirit.

This is what the Scholastic teachers[10] mean when they say in their highly obscure and entirely unintelligible way that there is no valid observance of the divine commandment unless it is formed by love. This word "formed" is a cursed word, for it compels one to think of the soul as if it remained the same after and before the outpouring of love and as if the form were added

---

[8] Augustine, *De spir. et lit.*, 4, 6.
[9] *Ibid.*, 14, 23.
[10] Duns Scotus, IV *Sent.*, d. 14, q. 2, n. 13; Ockham, I *Sent.*, d. 17, q. 3B; Biel, IV *Sent.*, d. 14, q. 1, a. 1, n. 3.

to it at the moment of action, while, as a matter of fact, it must be wholly mortified and made new before it becomes capable of deeds of love. (The same judgment applies to the distinction between a work that is good according to the substance of the deed and a work that is good according to the intention of the lawgiver).[11]

Also, the apostle agrees with this judgment when he says in I Cor. 13:2: "If I should know all mysteries and have all knowledge, and if I should have all faith, etc., and have not love, I am nothing." The plain conclusion, then, is that the mysteries and the whole gospel and every "spiritual" interpretation of the Scripture are "letter." For when they who teach this are dead, they also lack the Spirit, for "the Spirit gives life and the letter kills." Now they *are* killed and therefore they belong to the letter.

Blessed Augustine writes in the same book farther on in the twenty-first chapter:[12] "What else are the laws of God that are divinely written in our hearts than the very presence of the Holy Spirit who is the finger of God? By his presence, love is shed abroad in our hearts and this is the fulfillment of the law and the end of the commandment."

COROLLARY

Watch out scholars?

Great scholars who read much and abound in many books are not the best Christians. For all their books and their learning are "letter" and the soul's death. But people who do from a free and ready heart what the scholars read in books and teach others to do —they are the best Christians. But they cannot act from a free and ready heart unless they have love through the Holy Spirit. We must therefore dread it when, in our time, through the making of many books, people become learned scholars who do not know at all what it means to be a Christian.[13]

When, therefore, the question is raised why the gospel is called the word of the Spirit, a spiritual teaching, the word of grace and the clarification of the sayings of the old law and a knowledge that is hidden in mystery, etc., the answer must be that this is done only because it teaches where and wherefrom we can obtain grace and love, namely, from Jesus Christ whom the law promised and whom the gospel sets forth. The law commands that we should have love and that we should have Jesus Christ, but the gospel offers and presents both to us. Hence, it says in Ps. 45:2: "Grace is poured abroad in thy lips." When, therefore, we do not receive the gospel

---

[11] Cf. the discussion in connection with Rom. 4:7.
[12] Augustine, *De spir. et lit.*, 21, 36.
[13] *WA* 56, 338, 11 f.: "*Ideo nostro saeculo timendum est, ubi multiplicatis libris doctissimi fiunt homines, sed indoctissimi Christiani.*"

the Gospel

as gospel, it is nothing but "letter."[14] And it is gospel in the full sense of the word, where it preaches Christ; but where it rebukes and reproves and commands, it does nothing else but to shatter the presumptuousness of the self-righteous in order to make room for grace, so that they come to understand that they cannot fulfill the law by their own powers but only through Christ who shed the Spirit abroad in our hearts.

The real difference between the old and the new law is this: The old law says to those who are proud in their own righteousness: You must have Christ and his spirit; the new law says to those who humbly recognize that they lack all righteousness and who seek Christ: Behold, here is Christ and his spirit! They, therefore, that interpret the gospel as something else than "good news," do not understand the gospel. Precisely this must be said of those who have turned the gospel into a law rather than interpret it as grace, and who set Christ before us as a Moses.

"good news"

What shall we say then? Is the law sin? God forbid. But I do not know sin but by the law; **for I had not known concupiscence** *if the law did not say: Thou shalt not covet. But sin, taking occasion by the commandment, wrought in me all manner of concupiscence. For without the law sin was dead. And I lived some time without the law. But when the commandment came, sin revived, and I died. And the commandment that was ordained to life, the same was found to be death to me. For sin, taking occasion by the commandment, seduced me and by it killed me. Wherefore the law indeed is holy and the commandment holy, and just, and good. Was that, then, which is good made death unto me? God forbid. But sin, that it may appear sin, by that which is good, wrought death in me; that sin, by the commandment, might become sinful above measure. For we know that the law is spiritual; but I am carnal, sold under sin. For that which I do, I understand not. For I do not that good which I will; but the evil which I hate, that I do. If then I do that which I will not, I consent to the law, that it is good. Now then it is no more I that do it, but sin that dwells in me. For I know that there dwells not in me, that is to say, in my flesh, that which is good. For to will is present with me; but to accomplish that which is good, I find not. For the good which I will, I do not; but the evil which I will not, that I do. Now if I do that which I will not, it is no more I that do it, but sin that dwells in me. I find then a law, that when I have a will to do good, evil is present with me. For I am delighted with the law of God, accord-*

[14] *WA* 56, 338, 20: "*Ideo evangelium, si non recipiatur, ut loquitur, similiter est litera.*"

ing to the inward man. But I see another law in my members, fighting against the law of my mind, and holding me captive in the law of sin that is in my members. Unhappy man that I am, who shall deliver me from the body of this death? The grace of God, by Jesus Christ, our Lord. Therefore, I myself with the mind serve the law of God but with the flesh the law of sin. (Rom. 7:7–25.)

That, beginning with this passage until the end of the chapter, the apostle speaks in his own name and as a spiritual person and not at all as a carnal person, Blessed Augustine first asserts extensively and persistently in his book against the Pelagians.[15] Hence, he says in the twenty-third chapter of the first book of his *Retractations*,[16] where he deals again with his exposition of this passage: "When the apostle says: 'We know that the law is spiritual, but I am carnal' (Rom. 7:14), I did not want to understand this as in any way spoken by the apostle in his own name, because he was already spiritual, but with reference to a man who is subject to the law because he is not yet under grace. In this way I earlier understood these words, but later, having read several interpreters of the divine sayings whose authority impressed me greatly, I considered them more carefully and came to see that they can also be understood with reference to the apostle himself."

And in the second book against Julian, he writes:[17] "Behold, it is not, as you think, some Jew who says: 'I see a different law in my members, warring against the law of my mind,' etc. (Rom. 7:23), but according to Blessed Ambrose, it is the apostle Paul who speaks here in his own name." And, a little farther on, he quotes Blessed Ambrose from his book *On the Sacrament of Regeneration*:[18] "We must struggle against the flesh. Paul struggled against it. At last he says: 'I see a different law in my members, warring against the law of my mind.' Are you stronger than Paul? Have no confidence in the sedulous flesh and do not entrust yourself to it, since Paul exclaims: 'For I know that in me, that is, in my flesh, no good dwells: for to will is present with me, but to accomplish that which is good is not' (Rom. 7:18)."

Likewise, quoting the same author from the book *On Paradise*, he says:[19] "Again, at another place of the same work, the same teacher writes: Paul, he says, is assailed and sees the law of his

---

[15] Cf. Augustine, *Contra duas epistolas Pelagian.*, 1, 10, 17.
[16] Augustine, *Retract.*, I, 23.
[17] Augustine, *Contra Jul.*, II, 5, 13 (quoting Ambrosiaster, *De paradiso*, 12, 54).
[18] Augustine, *Contra Jul.*, II, 5, 14 (quoting Ambrose, *De sacramento regenerationis vel de philosophia*, a work that was lost).
[19] Augustine, *Contra Jul.*, II, 5, 13 (quoting Ambrosiaster, *De paradiso*, 12, 60.)

flesh warring against the law of his mind. Paul says: 'For the good which I will I do not; but the evil which I will not, that I do.' (Rom. 7:19.) And still you think that man is helped by knowledge in so far as it increases his displeasure at his transgression?" etc. And most clearly of all, he makes the same point in the same work from the sixth chapter to the end.[20]

But let us bring forth this same insight from the very words of the apostle: First, this whole passage clearly reveals disapproval and hatred of the flesh and love for the good and the law. Now such an attitude is not characteristic of a carnal man, for he hates and laughs at the law and follows the inclinations of his flesh.

Yet a spiritual man fights with his flesh and bemoans the fact that he cannot do as he wills. But a carnal man does not fight with it but yields and consents to it. Hence, this well-known judgment of Blessed Augustine: "The will to be righteous is a large part of righteousness."[21]

And in Wisd. of Sol. 9:15, the Preacher says: "The corruptible body is a load upon the soul, and the earthly habitation presses down the mind," i.e., the mind which "muses much" (i.e., which plans and devises many actions)—a Scriptural text that briefly expounds the entire passage that is before us. For the "mind"[22] here is the same "mind"[23] against whose law the apostle says the law of the members is warring. And where the Preacher says "muses much," the apostle says here: "With the mind I serve the law of God" (Rom. 7:25), and again: "When I have the will to do good, evil is present with me" (Rom. 7:21). And "For I am delighted with the law of God according to the inward man." (Rom. 7:22.)

The same thought that is expressed in this passage is to be found also in Gal. 5:17: "For the flesh lusts against the spirit, and the spirit against the flesh; for these are contrary to one another"; "that you do not do the things you would." And at another place: "I chastize my body and bring it into subjection, lest perhaps, when I have preached to others, I myself should be rejected." (I Cor. 9:27.)

The first word, then, which proves that a spiritual man is speaking here is this: **But I am carnal** (Rom. 7:14). Because it is characteristic of a spiritual and wise man that he knows that he is carnal, that he is dissatisfied with himself and hates himself, and that he

---

[20] Cf. *ibid.*, VI, 23 ff., 70 ff.
[21] Cf. Augustine, *Ep.* 127, 5. Cf. the discussion on Rom. 4:7, also the Corollary on Rom. 3:20.
[22] *"Sensus."*
[23] *"Mens."*

praises the law of God because it is spiritual. Conversely, it is characteristic of a foolish and carnal man that he thinks he is spiritual or that he is satisfied with himself and that he loves his life here in this world.[24]

A second word is this: **For that which I do, I understand not** (Rom. 7:15), which Blessed Augustine interprets[25] to mean "I do not approve," perhaps because a spiritual man who lives by the mind has sense only for what belongs to God; hence, he does not sense or understand the evil he does. Just as, conversely, he has a keen sense and understanding for what he does not do, namely, the good. "The carnal man, however, perceives not these things that are of the Spirit of God and he cannot understand them" (I Cor. 2:14), but he readily understands what he does, i.e., he approves of it, for, as we read below in Rom. 8:5: "For they that are according to the flesh, mind the things that are of the flesh; but they that are according to the Spirit, mind the things of the Spirit." Therefore, to turn this around, those who are according to the Spirit do not mind the things of the flesh, though they do them, and those who are according to the flesh do not mind the things of the Spirit.

But one can also interpret the phrase simply in this way, as I have done in the Gloss: "I do not understand" means: I am being deceived in so far as I am carnal, and sin seduces me when I do evil. For as a spiritual man I understand only the good, and yet I do what I neither care for nor want to do, namely, evil; in other words: It is not from intention or a considered choice that I do evil; I elect, rather, the good; nevertheless it happens that I do the opposite. A carnal man, however, has a full understanding of all this, for he wants to do evil because he plans, strives, and chooses to do it. And if he ever does anything good, he does so accidentally.

The third word: **For I do not that good which I will, but the evil which I hate, that I do.** (Rom. 7:15.) Yet the Scripture says of the carnal man: "Evil he has not hated" (Ps. 36:4). For if they had hated it, they would not perpetuate it by their action, but they would exert themselves in fighting against it.

The fourth word: **I consent to the law that it is good.** (Rom. 7:16.) The law wants the good, and he wants the good, and so they agree with one another. A carnal man, however, does not do this, but he always disagrees with the law and he would rather that there were no law (if this were possible). And so he does not want the good but evil. And even though he may do good (as I have said before), he does not really know it, because he acts from the

[24] Cf. John 12:25.
[25] Cf. Augustine, *Propos. ex ep. ad Rom.,* 43.

slavish compulsion of fear, always with the strong desire to do the opposite if he can get away with it.

From this we must not think that the apostle wants us to understand his statement that he does the evil he hates and that he does not do the good he wants to do, in a moral and metaphysical sense as if he did no good but only evil; to ordinary human understanding, this may seem to be the meaning of his phrase. But he wants to say that he does not do the good as often and to such an extent and as readily as he would like. For he wants to act from utter single-mindedness, freedom, and cheerfulness, unmolested by the resistance of the flesh, and this he cannot do. It is as with a man who seeks to be chaste: he does not want to be assailed by any excitement but he wants to realize chastity without difficulty. But the flesh does not let him do this; with its inclinations and drives, it makes chastity a most troublesome burden and it stimulates unclean desires however unwilling the spirit may be. He that sets out to watch, to pray, and to help his fellow man will always find that the flesh is rebellious and that it plots and desires something else.

Hence, we must take special note of the fact that the apostle makes a distinction between "to do" and "to accomplish," as Blessed Augustine extensively explains at the end of the third book against Julian.[26] "To do" he takes to mean here to try, to plot, to stimulate desires, to will, etc. Without letup, all these set the flesh against the spirit and the spirit against the flesh. For if he meant by "to do" "to fulfill by action," he could not possibly say: "The evil that I will not I do, but the good I will I do not," for in these words he describes very obviously the warring of the flesh against the spirit. For to say: he wants to do something else than he does means: he takes pleasure in the good and he has a will that is ready to do the good by the love that is diffused in it by the Spirit; and yet he cannot fulfill and accomplish what he wants to do, because the flesh resists and concupiscence opposes his will. If he could fulfill and accomplish what he wants, he would do the good cheerfully and without resistance, for this is what his will wants to do. But now he does not act in this way, for he does not do what he wants to do, but he does what he does not want to do.

Now a man who does not know what struggling is and who yields to the flesh and obeys its desires without putting up any resistance, does not say: "What I will not I do," for he does not take delight in the opposite of what he does but in what he does in fact. But "to accomplish" means to realize what one wants to

26 Augustine, *Contra Jul.*, III, 26, 62.

do or desires. So the spirit accomplishes the good it wants to do when it acts without protest according to the law of God. But this cannot be done in this life, for "to accomplish that which is good, I find not."

The flesh, however, accomplishes what it wants to do in so far as it fulfills its desires with joy and without any struggle and hesitation. This is the way of this life, nay, rather, it is a sign of death; it shows that the world is lost: it is so easy to do evil. Hence, I maintain that this word proves that Paul speaks here not as a carnal man but as a very spiritual man.

The fifth word: **It is no more I that do it, but sin that dwells in me.** (Rom. 7:20.)

So it is not he that sins, because his flesh covets without his consent; indeed, strictly speaking, he himself does not covet, because he does not agree with the coveting of his flesh. And yet he says: "The good that I will, I do not." For one and the same person is spirit and flesh; thus what the flesh does the whole man is said to do. And yet what resists is not the whole man but is rightly called a part of him. Both then are true: it is he that acts and yet it is not he.

It is as with a rider: When his horse does not trot exactly as he wishes, it is he and yet not he that causes it to trot as it does. For the horse is not without him nor he without the horse. But a carnal man does always what sin does, because he always agrees with the law of his members. For in this case, mind and flesh are held together not only by one person but also by one will.

The sixth word: **For I know that there dwells not in me, that is to say, in my flesh, that which is good.** (Rom. 7:18.)

Observe how he attributes the flesh to himself as a part of himself, as if he himself were flesh. This is why he said before: "I am carnal," and so he now confesses himself to be not good but evil because he does evil. Because of the flesh, he is carnal and evil, for the good is not in him and he does evil; because of the spirit, he is spiritual and good, for he does the good. *We must note, therefore, that the words "I will" and "I hate" refer to the spiritual man or to the spirit, but "I do" and "I work" to the carnal man and to the flesh.* Just because one and the same man as a whole consists of flesh and spirit, he attributes to the whole man both of the opposites that come from the opposite parts of him. Thus there comes about a *communio idiomatum:*[27] one and the same man is spiritual and carnal, righteous and sinful, good and evil. Just so the one person of Christ is at the same time both dead and alive,

---

[27] "Communion of proper qualities." Cf. E. Vogelsang, *Die Anfänge von Luthers Christologie* (Berlin, 1929), p. 178n.

both suffering and blessed, both active and inactive, etc., because of the *communio idiomatum,* even though there belongs to neither of his two natures what is characteristic of the other, for, as everyone knows, they differ absolutely from each other.

But this applies in no way to the carnal man; he is nothing but flesh in his whole person because the Spirit of God did not remain in him. The carnal man can therefore not say: "in me, that is to say, in my flesh," as if he were by his will something else than flesh, but he is identical with his flesh by virtue of his yielding to the desires of the flesh, just as man and wife are figuratively one flesh,[28] yet in the manner of harlots and fornicators.

In the light of this, we can better understand what the apostle meant before by his parable about the woman that is free when her husband dies. The application of this parable does not seem to fit, in view of the fact that he says that the soul itself, this is to say, the woman rather than the husband, must die in order to be set free, while the husband, i.e., the passions of sin, remains behind, but is being held captive, etc. However, the apostle who has respect for personal identity, sees in everybody a marital union, the flesh representing the woman and the soul or the mind, the man. When they agree in the same desiring, they are one flesh as Adam and Eve were. But when the mind, like the husband of the flesh, dies a spiritual death, then we become dead to the law in our whole person and thus are set free in our whole person. With respect to the flesh as well as to the spirit, we are one and the same, the husband who has become dead to the law and the woman who is freed from the law. And it is the law which produced this husband and this marriage, i.e., it stimulated desire and caused it to become stronger, and thus it furnished the occasion for the agreement between the mind and the flesh.

So then, on account of the flesh we are the woman, i.e., carnal, and, on account of the spirit, we are the husband who yields to the flesh, and thus we are at the same time dead and set free. For this double use falls to the whole person, even though the parts that bring it about are different. This is so because the parts communicate their individual qualities to the whole. Hence, the apostle says: "Therefore you also are become dead" (Rom. 7:4), even though it is only according to the inner man that we became dead and were set free from the law. This likewise belongs to the whole man on account of the inner man, and it is communicated also to the flesh or the outer man. For the flesh, too, is no longer enslaved

---

[28] In the moral exegesis of Gen. 2:18 ff., Lyra attributes to Augustine the comparison of the relation between reason and sensuality with that between husband and wife. (Cf., e.g., *De opere monachorum,* 32, 40.)

to the law or to sins, but it is freed from them because of the inner man who is set free. Together with him whose wife it is and was, it is one and the same man.

The seventh word: **For to will is present with me, but to accomplish that which is good I find not.** (Rom. 7:18.)

This "to will" is the readiness of the spirit which love brings forth. It is this promptitude which he means in saying: "The good that I will I do not" (Rom. 7:19), and it is meant also in Ps. 1:2: "He delights in the law of the Lord." But here he says: "To will is present with me," i.e., the good pleasure and delight in the good which the law commands, as he says farther on: "I delight in the law of God after the inward man" (Rom. 7:22), but because of the opposition of the flesh, he finds it impossible "to accomplish" this good of the law. He does not want to covet, and in his judgment it is good not to covet; nevertheless, he covets and thus he does not accomplish what he wills, and he fights with himself. But because spirit and flesh are so closely connected with each other that they are one, although they feel differently, he attributes to himself as a whole person what both are doing, as if he were at one and the same time wholly flesh and wholly spirit.

Yet he is clear in what he says here and he is able to meet the following objection: If you do not do what the law commands, and if, instead, you do what you do not want to do and do not what you want to do, in what way do you then not sin? For his answer is that he does the good but that he does not accomplish it, because he does not extinguish the coveting of the flesh.

How, then, can it be that a thoroughly carnal man, who prefers not to do the good, can have this kind of will, a will which the First Psalm attributes to a blessed man and which only the Holy Spirit gives through love? Only if one does extreme violence to this passage, can one make it say such a thing, indeed, only if one badly maltreats the words "I will," "I will not," "to will," etc.

The eighth word: **I find, then, a law that when I have a will to do good, evil is present with me** (Rom. 7:21), i.e., I find a contrary law within me when I am willing and ready to act according to the law of God. But one cannot say of a carnal man that he is willing. That is why it says in Ps. 112:1: "Blessed is the man that fears the Lord: he shall delight exceedingly in his commandments." Indeed, God has arranged it so that when this concupiscence resists a willing person and his good pleasure, it thereby makes this will all the more able to accomplish its end and inflames it to a hatred of all coveting that is greater than if it did not resist. For it causes the will to turn against it, and the more it resists and covets, the more it increases the hatred against itself. It is as with a man who is angry—the more the one who insulted him presses in upon him, the angrier he makes him. But a carnal man does not burn with such indignation, nor has he any resistance, because he lets himself be carried away and he follows along.

Nor does he know "that evil is present within him." For nobody knows the evil that is in him unless he is established in the good above evil, from where he can judge and discern the evil that is in him, just as we discern darkness only by the light, measure a contrast by the opposite, and judge what is worthless by that which we treasure. So then, if the spirit were not in the light, it would not see or bemoan the evil of the flesh that is present with it. This is made evident by those who are lost in the world and by the proud.

The ninth word: **For I delight in the law of God according to the inward man.** (Rom. 7:22.)

Observe that he says expressly that he has an inward man. But this is nothing else than the spiritual man, for without the spirit the whole man is "the old man" and the outward man. But the inward man is a clean mind and conscience and he takes his delight in the law of God. "I delight in the law of God," he says, i.e., "How sweet are thy words to me" (Ps. 119:103) and "The law of thy mouth is good to me" (Ps. 119:72). To a carnal man, however, they are bitter and harsh and utterly hateful, for a will that is afflicted with sin-fever detests them, even though it may seem to him as well as to others that he loves them from fear of punishment. As we have stated several times, this delight comes from the Holy Spirit through love, without which it is impossible to love the law and its righteousness; indeed, man detests righteousness more violently because he is in the law than he would if he were without the law, for he hates it that he is given to know what he does not desire, or, rather: the opposite of what he desires.

The tenth word: **But I see a different law in my members, warring against the law of my mind.** (Rom. 7:23.)

This shows that he speaks as a fighter who stands in between two opposite laws, but not as a defeated one for whom, as is the case with a carnal man, there is no longer a warring between the law of the members and the law of the mind, because the mind has surrendered. Indeed, he shows that he is dedicated in service to only one law and that he is withstanding another law that wars against him and that he refuses to serve it, or, rather, that he struggles with it. As everyone knows, one never hears of such a conflict or of a complaint about such a conflict in a carnal man.

The eleventh word: **Wretched man that I am! Who shall deliver me from the body of this death?** (Rom. 7:24.)

This shows even more clearly than the foregoing that a spiritual man is speaking here. For he sighs and grieves and longs to be delivered. Certainly no one will declare himself wretched except one who is a spiritual man. For perfect self-knowledge is perfect humility, and perfect humility is perfect wisdom, and perfect wisdom is perfect spiritualness. Hence, only a perfectly spiritual man can say: "Wretched man that I am!" A carnal man, however, does not long to be delivered and broken up, but he greatly abhors the dissolution of death and is unable to recognize his wretchedness.

So then, when Paul says here: "Who will deliver me from the body of this death?" he says exactly what he says elsewhere: "I desire to be dissolved and to be with Christ" (Phil. 1:23). For this reason, it is astonishing that it could have entered anyone's mind that the apostle speaks these words in the person of the old and carnal man, words which reflect such remarkable perfection, as if it were necessary for the apostle, like a hypocrite, to think and speak only well of himself, i.e., to praise himself and to deny that he is a sinner and thus not to praise grace but to deny its existence.

Indeed, it is a great consolation to us to learn that such a great apostle was involved in the same grievings and afflictions in which we find ourselves when we wish to be obedient to God!

The twelfth word: **Therefore, I myself with the mind serve the law of God, but with the flesh, the law of sin. (Rom. 7:25.)**

This is the most telling passage of all. Notice that one and the same man serves both the law of God and the law of sin, that he is righteous and at the same time he sins. He does not say: "My mind serves the law of God," nor "My flesh serves the law of sin," but he says, "I, this whole man, this person here, stand in this double servitude." He therefore gives thanks that he serves the law of God and he asks for mercy that he serves the law of sin.

Who can say of a carnal man that he serves the law of God? Notice, then, what I stated before: The saints in being righteous are at the same time sinners; they are righteous because they believe in Christ whose righteousness covers them and is imputed to them, but they are sinners because they do not fulfill the law and are not without sinful desires. They are like sick people in the care of a physician: they are really sick, but healthy only in hope and in so far as they begin to be better, or, rather: are being healed, i.e., they will become healthy. Nothing can harm them so much as the presumption that they are in fact healthy, for it will cause a bad relapse.

It is from this certain knowledge that, in the second chapter above,[29] the apostle speaks out so boldly against the self-righteous

[29] Cf. Rom. 2:1, 21 ff.

who set themselves up as judges over the evildoers while they themselves were no different, who preached that one must not steal while they themselves were thieves, etc. Though he did not know anything about their outward works, he was nevertheless very certain that as long as they are outside grace, they act inwardly in their hearts against the law. For if a spiritual man who wants to do what he should does not do what he should, how much more does a carnal man not do what he should, in view of the fact that he does not want but must be forced to do what he should! Thus "a spiritual man judges things, and he himself is judged of no man." (I Cor. 2:15.)

From here we can understand at last what David means when he says: "For this let everyone that is godly pray unto thee at the proper time" (Ps. 32:6), and why Christ repudiated his wife, the synagogue, on account of her ugliness.[30] For she does not want to acknowledge her wickedness and confess it to God's mercy, but she imagines herself to be righteous and holy. But we have dealt sufficiently with everything else, above in ch. 4 of the letter before us.

Without the law sin was dead. (Rom. 7:8.)

Blessed Augustine explains this passage together with the one that follows it with reference to the time of infancy when reason is not yet used. In the second book against Julian,[31] he says: "A little child that does not yet have the use of reason lives by his own will neither in the good nor in evil. But as he grows older and reason awakens, the commandment comes and sin revives, and, when it begins to fight him as he grows, then there will appear what was latent in the infant; it either conquers and will take domination over him, or it will be conquered, and he will be healed." The law comes to life and sin begins to appear when he begins to recognize the law; then concupiscence, which was latent in infancy, breaks forth and becomes manifest. And when it breaks forth in adolescence, then it brings fully to the fore what lay concealed in infancy. Just so, a young plant does not yet show what kind of fruit it will bear; but when it is in foliage and it bears fruit, one knows what kind of tree it is.

We can find a still profounder meaning in this: There are people who, in their mental attitude, are children, even if they are a hundred years old. They are those who let themselves be bewitched by a messenger of Satan that appears to them in the form

30 In medieval art, the church and the synagogue were often represented as two women, one ugly, the other beautiful, etc.
81 Augustine, *Contra Jul.*, II, 4, 8.

of a spiritual good. For this good they long more ardently than an adulterer longs for a woman or a miser for money, and so they forsake the law and the obedience of God, like the Jews, heretics, schismatics, individualists, and nonconformists[32] who have no sin because, as far as they are concerned, the law is not yet given. But if they knew the law against which they sin, they would doubtless recognize their sin at once, because they burn with pious zeal for the law. When, therefore, the law comes to them, sin is awakened in them. Then they long even more ardently for the realization of their special concerns and are even more strongly excited to anger against the law, so that they come to hate it because it prohibits to them what in their own imagination they have chosen to regard as law-conformity. So then when the law says: "You shalt not covet," all coveting is so strictly forbidden that whatever one covets besides God, even if it is coveted for the sake of God, is sin.

This is why many invite their own ruin when they love to practice piety and engage in prayers, studies, readings, devotions, meditations, and other such works as if they alone were good and well pleasing to God, but when they are called upon to render some mean service they get angry and provoked. Fools that they are, they do not know that it is not good works of some kind or number that God requires of them but a quiet and meek and obedient spirit. As it says in Ps. 51:16: *"For if thou hadst wanted it, I would have given sacrifice; with burnt offerings thou wilt not be delighted"* (i.e., thou dost not care for the good works, whatever they may be, that we have chosen to do). What then? *"A sacrifice to God is an afflicted"* (i.e., broken) *"spirit;*[33] a contrite" (i.e., broken) *"and humbled"* (i.e., contrite) *"heart, O God, thou wilt not despise"* (Ps. 51:17), i.e., a heart and spirit which are not hardened by an obstinacy of mind but can be guided and broken in to do thy will. People of such a spirit do not choose their work but they expect to be chosen for it whatever it may be. And all this in order that "he may open our lips and that our mouth shall show forth his praise" (Ps. 51:15). For people who choose on their own initiative what work they shall do cannot refrain from praising themselves. Instead of pleasing God and thereby themselves, they please only themselves even when they want to please God.

We should know that the devil disturbs everyone's mind in order to make void his vocation and in order to seduce and per-

[32] Cf. Ps. 80:13 and the discussion on *monius* (individualist) and *singularis* (nonconformist) in relation to Rom. 4:7.

[33] Luther depends here on Reuchlin's exegesis in *Septem psalmi poenitentiales, ad loc.*

suade him to something to which he is not called, as if God were
stupid and did not know whereto he wanted to call anyone. In
this way, the devil is always contending against the wisdom of God
and is trying to make God appear foolish in our eyes in order to
mislead us to the idolatrous notion that God wills what in fact
he does not want. These are certainly the gods of the house of Israel for whom altars have everywhere been set up at all street
corners throughout Jerusalem (Jer. 11:13).[34]

It is no more I that do it, but sin that dwells in me. (Rom. 7:17.) *anti-*
So then, is it not true that the treacherous metaphysics of Aris- *Aristotle*
totle and traditional philosophy have deceived our theologians?
For did they not believe to know that sin is done away with in
baptism or penance, so that they thought it absurd that the apostle
says: **"but sin that dwells in me"!** Thus it was chiefly this word
that gave them offense, so that they came to the false and noxious
opinion that the apostle was speaking here not in his own name
but in the name of a carnal man. And over against his various
and very emphatic assertions in many letters, they insist on talking nonsense by saying that he could not possibly have any sin.[35]

[34] Here is Luther's gloss on Rom. 7:9 (*WA* 56, 68, 5 ff.): "*I lived some time
without the law. But when the commandment came, sin revived.* So it is
with the proud heretics and the moralists. Because they do not know that
the law goes against them, it is impossible for them to know their sins.
Hence they are also incorrigible. But if they recognized the law, they would
immediately recognize their sin and it would revive, the same sin which
until now was dead to them."

[35] And here is Luther's gloss on Rom. 7:10 (*WA* 56, 68, 9 ff.): "*And the commandment that was ordained to life, the same was found to be unto death to
me.* One must not think, as Lyra and others say, that the apostle speaks here
in the name of a man who is in darkness and not in his own name. Neither
does he speak of a crass darkening of the mind that does not even superficially know the law. But he speaks in his own name and in the name of
all saints about that darkness in the very depth of our heart because of
which even the saints and the wisest of men do not have a perfect knowledge of themselves and therefore also not of the law. As David says, 'Who
can understand his errors?' [Ps. 19:12]. And who can, therefore, understand the law, inasmuch as it is impossible for anyone to understand the
law without discerning also every one of his sins? For the law touches every
sin, as Ps. 12:6 says, 'The words of the Lord are refined seven times.' Hence
if there is someone who thinks that he understands the law, at least with
respect to himself, as it says, 'Thou shalt not covet,' he is foolish and proud.
And this the heretics do! With the exception of Christ, it happens to every
man who is righteous, that as he progresses from concupiscence to purity,
he also progresses from ignorance of the law to an understanding of it.
Hence every saint must necessarily pray in the words of Ps. 25:7: 'Remember not the sins of my youth and my ignorances.' 'Of my youth,' i.e., the
hidden sins which also the spiritual man has who is already renewed. Only

This foolish opinion has led to a most harmful deception: people who are baptized or have received absolution think that they are at once without any sin; they become secure in the feeling that they have obtained righteousness and they do nothing because they are not conscious of any sin they should fight against and purge out under groaning and tears and with sorrowful effort.

But we should know that sin is left in the spiritual man for the exercise of grace, for the humiliation of pride, and for the restraint of presumptuousness. For if we do not earnestly endeavor to struggle against sin, we already have it, even though we have ceased to commit any sin for which we could be condemned. For we are not called to a life of ease but to labor against our passions.[36] And they would not be without guilt (for they really are sins and damnable, indeed) unless God in his mercy did not impute them to us. But he does not impute them to those only who, invoking his grace, resolutely attack their faults and fight against them. In the light of this we say that *when a person goes to confession, he must not think that he can put down his burden and live quietly, but he must know that by putting down his burden he becomes a soldier of God*[37] *and thereby assumes another burden, namely, to fight for God against the devil and his own faults.*

If he does not know this, he will soon relapse. *If therefore, he does not intend to fight henceforth against his sins, why does he pray for absolution and for his enrollment in the ranks of the soldiers of Christ?*

By the way, because they did not pay any attention to this, the interpreters[38] have misunderstood the apostle when he says in Heb. 12:1: "Let us put down every burden and the sin that surrounds us," etc. They took "burden" to mean the devil and "the sin that surrounds us" as evil works, while the apostle says that the works are the burden and the inward blemish of sin and the "tinder" "the sin that surrounds us."

We should note that the apostle does not mean to be under-

---

in faith, therefore, one can say, 'For I know my iniquity' [Ps. 51:3], in view of what follows: 'Thou hast made manifest to me the uncertain and hidden parts of thy wisdom' [Ps. 51:6]. These are the most hidden parts of the law: a way of knowing which we can never know entirely and which was revealed in order that we should believe it. He, therefore, that wants to confess only the sins he knows and that which is apparent to him, will confess only a few, and he cannot say: 'I acknowledge my sin unto thee,' etc. [Ps. 32:5]."

[36] *WA* 56, 350, 8 f.: "*Non enim ad ocium vocati sumus, sed ad laborem contra passiones.*"

[37] Lit., "*aggreditur militiam Christi*" ("He begins service as a soldier of Christ").

[38] Lyra interprets the "sin that surrounds us" as *occasiones peccati*, others, e.g., Thomas Aquinas (*ad Hebr.*), refer to the devil.

stood as saying that the spirit and the flesh are, so to speak, two separate entities. He understands them to be one whole just as a wound and the flesh are one. To be sure, the wound is something by itself and the flesh is something by itself, but because the wound and the flesh are one and because the wound is nothing else than wounded or weakened flesh, we can attribute to the flesh the properties of the wound. In the same way, one and the same man is at the same time spirit and flesh.[39] The flesh is his weakness or wound. In so far as he loves the law of God, he is spirit; but in so far as he covets, he shows the weakness of his spirit and the wound of his sin which must still be healed.[40] As Christ says: "The spirit is willing, but the flesh is weak." (Matt. 26:41.)

And Blessed Augustine says in the second book of *Against Julian*:[41] "When we speak of our faults we generally mean that which from the law of sin resists the law of the mind. When these faults are separated from us, they will not be somewhere else, but as soon as they are healed in us, they will be nowhere. Why do they not perish in baptism? Will you not admit that their guilt perishes but their weakness remains, not a guilt by which they themselves were guilty, but by which they made us guilty in the evil deeds to which they had drawn us? And their weakness does not remain as if they were something alive that has now become weak, but it is our own weakness." This beautiful authoritative work shows in what way concupiscence is that weakness in us which renders us unable to do the good. To be sure, it is guilty in itself, yet we become guilty by it only if we yield to it and commit a sin. This explains the remarkable fact that we are guilty and not guilty. For this weakness and we ourselves are inseparable;[42] hence, it is guilty and we are guilty until it ceases and is healed. Yet we are not guilty as long as we do act in accordance with it, for God in his mercy does not impute the guilt of weakness but the guilt of the will that yields to this weakness.

We can understand this dialectic[43] best in the light of the parable in the Gospel concerning the man who was left half-dead (Luke 10:30 ff.): When the Samaritan poured wine and oil on his wounds, he did not heal him right away but he began to get well. Just so the sick man of whom we are speaking is one and the same man who is weak and in process of being healed. In so far as he is healthy, he desires the good, but in so far as he is weak, he cannot help yielding to his weakness even though he does not want to.

[39] The *Gl. ord.* and Lyra.
[40] Lit., *"quod incipit sanari."*
[41] Augustine, *Contra Jul.*, II, 5, 12.
[42] *"Quia infirmitas illa not ipsi sumus."*
[43] *"Utrunque."*

ockham — see # 44

In the light of this we can see that the metaphysical theologians deal with a silly and crazy fiction[44] when they dispute about the question whether there can be opposite appetites in one and the same subject, and when they invent the notion that the spirit, i.e., reason, is something absolute or separate by itself and in its own kind an integral whole and that, similarly, opposite to it also sensuality, or the flesh, constitutes equally an integral whole. These stupid imaginations cause them to lose sight of the fact that the flesh is a basic weakness or wound of the whole man which grace has only begun to heal in his reason or spirit. For who can imagine that there are two such opposite entities in a sick person?—inasmuch as it is the same body that looks for health and yet is forced to conform to weakness; it is the same body that does both of these things. (*Against Julian*, Book 3, Chapter 20: "Concupiscence is an evil to such an extent that it must be overcome in actual combat, until, like a wound in the body, it will be healed by a perfect cure.")

sick person

In order to force these theologians, who love to deal with unrealities, to come to terms with a very concrete example, we ask: Suppose a house that had fallen to ruin is in process of reconstruction; is then its construction and standing structure one thing and its unfinished state something else? It is one and the same entity: we can rightly say of the same house which is being built that it is a house and that it is in process of becoming a house, but on account of its being unfinished, we can say at the same time that it is not yet a house and that it lacks the characteristics of a house. Thus "we who have the first fruits of the Spirit" (Rom. 8:23), and according to the apostle James "are become the beginning of God's creature" (James 1:18),[45] are "built up as a spiritual house" (I Peter 2:5). "And a building thus framed together grows into a holy temple of God." (Eph. 2:21.)

But that sin dwells within me. (Rom. 7:17.)

Blessed Augustine writes in Book 2 of *Against Julian*:[45a] "How can sin be dead in view of the fact that it works so many things in us despite our opposition? What are these many things except foolish and harmful desires which 'drown' those who consent to them 'in destruction and perdition'" (I Tim. 6:9), etc. "How, then,

---

[44] Ockham is the chief representative of the view that there is an essential difference between the potencies of the soul and that the *anima sensitiva* is separated from the *anima rationalis*. Gregor of Rimini, Gabriel Biel (II *Sent., d.* 16), and Trutvetter argue for the unity of the soul. Luther is here also dependent upon Lyra.

[45] Cf. Johann Haar, *Initium creaturae Dei. Eine Untersuchung über Luthers Begriff der "neuen Kreatur,"* etc. (Gütersloh, 1939).

[45a] Augustine, *Contra Jul.,* II, 9, 32.

can we say that this sin is put to death in baptism, and how can
we confess that it dwells in our members and works many desires
except in so far as it is dead with respect to that state of guilt in
which it held us and in which it rebels, even though dead, until
it is definitely buried and thus healed? However, it is now called
sin, not because it makes us guilty, but because it is the result of
the condition of guilt of the first man and because by its rebellion
it strives to draw us into this state of guilt."

This sin, then, is that original blemish of the "tinder," concerning which we have stated before that it would be better to say
that we die to it rather than that it dies to us and that while it continues in us, it is we who are turned away from it in this life by
grace, according to the saying of Ps. 81:7: "He turned his back
away from the burden."

(And in the twenty-third chapter of Book I addressed to Valer-
ian,[46] Blessed Augustine writes: "Concupiscence is no longer a sin
in the regenerate in so far as they do not consent to it, so that even
if one does not fulfill the word: 'You shall not covet,' one at least
fulfills the word: 'Go not after your lusts' [Ecclus. 18:30]. Yet it
is commonly called sin because, on the one hand, it came into being by a sin, and, on the other hand, it makes the sinner guilty
when it has vanquished him," i.e., it is sin with respect to its cause
and effect but not with respect to its essence.[47]

But to accomplish that which is good, I find not. (Rom. 7:18.)
There is a difference made here between "to do" and "to accomplish." Blessed Augustine writes at the end of Book 3 of *Against
Julian:*[48] "Remember what the apostle writes to the Galatians,
who were certainly baptized: 'But I say: Walk in the spirit and you
shall not fulfill the lusts of the flesh' (Gal. 5:16). He does not say:
'Do not have them,' because they were unable to be without them;
he says: 'You shall not fulfill them,' i.e., do not carry out their
works by consent of the will. For, if a man does not consent to the
lusts of the flesh, however real they are in their drives, they are
not fulfilled in works. Hence, when the flesh lusts against the
spirit and the spirit against the flesh, so that we do not do the
things we want to do, neither the lusts of the flesh are fulfilled,
however much they make themselves felt, nor are our good works
fulfilled, regardless of the extent to which they are done.

"For just as the concupiscence of the flesh is fulfilled when the
spirit consents to what it aims to do, so that it does not lust against
it but with it, so too our good works will be fulfilled when the

[46] Augustine, *De nupt. et concup.,* I, 23, 25.
[47] *"Causaliter et effectualiter, non formaliter."*
[48] Augustine, *Contra Jul.,* III, 26, 62.

flesh is ready so to consent to the spirit that it also does not lust against it. This is what we want in desiring to have the perfection of righteousness.

"But because we cannot accomplish this perfection in this corruptible flesh, he said to the Romans: 'To will is present with me, but how to accomplish what is good, I find not.' Or, as the Greek codices have it: 'To will is present with me, but not to accomplish the good,' i.e., it is not present with me to accomplish the good. He does not say 'to do' but 'to accomplish' the good. For 'to do good' is 'not to go after lusts' (Ecclus. 18:30), but 'to accomplish the good' is 'not to lust at all.'

"Therefore, to the word addressed to the Galatians: 'You shall not fulfill the lusts of the flesh,' there corresponds by way of contrast this word addressed to the Romans: 'How to accomplish [fulfill], I find not.' For neither are the lusts fulfilled in evil as long as they lack the consent of our will, nor is our willing fulfilled in the good as long as they continue to be active without our consent.

"The spirit therefore does a good work in not consenting to evil lusts, but it does not fulfill it, because it does not destroy the evil desires themselves. And the flesh feels an evil desire but does not fulfill it, because, in so far as the spirit does not consent to it, it does not achieve the realization of it that is subject to being damned."

From this passage we can derive the comforting thought that, even though the modern teachers[49] say the same thing about motives, about extinguishing the "tinder," about delight and consent, they speak with little authority, because they are not supported by the testimony of Scripture. But inasmuch as the ancient teachers[50] say the same thing much more plainly and in line with the apostles, we feel encouraged by the greater comfort they give us and also the readier help they offer us in the scruples of conscience, quite apart from the fact that, because of their presumption to speak with greater subtlety and clarity on this subject, the Scholastics obscured its meaning by too great a refinement of thought as they tried to translate divine speech into human form.

For this reason, it is nothing but futile and harmful imagination that they teach by way of interpreting Aristotle, and in words and metaphors that are utterly unenlightening, that virtues and vices stick to the soul like whitewash to a wall, like writing to a board, and like form to a subject. For by saying this they utterly failed to understand the difference between the spirit and the flesh.

[49] Trutvetter, among others, called Duns Scotus and Ockham *"recentiores doctores"* in contrast to Thomas Aquinas.
[50] *"Doctores antiqui"* are chiefly Augustine and Ambrose.

ROMANS, CHAPTER EIGHT

There is now therefore no condemnation to them that are in Christ Jesus, who walk not according to the flesh. For the law of the spirit of life, in Christ Jesus, has delivered me from the law of sin and of death. **For what the law could not do,** *in that it was weak through the flesh, God sending his own Son in the likeness of sinful flesh and of sin, has condemned sin in the flesh,[1] that the justification of the law might be fulfilled in us, who walk not according to the flesh but according to the spirit.* (Rom. 8:1–4.)

Where is free will now?[2] Where are those who try to make out that from our natural powers we can actually love God above all things? If only I said that we cannot fulfill the commandments, I should be subject to severe criticism. But here it is the apostle who says that it was impossible for the law to condemn sin, yes, that it was weak because of the flesh. This means, as I have repeatedly

[1] Luther's interlinear gloss reads as follows (*WA* 56, 74, 14 ff.): *"For what, when it was to liberate from the law of the members, but instead was weak, the law could not do,* namely, that it was to condemn and take away sin but instead increased it, *in that,* because it could not do it, *the law* itself *was* weak through the flesh, because it was not fulfilled. It can be strong only by the spirit of faith which is able to do what the law cannot do and thereby the law is made strong and established in its validity, according to the third chapter, above [Rom. 3:31]: 'We establish the law through faith': *God sending his own Son* by the incarnation *in the likeness of sinful flesh,* because he was not sinful flesh but, nevertheless, apart from sin, in all respects like us, as the serpent of brass in Num. 21:8–9 symbolizes, *and of sin,* i.e., through the punishment of sin which he bore for us, i.e., by the merit of his sin which was not in his flesh but which he took upon himself as he bore the punishment in his flesh, *he condemned,* i.e., he killed and destroyed *sin,* i.e., the tinder and sinful desire (concupiscence) *in the flesh,* that is to say: in our flesh."

[2] Cf. Luther's remarks on Rom. 4:7 ("*O Sawtheologen!*").

said above, that if we rely upon ourselves, we simply cannot fulfill the law and that it is no use to say that we can fulfill the law according to the substance of the deed but not according to the intention of the lawgiver, as if we could really produce from ourselves the willingness and ability to fulfill the law, but not in the way in which God wants it fulfilled, namely, in grace. If this is so, grace is useful, to be sure, but not necessary, and then also we do not carry a defect in our nature because of the sin of Adam but are sound in our natural powers. Thus philosophy stinks in our nostrils, as if reason could plead at all times for the best,[3] and we tell tall tales about the law of nature.

Now it is true that everyone knows the law of nature and that reason pleads for the best. But what best? It pleads for that which is best, not according to God's standards, but according to ours, in other words: it pleads for an evil kind of good. For it seeks itself and its own in all things but not in God. Faith alone does this in love.

Hence, all knowledge and virtue and whatever good we desire and search for in reliance upon our natural possibilities will turn out to be evil kinds of good, because they are not measured according to God's standard but according to that of the creature, i.e., according to our selfish ends. For how can one refer anything to God if one does not love him above everything else? And how can one love him if one does not know him? How can man know him if, by fault of the first sin, he is bound to darkness in all his thinking and feeling? So then, unless faith enlightens him and love sets him free, man cannot will or have or do anything good—he can do only evil even in case he does good.

COROLLARY

It is said that human nature has a general notion of knowing and willing good, but that it goes wrong in particulars.[4] It would be better to say that it knows and wills the good in particular things, but in general neither knows nor wills the good. This is so because it knows only its own good or what is good, honorable, and useful for itself, but not what is good for God and for others. Therefore it knows and wills mainly a good that is a particular good, indeed, that is good only for the individual self. And this is in agreement with the Scripture,[5] which describes man as curved

---

[3] Cf. Aristotle, *Eth. Nicom.* (ed. Bekker, I, 1102b, 15 f.).
[4] Luther has in mind the doctrine of synteresis and conscience. Cf. Biel, II *Sent., d.* 39, *q. un., a.* 1, *not.* 3E and *a.* 3, *dub.* 1; Trutvetter, *Physics* VIII, *Tract.* 1, *c.* 2, *De potentia intellectiva* (*synteresis, ratio, conscientia*).
[5] Cf. Isa. 2:9–22.

in upon himself to such an extent that he bends not only physical but also spiritual goods toward himself, seeking himself in all things.

Now this curvedness is natural; it is a natural defect and a natural evil. Hence, man gets no help from the powers of his nature, but he is in need of some more effective help from the outside. And this is love. Without it he constantly sins against the commandment: "You shall not covet," i.e., you shall not bend anything toward yourself or seek anything for yourself, but all your life, thought, and action shall be directed to God alone. Then he will know the good universally together with all particular goods, and he will judge everything (I Cor. 6:2).

In this sense, the commandment is impossible for us.

Hence, Blessed Augustine says in Chapter 16 of his book *On Grace and Free Will:*[6] "He commands what we cannot do in order that we should know what we shall ask of him. And this is faith which obtains by prayer what the law commands."

COROLLARY

Some think very highly of the light of nature and compare it to the light of grace,[7] but in vain, for it is darkness and the opposite of grace. This is why Job and Jeremiah curse it,[8] saying that it is an evil day and a very bad sight. For this light rose immediately after sin, as it is written: "And their eyes were opened" (Gen. 3:7)

For grace sets before itself no other object than God to whom it is moved and directs itself; it sees him alone; it seeks him alone and moves toward him in all things, and everything else it sees in between itself and God it passes by as if it did not see it, and simply turns to God. This is what it means to have a "right heart" (Ps. 7:10; 78:37) and a "right spirit" (Ps. 51:10).

Nature, on the other hand, sets before itself no other object than the self, to which it is moved and directs itself; it sees and seeks only itself and aims at itself in everything; everything else, even God himself, it bypasses as if it did not see it, and turns to itself. This is what it means to have a "perverse" and "wicked" heart (Ps. 101:4; Prov. 27:21).

As *grace* puts God in the place of everything else it sees, also in its own, and prefers him to itself, and seeks only what is God's

---

6 Augustine, *De gratia et lib. arb.*, 16, 32: *"Ideo iubet aliqua, quae non possumus, noverimus, quid ab illo petere debeamus. Ipso est enim fides, quae orando impetrat, quod lex imperat."*

7 Cf. Luther's exposition of Rom. 4:7. Duns Scotus, III *Sent.*, d. 14, q. 2, n. 4; Gabriel Biel, III *Sent.*, d. 14, q. un., a. 2L.

8 Cf. Job, chs. 31 ff.; Jer. 10:14.

and not its own, so *nature,* by contrast, puts itself in the place of everything, and even in the place of God, and seeks only its own and not what is God's. Thus it idolizes and absolutizes itself.[9] Then it turns God into an idol for itself, and the truth of God into a lie, and finally also all God's creatures and gifts. *Grace* is not content unless it sees God in and above all it sees, and it rejoices in wanting and wishing everything to have life and being in the glory of God. But *nature,* by contrast, regards everything it sees as worthless unless it serves to its advantage and makes itself available to it. It values only what it can use for its own enjoyment, advantage, and benefit.

This is spiritual whoring and wickedness and curvedness of the worst sort. One should therefore not call this kind of prudence light but darkness, and more correctly so, unless one wants to call it light because it observes and knows by reason and the senses. But in so far as it tends to turn all knowledge to itself, it is darkness in the full sense of the word. By its very nature it cannot help bending everything to itself. For it cannot love God and his law, as the apostle says here.

Here is the sign by which one can recognize all this: Nature is happy and content as long as it has everything it wants, but if this is not so, it is disturbed and disquieted. Not so grace. It remains neutral and loves and observes in everything only God's will, and it is content with itself and everyone else, no matter what may or does happen. Whatever God does and wills, it too wills, and it is glad in it regardless of how bitter it is. Indeed, it praises and blesses God at all times, also when something very troublesome and sad befalls it. It knows how to rejoice in sadness and to be sad in joy. The flesh cannot possibly do this in reliance upon its own powers.

For what the law could not do, **in that it was weak** *through the flesh.* (Rom. 8:3.)

Blessed Augustine comments on this text:[10] "The law was weak in so far as it did not fulfill what it commanded, not by its own fault, but 'through the flesh,' i.e., through men who, by seeking earthly possessions, did not love the righteousness of the law but preferred temporal advantages to it."

Now this happens when one observes the law for fear of punishment or from love of advantage, without having one's heart and mind in it, in other words: when one observes the law not because God so commanded and willed but because it promises something good and threatens with something evil.

[9] *"Ideo idolum est ipsa sibi primum et maximum."*
[10] Augustine, *Propos. ex ep. ad Rom.,* 48.

Only an utterly unrestrained readiness to love[11] performs an act or refrains from it, because this is God's good pleasure, without regard for any other good or without any fear for anything evil, apart from God's wanting it so. Nature is not capable of this, but only grace is, namely, the grace that is given by faith in Christ through the Holy Spirit.

COROLLARY

The phrase "the law was weak" must be referred to the heart and the inner disposition rather than to outward action. For people observed the law outwardly by their action, but inwardly in their heart they hated it, according to the saying of the psalm: "That speak peace with their neighbor but have mischief in their hearts" (Ps. 28:3), in other words: in themselves inwardly they cannot be as good as they outwardly appear to be.

Because he was aware of this, the apostle asserted so bluntly in the second chapter of this letter, as I have already pointed out, that those who taught that one must not steal were themselves thieves, etc. He knew with certainty that without grace they would not fulfill in their will what they taught by word of mouth and what they showed forth outwardly in their actions, in view of the fact that without grace all belong equally to that "mass of perdition"[12] of which it is written in Gen. 8:21: "The imagination and thought of man's heart are prone to evil from his youth" (and in no way to the good which the law commands).

God sending his own Son in the likeness of sinful flesh and **of sin, has condemned sin** *in the flesh.* (Rom. 8:3.)

Blessed Augustine comments on this passage:[13] "This is what our Lord's death accomplished: We no longer fear death and therefore we do not seek temporal goods nor fear temporal evils. This was the aim of the wisdom of the flesh on account of which the commandments of the law could not be fulfilled. But the Christian who is rid of this wisdom can fulfill the righteousness of the law, for he does not walk according to the flesh but according to the Spirit."

These words clearly show that we must take "sin" and "the wisdom of the flesh" to mean the same. For "to condemn sin" (Blessed Augustine says) is the same as "to be rid of the wisdom of the flesh." A man who is thus freed no longer fears death, nor does he love life. And because he loves only God, he fulfills the law. For

---

[11] Ellwein (p. 281) translates *"Solus amor voluntatis liberrimus": "Nur der vollkommen freiwillige Liebeswille."*

[12] Cf. Augustine, *De gratia et pecc. orig.,* 2, 29, 34.

[13] Augustine, *Propos. ex ep. ad Rom.,* 48.

a man who for God's sake does not fear death, and who does not love life more than God and thus hates himself in his heart, really loves God above everything. He that loves God more than himself certainly loves God above everything, for man loves nothing so much as himself. But this is an impossibility for the flesh; for it is the way of the wisdom of the flesh that man loves himself above everything, even above God.

If it were possible for the flesh to love God, "Christ died in vain" (Gal. 2:21), for then it would be whole and it would be a friend of God and the apostle would be mistaken in saying: "The wisdom of the flesh is not subject to the law of God, neither can it be" (Rom. 8:7). Thus we can once more refute the Scholastics who say that from purely natural powers the will can produce an act of the true love of God.[14] Moreover, it is an invalid argument of theirs to say that whatever the intellect can dictate as something that must be willed and done the will can will, and that therefore, in case the intellect dictates that God must be loved above everything, the will can will this.[15] We reply to this as follows: The conclusion is not correct nor is that which is subsumed under it. The conclusion should be this: Therefore, as it was told, the will can will that God must be loved above everything. But it does not follow from this that it is able to love God above everything, but it wills only with a feeble motive that this should be done, i.e., there is available only a tiny bit of that will that would be needed in order that what was commanded actually be done.

If this were not so, it would be meaningless to say, as everybody does, that the law was given in order to humiliate the proud who presumptuously rely on their own power to do good.

How, then, did Christ "condemn sin because of sin" or how did he bring it about by his death that we do not need to fear death and how did he rid men of "the wisdom of the flesh"? Only by the merit of his death! For it was by it that he earned for us the gift of the spirit and our liberation from "the wisdom of the flesh."

It is the spirit that kills "the wisdom of the flesh" and quickens the inner man and enables us to despise death and to give up life and to love God above everything, in accordance with the saying of The Song of Solomon: "For love is strong as death and jealousy as hard as hell" (S. of Sol. 8:6). (The Spirit also brings it about

---

[14] *"Voluntatem posse elicere actum dilectionis Dei super omnia ex puris naturalibus."*

[15] In part lit., according to Ockham I *Sent.*, d. 1, q. 2, concl. 1. Cf. Biel, II *Sent.*, d. 28, q. un., a. 2, concl. 1 and 2; Pierre d'Ailly, I *Sent.*, q. 2, a. 2 f. Cf. also Lyra's use of the term *"dictamen rationis, dictamen legis naturalis."*

that the concupiscence that is in us is condemned. For it is not our achievement but the gift of God that we hate ourselves and condemn all coveting and choose love. This is why the apostle says that it is God who has condemned and destroyed sin in our flesh. And he enables us to destroy it through faith in Christ by his Spirit that is shed abroad in our hearts [Rom. 5:5].)

Take note also of the fact that he does not say: "And on account of the sin in the flesh he condemned the sin in the flesh" (but rather, "on account of sin he condemned the sin in the flesh"), for he makes a distinction between sin and the sin in the flesh. For the sin by which the sin in the flesh is condemned is that punishment of sin which Christ took upon himself in his flesh. His flesh was without sin, yet it bore the likeness of the sin of the flesh for the sake of the punishment of sin. Thus it was that on account of the sin of him in whose flesh there was no sin, the sin which is in the flesh of everyone else was condemned.

For what the law could not do. (Rom. 8:3.)

The apostle says, "what the law could not do," rather than, "what we could not do," even though this inability is ours alone because we were too weak and powerless to fulfill the law. He does this because it is his way of speaking and because the occasion of his writing to the Romans demanded it. For he argues primarily against those who, relying on their natural powers, thought that, in order to obtain righteousness and good works, they were in need of no other help than the knowledge of the law, as the Jews did and as all who are proud do to this day. Out of the same haughtiness they all can say the words of Ex. 20:19: "Speak thou with us and we will hear" and of Ex. 19:8: "All that the Lord has spoken, we shall do." They all think that the law suffices them, and they are the more culpable in their error the more they think that the law can be fulfilled merely by outward deeds.

It is this empty confidence in the law and in their knowledge of it which the apostle reproves by saying that the law could not possibly accomplish what in their presumptuousness they assumed it could, namely, the abolition of sin and the attainment of righteousness. But this is not the fault of the law but of their foolish and empty regard for and trust in the law. For in itself the law is very good. It is just as with a sick man who wants to drink some wine because he is of the foolish opinion that he will thus be cured. When then the physician, not meaning to say anything at all against wine, tells him: "The wine cannot possibly cure you; it will only make you sicker," he does not put any blame on the wine but only on his foolish patient. For he needs some other kind of remedy in order to get well so that he can drink wine. So also our corrupted nature is in need of another medicine than the law, in order to become whole so that it can fulfill the law.

For they that are according to the flesh, mind the things that are of the flesh; but they that are according to the spirit, mind the things that are of the spirit. For the wisdom of the flesh is death; but the wisdom of the spirit is life and peace.[16] *Because* **the wisdom of the flesh is an enemy of God,** *for it is not subject to the law of God, neither can it be. And they who are in the flesh cannot please God. But you are not in the flesh, but in the spirit, if so be that the Spirit of God dwell in you. Now if any man have not the Spirit of Christ, he is none of his. And if Christ be in you, the body indeed is dead, because of sin; but the spirit lives, because of justification. And if the Spirit of him that raised up Jesus from the dead dwell in you, he that raised up Jesus Christ from the dead shall quicken also your mortal bodies, because of his Spirit that dwells in you. Therefore, brethren, we are debtors, not to the flesh, to live according to the flesh. For if you live according to the flesh, you shall die; but if by the Spirit you mortify the deeds of the flesh, you shall live.* (Rom. 8:5–13.)

It would be more appropriate to use uniformly throughout this chapter of the letter before us the word "prudence" rather than "wisdom" (as also Augustine and the Greek text have it).[17] All agree that prudence is directed to what one must do, but wisdom to what one must think about. And the apostle speaks here in the moral meaning and about what one must do.

Now, one practices prudence by choosing the good and by seeking to avoid evil. This is something twofold; therefore he describes here a twofold kind of prudence.

---

16 Luther's marginal gloss reads as follows (*WA* 56, 75, 21 ff.): "Gal. 5:19 ff.: 'Now the works of the flesh are manifest, which are these: fornication, uncleanness, lasciviousness, idolatry, sorcery, enmities, strife,' etc. 'But the fruit of the spirit is love, joy, peace,' etc. We should note that 'spirit' is here taken to mean the inner man, as the contrast between flesh and spirit shows. And farther down we read: 'The Spirit is life because of righteousness' [Rom. 8:10]. But the spirit, i.e., the inner man, must have the Holy Spirit. One may therefore regard these fruits of the spirit as fruits of the Holy Spirit. Hence it is more appropriate to understand by 'spirit' the inner man as if it were a good tree that brings forth good fruit and by 'flesh' a corrupt tree that brings forth evil fruit [Matt. 7:17]. It is also more appropriate to say that the Holy Spirit creates the good tree rather than that it is a good tree by itself."

17 Augustine, *Propos. ex ep. ad Rom.,* 49. Faber reads Rom. 8:7: *"sapientia"* (wisdom) for *"prudentia"* ("prudence"). The distinction was of some importance to the Scholastics. Cf. Biel, *Prolog. Sent., q.* 12, *a.* 2, *dub.* 1, where reference is made to Aristotle, *Eth. Nicom.,* VI, 3 ff.

The "prudence of the flesh" chooses what is to selfish advantage and it avoids what is harmful to the self. Moreover, it rejects the common good and chooses what harms the common spirit. This is the prudence that directs the flesh, i.e., concupiscence and self-will. It enjoys only itself and uses everyone else, even God; it seeks itself and its own interests in everything: it brings it about that man is finally and ultimately concerned only for himself. This is the idolatry that determines all he does, feels, undertakes, thinks, and speaks. Good is only what is good for him and bad only what is bad for him.

In the Scriptures, this curvedness, depravity, and wickedness are exposed many times under the names of fornication and idolatry. As we have said in connection with the sixth chapter of this letter, they are in the hidden depths of our nature, indeed, they are nature itself in so far as it is wounded and in ferment through and through—and this to such an extent that, without grace, it is not only incurable but also wholly unrecognizable. In order that we may recognize it more clearly, let us designate the stages of its range in terms of the objects of its concern, the objects of its "inordinate enjoyment," as the saying goes.[18]

External goods { riches / power / honors } parents / friends / family relatives / children / wife *(objects of "inordinate enjoyment")*

Physical goods: health   strength   beauty

Goods of the soul: talent memory intelligence prudence

Knowledge and skills { physical / mental } virtues { natural / acquired, etc. }

Corporal, i.e., human, *wisdom* such as { liberal arts / philosophy, etc. }

Intellectual wisdom { in the knowledge of and with respect to the mysteries of } { Scripture / Creation }

Affectional grace in righteousness, devotions, the gifts of the Spirit, meditations

God in so far as he is known[19] in his divine attributes

[18] On this term, cf. Ockham, I *Sent.*, d. 1, q. 4C; Biel, I *Sent.*, d. 1, q. 4, a. 2, concl. 1.

[19] "*Deus affirmative*"; cf. perhaps Dionysius Areopagita, *De coelest. hierarch.*, 2, 3.

All this, God has given to us men, clothing us, as it were, in a garment of many folds. And the "prudence of the flesh" clings to all these gifts. To be sure, not all men range over all of them, nor are all equally interested in the same one of them, but one is more, and another less, versed in one and the same; and one in several of them, and the other in only a few. Man, I say, turns all of them to himself, seeks his own good in them, and horribly makes an idol out of them. This he puts in place of the true God, in so far as he does not refer them to God, and he is unhappy when he is deprived of them. Hence, one cannot take any away from him against his will.

So there are some who refuse to give up even that of the lowest rank, say, riches; others are ready to part from riches but are unwilling to give up honor, and if they are, they refuse to part from children, parents, friends, etc.; but if they do renounce them, then they refuse to surrender health, beauty, or life—and so one could go on and notice the many very tight traps in which men are caught and their endless searchings. Human nature cannot disentangle itself from the smallest of these traps, and much less from all or from the larger ones. But grace will quickly set it free, as the Scripture says: "He will pluck my feet out of the snare" (Ps. 25:15). These human possibilities are "the snare of the fowler" (Ps. 91:3), not as if they turned into snares because this is their nature (for they were created good), but they become so by fault of the prudence of the flesh.

The "prudence of the spirit" chooses the common good and seeks to avoid what can harm the common life. It rejects self-interest and chooses what is disadvantageous to the self. For it directs the love that "seeks not its own" (I Cor. 13:5) but that which belongs to God and all his creatures. It regards as good only what is good to God and everyone and as evil what is evil to God and everyone. For its concern is only God as he is in himself and it is interested in anything only in relation to God.[20] Hence, it enjoys everything in God and with God.

How this can be, can easily be stated in words, but only the Holy Spirit can actually bring it about and only one who experienced it has any knowledge of it. It is the Spirit that causes so many things suddenly to disappear and to vanish into nothingness and to be regarded as worthless by the soul. And the soul that has inwardly turned away from everything seeks with Mary only the one thing needful (Luke 10:38). But as Martha passes through all this

[20] "Quia non habet obiectum aliud nisi Deum negative et omnia cum Deo negative."

and struggles with it, she is troubled about many things, "forgetting the things that are behind and stretching forward to the things that are before" (Phil. 3:13).

Now there are men who have renounced riches and profess poverty: their soul has really gotten out of this trap. But lo and behold, it falls into a worse one, namely, into self-will in connection with devotions or right living or in connection with learning and study or, what is not quite so bad, it falls into vainglory and the desire to be honored, etc. Thus, much effort is required until the "prudence of the flesh," entangled as it is in so many snares, is overcome by the "prudence of the spirit" under incessant prayers and with many tears. *Humility*

These are the traps which Saint Anthony saw everywhere in the world;[21] he bemoaned them and said: "Who can escape them all?" And he got the reply: "Only humility can." Now I have here enumerated eight big traps, but if one divides them into their parts, they become very many. And it is really true that, when someone has escaped the trap of wealth-seeking in one respect, say in so far as he despises money, he gets caught in it in another respect, say in so far as he longs for the ownership of land or other goods; and so it is with everything else.

So then, that which by fault of the prudence of the flesh is a snare and a stumbling block to man helps him on his way to God, thanks to the prudence of the spirit.

Hence, the apostle says: "They mind the things of the flesh," i.e., carnal goods which are objects of enjoyment. All those we have enumerated are of this kind.

The term "prudence of the flesh" refers not only to carnal pleasures but to everything this side of God that one can have in this life; the life to come, however, cannot be had in the created world but only in the Creator, and he is the good that is the concern of the prudence of the spirit.

Blessed Augustine says on this passage:[22] "By 'enemy of God' we mean a man who does not obey the divine law and this because of the prudence of the flesh, i.e., because he longs for temporal goods and dreads temporal evils. According to the conventional definition, prudence is the desire for goods and the avoidance of evils." Then he quotes the words of the apostle: "The prudence of the flesh is enmity toward God" and goes on to show that "enmity" *prudence*

---

21 *Vitae Patrum III, Verba Seniorum,* 129 (PL 73, 785).
22 Augustine, *Propos. ex ep. ad Rom.,* 49. Luther abbreviates Augustine's passages, interspersing his quotations with summaries and comments of his own.

means "not to be subject to the law of God," lest some Manichee
might think that some nature originating, so to speak, in an opposite principle constitutes the enmity toward God.

"But one obeys the law of God when this prudence has been
extinguished in order that it should be followed by the prudence
of the spirit which prevents us from hoping for temporal goods
and fearing temporal evils. It is characteristic of one and the same
nature of the soul that it has prudence of the flesh in so far as it
longs for 'the lower,' as well as prudence of the spirit in so far as
it chooses and loves 'the higher.' Just as it is characteristic of one
and the same nature of water that it congeals as it freezes and that
it evaporates as it is heated. Hence, the saying: 'The prudence of
the flesh is not subject to the law of God, neither can it be.' But
when water as it is heated steams and boils, one can no longer call
it snow."

So also the Lord says in Matt. 12:33: "Either make the tree good
and its fruit good; or make the tree evil or its fruit evil," in other
words: If the "prudence of the flesh," which is an evil tree, is not
changed into the "prudence of the spirit," which is a good tree, it
cannot produce good fruit even though it appears to bear good
fruit. The fruit does not produce the tree but the tree the fruit.

Works and actions do not produce virtue, as Aristotle says,[23]
but virtues determine actions, as Christ teaches. For a second act
presupposes the first one, and the prerequisite of an action is
substance and power just as there is no effect without a cause.

Now temporal goods, so we must understand, are everything
that is outside God whether we comprehend it with the senses or
with the mind, or whether it is life or knowledge or right living,
as we have said before. Similarly, we must regard as evil everything
that is opposite to these goods, such as death, ignorance, sin, etc.
A man who is prudent in spirit has no fear of them, just as he has
no love or special appreciation for temporal goods. But a man
who is prudent in the flesh has a horrible fear of death, stupidity,
sin, etc.

So then, if you feel that you dread death, instead of loving the
thought of it, you can take this as a most certain sign that you are
still involved in the "prudence of the flesh." Similarly, if you are
scared of sin and the judgment to come and if you despair on
account of your sin, this indicates that the prudence of the flesh
is still alive in you. We should not dread sin and death, not because
they are not to be feared and abhorred at all but for the purpose
of putting the prudence of the flesh in its place by recognizing it
for what it is, so that the weak may get busy freeing themselves

[23] Aristotle, *Eth. Nicom.*, III, 7; V, 9; V, 10.

from this horror and by the grace of God receive the hope of security. Those who are weak in this way are still under the law, unless they longingly turn their face toward grace that they may be torn away from their troubles.

The "prudent in spirit," however, love the will of God and hail it because they conform to it. So they are not frightened in the knowledge that by the will of God the Last Judgment will come and fill everything with horror when he displays his wrath, but they look forward to it with joy and pray that it may come soon. What others dread with the greatest horror is for them the object of purest joy, because, with a perfect will, they will what God wills. Whenever such a will prevails, there is neither pain nor dread, but there is the fulfillment of all one longed for and wanted, and the quiet achievement of what one had desired. As it says in Ps. 97:8: "The daughters of Judah rejoiced because of thy judgments, O Lord." And our Lord, having predicted the terrible things of the Day of Judgment, went on to say: "But when these things begin to come to pass, look up, and lift up your head, because your redemption is at hand" (Luke 21:28).

It is, therefore, useless for people after the manner of men to feel pity for themselves or others on account of the misery that awaits them. For we must not try to think how we may escape from this misery through fear, nor must we preach about it in such a way that people are filled with fright and terror at the thought of it, except in the case of those who wallow in the filth of the world, for they need to be scared into penitence. But people who are already penitent and full of sorrow for their sins are in need of preaching that encourages them to learn to wait with joy for what is to come and to ask that that Last Day may come soon. We do not escape the wrath of God and the misery and horror of the Last Judgment by fearing them but by loving them, and our conscience is quieted when we conform to the will of God.[24]

Of what use is it to fear the Day of Judgment? For a man who fears it hates it and does not want it to come. But now, it cannot possibly be that it will not come, and it cannot possibly be that it will come to bring benefit and salvation to one who hates its coming. It is the will of God and his good pleasure that it will come. One who resists his will and fears the Day of Judgment will therefore rightfully be condemned as a "rebel against God" (Num. 14:9).

Hence, the apostle is right when he says in the last chapter of II Timothy: "[There is laid up for me a crown of righteousness

[24] *Conformitas voluntatis Dei* (a favorite phrase of Gabriel Biel, and also of Bernard of Clairvaux and Staupitz).

which the Lord, the righteous judge, will give to me at that day],
and not to me only, but also to them that love his coming" (II Tim.
4:8). And Peter says in the last chapter of his second letter: "Seeing
that all these things are to be dissolved, what manner of people
ought you to be in holy conversation and godliness?" (II Peter 3:11.)
And to Titus, the apostle says: "We should live soberly, and
justly, and godly in this world, looking for the blessed hope and
coming of the glory of the great God," etc. (Titus 2:12 f.) And our
Lord says in Luke 12:36: "And you yourselves be like men who
wait for their lord when he shall return from the wedding."

None has vanquished this fear but Christ alone. He has overcome death and all temporal evils and even eternal death. Those
who believe in him have absolutely nothing more to fear, but
with a blessed feeling of pride, they can despise all those evils
and laugh at them and rejoice in them, knowing that they will
not perish and be swallowed up but that they will experience and
live to see even with their own eyes the victory that Christ has
won over those evils. So they can say: "O death, where is thy
sting?" (I Cor. 15:55).

Therefore, we cannot overcome death and its evils by power
and strength and we cannot escape them by running away from
them in fear but only by bearing them patiently and willingly in
weakness, i.e., without lifting a finger against them. This is the
lesson Christ teaches us by his example: he went confidently to
meet his Passion and his death.

**For whosoever are led by the Spirit of God, they are the sons
of God. (Rom. 8:14.)**

"To be led by the Spirit of God" means freely, promptly,
gladly to mortify the flesh, i.e., the old man in us, i.e., to despise
and renounce all that is not God, even ourselves. It means "not
to be afraid of death or of its friends, the savage race of penalties"[25]
and "to give up the vain joys of earth and its dirty, sordid fields"[26]
and readily to abandon all good things and to embrace evils instead. This is not the achievement of nature but of the Spirit of
God in us.

**For you have not received the spirit of bondage *again in fear;
but you have received the spirit of adoption of sons, whereby we
cry: Abba, Father.* (Rom. 8:15.)**

---

[25] Quoted from the hymn *"Virginis proles"* in the Breviary of the Augustinian Hermits. (Cf. Ficker, p. 366, n. 16.)
[26] This too is a line from a hymn of the Augustinian Breviary (*"Jesu corona
celsior, commune confessoris non pontificis"*).

The apostle formulates an antithesis, i.e., he puts one thing over against another and makes a comparison or a contrast. For "servant" and "son" are here put against one another as in John 8:35: "The servant abides not in the house forever, but the son abides forever." In the same way, the spirit of bondage is contrasted with the spirit of sonship and the fear of the servant with the love of the son. Hence, the term "bondage" must here be understood in an abstract sense as if, if one may say so, bondage were derived from "bond servant" as "sonship" is from "son."

"Bondage" must here be taken to mean "bondage to sin," as in John 8:34: "Everyone that commits sin is a servant of sin." The law could not liberate anyone from this bondage. For, by instilling the fear of punishment, it only compelled men to do the works of the law and thereby it did not mortify the doings of the flesh but rather increased them, for it deepened the hatred against the law and also the inclination and desire to transgress it.

This spirit is called the spirit of "fear" in two respects: First, because, as we have stated, by threatening people with punishment, it compelled these against their will to do the works of the law— with the result that (because one cannot but hate what one fears) they turned away inwardly from the intent and purpose of the law to the same degree by which they were forced to comply with it. This is symbolized in Ex. 20:18, where the people of Israel stood afar off, trembling with fear to draw near to the mountains. For when the heart and man's better part turn away from God and his law, it is of no significance if one practices outward obedience with the lesser part, i.e., the body, by doing good works and observing religious ceremonies. As our Lord says to the hypocrites: "This people honors me with their lips, but their heart is far from me." (Matt. 15:8; Isa. 29:13.)

Secondly: This spirit is called the spirit of fear, because at the time of trial and testing this slavish fear compels man to neglect even the outward compliance with the law. To be sure, this fear should be called a worldly fear rather than a slavish one, for it is not the fear that the law may not be fulfilled but the fear that temporal goods may be lost or that evils may impend, and it is therefore even worse than slavish fear. John refers to the slavish fear when he says (I John 4:18): "There is no fear in love, but perfect love casts out fear."

Notice how profound the words of Scripture are! We are never or rarely without fear, because none of us is without concupiscence or the flesh or the old man in him. But coveting is never without the fear that one may lose what one covets. Thus, none of us is endowed with perfect love. Similarly, the saying: "Everyone that commits sin is the servant of sin," seems, at first glance, to express a judgment that does not apply to many, but if one looks more closely into it, one finds that it applies to all: for we all are the servants of sin, because we all commit sin, if not by deed, then surely by desire and inclination—as we have sufficiently explained before.

All are sinners

According to Blessed Augustine's comment on this passage,[27] the "spirit of fear" is "he who has the power of death" (i.e., the devil) "and it is given to those who cannot fulfill the commandments of the law because they serve the desires of the flesh."

But it is much better to say that it is that stirring of the dread of the law in the prudence of the flesh which arises when the law is proclaimed and acknowledged, for as long as one does not know the law, it is quiescent. This is symbolized in Ex. 4:3, where Moses fled in horror when the rod he had cast on the ground became a serpent. The same thing happens when a man who is ignorant of the law, and is therefore wont not to observe it, is informed of the law: he becomes surly and loathes the law, and he looks back with sadness to the liberty from which he is now cut off. Such is the spirit of fear.

Luther does not always agree exactly with Augustine

The apostle says: "You received not the spirit of bondage **again unto fear,**" in other words: formerly you were in the spirit of fear and under a taskmaster, namely, the law, that drove you on, but now that you are free you have not again received the spirit of fear but, rather, the spirit of sonship which is the spirit of trusting faith. To this faith he gives most significant expression in the words: **whereby we cry: Abba.** In the spirit of fear, we can hardly open our mouth to mumble something and we certainly cannot cry. But a trusting faith opens the heart wide and releases feelings and speech, whereas fear draws them together and tightens them, as experience amply proves. Neither does it say: "Abba," but instead it hates God and flees from him and mutters against him as if he were an enemy and oppressor. For those who are in the spirit of fear and not in the spirit of adoption do not taste how sweet the Lord is (Ps. 34:8; I Peter 2:3), but he appears hard to them and difficult to please. In their heart they call him a tyrant, though with their mouth they say, "Father," just as did that servant in the Gospel (Matt. 25:24) who hid the money of his lord and said: "I know that you are a hard man, reaping where you did not sow," etc.

Of this sort are the people who are displeased that the Lord does not accept the merits of any man but has compassion on us freely. Hence, they say: Thou hast given no commandments that are impossible to fulfill; thou hast not given us grace but only

27 Augustine, *Propos. ex ep. ad Rom.,* 52.

knowledge; I have it still and now I give it back to thee! Instead
of feeling thus, they should rejoice that he has not placed our hope
in us, but in himself, in his mercy. All who are minded as they
are, say secretly in their heart: God acts like a tyrant; he is not
our father but our enemy. And this is true. But they do not know
that one must agree with this enemy and that thus and only thus
he becomes a friend and father. For he will not yield to us and
change himself in order that we may be his friends and children.
Therefore we do not need to fear him or anything he wills or
loves. But this cannot happen unless we have his spirit, so that
we love what he loves with the same spirit and hate what he hates
in the same way he does. We cannot love what God loves, unless
we have his loving will and spirit. For if there must be conformity
in what one should love, there must also be conformity in the
feeling of love. Such people are called godlike men and sons of
God because they are led by the Spirit of God.[28]

The difference between these two sorts of men is signified, on
the one hand, by those who gave Christ in his Passion vinegar to
drink or wine mixed with gall and hyssop (Matt. 27:34; John
19:29) and, on the other hand, by those who, after the resurrection,
gave him a piece of broiled fish and a honeycomb (Luke 24:42 f.).
The first ones signify that, in their eyes, God is bitterer for them
than gall and hyssop. This is why they give him of their own,
namely: a bitter and unwilling heart; a sour, i.e., a desperate,
heart. When the Lord tastes it, he does not want to drink it. The
others, however, in whose eyes God is sweet as honey, give him
this honey-sweet joy of their hearts, and he takes it and eats it all
before them (Matt. 27:34). With respect to the former, Jer. 15:10 f.
says: "All curse me, says the Lord." And Isa. 8:21: "They shall
curse their king and their God." Or does it not mean to curse God
if one thinks in his heart that God is an enemy and adversary; if
one opposes him in one's feeling and willing and tries with all
one's powers to accomplish the opposite of what God wills, indeed, tries to undo God and his will and to change it into one's
own, i.e., into nothing? To wish that someone be turned into
nothing is the worst of all curses. And it is this that all the damned,
all who have the prudence of the flesh, wish of God!

Now that this cry is not merely a passing sound, but a true
confession of the heart, is shown by Gal. 4:6 f.: "And because you
are sons, God has sent the Spirit of his love into your hearts,
crying: Abba, Father. Therefore he is no longer a servant, but a
son, but if a son, then an heir through God." These words sound

[28] Cf. Faber ad v. 15 f.: "Haec est conformitas filii Dei . . . Christi esse conformes, imo esse Christiformes."

exactly like the text of this passage and they obviously say the same thing.

For the Spirit himself gives testimony *to our spirit, that we are the sons of God,*[29] *and if sons, heirs also; heirs of God and joint heirs with Christ; yet so, if we suffer with him, that we may also be glorified with him. For I reckon that the sufferings of this time are not worthy to be compared with the glory to come that shall be revealed in us.* (Rom. 8:16-18.)

In his "Sermon on the Annunciation," Blessed Bernard, filled with the Holy Spirit, shows most clearly[30] that this testimony is nothing else but the trusting faith of our heart in God.[31] In the first chapter he says: "I believe that this testimony consists of three parts. First of all, you must believe that you can have the forgiveness of sins only by the kindness of God. Secondly, you cannot call a single good work your own that God has not given to you. Lastly, you cannot earn eternal life by any works, unless it, too, is given to you freely." Yet all this is by no means sufficient; we must regard it, rather, as some sort of beginning of faith, or, as it were, as its foundation. For, if you believe that only God can take away your sins, you have the right faith, but from here you must go on to believe, and *you yourself must believe* (and it is not you that can do this but the Holy Spirit must enable you to believe), "that through him you really have the forgiveness of your sins. This is the testimony of the Holy Spirit in our hearts that he says to us: Your sins are forgiven to you."

And this is what the apostle means when he says that a man is justified by faith[32] (you must firmly believe that it applies to yourself, and not merely to the elect, that Christ died for your sins and gave satisfaction for them).

[29] Here is Luther's gloss (the marginal gloss under numbers 1 and 2) (*WA* 56, 78 f., 13 ff.): "*The Holy Spirit himself,* who is bestowed on us *gives testimony to our spirit* by strengthening our trust in God *that we are the children of God* (1-2). For we are and have as much as we believe. Whoever, therefore, believes with a full faith and is confident that he is a son of God, is a son of God, for in Mark 11:24 it says, 'All things whatsoever you pray and ask for, believe that you receive them and you shall have them,' and in Matt. 9:29, 'According to your faith be it done unto you.'"
"(1) For whosoever by strong faith and hope is confident that he is a son of God is a son of God. But none can do this without the Spirit.
"(2) Against Eccl. 9:1, 'Man knows not whether he is worthy of hatred or of love.'"

[30] Luther quotes with interruptions from Bernard of Clairvaux, *Sermo in festo annunciatonis b. Mariae virg.* 1.

[31] "*Fiducia cordis in Deum.*"

[32] Bernard does not use the expression *"iustificari per fidem,"* but he says *"gratis iustificari."*

"It is the same with merits: it is not enough that you believe that we can have them only through Christ. Your faith is whole only if the Spirit of truth gives testimony in your heart that you yourself have them through him," and this becomes a fact when you firmly believe that the works you do are acceptable and agreeable to God whatever they may turn out to be in the long run. And you have this faith that they are agreeable to God if you feel that you are nothing before God on account of these works even though they are good and done from obedience and because you do no evil works. When good works are done with this humility and with this feeling of compunction, they become acceptable in God's sight. "It is the same with eternal life: it is not enough to believe that God gives it by grace, but you must have the testimony of the Spirit that you yourself are about to obtain it by God's favor."

The text shows clearly that the apostle has these three points in mind. For he says: "Who shall accuse against the elect of God?" (Rom. 8:33.) In other words: we are certain that our sins will not be laid to our charge. Likewise, he says of merits: "We know that to them that love God he will work together all things for good."[33] (Rom. 8:28.) Likewise, he says of eternal glory: "I am persuaded that neither things present nor things to come, etc., shall be able to separate us from the love of God which is in Christ." (Rom. 8:38.)

For the expectation of the creature *waits for the revelation of the sons of God.* (Rom. 8:19.)[34]

The apostle philosophizes and thinks about the things of the world in another way than the philosophers and metaphysicians do, and he understands them differently from the way they do. For the philosophers are so deeply engaged in studying the present state of things that they explore only what and of what kind they are, but the apostle turns our attention away from the consideration of things as they are now, and from what they are as to essence and accidents, and directs us to regard them in terms of what they will be. He does not speak of the "essence" of the creature, and of the

---

[33] Following Faber, Luther reads *"cooperatur"* ("he works together") instead of *"cooperantur"* ("they work together"). He comments in the Gloss (*WA* 56, 83, 16 ff.) : "The Greek text has 'he works together,' and this is better, for the reference is to the Spirit. The meaning, therefore, is this: It is not strange that he makes intercession for us, for he works together with the saints in all they do. The term 'he works together' is an explanation of 'he makes intercession.' In other words: He intercedes for us just as he works everything else together with us."

[34] Luther's glosses on Rom. 8:18–30 (*WA* 56, 79, 10 ff.) are given in full at the end of our translation of the Scholia on Chapter VIII.

way it "operates," or of its "action" or "inaction," and "motion," but, using a new and strange theological word, he speaks of "the expectation of the creature." By virtue of the fact that his soul has the power of hearing the creature waiting, he no longer directs his inquiry toward the creature as such but to what it waits for. But alas, how deeply and painfully we are caught up in categories and quiddities, and how many foolish opinions befog us in metaphysics! When shall we learn to see that we waste so much precious time with such useless studies and neglect better ones? We never cease to live up to the saying of Seneca:[35] "We do not know what we should know because we have learned superfluous things; indeed, we do not know what is good for us because we have learned only what harms us."

Indeed, I believe that I owe this duty to the Lord of crying out against philosophy and turning men to Holy Scripture. For, perhaps, if someone else who had not been through it all were to do it, he would either be scared to do it or he would not be believed.

But I have been in the grind of these studies for, lo, these many years and am worn out by it, and, on the basis of long experience, I have come to be persuaded that it is a vain study doomed to perdition.

For this reason, I admonish you all as earnestly as I can: Be quickly done with these studies and let it be your only concern not to establish and to defend them, but, rather, to deal with them as with bad skills that we learn only in order to get rid of them or as with errors that we take up in order to refute them. So we undertake these studies only in order to reject them, or, at least, for the purpose of getting acquainted with the manner of discourse of those with whom we have to maintain relations. It is high time that we be transferred from other studies and learn Jesus Christ "and him crucified" (I Cor. 2:2).

So then, you will be the best philosophers and the best explorers of nature[36] if you learn from the apostle to consider the whole creature as it waits, groans, and travails in pain, i.e., as it turns with disgust from what now is and yearns for what is to come. Then the science of the essence of things and of their accidental qualities and differences will soon become worthless. Thus, the foolishness of the philosophers is like that of a man who stands by a builder and marvels at the way the pieces and boards of wood are being cut and hewn and measured and who remains stupidly content with it all, utterly unconcerned about what the builder

---

[35] "Quia philosophi oculum ita in presentiam rerum immergunt, ut solum quidditates et qualitates earum speculentur."

[36] Seneca, ep. 45, 4.

finally plans to accomplish by all his labors. This workman is an empty-head, and his work is pointless. In the same way, the fools of philosophers look at God's creature: it is constantly being prepared for the glory that is to come, but they see only what it is in itself and how it is equipped but have no thought whatsoever for the end for which it was created.

Would it, then, not be sheer madness on our part to sing the praises of philosophy? For is it not so that, while we think highly of the science of the essences and actions and inactions of things, the things themselves loathe their essences and their actions and inactions and groan under them? We take pleasure and we glory in our knowledge of the created world and yet it mourns over itself and is dissatisfied with itself! Or do we not call a man mad, I ask you, who, on seeing someone moaning and weeping, laughs and glories in the fact that he sees him merry and happy? Such a man is everywhere rightly regarded as a crazy maniac. It would be tolerable if only uneducated folk who do not know better regarded philosophy as important and if it were they that do not know how to interpret the sighing of things. But now it is the scholars and the theologians who, infected as they are by the same "prudence of the flesh," derive a happy science from the mourning things of the world and laughingly gather knowledge from the sighings of creation—and all this with a marvelous display of intellectual power.

The apostle is therefore right when, in Col. 2:8, he speaks up against philosophy and says: "Beware lest any man cheat you by philosophy and vain deceit according to the tradition of men." If the apostle had wanted to understand any philosophy as something good and useful, he certainly would not have condemned it so unequivocally! We conclude, therefore, that *anyone who searches into the essences and functionings of the creatures rather than into their sighings and earnest expectations is certainly foolish and blind. He does not know that also the creatures are created for an end. This passage shows this clearly enough.*[37]

For the creature was made subject to vanity, *not willingly, but by reason of him that made it subject, in hope.* (Rom. 8:20.)

Most exegetes take the term "creature" in this passage to mean man, because he has a share in everything created. But it is better to understand man through the word "vanity," as it says expressly and very rightly in Ps. 39:5: "Surely every man living is altogether vanity." For it is certainly true that, if man, the old

[37] *"Rerum speculatores."*

man, were not, there would be no vanity. For all that God made "was very good" (Gen. 1:31) and is good to this day, as the apostle says in I Tim. 4:4: "Every creature of God is good," and in Titus 1:15: "To the pure all things are pure." It therefore becomes vain, evil, and noxious, etc., without its fault and from the outside, namely, in this way: Because man does not judge and evaluate it rightly and because he enjoys it in a wrong way, he regards it more highly than fact and truth allow, inasmuch as man who is able to grasp God and to find his fulfillment in God alone[38] (as far as his mind and spirit are concerned) presumes to possess this peace and satisfaction in created things. It is to this vanity, therefore (i.e., to this wrong enjoyment), that the creature is subjected, just as grass is in itself something good and not something worthless; indeed, it is good, necessary, and useful for cattle, but to man it is worthless and useless as a food, yet if it were used as human food, it would be regarded and valued more highly than its nature allows. So do all who do not love God from a really pure heart and who do not fervently thirst for him. This is characteristic of every man who is born of Adam and lives without the Holy Spirit. Hence, it is said of all in Ps. 14:3: "They are all gone aside," i.e., they have become vain. And through man the whole creature becomes vanity, though, to be sure, against its will. As the Preacher says: "Vanity of vanities, and all is vanity. What has a man more" (than vanity) "of all his labor that he takes under the sun?" (Eccl. 1:2 f.) He says significantly that man has no other profit than vanity. For created things are good in themselves, and those who know God know also the things of nature not as something vain but as they are in truth; and they use them but do not take advantage of them. Hence, it says in Titus 1:15: "To the pure all things are pure," but to the impure nothing is pure. So then, the same things are pure and impure on account of the fact that they to whom they are either pure or impure differ from one another.

Because **the creature also itself shall be delivered** *from the servitude of corruption into the liberty of the glory of the children of God. For we know that every creature groans and travails in pain, even till now. And not only it, but ourselves also, who have the first fruits of the Spirit, even we ourselves groan within ourselves, waiting for the adoption of the sons of God, the redemption of our body.* (Rom. 8:21–23.)

He says two things: *First,* the creature will be delivered, namely, from vanity, when the wicked will have been damned and taken away and the old man abolished. Such deliverance happens even

[38] *"Qui Dei capax est et solo Deo saturari potest."*

now every day in the saints. *Secondly,* it will also no longer be either vain or corruptible. Hence, the saying of Isa. 30:26: "And the light of the moon shall be as the light of the sun, and the light of the sun shall be sevenfold, as the light of seven days."

Here many say[39] that, in the first seven days when the world was created, the sun was much brighter than it is now, but that it became darker by fault of the sin of man who fell into sin on the seventh or sixth day; they say also that, in the world to come, it will be seven times brighter than it was then. This opinion cannot be proved from Scripture, though in a certain sense it can be sustained. Nor does the word of Isaiah demand this exegesis. For we can understand it by explaining it in this way: "The light of the sun will be sevenfold," i.e., "like the light of seven days," i.e., as if the brilliance of seven days were one brilliance, i.e., the brilliance of all seven days together.

For we are saved by hope. **But hope that is seen is not hope.** *For what a man sees, why does he hope for? But if we hope for that which we see not, we wait for it with patience.* (Rom. 8:24–25.)

Grammatically, this way of speaking may be figurative, yet, theologically understood, it expresses a most intense feeling in a most direct and telling way. For it is ever so that when the hope that rises from the longing for a beloved object is delayed, love is made all the greater. And thus what is hoped for and the hoping person become one through tense hoping, or as Blessed Augustine[40] puts it: *"Anima plus est, ubi amat, quam ubi animat"* ("The soul is more where it loves than where it lives"). In the same way, we say in common speech: My flame is here! And the poet says:[41] "You are my flame, Amyntas." And Aristotle says in Book 3, *On the Soul,*[42] that the intellect and what it understands, sensory perception and what it perceives, and, generally, potentiality and its object become one. In the same way love changes the lover into the beloved.

[39] Cf. *Gl. ord. ad loc.*
[40] According to Ficker (p. 374, n. 10), the saying must be attributed to Bernard of Clairvaux, *De praecept. et dispensat.,* 20, 60: *"Neque enim praesentior spiritus noster est ubi animat, quam ubi amat."* Luther quotes the saying as Tauler, who attributes it to Augustine, cites it: *"De seel ist vil meer da sy liebt dann sy in dem leib sey"* (*Sermones,* Augsburg, 1508, 12b.). John von Paltz (*Celifodina,* Leipzig, 1511, J III) attributes the saying to Hugh of St. Victor and quotes it in the following form: *"Anima ibi plus est ubi amat quam ubi animat"* ("The soul is much more at home where it loves than where it lives").
[41] Vergil, *Bucol. Ecl.,* 3, 66.
[42] Cf. Aristotle, *De anima,* III, 1; 2; 5; 7.

Accordingly, hope changes him who hopes into what he hopes for, but what he hopes for is not apparent. Hope therefore transfers him into the unknown and hidden, into an inward darkness,[43] so that he does not know what he hopes for and yet knows what he does not hope for. Thus, then, the soul that hopes has become hope and, at the same time, what it hopes for, because it is staying with what it does not see, i.e., hope. For if hope were seen, i.e., if he that hopes and what he hopes for mutually recognized each other, he would not thus be transferred into what he hopes for, i.e., into hope and the unknown, but he would be carried away to what he would see, and he would enjoy what he had come to know.

Likewise the Spirit also helps our infirmity. **For we know not what we should pray** *for as we ought, but the Spirit himself asks for us with unspeakable groanings. And he that searches the hearts, knows what the Spirit desires, because he asks for the saints according to God.* (Rom. 8:26–27.)

CONCLUSION

It is not a bad but a very good sign if the opposite of what we pray for appears to happen. Just as it is not a good sign if our prayers eventuate in the fulfillment of all we ask for.

This is so because the counsel and will of God far excel our counsel and will, as it says in Isa. 55:8: "For my thoughts are not your thoughts, neither are your ways my ways, says the Lord. For as the heavens are higher than the earth, so are my ways higher than your ways and my thoughts than your thoughts." And in Ps. 94:11: "The Lord knows the thoughts of men that they are vain." And in Ps. 33:10: "The Lord brings to nought the counsels of nations, and he rejects the devices of people and casts away the counsels of princes."

Hence, it comes about that when we pray to God for something, whatever it may be, and he hears our prayers and is about to fulfill them, he does so in such a way that he contravenes all our conceptions, i.e., devices, so that it seems that he is more offended by us after our prayers than before and that what we pray for is being less fulfilled than before. God does all this because it is his nature first to destroy and to bring to nothing whatever is in us before he gives us of his own,[44] as it is written: "The Lord makes poor and makes rich; he brings down to hell and brings back again" (I Sam. 2:7,6).

By this his most blessed counsel he makes us capable of receiv-

---

[43] Cf. Dionysius Areopagita, *Myst. Theol.,* 1, 3. *Opera Dionys.*
[44] Here Luther appears to follow the teaching of the German mystics, especially Tauler.

ing his gifts and his works. Only then we are fit for his works and counsels, when we have stopped making plans, let our hands rest, and have become purely passive in relation to God in our inner as well as our outer doings. This is what he means when he says: "My thoughts are not your thoughts and my ways are not your ways" (Isa. 55:8).

When, therefore, everything about us seems to be hopeless and all that happens goes against our prayers and wishes, then those "groanings" commence "that cannot be uttered." And then "the Spirit helps our infirmities," for without the help of the Spirit we could not possibly bear up under God when he acts in this way to hear and fulfill our prayers. Then the soul is told: "Expect the Lord, do manfully, and let thy heart take courage and bear up under God" (Ps. 27:14). And again: "Be subject to the Lord and pray to him," "and he will bring it to pass." (Ps. 37:7,5.) Then there comes about what is said in Isa. 28:21: "He does a strange work in order to perform his own work."[45] And in Ps. 103:11: "As the heavens are high above the earth" (i.e., not in accordance with our thoughts), "so great has been his loving kindness toward us," etc.

We can understand that people who do not know God and his will in this way find themselves in the situation of those of whom it is said in Ps. 106:13,24: "They did not bear up under his counsel" and "regarded the desirable land as nothing." They rely on their own good and godly intention and think in their presumptuousness that all they seek and want and pray for is right and proper. But when things do not turn out as they thought, they immediately go to pieces and give up in despair, thinking that God wants neither to hear nor to fulfill their prayers. When everything seemingly went against their intentions, they should instead have hoped all the more confidently precisely for this reason, for they must know that "they are dust and that man is like grass" (Ps. 103:14-15). But they want to be like God and, in their thinking, they want to be, not beneath God, but beside him, as if their minds were perfectly conformed to his.[46] This is as possible or, rather, as little possible as that a piece of clay which, according to its nature, is fit for a pitcher or some kind of vase can in its present shape correspond to the form or artist's conception after which the potter intends to mold it.[47] People of this sort are rather stupid; in their pride they know neither God nor themselves.

---

[45] "Alienum est opus eius ab eo, ut operetur opus suum."

[46] WA 56, 376, 19 ff.: "Ipsi vero sicut Deus esse volunt et cogitationes suas non esse infra, sed iuxta Deum, omnino conformes scil. atque perfectas."

[47] Cf. Luther's marginal notes on Tauler's Sermones, which were perhaps written at the same time when he worked on these lectures. WA 9, 102, 17 ff.

Now Isaiah says this: "But now, O Lord, thou art our Father; we are the clay and thou our potter, and we all are the works of thy hand." (Isa. 64:8.) People, therefore, who do not have the Spirit, run away from God's working and do not want to let it happen to them, but they want to shape themselves and their own lives. But people who have the Spirit are helped by him. Hence, they do not despair but they remain confident when they feel that the opposite of what they have so sincerely prayed for happens. For God's working must be hidden and we cannot understand its way.[48] For it is concealed so that it appears to be contrary to what our minds can grasp. This is why Gabriel said to the Virgin: "The Holy Spirit shall come upon thee," i.e., something that will be beyond your thought will come, "and the power of the Most High shall overshadow thee" (Luke 1:35), i.e., you will not understand it, therefore do not ask how it can come about.

In this way he acted in his own proper work, in that which is the foremost of his works and the pattern[49] of all of them, i.e., in Christ. When he wanted to glorify him and establish him in his Kingship, he made him die, he caused him to be confounded and to descend into hell, contrary in the utmost to what all his disciples fervently wished and hoped for in their devoutest thought.[50] So he dealt also with Blessed Augustine when he let him fall deeper and deeper into error despite the prayer of his mother, so that he might grant it to her beyond her asking. And so he deals with all saints. This is what is meant in Ps. 16:3: "To the saints who are in his land, he has made wonderful all my desires in them." And in Ps. 4:3: "Know that God has made his holy one wonderful," namely, "because the Lord will hear me when I shall cry unto him." And in Ps. 111:2: "The works of the Lord are great, sought out according to all his wills." For how can he be more wonderful than by letting a man who prays for chastity fall into the greater temptation of sensuality, than by letting a man who prays for strength slip into greater weakness? Yet, if one bears up under him, he accomplishes more than one had asked for. This is meant by what it says in Eph. 3:20: "Now unto him that is able to do exceeding abundantly above all that we ask or think," etc., and in II Cor.

---

[48] Lit., "God's work must be hidden, and one cannot understand it when it happens."

[49] On the significance of *"exemplar,"* cf. L. Thimme, *Christi Bedeutung für Luthers Glauben* (Leipzig, 1933), pp. 19 ff.; E. Seeberg, *Luthers Theologie,* Vol. II: *Christus* (Stuttgart, 1937).

[50] Cf. E. Vogelsang, *Die Anfänge von Luthers Christologie* (Berlin, 1929), p. 99n.

9:8-9: "And God is able to make all grace abound unto you, as it is written: He has scattered abroad, he has given to the poor" (i.e., to those who kept themselves passive toward him).

COROLLARY
As a rule, we understand our own work before it is done, but God's work we do not understand until it has been done; Jer. 23:20: "In the latter days you shall understand his counsel," in other words: in the beginning or at first, we understand only what we plan, but in the end we understand what God has in mind. (John 14:29: "When it shall come to pass, you may believe.")

As I have said before, it is as when an artist comes upon some material that is fit and suitable to be formed into a work of art. This fitness of the material is, as it were, an unfelt prayer for the form which the artist understands and fulfills as he gets ready to make what in its suitableness it longs for. So also God comes upon our feeling and thinking[51] and sees what we pray for, what we are fit for, and what we long for. And then he grants the prayer and he proceeds to shape us into the form his art has planned. Thereby the form and idea of our designing are necessarily undone. So it is written also in Gen. 1:2: "The Spirit of God moved upon the waters, and darkness was upon the face of the deep." Notice that it says "upon the face of the deep" and not "upon the deep," for, as far as we can see, all seems to go against us when the Holy Spirit comes over us and is about to do what we ask for.

About this endurance and sufferance of God, I refer you to Tauler. He has written in German about this matter and more enlighteningly than anyone else.[52]

This then, yes, this is what is meant by the word "We do not know how to pray as we ought." Hence, we need the Spirit to help our infirmities. Who would believe that these words could be so profound!

Christ says to his disciples in John 14:16: "I shall pray the Father, and he shall give you another Paraclete," etc. Now "Paraclete" means "comforter" and "advocate." This one word confirms sufficiently what the apostle says here: "We do not know what we must pray for." A man who looks for an advocate shows thereby that he does not know what he should say or ask for, and one who needs a comforter admits thereby that he is desperate and dejected. This is how it is with us when God grants our prayers.

---

[51] *"Affectus"* ("feeling") and *"cogitatus"* ("thinking") are nominalistic psychological terms.

[52] Cf. Tauler, *Sermones* (Augsburg, 1508), *Serm.* 62, 73, 82. Cf. Ficker (p. 378, n. 13).

For if we pray only for what is good and advantageous for us and
the opposite comes about, we are necessarily made sad and down-
cast. Everything about us is then despair and damnation. Then
another must intervene—one who understands this and prays for
us and strengthens us in the meantime, lest we lose heart.

COROLLARY

Toward the first grace as well as toward the glory of eternal
life we must always hold ourselves passive just as a woman does
when she conceives.[53] For we too are the bride of Christ. Hence,
we may engage in prayer and petitions before we receive grace,
yet when grace comes and the soul is about to be impregnated with
the Spirit, there must be neither prayer nor any action on our
part but only a keeping still. This is certainly a hard thing to do
and casts us into deep affliction. For not to think and to will is for
the soul the same as to go into darkness as though it were to be
ruined and reduced to nothing, and this it seeks violently to avoid.
So it comes about that it frequently deprives itself of the noblest
gifts of grace.

I call "first grace" not that which is infused at the beginning of
conversion, as in baptism, contrition, and remorse,[54] but all sub-
sequent and new grace which we call a degree and increase of
grace.

For God gives first operating grace; he lets it be used and he lets
it co-operate until he is ready to infuse another one; and when it
is infused, he again lets it become a co-operating grace, although
when it was infused it was an operating and first grace, even if
with respect to the previous one it is a second one. It is called
"first" grace always with respect to itself, because it is first operating and then, secondly, co-operating. For this reason simpletons
have not learned, as we say in the proverb, to salute God when
they meet him[55] and to take the gifts he offers to them. But the
prudent take them readily and gladly. For here we need greatest
prudence in order that we do not set our minds on that which is
apparent (for then we shall fall into despair) but on that which
is to come and is unknown and not apparent (Heb. 11:1).

For this reason, the apostle uses a very telling word in this

---

[53] Cf. John von Staupitz, "Von der nachfolgung des willigen sterbens Christi"
XI (*Opera,* ed. Knaake, Potsdam, 1867, Vol. I, 78).
[54] Cf. Gabriel Biel, IV *Sent.,* d. 9, q. 1, a. 1, n. 2: "*Gratia iustificans, i.e.,* ...
prima gratia. ... *Sacramenta per quae confertur prima gratia:* ... *baptismus
et penitentia.*"
[55] "*Wenn Gott grüsst, soll man danken.*" The meaning of this proverb is:
One must use an occasion as is offers itself. Cf. Ernst Thiele, *Luthers Sprichwörtersammlung* (Weimar, 1900), 180.

passage. Where our text[56] reads: **He . . . knows what the spirit
longs for** (Rom. 8:27), the Greek text[57] has: "He . . . knows what
is the prudence of the spirit." For *phronēma* means prudence, as
in the verse: "The prudence of the spirit is life and peace" (Rom.
8:6), for the same word is used also here.

We must note that when the apostle says: "We do not know
what to pray for," he does not mean to suggest that saintly and
devout men should pray for something that goes against them and
is harmful to them but, rather, that they pray for things that are
too small, lowly, or insignificant in comparison to what God wants
to give. Hence, he speaks of "our infirmity" rather than of "our
wickedness." For we are too weak and impotent to pray for something big. Hence, when God hears our prayers and is about to
grant them, he does away with the insignificant request we thought
of in our weakness and instead gives us what the Spirit asks for us.
It is like this: A son sends a letter to his father and asks him for
a little sum of silver,[58] whereas the father is disposed to give him a
large amount of gold.[59] When the father reads the letter he throws
it away and disregards it. But when the son hears about this and
when he realizes that he will not get the little sum he asked for,
he becomes surly.

This is why the Lord said to the sons of Zebedee in Matt. 20:22:
"You know not what you ask," and yet they asked for something
good. But then there follows the question: "Are you able to drink
the cup that I am about to drink?" in other words: Your prayer
will not be fulfilled in the way you expect. You do not ask for
the cup and yet you will drink it. You pray for less than you ought.
Therefore, this weakness will be crucified in you by the cup of
suffering, and you will become strong. And, in John 16:24, he
says: "Hitherto you have asked nothing in my name; ask and you
shall receive that your joy may be made full." How can this be
true, inasmuch as he taught them to pray: "Our Father"? But they
prayed in their name, not in the name of Christ, and therefore for
something less than Christ, not in the Holy Spirit, but according
to the flesh. Hence, he goes on to say: "In that day you shall ask
in my name" (John 16:26). For that man prays in the name of
Christ, who also prays in sufferings.

Let us come to a conclusion. There is no better proof that we
do not know what to pray for than that we do not accept as we
ought what the good God offers to us, but that because of our in-

---

[56] I.e., the Vulgate.
[57] Faber.
[58] Lit., *nummum* = a silver coin, the Roman penny.
[59] Lit., *milia aureorum* = thousands of goldpieces.

firmity we get scared and want to run away from it unless the Spirit prays for us and helps us in our infirmity. For one who does not accept as he ought what is offered to him certainly gives thereby conclusive proof that he did not know what to pray for. He deserves to be told: You fool, why did you pray at all if you do not want to accept what you prayed for? We should therefore accept the fright that overcomes us when God gives his gifts, with a joy that is greater than the longing with which we asked for them.

But do we not preach far and wide that God's power, wisdom, goodness, righteousness, and mercy are great and marvelous, yet can it be that we do not understand what they are? No, we do not understand what they are, because we understand them metaphysically, i.e., in accordance with our tendency to comprehend them as apparent and not as hidden, while as a matter of fact he has concealed his power only under weakness, his wisdom under foolishness, his goodness under austerity, his righteousness under sin, and his mercy under wrath.

This is why many do not recognize God's power when they see his weakness, etc. It says in Ps. 81:7: "I heard thee in the hiddenness of the tempest." Notice that it says "in the hiddenness," which means: when the fury of his wrath hides the sweetness of his mercy, i.e., when he grants our prayers by doing the opposite of what we look for. We pray for salvation, and he places us under greater damnation in order thus to save us, and, in such a tempest, he hides his way of granting our prayers. This is symbolized in Ex. 5:5 ff., where we are told that when God was about to set his people free, he caused Pharaoh to increase his oppression of them in order to make it seem that he did not want to set them free at all. And in the psalm it says: "O how great is the multitude of thy sweetness," i.e., of thy goodness, "which thou hast hidden from them that fear thee," i.e., which thou hast not shown publicly, "which thou hast wrought for them that take refuge in thee, before the sons of men," etc. (Ps. 31:19).

We know that to them that love God, he will work together all things for good, even to them that, according to purpose, *are called saints. For whom he foreknew, he also predestinated to be made conformable to the image of his Son, that he might be the first-born among many brethren. And whom he predestinated, them he also called. And whom he called, them he also justified. And whom he justified, them he also glorified. What shall we then say to these things? If God be for us, who can be against us? He that spared not even his own Son, but delivered him up for us all, how has he not also with him given us all things? Who shall*

accuse against the elect of God? God that justifies. Who is he that
shall condemn? Christ Jesus that died, yea, that is risen also again;
who is at the right hand of God, who also makes intercession for
us. Who then shall separate us from the love of Christ? Shall trib-
ulation, or distress, or famine, or nakedness, or danger, or perse-
cution, or the sword? As it is written: For thy sake we are put to
death all the day long. We are accounted as sheep for the slaughter.
But in all these things we overcome because of him that has loved
us. For I am sure that neither death, nor life, nor angels, nor prin-
cipalities, nor powers, nor things present, nor things to come, nor
might, nor height, nor depth, nor any other creature, shall be able
to separate us from the love of God, which is in Christ Jesus our
Lord. (Rom. 8:28–39.)

On this text hangs the whole passage that follows to the end of
the eighth chapter of the letter before us. For the apostle wants to
show that to the elect who are loved by God and who love God,
the Spirit makes all things, even though they are evil, work together for good. He approaches here the subject of predestination
and election, indeed, he discusses it from now on. This subject is
not so unfathomable as one commonly believes; we should, rather,
say that it is full of sweet comfort to the elect and all who have the
spirit, but bitter and hard beyond measure to the prudence of the
flesh.

The only reason and cause why so many adversities and evils
do not separate the saints from the love of God is that they are
called, and not merely called but "called according to purpose."
To them alone, therefore, and to no others "he makes everything
work together for good."

If there were not the divine purpose, and our salvation rested
upon our will and our works, it would be based on chance. How
easily could—I shall not say: all those evils at once, but—merely a
single one of them hinder or overturn this chance!

But by saying: "Who shall accuse? Who shall condemn? Who
shall separate?" the apostle shows that the elect are not saved
contingently but necessarily. Hence, it is obvious that neither
mere chance nor wonderfully contrary resistance to so many evils
can obstruct it. The reason why this is God's way of salvation and
why he exposes his elect to as many rapacious graspings as there
are evils—he enumerates them here, and they all try to pull the
elect into damnation so that they will not be saved—the reason
why God chooses this method of salvation is that he wants to show
that he saves us not by our merits but by sheer election and his
immutable will, and thus he renders vain the efforts of so many
grasping and very fierce adversaries. For if he did not lead us

through so many terrors, he would give us much leeway to think highly of our merits. But now he makes plain that we are saved by his immutable love. And he proves through all this not our freedom of decision but the inflexible and firm will of his pre-destination.

For how could a man possibly break through all these things in which he would despair a thousand times, unless the eternal and steady love of God led him through and the Spirit helped our infirmities by his presence and made intercession for us with unutterable groanings? For in such a situation man does not know what he should do and what he should pray for. Indeed, he would pray that he get out of it, and this would be foolish, because it would go against his salvation. And so we do not know what we should pray for, especially in situations of weakness, i.e., in such sufferings.

Where, then, is now our righteousness? Where are the good works, and the freedom of decision, and the contingency of things? For so one must preach! This is right preaching! This means to cut the throat of the "prudence of the flesh." Up to this point, the apostle cut off its hands and feet and its tongue, but now he cuts its throat and kills it. For now everyone must see that he is nothing in himself but that he can find all his good only in God.

Our theologians, to be sure, subtle as they are, imagine they have accomplished something, though I do not know what it could be, when they adduce in this context their notion of the "contingent." They say that the elect are necessarily saved, namely, by the necessity of the consequence but not by consequent necessity.[60] This is nothing but empty talk, especially in view of the

---

[60] Cf. Duns Scotus, I *Sent.*, d. 39, q. 5, n. 35; Gabriel Biel, III *Sent.*, d. 20, q. *un.*, a. 1B. The "consequent necessity" (*necessitas consequentis* or *absoluta* or *simplex*) means immutability and is generally attributed to God and his attributes. The *"necessity of the consequence"* (*necessitas consequentiae* or *conditionis*) is the necessity that is determined by a cause that once in effect can no longer be changed, but it could have been different. Luther discusses the same problem in *De servo arbitrio* (*WA* 18, 614–618). It may be helpful to quote a key passage, except for a few phrases, according to the translation of J. I. Packer and O. R. Johnston, *Martin Luther on the Bondage of the Will* (James Clarke & Company, Ltd., London, 1957), pp. 81 f.: "This is a point over which the Sophists have toiled for many years now (and have been defeated at last, and forced to give in): they maintained that *all things take place necessarily*, but *by necessity of consequence* (as they put it), *and not by consequent necessity.* By this distinction they eluded the force of their own admission—or rather deluded themselves. I shall not find it hard to show how unreal the distinction is. By *necessity of consequence* they mean, roughly speaking, this: If God wills something, it must needs be; but that which thus comes to be is something which of itself need not be; for only God exists necessarily, and everything else can

fact that they want to understand or at least give occasion to understand the concept of "consequent contingency" to mean that salvation can or cannot come by our decision. Thus I, too, once understood the matter.[61]

This concept of "the contingency of the consequent" is irrelevant to the theme under discussion. Moreover, it is meaningless to ask whether this "consequent" is contingent, as if (and this is implied in the question) it could be necessary, inasmuch as only God is necessary in this sense. Therefore, it is a ridiculous addition if one says: The elect are necessarily saved by the necessity of the consequence, but not by consequent necessity, i.e., the consequent is not God, or: because it is not God, therefore salvation is by the necessity of consequence. What else does "to be contingent" mean than "to be a creature" and not God? They twist the understanding by turning the necessity of an occurrence into the necessity of the essence of a thing. This equivocation is here out of place. For no one raises the question or doubts whether a created thing is contingent in its being, i.e., whether it is mutable or whether it is God and thus immutable. But the question is about the necessity of the sequel or whether what God has predestined will necessarily happen, and they concede that it will. And yet they make this superfluous addition, after they have said all that can be said. For if you know that something will definitely happen by the necessity of the consequence, what does it matter if you know further whether, at this particular place, it is contingent or not?

This is as absurd as if, in case you were asked: If a son necessarily kills his father, must this necessarily happen? you would answer by saying: It will happen by the necessity of the consequence and then add that the son is not father, or the father has no son.[62] They

---

cease to be, if God so wills. This is to say that God's action is necessary, if he wills it, but the thing done is not in itself necessary. But what do they establish by this play on words? This, I suppose—the thing done is not necessary; that is, it has no necessity in its own essential nature: which is just to say, that the thing done is not God himself! Nevertheless, it remains true, that each thing *does* happen necessarily, if God's action is necessary or there is a necessity of consequence, however true it may be that it does *not* happen necessarily, in the sense that it is not God and has no necessity of its own essential nature. . . .

"So their absurd formula, *all things take place by necessity of consequence but not by consequent necessity* amounts merely to this: everything takes place by necessity, but the things that take place are not God himself. But what need was there to tell us that? . . . So our original proposition still stands and remains unshaken: all things take place by necessity."

[61] Cf. Luther's notes on Peter Lombard, II *Sent.*, d. 26, c. 3 (*WA* 9, 71, 5 ff.).
[62] "*Fiet necessitate consequentiae, sed filius non est pater, vel quia non habet filium.*"

who raise this question are asking therefore whether a contingency can hinder the necessity of a chain of events, and they make the presupposition that they know the contingency, and you teach by a *petitio principii* that there are contingent things and that they do not hinder the necessary occurrence of a sequence of events. Your answer is correct, but what you teach is superfluous and irrelevant.

Simple people put the question as least in this way: Does the contingency of an event constitute an impediment of the certain predestination of God? The answer must be: With God there simply is no contingency, but only with us, because not even a leaf of a tree falls to the ground without the will of the Father. Just as the essence of things, therefore, also the times are in his hands. When one relates the concept of necessity now to the subject and now to the connecting clause, one is guilty of equivocation, inasmuch as the question concerns only the contingency of the connecting clause or of time but in no way that of the subject.

We shall deal with this matter in three sections. First, we shall gather the proofs of immutable predestination from the words of Scripture and the works of God. Secondly, we shall critically analyze the objections and exceptions, and the arguments and reasons of those who shift guilt to God. Thirdly, in order to provide comfort to those who are frightened by all this, we shall bring out also its more pleasant aspects and thus induce them to hope.

I

In this and the following chapter of this letter, the apostle deals thoroughly and almost word for word with the first theme, and he begins, as I have already pointed out, with, "We know that those who love God," etc.

Accordingly, he says, first: **who are called according to purpose.** It plainly follows, therefore, that others are not called according to the purpose. "Purpose" means here God's predestination or free election or deliberation or counsel. In Book I of the *Confessions*, Blessed Augustine says about this:[63] "Thou art wonderful, O God; thou changest thy opinion, but thou dost not change thy counsel."

Second: In the following chapter (Rom. 9:8 ff.), the apostle illustrates predestination by the two stories of Isaac and Ishmael, and of Jacob and Esau. He says expressly that these differed from one another only by election.

Third: At the same place, he quotes two Scriptural passages on it; one refers to the elect: "I will have mercy on whom I have mercy" (Rom. 9:15), and the other one to the rejected: "For this

[63] Augustine, *Confessiones*, I, 4, 4.

very purpose did I raise you up," etc., and he concludes: "So then, he has mercy on whom he will, and whom he will, he hardens," etc. (Rom. 9:17–18). It is clear that he argues in the same way in chs. 10 and 11.

Fourth: Predestination is proved by the following quotation from John 10:29: "No one can snatch them out of the hand of my Father."

Fifth: John 13:18: "I speak not of you all; I know whom I have chosen." And John 6:44: "No one can come to me, except the Father that sent me draw him." And at the same place: "They shall all be taught of God." (John 6:45.)

Sixth: Ps. 115:3: "He has done all things whatsoever he would." And II Tim. 2:19: "The foundation of God stands firm, having this seal: the Lord knows who are his."

A further proof are God's works: First, what, according to the following chapter, he did with Ishmael and Esau and with Pharaoh and the Egyptians.

Second: Predestination is shown by the fact that God exposes his saints to so many evils, all of which are like rapacious hands, and yet he does not let them get lost. Thereby he amply shows the firmness of his election: no creature can impede it, despite the fact that he leads the whole creature up against it, as he shows by the example of Pharaoh, who was hardened.

Third: Election is shown by the fact that he permits many to live a good life from the beginning and to do many good works and yet they are not saved; while, conversely, he lets many commit great evils who are nevertheless suddenly changed and saved. This is exemplified by Saul (I Sam. 13:13; 15:26 f.; 16:1) and Manasseh (II Kings 21:1 ff.), and likewise by Judas the Traitor (Matt. 26:14, 47 ff.), and by the thief of the cross (Luke 23:33 ff.), and so forth, and by many harlots and crude sinners. By way of contrast, he rejects those who think they know everything and those who try to shine with good works. Thus he rejected one of the forty martyrs.[64]

II

There are many reasons that can be advanced against predestination, but they proceed from the "prudence of the flesh." Hence, whoever does not deny himself and has not learned to submerge his questions in the will of God and to subject them to it will

---

[64] A martyrdom under the Emperor Licinius in Armenia Minor. One of the forty became scared and fled. Ficker (p. 384, n. 30) points out that the Missal of the Augustinians refers to this legend on the Day of the Forty Martyrs (March 9).

always ask why God wills this or does that, and he will never find
an answer. And rightly so. For this foolish prudence places itself
above God and passes judgment on his will as upon something
inferior, while, as a matter of fact, it is about to be judged by him.
The apostle, therefore, destroys all its reasons by one brief word.
First, he restrains our temerity lest we sit in judgment on God's
will. He says: "O man, who are you that you reply against God?"
(Rom. 9:20); in other words: You are subject to the will of God;
why, then, do you presume to reply to it and to argue with it?
And then he advances the decisive reason: "Has not the potter a
right over the clay?" (Rom. 9:21).

So then, the first objection, which is also the least weighty one,
is this: Man has been given free will and thus he can earn merits
or demerits. We answer to this as follows: The power of free decision in so far as it is not under the sway of grace has no ability
whatsoever to realize righteousness, but it is necessarily in sins.
Hence, Blessed Augustine is right, when, in his book against
Julian,[65] he calls it "the enslaved, rather than free, will." But
when it has received grace, the power of decision really becomes
free, at all events in respect to salvation. To be sure, it is always
free according to its nature, but only with respect to that which is
in its power and is inferior to it but not with respect to that which
is superior to it, since it is held captive in sins and then cannot
choose the good according to God.

A second objection: "God will have all men to be saved" (I Tim.
2:4), and he gave his Son for us men, and he created man for
the sake of eternal life. And likewise: Everything is there for man's
sake and he is there for God's sake in order that he may enjoy him,
etc. But this objection and others like it can just as easily be refuted
as the first one: because *all these sayings must be understood only
with respect to the elect,* as the apostle says in II Tim. 2:10:[66] "All
for the elect." Christ did not die for absolutely all, for he says:
"This is my blood which is shed for you" (Luke 22:20) and "for
many" (Mark 14:24)—he did not say: for all—"to the remission
of sins" (Matt. 26:28).

A third objection: God condemns none who is without sin.
And a man who is necessarily in sin is wrongly condemned. To
this I reply: We are all necessarily in sin and under condemnation,
but nobody is a sinner by coaction and against his will. For whoever hates sin is already outside sin and belongs to the elect.
But those whom God hardens, they are the ones to whom he gives
the will voluntarily to be and to stay in sin and to love wicked-

---

[65] Augustine, *Contra Jul.,* II, 8, 23.
[66] Augustine, *Enchiridion,* XXVII, 103.

ness. Such are unavoidably in sin by the immutability of necessity *?*
but not of coaction.

A fourth objection: Why does he issue commandments and then
does not want to see them fulfilled? And, what is worse, why does
he harden men's will so that they want even more to act against
the law? The cause, therefore, why men sin and are damned, lies
in God. This is the strongest and chief objection. And the apostle
replies to it mainly by saying: God wills it so and because he wills
it so, it is not wicked. For everything is his as the clay is the potter's! He, therefore, gives his commandments in order that the
elect fulfill them and the reprobate get entangled in them. And
thus he shows his wrath as well as his mercy.

Here the prudence of the flesh speaks up and says: It is cruel and
miserable of God that he seeks his glory in my wretchedness. Listen to the voice of the flesh! "My, my [wretchedness]," it says!
Take away this "my" and say instead: "Glory be to thee, O Lord!"
and you will be saved! Thus the prudence of the flesh seeks only
its own; it fears its own misery more than a desecration of God,
and, for this reason, it follows its own will rather than God's.

We must, therefore, have a mind about God different from
that which we have about man. For he does not owe anyone anything. To Job he says: "Who has given me before that I should
repay him? All things that are under heaven are mine." (Job
41:11.) This is the word which the apostle quotes at the end of
ch. 11 of this letter, where he says: "Who has first given to him,
and recompense shall be made to him?" (Rom. 11:35).

III

This subject of predestination tastes very bitter to the prudence
of the flesh. Indeed, it is so offended by it that it lets itself be carried away to the extreme of blasphemy, because here it is utterly
destroyed and reduced to nothing. For it is forced to recognize
that its salvation consists in no way of its own action, but that it
can be found only outside itself, namely, in the election of God.
But all who have the "prudence of the spirit" delight in this subject and they are filled with an ineffable happiness, as we can see
here in the apostle and in Hannah, the mother of Samuel (I Sam.
2:1 ff.). In between these there stand those who are just beginning
to turn away from "the prudence of the flesh" or who are on the
way toward "the prudence of the spirit." They are ready and willing to do the will of God, but they are fainthearted and they tremble when they hear about the teaching on predestination.

And so it is that, though these words, which are the best and
most wholesome food for the soul, do not as yet give them direct

pleasure, they nevertheless find them comforting and consoling, and by *antiperistasis*,[67] i.e., by a condition of contrast. Namely, in this way: there are no words that can more effectively shake up and humble the pride of men and undo the presumptuousness of the reliance on merits. People, therefore, who fear these words and are scared by them can take this reaction as a very good and happy sign, for the Scripture says: "Upon whom does my spirit rest except upon him that is humble and that trembles at my word" (Isa. 11:2; 66:2). Also Christ says to them: "Fear not, little flock, for it is your Father's good pleasure to give you the Kingdom." And Isa., ch. 40:[68] "Say (to them that are of a fearful heart: Be strong, fear not: behold, your God will come)." If he had not noticed that they thought the opposite, indeed, that they were afraid to the point of despair that the Kingdom of God would not come, he would certainly not have said: "You fainthearted, be comforted, for behold, your Lord will come." And again: "Blessed is the man that fears the Lord." (Ps. 112:1.) Everywhere in the Scriptures, people of this sort who are terrified by the word of God are encouraged and comforted. For they despair of themselves, and the word of God does its work in them by causing them to tremble before God. Just as those who are hardened toward the word of God and rely on themselves have a very bad sign in that they are of this mind, so they who stand in anxious fear of it have a very good sign precisely in this their attitude, as it is written in Ps. 144:6: "Shoot out thy arrows and thou shalt trouble them."

Therefore, if a man is overwhelmed by the fear that he is not one of the elect or if he is assailed and troubled about his election, let him give thanks for such fear and let him rejoice over his anxiety: he can be confident in the knowledge that God cannot lie who said: "The sacrifice of God is a troubled," i.e., a desperate, "spirit; a broken and a contrite heart, O God, thou wilt not despise" (Ps. 51:17). Now, he himself is aware of the fact that he is "troubled." He should be bold, therefore, and unhesitatingly rely on God's truthfulness and accept his promise and thus free himself from his former notion that God only frightens, and thus he will be saved and elected.[69]

It is certainly not characteristic of the reprobate, at least in this life, that they tremble at the hidden counsel of God, but this is

---

[67] *"Per antiperistasin,"* i.e., *contrarii circumstantiam.* Cf. Aristotle, *Physics,* VIII. Webster calls "antiperistasis" a term of Old Physics and defines it as an "opposition by which the quality opposed acquires strength."

[68] Luther actually thinks of Isa. 35:4.

[69] *"Ergo in veritatem promittentis Dei audacter ruat (se transferat) de prescientia terrentis Dei, et salvus et electus erit."*

characteristic of the elect. For the reprobate despise it and do not pay any attention to it. Or they say with the presumptuousness of despair: If I am damned, all right, let me be damned.

Now there are three ranks in the company of the elect.

To the *first* one belong those who are content with the will of God, whatever it is; they do not grumble against it, but trust, rather, that they are elected, and they do not want to be damned.

To the *second* one, which is higher, belong those who have re- signed themselves to God's will. They feel content in it or at least they yearn for such a feeling, in case God should not want to save them but place them among the rejected.

To the *third* and the best and highest rank belong those who in actual reality resign themselves to hell if God wills this, as it happens perhaps with many in the hour of death. These are per- fectly cleansed of their own will and of the "prudence of the flesh." They know what it means that "love is strong as death and jealousy as hard as hell" (S. of Sol. 8:6). A wonderfully strange comparison! Love is compared with the bitterest things, inasmuch as it is seemingly something soft and sweet. But it is true: love that finds pleasure in another is sweet, because it enjoys the beloved. In this world, God gives such a love to his elect briefly and spar- ingly, for to possess it richly and for long is, indeed, a most dan- gerous thing, "for they have received their reward" (Matt. 6:2). But a love that is full of longing, such a love is really as hard and as strong as hell, and, in this life, God exercises his elect in it in wonderfully strange ways. So the bride says in the Song of Solo- mon: "I am sick with love." (S. of Sol. 2:5.)

Hence, we must always take the word "love" to mean a cross and suffering, as this passage shows. Without these the soul becomes languid and tepid; it ceases to long for him and does not thirst for him, the living fountain. This love is sweet, to be sure, not when it passively receives, but when it actively gives, or, to put it crudely, it is sweet to its object, but it is bitter to its subject. For it wishes others everything that is good and gives it to them, but it takes upon itself the ills of all as if they were its own. For "it seeks not its own and bears all things and endures all things." (I Cor. 13: 5, 7.)

GLOSSES ON ROM. 8:18–30

[The interlinear gloss on Rom. 8:18–30 is given first, and the mar- ginal glosses are indicated by numbers within parentheses.]

For I reckon, inasmuch as they are really not worthy, **that the suffer- ings (1),** i.e., tribulations, **of this time,** because they are so small and insignificant, are not worthy to be compared with the glory already prepared with God, but not yet revealed, which shall be revealed in us, the elect. For the earnest expectation (because of the fact that, held captive as it were, it serves the unworthy) of the creature, i.e., of what is in process of being formed as the work of the maker, which is the whole world, waits (2) for the revelation (in the resurrection and glorification) of the sons of God. It longs for it. But, we ask, why does it long for it? For the creature was made subject to, i.e., it serves, vanity, i.e., the vain use of the wicked, not willingly, not by its own will but from necessity, but by reason of him, God, who has subjected the same, i.e., has caused it to serve unworthy men, (3) in hope, because the creature itself (Matt. 24:35: "heaven and earth shall pass away") (4) also shall be delivered from the bondage of corruption, in which it serves corruptibly, into an incorruptible bondage, yes, into liberty, namely, into the liberty of glory, (5) i.e., to the glory of the children of God. For this its bondage shall become its liberty, just as we must say of the righteous that they are transferred from the bondage of sin into the bondage of righteousness, or, rather, into the liberty of righteousness. For to be in bondage to God means to rule like a king. (*Quia servire Deo regnare est.* Cf. Augustine, *Enarr. in Ps.* 55:2; *De vera relig.*, 44, 82.) For we know that the whole creature, because, as it is said farther on (Rom. 8:28), "to the elect all things work together," groans for the redemption and the glory of the children of God and its own (6) and travails in pain (7) until now, but has not yet brought them forth. And not only it (this is not in the Greek text) but ourselves also, the believers, the elect, who have the first fruits of the Spirit (8) but not yet the fullness of it and the whole harvest or vintage, because we are "the beginning of his creatures" (James 1:18). For we shall be the perfect that is to come, according to I John 3:2: "Now we are the sons of God and it has not yet appeared what we shall be. We know that, when he shall appear, we shall be like him, for we shall see him as he is," even we ourselves groan, i.e., groaningly ask and pray within ourselves, i.e., in ourselves, where only God can see, for the adoption (of the sons of God) (this is not part of the text) waiting, weary of the present life and longing for the life to come; for the redemption of our body (9) from mortality to immortality, from corruption into glory. For we are saved by the hope in which "we wait." But hope unto eternal salvation, that which we wait for by hoping, (hope, I say,) that is seen is not hope (hence, he explains himself,) for what a man sees, why does he hope for?, for he has and holds it in his hands. But if we hope for that which we see not and neither have nor hold, then we wait with patience for it, for hope that is deferred discourages the soul. Likewise the Holy Spirit also helps, by causing us to pray with deep groanings, our infirmity (10) (the Greek text reads: "our infirmities"), our impotence and inability. For we know not (as we read in Matt. 20:22: "You know not what you ask," and in John 13:7: "What I do, you now do not know") what, in so far as the object of our prayer is concerned, we should pray for as we ought, in so far as the attitude and manner of our prayer are concerned; **but the Holy Spirit asks for us,** makes intercession for us, **with groanings that cannot be uttered,** that no man can express in words and none except God can feel. (11) This does not apply in the same way to everyone. But God alone, i.e., *he that searches* the hearts of men, *knows* and recognizes our inmost selves even more than we ourselves do, and he senses and approves (12) **what the Holy Spirit longs for** (and to him they are not unutterable). He knows, I say, **because he asks,** makes intercession, **for the saints according to God,** i.e., because this is pleasing to God according to his will, for, as he said before, the whole creature and we ourselves and the Holy Spirit groan together for the saints; this he proves now by saying: **And we know,** I say this lest it appear strange that the Spirit himself intercedes, **that to them that love God all things,** good as well as bad ones, **work together** (13) **for good,** i.e., for the coming of salvation, **to them who according to the purpose** (14) **are called,** according to predestination, for not all are called according to predestination, because "many are called, but few are chosen" (Matt. 20:16) **saints** (this is not in the Greek text). According to his purpose, then, they are called, **for whom he foreknew,** whom he knew before they came into being, **he also predestinated,** (15) predetermined, singled out, selected, proposed **to be conformed** (16) in glory and splendor just as also in suffering and shame **to the image** and likeness (exemplar) **of his Son Jesus Christ, that he might be the first-born,** the chief first fruit, the likeness, the image of all **among many brethren,** i.e., among all the elect who are many (17) in so far as he is man, for, in so far as he is God, he is the only-begotten one who has no brethren. **Moreover, whom he predestinated,** proposed or elected, **them he also called** by the word of faith, **and whom he called, them he also justified** (18) by the spirit of faith; **and whom he justified, them he also magnified** (which means "glorified"), i.e., glorified in eternal life.

(1) The sufferings are worthy or unworthy, not because we estimate them to be so; but our judgment of them is then right and true when we evaluate them in terms of what they really are. And this the proud do not do.

(2) He speaks of the creature, as if, alive and able to have sensations, it felt pain at being forced for such a long time to serve the wicked in misuse and ingratitude toward God, while in fact it was created to the end that, through it and in it, the saints might glorify God. It is for this its end (*"finem"*) that it naturally (*"naturaliter"*) waits.

(3) Matt. 5:45: "For he makes his sun to rise on the good and the evil and sends rain on the just and the unjust."

(4) This is the same as to say, "Heaven and earth shall pass" (Matt. 24:35), not in terms of their substance but in terms of their corruptibility. The philosophers may see how they can understand this! I understand the text to say: not in terms of their substance, i.e., not that they may cease to be, but that they may no longer be corruptible, but that they may be glorious. The word "they will pass," i.e., "they will be changed" (cf. Ps. 102:26), indicates this. Just as Christ passed

through his Passover (*"transiit phase suo"*), i.e., as he was changed into the glory of immortality, so all saints are called Galileans, i.e., those that pass, i.e., those that are to be changed into glory. As it says in II Peter 3:13: "We look for a new heaven and a new earth," etc. And in Isa. 65:17: "For behold, I create new heavens and a new earth"; and in Ps. 102:26 and 27: "They shall perish . . . and thou shalt change them, and they shall be changed."

(5) Again he contrasts (as is his wont) "the bondage of corruption" and "the liberty of glory," for it now serves in its corruption to the misuse of the wicked, but then, when it will be set free from corruption, it will serve "to the glory of the children of God."

(6) Note here what a great prayer is continuously said for the righteous and against the unrighteous, as the whole creature groans for its own deliverance and that of the righteous, thereby crying out against the unrighteous; then we come and groan, and finally also the Spirit himself.

(7) "It travails," i.e., it strives anxiously for the end of corruption, in order to bring forth glory, just as a woman in labor has sorrow, but when she has delivered her child, she does not remember her anguish (cf. John 16:21).

(8) He speaks here in a metaphor suggested by the first fruits of the produce of the earth—the beginning of the harvest, as it were, or the foretaste of the vintage that is to come.

(9) Those who have the spirit of fear do not understand all this, but they dread it and do not want it to happen.

(10) Because man, no matter how righteous he is, does not wish fervently enough, in reliance on his own powers, for the glory that is to come. Therefore, the Spirit asks in their stead with hidden sighs for what men cannot pray for. For also when we pray for eternal glory and ask that it may come soon or that it may be given thus and so, we do not know what to pray for, in view of the possibility that when it is given as we ask or if it comes soon, it may cause us a great loss. How much more does this apply to prayers for temporal things!

(11) In other words: the groaning is so heavy that only God can weigh it and properly sense it, as it is said in Ps. 38:9: "All my desire is before thee, and my groaning is not hid from thee."

(12) As in Ps. 1:6: "For the Lord knows the way of the righteous."

(13) The Greek text reads "he works together," in the singular, and this is better, because the reference is to the Holy Spirit. The meaning, then, is this: it is not strange that he intercedes for us, because he works all things together with the saints in all they do. The word is an explanation of the preceding: "he intercedes." In other words: he prays with us just as he acts together with us in everything else.

(14) He says simply "according to the purpose," without adding "of God" or "his." For there is, indeed, only one purpose, namely, God's, as all who know God understand. For only God's and no one else's purpose is realized and accomplished. The whole creature must be con-

formed to him, according to Judith 16:14: "Let thy creation serve thee."

(15) God does not create and save with his eyes closed as Jacob saw his father do in the prefiguration of his predestination (Gen. 48:17 ff.).

(16) The passage must be read as follows: Whom he foreknew to be conformed, them he also predestinated to be conformed. If he had meant to say that God had foreknown that they would become such by their own merits, he would have written: For of whom he foreknew that they would become conformed.

(17) "Many" is here said with positive emphasis. It must not be taken to mean that Christ is the first-born among many brethren but not among all. For it is written in Ps. 89:6: "Who among the sons of God is like God?" The meaning, then, is this: He is the first-born among all his brethren, who are very many as it says above in Rom. 5:19: "The many shall be made righteous."

(18) He does not glorify all whom he justifies, and he does not justify all whom he calls, and he does not call all whom he has foreknown. Hence, the apostle fashions this sequence here only with respect to the predestined, namely, with respect to those "whom he foreknew to be conformed."

ROMANS, CHAPTER NINE

I say the truth in Christ, I lie not, my conscience being witness with me in the Holy Spirit, **that I have great sorrow and pain in my heart.** (Rom. 9:1-2.)

This passage shows clearly that love proves itself not so much in sweetness and delight, but in very great sorrow and bitterness. Indeed, it finds delight and sweetness in bitterness and sorrow, because it takes upon itself the misery and suffering of others. Thus Christ was aflame with love in the very great agony of his death. Indeed, according to Blessed Hilary,[1] he was filled with greatest joy that he suffered the greatest pain. This is God's way: "He is wonderful in his saints" (Ps. 68:35), by causing them to rejoice most when they suffer the greatest pain.

For I could wish that I myself were anathema *from Christ for my brethren's sake, my kinsmen according to the flesh, who are Israelites, whose is the adoption, and the glory, and the covenants, and the giving of the law, and the services of God and the promises, whose are the fathers, and of whom Christ is according to the flesh, who is over all, God blessed forever.* (Rom. 9:3-5.)

Many[2] want to understand this, I do not know why, to refer to the apostle before his conversion, when he was still outside Christ, indeed, against Christ. But this interpretation is untenable for many reasons. *First:* He says, "I could wish." Yet only he wishes something whose wish is not yet fulfilled. But he was then already anathema. *Second:* He wishes to be anathema from Christ. Hence, we must understand him to be with Christ when he says this. *Third:* In a similar way we must understand "anathema,"

---

[1] Cf. Hilary, *De trin.,* X, 45.
[2] Cf. *Gl. ord.,* also Lyra and Faber.

i.e., excommunication, execration, rejection, when he says, "I could wish to be anathema," he must therefore be in communion with Christ, consecrated to him and accepted by him. *Fourth:* He says, "for my brethren's sake." But then, he was not cursed and execrated for their sake but together with them. Then he did not want to be there for their salvation but he wanted to perish with them.

This leads immediately to the next point. *Fifth:* The whole context of the passage indicates that he is most fervently concerned for their salvation. He wants to bring Christ to them. And this he certainly did not do earlier. He appealed to them with a sacred oath, because it seems unbelievable that a man should want to be damned in order that the damned might be saved.

And *sixth:* He alone wishes to be anathema from Christ. This is milder. But before his conversion, he wished instead that Christ and all who belonged to him should be anathema from the whole world, that Christ should be separated from him and everyone else and not he from Christ. Indeed, he wanted to be against Christ, because he was of one mind with the Jews who had excommunicated Christ, excluded him from their city and community, and killed him, while they maintained themselves, believing themselves to be elected. This is why Christ is called "Hermon" in Ps. 133:3: "As the dew of Hermon which descends upon Mount Zion." And in Ps. 42:6, the church is called together with him "Hermoniim": "I will remember thee from the land of Jordan and Hermoniim, from the little hill." In Greek, "Hermon" means "anathema" and "Hermoniim," "anathemas."[3] And "anathema" means to be expelled and set apart as the lepers and the unclean are set apart. In this sense, Christ made the prediction to his disciples: "They shall put you out of the synagogues" (John 16:2), i.e., you will be Hermoniim and anathemas, i.e., the rejected and the cursed among the peoples.

This word "I could wish," etc., is therefore the expression of a most excellent and truly apostolic love for Christ as well as for the Jews. For because of a deep love for him, he wishes that great glory should come to Christ from the Jews. For this reason, he is gladly willing to be separated from him but without hating him. Now this inverted love is the strongest and utmost kind of love: utter self-hatred becomes the sign of the highest love for another.

So then, he wants to see the Jews really saved, and in order that they may achieve this, he is ready to forego his own salvation. He

[3] Luther is here dependent on the *Gl. ord.* and on Jerome's Biblical Commentary.

does the same elsewhere in II Cor. 12:15, where he says: "And I will most gladly spend and be spent for your souls."

We should note that these words will appear strange and even foolish to those who regard themselves as holy and who love God with a covetous love, i.e., for the sake of their own salvation and eternal rest and for the purpose of avoiding hell, in other words: not for God's sake but for their own sake. They are the ones who babble that ordered love[4] begins with itself and that everyone must first of all wish his own salvation and then his neighbor's as his own. Such notions show that they do not know what it means to be saved and blessed, unless, of course, they take this to mean a happy and good life as they like to imagine it for themselves. But as a matter of fact, to be blessed means to seek in everything God's will and his glory, and to want nothing for oneself, neither here nor in the life to come.

Now, all who truly love God and revere him as a father and friend, not from natural capacity but only through the Holy Spirit, will think these words very beautiful and they will take them as evidence of a truly perfect example: for they submit freely to the will of God whatever it may be, even for hell and eternal death, if God should will it, in order that his will may be fully done; they seek absolutely nothing for themselves. And yet, inasmuch as they themselves so purely conform to the will of God, they cannot possibly remain in hell. For one who surrenders his own self completely to the will of God cannot possibly be forever outside God. For he wills what God wills. Therefore he pleases God. And when he pleases God, he is loved by him and by this love he is saved.

Now, if someone asks whether God has at any time willed or may ever will that a man should resign himself to hell and that, for the sake of his will, he should let himself be damned or be anathema from Christ, I answer: Yes, in the case of most men and chiefly of those who are still imperfect in love or in the pure devotion to God. For, in their case, the covetous love that is so deep-rooted needs to be extirpated. But it cannot be extirpated except by a superabundant infusion of grace or by this most difficult resignation of which we are speaking here. "For nothing unclean shall enter into the Kingdom of God." (Rev. 21:27.)

But now no one knows whether he loves God with a pure heart unless he experiences in himself that should God want it so, he does not wish to be saved or refuse to be damned. For the damned suffer such great torments because they do not want to be damned

---

[4] Cf. Duns Scotus, II *Sent.*, d. 29, *q. un.*; Gabriel Biel, III *Sent.*, d. 29, *q. un.*, a. 2, *concl.* 4.

or resign themselves to this will of God. And without the grace of God, they cannot do so.

If this is the pain of purgatory (as it seems to me to be), that souls of an imperfect love recoil from the actuality of this resignation until they take it upon themselves and consent to be anathema from God, we are miserable fools[5] in so far as we defer the task we should eagerly pursue in this life, namely, to love God perfectly, and, instead, look forward to such a crude distress in the future. Yet no one can be purged unless he is resigned to hell.

But the true saints actually achieve this resignation, because their hearts overflow with love, and they do this without great distress. For they are so completely dedicated to God that nothing seems impossible for them to do, not even the suffering of the pains of hell. And because of this very readiness, they escape from such a punishment. Indeed, they do not need to fear that they will be damned, because they submit gladly and willingly to damnation for God's sake. But it is those who want to escape from damnation that will be damned.

For even Christ suffered damnation and dereliction to a greater degree than all the saints. And his sufferings were not, as some imagine, easy for him. For he really and truly offered himself for us to eternal damnation to God the Father. And in his human nature, he behaved in no other way than as a man eternally damned to hell. Because he loved God in this way, God at once raised him from death and hell and thus devoured hell. All his saints must imitate him in this, some more and some less; the more perfect they are in love, the more readily and easily they will be able to do so. But Christ underwent all this with the most painful suffering of all. Hence, he complains in so many passages of the pains of hell.[6]

Those, then, who refuse to accept this interpretation let themselves be guided by the imagination of the flesh. They think[7] that "to love oneself" means primarily to want and desire something good for oneself, but they do not know what this good is and they cannot know what it means to love. "To love" means to hate and condemn oneself, to desire something that is bad for one, in accordance with the word of Christ: "He that hates his life in this world shall keep it unto life eternal" (John 12:25). (If someone were to say: But I do not love my life in this world, because I seek what is good for it in the world to come, I answer him as follows:

---

[5] Luther shares this spiritual conception of purgatory with German mysticism. Cf. *Theologia Deutsch*, 11.

[6] Luther thinks here of the psalms, Christologically interpreted.

[7] Cf. Gabriel Biel, III *Sent.*, d. 32, *q. un.*, *a.* 1, *n.* 1.

You do this from self-love, which is a love of this world; therefore, you thereby still love your life in this world.) One who loves himself in this way, practices a true self-love. For he loves himself not in himself but in God, i.e., in accordance with the will of God, and he hates, condemns, and maligns all sinners, i.e., every one of us.

For our good is hidden and that so deeply that it is hidden under its opposite. Thus our life is hidden under death, self-love under self-hatred, glory under shame, salvation under perdition, the kingdom under banishment, heaven under hell, wisdom under foolishness, righteousness under sin, strength under weakness. And generally, every yes we say to any good under a no, in order that our faith may be anchored in God,[8] *who is the negative essence and goodness and wisdom and righteousness and whom we cannot possess or attain to except by the negation of all our affirmations.*[9]

Thus "the Kingdom of Heaven is like unto a treasure hidden in the field." (Matt. 13:44.) The field is something dirty and is trampled upon, in contrast to the treasure which is singled out. And yet, the field hides the treasure. So also "our life is hidden with Christ in God" (Col. 3:3), i.e., in the negation of all we can feel, have, and comprehend. Likewise, our wisdom and righteousness are not at all apparent to us but are hidden with Christ in God. Only their opposites are apparent, namely, sin and foolishness, in accordance with the word of the apostle: "Who is wise among you, let him become a fool that he may become wise" (I Cor. 3:18), i.e., let him become wise and rich in God and not in himself; may all wisdom be taken from him and nothing remain but foolishness. The same applies to all other goods.

Of this kind, then, are the goods we must wish for ourselves (i.e., everything that is bad). For only thus we are conformed to God, and he does not recognize and take account of anything good in us. But we are already good by recognizing only God's good as good and our good as evil, for one who in this way is of one mind with God is wise and good. He knows that outside God there is no good and that all good is in God, as Christ says: *"The Kingdom of God is inside you"* (Luke 17:21), *i.e., outside you is exile. Everything that can be seen and touched is outside you. But everything that only faith can believe is inside you.*

Hence, it is very dangerous of these people to dispute about a good that is deduced from philosophy, inasmuch as God has turned this good into evil. For although everything is very good (Gen. 1:31), for us nothing is good, and though there are no things that are evil in every respect, yet they are all evil for us, and all this

---

[8] *"Ut fides locum habeat in Deo."*
[9] Cf. Dionysius Areopagita, *Myst. Theol.*, c. 3–5.

because we have sin in us. Therefore, we must shun the good and take evil upon ourselves. And this very thing we must confess not merely by word of mouth and from a deceitful heart but with our whole mind, wishing that we be damned to perdition. For we must act toward ourselves as one does when he hates another. One who hates desires not falsely but seriously to destroy, kill, and damn the one he hates. If we, therefore, sincerely impose destruction and persecution upon ourselves and are ready to go to hell for the sake of God and his righteousness, we shall thereby already satisfy his justice, and he will have mercy on us and set us free. "If we could judge ourselves, we should not be judged by the Lord." (I Cor. 11:31.)

People of this sort have only the one concern to wash away their guilt and to restore the grace of God whom they have offended; they do not seek the Kingdom; they are ready to forego salvation and are freely willing to suffer damnation. But thanks to the grace of God who is already placated, they do not fear punishment but only their enmity against God.

This is contrary to the ways of those who imagine that they have merits and who picture these to themselves while they seek their own kind of good; they shun evils but deep in their hearts they have nothing. For they go along blindly, wholly absorbed in the good they conceived and wished for themselves.

But it is not as though the word of God had come to nought. For they are not all Israel that are of Israel, neither, because they are Abraham's seed, are they all children, but "in Israel shall your seed be called." That is, it is not the children of the flesh that are children of God, but the children of the promise are reckoned for a seed. For this is a word of promise: According to this season will I come, and Sarah shall have a son. (Rom. 9:6–9.)

This word is spoken against the presumptuousness of the Jews and on behalf of grace, so that all proud confidence in righteousness and good works may be undone. For the Jews want to be regarded as the children of the Kingdom because they are the children of Abraham. The apostle reasons against them by an argument that is irrefutable, chiefly because they themselves cannot deny its validity. For if their presumptuous opinion of themselves were correct, also Ishmael and the sons of Keturah (Gen. 25:1 ff.) would be heirs of Abraham and deservedly of the same status with Isaac, but the text says plainly just the opposite. It is, therefore, a vain contention of theirs that they are of the same status with Isaac because they, too, are the sons of Abraham. For this does obviously not follow. If they object and say that Ishmael and the others do not deserve to be of the same status as Isaac, not only because they were evil and deserved to be deprived of their status on account of their sin, but also because they were not the children of the same mother Sarah, he counters with another example without refuting their objections, indeed, by quasi conceding them as valid, although one can read nowhere that the other children had sinned and it is written of Ishmael that he did so only once.

But if one concedes that they did not have the same mother, what, then, about Rebecca? First, there is the same mother; second, they have the same father; and third, there are two brothers of whom neither is as yet good or evil and yet, without desert, one of them is called to sonship and the other to servitude. Hence, it follows irrefutably: one does not become a son of God and an heir of the promise by descent but by the gracious election of God. Thus and only thus, the Spirit and the grace of God can arise as the pride of the flesh is put down.

So then, why does man take pride in his merits and good works? They cannot in any way please God, because they *are* good and meritorious, but only because God has elected from eternity that they would please him. We do the good only on the basis of gratitude, because our works do not make us good, but our goodness or, rather, the goodness of God makes us good and our actions as well. For what we do is not good in itself, but only because God reckons it to be so. Our deeds are good or not good only to the degree in which God does or does not regard them so. Hence, our reckoning or nonreckoning is worth nothing. A man who is aware of this is always trembling in fear and expectation of the divine reckoning. He therefore does not know anything about being proud and contentious in the way of the proud moralists[10] who are certain of their good works.

It is therefore wrong to define virtue in the way of Aristotle:[11] It makes us perfect and produces laudable acts only in the sense that it makes us perfect and causes our acts to be praiseworthy before men and in our own eyes. Before God this is abominable, and the opposite would please him much more.

And not only so, **but Rebecca also having conceived by one,** *even by our father Isaac.* (Rom. 9:10.)

Even though the Greek text can be read in both ways: "Rebecca having shared the bed with one, even with our father Isaac" and

_____

10 *"Iustitiarii."*
11 Cf. Aristotle, *Eth. Nicom.*, I, 12.

"having shared the bed with one, even the bed of our father Isaac,"[12] the second reading is the better one, so that nobody may cast aspersions on Sarah by thinking that Rebecca conceived by one husband and Sarah by many. The meaning of the text is this: Flesh and physical descent are of so little significance for the adoption to sonship that even Rebecca, the holy woman, having shared only the bed of the holy man Isaac, the father of all the Children of Israel, received the divine promise for only one of her sons in order that only he and not the other one should possess and inherit the promise. Hence, every one of these words must be specially emphasized: "having shared the bed of Isaac, our father," i.e., it was of no advantage to Esau that he had such a father and such a mother and that, like Jacob, he was so chastely conceived and born according to the flesh and even that he was the first-born. Of how much less advantage will it be to the unbelieving Jews, who were born so much later, that they are the sons of the patriarchs by physical descent if they are found to be without faith, i.e., if they were not elected by God!

Finally, we must note that the apostle, writing in Greek, speaks with much more modesty than his translator, for he says "bed" but the latter, "coition."[13] Thus he caused many to understand the apostle as if he had wanted to say that Rebecca conceived twins at one coition.

For the children being not yet born, **neither having done anything good or bad,** *that the purpose of God according to election might stand, not of works but of him that calls, it was said to her: The elder shall serve the younger. Even as it is written: Jacob I loved, but Esau I hated.* (Rom. 9:11–13.)

He puts it well when he says "neither *having done* anything good or bad" rather than "neither *being* good or bad," for there can be no doubt that both were bad in virtue of original sin, even though some think that Jacob was sanctified in his mother's

---

[12] Lit., *"Ex uno cubile habens."* The Vulgate reads *"patris nostri."* Erasmus prefers *"patre nostro."*

[13] The Greek term is *koitēn* which, in the Vulgate, is translated *concubitus.* Faber has *cubile.* Erasmus discusses both terms.

It is to be noted that, from here on, Luther constantly refers to Erasmus. At the end of February, 1516, the printer Froben of Basel published Erasmus' Greek edition of the New Testament and also Erasmus' *Annotationes Novi Testamenti.* Ficker surmises (p. XXIX) that Luther began his lectures of the summer semester, 1516, with an exposition of the ninth chapter of the letter to the Romans, having been occupied with chapters 1 to 8 during the two preceding semesters. It is obvious, therefore, that Luther began to use the work of Erasmus almost immediately after publication.

mass of perdition cf p273 cf p. 276

womb.[14] But according to their own merit they were alike and equally belonged to the same mass of perdition.

What shall we say then? **Is there injustice[15] with God? No.** (Rom. 9:14.)

The apostle furnishes no other proof for the statement that there is no injustice with God than that he says: "I will have mercy on whom I have mercy" (Rom. 9:15), which is the same as to say: I will have mercy to whom I intended to be merciful or to him who was predestined to receive my mercy.

proof vs humble

This is hard to take for the proud who claim to know everything, but it is sweet and welcome to the meek and humble, for they despair of themselves and this is why the Lord accepts them.

For there is no other reason for his justice and there can be no other than his will. Why, then, does man grumble about the impossible, namely, that God does not act according to the law? Could it be possible that God is not God? Moreover, inasmuch as his will is the highest good, why are we not ready and eager to see it done, especially in view of the fact that it cannot possibly be evil? And if you say: But to me it is evil, I answer: No. It is evil to no one. But the fact that his will cannot be managed and that men cannot cause it to be done, this is an evil to them. If one wills what God wills, even if this means to be damned and rejected, one has no evil. Then one wills what God wills and patience enables one to bear it.

cf p. 261f

For he says to Moses: **I will have mercy to whom I have been merciful** *and I will have compassion on whom I will have compassion.* (Rom. 9:15.)

The Greek text reads:[16] "I will have mercy on whom I have mercy and I will have compassion on whom I have compassion," i.e., to whom I have mercy in the moment of predestination, to him I shall be merciful in fact also later. The present tense "I have mercy" signifies the intrinsic mercy of him who predestines, and the future tense, the mercy that is given to the predestined one. The same applies to the phrase "I will have compassion."

The Hebrew text reads: "I will have mercy on whom I will have mercy, and I will be gracious to whom I will be gracious." (Ex. 33:19.) This is, as it were, indefinitely put. It speaks of mercy more

---

[14] Cf. *Gl. ord. ad* Hos. 12:3, which reads as follows (in the Vulgate): "In the womb he supplanted his brother, and by his strength he had success with an angel."

[15] The Vulgate has *"iniquitas"*; Luther reads *"inustitia."*

[16] Luther follows Erasmus' translation.

in terms of a chance without specific reference to predestination. In the same way he says in Ex. 3:14: "I am who I am" or "I shall be who I shall be."

He uses this mode of expression apparently in order to rebuff people who anxiously inquire about their own and others' predestination (as if he wanted to keep them back from all thinking and inquiring about predestination). As we commonly say: I get it when I get it, and when it hits me, it hits me,[17] i.e., nobody can know on whom I will have mercy and on whom I will have compassion. Nobody can be certain about it because of his merits or works or anything else. Hence, this is a saying that instills fear and humiliation.

We must note, therefore, that in Hebrew, the first mentioned word "I will have mercy" means "having mercy on someone" in the sense that he who has mercy bestows a gift or a benefit upon another, even one who has given no offense or committed no sin, but is merely poor and in want. Hence, "Hannan" (which, in Hebrew, means "one who has shown mercy") signifies "one who has given a benefit." Hence, "Hanna" means "grace" or "benefit" or "good gift." The same is true for Johannan or Johannes with the Greek ending.

"I will be gracious" or "I will show compassion" means "to forgive" or "to be gracious." This can become real also without the gift of grace in the case of one who has committed an offense that deserves punishment. Thus, when God remits the penalty of hell and forgives sin, he shows compassion, but he is merciful to one on whom he bestows the gift of grace and the Kingdom of God. The Hebrew word for this is "richem."[18]

So then, it is not of him that wills, nor of him that runs, *but of God that has mercy.* (Rom. 9:16.)

We must not understand this to mean: The only thing that matters is God's mercy and therefore it is not necessary for anyone to will and to run, but we must take it to say: A man owes his ability to will and to run, not to his own power, but to the mercy of God who gave him this power to will and to run. Without it, man could neither will nor run. As the apostle says in Phil. 2:13: "It is God who achieves in you both to will and to work." Here he expresses exactly the same meaning, but in different words: "It is not of him that wills nor of him that runs," i.e., who achieves, "but of God that has mercy," i.e., who gives the gift of his grace.

[margin note: we owe power to God.]

---

[17] Luther uses the German expression: *"Wem es wirt, dem wirt es; wen es trifft, den trifft es."*
[18] Cf. Faber and Erasmus.

So it says also in Ps. 119:32: "I have run the way of thy commandments," i.e., I have achieved, "when thou didst enlarge my heart," i.e., when thou enablest me to run. And in Ps. 1:2: "And his will is in the law of the Lord." (If someone should ask what it means "to run," I should answer that it means "to live and have one's being in God." This is why the life of the righteous is called a "way," as in Ps. 1:6: "For the Lord knows the way of the righteous.")

So also in Jer. 10:23: "I know, O Lord, that the way of a man is not his; neither is it in a man to walk and to direct his steps." Now all these sayings contain a contradiction of a sort. For if a man's way is not his way, why, then, does it say "his way"? The way of man is not his way. So also here: The race is not of him that runs" nor the will "of him that wills." It is a strange thing! The will is not his that wills and the race is not his that runs, but God's who gives and creates it. In the same way, the apostle says in Gal. 2:20: "I live, yet not I." And Christ says: "My teaching is not mine." (John 7:16.) And Eccl. 9:11: "I saw that the race is not to the swift, nor the battle to the strong, nor bread to the wise, nor riches to the learned, nor favor to the skillful." Whose is it then? Is the race, then, to those that sit and yawn? And the battle to the weak? Certainly not! But they all are the instruments of God who "works all in all" (I Cor. 12:6). Similarly, cutting wood is not the doing of the ax but of the cutter, and beating a dog is not the doing of the stick but of him that wields it. Hence, the word of Isa. 10:13 ff. is directed against people who boast of the strength that enables them to inflict damage and injury upon others: "The king of Assyria said: By the strength of my own hand I have done it," etc. And then there follows this: "Shall the ax boast itself against him that cuts with it? Or shall the saw exalt itself against him by whom it is drawn? As if a rod should lift itself up against him that lifts it up, and a staff exalt itself which is but wood!" And, farther on, in Isa. 41:23, he laughs at them and says: "Do good or evil, if you can," i.e., let us see whether, without my help, you do good to anyone in need. Experience plainly shows that nobody can heal or help those whom God punishes.

The same applies also to the opposite: doing evil, i.e., inflicting injury upon others. To be sure, many attempt to do great things, but they do not succeed because God resists them or refuses to cooperate with them. This is plainly apparent in the case of Pharaoh. He wanted to inflict injury on the Children of Israel and could not do so. And thus God demonstrated his power in him: he could not will it, because he was hardened; and he could run even less than he could will.

imp. of human willing

Now it does not follow from this text that a man's running and willing amount to nothing, but what follows from it is that they do not come from his own strength. For the work of God is not nothing. And a man's willing and running is God's work. Indeed, the apostle speaks here about a willing and running according to God, i.e., about a life of love and divine righteousness. But there is a willing and running that is vain—namely, that of those who do not will and run in the way of God, though they may will great things and run strongly. For what they do is not from God and does not please him. It is of these that Isa. 41:24 says: "You are of nothing and your work of that which has no being."

Yet I want to give here this warning: No one whose mind has not yet been purged, should plunge into these speculations, lest he fall into an abyss of horror and despair. He must first purge the eyes of his heart in meditating on the wounds of Christ.[19] Nor would I talk about this, did not the order of the lectures and necessity compel me to do so. For this is very strong wine and the most wholesome meal and solid food for the perfect, i.e., it is theology in the best sense of the word,[20] about which the apostle says: "We speak wisdom among the perfect" (I Cor. 2:6). I myself am still a little one in Christ that needs milk and not solid food. (I Cor. 3:1–2.) Let him who is as I am do likewise. The wounds of Christ, "the clefts in the rock," are safe enough for us.[21]

theology in the best sense of the word

Those that are strong and perfect may discuss the first book of the Sentences, which properly should not be the first but the last book.[22] But nowadays many read this book hurriedly and heedlessly—with the result that they become strangely blinded.

Thou wilt say then unto me: **Why does he still find fault?** *for who resists his will? Nay, but, O man, who are you that reply against God? Shall the thing formed say to him that formed it: Why didst thou make me thus?* (Rom. 9:19–20.)

Some, like Laurentius Valla, take this phrase[23] to be passive; Stapulensis understands it as referring to a person; but Erasmus

---

[19] Ficker (p. 400, n. 3) points out that these ideas of Luther's, which seem to be under the influence of Bernard of Clairvaux, are reflected in the penitential practices and in the religious art of the Middle Ages.

[20] *"Excellentissima theologia."*

[21] In the *Gl. ord.*, and also the commentaries of Lyra and Faber, *"in foraminibus"* ("in the clefts of the rock") is interpreted as in *"vulneribus Christi"* ("in the wounds of Christ").

[22] *I Sent., d.* 35, where predestination and the problems of the divine will are discussed.

[23] *"Queriter"* ("find fault").

says that all Greek interpreters take it as a deponent, and he agrees with them.[24] Now one must know that the apostle cites this word in the name of people who contend against God in their ungodly pride and indignantly grumble against him as if he were an evildoer and someone like them. This is why the Greek text does not say as ours does: "Who are you that you reply to him?" but "that you reply against" or "in opposition to" him;[25] in other words: you make bold to quarrel with your Creator and to oppose him and speak up against him and you are not willing to yield him an inch of ground.

Now, it would not be a sin at all if someone were to say to God fearfully, humbly, and devoutly: "Why didst thou make me thus? Even if he would blaspheme God while under the overwhelming power of an assault upon his faith,[26] he would not perish because of this. For our God is no impatient or cruel God, even toward the ungodly. I say this in order to comfort those who are constantly plagued by blasphemous thoughts and are in very great trepidation. Indeed, because it is the devil that forcibly extorts such blasphemies from men against their will, they are sometimes more agreeable to God than the sound of a hallelujah or an anthem of praise. For the more horrible and horrid a blasphemy is, the more agreeable it is to God if only the heart feels that it does not want to utter it, because it has not freely brought it forth from itself. If a man is filled with fear and trembling because he has uttered a blasphemy, this is a sign that he did not really want to do it and that he did it innocently. *This dread of evil is an evident sign that one has a good heart.* Hence, the best cure for such thoughts is not to be concerned about them.

As an example, take Job, who was a great saint. The Holy Spirit was his witness that he had not sinned against God with his lips or said anything foolish against him in all his trials.[27] Yet more than once he spoke up against God in this way: "What is man that thou shouldst magnify him, or why dost thou set thy heart upon him? How long wilt thou not spare me, and why dost thou not let me go?" (Job 7:17, 19). And again: "Against a leaf that is carried away with the wind thou showest thy power and thou pursuest a dry straw." (Job 13:25.) But his plainest word is this: "Why didst thou bring me forth out of the womb?" (Job 10:18). Jeremiah and Habakkuk raise the same complaint against God.[28]

---

[24] Cf. Laurentius Valla, *Annotationes in Novi Testamenti interpretationem* (ed. Erasmus), Paris, 1505, f. 28. Also, Faber and Erasmus.
[25] Luther follows Erasmus.
[26] "*Si ex abundanti tentationis violentia blasphemaret.*"
[27] "*Tentationibus.*"
[28] Cf. Jer. 20:18. There is no saying of this kind in Hebrews.

For the Scripture says unto Pharaoh: *For this purpose did I raise thee up, that I might show thee my power, and that my name might be declared throughout all the earth.* (Rom. 9:17.)

If we ask: Is the apostle in saying this consistent with what he stated before? we must answer that he speaks in a most orderly fashion. For he had stated that everything happens according to God's election: Jacob was loved by God because he was chosen; and he obtained mercy because it thus pleased God from eternity. As he said to Moses: "I will show mercy," etc. (Ex. 33:19.) To these statements he properly adds the corollary which is plainly implied in them, namely, that it is only because of the mercy of God that someone is beloved and righteous, inasmuch as all belong to the same mass of perdition and none is righteous before God, unless he has mercy on him. And then there follows the sentence: "For the Scripture says." Its meaning is this: that all depends on God's mercy and not on anyone's willing is plainly shown by the fact that in order to demonstrate this and to let man know that his willing and running is not due to his running but to the divine mercy, God set Pharaoh over the Children of Israel, driving them into utter despair so that they would understand that they could not escape from Pharaoh by their own strength but only by the power of the merciful God. Thus their escape was not their own achievement but that of the Lord who led them.

Today, he deals with his elect in the same way: In order to humble them and to teach them to rely on his bare mercy, putting down all presumptuous confidence in their own willing and doing, he lets them be afflicted to the point of desperation and causes them to be persecuted by the devil, the world, and the flesh. Indeed, again and again and particularly in this our time, he incites the devil to drive his elect into horrible sins and to have dominion over them for a time, or at least constantly to obstruct their good intentions, so that they do the opposite of what they want to do, and all this to such an extent that they even take pride in not being able to will or to do anything good. And yet, through it all, God continues to be their guide: he finally sets them free when they become hopeless and find themselves driven to despair over the fact that they want to do and actually do so much evil and that they do not have the will or intention to do any of the good toward which they aspire. Thus, yes, thus it comes about that "he shows his power and that his name is declared throughout all the earth."

Note that *"virtus"* (power) means the same as *"potentia"* (power), a word that is used in the passage that follows a little farther on (Rom. 9:22): "to make his power known." Our translator, strangely enough, translates the word *"virtus"* in various ways[29] using interchangeably such common terms as *fortitudo* (strength), *imperium* (dominion), *virtus* (power), *potentia* (power), *potestas* (power). But there is a great difference between them. For the Greek word *dynamis,* the Hebrew word *gebura,* and the Latin words *vis, vires, robur,* and, very characteristically, *virtus* signify that by which one is strong enough actually to conquer and break down what one tries to break down. The opposite is called in the Scriptures *"infirmitas"* (weakness), and not *aegritudo* (sickness) or *morbus* (disease). For example, it says: "Power is made perfect in weakness."[30] (II Cor. 12:9.) And again: "It was weakened, but thou hast made it perfect." (Ps. 68:10.) And Ps. 6:2: "Have mercy on me, O Lord, for I am weak," or, as we say in German: *Crafftlos, machtloss* (powerless), the opposite of *Crefftig, mechtig* (powerful) in the sense of *Er vermag vill* (he can do much), *vermags nit* (he is not able to do much), *er kans woll thun* (he is able to do it).[31] Thus we say also of God: "God is able to perform" (Rom 4:21) and likewise: "God is mighty in battle" (Ps. 24:8).

But the Greek word *exousia* signifies "power" (*potestas*) in the sense of a free faculty and license to dispose of something. It signifies a power of peace, so to speak, while the other (*potentia*) is a power of war. For with respect to what we possess and own, we have the free faculty and power of disposal, but, with respect to what we oppose, we are powerful and strong.

In Hebrew, there is still another word for strength (*fortitudo*). It is *ethan,* i.e., hard, robust. Strictly speaking, it signifies a passive power, i.e., a power that is capable of sustaining an active power. In German, we say *fest* (strong). Numbers 24:21: "Thy habitation is indeed strong," just as rock is strong or a castle or the city about which the Lord says in Isa. 50:7: "I have set my face on a very hard rock." In the same way, we call someone strong who cannot be twisted or put down. We also call a stiff-necked person strong, one who does not let himself be persuaded, but then we mean something opposite to *gebura.* As we say in the proverb: "Two hard stones cannot grind."[32] For when *gebura* (*virtus*) and *ethan* (*fortitudo*) balance each other, they cannot do anything. For when two are equally balanced, there can be no action between them.

But to return to our text: God raised up Pharaoh in order to

---

29 Faber and Erasmus explain *virtus* as *potentia;* Faber also uses *potestas.* Cf. Biel, III *Sent., d.* 23, *a.* 1, *n.* 1.

30 *"Virtus in infirmitate perficitur."*

31 Luther uses his own spelling for *kraftlos, machtlos; er vermag viel; er vermag's nicht; er kann's wohl tun.*

32 *"Duo lapides fortes non molunt"* (*"Zwei feste Steine mahlen nicht"*). Cf. E. Thiele, *Luthers Sprichwörtersammlung,* Nr. 463.

demonstrate his power. For he cannot demonstrate his power in his elect, unless he first shows them their weakness by concealing their power and reducing it to nothing so that they cannot glory in their own power. But he could not accomplish this unless he raised up against them one stronger than they to reduce their power to nothing, so that then only God's power might become manifest in the fact that they are free. The meaning of the passage, then, is this: I have raised you up in order that you should put down the proud presumption of my people so that they will cry unto me out of their oppression and so that my power may be magnified in them and in you. This is the meaning I have followed in the Gloss.[33]

We can also read the text differently: perhaps it would be better to understand the term "power" with reference, not to our salvation, but to the destruction of others. In this case, the sense of the whole passage would be this: Jacob, who was made good because God had mercy on him, is the chief example of the fact that everything depends solely on God's being merciful and not on anyone's willing and running; and Pharaoh is an example of the fact that no one can become good if God is not merciful to him. We have then an example for both possibilities: it is of God who has mercy if someone runs, and if he does neither will nor run, this is not of God who has mercy but of God who hardens: I like this interpretation because, from either example, one can at once conclude that "he has mercy on whom he will, and whom he wills he hardens" (Rom. 9:18). Moreover, I like this interpretation also in the light of the saying: "That I might demonstrate in you my power" (Rom. 9:17). He wills that his power should be magnified in man's perdition.

Or has not the potter a right over the clay, *from the same lump to make one part a vessel unto honor and another unto dishonor? What if God, willing to show his wrath and to make his power known, endured with much patience vessels of wrath, fitted for destruction, that he might show the riches of his glory on the vessels*

---

[33] In the Gloss, Luther interprets Rom. 9:17 as follows (*WA* 56, 92, 15): "The power to save is mine alone, and it does not lie in anybody else's power, merit, or righteousness, or in any other good. It is this I wanted to demonstrate and call to your attention by the fact that I hardened you and that I freed Israel. In other words: I cause and did cause all this to happen, in order to show that the election of my grace brings salvation and that those who were elected are saved but that those who were not elected are rejected. This knowledge of grace would not come about if God did act in this way, but if everyone persisted presumptuously in believing in his own righteousness as if he could be saved by his effort and not by the mercy of God."

*of mercy, which he has prepared unto glory? Even us whom he has
also called, not only of the Jews, but also of the Gentiles. As in
Hosea he says: I will call that which was not my people, my people;
and her that was not beloved, beloved; and her that had not obtained mercy, one that has obtained mercy. And it shall be, in the
place where it was said unto them: You are not my people; there
they shall be called the sons of the living God.* (Rom. 9:21–26.)

Blessed Augustine writes in Chapter 99 of the *Enchiridion*:[34]
"The whole human race was condemned in its apostate root by a
divine judgment so just that not even if a single man were saved
from it, no one could possibly rail against God's justice. And those
that are saved had to be saved on such terms that it would show,
by contrast with the greater number of those not saved but abandoned to their wholly just damnation, what the whole mass deserved and to what end God's merited judgment would have
brought them, had not this undeserved mercy intervened, so that
'every mouth' of those disposed to glory in their own merits 'would
be stopped' (Rom. 3:19), and that 'he that glories may glory in the
Lord' (I Cor. 1:31)."

This is a significant statement that should be carefully considered, for it makes us humble and has a deterrent effect upon us.
Indeed, Blessed Augustine shows admirably why the apostle spoke
as he did, namely, in order to instruct us in humility. It is plainly
not the purpose of his words to lead us to the horror of despair
but to induce us to praise grace and to put down all presumptuous pride. This is a salutary despair. Hence, Blessed Augustine says
in Chapter 98 of the same book:[35] "Indeed, referring everything
to a very profound and salutary mystery, and looking the Holy
Scriptures straight in the eye, so to speak, the apostle seems to give
the admonition that 'he who glories should glory in the Lord' "
(I Cor. 1:31). And again he writes in the same place:[36] "God shows
mercy out of his great goodness and hardens out of no wickedness,
so that he who is saved has no basis for glorying in any merit of his
own and he who is damned no basis for complaining of anything
except what he has fully merited. For grace alone separates the redeemed from the lost, all having been mingled together in the one
mass of perdition arising from a common cause which leads back
to their common origin."

Such words cause a man to recognize his damnation and to despair of the possibility that he can be saved by his own powers.
Ordinarily, the idea that he is fallen in Adam leaves him cold, for

[34] Augustine, *Enchiridion*, 99.
[35] *Ibid.*, 98.
[36] *Ibid.*, 99.

he hopes, indeed he presumes, to be able to raise himself by his own free will. But here he is given to understand that grace raises him up before and beyond all his free will.

And Isaiah cries concerning Israel: If the number of the Children of Israel be as the sand of the sea, it is the remnant that shall be saved. (Rom. 9:27.)

The term "remnant" and similarly the idea expressed in this particular saying can be found frequently in the books of the Prophets. For example, in Isa. 4:3: "And it shall come to pass that everyone that shall be left in Zion and that shall remain in Jerusalem shall be called holy, everyone that is written in life in Jerusalem." And Isa. 46:3: "Hearken unto me, O house of Jacob and all the remnant of the house of Israel." Isaiah 65:8: "As if a grape be found in a cluster, and it be said: Destroy it not, because it is a blessing, so will I do for the sake of my servants that I may not destroy the whole. And I will bring forth a seed out of Jacob," i.e., a remnant, etc. And Amos 3:12: "As if a shepherd should get out of the lion's mouth two legs or the tip of an ear: so shall the Children of Israel be taken out." Micah 2:12: "I will bring together the remnant of Israel." And Micah 5:7: "And the remnant of Jacob shall be in the midst of the nations as a dew from the Lord."

In this way, then, and in many other places, the apostles and the faithful among the Jews are called "the remnants" or "the remains," even "the dregs" of the people of Israel, as if the better part of them had to perish. As we read in Isa. 49:6: "It is a small thing that you should be my servant to raise up the tribes of Jacob, and to convert the dregs of Israel. Behold, I have given you to be a light," etc. And in Ps. 78:31 it is said: "And he slew the fat ones among them and brought down the chosen men of Israel," i.e., the dregs and the lowly ones are saved, but the nobler ones are made blind. Just as when a whole cluster of grapes is thrown away and only one berry is left over.

This remnant is represented by the few poor people who were left behind in the country at the time of the exile to Babylon, when the king and queen and the prophets, i.e., the powerful, the wise, and the saints, had to go away (II Kings 24:12 ff.). In this same way, the Jews of today have migrated to the true Babylon of unbelief; all the nobler ones have done so with the exception of the few they left behind. It is this migration which Jeremiah deplores in his Lamentations (Lam. 1:3 ff.). In spirit he sees that what happened then really signifies what is occurring today.

They are also symbolized by the Amalekite boy in I Sam.

30:11 ff., who was left behind by his master that had gone on with his troop and his spoil. This is why Isaiah says of the few who were left behind in Israel (Isa. 10:17 f.): "And Israel shall run away through fear, and they that remain of the trees of the forest shall be so few that they shall easily be numbered, and a boy shall write them down." The trees of the forest are the people of the synagogue, very dense and tall in the boastful multitude of the Children of Israel.

They are called a "remnant" because they are left over, as one can plainly see here in the prophecy of Isaiah. For while God gave the others up to destruction, he kept only these for himself as a seed for another people.

For the Lord shall consummate his word and cut it short in righteousness; *because a short word shall the Lord make upon the earth. And as Isaiah foretold: Except the Lord of Sabaoth had left us a seed, we had been as Sodom and Gomorrah. What, then, shall we say? That the Gentiles who followed not after righteousness have attained to righteousness, even the righteousness which is of faith? But Israel, which followed after the law of righteousness, has not attained to the law of righteousness. Why so? Because they sought it not by faith but, as it were, by works.* (Rom. 9:28–31.)

The words "he shall consummate and cut short" refer to the Spirit and the letter, for the flesh and the wisdom of the flesh are in no way capable of comprehending the righteousness and wisdom of God. Therefore, this word of righteousness and wisdom, which is the word of faith, must be contracted and shortened so that it can in no wise be extended to the flesh and its wisdom and righteousness, and neither comprehends it nor is comprehended by it. Hence, carnal persons must necessarily take offense at it and find themselves standing outside it and cut off from it.

For before this word of faith, the word of the Spirit, was revealed, everything was veiled in sign and shadow on account of the slowness of the Jews; the word was incomplete and imperfect and therefore easily intelligible to all, because it spoke in signs about things that are accessible to the senses. But as soon as God turned away from the sensible and from signs and began to speak the word of the Spirit, the word of faith which is hidden, and thus brought forth the complete and perfect word, it had neccessarily to be cut off from everything that can be perceived by the senses and from all signs and symbols. Thereby all who wanted to hold on to sense and symbol were also cut off, or rather: the word was cut off from them.

It is on account of these people who have fallen that the apostle says "he will cut short the word" rather than the reality manifested by the word. For, having rejected what can be seen and withholding what is yet to come and cannot be seen, he placed only his word in their midst. Whosoever does not believe, therefore, will perish. (Isa. 7:9.) For an unbeliever is not content with the word and is indignant at the fact that the reality it expresses is denied to him.

To those who "cut" themselves "short" and "consummate" themselves, this shortened and consummated word will bring righteousness, but to all others, sin and unrighteousness because of their unbelief. For it is "a word that is consummated and cut short in righteousness," i.e., all who believe in this word are righteous. But no one believes unless he keeps his thinking bound to the invisible and unless he cuts himself off from the contemplation of all that is visible.[37] For the word is "cut short" also in this sense that it is cut off and separated from all that can be seen. It promises and exhibits nothing visible but rather abnegates it and cuts it off. It teaches that one must renounce the visible. And this because it is the "consummated," i.e., perfect, word that cannot signify anything else but the perfect and complete.

Every word, namely, that signifies and proclaims something visible and created, is on this account not complete and perfect, because it proclaims a part and not the whole, i.e., something that does not satisfy the whole man, but only titillates a part of him, his flesh and the senses. But if it is to proclaim the perfect that satisfies the whole man, it must not proclaim anything that satisfies the flesh, i.e., something created or visible, but God alone. Hence, it is cut short precisely in being consummated, and, conversely, in being cut short it is consummated. For it is consummated on behalf of the Spirit, because it proclaims what is good for the Spirit. Its being cut short, however, is directed against the flesh, because it rejects all that is good for the flesh.

The word of the letter or of the old sign was thus, by contrast, imperfect and incomplete because it had to be understood with respect to temporal goods and promises, and, for this reason, it was prolonged and extended rather than cut short. For it caused the Spirit to be more and more removed and separated from his goods or from the understanding of his goods.

To summarize briefly:

As the word of the law carnally understood was an imperfect, dilated, or extended word, so the word of the Spirit, i.e., of the law spiritually understood, is a consummated and abbreviated word.

It was imperfect because it signified something but did not ac-

[37] *"Ab intuitu omnium visibilium."*

tually display what it signified. On this account, it was dilated and
extended, for it led more and more to the imperfect and carnal,
inasmuch as it is impossible to display the spiritual as long as one
regards and understands it as something carnal. So it is also with
a sign: as long as one takes it for that which it signifies, one does
not really have what it signifies. So also this word did not lead in
the end "to righteousness," but to wickedness, deceitfulness, and
vanity.

On the other hand, the word of the gospel is complete, because it
actually makes available what it signifies, namely, grace. For this
very reason, it is also abridged, for it does not defer the actualization of what it announces. Indeed, it cuts itself off from everything that postpones and impedes its actualization. Therefore, it
is also "cut short in righteousness," for it avails righteousness to
those for whom it is consummated and abridged, and this happens
through faith.

COROLLARY

The word of the old and the new law is the same. Hence, it can
be called perfect or not perfect, short or long, only in terms of our
understanding or lack of understanding. Those, therefore, who
understand the most sacred gospel in terms of pride or error (as the
heretics and individualists[38] do) fashion for themselves from the
consummated and abridged word an imperfect and long one, i.e.,
a vain, useless, and deceitful word.

For no one can receive the word of Christ unless he abjures
everything else and rids himself of it, i.e., unless he humbly surrenders also the sovereignty of his reason and his whole mind.[39]
But because most people, persisting in their pride, do not take hold
of the word or, rather, are not taken hold of by it, hardly a remnant is saved; the word is cut short in those who perish and consummated in those who believe.

This is the allegorical "abridgment and consummation," i.e.,
this is what the letter means in so far as it signifies the spiritual
word. But the same meaning can be found by the moral interpretation. For because the word of the Spirit pronounces a "No" upon
all pride and self-will, it must equally pronounce a "No" also upon
all who are proud and sufficient to themselves in their own knowledge, and it must cut itself off from them. Thus the tropological
"abridgment" implies the allegorical one. For because the word
consummates and perfects humility and a willing obedience, it

[38] "Monii" ("singulares"); cf. Luther's comments on Rom. 4:7 and Rom. 7:8.
[39] WA 56, 408, 23 ff.: "Quia verbum Christi non potest suscipi nisi abnegatis
et precisis omnibus, i.e., etiam intellectu captivato et omni sensu humiliter
submisso."

also consummates and perfects all men who are humble and ready
to obey. And so the moral "consummation" implies also the allegorical one.

Faith, then, is the consummation and abridgment and compendium of salvation. For the word that is abridged is nothing
else but faith. How can we prove this? The word is abridged only
for one who understands that it is abridged. But one can have the
understanding only by faith. Hence, faith is life and the living
word that is abridged.

Notice that it is a short "evidence of things not seen" (Heb.
11:1), i.e., how it cuts one off and separates one from everything.
In the same way, the believer also cuts himself off from everything
by his faith, so that he has his being in that which is not apparent.
Then faith is a consummation, because it is "the substance of
things hoped for" (Heb. 11:1), i.e., mastery and power over the
things of the future which are eternal,[40] but not of the things of
the present; from them it cuts one off.

The apostle adds in equity[41] or "righteousness." For also the
word of the dead letter is consummated and abridged, but in the
opposite way, namely, in unrighteousness. Just as the word of the
Spirit consummates humility and the humble, and cuts short pride
and the proud—i.e., perfects those that are spiritual and destroys
those that are carnal, perfects the wisdom of the Spirit and does
away with the wisdom of the flesh, builds up Jerusalem and destroys Jericho[42]—so, by contrast, the word of the dead letter consummates and hardens the proud and destroys the humble,
perfects the wisdom of the flesh and does away with the wisdom of
the spirit, destroys Jerusalem and builds up Jericho. Thus one is
the word that is consummated and abridged "in righteousness"
and the other that which is consummated and abridged "in unrighteousness."

It is, then, sufficiently plain that these two terms refer to different things: "consummated" to the *terminus ad quem*, "cut short"
(or abridged) to the *terminus a quo*. "Consummated" indicates
where this word leads to, namely, to the perfection of righteousness, but "cut short" what the word turns one from, namely, from
the wisdom of the flesh and unrighteousness. From those who want
neither of these two, the word remains entirely cut off, leaving
them in the flesh and in unrighteousness.

This word can be likened to a coat or a cover that is too short:

---

[40] "*I.e., possessio et facultas futurarum verum, quae sunt eternae.*" Cf. Luther's
comments on Heb. 11:1 in his commentary (*WA* 57, 228).
[41] The Vulgate has "*in aequitate.*"
[42] In the moral interpretation of Josh., ch. 6, Lyra takes Jericho to mean "the
city of the devil" and Jerusalem "the city of God."

it covers one but leaves the other naked; Isa. 28:20: "The bed is
so narrow that the other one must fall out, and the coat so short
that it cannot cover them both." The word of faith is just as
narrow, so that two cannot rest in it, but one, namely, the "old
man" in us must fall out, because he does not lay hold of it. And
one and the same coat cannot cover them both, but only the "new
man" in us. The word is then perfect and consummated indeed,
because it consummates man wonderfully and exceedingly well,
but it is short indeed, because it consummates no one who is an
"old man," but it cuts him off from everything. In other words:
God will bring about a consummation, but one that is very short
and narrow. For in the case of most men, it will be abridged in so
far as it will cut off the whole old man in accordance with the perfection of the consummation; hence, the extent of the "abridgment." Now almost the entire people of Israel were carnal and
gloried in the flesh; hence, the abridgment that happened among
them was a vehement one in proportion to the multitude of carnal
men. Nor would it have been strange if all had been cut off (for
they were all children of the flesh, and as to the old man in them,
all were the descendants of their fathers), if the Lord had not left
a seed.

Therefore, "the consummation abridged shall overflow with
righteousness." (Isa. 10:22.) It is a strange thing, this consummation overflowing with righteousness which is nevertheless short
and narrow. Who has ever seen a narrow flood? And who has seen
a "being consummated" which is at the same time a "narrowing,"
a becoming perfect that is at the same time a being diminished,
something that is simultaneously minimized and magnified, simultaneously filled and emptied. Yet here it happened: What is wonderfully clothed and covered is yet almost entirely naked and bare.
What God has promised is fulfilled and yet at the same time cut
off from nearly everything. But where it is fulfilled, it is overflow-
ingly consummated in righteousness.

*They stumbled at the stumbling stone. As it is written: Behold,
I lay in Zion a stumbling stone and a rock of offense. And* **he that
believes in him shall not be confounded.** *(Rom. 9:32–33.)*

The Hebrew text reads: "He that believes, let him not hasten."[43]
The discrepancy between the two versions can be straightened out
in this way: One who believes in Christ is secure in his conscience;
he is righteous and, as the Scripture says, "bold as a lion" (Prov.
28:1). And again: "Whatever shall befall the righteous shall not
cause him anxiety" (Prov. 12:21), while "the wicked man flees

[43] Isa. 28:16 (Vg.): *"Qui crediderit, non festinet."*

[margin note: Scripture interprets Scripture]

when no man pursues" (Prov. 28:1)! And again (Isa. 57:20): "The wicked are like the raging sea which cannot rest." "There is no peace to the wicked, says the Lord." (Isa. 57:21.) And Ps. 1:4: "Not so the wicked: they are like the dust which the wind drives away." Leviticus 26:36: "The sound of a flying leaf shall terrify them." And Isa. 30:15 ff.: "Thus says the Lord God, the Holy One of Israel: If you return and be quiet, you shall be saved; in silence and in hope shall be your strength. And you would not. But you have said: No, but we will flee to horses; therefore shall you flee. And we will mount upon the swift ones, and therefore shall they be swifter that shall pursue you. A thousand men shall flee for fear of one," etc.

All this means: One who believes in Christ does not hasten or flee; he is not frightened, because he fears nothing; he stands quiet and secure, founded upon a firm rock, according to the teaching of the Lord in Matt. 7:24. But one who does not believe in him will really "be in a hurry," i.e., he will flee, yet he will not be able to escape when tribulation and anxiety and, above all, the judgment of God assail him. For this is the punishment of the damned and the unending restlessness to which they are condemned that they flee from God and yet cannot escape him. This is also the state of every evil conscience that has forgotten Christ, according to Deut. 28:67: "In the morning you shall say: Who will grant me evening? and at evening: Who will grant me morning? for the fearfulness of your heart wherewith you shall be terrified." "For the Lord will give you a fearful heart and a soul consumed with longing." (Deut. 28:65.)

Such a horror and such a flight of the conscience that quickly wants to get away is the confusion of conscience. It is as Pliny says:[44] "For no living being is fear more confusing than for man." How aptly, therefore, our translation corresponds to the Septuagint![45] The Seventy say: "He shall not be confounded"; thereby they want to signify the confusion and disturbance of the conscience that result from terror and fear; then a man is incapable of orderly thought and planning; he only wants to get away from it all and yet cannot do so. It is just like the confusion that occurs in tumults of war: when fear and terror strike, everyone runs to and fro and is confounded. Such is the penalty of all who die or, rather, suffer outside Christ; they are so perturbed that they do not know what to do.

[44] Pliny, *Nat. hist.*, VII, 5.
[45] Cf. n. 43. Cf. Jerome, *Comm. in Isaiam*, 9, 28. Erasmus (in the *Annot.*) compares both versions. He himself makes the text read neither *festinet* nor *confundetur*, but *"pudefiet"* ("he will be ashamed").

Blessed Jerome,[46] whom Lyra follows, says: "He does not hasten," i.e., the Advent of the Lord does not seem near to him, just as, by contrast, the Thessalonians were upset and terrified as if the Day of the Lord would momentarily come (II Thess. 2:1 ff.). In other words: one who believes in Christ is not so fearful that he thinks that the Day of Judgment has come whenever some kind of tribulation befalls him. But I do not understand this translation. Although I do not reject it, I do not want to take the time to discuss it further.

Still another interpretation is possible, one that I formerly used to advance, but it is a little too forced, namely: One who believes in Christ does not hasten with foolish zeal and does not walk about like the noonday devil[47] in order to judge others and to excuse himself, but he is of a humble mind and teachable and willing to be led. For in the fervor of the novitiate many hasten toward heaven and toward righteousness and wisdom with an excessive, burning zeal. It is the devil who excites this in them, so that, exhausted from the first run, they afterward become useless, because their mind is full of disgust at every good effort and they have a lukewarm and languid attitude toward all that is good, because at the very start they spent themselves like water. Thus "the inheritance that is gotten hastily in the beginning, in the end shall be without a blessing." (Prov. 20:21.) And Blessed Augustine says in his book *On the Blessed Life*:[48] "What one begins with too much eagerness commonly ends and gets lost in a great disgust."

Some, then, are quick and eager to judge others and to instruct them, demanding to be heard, but they are slow in letting themselves be judged and taught and they do not want to listen. But one who believes in Christ is not of this sort; he is like the one of whom Blessed James says: "Let every man be slow to speak but swift to hear" (James 1:19). The Jews, however, did not want to hear, because they hastened in their heart, etc.

The Greek equivalent of the word *"confundetur"* ("he shall be confounded") does not have this specifically Latin and proper meaning, suggesting, as was stated above, the sense of "confusion" or "being disturbed," etc., but *"confundetur"* is taken to mean "he will be ashamed" or "he will blush with shame." In this case, the haste we have spoken of and this blushing with shame are

46 Cf. Jerome and Lyra *ad loc.*
47 Cf. Ps. 90:5 f. (Vg.): "Thou shalt not be afraid of the terror of the night, of the arrow that flieth in the day, of the business that walks about in the dark, of invasion, or of the noonday devil." (The King James Version reads [Ps. 91:6]: "Nor for the pestilence that walketh in darkness; nor for the destruction that wasteth at noonday.")
48 Not to be found in *De beata vita* or elsewhere in Augustine.

brought into accord with one another in this way: one who is ashamed dreads to show himself; he wants to flee and to go into hiding. As the saying goes: "Fall upon us, mountains" (Hos. 10:8; Luke 23: 30). Thus his confusion causes him to hasten, i.e., to flee in fright. But one who believes in Christ does not do anything of this kind; he is not confounded and he does not blush with shame, because Christ has made him secure.

Either translation has, then, the same meaning, but the Septuagint expresses the cause and the Hebrew version[49] the effect, as it is frequently the case also elsewhere. For upon being confounded and upon being put to shame, there follows hurried flight, because one dreads to be seen.

[49] I.e., Jerome's correction of the Septuagint.

ROMANS, CHAPTER TEN

Brethren, my heart's desire and my supplication to God is for them, that they may be saved. For I bear them witness that **they have a zeal for God, but not according to knowledge.** (Rom. 10:1–2.)

This is something monstrous: it constitutes the most telling single opposition to faith; it refuses obedience and makes men stiff-necked and incorrigible, as heretics and schismatics plainly demonstrate. For as if they could not possibly be mistaken, they stay put on their good intention with unyielding obstinacy and they stake their salvation on the fact that they are engaged in religious pursuits with a divine zeal. The Scripture characterizes such people as being of a twisted and bent heart and of a corrupt mind, even though they are not corrupt in the flesh or in corporeal vices. Yet they are spiritually corrupt in so far as they obstinately persist in their own opinion and in their own way in pursuing the spiritual good. Such people are reproved by the Holy Virgin as she says: "He has scattered the proud in the conceit of their heart" (Luke 1:51).

Excellent

Today there belong to them those higher clergymen and princes who, under neglect of their proper duties, devote themselves to other affairs out of a zeal for God and with an upright intention,[1] and also everyone else who forsakes the lesser good he ought to do in order to pursue a greater good, i.e., a good that, by deceit of the devil, has the appearance of being greater. For the devil is the mind and head of the serpent of old and the cause and source of all discord, the father of pride, and obstinacy, and unbelief. Giving himself the appearance of acting on behalf of salvation, he blocks salvation.

[1] *"Pia intentione."*

We must note, therefore, that "to have a zeal for God according to knowledge" means to have a zeal for God in devout ignorance and in mental darkness;[2] in other words: to regard nothing as so wonderfully good, even if it seems to be God himself in all his glory, so as not always to be ready, with fear and trembling, to be led and guided to any kind of lesser good in order to be instructed by it. Not claiming to know, feel, or think anything, one must be indifferent to everything, whatever may be required of him either by God or by a man or by any other creature. For one does not claim to be able to know what to choose, but one expects to be chosen and called. Hence, Ps. 18:26 says: "With the chosen thou wilt be chosen," but it does not say: By choosing, you will be chosen.

Such people are soft and teachable, like gold that can be shaped and fashioned in any form. Hence, we find that, in the Holy Scriptures, a distinction is made between "upright" and "good," as, for example, in Ps. 125:4 f.: "Do good, O Lord, to those that are good, and to the upright in heart. But such that turn aside into bonds" (i.e., into crooked ways, against and away from uprightness) "the Lord shall lead forth with the workers of iniquity," i.e., with those who do a good they value in terms of the vain standards of their crookedness.

This word "uprightness"[3] is usually interpreted as "equity"; correctly understood, this means that the right kind of righteousness is the right good and that the wrong kind of righteousness or self-righteousness is a wrong and perverted good. Ecclesiastes 1:15: "The perverse are difficult to correct." Hence, Ps. 45:6 speaks of the "scepter of equity" or a staff that gives "direction," i.e., a staff of uprightness, which is "the scepter of thy Kingdom."[4] For "it directs the meek in judgment," i.e., those who do not know anything and do not direct themselves according to their own judg-

---

[2] In his lectures, so it seems, Luther reduced what follows to these sentences (*WA* 57, 207, 10 ff.): "It is to be noted, therefore, that 'to have zeal for God according to knowledge' means to have zeal for God in devout ignorance and in mental darkness. For the highest knowledge is to know that one knows nothing; true faith accomplishes this knowledge. Men of this knowledge are those who regard nothing as so wonderfully great, even if it seems to be God himself and all his glory, as not always to be ready, with fear and trembling, to be drawn and led to some less important good. And so they are disinterested in everything, having no specific knowledge of anything and no mind of their own. For they themselves do not choose, but they look forward to be chosen and called. Hence it says in Ps. 18:26: 'With the chosen one you will be chosen.' It does not say, 'With the one who chooses you will be chosen.'"

[3] "*Rectitudo.*"

[4] Luther here follows Faber in the *Psalterium Quincuplex.*

ment and conceit. "To have zeal according to knowledge" means, therefore, not at all to know what one has a zeal for. *For to know that one does not know*[5] is a kind of knowledge on which the Jews do not base their zeal. For they know that they have knowledge. But one who knows that he does not know is gentle and willing to be directed; he is not obstinate but ready to give his hand to everybody.

For, being ignorant of God's righteousness, and seeking to establish their own, they did not subject themselves to the righteousness of God. For Christ is the end of the law unto righteousness to everyone that believes. For Moses writes that the man that does the righteousness which is of the law shall live thereby. But the righteousness which is faith speaks thus: Say not in your heart: **Who shall ascend into heaven?** *(that is, to bring Christ down), or: Who shall descend into the abyss? (that is, to bring Christ up from the dead). But what says the Scripture? The word is nigh you and in your heart, that is, the word of faith which we preach. For if you confess with your mouth the Lord Jesus, and believe in your heart that God has raised him up from the dead, you shall be saved.* (Rom. 10:3–9.)

Moses writes these words in Deut. 30:12, and he does not have the meaning in mind they have here, but his abundant spiritual insight enables the apostle to bring out their inner significance. It is as if he wanted to give us an impressive proof of the fact that the whole Scripture, if one contemplates it inwardly, deals everywhere with Christ, even though in so far as it is a sign and a shadow, it may outwardly sound differently. This is why he says: "Christ is the end of the law" (Rom. 10:4); in other words: every word in the Bible points to Christ. That this is really so, he proves by showing that this word here, which seems to have nothing whatsoever to do with Christ, nevertheless signifies Christ.

There are several ways to expound this passage. *First,* there is the exposition as I gave it in the Gloss:[6] The apostle compares two kinds of righteousness with each other: he attributes the good work to the righteousness of the law, but the word to the righteousness of faith. For the law requires a deed, but the word requires faith (the deed requires the law in order that one may know what one must do, but faith requires the word not in order that one may know but that one may believe). The first kind of righteousness depends on the good work one does, but the second kind

---

[5] Cf. Tauler, *Sermones (Serm. 6).*
[6] The exposition that follows is practically identical with the one Luther offers in the Gloss.

depends on the word one believes. Now what this word is he makes plain by saying: **Say not in your heart: Who shall ascend into heaven?** or, in other words: The word that one must believe is nothing else but this: Christ died and he is risen.

This is why these negative and questioning forms of expression contain very strong affirmations. For example, the question: Who shall ascend into heaven? means: Say constantly in your heart: Christ is ascended into heaven, and you will be saved. Do not doubt in the slightest that he ascended. For this is the word that will save you. This is what the righteousness of faith teaches. This is the short way to salvation, the way of the compendium! But the righteousness of the law is a long, winding, and roundabout way, as it is symbolically represented by the people of Israel in the desert.

Second: Faber Stapulensis[7] thinks that by these words Moses insinuated the righteousness of Christ and his descent into hell and his ascent into heaven. Hence, he translates as follows: "But of the righteousness which is of faith he speaks thus: Who shall ascend into heaven? This signifies the descent of Christ. Or: Who shall descend in the abyss? This signifies Christ's restoration from the dead." He therefore relates the phrase "this is" or "this signifies" to the interrogatory sentences: "Who shall ascend?" and "Who shall descend?" but not to the phrase "Say not in your heart." But this exposition is so labored, and he himself is so uncertain about it that one cannot find any meaning in it.

Third: Erasmus[8] thinks that there is no difficulty here and that the expositors struggle with it in vain, because, in his opinion, the apostle means to say that by these words Moses wanted to curb those who do not believe unless they see direct evidence. The meaning of the question, "Who shall ascend into heaven?" then would be: Say not in thy heart: Christ is not in heaven; even though you do not see him, at least believe it. For one who does not believe this and says: "Who shall ascend into heaven?" does the same as one who denies that Christ is there or who demands that he be given proof and evidence for this faith.

But however this may be, the apostle means to say that the whole righteousness of man leading to salvation depends on the word apprehended by faith and not a work based on knowledge. This is why God causes all his prophets to reprove the people for nothing so much as that they do not want to hear his voice. Hence, he committed to his prophets not works, but words and sermons. Jeremiah says expressly: "Thus says the Lord of hosts, the God of

[7] Cf. Faber's *Comm., ad loc.*
[8] Erasmus, *Annot., ad loc.*

Israel: Add your burnt offerings to your sacrifices and eat the flesh. For I spoke not to your fathers, and I commanded them not, in the day I brought them out of the land of Egypt, concerning the matter of burnt offerings and sacrifices. But this thing I commanded them: Hearken to my voice, and I will be your God and you shall be my people." (Jer. 7:21 ff.) And Isa. 1:10 f.: "Hear the word of the Lord, you rulers of Sodom; give ear to the law of your God, you people of Gomorrah. To what purpose do you offer me the multitude of your sacrifices?" And then there follows the word (Isa. 1:19): "If you be willing and will hearken to me, you shall eat the good things of the earth." And, at the end of the book, he says: "But to whom shall I look but to him that is poor and little, and of a contrite spirit, and that trembles at my words? He that sacrifices an ox is as if he slew a man; he that burns incense is as if he blessed an idol. . . . All these things they have chosen in their ways," etc.

Only faith can accomplish this. It extinguishes all wisdom of the flesh and all insistence on knowledge and makes one ready to be taught and led and willing to listen and to yield. For God does not require a magnitude of works but the mortification of the old man in us. But he cannot be mortified except by faith, which humbles our self-will and subjects it to that of another. For the whole life of the old man is concentrated in the thinking or mind or wisdom and prudence of the flesh just as the life of the serpent is centered in its head. If this head is crushed, the whole old man is dead. And, as I have said before, faith in the word of God brings this about; faith not only in the word that sounds forth from heaven but in that word which also proceeds from the mouth of any good man, especially that of an ecclesiastical superior.

This is why unbelievers are contentious and always take offense at the word of faith. For when they are asked to have faith, they demand visible proof, because, in their presumptuousness, they think that they are able to tell what is right and that all others are mistaken. It is absolutely certain that Adam and the old man are still alive in a man who does not yield and who thinks that he is always right. In such a man Christ is not yet risen.

Hence, God conceals obedience, which, in his eyes, is of greatest value, under works great and small alike. He does not consider the difference between works but only the value of obedience. But the prudence of the foolish always regards the work as more important than the word and tends to judge the worth of the word in terms of the worth or unworth of the works. Where the work has proved itself to be mean and lowly, it immediately judges also the word to be mean and lowly and despises it. For the "prudence of the flesh" that distinguishes between good and evil is as alive today as when it originated in the first sin at the tree of the knowledge of good and evil (Gen. 2:9, 17; 3:6 f.).

By contrast, the prudence of spiritual men knows neither good nor evil. It always looks at the word and not at the work, and it judges and weighs the worth of the work by the word. Hence, even though a work may be the meanest of all, it regards it as most precious, because it always regards the word as that which is of all things the most precious.

By this trick the serpent of old deceived Eve, but not Adam, and, by the same trick, it deceives to this day all the proud. For right away he called Eve back from the word to the work by saying to her: "Why has God commanded you?" etc. (Gen. 3:1). Made aware of the littleness of the work, she then at once proceeded to despise also the word. Thus also Saul neglected the word of God for the sake of the great number of animals that were to be offered as sacrifices. (I Sam. 15:1 ff.) And so, too, the moralists,[9] who rely on their good works, hope to this day to obtain salvation of a kind that corresponds to their works. But the fact that they are interested only in the size and extent of their works is the most certain sign by which one can recognize them as unbelievers who, in their pride, despise the word. For a man who lets himself be tempted to perform great good works, so that he despises and turns away from a little one but pants to do the great ones, he is the one who, together with the Jews and the heretics, stumbles at the stone of stumbling. For when something of this sort happens, Christ stays with the mean works that are enjoined by the word, and he forsakes those who long to do only the great works that the devil suggests to them through the prudence of the flesh.

Hence, we must do nothing else but listen to the word with all our mind and all our strength, simply keeping our eyes closed and directing all our prudence only to it. And whether it enjoins something foolish or bad, something large or small, we must do it, *judging what we do in terms of the word and not the word in terms of what we do.*

One can recognize unbelievers by still another sign, namely, by the way in which they seize upon works which are regarded as great before men and are admired by the crowd. But as soon as people cease to admire them and begin to regard them as worthless, they who do them tire of them and lose interest in them, so that it is apparent that in doing them they were not concerned for good works or for God, but for their own vainglory. Thus, they have no interest in works that are of no value and that are not

9 *"Iustitiarii."*

highly regarded by men; but it is precisely such works that we should be eager to do in case we have to act without the word.

Now, this is what the unlearned preachers are concerned about, with the result that they mislead the common people. They either preach or read aloud about the great works' that are told in the legends of the saints and impress only them upon the people by making them important. Then the common folk, who listen to them, conclude that there is something to good works and they turn immediately away from everything else and eagerly try to imitate the saints—and this is where so many grants of indulgences come from and so many permits for the building and decoration of churches and for the multiplication of ceremonies, and in the meantime no one cares one bit about what everyone owes to God according to his calling.

And the pope and the higher clergy, who are so liberal in granting indulgences for the temporal support of the churches, lack all feeling for what is right if they are not equally liberal, or even more so, in their concern for God and for the salvation of souls. They freely received all they have and freely they should give it. But "they are corrupt and are become abominable in their ways" (Ps. 14:1); being themselves misled, they lead the people of Christ away from the true worship of God.

In this connection, I am reminded of an amusing story I once heard: There was once a simple fellow who heard a preacher say— one who made a big noise about the examples one should follow— that, according to the example of Simeon Stylites in the *Lives of the Pillar Saints*,[10] one must do something really great for God's sake. Now in order to ridicule the silly talk of pulpit-performers[11] of this sort, and in order to demonstrate what the result would be if men obeyed this frivolous nonsense, he decided by the will of God and out of love for God, not to make water. After he had done this for a few days, he became so sick that he almost died. When others tried to dissuade him from what he was doing, he paid no attention. But now observe how, by another counsel of God, he was freed from his undertaking: A shrewd fellow, who, by the influence of God, was informed about everything, stepped up to him and confirmed him in his undertaking and urged him to continue with it. He said: Why, certainly! You are right, brother! Just go on doing what you are doing! I myself shall do what you are doing, just in order to show all my friends that I do not care for them. For they do not like me, just as yours do not like you. When the fellow heard that what he was doing meant so little and that,

---

[10] Cf. *Vitae patrum* I: *Vita S. Simeonis Stylitae,* 5 (PL 73, 528).
[11] *"Ambonistae,"* a sarcastic word of Luther's own making.

in the opinion of people, it did not amount to anything, indeed, that they said that he did what he was doing not because he liked them but because he disliked them, he became well immediately, and he said: If they think that this is the reason why I am doing it, I shall not do it. He did what he did for the sake of men! This was the deadly ulcer in his heart. But as soon as it was cut out, he became well. O what a really wise counsel he received; only a teacher like God can give it! How directly it touched his sickness!

The moral of the story is this: One must not preach the works of the saints as such, i.e., one must not encourage people to imitate them without adding: See here, in his own station in life this man lives in this way or that as an example for you, in order that you should do likewise in your station in life but not in order that you should do the same as he by giving up your station and leaping over to his.

For with the heart man believes unto righteousness. (Rom. 10:10.)

It is just as if he wanted to say: One cannot obtain righteousness by any works, any wisdom, or any effort, nor by riches or honors, even though today many think that they can obtain release from sin by paying two pennies. And many regard themselves as righteous because they are great scholars and teachers or because they have a high title or position and are ministers of sacred affairs. But this is a new way to obtain righteousness, a way that goes against Aristotle[12] or beyond him, since, according to him, righteousness is brought about by actions, even if they are entirely outward, if only they are repeated often enough. But this is political righteousness, a righteousness that cannot prevail before God.

But true righteousness comes about only if one believes the words of God with his whole heart, as he says above in ch. 4:3 of this letter: "And Abraham believed in God, and it was reckoned to him for righteousness." But if one divides righteousness, as the philosopher[13] understands it, into a distributive and a commutative righteousness and then also a general one,[14] this is an effect either of mental blindness or of that human wisdom which is intent only upon earthly matters that must be dealt with in terms of reason, where it can happen, for example, that one is in debt and obligation to none, another to several, and still another to many.

[12] Aristotle, *Eth. Nicom.,* II, 1; III, 7; V, 9, 10.
[13] Cf. Aristotle, *op. cit.,* V, 5.
[14] Gabriel Biel, III *Sent., d.* 34, *a.* 1, *n.* 3 (according to Duns Scotus, III *Sent., d.* 34, *q. un., n.* 17).

But in the righteousness of God, man is a debtor to everyone because "he is guilty to all" (James 2:10). To the Creator, whom he has offended, he owes glory and a blameless life, and to the creature, good use and co-operation in the service of God. And he cannot pay this debt unless, taking the lowest seat, he humbly takes all this upon himself and seeks nothing for himself in anything. As the lawyers say: "One who has given up all his goods has made satisfaction." A man, therefore, who submits to God and his creatures, even if it should cost him his life, who is ready and willing to walk into nothingness and death and damnation, and who does not regard himself as worthy to share in any of these goods, such a man has truly satisfied God and is righteous. For he kept nothing for himself but yielded everything to God and his creatures. This is accomplished by faith. Then man lets his mind be captive to the word of the cross and denies himself and renounces everything, having died to himself and everything else. Thus he lives to God alone, "to whom all live," even the dead.

But with the mouth confession is made unto salvation. (Rom. 10:10.)

In other words: the faith that leads to righteousness does not reach its goal of righteousness or salvation if it does not arrive at confession. For confession is the principal work of faith: Man denies himself and confesses God and he does this to such an extent that he will deny even his life and everything else before affirming himself. For by confessing God and denying himself, he dies. And how can he better deny himself than by dying in order to confess God? For then he forsakes himself, in order that God and the confession to him may stand.

For there is no distinction between Jew and Greek: for the same Lord is Lord of all, and is rich unto all that call upon him. (Rom. 10:12.)

A new form of expression! For he could have said "ready," "willing," or, as the law says: "merciful to them that cry unto him and compassionate to hear them" (Ex. 22:27; Joel 2:13), just as it says in Ps. 86:5:[15] "For thou, O Lord, are sweet and mild, and plenteous in mercy to all that call upon thee." But the apostle wanted to emphasize what he says also elsewhere, namely, that God gives to those who call upon him beyond what they ask for, so that, compared with what they receive, what they ask for is poor and modest. No one would think of such great gifts when he prays, much less ask for them. As he says in Eph. 3:20: "He is

[15] Luther writes: Ps. 43.

able to do all things more abundantly than we can ask or think."
And above in Rom. 8:26: "We do not know what we should pray
for as we ought." And in II Cor. 9:8: "God is able to make all grace
abound in you."

God, therefore, is rich as he hears our prayers, but we are poor
as we call upon him. He is strong when he fulfills our prayers,
but we are hesitant and weak when we pray. For we do not pray
for as much as he can and wants to give to us; in other words: we
do not pray in proportion to his power, but far below his power
in proportion to our weakness. But he cannot give except according to his power. Hence, he always gives more than he is asked
for. Therefore, he says: "Open your mouth wide and I will" (not:
drop something into it, but) "fill it" (Ps. 81:10), i.e., pray for as
much as you can and I shall give more, for my giving is more
powerful than the strength of your praying. Hence, "the spirit
helps our infirmity" (Rom. 8:26) when we pray.

Now this "being able or potent," which is here asserted with
respect to God, is not to be understood, as in logic, as the contingent and free ability and faculty of acting when and where one
wants to. The Greek word is *"dynamenō,"* "to him that is able."[16]
This signifies that ability which I have defined above as "strength"
or "powers" or "power," so that its meaning is this: When God
gives, he gives so potently and strongly that his giving far exceeds
what we could have imagined it would be. For he is so able, i.e.,
so very powerful and strong, that he gives more than our weakness
asks for. But he adds: "according to the power" (in Greek:
"dynamin") "that works in us." Thereby he excludes the power
of the flesh. For he does not work in us or hear us according to the
power of the flesh, but according to spiritual power. This is what
is meant by "beyond what we can think," in Greek *"noumen,"*
i.e., what we feel and know, from *noys*[17] mind, thought, judgment.

For his way of granting our prayers goes beyond all our thinking,
i.e., it is not as we preconceived it, thought it out, and prudently,
so it seemed to us, chose it. For we choose weakly and impotently,
or in other words: if what we ask for were given to us in proportion
to our weak way of asking, it would be weak and impotent, for it
could not transcend the limits of our understanding, and hence
we would immediately tire of it as of something temporal. In the
same way he says in Phil. 4:7: "And the peace of God which surpasses all thought" (i.e., *"noun"*), i.e., knowing, feeling, understanding, as we said before, "keep your hearts and minds," i.e.,

16 Cf. Eph. 3:20. Luther follows Faber.
17 Instead of *nous.*

"noēmata," i.e., what you feel and think by reason and mind, or as we would say, "your thoughts."[18]

For whosoever shall call upon the name of the Lord, shall be saved. How, then, shall they call on him in whom they have not believed? *Or how shall they believe in him of whom they have not heard? And how shall they hear without a preacher? And how shall they preach except they be sent?* (Rom. 10:13–15.)

People who are of a proud mind, such as the Jews, the heretics and schismatics, arrogate to themselves these four propositions, one by one; for they are all deceived by what appears to be piety. For these four statements are so related to one another that one follows from the other and the last one is the antecedent cause of all others. In other words: one cannot preach if one is not sent; it follows from this that one cannot hear if one is not preached to; and from this, that one cannot believe if one does not hear, and then, that one cannot call upon God if one does not believe, and, finally, that one cannot be saved if one does not call upon God.

The whole source and origin of salvation, therefore, is in God's sending. If he does not send them, the preachers preach falsely, and such preaching is the same as no preaching; indeed, it would be better for them not to preach at all. And the hearers hear falsely, and it would be better for them not to hear at all. And they who believe them believe falsely, and it would be better for them not to believe at all. And those who thus invoke God do not call upon him at all, and it would be better for them not to do so at all. Since preachers of this kind do not preach, the hearers do not believe, those who invoke God do not call upon him, and those who are to be saved are damned. Proverbs 1:28: "Then they shall call unto me, and I will not hear them." (Psalm 110:2: "The Lord will send forth the scepter of your power out of Zion." And then: "Rule!" i.e., act strongly, "and your preaching shall be effective in the midst of your enemies." But those people rule in the midst of their friends and they attract them to themselves by flattering them.) And Ps. 18:41: "They cried, but there was none to save them, to the Lord, and he heard them not." Therefore, they are like reflected images before God; they have ears but do not hear; they have a mouth and do not speak, etc. (Ps. 115:5 f.; Ps. 135:15 f.). Why? Because they are not from God. For when God sends forth his word, *sso geets mit gewalt* (it goes forth with power), so that it converts not only its friends and those who applaud it but also its enemies and those who oppose it.

Hence, we must see to it, before everything else, that a preacher

18 Here Luther follows Erasmus.

is sent as John was sent (John 1:6). We can recognize this if he proves by miracles and a testimony from heaven that he was sent (as the apostles were) or if he proves that later he is sent by apostolic authority confirmed from above and that he preaches in humble submission to this authority, always ready to stand under its judgment and to speak only what is commanded to him and not what he likes or has invented. (As it says in Zech. 13:3: "And it shall come to pass that when any man shall prophesy any more, his father and mother that brought him into the world," [i.e., his ecclesiastical superior and the church][19] "shall say to him: You shall not live" [i.e., you shall be condemned and excommunicated] "because you have spoken a lie in the name of the Lord. And his father and his mother, his parents, shall thrust him through when he shall prophesy.") This is the very sharp spear by which the heretics will be pierced. For they preach without the testimony of God or without divinely confirmed authority, but from their own initiative, and they are elevated to their position by a semblance of religiousness.

We read in Jer. 23:21: "They ran and I did not send them." And yet they dare say: We shall be saved because we have invoked the name of the Lord; we believe because we hear; we hear because we preach. But what they cannot say is this: We preach because we are sent. Here, at this point, they go down! Here is all that matters for salvation. Apart from this, everything is wrong, even if they do not think so. This is what the apostle emphasizes so strongly in Rom. 1:2, lest one think that the gospel came into the world through a man. First, it was promised long before it came; it was no new invention. Furthermore, it came into the world not by one but by many, by the prophets of God and not only in form of the spoken word but also in form of the Holy Scriptures. A heretic must present this kind of testimony for his heretical doctrine. He must also show where it was promised earlier and by whom, and then also by whom it was taught, and, finally, in what Scriptures it is to be found so as to produce also writings as witnesses. But they are not in the least concerned about this and they say foolishly: We have the truth; we believe; we hear; we call upon God —as if it were sufficient proof that something is from God if one imagines it to be so, and as if it were not necessary for God to confirm his word and to work with it by signs that follow upon it later and by promises and prophecies that precede it.

And so the ecclesiastical authority was established which the Roman Church maintains to this day: only they preach safely who preach the gospel without defects that come from somewhere else.

19 Cf. Lyra's exposition of the passage.

Now the word which the heretics preach gives them great satisfaction[20] because it sounds as they want it to sound. They aim at the highest religiousness[21] (so it seems to them). And so their own thinking remains unchanged and their will unbroken. For the word does not come to them counter to or beyond what they think but according to their own ideas, as if they were its equal or even its judges.

But, in reality, the word of God comes, when it comes, in opposition to our thinking and wishing. It does not let our thinking prevail, even in what is most sacred to us, but it destroys and uproots and scatters everything. As we read in Jer. 1:10 and 23:29: "Are not my words as fire and as a hammer that breaks the rock in pieces?"

Hence, it is an infallible sign that one really has the word of God and that he carries it in his heart if he is not satisfied but only dissatisfied with himself and if he is troubled in all he knows, says, does, and suffers, finding pleasure only in others or in God.

Conversely, it is a most evident sign that the word of God is not in one if he is satisfied with himself and rejoices in what he says, knows, does, and suffers, as if he had produced it all.

This is so because the word of God "crushes the rock"; it destroys and crucifies all our self-satisfaction and leaves in us only dissatisfaction with ourselves. Thus it teaches us to have pleasure, joy, and confidence in God alone and to find happiness and well-being outside ourselves or in our neighbor.

Even as it is written: **How beautiful are the feet of them that preach the gospel of peace,** *of them that bring glad tidings of good things.* (Rom. 10:15.)

First, they are called "beautiful" because of their purity, since they do not preach the gospel for the sake of advanatge or vainglory, as it is done everywhere today, but only from obedience to God and for the sake of the salvation of their hearers.

Secondly, in terms of its specific meaning in Hebrew, "beautiful" means "desirable"; it refers to something that is favored or worthy of love and affection, or as one would say in German, *lieblich und genehm* (lovely and agreeable). And so the meaning of the text is this: For those who are under the law, the preaching of the gospel is lovely and desirable. For the law lays sin open, makes guilty, and tightens the conscience with dread, but the gospel announces the desired remedy to those who find themselves in these narrows. Hence, the law proclaims something bad, but

[20] *"Suaveplacentiam,"* perhaps a translation of *Wohlgefallen* (good pleasure).
[21] *"Summam pietatem."*

the gospel, something good; the law proclaims wrath, but the gospel, peace. The law says (according to the quotation of the apostle in Gal. 3:10):[22] "Cursed is everyone that does not abide in all things which are written in the book of the law to do them." But nobody abides in them to do them, as it is stated in the same place: "For as many as are of the works of the law are under a curse."

But the Gospel says: "Behold the Lamb of God, behold him who takes away the sins of the world." (John 1:29.)

The law oppresses the conscience through the sins it uncovers, but the gospel sets it free and gives it peace through faith in Christ.[23]

This is what it says above in ch. 10:5 of the letter before us: "Moses writes that the man that does the righteousness which is of the law shall live thereby," and the apostle says: None does it, hence none shall live thereby. Hence, once more, Gal. 3:11: "But that no man is justified in the law before God, it is manifest: because the righteous shall live by faith. But the law is not of faith, but he that does those things shall live in them." And, above in ch. 2:13 of this letter he said: "For not the hearers of the law are righteous before God, but the doers of the law shall be justified." In other words: before God all who are outside faith are only hearers, for "he that does these things, shall live." But none does. Why else would faith be necessary?

In the phrase "of them that preach the gospel," the Spirit gives expression to something that goes beyond what we have stated in the Gloss,[24] namely, that the "peace" and the "good things" that are mentioned here cannot be seen and that they do not correspond to anything that is in the world. They are so concealed that they can be made known only by the word and apprehended only by faith in the word. These good things and this peace are not within the reach of direct apprehension, but they are pro-

22 Cf. Deut. 27:26.
23 "Fides Christi."
24 Luther's marginal gloss reads as follows (WA 56, 102, 19 ff.): "The apostle proves by this one term 'of them that preach the gospel' that one cannot preach unless he is sent. For 'to preach the gospel' is the same as 'to proclaim it.' But nobody can proclaim the word of God and be its messenger, whom God has not sent and upon whom he has not laid his word. For one cannot seize the word of God; it must be received from God as he commits it to one and sends him to preach it. Any preacher who preaches on a condition other than this most certainly speaks a lie even if he appears to speak the truth. Then too, he defines by this term the nature of peace and of good things, namely, that they are of such a nature that they can only be heard through the word and that they must be comprehended by faith. They cannot be exhibited to sight, as the Jews expect."

claimed by the word and thus are perceivable only by faith, i.e., they cannot be experienced until the future life comes.

Now the expression "good things" refers to the granting of the gifts of grace and the word "peace" to the removal of evil. Hence, the apostle puts peace ahead of "good things." These "good things" are to be found under the cross, for none can receive this peace and its goods unless he has first renounced the peace and the goods of the world and unless he patiently bears the evils and troubles of this world and of his conscience for the sake of faith.

And what is the meaning of "feet"? According to a first interpretation, they signify the inner attitude of those who preach: it must be free from all desire for gain and glory.

But according to the Hebrew text and a more adequate exegesis,[25] we must say the following: Even though one can interpret "feet" literally in the sense that the coming of the preachers of good things is eagerly awaited by those who are in anguish of sin and an evil conscience, they signify more correctly their very words or the sound and the syllables or pronunciation of their words and preachings. For voices are like feet and vehicles or wheels by which the word is conveyed, carried, or moved to the ears of the hearers. Hence, it says: "Their sound has gone forth into all the world." (Ps. 19:4.) If it went forth, it must have feet. And again: "His word runs swiftly." (Ps. 147:15.) What runs has feet. The spoken word runs and therefore has feet, and they are the diction and the sounds of words. This must be so, for otherwise the saying of Isa. 32:20 would be absurd: "Blessed are you that sow upon all waters, sending thither the foot of the ox and the ass." And Ps. 91:13: "You shall walk upon the asp and the basilisk, and you shall trample underfoot the lion and the dragon." This can be done only by the word. For while the hearer sits quietly and receives the word, the "feet" of the preacher run over him and he tramples him underfoot as he betters him. As we read in Micah 4:13: "Arise and tread, O daughter of Zion, for I will make your horn iron, and your hoop I will make brass, and you shall beat in pieces many peoples." "Treading" here means the same as when an ox thrashes with his feet. The feet of the church as she preaches are, therefore, the utterances and words by which she strikes and shakes up the peoples and "beats them to pieces." And she does this with nothing else than her words and utterances. But they are "beautiful" and desirable to those who are depressed by a sinful conscience.

Two couples of terms are therefore put in opposition to each other:

[25] Luther is dependent on Erasmus' *Annot.*

Law-sin: The law uncovers sin; it makes the sinner guilty and sick; indeed, it proves him to be under condemnation.

Gospel-grace: The gospel offers grace and forgives sin; it cures the sickness and leads to salvation.

But all do not obey the gospel. *For Isaiah says: Lord, who has believed our report? Faith, then, comes by hearing, and hearing by the word of Christ. But I say: Have they not heard? Yes, verily, their sound has gone forth into all the earth, and their words unto the ends of the whole world.* (Rom. 10:16–18.)

This has reference to what was said before; it is to confirm those four propositions that followed one another in order. First of all, we must relate to what he says here the saying: "Whosoever shall call upon the name of the Lord shall be saved" (Rom. 10:13; Joel 2:32). For if "they all did not obey the gospel," why do they presume to call upon the name of the Lord according to the word of the prophet? How could they all call upon him if they did not believe in him? But obviously they did not all believe, for Isaiah says: **Lord, who has believed what we have heard?**

Secondly, also, this other sentence is confirmed: "How shall they believe in him of whom they have not heard?" (Rom. 10:14). For he says: **Hence, faith comes by hearing:** in other words: if they do not hear, they cannot believe, just as it is stated in the word of Isaiah.

Thirdly, he confirms also the proposition: How shall they hear without a preacher? For hearing comes through the word of Christ.

Fourthly, the same interpretation applies to the saying: "How beautiful . . ." as we have sufficiently explained.

"What we have heard"[26] here means "hearing"[27] (i.e., the perception of the word heard), listening to its sound and voice. He says: "what we have heard," because only they received it. And he speaks of the gospel whose sound has gone forth throughout the world and that has been heard or is being heard. The meaning of the saying is then very clearly this: O Lord, who has believed what we now hear being spoken and preached throughout the world or what is now being heard. Now, it is not without reason that the apostle expresses himself in this way, for he could have said: Who has believed the gospel? inasmuch as he says in this passage: "They all do not obey the gospel." But he expresses himself here in the way he does in order to make plain that the word is of such a character that unless it is received by hearing and by faith, none can grasp it. At this the Jews were offended, for they strove after signs and wonders.

---

[26] *"Auditus"* ("what we have heard"; "report").   [27] *"Auditio"* ("hearing").

But I say: Has not Israel known? First, Moses says: I will provoke you to jealousy **by that which is not a nation; by a foolish nation** *I will anger you. But Isaiah is bold, and says: I was found by them that did not seek me. I appeared openly to them that asked not after me. But to Israel he says: All the day long have I spread my hands to a people that believes not and contradicts me.* (Rom. 10:19–21.)

These are words of grace, i.e., they are spoken in order to praise grace: God saves only sinners; he instructs only the foolish and the stupid; he enriches only the poor; he quickens only the dead; and, indeed, he saves, etc., not those who merely imagine and consider themselves to be sinners, etc., but those who really are such and acknowledge themselves as such. For it was really so that the heathen were not God's people and that they were a foolish nation, so that, being saved without any merits and effort of their own, they might acknowledge God's grace.

The proud, however, who trust in their own merits and wisdom, become angry and grumble when others, who do not deserve it, are given freely what they themselves have been seeking with so much zeal. In the Gospel, Christ speaks of this in parables with respect to the elder brother (Luke 15:28), who turned away from his prodigal brother and did not want to let him come in, and also with respect to those who, having received one shilling for a whole day, grumbled about it that the Lord made the last equal with the first (Matt. 20:11).

Now these are the ones who are "foolish." Instead of rejoicing in the salvation of others, they advance presumptuous claims in their own behalf. Thereby they show that they were not seeking God for God's sake but for their own sake, namely, from self-love and from a desire for personal advantage (i.e., impurely). And then they even go so far as to be proud of this impurity and loathsomeness of theirs and are therefore twice as loathsome as those on account of whom they are offended. If they were really seeking God, they would not be offended at the salvation of others, but they would rejoice in it; they would be very well pleased at seeing God so well pleased, for we must love his good pleasure above everything.

It is, then, in opposition to their vain high estimation of their own merits that Isaiah is so bold as to say: **I was found of them** that sought me not, etc. (Isa. 65:1), i.e., I became known to them by my grace and not by anyone's effort and merits. Why, then, do you presume in your pride that your merits are so great that you *must* find me?

Of this sort was the hermit of whom the story is told[28] that when
he saw a robber being taken to heaven, he indignantly returned
to the world. Of the same kind was that other hermit who said
to a repentant robber as he expressed the wish that he might be
like him: "That is fine! You can wish to be like me. But O that
you were!" And he was damned. Of the same kind was also a certain nun who, as she lay on her deathbed, heard the people that
stood about her speaking well of her. Then she began to compute
with her fingers the day of her death on which her feast would be
celebrated. It is true, then, that "whosoever shall exalt himself
shall be humbled" (Matt. 23:12).

All this, therefore, is spoken, written, and done in order that
the proud presumptuousness of men might be humbled and the
grace of God commended so that "he that glories may glory not
in his own race but in the mercy of the Lord" (I Cor. 1:31).

What will a proud man say, one who has accomplished much in
his life, if God prefers some poor little woman and mother to him
and says: Behold, she has served me only by bearing children,[29]
and I gladly prefer what she has done to all your great accomplishments! What will he say then? All works have only as much worth
as God reckons them to have, and he can put much value on
something that is very unimportant and very small, and he can
reject what is very great and important. Shall we, then, *not* do the
good? No. But we must do so with humility; then God will not
reject it. Those people of today, therefore, are wonderfully strange
fools as they pile up what they regard as many and grand good
works in the belief that they are good because they cost them much
labor and because they appear to be good to *them*. But all this is
in vain. Only the works of humility are good works. And these
people do not even know what humility is!

Who has believed our hearing? (Rom. 10:16.)

The Scripture or rather its translator frequently uses "hearing"
and "seeing" for "that which was heard" and "that which was
seen," as we have stated in the Gloss.[30] This is so, first, because
that which is proclaimed is invisible and can be perceived only by
hearing and believing, and, secondly, and more appropriately so,

---

[28] This and the following story are to be found in *Speculum exemplorum*.
(Cf. Ficker, p. 427, n. 26.)

[29] Cf. I Tim. 2:15, a passage frequently quoted by Augustine, e.g., *De trin.*,
XII, 7, 11.

[30] In the Gloss, Luther quotes several Scripture passages to prove his statement, e.g., Ezek. 7:26; Obad. 1:1; Ps. 16: 45; 110:7; Heb. 3:2; Isa. 1:1.

because the word of God is very good in itself but as it is spread
to men it becomes something diverse, and, being itself without any
variety, it must undergo variation.[31] It is life to good men and
death to evil ones; it is good to the good and evil to the evil.

Now, it is capable of this differentiation only in so far as it is
preached and heard. The righteous wish to hear it. Filled with
sorrow and amazement that the wicked do not listen to such a
good word, they say: Who has believed what we have had heard?
In other words: Why do not also others believe that very good
report[32] which we hear and believe?

[31] *WA* 56, 428, 18: *"Verbum Dei in seipso est optimum, sed diffusum ad
homines fit varium et patitur differentiam ipsum indifferens."*
[32] *"Auditio."*

ROMANS, CHAPTER ELEVEN

I say then: Did God cast away his people? God forbid. **For I also am an Israelite,** *of the seed of Abraham, of the tribe of Benjamin. God did not cast away his people which he foreknew. Know you not what the Scripture says of Elijah? How he calls on God against Israel: Lord, they have slain thy prophets, they have dug down thy altars; and I am left alone and they seek my life.* (Rom. 11:1–3.)

The apostle establishes something less important in order to prove the validity of something more important; i.e., he argues from the lesser to the larger. For if God had cast away his people, then above all he would have cast away the apostle Paul who fought against him with all his strength. But in order to show that he does not reject his people, God accepted even him who was hopelessly lost, proving thereby how firm his predestination and election are. It cannot be obstructed even by such hopeless desperation. Hence, he adds quite rightly: **God has not cast away his people which he foreknew.** In other words: he has proved this in my own case, for he did not cast me away; much less he cast away the others who did not depart from him as far as I did.

But what says the answer of God to him? **I have left me** *seven thousand men who have not bowed their knees to Baal.* (Rom. 11:4.)

They are called a "remnant" in the sense of being left over, for God left them for himself. This word implies a wonderful commendation of his grace and election. The apostle does not say "they remained," although this would be quite true; but this "remaining" was not the decision of them that remained but of God who kept them back so that "it was not of him that runs, but of God that has mercy" (Rom. 9:16).

Indeed, he indicates by the same word indirectly that he is the author of the reprobation of the others, just as it was he who then and there drove Israel into the Babylonian exile (II Kings, ch. 25). Now by saying, "I have left me," he means to say this: When I myself cast them all away, I left for myself seven thousand men. He does not say: When they were all cast away, seven thousand men were left over, or: When Nebuchadnezzar or the devil took them away, he left me seven thousand men, but: I myself kept them back, I who took them, i.e., the others, away. This is said in order definitely to establish what was stated before: "Has not the potter power over the clay, of the same lump to make one vessel unto honor and another unto dishonor?" (Rom. 9:21). And also this: "I will have mercy on whom I will have mercy." (Rom. 9:15.)

To Baal (Rom. 11:4.)

Baal was an idol. I do not know by what rites he was worshiped. I know only what the book of Kings tells about this (I Kings 18:26,28), namely, that he was worshiped by kissing the hands, by dancing around altars, and by cutting the skin with knives and lances. Yet the same passage shows plainly that all this was done from devoutness and under the pretext and with the zeal to render true worship to the God of Israel. It was for this reason that Ahab called Elijah one who troubled Israel (I Kings 18:17). He seemed to oppose the worship of God when he hindered the people from following Baal. But, also, in Hos. 2:16, the Lord says that they called him Baalim: "She shall call me: My husband, and she shall call me no more Baalim."

So then, they were worshiping the true God, but under a superstitious rite and name; and this was forbidden to them. They were not to make themselves any graven image or picture. But, misled by a foolish zeal, they thought that a graven image was forbidden only if it was the picture of a strange God, but that if they attributed it to the true God and worshiped it in his name, they were doing right. Out of this same zeal they killed the prophets as if they were godless, because they said that any kind of picture was forbidden. And this was done from the intention of being devout and out of a zeal for God.

Now, Baal represented a dreadful righteousness and a superstitious religion. Both have prevailed widely until today. They are to be found among the Jews, the heretics, and the nonconformists,[1] i.e., those conceited individualists who worship the true God according to their own mind. In their exceedingly foolish zeal and

[1] "Monii."

eccentric religiousness,[2] they are worse than the ungodly: for the sake of God, they are enemies of God; because of the fear of God, they despise him; for the sake of religion, they become ungodly; for the sake of peace, they disturb the peace; because of love and saintliness, they become jealous and profane; and because of their humility, they are proud.

Now "Baal" means "man" or "lord." Hence, "Beelzebub" means "lord of the flies," and "Beelphegor" "lord of the corpse."[3] "Man" here stands for hero, leader, head, prince, commander, a person of power. We are dealing here with the fancied piety of a willful mind and with fanatical religiousness;[4] it worships what it has itself established as worshipful; it follows its own leading on God's way; it is its own teacher toward God, toward righteous salvation and every good. It refuses to perform true obedience, does not heed the word of true teaching, and despises God and all who speak, act, and rule in his name. It ridicules them as mistaken fools; indeed, it treats them as if they were crazy.

Thus they worship this idol of the heart as if it represented God himself and as if it were the very truth and righteousness. How? They kiss the hands, i.e., they take complacent satisfaction in their own works and entertain a high opinion of their own righteousness.[5] Then they dance with wild excitement and rejoicing around their own striving and accomplishments; and, finally they cut themselves with knives and lances, i.e., each of them accuses himself with words of humility and penitence, saying: O most miserable sinner that I am! I am not worthy to go to heaven! Have mercy on me, O God, etc. And so he busies himself with grand efforts in pursuit of righteousness and he makes them the more fervently, the more he hopes that they will be highly esteemed before God and men. For if he knew that they might be ignored, he would not trouble himself about them in any way whatsoever. So great are his pride and his vain imagination! It does not occur to him that his religious efforts might be as unclean "as a polluted garment" (Isa. 64:6), for then he would be compelled to identify himself with the sinners. But just this he tries to avoid by all means.

Even so, then, at this present time also, there is a remnant saved according to the election of grace. (Rom. 11:5.)

2 *"Nimia pietate."*

3 Cf. Reuchlin, *Lex. heb.* Erasmus (*Annot., ad loc.*) translates "Beelphogor" and "Beelzebub" *"cadaveris"* and *"muscarum idolum."*

4 *"Hic est enim obstinatae mentis opiniosa pietas et induratae cervicis religiosa sapientia."*

5 *"Magniputatione iustitiae suae."*

The Greek text reads: "Even so, then, at this present time also, there is a remnant according to the election of grace." This means: Just as there could be found then a remnant, while others perished, so also there can be found today a remnant according to the election of grace. Thus the word "there is" must be related to the phrase "at the present time." In other words: just as there was then a remnant, so there is one now. At both times, God left for himself some according to the election of grace. For he explains the phrase "I have left for myself" by reference to the expression "according to the election of grace." As I have said above, this "I have left" implies, indeed explains, the election and it commends grace.

But if by grace, it is not now by works, otherwise grace is no more grace. What then? That which Israel sought, he has not obtained, **but the election has obtained it** *and the rest have been blinded.* (Rom. 11:6–7.)

"Election" must here be taken in the passive sense and as a collective term, i.e., meaning "the elect" in a way that corresponds to that which Abraham is told in Gen. 12:2: "I will bless you and you shall be a benediction." And Isa. 19:24–25: "In that day Israel shall be a benediction in the midst of the land, which the Lord of hosts has blessed." And Isa. 65:8: "As if a grain be found in a cluster and it be said: Destroy it not, because it is a benediction."

According as it is written: **God gave them a spirit of compunction,** *eyes that they should not see, and ears that they should not hear, unto this very day.* (Rom. 11:8.)

"Compunction" is of two kinds.[6] One is salutary. About it, it says in Ps. 4:4: "On your beds you will be sorry."[7] It causes man to be displeased with himself and to be pleased with everything else, in accordance with the word of Titus 1:15: "All things are clean to the clean." The other kind is detestable. It causes man to be pleased with himself and to be displeased with everything else, in accordance with the same word: "But to the unclean, nothing is clean; but both their mind and their conscience are defiled." The cause of both is the light of the Spirit. If it is not there, it causes the second kind of compunction; if it is there, the first kind. For man knows himself only if God is his light. Apart from him, he cannot know himself at all; apart from him, he, therefore, is also not displeased with himself.

---

[6] Cf. Faber, *ad loc.*

[7] Translated from the Vulgate, the verse reads: "The things you say in your hearts, be sorry for them [*compungimini*] upon your beds."

"Spirit" must here not be taken to mean some created or infused spirit, but the soul or will of man, as it says in I Cor. 2:11: "No one knows the things of a man but the spirit of a man that is in him." And at another place (Matt. 27:50): "and yielded up his spirit," i.e., his soul, and "the spirit must return to God who gave it" (Eccl. 12:7). Psalm 104:29: "Thou shalt take away thy spirit and they shall fail." Genesis 6:17:[8] "Wherein is the spirit of life."

The apostle is quoting Isaiah but makes additions of his own at the beginning and at the end. Moreover, as I have said in the Gloss,[9] he quotes the sentence in between according to its meaning but not literally: "God gave them a spirit of compunction, *eyes that they should not see, ears that they should not hear,* unto this very day."

And David says: "Let their table be made a snare, and a trap, and a stumbling block, and a recompense to them. Let their eyes be darkened, that they may not see and bow down their back always." (Rom. 11:9–10.)

This "snare" is the divine Scripture itself, in so far as it is understood and handed down in a deceitful manner, so that under the semblance of pious instruction the souls of the deceived and the simple are ensnared. Psalm 91:3 speaks of this: "He delivered me from the snare of the hunters," i.e., from the treacherous teaching of the learned who are on the hunt for unstable and fickle souls. In this sense, Blessed Augustine in the *Confessions*[10] calls the Manichee Faustus the snare of the devil. "Trap" can, in this place, be taken to mean "deception,"[11] or, better yet, "hunt."[12] For on a hunt, one makes catches with a trap. Although, in the Greek text, the apostle does not add the words "unto them," in the psalm this addition is made most appropriately in order that one should understand that from the same table, from the same Holy Scripture,[13] one takes death, and another life; one honey,

---

[8] Luther writes "Gen. 1."

[9] Luther's marginal gloss reads as follows (*WA* 56, 108, 20 ff.): "Isa. 6:9: 'Go, and thou shalt say to this people: Hearing hear and understand not, and see the vision and know it not.' The apostle, however, quotes only the meaning of these words. For 'hearing hear' means 'to hear those that have ears' and 'not to understand' means 'not to hear.' And 'to see a vision' means 'to have eyes'; 'not to know' means 'not to see.' Thus he expresses the way by which they became blind, namely, by seeing and hearing what they hated and by not seeing what they liked."

[10] Cf. Augustine, *Conf.*, V, 3.

[11] *"Decipula"* = *"deceptio."* Cf. Erasmus, *Annot.*

[12] *"Venatus."*

[13] This is the common medieval exegesis.

another poison, just as from one and the same rose or flower the spider gathers poison, and the bee, honey.

The "stumbling block" consists in this, that the trapped continually take offense. For they are trapped in that which they understand wrongly. They cling to this wrong understanding because they find pleasure in it, and thus they let themselves be trapped without realizing it.

Now, what they take offense at is the truth that is held up before them. But they turn away from it, and if they cannot escape from it, they distort it and deny that it must be understood as they are told. The "snare," therefore, means that they do not know the truth; the "trap," that they want to accept as true only what they regard as true; the "stumbling block" that they turn away from what is held up before them as true and from everything that goes counter to their own conceit. As it says in another psalm (35:8): "Let the snare, which he knows not, come upon him, and let the trap, which he has hidden, catch him."

Thus, every proud heretic is caught first in his ignorance of the truth; as soon as he despises it, he is already ensnared. Then he accepts what appears to him to be true; and again he is trapped, because he thinks that everything is in order, as if he had the truth and were in no danger of being ensnared and entrapped. Finally, he takes offense at everything that goes against him and he refuses to listen to anyone. And, at last, growing indignant, he fanatically defends the figments of his mind, all the while heaping persecution, detraction, and harm upon his opponents. And then he gets the "recompense" he deserves.

Then finally their eyes are darkened, so that, whereas everybody else is able to see, they do not even move to open their eyes, and while all others stand erect, they remain bent down upon their own understanding.[14]

I say then: Have they so stumbled that they should fall? God forbid. **But by their offense salvation is come to the Gentiles to provoke them to jealousy.** *Now if their offense is the riches of the world and their diminution the riches of the Gentiles, how much more their fullness!* (Rom. 11:11–12.)

This means: salvation has come to the Gentiles by the fall of the Jews in order that their fall might not be entirely fruitless and

---

[14] Luther's marginal gloss on Rom. 11:10 (Ps. 69:23) reads as follows (*WA* 56, 110, 23 ff.): "This is to be understood metaphorically: When one bends his back, he cannot look up. Therefore he does not see the righteousness that shines from heaven but only his own earthly one. On it he depends and relies."

this evil not without good: inasmuch as all things work together for good to the saints (Rom. 8:28), how much more must evil serve Christ and God for good! Indeed, evil serves the good in an abundantly rich measure when God is at work, for then it brings forth not only the good of others but also of him whose evil it is. In this sense, their fall is the salvation of the Gentiles; yet this was not its final purpose, but the fact that they fell was to induce them to emulate the good of those who rose up.

For the most drastic remedy of a good and loving father is this: if he has given his son admonitions, commandments, prohibitions, and even punishment, but without results, he proceeds to give his inheritance to someone else before the eyes of his son, so that he, the son, being greatly grieved at this sight, eagerly rushes upon it in order to obtain it. In this same way, God wanted the fall of the Jews to be to their own advantage. He let the Gentiles reap the advantage of it, in order to provoke the Jews to jealousy by the realization that, by their fall, they had lost the grace with which the Gentiles were now provided before their eyes.

Exactly the same happens (and this is the moral interpretation) when God lets a man fall into grave sin in order that fallen he may recognize his loathsomeness, whereas, before his fall, he regarded himself as excelling others in purity.

For I say to you, Gentiles: as long, indeed, as I am the apostle of the Gentiles, I will glorify my ministry, *if by any means I may provoke to jealousy them who are my flesh and may save some of them. For if the casting away of them is the reconciliation of the world, what shall the receiving of them be but life from the dead.* (Rom. 11:13–15.)

How does he glorify his ministry? By glorying in the fact that, after the fall of the Jews, he is proclaiming the riches of Christ to the Gentiles. For he seems to reprove the Jews because they refused the gift and because they were made poor, small, and sinful, while the Gentiles were made rich and this by his ministry. If, then, such a great good came to the Gentiles by his ministry, whereas it was taken away from the Jews, then he certainly proves thereby the glory of his ministry in an impressive way. But he does not glorify it for the sake of personal satisfaction but for the sake of the salvation of others: on hearing that, by their fall, the Gentiles had been made rich, the Jews should be stimulated to seek the riches of his ministry. But they would not let themselves be so stimulated if he said that he had given the Gentiles something worthless or that the Jews had not lost anything.

Here one can see that glorying is allowed if it is done for the benefit of others, i.e., from brotherly love, out of a concern for the salvation of others and not for the sake of one's own vain satisfaction.

But, secondly, he says this chiefly in order to explain why he, himself one of the Jews, says only bad and damaging things about them and why, inasmuch as he is not a Gentile, he speaks only of their excellence and riches, indeed, why he exalts these and magnifies their gifts, and why he disparages the Jews, deploring, so to speak, the evil that befell them. His answer is that he does this because his office requires it of him, since as the apostle to the Gentiles he cannot say that he proclaimed something insignificant and worthless to them, lest none of them receive him and his ministry bear too little fruit among them. For who appreciates a gift which the giver himself does not think is worth giving? But, apart from this, the Jews shall also be provoked to jealousy by this, so that he may obtain a twin result from his ministry: the Gentiles multiply on account of the excellence of the good offered to them by his ministry, and the Jews, seeing how the Gentiles increase and how eagerly they receive these goods, are stimulated thereby to pursue the same goods.

Hence, he says: "For I say to you, Gentiles," i.e., to your glory that you have received riches. But he would not dare speak to the Jews in this way lest they be even worse offended.

For if the first fruit is holy, *so is the lump also, and if the root is holy, so are the branches. But if some of the branches be broken off and you, being a wild olive, are ingrafted in them, and not made partaker of the root and of the fullness of the olive tree, boast not against the branches, but if you boast, it is not you that bear the root but the root you. You will say then: the branches were broken off that I might be grafted in.* (Rom. 11:16–19.)

The word *"delibatio,"* which the Vulgate here uses, means in Greek *"aparchē,"* i.e., first fruit or that which is offered from the first and best fruits. And this reflects much more fittingly what the apostle has in mind than *"delibatio."* In other words: if the apostles are holy who have been taken from Israel as the first fruit, so to speak, and as the best part, then also the whole people to which they belong is holy. Hence, one must not despise them on account of their unbelief.

Well, by their unbelief they were broken off, but you stand by faith. **Be not high-minded,** *but fear, for if God has not spared the natural branches, fear lest perhaps he also spare you not.* (Rom. 11:20–21.)

This translator[15] displays a strange inconstancy in rendering this word *"sapere"* (to be of a mind to), of which the Greek equivalent is *phronein*. For, above, in ch. 8:5 ff., of the letter he gave the translations: "they are of a mind" as well as "they feel." In the same connection, he uses "wisdom of the flesh" as well as "prudence of the flesh" and "prudence of the spirit." In this chapter, he again uses *"sapere"* in the sense of "to be wise" (Rom. 11:25) and likewise in the following chapter: "I say, by the grace that is given me, to everyone that is among you, not to be more wise (*sapere*) than it behooves to be wise, but to be wise unto sobriety" (Rom. 12:3).

Now this word means something else than what is commonly called "wisdom" (*sapientia*, in Greek, *sophia*) and "prudence" (*prudentia*), which in Greek is called *euboulia* or *promētheia*. Its correct significance is "to be mindful of something with a certain self-complacency";[16] hence, it means in Greek sometimes "to be minded," sometimes "to glory in," and sometimes "to exalt." It has reference to an inward disposition rather than to the intellect.[17] It is commonly applied to persons "who think themselves to be something they are not" (Gal. 2:6; 6:3). Hence, *phronēsis* means a complacency of this sort; *phronēma*, the sense and actualization of this *phronēsis;* and *phronimos* means one who feels complacent. Hence, if one wants to translate *"sapere"* in a uniform way, it would be better to use the translation of "to feel" (*sentire*) and this would have to be understood as describing an attitude of mind.[18] We have the common expression "to do as one likes"[19] or in German: *gutdüncken*. This is commonly said of the proud. But sometimes it is taken in a good sense, as when we say: "This is how I feel, this is what I have a mind to do."[20] But this does not fully express the forcefulness of the Greek word, as is shown in the passage before us: "Do not be wise in your own conceit," i.e., do not be self-complacent in your thinking, do not feel yourselves superior.

Behold, then, the goodness *and severity of God: to them that fall, severity, but toward you, God's goodness, if you continue in his goodness, otherwise you also shall be cut off.* (Rom. 11:22.)
The lesson of this passage is this: when we see the fall of the

---

15 I.e., the Vulgate.
16 *"Cum quadam sui complacentia sapere."*
17 Cf. Erasmus, *Annot. ad Rom.* 11:25.
18 *"De sensu mentis intelligendo."*
19 *"Bonum videri."*
20 *"Ego sentio, sic sapio."*

Jews or the heretics or others, we should not concentrate our attention on the person that fell but on the work that God performs in them, so that we may learn to fear God by the example of the misfortune of someone else and not entertain any presumptuous pride with respect to ourselves. Moreover, it is noteworthy that the apostle teaches us here that we give consideration to the one who performs this work rather than that we make a comparison between others and ourselves.

In opposition to this, many display an amazing stupidity when they are so presumptuous as to call the Jews "dogs" or accursed or whatever they choose to name them, though they themselves do not know who or of what sort they themselves are before God. They should feel compassion for them fearing that they themselves may have to take similar punishment, but instead they rashly heap blasphemous insults upon them. Indeed, as if they could be certain about their own destiny as well as that of these others they are so bold as to call themselves blessed and them accursed. Today the theologians of Cologne are this kind of people: They are so utterly stupid in their zeal that, in their articles or, rather, in their inarticulate[21] and inept literary products, they unblushingly call the Jews accursed.[22] Why? Because they have forgotten what is said in the following chapter: "Bless and curse not" (Rom. 12:14) and at another place: "Being reviled, we bless; being defamed, we entreat" (I Cor. 4:12–13). They want to convert the Jews with force and invective. May God be against them!

And they also, if they do not continue in their unbelief, shall be grafted in, for God is able to graft them in again. For if you were cut out of that which by nature is a wild olive tree, and were grafted contrary to nature into a good olive tree, how much more shall these, which are the natural branches, be grafted into their own olive tree! **For I would not, brethren, have you ignorant** *of this mystery, lest you be wise in your own conceits, that a hardening in part has befallen Israel, until the fullness of the Gentiles shall come in, and so all Israel shall be saved, even as it is written: "There shall come out of Zion the deliverer; he shall turn ungodliness from Jacob; and this is my covenant unto them, when I shall take away their sins."* (Rom. 11:23–27.)

[21] *"Inerticulis."*

[22] The reference is to such writings as Arnold von Tungern, *Articuli sive propositiones de iudaico favore nimis suspecto ex libello theutonico domini Ioannis Reuchlin,* 1512. The occasion that called forth books of this sort was the controversy between Reuchlin and the Theological Faculty of Cologne about the anti-Semitic writings of Pfefferkorn. (Cf. Ficker, p. 436, n. 18.)

It's no more than many others that he has expounded! obscure that [handwritten marginal note]

This text is the basis of the common opinion that, at the end of the world, the Jews will return to the faith. However, it is so obscure that, unless one is willing to accept the judgment of the fathers who expound the apostle in this way,[23] no one can, so it would seem, obtain a clear conviction from this text. Yet also our Lord agrees with the saying of the apostle, for he says in Luke 21:23–24: "There shall be great distress upon the land, and wrath upon this people. And they shall fall by the edge of the sword, and shall be led captive into all the nations; and Jerusalem shall be trodden down by the Gentiles, until the time of the Gentiles be fulfilled." This is exactly what he says here: **until the fullness of the Gentiles shall come in.** And Moses says in Deut. 4:30, after he has prophesied that they must be led through all nations: "In the latter days, you shall return to the Lord your God and harken unto his voice, for the Lord your God is a merciful God." Likewise, Hos. 3:4 f.: "The Children of Israel shall sit many days without kings, and without princes, and without altar, and without ephod, and without teraphim. And after this, the Children of Israel shall return to the Lord their God and David their king; and they shall fear the Lord and his goodness in the last days." The same prophet says in Hos. 5:12: "I will be like a moth to Ephraim and like rottenness to the house of Judah." And farther on: "I will go and return to my place until you are consumed and seek my face." (Hos. 5:14.) And again, the Lord says in Matt. 23:38–39: "Behold, your house shall be left to you, desolate. Verily, I say to you, you shall not see me henceforth till you say: Blessed is he that comes in the name of the Lord."

Accordingly then, the apostle means to say this: I would not, brethren, that you should be ignorant of this mystery, i.e., Be not proud! It is a holy secret why the Jews fell, a secret that no man knows, namely, this: The Jews who are now fallen will return and be saved, after the Gentiles are come in, according to the fullness of the election. They will not stay outside forever, but they will return in their own time.

This is very clearly represented by Joseph, the figure of Christ: he was sold by his brethren to Egypt (Gen. 37:28), and there he was elevated to be a ruler, but, in the end, he was unexpectedly recognized by his father and his brothers, as the book of Genesis so beautifully tells in its last part (Gen. 45:3; 46:29).[24] In the same way, it will happen that the Jews who expelled Christ to the Gentiles, where he now reigns, will come to him in the end.

[23] Chrysostom, *Hom. in ep. ad Rom.*, 19, 7. Ambrosiaster, *ad loc.*
[24] Cf. Gen. 45:3; 46:29. The parallel between Joseph and Christ is to be found in the *Gl. ord.*

Hunger for the word will force them to do so, and in the midst of the Gentiles they will receive him.

This is what the apostle indicates when he quotes Isaiah in connection with his statement: **And so all Israel shall be saved.** In our translation[25] the passage of Isa. 59:20 reads as follows: "There shall come a redeemer to Zion and to them that turn back from iniquity in Jacob." But only those who are in iniquity, as the Jews now are, will turn back from it. Now "ungodliness" or "iniquity" (in Greek: "*asebeia*") do not signify any kind of sin, but the sin against the service of God, i.e., against faith, through self-righteousness.[26] In Hebrew it is called "*rāsha'*." Ecclesiastes 8:8: "Ungodliness shall not save the ungodly," i.e., self-righteousness will not save a man (as he might think), for it is not righteousness but ungodliness.

The additional part of the sentence: **when I shall take away their sins** is not a part of the passage of Isaiah; it is either an addition of the apostle or a quotation from other prophets.[27] But he indicates thereby the difference between the two testaments. Where we increased sin, there was the earlier testament. But where God has taken sin away, there is the new testament. Hence, he intends to say: This is the testament of the remission of sins, in which "he will turn ungodliness away from Jacob," just as the other one is the testament of the commission of sins in which one is turned to ungodliness.

Christ, therefore, has not yet come to the Jews, but he will come to them, namely, in the Last Day, in accordance with the Scripture passages we have quoted. It is in this sense that one must interpret the apostle: he speaks about Christ's mystical advent to the Jews. Otherwise, this word of Isaiah was clearly fulfilled by the physical advent of Christ. This is why I said earlier that the apostle speaks obscurely and that we should not be able to elicit this meaning from the text unless we accept the interpretation of the fathers. So then, now "blindness in part has befallen Israel," but then Israel will be saved not in part but in its entirety. Now only part of them are saved, but then all will be saved.

COROLLARY

The word "mystery" in this passage must be understood without qualification as something that is unknown. It must not be understood according to common usage in terms of its figurative and literal meaning, as we speak, for example, of a "mystical meaning"

---

25 I.e., the Vulgate.
26 Both Faber and Erasmus use the term *impietas*.
27 The words were perhaps suggested by Isa. 27:9.

and then distinguish between a meaning of the surface and another of depth. But what has been concealed from all is a mystery in the abolute sense, namely, that the fullness of the Gentiles would enter in by the fall of a certain number of Jews. The apostle says the same elsewhere, as, for example, farther on in ch. 16:25 of this letter: "according to the revelation of the mystery which was kept secret from eternity." And also in Col. 1:26.[28]

Throughout the whole passage, it is his purpose to persuade this people to turn back. To understand the apostle rightly, we must know that what he says extends over the lump of the Jewish people and has reference to the good ones among them of the past as well as of the present and the future. Even if some among them are rejected, the whole lump must be honored because of the elect, just as any community must be honored because of the good ones among its members, even though the wicked outnumber them.

Hence, there applies here one certain rule about the understanding of Scripture, namely, that it speaks at one and the same time of the good and the wicked that exist in the same mystical body. In this sense, the Jewish people is a "holy lump" because of the elect but "cut off branches" because of the rejected. Thus the Jews are "fullness" and "diminution," and, likewise, they are "enemies for the sake of the Gentiles" and "yet greatly beloved for the sake of their fathers." Again and again, the Scripture says diverse things about them on account of the diversity that prevails among them. This sounds as if the apostle wanted to regard them one and all personally as enemies and beloved friends, inasmuch as, though he distinguishes between individual persons, he emphasizes that they belong to the same lump. The reason why he calls them "lump" is that he wants to indicate that he does not speak of particular persons but of the whole race in which there may be many who are not holy.

As touching the gospel, they are enemies *for your sake, but as touching the election, they are beloved for the Father's sake.* (Rom. 11:28.)

The word **enemies** must here be taken in a passive sense, i.e., they deserve to be hated; God hates them, and, therefore, also the apostles and all who belong to God hate them. This is clearly indicated by the opposite: **but beloved;** in other words: they are hated and yet loved, i.e., the whole lump of them is loved and hated "according to the gospel for your sakes," i.e., because you

[28] "The mystery which has been hidden from ages and generations, but now is manifested to his saints."

are beloved according to the gospel, they are hated according to the gospel; and yet they are beloved **for the sake of the fathers as touching election,** i.e., because the election adopts some of them to this day. Hence, they are beloved for the fathers' sake, because they, too, are friends.

For the gifts and the calling of God are without repentance. *For as you in times past were disobedient to God but now have obtained mercy by their disobedience, even so have these also now been disobedient, that by the mercy shown to you they also may now obtain mercy. For God has shut up all unto disobedience that he might have mercy on all.* (Rom. 11:29–32.)

This is an excellent statement. For God's counsel cannot be changed by anyone's merit or lack of merit. God does not repent of his gift and of the calling he has promised, because the Jews are now unworthy of them and you worthy. He does not change when you are changed. Hence, the Jews will turn back and they will at last be led to the truth of faith. (This is why the Greek text reads: "God's gifts are . . . *ametameleta*, i.e., *"impoenitibilia,"*[29] irreversible. The reference, then, is not to our repentance but to God as he lets it repent him concerning what he changes and destroys.

O the depth of the riches of the wisdom and of the knowledge of God! *How incomprehensible are his judgments and how unsearchable his ways![30] For who has known the mind of the Lord, or who has been his counselor? Or who has first given to him and it shall be recompensed to him again? For of him, and through him, and to him are all things. To him be glory forever. Amen.* (Rom. 11:33–36.)

Of the wisdom and of the knowledge! According to Blessed Augustine,[31] this is the correct distinction. The contemplation of eternal things pertains to wisdom, but the acquaintance with tem-

[29] Cf. Erasmus, *Annot., ad loc.*
[30] Luther's marginal gloss reads as follows (*WA* 56, 115, 19 ff.): "This word of the apostle is to make us aware of the fact that, in the conclusions stated above, there is something hidden that is too deep for us to understand. For he had said: 'Until the fullness of the Gentiles be come in' [v.25], 'That they also may obtain mercy' [v.31], 'That he might have mercy upon all' [v. 32]. All of this suggests that God wanted evil to happen in order to make something good from it. But why he does this in this special way or why he lets it happen in them and why he does not at the same time do good and evil to the same people, this is 'incomprehensible.' The following propositions are strange indeed: 'They fell in order that they might be saved'; 'they do not believe in order that they may believe.'"
[31] Augustine, *De trin.,* XII, 15, 25.

poral things to knowledge. Created wisdom thus deals with what we cannot see or understand except by faith alone or by being translated into heaven.[32] And knowledge deals with what is outside God and created. Hence, the wisdom of God is that wisdom by which he contemplates in himself all things before and above and within their happening,[33] and his knowledge is the knowledge by which he knows them as they happen; hence, it is called the "knowledge of sight."[34]

[32] Luther says, *"raptu anagogico."*
[33] *"Antequam fiant et supra quam fiant et intra quam fiant."*
[34] On *scientia visionis,* cf. Gabriel Biel, I *Sent., d.* 39, *a.* 1, *coroll.* 3.

ROMANS, CHAPTER TWELVE

I beseech you, therefore, brethren, by the mercies of God.
(Rom. 12:1.)
The apostle is about to teach a Christian ethic.[1] From here to

[1] In the marginal gloss, Luther writes (*WA* 56, 116 f., 21 ff.): "In the preceding chapters, the apostle laid 'the true foundation which is Christ' (I Cor. 3:11), or 'the first rock,' upon which the wise man builds (Matt. 7:24), and he destroyed the false foundation, namely, man's self-righteousness and merits, which are as 'the sand' upon which the foolish man builds (Matt. 7:26). Here now he proceeds to 'build upon this foundation gold, silver, and precious stones.' (I Cor. 3:12). Good works, which are the building, must above all have a sure and dependable foundation on which the heart can purpose to stand and to rely forever, so that, even in case it may not yet have built upon it, the site is ready for it to do so. The moralists ['*iustitiarii*'] do the opposite of this with their good works. They seek to put their trust in their conscience and, when they have performed many good works, they think they have done enough for themselves, so that they can feel secure. This is nothing else than to build on sand and to reject Christ. The apostle tries hard to prevent this; this is the purpose of all his letters. To say, as is commonly done [cf. the *Gl. ord.* and Lyra], that 'sand' means the riches of the world is a superficial and weak exegesis. For Christ speaks here of people who build (i.e., who do good) and not of misers and worldlings, who rather destroy themselves than build up anything.

"Hence, it is good works that he calls sand. And it is upon this foundation that these people try to build their righteousness in order to obtain a dwelling place for their conscience and peace of mind. But, as a matter of fact, only Christ is this foundation—and before all good works. For even before we think of doing enough or building up ['*praeveniens omne nostrum satisfacere vel aedificare*'], he has given us the foundation as a free gift, namely, a quiet conscience and a trusting heart. Has there ever been a builder stupid enough to lay also the foundation? Do not the builders look for the foundation that is already laid in the earth or do they not accept what is offered to them? So then, just as the earth offers us a foundation without our effort, so Christ offers himself without us as our right-

320

the end of the letter his chief concern is, therefore, the uprooting of man's own prudence and self-will. And so he deals with this pest right at the start. It is the most noxious of all because, under the artful disguise of bringing forth goods, it alone causes the birth in the Spirit to be undone again; indeed, it gradually brings it to fall by its own good works. He does this not only in this letter but also in all the others, and with greatest care, because he knows that good works are nothing apart from unity, peace, and humility, to all of which this prudence brings instantaneous death.

Hence, he says in Phil. 2:1 ff.: "If there are any bowels of commiseration, make full my joy that you be of one mind, having the same love, being of one accord, agreeing in feeling. Let nothing be done through contention, neither by vainglory; but in lowliness of mind let each esteem others better than himself, each one not considering the things that are his own but those that belong to others. Have this mind in you," etc. In the same vein he writes in II Cor. 6:1: "Helping you, we exhort you that you do not receive the grace of God in vain." So he says also here: "I beseech you by the mercy of God," i.e., which you have been given; see to it that you do not receive it in vain but, rather, "present your bodies as a sacrifice." Moreover, what it means to "present a sacrifice" he explains by saying in II Cor. 6:4 ff.: "in much patience, in much fasting, in watchings, in labors," etc.

And be not conformed to this world, **but be reformed** *by the renewing of your mind, that you may prove what is the good and acceptable and perfect will of God.* (Rom. 12:2.)

The apostle speaks of progress, for he addresses people who have already begun to be Christians, whose life is not static[2] but in movement[3] from good to better, just as a sick man moves from sickness into health, as our Lord shows in the half-dead man whom

---

eousness, peace, and security of conscience in order that from then on we can continually build upon him in doing good.

"So far the apostle has spoken about what it means to become a new man, and he has described the new birth which bestows the new being ['*dat novum esse*'] (John 3:3 ff.). But now he speaks about the works of the new birth; one who has not yet become a new man presumes that he is doing them—but in vain. For being comes before doing, but being-acted-upon comes even before being ['*Prius est enim esse quam operari, prius autem pati quam esse*']. Hence becoming, being, acting, follow one another." (Note by ed.: This is the Aristotelian "*progressio a non esse ad esse*.")

2 "*In quiescere.*"
3 "*In moveri.*"

the good Samaritan took care of (Luke 10:34). In the same way, in Gen. 1:2, the Spirit of God did not rest but "moved upon the face of the waters." And in Deut. 32:11 it says: "As the eagle enticing her young to fly and hovering over them" and, in Ps. 18:10: "He ascended and flew; he flew upon the wings of the winds."[3a] This is why Blessed Bernard writes: "As soon as you do no longer want to become better, you cease to be good."[4] It is of no use for a tree to grow green and to blossom if the blossoms do not turn into fruit. Hence, many perish when they are in blossom.

For just as there are five stages of natural growth, according to Aristotle: not-being, becoming, being, action, and being acted upon, i.e., privation, matter, form, operation, and passion,[5] so it is also with the Spirit: not-being is something without a name and man in sins; becoming is justification; being is righteousness; acting is to act and live righteously; to be acted upon is to be made perfect and complete. These five are somehow always in motion in man. In whatever way the nature of man may be explained—and leaving out of account the first "not-being" and the last "being," for in between these two: "not-being" and "being acted upon," the other three, namely, "becoming," "being," and "acting" are always in motion—by the new birth he passes from sin to righteousness and thus from "not-being" through "becoming" to "being." Thereupon he acts righteously. But from this "new being" which is really a "not being," he proceeds and passes into another "new being" through "being acted upon," i.e., through becoming new, he passes into being better and from there again into being new. For it is really so that man is always in privation, always in becoming or in the state of potency and matter, and always in action. In this way, Aristotle philosophizes about these matters and he does it well, but he is not well understood.

Man is always in not-being, in becoming, in being; always in privation, in potency, in act; always in sin, in justification, in righteousness, i.e., always a sinner, always penitent, always righteous. For by repenting he becomes righteous from being unrighteous. Repentance is, therefore, the medium between unrighteousness and righteousness. And thus he is in sin as the *terminus a quo* and in righteousness as the *terminus ad quem*. If, therefore, we are always repenting, we are always sinners, and precisely thereby we

---

[3a] One must remember that Luther read these words with the understanding that they speak of Christ.

[4] Cf. Bernard of Clairvaux, *Ep.* 91 (cf. Luther's exposition of Rom. 3:11).

[5] All these terms are derived from Aristotle, though they cannot all be found in one specific passage of his writings. Luther depended upon the medieval handbooks of physics. Cf. Ockham, *Summule in lib. physicorum,* c. IX; c. XXV f. (Ficker, p. 441, n. 23.)

are righteous and being made righteous; we are partly sinners and partly righteous, i.e., nothing but penitents.

Just so, by contrast, the ungodly who deviate from righteousness hold the middle between sin and righteousness, but they move in the opposite direction. This life, therefore, is a road to heaven and to hell. None is so good that he cannot become better, and none is so bad that he cannot become worse, until at last we become what we are to be.[6]

The apostle treats this with great sensitiveness. He does not say: be reformed to the renewal but: *"in the renewal"* or "through the renewal," or better yet, as in the Greek: "Be reformed by the renewing of your mind." He adds "by the renewing" in order that one should see that, in connection with this transformation, he does not teach an instability of mind (or a renewal of the external cultus) but, rather, a renewing of the mind, day by day, that is to become greater and greater, in accordance with the words of II Cor. 4:16: "The inward man is renewed day by day," and of Eph. 4:23: "Be renewed in the spirit of your mind," and of Col. 3:10: "Put on the new man, which is renewed."

Present your bodies a living sacrifice, holy, acceptable unto God, which is your reasonable service. (Rom. 12:1.)

The true sacrifice to God is not outside us or outside what belongs to us, nor is it a matter of time confined to a certain hour of the day, but we ourselves are this sacrifice (forever, according to the word of Ps. 110:4: "You are a priest forever" and hence, Christ has the eternal priesthood [Heb. 7:17]), as it says in Prov. 23:26: "My son, give me your heart." It says a *"living"* sacrifice, in contrast to the sacrifices of animals which in former times were offered up dead (as Lyra[7] says and as also Blessed Gregory[8] explains). But it is better to interpret the term in relation to the spiritual life in so far as it is to bring forth good, "in order," as it is said above in ch. 6:6 of this letter, "that the body of sin may be done away." For before God the "body of sin" is dead. But good works which are done by the morally defiled are worth nothing. Hence, there follows the phrase "Holy." Lyra translates it to mean "firm" and "persevering." This is a proper but not a suitable translation. For, in the Scriptures, "holy" does not mean "something firmly established" or "inviolable," nor is it something that is "without earth," something quasi *"ageos,"* as the

---

[6] *"Usque dum ad extremam formam perveniamus."*
[7] Luther seems to refer not to Lyra, but to the *Additio* I of Paul of Burgos, where something of this sort is said.
[8] Cf. Gregory, *Hom. in Ezech.*, II, 10, 9.

term goes that has been derived from the Greek.[9] But this is pure imagination. The "holy" is something separate and set apart, something kept away from the profane, something that is detached from other use and is attached only to sacred use worthy of God, something sacred that is dedicated, as in Ex. 19:10: "Sanctify the people today and tomorrow and let them wash their garments," etc. and in Josh. 3:5: "Sanctify yourselves, for tomorrow the Lord will do wonders among you"; and I Sam. 21:4 ff.: "If the young men be clean, especially from women, they shall eat. And David answered: Truly, as to what concerns women, the vessels of the young men are holy," i.e., clean and chaste. Then the text goes on to say: "Now this way is defiled, but it shall also be sanctified this day. And the priest gave them hallowed bread."

"Holy" is then obviously the same as "clean," "chaste," "separate"; it signifies mainly that purity which we owe to God. Blessed Gregory says in the *Homily on Ezechiel*:[10] "A living sacrifice is the body, in so far as it under affliction for the Lord's sake. It is called a *living sacrifice* because it is alive in virtues and dead to vices; it is a sacrifice because it is already dead to this world and does no wrong; it is living because all its actions are good."

The apostle, then, understands "holy" as "chaste" in the sense that our bodies must not be defiled by dissipation, as he says in ch. 6:19 of this letter: "Present your members to serve righteousness, unto sanctification," and I Cor. 7:34: "that she may be holy both in body and in spirit." Briefly, then, "holy" is the same as "sacred," "pure and clean before God." It is something else than the cleanness or neatness observed in human relations. Nevertheless, there prevails a strange confusion about the distinction between "holy" and "sacred," "sanctify" and "sanctification." It is right, therefore, that, in German, we say *heilig* rather than *rein*.

Now, doing good and living cleanly are not worth anything if one takes pride therein. Hence, the apostle goes on to say: **acceptable unto God**. He says this by way of criticizing the vainglory and pride that commonly undermine the good. For just as envy doggedly pursues somebody else's happiness, so pride and vainglory dog one's own. Thus people become foolish virgins (Matt. 25:3):

---

[9] This derivation, which was attributed to Beda, is mentioned by Lyra in connection with Luke 1:49 ("Because he that is mighty has done great things to me, and holy is his name"). In the *Catholicon* of John Balbus de Janua, Hugh of St. Victor is named as the originator of the etymological suggestion. In his *Vocabularius brevil.*, Reuchlin states (in dependence on the *Catholicon*): *Agios graece*, i.e., *sanctus latine et dicitur ab a quod est sine, et gē, quod est terra* (the Greek word *hagios* [holy], which in Latin is *sanctus*, means *a* [= without] *gē* [= earth], without earth).

[10] Gregory, *Hom. in Ezech.*, II, 110, 19.

they have lamps, i.e., they live holy lives, but they have no oil, because they seek to be acceptable to men. Now, to be acceptable only to God is something greater than to be holy. For people who have something, such as sanctity, wherewith they feel they must become acceptable, find it most difficult to be displeased with themselves and to be unconcerned for the criticism of others.

Which is your reasonable service. Lyra interprets this to mean a "discreet and moderate" service, lest man destroy his whole body instead of keeping it only under control with respect to its desires. Though this is good and very wholesome advice, it is not handed down to us in this passage by the apostle. Indeed, in the Greek, he separates this particular phrase from the foregoing by using the article, for he says: *"tēn logikēn latreian hymōn,"* as if he wanted to give a reason why, as he had just been saying, their bodies should be offered as a sacrifice; in other words, he means to say: I tell you this because I want to point out that, in terms of the new law, you owe God a reasonable sacrifice and not one of beasts. *Logikos* means "reasonable" as *alogos* means "unreasonable." And "service" or *"latreian"* means the sacrifice as such or the actual presentation of this living sacrifice. In short, he wants to say: Present your reasonable service, namely, your bodies as a living sacrifice.

That you may prove what is the good and acceptable and perfect will of God. (Rom. 12:2.)

Some interpreters[11] relate **good** to the beginners, **acceptable** to the advanced, and **perfect** to the perfect. This application of the text is not unreasonable. One can relate it also to the three aforementioned terms "living, holy, acceptable to God." For it is the "good" will of God that one should do good; and to live cleanly and to be abstinent is his "acceptable" will; and wanting to be acceptable only to him is his "perfect" will.

However, by saying that the proving of this threefold will of God comes from being transformed to a new mind, the apostle hints at something that is deeper than written words can convey, something that one can come to know only by experience. This is why those "who are led by the Spirit of God" (Rom. 8:14) are flexible in mind and thought. "The right hand of God leads them wonderfully" (Ps. 45:4) whither they neither want[12] nor think to go, and beyond all understanding. As they are thus led, the will of God seems to go against them; it is harsh and displeasing and utterly hopeless. But they yield to such a leading in humble resig-

11 Lyra.
12 Cf. John 21:18.

nation and are patient in faith. Only when they have been most severely tried, they understand how good this will was, though they did not, indeed could not, know this while it was in process of being done.

But unbelievers "do not wait for the counsel of God" (Ps. 107:11). They act and want to see action done according to their own set mind and they refuse to give up their own thinking; neither do they want to have it changed. Hence, they do not "prove what is the good will of God," but they are "conformed to this world" because they rely only on their own feelings and experience. It cannot be otherwise, for only faith transforms the mind and leads it to the recognition of the will of God. The apostle expresses a similar thought in Eph. 3:18, where he says: "That you may be able to comprehend with all the saints what is the breadth and length and height and depth that you may be filled unto all the fullness of God." And then he goes on to say: "Now to him that is able to do exceeding abundantly above all that we think," etc.

Whenever God gives us a new degree of grace, he gives it in such a way that it conflicts with all our understanding and our planning. A man, therefore, who then does not yield and is not willing to change his mind and to wait but is scornful and becomes impatient can never obtain this grace. Hence, this transformation of our mind is the most useful of all knowledge for Christ's believers. And the clinging to our own mind is the most hurtful resistance to the Holy Spirit. For example: when Abraham received the command to go out from his own country (Gen. 12:1 ff.), not knowing whither he went, this was against his own mind. Likewise, when he was ordered to sacrifice his own son (Gen. 22:2 ff.), this was an exceedingly great transformation of his mind, as Rom. ch. 4, proves,[13] and the will of God concerning Isaac seemed harsh and unacceptable to him to the point of despair; and yet it was afterward proved to have been very good, very acceptable, and perfect in every way. Similarly, one could point to David[14] and the Virgin Mary[15] as other examples. But everyone needs to have here his own experience, and he must carefully observe the visitation that comes upon him.

Certainly self-will is here a very great hindrance, especially because it leads to differences with others. Moreover, it causes one to have his own mind in opposition to his superiors and those by whose words or action God wants to demonstrate his will. Hence,

---

[13] Luther probably thinks of Heb. 11:17 and James 2:21 ff., where Gen. 15:6 (which Paul quotes in Rom. 4:3) is related to the sacrifice of Isaac.
[14] Cf. I Sam. 17:33.
[15] Cf. Luke 1:28 ff.

the apostle goes on to say: "For I say. . . to every man that is among you, not to think of himself more highly than he ought to think." (Rom. 12:3.) For in the church, God does nothing else than transform men's minds. But people who are self-complacent resist being so transformed; they disturb everything and cause schisms and heresies. They are "men corrupted in mind," as he calls them elsewhere (II Tim. 3:8).

Therefore, just as the wisdom of God is hidden under the disguise of foolishness and truth under the form of a lie, so also the word of God comes, whenever it comes, in a form that is contrary to our own thinking in so far as it pretends to have the truth by and from itself. Hence, when the word goes against us, our mind condemns it as a lie and this corresponds to the fact that Christ called his word our adversary: Matt. 5:25:[16] "Agree with your adversary," and Hos. 5:14: "For I will be like a lioness to Ephraim and a lion's whelp to the house of Judah," i.e., I will be an adversary.

So it is also with the will of God. In its nature, it is really "good, acceptable, and perfect." But it is so hidden under the disguise of evil, unacceptableness, and hopelessness that it seems to our will and so-called good intention[17] to be nothing but a very bad and desperate will and in no way the will of God but rather that of the devil, except in case man abandons his own will and good intention and undergoes a total denial of his preconceived notions of righteousness, goodness, and truth. If he does this, all that previously was very bad for him, greatly displeased him, and seemed lost to him will taste very sweet to him, and it will be most acceptable to him, and he will recognize it as perfect in every way.

Thus the Lord says to Peter: "When you were younger, you girded yourself and walked where you would. But when you are old, another shall gird you and lead you whither you would not." (John 21:18.) *How amazing! Peter is led whither he will not, and yet unless he wills this, he will not glorify God but fall into sin. At the same time, therefore, he wills and wills not. In the same way, Christ in the agony of his death perfected his not-willing (if I may say so) by a most fervent willingness.*[18] *Thus God acts in all his saints: he makes them do very willingly what they do not want to do at all.* This contrariety astounds the philosophers, and men do not understand it.

This is why I said that unless one becomes acquainted with it

---

[16] The Gloss interprets *adversarius* to mean *sermo divinus.*

[17] Cf. Gabriel Biel, II *Sent.*, d. 40, q. *un., n.* 2.

[18] "*Sic Christus in agone suo voluntatem suam (ut sic dixerim) ferventissima voluntate perfecit.*"

through practical experience, he will never understand it. And certainly, if practical experience is necessary in law which teaches a shadowy righteousness, how much more necessary it is in theology. *Every Christian, therefore, should rejoice most, precisely when something is done against his will and intention, and he should be very apprehensive when he has his own way. I say this not only with respect to the desires of the flesh, but also with respect to our greatest achievements of righteousness.*

This is why, nowadays, the lawyers give very dangerous counsel when they advise without hesitation that what, according to their knowledge of the law, is just must be carried out. In this way, they advised Pope Julius, and people called him blessed. In this manner, they counseled Duke George. Indeed, almost the entire world is carried away by this error—cardinals, bishops, and princes, just as the Jews once were when they opposed the king of Babylon (II Kings 24:20; 25:1 ff.)

All of them insist on their particular rights; therefore they do not settle anything but get ruined. For God rules the world by a universal right[19] by which what ought to be is done in all and by all and through all. But they are so blind and foolish as to proceed according to a particular right. In this matter no lawyer is of any use. They are all alike: they are so utterly foolish that they are not ashamed to make proposals so silly that not even peasants would dare to advance them. For example, they say: This man here is right, even before God, but that man there is not right, either according to divine or human law; then they proceed with greatest assurance along the lines of their "good intention" and of their great concern for justice.

Meanwhile, it occurs to none of them that one may be right in one single part but perhaps wrong before God in all other, or at least in several other, parts. Then God must be ready to help him as if he were righteous, and all the while God is expected to ignore all his wrong acts and prefer this single point of his being right to the whole mass of his wickedness.

For example (and I say this in order to give a practical exposition of what the Scripture means so that in similar cases you can form a similar judgment): when Duke George was advised to insist upon his right in Frisia,[20] there was none that dared say to him: Good prince, your merits and those of your entire people are not such that God should not rightly punish you by chastening you through this rebellious and unrighteous fellow. Therefore, calm

---

[19] *"Iustitia universali."*

[20] Luther here refers to the feuds between Duke George of Saxony and Count Edzard of East Frisia. George invaded Frisia in 1514.

down and recognize in this wicked act the gracious will of God. You had better submit to his will!

Just so, someone should have advised Pope Julius by saying to him: Holy Father, the Roman Church of today is not so holy that it would not deserve something much worse than this injury the Venetians now inflict upon it. Be still, this is the will of God. But he was the sort of person who would say: No, no, we must get justice.

In the same way, some one should counsel our own bishop of Brandenburg[21] and say to him: Reverend Father, you, too, have often sinned universally. Please tolerate this particular case of injustice. And you, Prince Frederick, you have so far been protected by a good angel. If you would only acknowledge this! How often have you been provoked by wrongs and how often would you have gone to war for just causes! But you have quietly endured it all. Yet I do not know whether you did so from a sincere confession of sin or from fear that you might sustain a loss.

This is why (if I may speak of myself) I detest this word "justice." To hear it pains me more than if someone were to rob me. And yet, the lawyers have it constantly on their lips. No group of people on this earth are more unteachable in this matter than the lawyers and the folk who harp upon their "good intention"[22] or consider themselves to be of superior intelligence. For I have often had the experience with myself and many others that when we were right God laughed at us in our rightness. And yet I know people who dared say: I know that right is on my side. But God does not pay any attention to this. And it is really so, right is on his side but with respect to a particular case. But God does not care how right it may be.

The universal right or justice is then humility. It subjects everyone to everyone else and thereby gives everyone everything, as Christ said to John the Baptist: "So it becomes us to fulfill all justice."

Thus, in Dan. 3:27 (Vg.), Azarias confesses it to be altogether right that he and those with him should suffer, even though wrong is being inflicted upon them, namely, by the wicked king. For even though one who inflicts wrong is in the wrong, he does not do wrong to him who must suffer it, for he suffers justly. By what right does the devil take possession of men? Or by what right does an evil hangman hang a thief? Certainly not by his own right, but by that of the judge. Thus men who boast of their own rightness

---

[21] This seems to be a reference to Jerome Scultetus (Schultz), who was chancellor of the Elector of Brandenburg.

[22] "Boneintentionarii."

refuse to direct their attention to the supreme Judge but they mind only their own judgment. And so they take themselves to be innocent in all respects, when in fact they are innocent only in relation to him who did them wrong.

Inasmuch, therefore, as there is none righteous before God, no injustice can be done to anyone by any creature, even though right may be on his side. Hence, all men are rid of the cause of contention.

Therefore, whenever you are being wronged and evil befalls you while you are doing good, turn your eyes away from this evil and consider how much evil you have yourself done in other ways. Then you will see how good the will of God is in this evil that befalls you. This is what it means to be changed by the renewing of your mind and to be concerned for what belongs to God.

We can then be sure that Peter would not have glorified God if he had girded himself and gone whither he himself would, even though he were not to walk on evil paths but on the very best road to righteousness. Indeed, our Lord put a damper on him when he wanted to demonstrate his great righteousness. And when, thereupon, he went whither he would not but whither another led him, he did glorify God.

Thus we, too, cannot glorify God unless we do what we do not want to do, even if we think we are right, indeed, most of all if we think we are right in what we plan and in the good we do. So then: "to take up your cross" and "to become Christ's disciple" (Luke 14:27) and "to be transformed by the renewing of your mind," etc., is the same as to hate yourself, to will against your own will, to mind what transcends your comprehension,[23] to concede over against the objection of your own righteousness that you are sinful, and to give an ear to foolishness against the objection of your own wisdom.

Hence, we must note that the terms "good," "acceptable," "perfect" do not refer to the will of God as such but as it is in relation to its object.[24] For it is not our proving that makes the will of God good, acceptable, and perfect, but in our proving we recognize that

---

[23] *"Sapere contra suum sapere."*

[24] *"Non formaliter, sed obiective."* Cf. Luther's interlinear gloss on Rom. 11:8 (*WA* 56, 108, 3 ff.): *"God has given them* through the word of the gospel that was received by others *the spirit of compunction,* because of their unbelief and their presumptuous pride in their own righteousness."

In the marginal gloss, he comments as follows (*WA* 56, 108, 9 ff.): "God gives them this spirit in order to make them indignant by doing what they do not want him to do and by completely undoing what they want. Thus he gives them in fact (*'obiective'*) the spirit of envy, but not because it is his purpose to make them envious or because he is envious in himself (*'non effective seu formaliter'*). If one understands that God gives them this

it is so; it becomes "good" to us means, therefore, that it is being recognized as good; and it is acceptable because it proves to be highly acceptable, and "perfect" because it perfects everything, i.e., it becomes "good, acceptable, and perfect" to us. *Consolation*

These words overflow with consolation. For precisely when evils ↓ befall us we must be of good courage, for therein God shows his good will. We should be best pleased when something happens to us that is most unpleasant to us, for there is in it most certainly the acceptable will of God, i.e., a very gentle and pleasing will. And we should be most confident when something desperate and hopeless befalls us, for the perfect will of God is in it, perfecting everything and bringing full salvation.

For it is the nature of the divine will, according to I Sam. 2:6, that "it kills and makes alive, that it brings down to hell and brings back again." This means: it does good by doing us harm, it is most acceptable when it causes our displeasure, and it perfects while it destroys. We must, then, not become foolish and "be conformed to this world" which judges according to its sense and understanding (and it understands only what it experiences here and now), but we must be more and more renewed. For this is what it means to prove the will of God: not to form our judgments on the basis of what we feel and experience but to walk in darkness.

Now those who do not want to be transformed will find out what is the evil and unacceptable and destructive, wrathful will of God. It is evil, because it inflicts injury and harm; it is unacceptable, because it causes men to resent this affliction and renders them incapable of bearing it patiently; and it is destructive, because it causes the impatient and resentful to fall into obstinacy and damnation where they live or rather die uttering blasphemies and curses.

However, the will of God is "good," because it brings forth good from evil; it is acceptable, because it causes men to love this good cheerfully and to find good and real pleasure in it, and not only in it but also in the evil we spoke of before. It is perfect, because it brings those who rejoice in it to completion, perfecting what has here been begun.

Yet all this is addressed only to those who have the power to

---

spirit incidentally, so to speak, or by his permission, he has the correct understanding. Not that God does not want them to be of this mind, for he wants them to realize that they are being punished, but he acts as he does, according to Ps. 112:10, 'in order that the sinner shall see and be angry, that he shall gnash his teeth and pine away' and that 'the desire of the wicked shall perish.' By giving others something good, he thus gives them an evil that they hate and must pursue."

act and who are responsible for themselves. But the matter is different in the case of those who are set over others, for they are not
their own agents but the agents of God. Hence, it is their responsibility to rule their subjects with justice and not to permit them to
inflict wrong upon one another. They are not empowered to tolerate everything, and patience is out of place for them. For God
expects of them, not humility and patience and submission, but
readiness to pass judgment, to exercise power, and to impose punishment. They are his representatives. Yet if it is possible for any
one of them to make concessions without violating his trust, he
must do so, as we have said before, even if this entails harm and
trouble for him.

For I say, through the grace that was given me, to every man
that is among you, not to think of himself more highly than he
ought to think, but so to think as to think soberly, according as
God has divided to each man the measure of faith. (Rom.
12:3.)

"Measure of faith" can be understood, first, as the measure or
mode according to which faith is given, in distinction from all
other gifts. But here it cannot be taken in this sense, because the
apostle plainly states that different gifts are given according to
this measure.

The term "measure of faith" must, therefore, be taken to mean,
secondly, the measure of the gifts of faith. In other words: there
are many gifts in faith, and though believers live by one and the
same faith, they have a different measure of gifts. Now the apostle
calls this a measure of faith, because those who act without faith
do not have these gifts and this measure. It is certainly true that
there is one faith, one baptism, one church, one Lord, one Spirit,
one God (Eph. 4:4 ff.). Nevertheless, there are diverse gifts in this
one faith, in this one church, in this one Lordship, etc. It is just
like saying: Everyone is entitled to the measure of the town or
the measure of the house that the prince has assigned to him, i.e.,
the measure that prevails in a given house or town.

Or better still: faith is all of this, for faith is nothing else than
the obedience of the spirit. But there are different degrees of the
obedience of the spirit. For one of us exercises his obedience and
faith here and another there, yet we are all of one faith. Just so
there prevails in a town one obedience to the prince, yet there are
diverse ways of practicing this obedience; nobody can presume to
adopt someone else's way and neglect his own responsibility, for
then confusion, sedition, and rebellion would develop in the com-
monwealth.

For as we have many members in one body, but all the members have not the same office, so we who are many are one body in Christ, and every one members one of another. And having gifts differing according to the grace that is given us, **either prophecy, to be used according to the rule of faith, or** . . . (Rom. 12:4–6.)

So far the apostle has shown how we must behave toward God, namely, by the renewing of our mind and the sanctification of our body so that we may prove what is the will of God. But from here on to the end of the letter, he teaches us how we must behave toward our neighbor and he explains the commandment of the love of the neighbor in great detail. It is strange, indeed, that there is not more concern among us for such an important teaching of so great an apostle, a teaching which is manifestly that of the Holy Spirit. Instead, we occupy ourselves with matters that are trifling by comparison: we build churches; we expand ecclesiastical property; we accumulate money; we provide the church with more and more ornaments and vessels of gold and silver; we install organs and other ostentatious pieces of display. We practice all our piety in activities of this kind and are not a whit concerned about what the apostle here commands. And I have not even mentioned the monstrous display of pride, ostentation, greed, dissipation, and ambition that is connected with all these enterprises!

So then, he turns first against the false prophets. For prophecy must be practiced "according to the rule of faith." And this is violated by those who prophesy on the basis of human thought or according to conjectures of probability derived from actions and signs of the creature, as, for example, by people who foretell God's plan by the stars or some other guess of probability that they may have. But God-given prophecy comes in such a way that it goes against all human sense just as though it proclaimed something impossible. Hence, it provokes most people to unbelief, inasmuch as everything pertaining to the truth of this kind of prophecy appears to be beyond hope, leading one to expect its opposite. Such was the prophecy of Jeremiah (Jer. 32:15). During the siege of Jerusalem, when everything was quite hopeless, he prophesied saying: "Thus says the Lord: Houses and fields and vineyards shall be possessed again in this land." Yet all was already laid waste, and the people of the city were already moving away. This is why Jeremiah exclaims then and there: "The Lord is great in counsel and incomprehensible in thought." However, when he prophesied the destruction of the city and the exile of its people, one did not believe him, inasmuch as there were no signs pointing to such an eventuality. Everything spoke against it: fortifications; armed strength; auxiliary power, so that the destruction of Jerusalem seemed to be impossible—so much so that, on the basis of these indications, Ananias dared to prophesy the opposite (Jer. 28:1 ff.), and he, too, was a prophet. For it was not only the false prophets who prophesied wrongly; also true prophets became false precisely when they forgot to prophesy "according to the rule of faith." Thus Nathan certainly erred when he advised David to build the Temple (II Sam. 7:3 ff.). And, according to Num. 22:21 ff., Balaam erred and became a false prophet despite the fact that he foretold such extraordinary things. Thus (at the end of the book of I Kings) also Micah prophesied contrary to the common feeling that Ahab would perish, although everywhere there were only the strongest indications that certain victory was at hand. This was the reason why Zedekiah, who relied on these indications, prophesied against him.

A prophecy, therefore, is not true because it is based on experience or human proof. Hence, it says, in the passage before us, "according to the rule of" or "by comparison with" faith. For some interpreters[25] take the Greek word *"analogia"* to mean "rule," "comparison," "proportion," or "similarity." The apostle is then saying: If you want to prophesy, prophesy in such a way that you do not exceed faith, so that your prophesying can be in harmony with the peculiarity of faith. In German we say: *Es ellicht ym. Es sihet ym gleich,*[26] i.e., "it has the same characteristics," "it resembles it," "it is like it."

For example, if you see a monastery that resembles a castle, you can say that it is analogous to a castle, i.e., it has the proportion, peculiar character, and location that a castle would have. In the same way, the apostle wants to say here that prophecy must be in harmony with faith: It must be concerned with "things that are not seen" (Heb. 11:1), lest it become a wisdom of the world which, with respect to its cause as well as its effect, is part of the things that are apparent. And this word is noteworthy.

So then, an analogy is an assimilation, not one that is produced by the intellect, but one that is contained in the matter itself, or, rather, it is neither of the two, but that in virtue of which one thing agrees with another in its peculiar characteristics and becomes like it. To be sure, one may prophesy something new but, in doing so, one must not transcend the characteristic nature of faith. In other words: what one prophesies must not be provable by experience; it must only be a token of things that are in no way apparent either by signs or other indications. Otherwise, faith

---

25 Cf. Faber and Erasmus.
26 A Middle High German expression, meaning: *Es ähnelt ihm; es sieht ihm gleich.*

will be destroyed by prophecy and become a plain kind of wisdom
that any knowledgeable man can understand and comprehend and
by which he can construe a similar prophecy. In such a case, prophecy is no longer prophecy but a factual demonstration and an evidence of experience.[26a]

Ministry, in ministering. (Rom. 12:7.)

In Greek, these words read *"diakonian"* and *"in diakonia,"*
i.e., "in ministering." Ministers are all those who serve in ecclesiastical offices, such as a priest, a deacon, a subdeacon and whosoever has to do with sacred things, with the exception of the
administration of the word of God, and also those who assist a
teacher, just as the apostle often speaks of his helpers.

This rule is being violated, first of all, by ambitious men who,
because they dislike their office, want to teach, though they are not
only untrained, which is something that could be tolerated, but
also lack the gift of teaching. For it is not enough to be learned
and intelligent, but the gift of grace, too, is required in order that
one be chosen by God for teaching. But today all of us rush forward eagerly in order to teach the whole world, even if we ourselves do not understand what we teach, and even if, in case we
have this understanding, we lack the gift of grace or the mandate of
God who must send us. In this sense he says: You have no right to
send, because you are servants and not masters. "Pray ye, therefore,
the Lord of the harvest that he send forth laborers into his vine-
yard." (Matt. 9:38.) For this reason, let him be content with his
ministry who does not know how to preach or is not yet called to
preach, even though he may know how to do so. (Matthew 25:14:
"He called his own servants and delivered unto them his goods,"
but first he called them.)

It is certainly strange to see to what an extent the "good intention" is at work here: It imagines that by preaching it can produce heavens knows how much fruit, though, in the first place,
it may be untrained, and, secondly, trained but not called, and,
thirdly, trained but not provided with the gift of grace. For when
God extends this call to preach, he either calls men who already
have this gift, or he grants the gift with the call.[27] And if someone
preaches without a call, "he beats the air" (I Cor. 9:26) or the
fruit he boasts of exists only in his foolish imagination.

I refrain from saying anything about the utterly stupid and
incompetent persons whom bishops and abbots nowadays promote
everywhere to the pulpit. We really cannot say that they are

[26a] *"Experimentum."*
[27] Lit., *"Nam vocatio vel invenit gratiam vel confert eam."*

called and sent, even if we wanted to, because in this case incompetent and unworthy men are given the call. This is the work of God's wrath, for it is he who withdraws his word from us on account of our sins and he increases the number of vacuous talkers and verbose babblers.

Or he that teaches, in doctrine. (Rom. 12:7.)
Many have the gift of teaching, though they do not possess great learning. Others have both, and they are the best teachers, as, for example, Saints Augustine, Ambrose, and Jerome. A man, therefore, who does not use this gift but gets involved in other matters, sins against this mandate of the apostle, indeed, against the mandate of God. This concerns especially those who have been called and put into teaching positions, even though they may not yet be called by the title of teachers. For "tender ears do not want to listen to a truth that bites."[28] But the apostle deals chiefly with those who have been called. In his letters, he therefore always emphasizes his own call, because without the divine call neither the office of the ministry nor teaching can prosper. Hence, it is due to the instigation of the devil that as ministers arrogate the teaching office to themselves so, by contrast, teachers flee the teaching office, with the result that thus the work of God is hindered in both ways. To be sure, in this passage as well as in I Cor. 12:28, the apostle puts the order of the teachers in the third place.

He that exhorts, in exhortation. (Rom. 12:8.)
Teaching and exhortation differ from each other in this, that teaching is directed to the ignorant but exhortation to those who have knowledge. The teacher lays the foundation and the exhorter builds upon it. The teacher transmits knowledge; the exhorter stimulates and sees to it that the transmitted knowledge bears fruit. The one plants and the other waters. As the apostle says in I Cor. 3:6: "I have planted, Apollos watered," and also farther on (I Cor. 3:10): "As a wise master builder, I have laid the foundation, and another builds thereon." In our age, almost all preachers find themselves in this situation: they are watering a faith that is already planted unless they are preaching where there has not been any preaching before. Therefore those who possess this gift and are called should not take time for other things. Yet today, this gets to be a common practice—in the same way in which the heathen Horace was acquainted with it: "The lazy ox desires the saddle, while the horse yearns for the plow,"[29] and "Nobody is con-

[28] Cf. Persius, *Satira*, I, 108.
[29] Horace, *Ep.* I, 14, 43: *"Optat Ephippia bos piger, optat arare Caballus."*

tent with his lot but he praises those who follow strange trails."[30] And Terence says:[31] "Most of us are of such a mind that we are not satisfied with what we have." Those who are fit to do a certain piece of work detest it, and the incompetent pant for it.

He that gives, with simplicity. (Rom. 12:8.)

Just as everybody else is tempted in his state of grace by his particular devil, so that he cannot purely and faithfully cultivate his divine gift for his God, so also he that gives does not lack his special devil. This means that this commandment is here broken in two ways.

First, when one gives on condition and not freely, i.e., with the expectation that he will get his gift back with interest. Today, one can often find this way of behavior among Christians, and a common proverb describes it as follows: "Nowadays people are wont to give a piece of bread to one who has plenty to eat."[32] In German, we say: *Geschenk unnd eer.*[33] Thus those of lower rank give to those of higher rank, i.e., to the princes, prelates, bishops, and to the rich and powerful. But these would not get anything given to them if everyone gave with simplicity, i.e., without the expectation of getting something in return. Strangely enough, this evil is today widely spread. Here the saying of Luke 14:12 ff. is relevant: "When you make a dinner or a supper, call not your friends nor your brethren, nor your kinsmen, nor rich neighbors, lest perhaps they bid you again and a recompense be made you. But when you make a feast, bid the poor, the maimed, the lame, the blind, and you shall be blessed, because they have not wherewith to recompense you; for you shall be recompensed in the resurrection of the righteous." If only this were observed, how many monstrous evils would the church then be spared today! Would the lawyers then get such large gratuities and tips? This practice of buying favors is widely current in all ranks of society. To be sure, this kind of payment can sometimes give great joy, but getting it repaid is always a much greater joy. This applies particularly to subordinates in relation to their superiors.

The commandment of the apostle is broken, secondly, when those who belong to the upper ranks give to those who are below them or when persons of equal rank give to each other. This

---

[30] A free rendering of Horace' first satire.
[31] Terence, *Phormio,* I, 3, 20.
[32] "*Mos nunc est genti, quod panis praebetur habenti.*"
[33] I.e., "*Geschenk und Ehre.*" These words are probably pointers to German proverbs, corresponding to the Latin ones quoted in the text, which Luther intended to cite in his lectures.

gives much greater delight, because it is the occasion for boasting and vainglorying. Here, indeed, "it is more blessed to give than to receive" (Acts 20:35)! In their pride, they think they are like God himself!

(This exposition does not seem right to me. For the apostle speaks of the tribute to which the teachers of the word and the leaders of the churches are entitled. As he says in Gal. 6:6: "Let him that is instructed in the word communicate to him that instructs him in all good things." To be sure, this must be done in the spirit of simplicity and not in that of hypocrisy, just as the Children of Israel were commanded "to take heed not to forsake the Levites" [Deut. 12:19]. Hence, he goes on to say in Gal. 6:7: "Be not deceived; God is not mocked." It is this gift, I think, which he has in mind in I Cor. 12:28. There he speaks of "gifts of healings" or "subsidies"[34] that are due to the leaders and teachers who devote themselves to the word and to prayer. For "the Lord is their portion" [Num. 18:20; Ps. 73:26] and thus "the laborer is worthy of his reward" [I Tim. 5:18; Matt. 10:10].)

The common people call this *eyn gnade adder fruntschafft*.[35] I do not know whether I should number among them the foundations and anniversary endowments[36] that have become so common in our age. For the people who contribute to them seem to be chiefly concerned in obtaining honor and glory, indeed, not only glory but also temporal as well as eternal repayments—I mean, when they press certain burdens upon those who are obligated to them. Then there are those who give for the sake of future glory. They believe that they give simply and they are really more sincere than the ones just named. (For they do not appear to give temporal goods in order to obtain eternal ones. But they make arrangements for the singing of choirs in a certain way as if they did not get their due when the singing is arranged in a way different from that which they had determined or when there is less of it than they had anticipated. Formerly, however, the choirs were not established in the name of certain persons, as one can see in the practices of the collegiate churches.[37]) But they, too, make their contribution, not simply for the sake of the glory of God, but for

---

34 This is the translation of Erasmus.
35 *"Eine Gnade oder Freundschaft"* ("a gracious gift or friendly act").
36 Luther may think here of the endowments which the Elector Frederick the Wise gave to the Chapter of All Saints in Wittenberg.
37 Luther here apparently refers to the practice, which, at the end of the fifteenth century, became more and more common in Germany, to provide for the singing (by choirs) of a certain number and kind of hymns in the church services. Donors established foundations or provided funds for this purpose. Luther may have thought of the institution of such choirs at the Church of All Saints in Wittenberg or of the establishment of the "eternal

the sake of their own future advantages in heaven, and they would not make a gift if they did not hope to gain advantage. But this is a vain hope, because they are not free from duplicity. However, they give no thought to this but go securely along as if they could count with certainty on a remuneration, and they are unmindful of the fact that they have received their reward (Matt. 6:2; 5:16).

To be sure, I can hardly believe that they do this for the glory of God, inasmuch as they would then prefer to cultivate old foundations or restore such as are already sufficiently endowed but have been permitted to break down. But the worship and the service of God have become a market place.

He that rules, with diligence. (Rom. 12:8.)
But today it is like this: he that rules, whether in a spiritual or secular office, does so with luxury and ease, riches and pleasure, glory and honor, power and terror. (Of such, Ezek. 34:2 ff. says: "Woe to the shepherds of Israel that fed themselves. You ate the milk and you clothed yourselves with the wool, and you killed that which was fat; the weak you have not strengthened and that which was sick you have not healed and that which was driven away you have not brought again, neither have you sought out that which was lost. But you ruled over them with cruelty and a high hand." Should these words not cause one to tremble, and make one's hair stand on end?) It is fellows of this sort that violate this commandment. They do not ascend in order to descend as the angels did on Jacob's ladder (Gen. 28:12). For to ascend means to rule, and to descend means to be diligent. They do not rule in order to serve, although everyone who is exalted is exalted in order that he seek nothing for himself nor live for himself, but in order that he should recognize that he was made the servant of his servants.

The clear and distinct norm of every rulership is diligence, as the apostle here states. Moreover, only he can be diligent in relation to others who is not concerned for himself and his own. For diligence makes one unconcerned, the wrong kind of diligence in the wrong way and the right kind in the right way. Therefore, then, let him who rules do so with diligence, i.e., with no concern for himself.

He that shows mercy, with cheerfulness. (Rom. 12:8.)
Second Corinthians 9:7: "not grudgingly or of necessity: for

---

choir" in the cathedral of Meissen in Saxony. The singing of this choir was conceived by its founders as a perpetual memorial commemorating their ancestors.

God loves a cheerful giver." This is different from what he said before: "He that gives, let him do so with simplicity." For in that case one gives to those from whom one can expect to be repaid, but here one gives to the poor and needy.

Now I think that one can safely ignore the question about which Lyra is so much concerned, namely, why the good works of this list are ranked in a certain order. For we may lose the true understanding of the whole text if we base it on an imagined construction of its parts. This happens to Lyra whenever, as he likes to do, he divides the Scripture into parts, as he brings his great learning to bear upon it in the belief that he is expounding it most excellently.

A man who feels obliged to help the needy because he feels ashamed or senses some kind of danger does not show mercy with cheerfulness. Thus, today, many contribute to collections of alms, but they do not earn any merits thereby, because they do so against their will and without joy. The same is true of those who give alms lest they be regarded as miserly, heartless, or merciless.

Let love be without dissimulation. (Rom. 12:9.)
The connection between these two terms is a necessary and most significant one. For just as there is nothing that must be purer and freer from dissimulation than love, so there is nothing more easily defiled by dissimulation. Nothing abhors dissimulation so much as love does and nothing must suffer so much dissimulation as love must bear. This is why there is on everybody's lips the proverb: "You cannot trust anyone,"[38] and also the saying of the Preacher:[39] "Who can find a faithful man?" Everything is covered with rouge and concealed under the disguise of friendship.

Indeed, there are two kinds of simulated love. First, there is that kind which outside displays itself as love but hides a veritable hatred inside. (This kind is characteristic of the relation of subordinates to their superiors and of the relation between equals.) Here we must make a twofold distinction: There are some who, like Joab over against Abner (II Sam. 3:27), do this knowingly. Here belong also the detractors, the deceivers, the scandalmongers, and the double-tongued traitors. But this is such a crass kind of simulation that I cannot believe that it is what the apostle here speaks of. Today, however, this vice is spread everywhere, overflowing everything with its dirt.[40]

---

[38] *"Nusquam tuta fides."*
[39] Luther writes *"Ecclesiastis,"* but the quotation is from Prov. 20:6.
[40] *"Quamquam toto gurgite hoc vitium grassatur hodie."* Ficker thinks that this term "whirlpool" (*gurges*) was part of the apocalyptical speech of

Then there are others who do this unknowingly. They are not aware that they love falsely until trial and adversity befall the one they love. As Ovid says: "When you are happy, you will have many friends, but in times of trouble, you will find yourself alone."[41]

Even the apostles were of this sort at the time of Christ's Passion, and so also were many other saints. This dissimulation is so deep that there is hardly anyone who recognizes it in himself. Indeed, I dare say, even though many do not think so, that nobody is free from this dissimulation. Who would be more perfect than the apostles who were made strong by the fact that they lived together with Christ?

Secondly, there is the kind that does not conceal a wrong love or shows itself as true hatred. (This kind is characteristic of the relation of superiors to their subordinates and of the relation between equals.)

This love, too, is of two kinds. There are some who see with their own eyes that their neighbor commits a mistake or a sin, i.e., that he does himself great harm, but though they have the power to do so, they do not reprove or admonish or correct him. But also this kind of simulated love is so crude and gross that it is unbelievable that the apostle had it in mind when he wrote this passage of his letter. However, there are many who practice this dissimulation even if it goes against their conscience.

Others show this kind of simulated love unknowingly: they admire and praise the vices of others as if they were virtues. They have achieved a high degree of humility and are therefore all the more ready to interpret an apparent evil as a good. They are quick to praise but slow to reprove, even if they happen to encounter a very great vice, if only it is covered by a thin disguise of good so that, even though one cannot actually see any evidence of good, one can nevertheless find something to appreciate. In this case, one does not test all things in order to hold fast that which is good (I Thess. 5:21), but one is satisfied with a superficial impression and is quick to pronounce things good and to make friends.

So then, people of the first kind do not do the good, and those of the second kind do not do the evil, which love requires them to do. But the former do evil and the latter good, each going against love.

In between these two, the neutralists[42] have their way. Like

---

Luther's day. He quotes an expression that refers to Rome as *"quasi gurges flatitiorum."*

[41] Ovid, *Tristia*, I, 9, 5.

[42] *"Neutrales."*

Absalom (II Sam. 13:22), they speak or do neither good nor evil. Such are the theologians of today. They stand firm and secure in their "elicited acts"[42a] and never come through with an effective deed. They think that they have done more than enough when they wish their neighbor well and hope the best for him and when they reject, detest, and deprecate the evil of their fellow man, and all this they do by "elicited acts." Otherwise, they do nothing or they behave like the aforementioned simulators. (Furthermore, I do not hesitate to say that it is simulated love to say that to love means to wish someone well by an "elicited act.") As if to expose the deceitfulness of such a dissimulation, he therefore goes on to say:

Hating that which is evil, cleaving to that which is good. (Rom. 12:9.)

There is not one man who would say that he loves that which is evil and that he hates that which is good. Nevertheless, the apostle gives this commandment and certainly not in vain, for man is inclined toward that which is evil and he is reluctant to do good. Dissimulation, therefore, finds its defense in the ignorance of good and evil, in view of the fact that everyone calls good what pleases him and evil what displeases him. What he means to say, therefore, by his commandment that "we test all things and hold fast to that which is good" (I Thess. 5:21) is only that we should beware of taking hold of the good through its immediate outward appearance.

For here he understands the good to be that of the new man and evil also that of the new man. Now this good is something twofold, and so also is this evil. The one is invisible, and man can keep it only by faith: it is God. The other is visible: it is all that which is bad for sensuality and opposes the old man in us, for example: the chastisement of the old man in us and the exercise of good works. Just so, by contrast, the visible evil is all that is good for the old man in us and agreeable to him, as, for example, the license of the flesh and the neglect of the spirit.

Both are twofold in so far as they are related, on the one hand, to one's own person, and, on the other hand, to the neighbor. It is of the latter that the apostle speaks here, for in order that our "love be without dissimulation," we must hate in our fellow man whatever is evil, without fear or favor,[43] and cleave to that in him which is good, without fear or favor.[43a]

[42a] *"In actibus elicitis."*

[43] *"Sine adulatione et timore."*

[43a] *"Sine simulatione et favore."*

(By using the expression "hating" that which is evil, he means to say that there will always be evil and that not every evil is in your power. Therefore, hate the evil you are trying to avoid and do not side with the evil of someone else, but align yourself with the good of someone else. Cherish and favor, promote and preach, the good, but hate and hinder evil where you can. But often one can do nothing else but hate that which is evil and love that which is good, as in the case of heretics and other unteachable persons who rage against the people of the church who keep the peace.)[43b]

(If there were such men, i.e., who hate evil, at the courts of the higher clergy and of the princes, the church would be fortunate. But just the opposite is the case today. Hence, the church is in a miserable state, not so much because they themselves are evil, but because they do not hate the evil that can be found in the church.)

Yet hatred or good will directed toward an individual person overthrows this judgment entirely, as one can see today, for example, in the case of John Reuchlin and the theologians of Cologne.[43c] When we give our love to a person with unreserved assurance and devotion, we are ready and eager to cherish and defend whatever he may happen to think, but we do not ask ourselves how we can recognize what is good or evil in him, because we do not want to make it appear that this kind of person has good or evil in him. Hence, it is the nature of simulated love that it hates what is good and cleaves to what is evil. Indeed, a characteristic of every kind of love is that it makes blind. Who, then, is not blind? For who is without love—without sensual love, I mean, except one who is not alive?

Loving one another with brotherly love. (Rom. 12:10.)
One Greek version of the text reads "brotherly love": *"philadelphia"*; hence, *"philadelphos"* means "lover of the brethren" or "one who loves his brother." Thereby the apostle means to say that, among Christians, love must be of a special kind and more perfect than the love one shows to strangers and enemies. Thus he says in another passage (Gal. 6:10): "Whilst we have time, let us do good unto all men, but especially unto them who are of the household of faith." And where, in our translation, we have "loving" (*diligentes*), we read in the Greek text (*"philostorgoi"*; *philos = amor*).[44] Now *storgē* means "affection" or "sympathy" as we say in common speech. *Philostorgos,* therefore, is one who is

[43b] *"Ut in haereticis et obstinatis contra catholicos et mites furentibus."*
[43c] Cf. Luther's comment on Rom. 11:22.
[44] The translation of *philos* into *amor* was common in the Middle Ages.

tenderly affectioned toward someone else whom he is to love with *philadelphia*. The apostle speaks, then, with great emphasis, by quasi superfluously putting together these two words that mean love, saying *"philadelphia estote philostorgoi,"* i.e., "in brotherly love be tenderly affectioned one to another."

With honor preferring one another. (Rom. 12:10.)

In Phil. 2:3 he says: "in humility each counting the other better than himself." And our Lord says in Luke 14:10: "When you are invited, go, sit down in the lowest place." He speaks here of that inward honor which is represented by a high regard and esteem for one's fellow men. For outward honor is, in most cases, simulated and mercenary. One bestows it in order to receive a higher one in return. And if it is not returned, one becomes indignant and ceases to bestow honors. This is what he means by "counting the other better than himself." He does not say: "each placing himself higher than the other."

However, you cannot bestow this honor upon someone else without self-denial. Moreover, you must judge yourself worthy to be put to shame, but must regard others as worthy to be honored in preference to yourself. In other words: only a humble man can prefer another in honor.

Pride, too, bestows honors, but it follows after others in bestowing its honor, just as humility precedes them in doing so. Pride expects that one goes before it, but humility does not even wish the others to come after it, believing that its only duty is to go before others. What a great service it is to yield honor to someone else! It is easier to give and do service with one's body than to make nothing of oneself and to think highly of all others.

Some are prompt in returning an honor or, in the way of a mercenary, in bestowing honors with the expectation of being honored in return. But this also the Gentiles do; the Roman Domitius[45] said, for instance: "Why should I recognize you as a prince if you do not recognize me as a senator?" This is not a Christian but a heathen saying. For we must give honor to one another without asking who comes first or last in honor.

In diligence not slothful. (Rom. 12:11.)

I.e., in Greek: "in diligence," "in zeal," "in service," "in application."

Notice how love does not keep anything for itself but how it is concerned only for that which belongs to others. In the preceding,

---

[45] This story goes back to Cicero (*De orat.*, 3, 4). It is reported by Jerome, on whom Luther probably depends (cf. *Ep. ad Nepot.*, 52, 7 [PL 22, 533 f.]).

the apostle taught us how we must direct our substance and faculties to others by giving them gifts and by showing them mercy and diligence, etc., and, then, how we must give them the honor and esteem we have for ourselves. Now he teaches us that we must also give ourselves, and he says that the helping action of one's own person, so to speak, on behalf of those in need is the help, service, and succor we must give to them. The Absalomites do the opposite, i.e., "the fathers of peace"[46] and those who do not want to be disturbed by serving others. Yet if they do help someone, they do so unwillingly and sullenly, as, for instance, in court cases, legal actions, and similar undertakings.

Fervent in spirit. (Rom. 12:11.)
This commandment is broken by those who are asleep and lazy and without interest in anything they do. Whatever work they undertake proves to be wasted. Proverbs 18:9: "He that is loose and slack in his work is the brother of him that wastes his own works." People of this sort are irksome also to men, to say nothing of God. So it is nowadays a common experience that the artisans one has hired do their work as if they were asleep. It is an actual fact that monks and priests are fast asleep during prayers, even physically. I shall not say anything about their mental laziness. Whatever they do, they do slothfully.

It is this capital sin of sloth or boredom in the performance of good works that the apostle criticizes in this passage. The Greek work *akēdia* or *acēdia* means being "bored" or "morose" or "indifferent."

This evil is so widespread that scarcely anyone deems it worthwhile to exert himself. Now, if one does not want to be fervent in spirit, one cannot help being fervent in the flesh. For one of the two must burn with passion, either the spirit or the flesh. And when the one glows fervently, the fervor of the other cools and becomes dead, except in times of temptation, when God lets the spirit continue to be fervent in the midst of physical ardor. A man, therefore, who performs his tasks without ardor cannot help being fervent in the flesh; hence, he will necessarily "waste the work" he does, namely, by the fervor of the flesh. For example: a lazy cook who is about to get a meal ready proceeds in such a way that the food gets cold while it is being served. Who would not detest him, and rightly so?

46 The interpretation of Absalomites as "fathers of peace" is of an etymological character (cf. Augustine, *Enarr. in Ps.*, 3, 7). Cf. also Luther's reference to Absalom in his comment on Rom. 12:8. There he has in mind II Sam. 13:22: "Absalom spake unto Amnon neither good nor bad, for Absalom hated Amnon."

Serving the Lord. (Rom. 12:11.)

This is directed not only against those who serve avarice, or the world, or their own belly, but also, and emphatically so, against those who stubbornly persist in doing a good work when obedience calls them to some other task. They are like the people of the Gospel who have an ass under yoke and do not want to let him loose in order that it may serve the Lord (Matt. 21:2 ff.; Mark 11:2 ff.; Luke 19:30 ff.); i.e., they wear themselves out in their own pursuits and do not let themselves be called to something else by any religious task or even by a divine cause. Hence, they serve themselves rather than the Lord. For they are not ready to do whatever God wills unless they can choose what it shall be. They excuse themselves and say: It would not be right that I leave what I am doing now in order to work somewhere else. I doubt whether I am wrong in saying that among people of this kind there must also be numbered the princes who are constantly in church and the higher clergy who cannot absent themselves from court.

This applies also to our Duke Frederick[47] and his officials. When one asks for them, they are unavailable. God called them away and they say: Ah, I must pray and serve God! What fools they are! For the sake of serving God they decline to serve God. They do not know that to serve God means to be indifferent about whereto the Lord may have called one and not stubbornly to stay put in one place.

Rejoicing in hope. (Rom. 12:12.)

This means: do not rejoice in present experience and knowledge. For joy is of two kinds. First, there is the joy in visible things, i.e., what we have somehow come to know inwardly or outwardly. But this is a vain joy because it is transitory. Then, there is the joy in invisible things, i.e., in that which we cannot know but can only believe. And this is true, eternal, and abiding joy. Yet without hope this joy cannot be real. For who can rejoice in something that he despairs of or doubts he can ever obtain? The apostle means to say, therefore, that Christians should always be joyful, but not with respect to any specific thing. For "blessed are they that mourn" (Matt. 5:4), about something specific, here and now, for they rejoice in hope. But we can have hope and therefore also joy through hope only if we renounce everything and have nothing to desire, to rely on, and to delight in. Moreover, we are beset by so much trouble that we cannot rejoice in any earthly good. If we bear all this willingly, we shall obtain hope and through hope, joy. Therefore he goes on to say:

[47] I.e., Luther's prince, Frederick the Wise, Duke of Ernestine Saxony.

Patience in tribulation. (Rom. 12:12.)

Romans 5:3 ff.: "Tribulation works patience, and patience trial, and trial hope, and hope does not confound," i.e., it rejoices and is cheerful and confident. But our theologians, subtle as they are, have limited hope to "elicited acts."[48] This is why none of them has any understanding of what hope is, although the word is on everybody's lips. They say that we can induce an act of hope, even though everything about us on which we depend and rely is in good order. But by such an "induced act" we shall never get even a taste of hope. For hope strips a man, at least in his inner being, of all the goods he relies on and it surrounds him with all sorts of evil. Then "patience is necessary," and it works hope.

Instant in prayer. (Rom. 12:12.)

This is directed against those who merely read off the psalms during prayer and who do not have their heart in what they read. And indeed, I am afraid, that today the prayers in church are more a hindrance than a help. First, because we offend God all the more when we read them off and our heart is not in what we read, for he says himself: "This people honors me with their lips, but their heart is far from me" (Matt. 15:8; Isa. 29:13). And, secondly, because, letting ourselves be deceived by this pretense, we feel safe and at peace, as if we had really prayed. And thus we never gird ourselves for the effort of true prayer, but having said our prayers in this superficial way, we think we have really prayed and are no longer troubled about anything. This exposes us to a terrible danger. And in return for this, we then consume at leisure and in safety the taxes, pensions, and subsidies of the people!

This is why the word "instant" is a call to order and vigilance that everyone but especially the clergy must hear and fear. For it means that praying must be a constant effort. Nor is this a useless call, for as the ancient fathers said: "No labor is so hard as prayer."[49] One who wants to enter the priesthood should first consider, therefore, that he must perform a labor that is harder than every other labor, namely, prayer. For it requires a subdued and broken mind and a high and triumphant spirit. But at this point the legalists[50] introduce a nice explanation: they say that it is not prescribed that they pray the hours[51] but that they "read" or "say" them. Thus they weigh every word of the canon so that they can doze in safety.

---

[48] Cf. Ockham, III *Sent.*, q. 8, *H ad tertiam;* Pierre d'Ailly, III *Sent.*, d. 26, q. un., Gabriel Biel, III *Sent.*, d. 26, q. un., a. 2, concl. 3.
[49] Cf. *Vitae Patrum V, Verba Seniorum* XII, 2 (PL 73, 941).
[50] *"Iuristae."*
[51] *"Orationes horarias."*

However, quite apart from the canonical hours, we must say something else about prayer.

Prayer is of two kinds: it is vocal or mental.[52]

It is now customary to say that for "vocal prayer" a "virtual intention"[53] is sufficient. A nice cover for laziness and indolence! For one takes this to mean that one must first wrest from himself the good intention of praying, and that, in reliance on this, one can then give up any further effort.

The attentiveness practiced in vocal prayer is threefold: There is the *material* (or sensual) attentiveness. Here one pays attention only to the words. Monks[54] pray in this way, but also others such as simple lay people who do not understand even the Lord's Prayer. This is prayer no more than "matter" is the real thing, i.e., as to its nature, it is not praying strictly so-called, but it is prayer only in an extrinsic sense, in terms of which every other good work can also be called a prayer. To pray in this way is nothing else than to perform an act of obedience. And this obedience is supposed to make it acceptable in God's sight.

Such a prayer is not to be despised, for, apart from the fact that it constitutes an act of obedience, it is good in many respects. *First:* it drives the devil away if only it is spoken aloud in the spirit of simplicity (i.e., if it is "sung in the Spirit" (I Cor. 14:15), thus procuring the presence of the Holy Spirit. (This is symbolized by David playing the harp before Saul.) For, as we can learn from many examples, the devil cannot bear it that the word of God is spoken aloud (I Cor. 14:2: "For he that speaks in a tongue speaks to God"). *Secondly:* the divine word affects the soul (this is its nature) even if one does not understand it. For it is a word of grace, according to Ps. 45:2: "Grace is poured upon your lips" and "Your lips are like a dropping honeycomb" (S. of Sol. 4:11). *Thirdly:* it offers the intellect and the feeling an occasion they would not have otherwise (this is symbolized in Elisha's playing).[55] *Fourthly:* even though people who pray in this way do not comprehend the feeling-tone[56] characteristic of the words they recite,

---

[52] The Scholastics distinguished between *oratio vocalis* and *oratio mentalis.*
[53] Cf. Garcia, *Lex. scholast.,* 359 ff.
[54] *"Moniales."*
[55] Cf. II Kings 3:15. If Luther meant to refer to this passage, he probably had in mind Lyra's comment on it. Lyra explains that the spirit of prophecy did not always touch the heart of the prophets. This, he says, could be brought about only by the lifting up of the heart in devotion. This devotion, again, could be induced by certain prescribed melodies as they were played on various instruments to the praise of God. Elisha asked for such a playing of music. Cf. Ficker, p. 467, n. 13.
[56] *"Affectum."*

many have, nevertheless, a general impression of it, and this means that their spirits are lifted up to God.

There is also the *intellectual* attentiveness. Here the attention is directed to the meaning and significance of the words spoken in prayer. All educated and intelligent people are obliged to practice this. For everyone must return his talent to God (Matt. 25:14 ff.).

Then there is the *spiritual* or affectional attentiveness. Here one directs his attention to the feeling-tone or spirit of the words used in prayer, sighing with those that sigh; rejoicing with those that rejoice; shouting for joy with those that exult, adapting himself to every movement of the words. This is true prayer.

Of these two the apostle says in I Cor. 14:15: "I will sing with the spirit; I will sing also with the understanding." He calls "singing with the spirit" that sensual attentiveness which does not achieve understanding but is not without emotional alertness; devout nuns and unlearned folk practice it. "Singing with the understanding" means intellectual attentiveness. It can be achieved without as well as with the spirit.

Mental prayer is the ascent of the mind,[57] or rather of the spirit, to God.

This, then, is the prayer with respect to which the apostle says here: "Instant in prayer." He means to say by this that Christians must practice prayer frequently and with diligence. For "to be instant" does not only mean "to be constantly engaged in something" but it means also "to press on," "to quicken one's pace," "to demand earnestly." So then, as there is nothing that Christians must do more frequently than praying, so there is also nothing that requires more labor and effort and, for this reason, is more effective and more fruitful. Here "the Kingdom of God suffers violence, and the violent bear it away" (Matt. 11:12). In my judgment, prayer is indeed a continuous violent action of the spirit as it is lifted up to God. This action is comparable to that of a ship going against the stream. This is why it is said in praise of Blessed Martin that he had an invincible spirit, for he never relaxed from prayer.[58]

To be sure, this violent action becomes milder and even ceases whenever it happens that the Spirit draws and carries our hearts

---

[57] This definition of prayer was common in the Middle Ages. It was derived from John of Damascus.

[58] In the *Responsorium* on the Feast of St. Martin, the following words were said: "*Oculis ac manibus in caelum semper intentus. Invictum ab oratione spiritum non relaxabat.*" ("With eyes and hands he was always intent upon heaven. He never relaxed his invincible spirit from prayer.") Cf. Ficker, p. 468, n. 8.

upward through grace or, in any case, when a pressing and growing
anxiety forces us to seek refuge in prayer. Without these two,
prayer is a very difficult and most wearisome thing. But its effect
is tremendous. For true prayer is omnipotent, as our Lord says:
"Everyone who asks, receives," etc. (Matt. 7:8). Everyone, therefore, must do violence, out of the awareness that he that prays
fights against the devil and the flesh.

Now with respect to the prayer of hours, the question is raised,
In what way is it prescribed? The answer is as follows: The church
requires only sensual attentiveness (i.e., the individual words must
be spoken aloud) but not intellectual or affectional attentiveness
—at any rate, not a personal involvement. For the church requires
and presupposes a common disposition. And it is not in its power
to command that one should have an understanding and a personal
experience of prayer, but by its prescription it only provides the
occasion therefor.

For this reason, it is nothing but foolishness if nowadays people
make endowments for canonical hours. They do this in the superstitious belief that they do not need to be concerned about what is
being prayed but only that there should be much of it, inasmuch
as they want to have the prayers said for themselves. Moreover,
they themselves prescribe the prayer as if it were in their power to
buy prayer. How much better it would be if they gave their gifts
without any condition, so that prayers would be said for them
when the one who does the praying would be able to do so!

But they think that they must imitate the old foundations.

But I say: No, this is impossible, for our ancestors sought to
glorify God with them; they did not merely try to gain an advantage from prayer.

Thus also the documents by which our foundation here was
established state specifically that this was done "for the salvation
of our souls."[59] Could God not have known for what purpose the
gift was made? Or could he not have given you sufficient recompense if you had given your gift purely for his sake, and if you
had not prescribed to him for what purpose you wanted to make
your gift, and if you had not blown your own horn in the presence
of your fellow men? What if you deceive yourself? What if you
are not at all concerned about the glory of God? Would God that
I turn out to be a false prophet, but I fear that this monastery will
yet bring great misery upon its unfortunate founder and likewise
upon the Church of All Saints.[60]

[59] This formula appears frequently in the documents relating to the endowments of the Wittenberg Chapter of All Saints.
[60] Luther probably is thinking of the new buildings which, in 1513–1514, the

Communicating to the necessities of the saints. (Rom. 12:13.)
Today we understand the "saints" to be the blessed ones who
have been glorified; the apostle, however, and, indeed, the whole
Scripture, call "saints" all who believe in Christ. This is perhaps
the reason why nowadays one does not readily communicate to the
saints; one believes that there are no longer any. Why, then, does
the apostle say in Rom. 1:7: "to all that are . . . called to be saints"
and in I Cor. 7:14: "The unbelieving husband is sanctified by the
believing wife" and in I Peter 1:16: "You shall be holy, for I am
holy," the Lord, your God?

He speaks here of the feeling of compassion, urging Christians
to make the needs of the saints a common concern of theirs
through compassion, according to Heb. 10:33 f.: "On the one
hand, by reproaches and tribulations, you were made a gazing
stock; and on the other, became companions of them that were
used in such sort. For you had compassion on them that were in
bands," etc. This is disregarded by people who blush when they
see the needs of the saints and are ashamed of them.

However, one can understand this passage also in the sense that
it refers to the effect that is produced by helpfulness. Then it
means something else than the commandment with which we have
dealt before, namely: "He that shows mercy, with cheerfulness"
(Rom. 12:8). For there, the apostle spoke generally of the miserable and needy whether they were saints or not. But here he speaks
of those who are being persecuted, who are being deprived of their
possessions and to whom one can give nothing except sympathy,
as Saint Anastasia and Saint Natalie did in their time when they
visited the prisons and encouraged the martyrs.[60a] If it was possible
that one could contribute something to them, it was not so much
because they lacked anything but because they suffered need for
the sake of righteousness, for they were needy only because they
were victims of persecution.

But today, the saints live in obscurity and their needs are therefore unknown. Yet people who are oppressed by want but keep it
secret and who are ashamed to beg or to disclose their poverty in
public can be thought of as taking the place of the martyrs of old.
But all this relates to temporal necessities.

Others are in spiritual straits: They find themselves in great
trials of temptation which are inflicted upon them either by a
fellow man or by the devil. We must defend and console them, for
they too suffer harm. This word here therefore says something else

---

Elector Frederick ordered to be built both for the Chapter and the Augustinian monastery in Wittenberg.
[60a] Cf. Ficker, p. 470, n. 11.

than what is enjoined in the saying: "He that shows mercy . . ."
For there the apostle speaks of needy folk who are spared suffering,
but here he is concerned about those who must suffer quite apart
from poverty.

Pursuing hospitality. (Rom. 12:13.)

In the letters to Titus and Timothy, the apostle commends this
duty specifically to the bishops (Titus 1:8; I Tim. 3:2), but here
he enjoins it generally to everybody. Hebrews 13:2: "Do not forget
hospitality, for by this some have been pleased to entertain angels,"
or, according to another version: "For thereby some have entertained angels unawares,"[61] i.e., they were not aware that they had
entertained angels; for example, Abraham and Lot (Gen. 18:2 ff.;
19:2 ff.). Thus it can happen also today that we give or refuse
hospitality to saints without being aware of it. Furthermore, the
apostle has here in mind a "hospitality" that is freely extended
and not one for which one must pay an innkeeper; hence it is
called in Greek *philoxenia,* which means "love of strangers" or
"loving to take care of strangers," as *philoxenos* means "one who
loves strangers." So then the apostle commends here those who
extend hospitality from the free love of their heart and not those
who are hospitable for mercenary reasons. For this also the heathen
do. Nevertheless, it is no "evil work"; properly done, it too is
meritorious.

*Bless them that persecute you; bless and curse not. Rejoice with
them that rejoice; weep with them that weep. Being of one mind
one toward another.* **Not minding high things, but consenting to
the humble.** (Rom. 12:14–16.)

The apostle speaks of "high" and "humble" things and not of
"high" and "humble" persons. So he does also in I Cor. 1:27 and
25: "God chose the weak things of the world that he might confound the strong" and "the foolishness of God is wiser than men."
What he wants to say is this: Do not set your minds on high things,
i.e., do not find satisfaction in any relation with those who hold
high positions in the world and do not be displeased to have dealings with them that are despised, but have a cordial interest in the
humble and take satisfaction in relating yourselves to them. Do
this in accordance with the rule of Blessed Augustine: "Do not
glory in the high rank of wealthy parents but in the company you
keep with your poor brethren."[62]

---

[61] Faber preferred the version: *"Per hanc enim quidam latuerunt angelis
hospicio receptis."* Erasmus rejected this and read *placuerunt* instead of
latuerunt. Luther agreed with him.
[62] Cf. *Regula Augustini,* c. 5 (PL 32, 1379).

We must take note of the fact that our translation uses the word *"humile"* ("humble") indiscriminately, while in Greek it is one thing to say *tapeinōsis* and another *tapeinophrosynē*. *Tapeinōsis* means "humility" and *tapeinos* "humble" or "low," so that *"tapeinōsis"* must be translated by "lowliness" if one wants to pay close attention to the sense of the Latin where *humilis* means the opposite of "high" or "noble." *Tapeinophrosynē* is derived from *tapeinos* and *phronein;* it means "to be mindful of humble things."[63] It signifies humility or the readiness to accommodate oneself to that which is inferior or not to despise that which is lowly, i.e., it is characteristic of one who has a concern for what is base and exposed to contempt and who avoids all that is highly regarded. A man who is of this disposition has humility or, as we say, the virtue of humility. So we read, on the one hand: "because he has regarded the humility" (in Greek: *"tapeinōsin"*) "of his handmaiden" (Luke 1:48), and, on the other hand, in Phil. 2:3: "In humility let each esteem others better than himself" (here the Greek word is *"tapeinophrosynē"*) and in Eph. 4:2: "with humility and mildness" (in Greek: *"tapeinophrosynēs"*).

One can also interpret the words *"alta"* ("high things") and *"humilia"* ("humble things") in such a way that they are strictly taken as things (in terms of the neuter and not the masculine gender). Then the meaning of the passage would be: one should not strive after something high in order to attract attention and to be regarded as someone important but, rather, after something lowly so that one can remain unnoticed and even despised. Thus interpreted, the saying would be directed against ambitious men who want to make an impression by their involvement in high affairs.

It is superfluous to allude here to the disagreements and animosities that prevail now in the kingdoms, duchies, and towns in their relations with one another, to a greater degree, it would seem, than among the heathen. I refer to the Venetians, the Italians, the French, and the Germans. The Germans give preference to German poets, and the French to French ones. And all this is regarded as being highly virtuous, and one has almost forgotten that we are Christians. Thus the word of Christ is being fulfilled: "Nation shall rise against nation and kingdom against kingdom" (Mark 13:8).

Be not wise in your own conceits. (Rom. 12:16.)
This is directed against opinionated, hardheaded, stiff-necked

---

[63] All these grammatical distinctions seem to be derived from Erasmus' *Annotationes*.

folk whom, in common speech, we call "standpatters,"[64] but the Scripture calls them "stiff-necked" and "unbelieving" (Ex. 32:9; Deut. 9:13). We all have a strange proneness and propensity toward this fault; and a man who does not have it is very rare indeed. In German, we say *"Steifsynnig."*[65] People of this sort refuse to change their minds, even if they have been refuted by every kind of reasonable argument. Even if one uses the opposite method,[65a] they stand absolutely pat and wait for the chance to laugh at their opponents when their scheme breaks down. These people cause contention; they upset and disturb the peace; and they destroy spiritual unity. It is this which the apostle has in mind when he says in Eph. 4:3: "Be careful to keep the unity of the spirit in the bond of peace" and, in Phil. 2:2: "being of one accord and of one mind."

To no man rendering evil for evil. (Rom. 12:17.)
In Ps. 37:27,[65b] we read: "Depart from evil." In I Peter 3:9, Blessed Peter explains this to mean that one should not only do no evil but also not return evil for evil. In like manner, we must understand the injunction "Do good" (Ps. 37:27) to mean not only that we should render good for good but also that we should take the initiative in doing good. Also, Christ rebuked his disciples when they wanted to call down fire from heaven, saying, "Do you not know of what spirit you are?" (Luke 9:55). So we, too, are not born "to destroy souls but to save them" (Luke 9:56).

Providing good things, not only in the sight of God, but also in the sight of all men. *If it be possible, as much as is in you, have peace with all men. Revenge not yourselves, my dearly beloved, but give place unto wrath, for it is written: Revenge is mine, I will repay, says the Lord. But if your enemy be hungry, give him to eat; if he thirst, give him to drink.* (Rom. 12:17–19.)
In I Peter 2:12, we read as follows: "Having your conversation good among the Gentiles, that whereas they speak against you as evildoers, they may, by the good works which they shall behold in you, glorify God." And in I Tim. 5:14: "Give no occasion to the adversary to speak evil." And in Titus 3:1–2: "To be ready to every good work, showing all mildness toward all men." And in I Cor. 10:32 f.: "Be without offense to the Jews, and to the Gen-

---

[64] *Immansivos* (perhaps to be translated, "blockheads").
[65] *Steifsinnig* = of an unbending mind.
[65a] I.e., unreasonableness.
[65b] Luther writes: Ps. 33 (Vg.).

tiles, and to the church of God. As I also in all things please all men," etc., i.e., seek to please all men as far as I can.

From this saying stems the following famous word of Blessed Augustine's:[66] "A man who is not concerned to have a good reputation is lacking in good feeling. For you personally a good conscience is sufficient, but for your neighbor your good reputation is a necessity." It is strange to see how often this word is misused: People quote it in order to cover up their impatience, their contentiousness, and their pride. They understand Blessed Augustine to say that they must not take any insult and that they must not let anyone who disparages them go unpunished. But Blessed Augustine wants to express exactly what the apostle says here, namely, that one must not do anything that may cause offense by what to all appearances is evil, even though one has a good conscience about it.

At all events, if one has sustained an insult, one should excuse himself, speaking quietly and not angrily, and one should not fight back or get angry or acknowledge the insult as if it were justified. Just so that woman who was beaten seven times bore the wrong that was inflicted on her, but she did not acknowledge any guilt and she did not hurt her reputation, for she did not speak up, though inwardly in her conscience she knew herself to be innocent.[67]

In contrast to this, there is abroad today the shocking notion[68] not only of the liberty of conscience but, what is worse, of the liberty of intention or of the feigned conscience. Everywhere the higher clergy grant dispensations according to their liking. Merely on the evidence of the so-called "good intention," the lower clergy obtain the license to transfer, to exchange, or to combine ecclesiastical benefices and, under cleverly designed strange pretexts, to engage in fraudulent financial transactions.

For, doing this, **you shall heap coals of fire upon his head.** (Rom. 12:20.)

Blessed Augustine writes:[69] "We must understand this saying in the following way: we should induce a man who has done us harm to repent of what he did, and, in this way, we shall do him good. For such "coals," i.e., benefits, have the power to burn his spirit, i.e., to distress him. This is what is meant by the words of the

---

[66] Cf. Augustine, *Sermo* 355, 1, 1.
[67] The reference is to the unjust sentence imposed upon a woman during a persecution in Vercelli: The story is told by Jerome in *Ep.* 1.
[68] "*Monstrum.*"
[69] Cf. Augustine, *Propos. ex ep. ad Rom.*, 71.

Psalter: "The sharp arrows of the mighty, with coals that lay waste" (Ps. 120:4). Thus also God converts those whom he converts by showing them his goodness. And this is the only way to convert anyone: to show him love and kindness. For a man who is converted by threats or fear is never truly converted as long as he retains this character of his conversion, for fear will cause him to hate the one who converted him. But a man who is converted by love is ablaze with self-criticism and is angrier with himself than anyone else could possibly be with him, and he is greatly displeased with himself. Moreover, it is not necessary to forbid him anything or to watch him or to demand satisfaction from him, for love will teach him all he needs to do; as soon as he comes under its influence, he will go to seek out the one he offended.

So then, it is the benefactions one has performed for his adversaries that are the "coals of fire." But benefactions for friends are something else. For a friend does not feel about a good deed as an enemy does: he thinks that he is entitled to receive benefits and he is never satisfied by nor astonished at the good will[70] of his benefactor. But an enemy feels differently. He is conscious of his own unworthiness and is therefore drawn in his whole being toward his benefactor.

Thus God gave his only-begotten Son for us, his enemies, in order to kindle in us a great love for him and in order to arouse in us a deep hatred for ourselves. Christ is a furnace full of fire,[71] according to Isa. 31:9: "The Lord has said it, whose fire is in Zion and his furnace in Jerusalem." We heap "coals of fire" upon the head of our adversary, but God heaps the very fire upon it.

Be not overcome by evil but overcome evil by good. (Rom. 12:21.)

This means: see to it that he who hurts you does not cause you to become like him, namely, a wicked person, nor let his wickedness defeat your goodness. For a man who changes another man by causing him to become like him, while he himself remains unchanged, is a victor over that man. No, by doing good to him, you must make him into a good person who resembles you. Thus your goodness will overcome his wickedness and change him into you.

Now, to be sure, men commonly regard as the victor the one who has the last word and can deal the last blow, whereas, as a matter of fact, he who is the last to inflict pain is the one who is

---

[70] *"Gratiam."*

[71] *"Caminus totus est Christus."* Ficker (p. 474, n. 26) observes that this interpretation cannot be found in the *Gl. ord.* and in Lyra. It seems to be Luther's own.

worse off, for the evil remains with him while the other is done with it. In this sense, Blessed Gregory says: "It is more glorious to escape from anger by keeping silent than to overcome it by replying in kind."[72] Proverbs 26:4–5: "Answer not a fool according to his folly, lest you be made like him. But answer a fool according to his folly, lest he imagine himself to be wise."

Disregarding the truth we have just been trying to state, some wrongly use this word in order to cover up their own fury. They say it means that a wise man is allowed to answer a fool with foolishness and to render him evil for evil. And also many learned men allege with great erudition that in their judgment this appears to be the meaning of the word. He, therefore, that lets himself "be overcome by evil" and does not correct the fool but even falls victim to the same violent feeling answers the fool according to his folly and thus becomes like him. But one who "overcomes evil with good" answers the fool in such a way that he does not imagine himself to be wise, with the result that he recognizes his folly and detests and bewails it. For if you answer folly with folly, you will never cause the fool to see himself as he is, but your reply in kind will only make him still more of a fool.

But what does it mean "to answer and not to answer according to folly"? I believe that "according to"[73] is written here in place of "to"[74] or "against."[75] When one thing is put "against" another thing, we say: they are "put next to each other."[76] And to say "when opposites are put *next to* each other, each becomes more distinct" is the same as to measure them *against* each other or to relate them *to* each other. So also this expression "according to his folly" does not mean that one should answer a fool with the same folly, but that one should put something else next to it, by comparison with which one can recognize how abominable it is; and this must not be something which by its likeness to folly only enhances it, so that one knows even less how hideous it actually is. For as long as folly sees something like itself, it does not become dissatisfied with itself, but it becomes dissatisfied with itself only if it sees something that has no resemblance to it at all.

---

[72] This quotation cannot be located in the writings of Gregory I.
[73] "*Iuxta*."
[74] "*Ad*."
[75] "*Contra*."
[76] "*Iuxta*" can mean both "according to" and "next to."

ROMANS, CHAPTER THIRTEEN[1]

Let every soul be subject to higher powers, for there is no power but from God, and those that are, are ordained of God.[2]

[1] Luther writes in the marginal gloss (*WA* 56, 123 f., 16 ff.): "Here the apostle instructs the people of Christ how they should conduct themselves toward the higher powers that are without. And in contrast to the Jewish conception, he teaches that they must submit also to evil and unbelieving rulers. As it is also written in I Peter 2:13 ff., 'Be subject to every human creature, whether it be to the king, as excelling, or to the governors, as sent by him, for so is the will of God.' Even though the rulers are evil and unbelieving, the order of government and their power to rule are nevertheless good and from God. Just as our Lord said to Pilate, to whom he was willing to surrender in order to give us all an example, 'You could have no power against me, unless it were given you from above' (John 19:11). Christians should not refuse, under the pretext of religion, to obey men, especially evil ones. The Jews thought they should, according to John 8:23: 'We are Abraham's and have never been in bondage to anyone.' He commands them, therefore, that they should honor the higher power and not make the liberty of grace a cloak for their malice. As Peter says, 'As free, and not making liberty a cloak for malice.' (I Peter 2:16.)

"In the preceding chapter, he taught that one must not disturb the order of the church; in this chapter, he teaches that also the secular order must be maintained. For both are of God: it is the purpose of the former to give guidance and peace to the inner man and what concerns him, and it is the purpose of the latter to give guidance to the outer man in his concerns. For, in this life, the inner man cannot be without the outer one."

[2] In the marginal gloss, Luther writes as follows (*WA* 56, 124, 17 ff.): "The Greek text reads as follows: 'The powers that are are ordained by God.' Now this saying is being interpreted in different ways. Stapulensis reads it as follows: 'The powers that are of God are ordered' [*Comm. ad Rom.*]. Then he makes the comment that power is twofold, namely, ordered and disordered. But I do not like this comment. No power is disordered, but one aspires to it in a disorderly way and handles it in a disorderly way, just as all other goods do not lose their goodness through evil use; otherwise, money would become evil through theft. Hence the following is a better

Therefore, he that resists the power resists the ordinance of God. And they that resist purchase to themselves damnation. For princes are not a terror to the good work but to the evil. Will you, then, not be afraid of the power? Do that which is good, and you shall have praise from the same. For he is God's minister to you for good. But if you do that which is evil, be afraid, for he bears not the sword in vain. For he is God's minister, an avenger to execute wrath upon him that does evil. Wherefore be subject of necessity, not only for wrath, but also for conscience' sake. For therefore also you pay tribute. For they are the ministers of God, serving for this purpose. Render, therefore, to all their dues: tribute to whom tribute is due; custom to whom custom; fear to whom fear; honor to whom honor. Owe no man anything save that you love one another. For he that loves his neighbor has fulfilled the law. (Rom. 13:1–8.)

Why does he say "every soul" and not "every man"? Has he a hidden meaning in mind? Perhaps he intends to say thereby that the submission to the higher powers must be sincere and come from the heart. Another reason why he speaks in this way is that the soul is in between the body and the spirit. He wants to point out, therefore, that a believer is exalted once for all above all things and yet is subject to all things. Just as Christ does, he bears two forms in himself, for he is a dual being.[3] For, according to the Spirit, he is lord of all things. And all things "work together for good to the saints" (Rom. 8:28); also, as it says in I Cor. 3:22: "All things are yours whether it be the world, or life, or death." By faith the believer makes all these things subject to himself in the sense that he does not let himself be affected by them in any way and does not put his trust in them but compels them to serve him toward his glory and salvation. To serve God means to rule in this manner and to exercise the spiritual reign of which it is written in Rev. 5:10: "Thou has made us to our God a Kingdom, and we shall reign on the earth."

Now, there is no better way to triumph over the world and to subject it to spiritual rule than to despise it. But nowadays this spiritual Kingdom is so little known that there prevails the almost unanimous opinion that the temporal things that have been given to the church are spiritual ones. And so the spiritual rulers regard only these as important and exercise their government in them, except that they still administer jurisdiction, fulminate their de-

---

reading: 'The powers that are, are ordered of God,' i.e., because there are powers, they are ordered as they are by God alone. It is the same as to say, 'There is no power but from God.' Therefore, whatever powers exist and flourish, exist and flourish because God has ordered them."

[3] *"Gemellus"* = twin-born.

crees, and hold the power of the keys, but with much less care and zeal than they expend on these "spiritual," i.e., temporal, concerns of theirs.

The spirit of believers, therefore, is not or cannot be subject to anyone, but it is raised up with Christ in God and it has all these things under its feet. The symbolical representation of this is the woman of Rev. 12:1 who has the moon, i.e., temporal things, under her feet.

The "soul" is the same as man's spirit, but in so far as it is alive and active and occupied with the visible world and temporal things, it must "be subject to every human creature for God's sake" (I Peter 2:13). By being thus subject it obeys God and wills what he wills; thus it overcomes even now the temporal world.

Now let me digress a little.

One cannot but be amazed at the impenetrable darkness that prevails in our age. Nowadays nothing is more annoying to the spiritual rulers, i.e., these extravagant spendthrifts of the goods of the earth,[4] than a violation of the church's liberties and of its rights, privileges, and properties. They are quick to fulminate verdicts of excommunication against any whom they suspect of doing this and to proclaim them heretics, and they even have the astonishing audacity to label them publicly as enemies of God and the church and of the apostles Peter and Paul. Meanwhile, they are in no way troubled by the thought whether they themselves at least are God's friends or whether they might not be worse enemies of his than those they condemn. To such an extent they have come to identify obedience and faith with their custody, enlargement, and defense of temporal goods.

You may be guilty of pride and wantonness, you may be greedy and contentious, you may be given to anger and ingratitude and perhaps even call your own the whole catalogue of vices which the apostle lays down in I Tim. 3:1 ff.,[5] indeed all these vices of yours may cry to high heaven, yet you are a very good Christian if only you protect the rights and liberties of the church. But if you disregard them, you are no longer a faithful son and friend of the church.

Furthermore, the secular princes have bestowed rich properties upon the church and they have endowed her leaders with many privileges. Yet consider this remarkable fact: in the apostolic age, the priests paid taxes and were subject to the higher powers despite the fact that they were then most deserving of everyone's good will and favor. But today, when the life they lead is everything but a

---

[4] "Voragines amplissimae rerum temporalium."
[5] Luther writes "II Tim. 3."

life worthy of the priesthood, they nevertheless enjoy rights of special privilege. Are they then entitled to have what their early predecessors should have received as their desert but did not obtain?[6] And can the accomplishment of their predecessors take the place of what they themselves should accomplish? What a strange exchange this is! The leaders of the early church labored and earned their reward but did not receive it; now their successors enjoy this reward without having earned it by an effort of their own! I do not say that these rights are evil, but what I say is that rights that once only good men were entitled to are nowadays bestowed upon men that are evil and godless.

No wonder that laymen hate the clerics! (We all complain nowadays that the laymen are hostile to the clerics but we do not ask why this is so. Why, in times past, were they not hostile to the apostles and saints when these led them on into poverty, suffering, and death, and caused them to fall victim to all the evils of this life?) If someone says: You clerics were given privileges of law and rich benefices because of the duties of your office in accordance with the rule: *Beneficium propter officium,*[7] then they immediately reply by pointing to the murmuring of their prayers, and this is all they have to say. The duties of the priests consist in the observance of the canonical hours, including those that are perfunctorily mumbled and, indeed, those from which they are suspended and excused by special dispensation. Yet the apostle's description of priestly duties does not contain even a mention of prayer. And no one even thinks of translating into reality what he does say they are.

So then, as the priests, so the reward; as the office, so the benefice.[8] Clerics who are only the shadows of what they ought to be should get only the shadow of a reward. They are priests only in appearance; what they possess in the form of property should therefore also be proportionate only in appearance. How much more honest and right it would be if a man who wants to enjoy priestly privileges were to prove himself a good priest! And if he should not want to be a good priest, he should not contentiously insist upon his right inasmuch as he knows in his conscience that he does not deserve it in the sight of God. But if he demands it, insists upon it, and wants to lay hold of it, what else should he then receive but what he deserves?

The lawyers complain that it is a very bad thing not to execute

---

[6] *"An, quod illis debebatur, isti possident."*
[7] This was the legal principle on which all endowments of the church were based.
[8] *"Quales sacerdotes, talis et merces, quale officium, tale et beneficium."*

a last will and testament. But is there a priest nowadays who lives up to what the founders of endowments wanted done? Can it be that they are safe and cannot be interfered with because the founders failed to leave an instrument that states what they wanted done? Granted that the church is obliged to make provision for priests that are poor, not in return for the prayers they say but gratis, what about those who are insatiable in their greed for riches?

The Jews were destroyed when they did not want to be subject to the Romans; and the same happened to them under Nebuchadnezzar. Yet all the time they babbled exactly as we do now: "We are the servants of God in heaven" (Ezra 5:11); we do not need to be the servants of men. What this actually amounts to is that neither God nor men are being served. So it is also with us. We do not serve God, neither do we want to serve men, though men have freed us from the service we owe to them in order that we should serve God. Up to now, the laymen were ignorant; they could easily be talked into believing anything; and they did not understand what was happening, though they did not like it and were sore about it, and rightly so. But now, lo and behold, they certainly begin to fathom the mysteries of our wickedness[9] and to show some discernment about our duties. Therefore, unless we prove ourselves to them once more as true clerics, so that they are forced to believe in what we really are and take it seriously, we shall discover in the end that we can no longer deceive ourselves about our rights and privileges.

I am not sure, but I am inclined to think that the secular powers fulfill their office better and more happily than the ecclesiastical ones do. They are strict in punishing thefts and murders, except in so far as they let themselves be corrupted by insidious rights. But the ecclesiastical rulers! Except for the fact that they inflict excessive punishment upon all who seize the liberty, properties, and rights of the church, they foster rather than punish extravagance, greed, prodigality, and strife (so that it would be much safer if the temporal affairs also of the clergy were placed under the control of the secular rulers). Moreover, not only do they not prevent untrained, dull, and unfit persons from entering sacred offices, they even let them advance to higher positions! Knowingly, fully aware of what they are doing and with their eyes open, they ruin the church through these pestiferous men whom they have elevated to high positions—and yet they impose judgment on those who encroach upon their property and to whom they themselves offer ample opportunity for attack by the manner in which

9 "Mysteria iniquitatis nostrae."

they themselves invite hatred rather than friendliness. And if their attackers commit such a great sin by infringing upon their rights, how gravely do they themselves sin who, by the appearance of evil (I Thess. 5:22), indeed by the actuality of evil deeds done in defiance of the apostle, give so much occasion for attack!

And if there is no excuse, certainly for Christians, to let an occasion tempt them to do an evil deed, how can one find an excuse for those who knowingly, willfully, and needlessly offer a provocation and occasion of this kind? So then, the whited walls sit there and judge (Acts 23:3) the transgressors according to their laws while they themselves are the ungodliest transgressors. They are not one whit concerned about how they themselves might become blameless but only how they can rebuke others. They are strict taskmasters of the righteousness of others but the gravediggers of their own![10] If they, too, had to live in fear of others, how much more cautiously would they handle their affairs!

For example, here is this bishop who proceeds to execute the canon law and he harasses a whole city because of this disgusting affair.[11] Why can he get away with this? Because there is the tradition among men that the churches must not be profaned. Moreover, if he really wanted to carry out God's commandments, he would not even have to leave his own house. This particular action of his is not evil, but what is happening is that gnats are being strained out as one swallows a camel (Matt. 23:24).

The good Lord lets this and other transgressions happen in order to remind the bishops of the duties of their office and of the evangelical commandments. But they pay no attention to God's warning in connection with this affair; they burn with eagerness in their haste to inflict punishment and penance upon others and call them Pharaonic and Satanic or by even worse names than these—and all this only because they found a mote in their brother's eye and because they do not see the beam in their own eye (Matt. 7:3). Thus they themselves are as Pharaonic and Satanic and monstrous as Behemoth[12] but to an incomparably greater degree than others.

Would God that the time comes when laws of this sort will be

---

[10] "*Iustitiae alienae exactores, suae propriae vero pessundatores.*"

[11] Luther is thinking here of a notorious case that kept the city of Strassburg aroused. Hepp von Kirchberg, a canon of St. Thomas, had kidnaped the daughter of a Strassburg citizen. The city appealed to the bishop, demanding that the clergyman be put on trial. But the criminal had gone to Rome in the meantime and succeeded in persuading the Curia to issue a citation against three members of the City Council of Strassburg. Thus the city was placed in the position of the defendant. Cf. Ficker, p. 479, n. 11.

[12] "*Pharaonici, Satanici, Behemotici.*"

done away with and destroyed together with those who keep them intact as if they were holy![13] Take, for example, this one: That soul is dead which profaned sacred stones with the touch of a finger! But that soul is not dead which bursts with ambition but is without faith, and yet curses, judges, and condemns that other one!

I earnestly wish that no one would imitate me in what I say here because my distress compels me and my office requires that I do so. For a teaching is understood best if one sees its relevance to present conditions of life. At the same time, I must perform my duty as a teacher who holds his office by apostolic authority.[14] It is my duty to speak up whenever I see that something is done that is not right, even in higher places.

Consider this, for example: The Venetians committed a very grave offense against Julius II by abolishing small contributions to the church; and he recovered them for the church, earning a great merit thereby, by slaughtering and ruining a great many Christians. But the disgraceful utter corruption of the entire Curia and the monstrous collection of filth that can be found there, full of all sorts of prodigality, waste, and extravagance; greed, intrigue and sacrilege—this is no sin, of course. Blessed Bernard is therefore rightly sarcastic in saying in the fourth book of *On Consideration*:[15] "Is it not strange that the bishops have more than enough people available to whom they can entrust souls, but they cannot find anyone whom they can put in charge of their trivial secular affairs? They are obviously men of excellent judgment: to the least significant things they devote great care, but to highly important problems they pay little or no attention."

But enough of this. We must go back to the apostle.

I was saying that man is made up of body, soul, and spirit, the soul being the middle of the two others. The body is subject to the political power, but only with the ready consent of the soul and at the command of the spirit which is lord over everything. Here one can raise the following question: Why, then, does the apostle say in Gal. 5:13: "You have been called unto liberty, only make not liberty an occasion to the flesh"? And in ch. 2 of the same letter: "False brethren came in privately to spy out our liberty that they might bring us back into servitude." (Gal. 2:14.) And in another passage: "All things are lawful to me, but I will not be brought under the power of any man." (I Cor. 6:12.) And in I Cor. 7:23: "You are bought with a price; be not made bondslaves to men." One can cite many passages of his letters in which he

---

[13] *"Cum suis cultoribus."*
[14] *"Simul quia authoritate apostolicae officio docendi fungor."*
[15] Cf. Bernard of Clairvaux, *De consideratione*, IV, 6.

upholds liberty and rejects servitude. Yes, in I Cor. 9:19 f., he goes so far as to say: "Whereas I was free from all men, I made myself the servant of all that I might gain the more; and to the Jews I became as a Jew that I might gain Jews." And, a little farther on, he says: "I became all things to all men that I might save all." Now what shall we say to this? How do these statements agree with one another?

The answer is this: Just as the apostle has become all things to all men, so he also speaks to everyone in his own terms. Hence, he must necessarily become equivocal when he uses the words "liberty" and "servitude." When he addresses those that are slaves but freemen according to the law of nations,[16] he employs the appropriate terminology, as for example, where, in I Cor. 7:21 and in almost all his letters, he commands the slaves to obey their masters, adding that if they can, they may become free. But he has something else in mind in I Cor. 6:12 where he says: "All things are lawful to me, but I will not be brought under the power of any man," and in ch. 7:23 of the same letter, where he writes: "You were bought with a price; do not become the servants of men." These and similar passages deal with servitude in a metaphorical sense. What the apostle says here is this: A person loses his liberty if he engages with others in temporal matters and business transactions. He must stay with his business partners and clients and, if he wants to be honest, he must fulfill the mutual business obligations. Thus people of this sort are somehow one another's prisoners. Completely occupied with temporal affairs, they cannot devote attention to God.

There is still another kind of servitude and this he calls the best of all: "By love serve one another" (Gal. 5:13). It is this servitude he has in mind when he says that though he was free, he made himself the servant of all. This servitude is greatest freedom, because it needs nothing and takes nothing but is giving and outgoing. Hence, it is truly the best liberty, the liberty that is characteristic of Christian men. This is also what he has in mind when he writes in this chapter of the letter before us: "Owe no man anything but that you love one another" (Rom. 13:8). This, then, is the good kind of spiritual servitude: all things serve them that have it and all things work together for good to them, but they themselves are the servants of none, for, as I have stated, they are in need of none.

A fourth kind of servitude is equally spiritual, but it is a very bad kind. The apostle fights against it on behalf of the Christians with all his might. It is nothing else but to be subject to the law and all its burdens, i.e., to believe that outward works of the law

16 "*Ius gentium.*"

are necessary for salvation. People who are disposed to believe this remain unfree and will never be saved. For they are in the service of the law, and the law rules over them because of this foolish belief and conscience of theirs. All who want to be saved in some other way than by faith in Christ[17] are of this mind. Their greatest concern is how they can satisfy the law by the number of their good works and their deeds of righteousness. To be sure, the apostle and also spiritual men did and still do such works, not because they have to do them but because they want to do them; one need not do them but one may do them. Those hypocrites, however, are so bound up with these good works, as if they were necessary to salvation, that therefore they do them because they feel they must do them and not because they want to. They would rather that they were not necessary and yet it seems to them that they are. This servitude is nowadays pretty general.

In the light of this we can readily understand, on reading the book of Acts, why the apostle wanted to purify himself (Acts 21:26) and why he circumcised Timothy (Acts 16:3), though he was preaching everywhere the opposite of this. For anything outward is free to those who are in the Spirit.

But the apostle does not raise the question of liberty with respect to secular power. And, indeed, it does not embody that spiritual kind of servitude which we have just dealt with, inasmuch as it pertains to all men in the world; but this is not the case with respect to the works of the law.

For you shall not commit adultery; You shall not kill; You shall not steal; You shall not bear false witness; You shall not covet; and if there be any other commandment, it is comprised in this word: You shall love your neighbor as yourself. The love of our neighbor works no evil. **Love therefore is the fulfilling of the law.** (Rom. 13:9–10.)

The commandment: "Love your neighbor as yourself" (Matt. 19:19) or, as it is formulated in Lev. 19:18: "Love your friend as yourself" can be understood in a twofold way.

First, one can take it to mean that both are commanded: we shall love our neighbor and ourselves as well. But another way to understand it is that it commands us to love only our neighbor and this according to the example of our love for ourselves. This is the better interpretation, for because of the defect of his nature, man loves himself above everything else, he seeks himself in everything, and loves everything for his own sake, even when he loves his neighbor or his friend, for he seeks only his own therein.

17 *"Per fidem Christi."*

This commandment, therefore, is very profound, and everyone must carefully examine and test himself by it. For by the phrase "as yourself" every kind of simulated love is ruled out. Hence, he that loves his neighbor on account of his

money ⎤		poor ⎤	
honor ⎟	and would	lowly ⎟	would obviously
learning ⎟	not love	ignorant ⎟	have a
favor ⎬	him if	hateful ⎬	hypocritical
power ⎟	he were	dependent ⎟	love for him.
comfort ⎦		uncouth ⎦	

For, having his own advantage in mind, he does not love him as he is but he loves what he has and owns, and therefore he does not love himself "as himself," for he that loves himself loves himself also if he is poor, dull, and a complete nonentity.[18] For who is so useless that he hates himself? However, nobody is such a nonentity that he does not love himself, and the love he has for others is not like the love he has for himself.

Hence, this commandment demands something of us that is most difficult to accomplish as we can see if we consider it thoroughly. Nobody wants to be robbed, harmed, murdered, to have his marriage broken by adultery, to be lied to, to suffer through perjury, and have somebody else covet what he owns. But if he is not so disposed that he does not want his neighbor to suffer these wrongs either, he is already guilty of transgressing this commandment. Hence, this commandment includes the saying of Matt. 7:12: "All things whatsoever you would that men should do to you, do you also to them. For this is the Law and the Prophets." From a superficial point of view and taken in general terms, this rule may seem rather scanty, yet if we apply it to particular cases, we can gather from it an unlimited measure of salutary instruction and we can obtain from it most dependable guidance for everything.

But that people do not observe it and that they violate it innumerable times, even in ignorance, and, indeed, that people break it who do not think that they do so—all this stems from the fact that they do not apply this standard to their actual conduct but that they are satisfied with their good intention. For example: the rich provide the priests with large funds for the building of churches and memorials. But if they would put themselves in the place of the poor and then ask themselves the question whether they would not want that they, rather than the churches, be given

18 *"Penitus nihil."*

these gifts, they would easily know from themselves what they should do.

In a similar way, our prince and our bishop compete with each other in the traffic of relics.[19] Each wants the other to yield to him, yet both persist in what they are doing, carefully observing the show of piety, and neither yields to the other.

Likewise, the Observants[20] fight against one another for the sake of God, but they pay no attention to the commandment of love.

Now he that wants to take this commandment seriously and wants to apply it must not depend on "acts elicited" from within himself, but he must refer the works, words, and thoughts of his whole life to this commandment as to a rule, and he must always ask himself with respect to his neighbor: "What do I want him to do for me?" With this before him, he will immediately treat his neighbor in the same way. Then all wrangling, mutual disparagement, and discussion will cease at once and there will be there the whole host of virtues, indeed, every grace, every kind of holiness will be there, and, as he says here, "the fulfilling of the law."

This is how Moses taught the Children of Israel (Deut. 6:4 ff.): "These words which I command you this day shall be in your heart, and you shall tell them to your children and you shall meditate upon them sitting in your house, and walking on your journey, sleeping and singing." And then he goes on to say: "And you

---

[19] Frederick the Wise was greatly interested in increasing the collection of relics in the Church of All Saints in Wittenberg. Albrecht von Brandenburg, archbishop of Halle (when Luther wrote this, he was already also archbishop of Mainz, besides being the bishop of Halberstadt), similarly acquired ever new relics for the cathedral-chapter at Halle. (Cf. Ficker, p. 483, n. 25.)

[20] Luther may think here of his own experience in the Augustinian cloister at Erfurt. The monks there were "Observants," i.e., they advocated and practiced strict observance of the monastic rule, and they demanded that the entire Order do the same. As general vicar of the Augustinians in the Province of Saxony, John von Staupitz, Luther's teacher, predecessor (in the professorship at Wittenberg), and friend, had attempted to effect a reconciliation between the "observant" and "lax" cloisters in his charge. But he failed. The majority of the Erfurt Convent refused any compromise and persisted in their exclusivist position. They were opposed by a minority of other "Observants" (of whom Luther was one) who were ready to support Staupitz in the interest of unity. But, as Luther makes plain in many passages of these lectures, they also wanted to comply, fulfilling their monastic vow, with the requirement of obedience to the superiors. In this connection, it should be stated that Luther's criticisms of wrong Christian attitudes (pride, self-righteousness, nonconformity, stubbornness, and spite) as well as his constructive exposition of justification are not properly understood, unless one sees them against the background of his monastic experiences, concerns, and struggles.

shall bind them as a sign on your hand, and they shall be and shall move between your eyes. And you shall write them in the entry and on the doors of your house." Moses does not want us to wear pharisaical phylacteries,[21] but by saying: "These words shall become a sign in your hand," he means that we must do all our works as this commandment directs us to do them. "To have them before the eyes" means that all our thoughts must be guided by these words; and "They shall be written on the doors and the entry" means that all our senses and especially our tongue must be guided and directed by these words.

He that would do this would learn thoroughly to know his faults and to humble himself before God and fear him; otherwise, he would remain secure and holy in his own eyes. For example, he would discover himself not only as quite often indolent in helping his neighbor (though, regarding himself, he would find that he would want everyone to be affectionate, loving, and kindly disposed toward him) but also as an enemy and false brother toward his brethren, indeed, a slanderer and a person full of all kinds of sin.

We can say, then, that the apostle expresses the substance of this commandment when he says in Phil. 2:4: "Each one not considering the things that are his own, but those that are other men's" and in I Cor. 13:5: "Love seeks not its own," i.e., it causes man to deny himself and to affirm his neighbor, to put on affection for others and to put off affection for himself, to place himself in the position of his neighbor and then to judge what he would want him to do to himself and what he himself and others could do to him. Thus he will find by this infallible teaching what he must do. But if he disregards this teaching, the commandments will increase many times in number and he will not reach his goal.

As often as he desires and asks blessings only for himself, whether they be physical or spiritual (and he has a way to see to it that his wishes are fulfilled and perfectly so), he becomes entangled in faults by this wish, for he owes the same also to others; and then he finds that he does not want to do this to others. Or else he may hate himself and not desire anything good from others and then he on his part will not owe anything to others. And why is this so? Because he that is dead is righteous.[22] Do you see now how profound and far-reaching this commandment is?

And that knowing the season; that it is now the hour for us to rise from sleep. (Rom. 13:11.)

In I Cor. 15:34, it says: "Awake, you righteous, and sin not,"

---

21 *"Non vult Moses, ut Pharisaica philacteria faciamus."*
22 *"Quia, qui mortuus est, iustus est"* (cf. Rom. 6:7).

and in Eph. 5:14: "Rise, you that sleep, and arise from the dead, and Christ shall enlighten you." There can be no doubt that in these words, as also in this passage before us, the apostle speaks of that spiritual sleep in which the spirit is asleep when it lives in sins and is resting. From such a sleep Christ, too, arouses us many times in the Gospel as he commands us to be watchful (Matt. 26:41).

We should note that the apostle does not speak of those that are dead in the sins of unbelief or of believers who have fallen into mortal sin, but of Christians who are listless in what they are doing and have fallen fast asleep because they feel so secure. What he wants them to do is that they go forward but solicitously so. As it says in Micah 6:8: "I will show you, O man, what is good and what the Lord requires of you: Verily, to do justly, and to love mercy, and to walk solicitous with your God." For it is those who are not solicitous and not watchful from fear that are the ones who make a beginning but do not progress and put their hand to the plow and look back (Luke 9:62); they have the appearance of godliness but deny the power thereof (II Tim. 3:5); with their body they go out from Egypt and with their heart they go back to it; feeling secure and without the fear of God, they go their way, hardened, irreverent,[23] bereft of feeling. Blessed Bernard says with respect to them:[24] "He that does not incessantly hasten to do penance says thereby that he does not need to repent." If he does not need to repent, he is also not in need of mercy; and if he does not need mercy, he does not need salvation. But this is possible only for one who is without sin, like God and the angels.

Therefore the apostle speaks the right word when he admonishes the Christians that they should arise, even though, if they had not already risen, they would not be Christians. However, to stand still on God's way means to go backward, and to go forward means ever to begin anew.[25] (Hence, the Preacher does not say: When a man has gone forward but "when a man has done, then he shall begin" [Ecclus. 18:7].) Thus Saint Arsenius asked God in his daily prayer: "Help me, O Lord, that I may begin to live to thee."[26] And, certainly, just as the apostle said of knowledge that "if any man think that he knows anything, he has not yet known as he ought to know" (I Cor. 8:2), so we must also conclude with

---

[23] "Indevoti."

[24] Cf. Bernard of Clairvaux, Sermo II in vigilia nativitatis Domini (PL 183, 90).

[25] "Stare in via Dei, hoc est retrocedere, et proficere, hoc est semper de novo incipere."

[26] Vitae Patrum, Verba seniorum, III, 190, V, 15, 5. (PL 73, 801, 953.)

respect to the several individual virtues: he that thinks he has already apprehended and made a beginning does not yet know how he ought to begin.

Nowadays people of this kind can be found in surprisingly large numbers. They practice the repentance Christ calls for in the form of temporal and external works and when they have done these, they regard themselves as righteous. This is why it happens so often that when a confession is made in this spirit it results in the ruin of this wretched trust in oneself, because it does not take away what in their presumptuousness they think it should take away.

The word "sleep" is used in the Scriptures in several senses. In the first place, it denotes physical sleep, as in John 11:11: "Our friend Lazarus sleeps." And in the Old Testament, especially in the books of Kings and Chronicles, it is often said: "He slept with his fathers" (I Kings 2:10; 11:43, etc.; II Chron. 9:31; 12:16, etc.).

In the second place, it is used to denote a spiritual sleep, and this in two senses. First, in a good sense, as in Ps. 127:2: "He shall give sleep to his beloved," and in Ps. 68:13: "If you sleep among the midst of the lots," etc. And in the Song of Solomon, the bride says: "I sleep, and my heart watches" (S. of Sol. 5:2). To sleep in this way means: not to pay attention to earthly goods and to regard them as mere show and shadow rather than as real things, because one is concerned for things that are eternal, and one sees these with the heart when it is wide awake by the light of faith. Hence, sleepers of this kind are asleep in temporal affairs and they deal indifferently with them.

In the third place, the word is used to denote a spiritual sleep that is bad and the opposite of the one just mentioned. First Thessalonians 5:6 f. speaks about it as follows: "Therefore let us not sleep as others do, but let us watch and be sober. For they that sleep, sleep in the night; and they that are drunk, are drunk in the night." Here the word "night" denotes the spiritual night that is evil, as in Ps. 76:5: "They have slept their sleep, and all the men of riches have found nothing in their hands." "To sleep" in this sense means to pay no attention to eternal goods and to despise them. Sleepers of this sort act indifferently toward eternal goods because they are concerned only about temporal things, and these they see with a desire that is always awake. And so they are the opposite of the sleepers of whom we spoke before: what is night to these is day to the others, and what is waking to the latter is sleep to the former, and conversely. Just as their goods conflict with one another, so do also their attitudes of mind and hence also the people themselves. (One could say briefly that they are the sleep of nature, of grace, and of guilt, but such a distinction is somewhat obscure.)

The threefold distinction made in the Scripture about sleep is characteristic also of the way it speaks of night and day; indeed, it is characteristic of almost all the other metaphorical forms of expression it employs.

For example, spiritual day is faith and spiritual night is unbelief. Conversely, faith is night and unbelief is day, as in Ps. 19:2: "Day to day utters speech, and night to night knowledge," i.e., the carnal[27] man utters knowledge to the prudent; the fool of God utters speech to the fools among men, and one who is wise in Christ utters knowledge to the worldly wise. In the passage before us, the apostle, therefore, obviously does not speak of physical sleep or of the darkness and the night that one experiences with the senses. Of them he speaks farther down where he says: "Not in chambering and in impurities," i.e., in sleep and lust, and these are certainly done in the night.

The works of darkness, then, are the works of them that are asleep in the spirit, and this in the bad sense, i.e., the works of them that are asleep in the lusts of the world. Moreover, these works of darkness are not merely such as are commonly regarded as evil, but also such as are regarded as good but in fact are evil because of their inner darkness, i.e., because they are not done in a faith that is awake.

For now our salvation is nearer *than when we first believed. The night is passed, and the day is at hand. Let us therefore cast off the works of darkness and put on the armor of light.* (Rom. 13:11–12.)

What the apostle means by this he states in II Cor. 6:1–2 as follows: "And we helping do exhort you that you do not receive the grace of God in vain. For he says: In an accepted time have I heard thee, and in the day of salvation have I helped thee. [Isa. 49:8.] Behold now is the acceptable time; behold now is the day of salvation." What here, in the letter to the Romans, the apostle briefly touches upon in passing, he there works out in much greater detail, particularly as he fully describes what he means by **the armor of light** and **the works of darkness.** He says: "Giving no offense to any man that our ministry be not blamed, but in all things let us exhibit ourselves as the ministers of God, in much patience, in fastings." (II Cor. 6:3 ff.) Then, farther on, he says: "by the armor of righteousness on the right and on the left," etc. (II Cor. 6:7). What here, in the passage before us, is "the armor of

[27] Luther says "spiritual," but this is obviously a writing mistake.

light" is there "the armor of righteousness"; hence righteousness and light are the same.

Let us walk honestly, as in the day:[28] **not in reveling and drunkenness.**[29] (Rom. 13:13.)

As *Graecari* (to live in the Greek fashion) comes from *Graecus,* so *comissari* (to revel) comes, it seems, from *kōmos.* Now the Greek word *"kōmos"* means "banquet" or, rather, the luxury of a banquet and the lavish and wasteful preparation and celebration of a banquet. Indeed, the god of drunkenness is called Comus and his feast has the same name. In this the Greeks are superior to the Germans and to the whole world in that they spent so much time in reveling and drunkenness that they even fashioned a god for these as if this were the profitable thing to do.

What the apostle teaches here in a negative way he explains in positive fashion in II Cor. 6:4 ff. He wants us to devote ourselves to fastings and temperance and sobriety. And, indeed, a reader of historical books, or of Blessed Jerome at least, will find that the six vices of which the apostle speaks here in this part of the letter were not merely numerous in Rome at that time, but that they held sway over the city to the point of tyrannizing it—read Suetonius' *Lives of the Caesars!*—so that even the heathen Juvenal exclaimed:[30] "A fiercer enemy, namely profligacy, has settled among us and takes vengeance upon a defeated world."

The apostle therefore wants to frighten the faithful away so that they do not yield to these wild examples that godless Rome gives. Also Blessed Peter did not pass over in silence the riotousness of this city (I Peter 4:4); he is not satisfied to call it riotousness but he speaks of a "confusion of riotousness" or a collection of filth. Indeed, because of this, he does not hesitate to call this city a Babylon, in view of the fact that everything there is disorderly, also according to the testimony of Catullus:[31] "Everything goes, and wrong is mixed with evil ravings," so that it appears that, when it was at the point of the utmost extreme of riotousness, the city cried to heaven and called for either the apostles, and the foremost among them at that, or a punishment similar to that of Sodom and Gomorrah. Hence, it says in I Peter 4:3 f.: "For the time past is sufficient to have fulfilled the will of the Gentiles, for them who

[28] In the marginal gloss, Luther writes (*WA* 56, 128, 18): "This is the text from which ['*ex quo*'] Blessed Augustine was converted." (Cf. Augustine, *Conf.,* VIII, 12.)

[29] Vulgate, "*non in comessationibus.*"

[30] Juvenal, *Satyrae,* VI, 292: "*Sevior hostis luxuria incubuit victumque ulciscitur orbem.*"

[31] Catullus, *Propertius,* LXIV, 406.

have walked in riotousness, lusts, excess of wine, revelings, banquetings, and unlawful worshiping of idols; wherein they think it strange that you ran not with them into the same confusion of riotousness, speaking evil of you."

And in II Peter 2:13, it is written: "counting for a pleasure the delights of a day of[32] stains and spots, disporting themselves to excess, rioting in their feasts with you." So it is again today: Rome has reverted to its former ways and draws almost the whole world under the sway of its example. If only the Rome of today does not exceed the ancient city in a greater extravagance of luxury, so that the presence of the apostles may again appear to be required, but now with greater necessity! Would that they come as friends before they must enter as judges!

We must note in passing that *"luxuria"* ("wantonness") must here not be understood to mean "lust" (*"libido"*) but "reveling" or "immoderate profligacy," in the sense of the Greek words *"asōtia"* and *"asōtos."*

Attacking the same vice in I Tim., chs. 2 and 3 and also in Titus, chs. 1 and 2, the apostle commands that the bishop, the deacons, the man, the elders, the young men and women, should be sober, and to all of them he forbids drunkenness and reveling as though these were a pestilence. Thus, if we compare these passages with the one that is here before us, we gain a correct understanding of the apostle; here he indicates what he does not want and there he shows what he wants.

Not in chambering and unchastities. (Rom. 13:13.)

This means that they should be watchful and chaste. This is the same commandment of chastity and vigilance which, in the aforementioned passages, he gives chiefly to the bishop and then also to the elders and others.

This is indeed a fitting sequence. For reveling and drunkenness foment unchastity, or, as the Greek text says, lasciviousness.[33] Hence, the holy fathers[34] declared that he that wants to serve God must conquer above all the vice of gluttony. Just as it is the foremost of all vices, so it is also the one that is most difficult to overcome. If it is not extirpated, it makes the soul dull for divine things, even if it does not lead to chambering and licentiousness, as sometimes happens in the case of older men. Hence, fasting is

---

[32] The Vulgate Luther had before him read *"coinquinationis"* rather than *"coinquinationes."*

[33] This is Erasmus' translation.

[34] Cf. John Cassian, *De coenob. inst. lib.,* V, 1 ff.; *Collationes patrum,* 2 ff. (PL 49, 611 ff.).

one of the strongest weapons of Christian people, but gluttony is a most effective contrivance[35] in the hands of the devil. But you can find all this amply discussed in the writings of the saints.

Not in contention and emulation. (Rom. 13:13.)

In the foregoing the apostle instructs man with respect to himself: he should be temperate, watchful, and chaste. But here he instructs him with respect to his neighbor: they should live with one another in peace, amity, and love. Throughout all his letters, he enjoins this most emphatically just as he did in the preceding chapter. In I Tim. 2:8 he says: "I will, therefore, that men pray in every place, lifting up pure hands, without anger and controversy." And in the third chapter of the same letter (I Tim. 3:3) and in Titus 1:7 he commands the bishop that he should not be a striker. According to the interpretation of Blessed Jerome,[36] this means that he should not have a sharp tongue. He therefore wants Christians to be mild, kindly, considerate toward one another.

A "contention" is a gladiatorial combat that is fought with many words ("to contend" means "to fight with words"), in which each of the two contenders wants to be considered as truthful, right, and able to the point that he disapproves of everything else; it is a fight in which neither of the two yields to the other.

"Emulation" is a very broad term. "To emulate" means "to follow" and "to pursue." And just as one can take the terms "I pursue something" or "I follow something" in a good or a bad sense, so one can understand also the word "I emulate" in this way. Now "to emulate" does not quite mean "to imitate" but, rather, to pursue something in such a way that one reaches it, or gets hold of it, or surpasses it. It does not only express the mere following after something but also the attempt to surpass it. So then, he that emulates in the good sense of the word is one who imitates his teacher or whoever is his example in such a way that he tries to outdo him, which one does not do if he merely imitates someone. And he that emulates in the bad sense of the word is one who tries to overcome the one he contends with, or as we say in common speech, he wants to have the last word or to get in the last dig; in short, he wants to overcome evil with evil. If the other does or says something bad, he tries to do or say something worse. So then, emulation is the sister or maidservant of contention. Hence, we say *"aemulus"* and *"aemula"* ("rival") and we use these words either as nouns or adjectives.

[35] *"Machina diaboli."*
[36] Cf. Jerome, *Comm. in ep. ad Tit.* 1:7.

But by this the use of this word is not exhausted, even though it may suffice for this passage. For God is called *"Zēlōtēs"* and *"emulator"* (Ex. 20:5; 34:14): he is a jealous God. And the apostle says: "I emulate you with the emulation of God" (II Cor. 11:2), which means: "I am jealous of you with the jealousy of God." And in the Song of Solomon "emulation" (jealousy) is called "hard as hell," and this cannot be taken to refer, so it would seem, to a mutual contention.

Now, it is because everyone who emulates another wants to be the only one to realize what he contends for with the other that the husband competes against the adulterer, and God against the idol, and the wife against the adulteress or mistress, so that just as the husband wants to be the only one to possess his wife and therefore tries to keep another away from her, so God wants to be the only God, and so the apostle was jealous of the Corinthians because he alone wanted to be their teacher ahead of the rest of the apostles, begrudging others this glory, but with a holy envy. For he feared that their mind might be corrupted by the craftiness of the devil, even though he had betrothed them to Christ. He certainly feared the false apostles. Consequently, emulation, in the sense of jealousy, encloses the good one loves and thereby it excludes the sharing of it with someone else and, because of this, it is also a kind of hatred for the one who wants to share it and does not want to leave it to anyone for himself alone.

So then, jealousy hates and loves at the same time. Sometimes the object of jealousy is what one loves, sometimes it is that which one hates. Thus we say: "A husband is jealous of his wife," but we also say: "He is jealous of the adulterer," but the first way of speaking is the more appropriate one. In this sense, the apostle says in I Cor. 12:31:[37] "Be jealous for the better gifts."

Emulation as jealousy is loving envy or envious love; it is love and envy mixed together, bitter love as well as loving bitterness,[38] just as repentance is sweet sorrow and sorrowful sweetness. For the sweetness of his love makes the jealous person lively and willing, but the bitterness of his hatred makes him unwilling.

However, the term "emulation" is not always used in the sense of "jealousy" which is its proper meaning; quite often it stands for the mental effort by which one tries to surpass someone else and to maintain the advantage one has gained over him, but without hating him, as, for example, in I Cor. 10:22, which says: "Do we emulate the Lord?" i.e., Are we trying to surpass the Lord and to outdo him? Are we stronger than he?

[37] Luther writes "I Cor. 14" (the word here is *emulamini*).
[38] *"Amarus amor et amorosus amaror."*

But put you on the Lord Jesus Christ, **and make not provision for the flesh in its lusts.** (Rom. 13:14.)

I.e., lest evil desires[39] arise, but make good provision for its necessities and according to its necessities. The apostle wants to say that we should not favor or cherish the flesh, lest evil desires arise. For as Hugh of St. Victor[40] rightly says: "He that cherishes the flesh nourishes an enemy" and, on the other hand: "He that destroys the flesh kills a friend of his." One must not destroy the flesh but the vices of the flesh, i.e., its evil desires. Proverbs 29:21: "He that nourishes his servant delicately shall find him stubborn."

---

[39] *"Concupiscentias."*

[40] According to Ficker (p. 491, n. 27), these sayings cannot be found in the writings of Hugh of St. Victor, but he gives a reference to Gregory, *Hom. in Ezech.*, II, 7: "Sometimes our flesh is a helper in a good deed and sometimes it is a seducer to an evil one. If, therefore, we give it more than we should, we nourish an enemy. But if we do not serve its needs as we should, we kill a fellow citizen [*civem*]."

ROMANS, CHAPTER FOURTEEN[1]

Now him that is weak in faith take unto you, *not in dispute about thoughts. For one believes that he may eat all things; but he that is weak, let him eat herbs. Let him not that eats despise him that eats not; and him that eats not, let not him judge him that eats. For God has taken him to him. Who are you that judge another man's servant? To his own lord he stands and falls. And he shall stand, for God is able to make him stand. For one judges be-*

[1] Luther's marginal gloss reads as follows (*WA* 56, 129, 8 ff.): "In this chapter the apostle commands two things: first, that the strong and the weak in faith should not despise and judge one another, and, secondly, that the stronger ones should not give offense to the weak, as he says below: 'But judge this rather that you put not a stumbling block or a scandal in your brother's way.' This teaching is occasioned by the fact that, in the old law, many foods were forbidden and this was a symbol of what was to come. The weak and simple in faith, therefore, who could not understand that the symbol was no longer in force and that all things had become clean, or who believed that certain kinds of food could not be eaten because of their common use, these should be tolerated and not despised. On the other hand, those who had a clear understanding should not be condemned as if they did evil because they ate anything. About this question there arose then a very great controversy. The first church council was held about it (Acts 15:6 ff.); indeed, even Peter was rebuked by Paul on the same matter (Gal. 2:14).

"In all his letters, the apostle deals with this subject in opposition to the false apostles of Jewish extraction who taught that it was necessary to salvation that one observe these laws. For example, in I Tim. 1:7 he speaks of them as 'understanding neither the things they say, nor whereof they affirm.' And, in Titus 1:10, he calls them 'deceivers of minds.' But, elsewhere, he says of himself, 'I have become a Jew to the Jews and a Gentile to the Gentiles,' etc. [I Cor. 9:20–21].

"Meat offered to idols became a similar occasion for controversy to believers of Gentile origin, as one can plainly see on reading chapters 8 to 10 of I Corinthians. 'Whatever is sold in the shambles, eat' (I Cor. 10:25)."

378

tween day and day, and another judges every day; let every man abound in his own sense. He that regards the day regards it unto the Lord. And he that eats, eats unto the Lord, for he gives thanks to God. And he that eats not, to the Lord he eats not and gives thanks to God. For none of us lives to himself, and no man dies to himself. For whether we live, we live unto the Lord; or whether we die, we die unto the Lord. Therefore, whether we live or whether we die, we are the Lord's. For to this end Christ died and rose again that he might be lord both of the dead and of the living. But you, why judge you your brother? Or you, why do you despise your brother? For we all stand before the judgment seat of Christ. For it is written: As I live, says the Lord, every knee shall bow to me, and every tongue shall confess to God. Therefore every one of us shall render account to God for himself. Let us not therefore judge one another any more. But judge this, rather, that you put not a stumbling block or a scandal in your brother's way. (Rom. 14:1–13.)

"Weak" must here not be understood in the sense of "impotent" as in the passage of the following chapter where "the infirmities of the weak," i.e., impotent, are mentioned, but in the sense of feebleness which is the opposite of health or well-being. (For example: over against a man a boy is impotent but not feeble. The first word must be understood as a relative or transitive word but the second one must be taken absolutely.) Thus, if, in this letter, the apostle calls some weak and some strong in faith, he thinks of the weak as those who are anxious-minded[1a] or still somehow under the influence of superstition and who therefore believe that they must do something which in reality they are not required to do at all. We should note, however, that he does not speak on behalf of those who choose to hang on to superstition but on behalf of those who are still superstitious because of the weakness of their faith and who because of this are not yet in the state of salvation but close to it, so that they must be nourished and fed in order that they can reach their goal. Hence, he admonishes Titus: "Speak the things that become sound doctrine" (Titus 2:1); "the sound word that cannot be blamed" (Titus 2:2); "so that he may be able to exhort in sound doctrine" (Titus 2:9).

He says all this in opposition to that Jewish superstition which some of the false apostles taught by making a distinction between several kinds of food and between the days of the week. It is these he has in mind as he says in Titus 1:10, 13: "For there are many vain talkers and deceivers, especially they who are of the circumcision. . . . Wherefore rebuke them sharply that they may be

1a *"Scrupulosos."*

sound in faith." And in I Tim. 1:3 ff. he writes: "That you may charge some not to teach otherwise and not to give heed to Jewish fables. For the end of the commandment is love from a pure heart and a good conscience and an unfeigned faith. From which things some going astray are turned aside unto vain babbling, desiring to be teachers of the law, understanding neither the things they say nor whereof they affirm." And in the same manner, he writes in Gal. 4:8 ff.: "How turn you again to the weak and needy elements which you desire to serve again? You observe days, and months, and times, and years. I fear that I have labored in vain among you." And much more clearly he writes in Col. 2:16 ff.: "Let no man judge you in meat or in drink, or in respect of a festival day, or the new moon, or the Sabbaths, which are a shadow of things to come, but the body is of Christ. Let no man seduce you, willing in humility and in worship of angels, walking in the things he has not seen, in vain puffed up by the sense of his flesh, and not holding the head from which the whole body, being supplied with nourishment and knit together through the joints and bands, grows unto the increase of God. If, then, you be dead with Christ from the elements of the world, why do you subject yourselves to ordinances as though living in the world? Touch not, taste not, handle not, which all are unto destruction by the very use, according to the precepts and doctrines of men; which things have indeed a show of wisdom in superstition and humility, and severity to the body, but are not of any value against the indulgence of the flesh." Also in I Cor. 8:1 ff. and 10:6 ff., he gives a full discussion of the thoughts he expresses in the chapter before us.

What the apostle means to say, then, is that in the new law everything is free and nothing necessary for those who believe in Christ, but that love is enough for them, a love, as he says, "from a pure heart and good conscience and unfeigned faith" (I Tim. 1:5). And in Gal. 6:15 he says: "In Christ Jesus neither circumcision avails anything nor uncircumcision, but a new creature and the observance of the commandment of God."[2] And our Lord himself says in the Gospel: "The Kingdom of God comes not with observation; neither shall they say: Behold here or behold there. For lo, the Kingdom of God is within you." (Luke 17:20 f.) And in Matt. 24:11, 26, he says: "There shall arise many false prophets and false Christs and they shall seduce many. . . . If, therefore, they shall say to you: Behold, he is in the desert, go not out; Behold, he is in the closets, believe it not." (And in Isa., ch. 66, at the end of the chapter, it is written: "There shall be month after month and Sabbath after Sabbath." [Isa. 66:23]. And in the first chapter he says: "I

[2] The passage of Galatians is combined with I Cor. 7:19.

will not abide your new moons and your solemnities." [Isa. 1:13 f.]
In this whole book there are many such sayings.)

For it does not belong to the new law to set aside some days
and not others for fasting, as it was done by the law of Moses. Nor
does it belong to the new law to select certain kinds of food and
distinguish them from others, for example, meats, eggs, etc., as,
again, the law of Moses does (Lev. 11:4 ff.; Deut. 14:7 ff.). Nor
does it belong to the new law to designate certain days and not
others as holidays. Nor does it belong to the new law to build such
and such churches and to adorn them thus and so and to sing in
them in one way or another. Nor are organs, altar decorations,
chalices, or pictures required, and whatever else we now find in the
houses of worship. Finally, it is not necessary that priests and
monks wear tonsures and that they walk about in special habits as
they did in the old law. All these things are mere shadows and to-
kens of reality; indeed, they are childish things. On the contrary,
every day is a holiday, every kind of food is permitted, every place
is sacred, every time is suitable for fasting, every garment is allowed. Everything is free as long as there is practiced in it moderation and love and whatever else the apostle teaches.

Many false apostles have preached against this liberty which the
apostle proclaims. They tried to induce the people to observe all
those laws as if they were necessary to salvation. But the apostle
opposed them with amazing zeal.

What is the upshot of all this? Shall we now confirm the heresy
of the Picards?[3] For they adopted this rule. Shall we say that all
churches, and all the ornaments in them, all the holy offices that
are celebrated in them, all fast days and all feast days, and finally
all the distinctions between priests, bishops, and monks regarding
their rank, habits, and ceremonies, observed as they have been for
so many centuries to this very day, and also all the many mon-
asteries and foundations, the benefices and the prebends—shall
we say that all these must be abolished? This is what the Picards
do because, so they maintain, this is what the liberty of the new law
requires.

God forbid! For if one were to understand the apostle in this
way, the immediate consequence would be that one would raise
the following objection to his teaching: therefore, "let us do evil
that there may come good" (Rom. 3:8); let us stop doing good; we
shall get to heaven without having to lift a finger. It is obvious
that one can draw this conclusion. For if the apostle did reject all
these works we have just enumerated, all other works must likewise

[3] The Picardi were the most radical group of the Hussites. (Cf. A.R.G. 31
[1933], 102 ff.)

be rejected. For none of them is necessary to salvation. This is proved by the fact that infants and children, and also the sick or prisoners or poor people do not need or are not able to do these works of piety, at least not all of them. Indeed, nobody needs to or can do them all, but it is sufficient that one has "love from a pure heart," etc., as was stated before.

Over against this there stands the statement of the apostle himself, in I Tim. 5:12, 11, that certain widows "have damnation because they made void their first faith" and wanted to marry. Hence, they had to remain widows ("because they had grown wanton in Christ," i.e., sumptuous and fat). And, in the Gospel, our Lord said even of the smallest things: "These things you ought to have done, and not to leave those undone" (Matt. 23:23; Luke 11:42). And in Jer. 35:5 ff. he highly commends the house of the Rechabites because they did not drink wine and did not build houses, indeed, because they obeyed their father Jonadab in these things. And the apostle himself circumcised Timothy (Acts 16:3), offered sacrifices, and purified himself in the Temple (Acts 21:26).

We reply to the objection as follows:

It is true that according to the new law none of all these things is necessary, but this does not mean that because one does not have to do one thing, he is free to do the opposite or something else. But, as Hilary says:[4] "One must understand a statement in the light of the occasion that called it forth." Now the apostle speaks against the Jews and their kind who taught that the observance of the law was necessary in the sense that without it even the faith in Christ was not sufficient for salvation. Hence, according to Acts 15:1, they said even to believers who were already baptized in Christ: "Except you be baptized after the manner of Moses, you cannot be saved." And a little farther on, it is written that they said: "They must be circumcised and they must chiefly observe the law of Moses." (Acts 15:5.)[5] The same meaning is implied in Paul's question to Peter, according to Gal. 2:14: "How do you compel the Gentiles to live as do the Jews?" In other words: you compel them to believe, i.e., it is you who make them believe, that it is necessary for salvation that they abstain from the food of the Gentiles. (In the same chapter we read that "neither Titus, being a Gentile, was compelled to be circumcised" [Gal. 2:3].)

The same meaning is implied in the word "to judge" which he uses several times in this same passage. For whoever judges some-

<hr>

4 Hilary, *De trin.*, IV, 14.

5 The text of the Vulgate that Luther had before him read:"*Oportet eos circumcidi et* PRACIPUE [chiefly, instead of PRAECIPERE (and commanded)] *servare legem Mosis*" (Acts 15:5).

one else certainly believes that the one he condemns is doing something that goes against salvation and that he must therefore change his ways. So then, in the absence of this weakness of faith and of this superstitious belief, everyone is allowed, within the limits of the vow he has made, to observe even the whole law, indeed all commandments. In this sense, the early church was for a long time permitted to use the Jewish ceremonies. Blessed Augustine had a long controversy with Blessed Jerome about this, according to his letters 8; 9; 10; and 19.[6]

Therefore, as it was foolish then to regard these things as so weighty that one made salvation dependent upon them, meanwhile neglecting faith and love which alone are sufficient for eternal life (this was highly repugnant to Christ; hence he said: "You strain out the gnats and swallow the camel" [Matt. 23:24]), so it is foolish and preposterous also today and at any time to identify the Christian religion outwardly with this ostentatious display which (according to the modern custom) is practiced by the observance of distinctions between feast days, food, habits, and places while, in the meantime, the commandments of God and faith and love are utterly disregarded.

Although all this is now completely free, anyone may, nevertheless, for the sake of the love of God, bind himself by a vow to this or that. But now he is bound to it, not by reason of the new law, but by reason of the law that he has taken upon himself for the sake of his love of God. For who is so stupid as to deny that anyone can give up his liberty in deference to someone else and make himself a slave and bind himself to this or that place or to such and such a day or to such and such a type of work! Only he must have done this out of love and in such a faith that he is confident that he does not do it because it is necessary for salvation but from a spontaneous will and out of a sense of liberty.

Everything, therefore, is free, but it can be given up by a vow for love's sake. (Where this has actually occurred, one is bound to it not because of what one has vowed to do but because of the voluntary character of the vow. Hence, he must take care that he keeps his vow with the same love out of which he promised that he would keep it. Without this love the vow cannot be kept. For if it is kept without love, i.e., against one's will, it would be better not to make any vow. For one who does this is like a man who makes a vow and does not keep it; he keeps it outwardly but in his heart he has made reservations; he commits a sacrilege because he does not voluntarily keep his vow. This is why there are many

---

[6] This numbering is that of the older editions (e.g., *Liber epistolarum beati Augustini,* Basel, 1493). For us, the reference is to Letters 28, 40, 75, 82.

apostates who outwardly cannot be recognized as such.) However,
if one disregards love and directs his attention now to these and
then to those commandments because he considers them necessary
for salvation, as it now happens everywhere among priests and
monks and even among secular people who are preoccupied with
their statutes and human doctrines—then we have certainly returned to the Jewish superstition and restored the Mosaic servitude, especially if we do all this by forcing ourselves to do it and
in the belief that there is no salvation apart from these works and
that salvation can be achieved only through them.

But then what about the general rules of the church, the fasts
and the feast days? We answer this question as follows: What has
been imposed upon us by the ancient consensus of the whole
church and from the love of God and for adequate reasons must
certainly be kept, not because any of it is necessary and unchange-
able but because the obedience is necessary which for love's sake
we owe to God and the church. Nevertheless, the higher clergy
should see to it that they issue as few rules as possible, and, with a
view to changing them, they should watch out where, how, and to
what extent they further or hinder love. (For example, when they
fill the houses of worship with much noise and let the organs re-
sound and when they have celebrated mass with every conceivable
pomp and circumstance, they believe that they did good thereby
so that, by comparison, they regard any help that was given to the
poor as if it were nothing.) Moreover, nobody cares whether perjury, lies, or slanders are committed, even on holidays. But if
somebody eats meat or eggs on the sixth day of the week, people
are stunned. This is how silly almost everyone has become nowadays.[7] Hence, today the fast days and the many holidays should be
abolished. For the common people make it a point of conscience to
observe them, in the belief that there is no salvation without them.
But, nevertheless, almost everyone acts against this very voice of
conscience, again and again. The people have come to hold this
foolish belief because the preaching of the true word has been
neglected so that nowadays they once more need the apostles in
order to learn what true religion is.

Thus it would also be useful to purge and change almost the
whole book of decretals and to reduce the pomp and even more the
ritual of the prayer services and of the ecclesiastical vestments. For
every day these things become more and more lavish, and faith and
love decline proportionately, and greed, pride, and vainglory

---

[7] The sentences here put in parentheses were written by Luther on the margins of his sheets. They should be read not as organic parts of the argument,
but as notes.

are being fostered and, what is worse, people hope to be saved by it all and are no longer concerned about the inner man.

Is it, then, a good thing to become a monk nowadays? My answer is this: If you think that you cannot obtain salvation in any other way than by becoming a monk, do not go into the cloister. For what the proverb says is only too true: "Despair makes a monk," or rather, not a monk but a devil. He that puts on the cowl from sheer desperation will never be a good monk, but only he that does this for love's sake: seeing how great his sins are and wanting to bring God a great sacrifice by love, he voluntarily gives up his liberty, puts on that foolish garb, and subjects himself to degrading duties.

Hence, I think that to become a monk is a better thing today than it has been for the last two hundred years, and for this reason: up to now the monks drew away from the cross and it was something glorious to be a monk. But now people begin to dislike them again, even the good ones among them, on account of their foolish garb. For this is what it means to be a monk: to be detested by the world and to let oneself be taken for a fool. He that out of love submits to this kind of treatment does very well indeed. It does not scare me at all that the bishops and priests persecute us. This had to happen. But what displeases me is that we give them such a poor reason to dislike us.

Moreover, those who detest the monks for no reason at all but from mere prejudice are the best friends the friars have in the world. For the monks should be glad if they fulfill their vow by letting themselves be despised and put to shame for having taken this very vow for God's sake, for they wear their foolish garb in order to induce everyone to despise them. But nowadays they behave quite differently. They give only the appearance of being monks.

But I know in my heart that they would be the happiest men if they had love, and that they could feel more blessed than the hermits did that were in the desert, because of the fact that they are exposed to the cross and to daily disgrace. But alas! today there is no more arrogant class of people than they are!

But to return to the text: the apostle desires above all that the weak in faith should be tolerated and instructed by the strong and also that the weak should not make rash judgments. In this way he admonishes them to peace and unity. For although a weak faith does not suffice for salvation, as the Galatians show, weak believers must nevertheless be supported until they become strong, and one must not let them stay weak because one detests them and is concerned only for one's own salvation. (The apostle exemplified this teaching not only generally in his relations with men but particularly in his attitude toward the Galatians: he sent them a letter that he had written with his own hand.) Hence, the word "take on" ("*assumite*") means in Greek "join yourselves together with."[8] When therefore the apostle writes: "Join yourselves together with him who is weak in faith," he means to say: You must not reject him because you dislike him and leave him to himself, but you must draw him to yourselves and strengthen him until he too is whole. But if, instead, you despise him as if he were worthless, be on your guard lest God himself puts him on his feet. So then, he says to both of them: The strong should instruct the weak and the weak should let themselves be instructed; then peace and love will prevail among them both.

Not in disputes about thoughts. (Rom 14:1.)

This is not an entirely suitable translation. Where our version[9] says "in disputes," the Greek text has "in making distinctions."[10] Where our text says "thoughts," the Greek version has "*dialogismōn*."[11] This is more appropriate and means "making a decision" and "weighing reasons," in the sense of the phrase of Rom. 1:21: "They became vain in their thoughts," i.e., in what we commonly call "motives" and "reasons." The apostle means to say, therefore, that no one should judge another's decisions and reasons by which he is moved in this way or that. For a strong man has his own opinion and is moved by reasons of his own, and similarly a weak person has his own opinion. Hence, he says a little farther down: "Let every man abound in his own sense" (Rom. 14:5); in other words: leave him in peace and let him be content with his own motives or, to put the matter more plainly, let him stay firmly put in what his conscience directs him to do.

But this does not mean that nowadays we should tolerate these superstitious practices of religion or rather this show of piety[12] on the assumption that they are due to a weakness of faith, for, as a matter of fact, people perpetuate them from crass ignorance. They do not know that they themselves must first be changed, and not their works.

Yet the apostle admonishes the Galatians that "they should not

---

8 *Proslambanesthe.* Cf. Erasmus, *Annot.*
9 I.e., the Vulgate.
10 "*In diiudicationibus.*"
11 Erasmus explains the word *dialogismōn* (which occurs also in Rom. 1:21) as follows: "*Non simplex cogitatio, sed cogitatio ratiocinantis et expendentis et diiudicantis*" ("not thought as such, but the thought of one who reasons, weighs, and makes distinctions").
12 "*Superstitiosas istas pietates, immo species pietatis.*"

make this liberty an occasion to the flesh" (Gal. 5:13), as they do now in Rome where they no longer care about rules; for these are all swallowed up by dispensations. In the use of this kind of liberty they are masters. Completely disregarding the other commandments of the apostle, they use this liberty as "an occasion to the flesh" (Gal. 5:13) and as "a cloak for malice" (I Peter 2:16). They say that they are not bound by any rules, and this it true. But oh, how many would enter the monastic life or other spiritual professions today if they knew about this liberty? Indeed, how many would only too gladly give up their ceremonies, prayers, and rules if only the pope would annul them as he has the power to do! This is an indication of the fact that nowadays practically all fulfill their vocations[13] reluctantly and without love. If there are some who fulfill their responsiblity, they do so from fear, so that they put their trust in the miserable cross of their conscience that forces them to do their duty.

But perhaps God wants us today to be so bound to the various orders, and rules, and statutes that he may at least compel us to come in (Luke 14:23).

But if the liberty of which the apostle speaks should again be granted to us, that is to say, if fasts, prayers, compliance with ordinances, church services, etc., would be left to everyone's free decision and conscience so that he could do as much as the love of God would impel him to do, I believe that then all churches would be closed and all altars deserted within one year. And yet, if everything were as it should be, we should be engaged in all this as though we wanted to serve God freely and gladly and not from fear of conscience or punishment, nor in expectation of pay and honor.

For example, if the mandate were issued that, unless he wanted to, no priest would need to be without a wife, or wear a tonsure, or be dressed in a special habit, or be obliged to say the canonical hours, how many would there be, I ask you, who would choose the way of life they now observe? What would they do if, as the saying goes, they would let their conscience decide?[14] And yet it is precisely this that ought to be done: it should be left to everyone's free decision that he do as much or as little as his responsibility to God would allow him to do.

You will say: Who, then, would not want to be a priest? And I answer: By speaking as you do, you show plainly that you want liberty as an occasion to the flesh. You are in servitude against your will and you do not deserve any reward before God!

---

13 *"Agunt in suis vocationibus"* (!).
14 *"Nonne sicut dicitur: Wens bis auf die conscientz kumpt?"*

I fear that we shall all perish shortly. For who obeys this rule? And what about the people? What would they give if they were free to give what they would want to give? They are equally as foolish as anyone, for they prefer to make their contributions to hired servants, who must be compelled to do what they do, rather than to brothers who are free.

Therefore examine yourself closely when you say your prayers, when you make your sacrifice, when you enter the choir or when you do whatever else you have to do, whether you would do the same also if you had a free choice about it—and you will find out who you are before God. If you would not, if you would rather be free and untonsured, then what you are doing now is worth nothing, because you are only a slave and a hireling. (John 10:12 f.) However, I know of some who, inasmuch as they are aware of this, sit down in some corner and say to themselves: I shall arouse in me a "good intention" and a will if this is what is required. Meanwhile the devil standing behind him laughs in his sleeve and says: Primp yourself, little kitten, here comes company![15] Then he gets up, goes into the choir to pray, and says: O little owl, how beautiful you are! Where did you get the peacock feathers?[16] If I did not know (to use the language of the fable)[17] that you are an ass, I should think you were a lion—that is how you roar; but go on, wear your lion's skin: your long ears will betray you! Thereupon he gets bored and counts the pages and verses of his prayer book, wondering whether the prayer is almost over, and consoling[18] himself he says: Scotus[19] proved that a "virtual intention" is enough and that an actual intention is not required. Then the devil says to him: Fine! You are right! Now you can feel secure!

O God, what a laughingstock we are to our enemies! A good intention is not so easy as that! And (good God!) it is not in your power, O man, to arouse it in yourself as Scotus and the Scotists teach to our very great detriment. It is utterly pernicious for us to

---

[15] Luther uses a German proverb: "*Schmug dich, libs Ketzle, wir werden gesste haben*" ("*Schmück' dich, liebes Kätzchen, wir werden Gäste haben*").
[16] Here too, Luther uses a proverb (in this case derived from the well-known fable of the raven [or owl] and the fox). He has the devil (who is playing the monk) say, "*Sih, aulichen, wie schon bistu, hastu nu pfawenfedern?*" ("*Sieh, kleine Eule, wie schön du bist! Hast du nun Pfauenfedern?*").
    Ficker (p. 500, n. 23) suggests that Luther was perhaps thinking of a decorative design that the German printers of his time were using on the title pages of some of their books. It shows an owl that is being pecked by other birds. The design often carried the description: "All birds hate me" ("*Mich hassen alle Vögel*").
[17] Cf. Aesop, *Fab.* 141.
[18] "*Sibique consolator factus dicit.*"
[19] Cf. Duns Scotus, IV *Sent.*, d. 6, q. 6, n. 2.

presume that we can form "good intentions" from ourselves as if
we were capable of putting anything together in our minds by our
own power. This would be in contradiction to the clearly expressed judgment of the apostle. Hence, relying on our free will,
we feel secure and doze, for we think that it is in our power to
awaken in us a pious intention whenever we want to. Why, then,
does the apostle pray: "And the Lord direct your hearts and
bodies"[20] (II Thess. 3:5)? And why does the church pray: "May
our words always be spoken and our thoughts and works always
be directed to the end that thy righteousness be done"?[21] But
their thoughts are the snares of the unrighteous about which it is
written in Ps. 5:9: "Their heart is a snare,"[22] and in Prov. 11:6:
"The unrighteous shall be caught in their own snares."

No, you godless fellows, no! This is not the way![23] What you
must do it this: Go into your chamber and fall on your knees and
pray to God with all your strength that he give you the intention
that you so presumptuously tried to arouse in yourself. You cannot live by the security that you conceived from and in yourself
but only by that which in his mercy he gives to you in answer to
your expectant prayer.

The whole error with which we are here concerned is this: we
fail to take into consideration that, in order to be acceptable in
God's sight, we must do all this, not under the pressure of necessity
or because we are disturbed and agitated by fear, but so that it
may please God we must do it because we are animated by a joyful
and utterly free willingness. For he that does this in such a manner
that, if it were possible, he would not want to do it, in reality does
nothing, all things being equal: Yet he does do it and he thinks
that he did enough by having done it, and his conscience is clear.
But if he failed to do it, he has a bad conscience.

This fault can everywhere be found also among the monks.
They feel secure and are free from all compunction in what they
are doing, even if they do it without gladness but under compulsion or from necessity, fear, or sheer habit. But if they neglected to
do something they were supposed to do, they go to confession and
do penance. The only difference between these two attitudes is
this, that in the first case they cover up their wickedness by outward activity and do not recognize the weakness of their will that
underlies this activism. But in the other case, they do indeed rec-

---

[20] In the Pauline letter, the words "and bodies" are lacking. Luther quotes
from the Breviary, where the addition is used. (Cf. Ficker, p. 501, n. 10.)
[21] This too is a quotation from the Breviary.
[22] Quoted according to Col. Hebraeus of Faber's Quincuplex Psalterium.
[23] "Non sic, Impii, non sic!"

ognize their fault; only they repent more of what they failed to do than of the lukewarmness of their will.

In everything we do, therefore, we should not apply our mind to what we did or still must do, or to what we did not do or should not do, or to what good we did or did not accomplish, or to what evil we did or did not do, but we should be concerned about the quality and strength of the will and the depth and breadth of the joy in our heart that motivated everything we did and must inspire all we still have to do.

In this sense, the apostle says in the last chapter of First Corinthians that he had much entreated Apollos, though he could have compelled him. And yet he says: "I much entreated him to come to you, and indeed it was not his will." (I Cor. 16:12.) In the same way, he beseeches Philemon on behalf of his slave, though he could have given him orders, so "that your good," he says, "might nòt be of necessity but voluntarily" (Philemon 14).

But nowadays the children who are princes and the effeminate that rule the church[24] know nothing better to do than to coerce their subjects with severity and force, whereas they should prudently proceed in such a way that they would first make an effort to win their voluntary compliance, and only if they then refused, they would use means to shame and frighten them.

Now the substance of this whole error is the Pelagian belief. For although there are now none that profess Pelagianism and call themselves Pelagians, there are very many who in fact and in what they believe are Pelagians even if they are not aware of it. For example, there are those who think that unless one attributes to the freedom of decision,[25] before grace, "the power to do what is in him," one sins, in case he sins, because God forces him to sin so that he, therefore, sins necessarily. Even though it is altogther impious to think so, they are so sure of themselves and so bold as to reckon that if they form a good intention, they will infallibly obtain God's infused grace. Thereupon they go about with the feeling of great security and, of course, they are certain that the good works they do are acceptable to God. They do not feel that they need to implore grace, because they are no longer fearful or anxious. They are also free from any fear that by being of this mind they are perhaps in the wrong, but they are certain that they are right in what they are doing (Isa., ch. 44).[26]

---

[24] Cf. Isa. 3:4: "And I will give children to be their princes, and the effeminate shall rule over them." Albrecht von Brandenburg became archbishop of Magdeburg when he was twenty-three years old; a year later (1514), he became archbishop of Mainz and an elector of the empire.

[25] "Libertas arbitrii."

[26] Luther is thinking here of Isa. 44:20 (which he cites later on): "He will not say: Perhaps there is a lie in my right hand."

Why? Because they do not understand that God lets the ungodly sin even when they do good works. Certainly, they are then not forced to commit a sin, but they are doing only what they want to do according to their good intention. If they did understand this, they would be filled with the same fear that was in Job and they would say with him: "I feared all my works" (Job 9:28); and another again says: "Blessed is the man that is always fearful" (Prov. 28:14). Hence they that really do good works do not a single one of them without asking themselves: Does God's grace really act here together with me? How can I be certain that my good intention is from God? How can I know that what I am doing is really my doing or that what is in me is acceptable to God? These here know that man cannot do anything from himself.

Hence, it is utterly absurd and it means strongly to support the Pelagian error to hold the view that is expressed in the well-known statement: "God infallibly infuses grace in one who does what is in him"[27] if the phrase "to do what is in him" is to be understood to mean "to do or to be able to do anything." Hence, it is not to be wondered at that almost the whole church is undermined, namely, by the trust one puts into that which this one sentence expresses. Meanwhile, everyone goes ahead and sins, because at any time he can freely decide to do what is in him and therefore also obtain grace. Therefore, they go about without fear because they think that at the proper time they will do what is in them and obtain grace. It is with respect to them that it is said in Isa. 44:20: "Nor will they say: Perhaps there is a lie in my right hand," and in Prov. 14:16: "A wise man fears and declines from evil; the fool leaps over and is confident," i.e., he does not fear that "perhaps there is a lie in his right hand" and he is not afraid that his good is perhaps evil, but he is confident and feels secure.

This is why also the apostle Peter commands: "Fear God" (I Peter 2:17) and why Paul says: "Knowing therefore the fear of God, we use persuasion to men" (II Cor. 5:11) and again: "With fear and trembling work out your salvation" (Phil. 2:12). And the psalmist says: "Serve the Lord with fear, and rejoice unto him with trembling" (Ps. 2:11). How can one fear God or one's works if one does not regard them as bad and if one does not mistrust them? Fear comes from evil. Hence, the saints are full of anxious

---

[27] *"Facienti, quod in se est, infallibiliter Deus infundit gratiam."* Cf. Thomas Aquinas, *Summa Theol.,* II, 1; q. 112; a. 3: *"Videtur quod ex necessitate detur gratia . . . facienti quod in se est . . . homo infallibiliter gratiam consequitur";* Gabriel Biel, *Expositio canonis missae,* lect. 59P (Ficker, p. 503, n. 2); *Haec facienti Deus gratiam suam tribuit necessario* (quoted from Alexander of Hales, II *Sent., d.* 22, *q.* 2, *a.* 3, *dub.* 1).

desire for God's grace; they know that they must constantly implore it. They do not rely on their good intention or on the diligence with which they endeavor to do what is right, but they are in constant fear that their works may still be evil. Humbled by this fear they ask and sigh for grace and by this humility they win God's favor.

Worst of all, therefore, nowadays is that kind of preacher who preaches about the signs of present grace in order to make people secure, when as a matter of fact it is fear and trembling that is the surest sign of grace while, conversely, it is the most evident sign of God's wrath if one is secure and self-confident. And yet everyone yearns for just this with an amazing eagerness!

So then, it is only through fear that grace can found, and it is grace that enables man voluntarily to do good works; and if he lacks it, he is unwilling to do them. Yet it is this cheerless unwillingness (if I may say so) that makes him unafraid, hard, and secure, for, even though he lacks grace and therefore the ability freely to do the good, he is able outwardly to do what, in his own eyes and before men, appears to be good.

I know and am confident *in the Lord Jesus that nothing is unclean in itself.* (Rom. 14:14.)

This phrase "I am confident" must here not be understood in the sense of "hoping" but in the absolute sense, i.e., in the sense of "being secure and certain," yes, of "being bold" or "daring." In this sense, the apostle himself said above (Rom. 10:20): "But Isaiah is bold and says," i.e., he speaks confidently and boldly. Persons who are a little high-spirited are called in Latin *"confidentes"* ("confident") as, for instance, in Plautus;[28] in German we call them *"keck."* (Then too, the apostle says in II Tim. 1:12: "I know the truth in which I have believed and I am certain," i.e., I am not deceived.) By the words "I know and am confident," the apostle therefore means to say, as we would put it in German: *"Ich weys und byn keck, darffs kecklich sagen."*[29] Otherwise, i.e., if he wished that "to be confident" should be understood in terms of "to hope," he should have said: I have confidence in the Lord Jesus.[30] But what he does say is: "I am confident in the Lord Jesus,"[31] i.e., because of the fact that I am in Christ, I feel bold.

He uses this form of expression suggesting boldness on account

---

[28] Plautus, *Amphitr.,* I, 1, 1: *"Qui me alter est audacior homo, aut qui confidentior?"* ("What other man is more daring and more confident than I?").
[29] *"Ich weiss und bin keck; ich darf es kecklich* (= *kühnlich*) *sagen."*
[30] *"Confido in dominum Jesum"* (= accusative)
[31] *"... in domino Jesu"* (ablative).

of the anxiety of some who were timid and diffident with respect to the affirmation he makes here and then also because of the false apostles who taught the opposite.

I know and am confident in the Lord Jesus that nothing is common *of itself; but to him that esteems anything to be common, to him it is common.* (Rom. 14:14.)

"Common" is the same as "unclean." But according to the Hebrew way of speaking, this word is also the opposite of that which signifies something "holy," "separated," "set apart." In this sense, it says in Ps. 4:3: "The Lord has made his holy one wonderful." Some translate this as follows (according to Reuchlin's explanation of its proper meaning):[32] "God has set him apart to whom he gave his mercy and his grace and whom he sanctified." In this same sense, also, the apostle says in Rom. 1:1 that he was "separated unto the gospel of God," i.e., that he was sanctified away from a common occupation to the service of the gospel. For the same reason, it is figuratively said in the law: "Sanctify unto me every first-born" (Ex. 13:2), and again: "I have separated you from other people" (Lev. 20:24). The same expression is used there frequently. So then, what is not thus separated is called in Hebrew "common" or "mean." Hence, it was in connection with further use that the word "separated" came to mean "clean," "holy," "pure," and "mean," by contrast, "unclean," "profane," "impure." In this sense, it is written in Acts 10:15 and 11:9: "That which God has cleansed, do not call common." If "common" and "unclean" did not mean the same thing, the passage should read: That which God has cleansed, do not call unclean.

None lives to himself. (Rom. 14:7.)
The apostle argues from a major premise. For if we do not live to ourselves or belong to ourselves, and this is what is greater, how much less do we eat or drink to ourselves, or do or suffer anything to ourselves; but everything is the Lord's. Hence, he says in I Cor. 6:19: "Or know you not that your bodies are the temple of the Holy Spirit and that you are not your own?" And again: "Glorify God in your body and your spirit, which are God's" (I Cor. 6:20); and in Gal. 2:20: "And I live, now not I, but Christ lives in me."

Let every man abound in his own sense. (Rom. 14:5.)
The holy fathers and teachers wrongly use this saying here and there in support of the general opinion according to which every-

[32] Cf. Reuchlin, *Lex. Heb.* Cf. Ficker, p. 505, n. 2.

one must abound in his own sense as he tries to understand the Scripture.[33]

But the apostle means to say here something special: Every man should be content in his own thinking, or, as we commonly say, in his own feeling, and he should not judge another in his thinking and feeling, nor should the other despise him in return, lest perhaps someone who is weak in faith but has an understanding, feeling, or conscience of his own might be disturbed and scandalized by someone else's understanding and proceed to act counter to his own understanding and thus by changing his way of thought and action get into a conflict with himself. For although on account of his weakness he cannot judge otherwise than that this or that is not permitted, he nevertheless does now what the strong are doing in order that they should not despise him; yet according to his own judgment, he should not do it. The apostle deals with this in I Cor. 8:4, 7: "But as for meats that are sacrificed to idols, we know that an idol is nothing in the world. . . . But there is not knowledge in everyone. For some until this present, with conscience of the idol: eat as a thing sacrificed to an idol; and their conscience, being weak" (i.e., being unable to judge in any other way than that this is forbidden), "is defiled," because they eat against their own judgment.

The cause of this defilement is the pride of the strong: under the very eyes of the weak they eat the meats sacrificed to an idol, and in doing so they look upon them with contempt; instead, they should bear with them and instruct them or, in case they cannot take instruction on account of their weakness, they should become weak with them for love's sake and, like them, abstain from eating, meanwhile keeping their faith inwardly in their conscience.

For although one is free to do anything, he must not make a display of his freedom, and this for the sake of the salvation of his brother. It is better for him to be outwardly deprived of his freedom than that the weak brother should perish. For if one despises him because he has a weak conscience, this cannot mean anything else than that one tries to force him by this contempt to do what his judgment tells him he should not do. Because of the diversity of consciences, therefore, it can happen that one man sins and another does the right thing in one and the same action which, as such, is allowed.[34] In this sense the apostle says: "Let every man abound in his own conscience," i.e., let him be certain, quiet, and firm; the strong should not change his faith because of the

[33] Ficker says (p. 505, n. 22) that such an interpretation of this passage cannot be found in the exegetical writings of the fathers or the Scholastics.
[34] "Opere licito."

scruples of one who is weak; nor should the one who is weak act against his own judgment for the sake of the strong; he should let them do what they want and satisfy his own conscience.

I know and am confident in the Lord Jesus that **nothing is common of itself,** *but to him that esteems anything to be common, to him it is common. For if because of your meat your brother be grieved, you do not walk according to love. Destroy not with your meat him for whom Christ died. Let not, then, your good be blasphemed. For the Kingdom of God is not meat or drink, but righteousness and peace and joy in the Holy Spirit. For he that in this serves Christ pleases God and is approved of men. Therefore, let us follow after the things that are of peace, and keep the things that are of edification one toward another. Destroy not the work of God for meat. All things indeed are clean, but it is evil for that man who eats with offense. It is good not to eat flesh and not to drink wine, nor anything by which your brother is offended, or scandalized, or made weak. Have you faith? Have it to yourself before God. Blessed is he that condemns not himself in that which he allows. But he that discerns, if he eat, is condemned, because not of faith. For all that is not of faith is sin.* (Rom. 14:14–23.)

Nothing is common by itself. (Rom. 14:14.) We can relate "by itself," so it seems, either to "the Lord Jesus" or to "common." In other words, nothing is common by Jesus Christ or nothing is common by itself or according to its nature and inner substance, but only in someone's opinion and conscience. And this is more in accord with the following sentence which reads **but to him that esteems anything common, to him it is common.** For even if one were to understand the sentence to say that nothing is common by Christ, one would have to imply the thought that only to him that esteems it so is it common by Christ. Hence, the translator[35] should have avoided the ambiguity of the Greek text and should have said "as such" instead of "by itself," as Erasmus does.

So then, let us sum up this chapter. It contains two injunctions:
First: the strong must not despise the weak.
Second: they must not give offense to them.

Either one of these attitudes is contrary to love. For love bears the weak because it does not seek its own but the needs of the weak. The apostle exemplifies this in himself by saying: "My daily solicitude for all the churches: Who is weak, and I am not weak? Who is scandalized, and I am not on fire?" (II Cor. 11:28–29) and: "To the weak I became weak. I became all things to all men that

[35] I.e., the Vulgate.

I might gain all" (I Cor. 9:22). Now the passage before us clearly shows that he could be thus on fire (and he certainly did not let himself be scandalized together with the scandalized), for he speaks here in passionate words against those who do despise and scandalize the weak.

This is how he impresses the first part on their minds: I. He says: **God has taken him to him.** (Rom. 14:3.) With this very weighty word he checks them. They now have to face up to this, that he that despises or judges someone else despises and judges not merely a man but God. By administering such a strong shock to them, he wants to urge them on to practice humility and mutual forbearance.

II. **Who are you that judge another man's servant?** (Rom. 14:4.) It is against the law of nature and the ways of mankind[36] to judge another man's servant. Hence, their behavior is not only a defiance of God but it is also contrary to all human judgment and feeling.

And now he proceeds to demolish also their motives:

(1) that the one who is weak thinks that the one who is strong is falling, and that the strong one thinks that it is the weak one who has fallen. To this he replies: In what way does this concern you? **To his own lord he falls,** or if he stands, **he stands to his own lord** (Rom. 14:4). You are therefore not free to judge and despise another, even though what you think is true, because you are not allowed to spurn him.

(2) That they think: Who knows whether he will stand? To this he replies: **God is able to make him stand.** (Rom. 14:4.)

(3) All we do, are, and live for, we do, live, and are to God; therefore we must not despise one another. **For none of us,** he says, **lives to himself.** (Rom. 14:7.)

(4) **To this end Christ died and rose again that he might be the Lord of all.** (Rom. 14:3.) Hence, it is against Christ to claim the right to judge and to despise others.

(5) He faces them with **the judgment seat of Christ** (Rom. 14:10). For there we must all be judged. Notice, then, with what thunderbolts he frightens us away from despising one another and especially the weak! He points to God, man, Christ's Passion and Kingship, and to the Last Judgment—there is not anything that he does not bring to bear on his argument.

With similar sharpness he makes the second part convincing:

I. **For if because of your meat, your brother be grieved, you do not walk now according to love.** (Rom. 14:15.)

(1) Note here how he expresses the climax and how he makes his emphasis in the individual words. He says, "because of your

36 *"Contra ius naturae et omnes homines est."*

meat," that is, for so trivial a matter, you despise the eternal salvation of your brother. It would be less bad if you did so on account of money or honor or at least for the sake of your life and
the well-being of your body or for the sake of anything else that
is more desirable than food which is only for your present use and
enjoyment. These words, then, are a sharp rebuke: he that despises
his brother because of what he eats gets a severe scolding for his
lovelessness.

(2) He is equally emphatic in saying "your brother." He does
not say: "your enemy." Nor does he say at least "friend" or "acquaintance," but "brother," one to whom a Christian owes more
than to anyone else, since he is his brother, almost the same as his
neighbor. Why, then, should he be more concerned about his
belly and his gullet, which are bound to perish, than about his
brother who will live in glory forever?

(3) He is "grieved," disturbed, wounded in his conscience. This
is more than if he were deprived of his money or goods or even if
he were wounded. And this for the sake of meat! Furthermore,
notice that he does not say: if you grieve him, but "if he is
grieved." Thereby he skillfully rejects their excuse in case they
should say: It is not my fault; I have not done anything to him. I
have not grieved him; I am doing only what I have the right to
do. Have I not the right to do what I want with my own things?
This is exactly what the lawyers of today mean by justice as they
interpret or rather, pervert, their laws.

But it is not enough that you live according to your rights and
that you do what you want with your own things, unless, according
to God's commandments you also make provision for your brother.
Indeed, you do not have the right and the power to do what you
want with your own things, for they are no longer only yours when
your brother is offended by them. To be sure, they are yours
temporarily, but, spiritually, they belong to your brother because
he cleaves to them with his scruples of conscience. Hence, you act
according to an alien right, i.e., you commit a wrong, if you act
in such a way that your brother is grieved thereby. Thus also today
everybody is concerned only for what is his and what he is entitled to and not for what he owes to his neighbor and for that
which would be expedient both for him and his neighbor. "All
things are lawful to me," the apostle says, "but they are not all
expedient and they do not all edify." (I Cor. 6:12.)

(4) "You do not walk now according to love," in other words:
you walk in vain even though you move about in great and
wonderful affairs, for as it says in I Cor. 13:1–2: "If I have not
love, I am nothing." There is something terrifying about the fact

that because of a bit of food one can render all his good works useless. And yet, the world is full of fools who pay no heed to love but wear themselves out with many works in order that the saying of the Preacher may be fulfilled: "The labor of fools shall afflict them that know not how to go to the city" (Eccl. 10:15).

II. **Destroy not with your meat him** *for whom Christ died* (Rom. 14:15), in other words: it is comparatively insignificant that you hurt him, offend him, and deny your love to him; what is much more important is that you are also a cruel murderer, because you ruin your brother; indeed, and this is the height of cruelty, you are a fratricide. Furthermore, and this likewise surpasses every kind of cruelty as well as of ingratitude, you despise, in your brother, the death of Christ, for he died certainly also for him. This is what it means to despise your brother and to walk without love! First Corinthians 8:12: "You sin against Christ when you wound their weak conscience," and I Cor. 8:11: "Through your knowledge shall the weak brother perish, for whom Christ has died."

III. **Let not, then, your good be blasphemed.** (Rom. 14:16.) In other words: you sin against the church as well as against yourselves. For your good, i.e., what you are in God and what you have from God, will impress the heathen in such a way that they flee from it rather than desire to obtain it. Thus you will be the cause that many will perish who otherwise might be saved. It is a weighty and serious matter that not only your evil but also your good is blasphemed because of a little bit of food. What the apostle here calls "good" is everything we are through Christ. What he means to say, then, is this: Be careful that the heathen do not berate your faith, your religion, and all your Christianity, for its good reputation should attract them and its actual goodness should edify them—through you. In this sense, he says in II Cor. 6:3: "That our ministry be not blamed." We have sufficiently dealt with this in the twelfth chapter, under the heading: "Providing good things" (Rom. 12:17).

IV. **For the Kingdom of God is not meat and drink.** (Rom. 14:17.) In other words: you believe in vain that the Kingdom of God is yours if, as also frequently happens today, you disturb the peace because of what you eat and if you are so eager to defend meat and drink, as if the Kingdom of God consisted of them. Outward food stirs up disturbances to a greater extent than inward religion makes for peace, and they continue to prevail in times of peace and war. But with respect to God, the Kingdom of God is **righteousness,** which is realized by faith or trust; with respect to the neighbor, it is **peace,** which is realized through mutual love, forbearance, and caring one for another; with respect to oneself, it is **joy in the Holy Spirit,** which is realized through hope and by a hearty trusting in God, and not by what one does on behalf of the neighbor or for God's sake. In relation to yourself be agreeable; in relation to your neighbor be peaceful; but in relation to God be righteous. But nothing disturbs this peace so much as an act by which one offends and scandalizes his brother, especially with respect to things that wound the conscience. The word "peace" must here be understood, therefore, in several meanings:

(1) *"Peace with God,"* according to Rom. 5:1, for example: "Being justified, therefore, by faith, we have peace with God." This peace is broken by sinning.

(2) *"Peace with oneself,"* which one may have through joy in the Holy Spirit and by hope and patience, according to Rom. 12:12, for example: "rejoicing in hope, patient in tribulation." This peace is disturbed by impatience and by an impatient acceptance of tribulations, i.e., by the desire for a carnal and useless peace.

(3) *"Peace with one's neighbor,"* which one may have by satisfying and edifying one another in mutual love. This peace is broken by the contempt of another man's weakness and by the disturbance of conscience, namely, of the conscience of those who have peace with God and, through faith and patience, with themselves, but not with their neighbor, i.e., they do not leave others in peace. The apostle, therefore, wants us not only to be at peace, but he also wants us to make peace by being calm and unassuming in our relations with one another. This is why there follows now this sentence:

For he that in this serves Christ, pleases God (Rom. 14:18) (because of his righteousness) "and pleases men" (because of his peacefulness). Here he puts the joy in the Holy Spirit in the last place. For one must first seek God and then not what concerns one's own self but that which concerns one's neighbor. Hence, we commonly say of people who are restless and disturb others that "they have no peace," because they do not leave others in peace but upset them. In I Thess. 5:12–14, the apostle calls them unquiet; he says: "Have peace with them that are over you." "Rebuke the unquiet, comfort the fainthearted, support the weak, be patient toward all men." And in Acts 15:19, James, speaking in the same vein, says: "I judge that they who from the Gentiles are converted to God are not to be disquieted," namely, by being required to observe the law. And in Gal. 5:12, the apostle says: "I would they were even cut off who trouble you." And in II Thess.

3:6, he goes so far as to say: "Withdraw yourselves from every brother walking disorderly." Hence, this sort of people are "not approved of men" (Rom. 14:18) but, rather, displease them.

And now he says of this peace: **Therefore let us follow after the things that are of peace** (Rom. 14:19), i.e., the things that do not upset others but edify them and make them quiet. And what are these things? The only answer to this question is this: Love teaches us what they are as their own time and place demand. They cannot be specifically detailed.[37]

V. **Destroy not the work of God for meat's sake.** (Rom. 14:20.) The apostle means by "work of God" the brother as, for example, in I Cor. 3:9: "You are God's husbandry, you are God's building" and farther on, in the same letter, ch. 9:1: "Are you not my work in the Lord?" and in Heb. 3:6: "Christ is the Son in his own house, which house we are." And again in I Cor. 3:17: "The temple of God is holy, which you are. But if any man violate the temple of God, him let God destroy." And who else is it who does violate it but the know-it-all moralists.[38] It is with reference to them that the apostle then immediately goes on to say: "Let no man deceive you:[39] if any man among you seems to be wise in this world, let him become a fool that he may be wise" (I Cor. 3:18).

Understand, then, what it means "to destroy the work of God for the sake of meat": not merely to offend God, but also to fight against God and to destroy what he builds up, to be constantly engaged in a war with God (like the legendary giants who fought with the gods).

All that is not of faith is sin. (Rom. 14:23.)
(Cf. Blessed Augustine, *Against Julian*, Book 4, Chapter 3, letter F.)[40]

The apostle speaks here of faith in a very general sense, but in doing so he nevertheless alludes to that particular faith in Christ, apart from which there is no righteousness but only sin. Now faith is faith in God, it is faith in one's neighbor, and it is faith in oneself. By faith in God one is made righteous, because he acknowledges God to be truthful as he believes him and trusts in him.[41] And by faith in the neighbor, he comes to be regarded as

---

[37] *"Charitas haec pro tempore et loco docet. Non enim possunt particulariter tradi."*
[38] *"Sapientes iustitiarii."*
[39] Paul says: deceive "himself."
[40] Cf. Augustine, *Contra Jul.*, IV, 3, 24.
[41] *"Quia Deum verificat, cui credit et confidit."*

faithful, truthful, and trustworthy, because he stands in the same relation to his neighbor as God does to him. Nevertheless, faith in the neighbor is also called an active faith,[42] because it believes the neighbor. What characterizes this faith is this: if one's actions are different from one's faith or if one has doubts about his neighbor, he commits an offense against him, because he does not fulfill what he promised to him. In the same way, he sins also against God if he does not act in accordance with his faith in what he was told. In the same way, he believes also in himself and the dictates of his conscience; but he acts against it when he does not act according to what he believes; then he acts against his faith. Thus "everything that is not from faith, is sin," because it goes counter to faith and conscience. In view of this, one must take great care not to act against his conscience.

Now the question arises whether a godless person sins, when he does not believe, because he does not act from faith and therefore also not against his conscience or, rather, because he believes falsely. When he does something wrong from this false faith of his, does he then not sin?

Our answer is as follows: The word "Everything that does not come from faith is sin" means that everyone who does not want to sin must believe. For only faith is without sin. Therefore, he that does something he does not believe sins. For example, he that eats what he thinks is unclean sins, not so much because he sins against his conviction as because he lacks the faith by which he would know that it is not unclean. The fact that the faith he has is weak, and that he lacks a strong faith, causes him to sin if he eats. He that has no faith must, therefore, not eat, i.e., he must not do a work of faith. For an act of faith must proceed from faith. Otherwise, he will commit a sin when he eats, because he does not believe that it is allowed but thinks that it is forbidden (this is his lack of faith) and that he acts against his conscience. An additional inference from this would be the statement that everyone who lacks faith sins even when he does something good. This is what this saying means.

But if you object and say: If this means that a weak person sins not so much because he acts against his conscience as because he does not act from faith, then he sins whether or not he eats, because the deficiency of faith will always be there, I answer as follows: So it is indeed; he is always in sin, i.e., in lack of faith.

---

[42] The phrase is parallel to the term *iustitia activa* (active righteousness = the righteousness of good works), which is in contrast to *iustitia passiva* (passive righteousness = the righteousness of faith). The latter "receives" from without; the former actively goes out from within.

But, nevertheless, one must not stimulate him further so that he commits a still greater sin. For the weakness of his faith is a venial sin, because God does not reckon it to him as a mortal sin, although it is a mortal sin by its nature. For God has taken him up in order to render him perfect and whole just as the good Samaritan did with the man who was left half-dead (Luke 10:33 ff.). Therefore one must not stimulate him to act according to this weakness of faith, but he must be cared for and nourished in order that he may grow in the knowledge of our Lord Jesus Christ, according to what Saint Peter says in concluding his second letter: "Grow in grace and in the knowledge of our Lord Jesus Christ" (II Peter 3:18).

This corresponds exactly to the situation of one who is baptized or is doing penance and yet remains in the weakness of concupiscence. Though his weakness violates the law "You shall not covet" and certainly is a mortal sin, God in his mercy does not reckon it as such because of the fact that he has begun to heal the sinner. He is, therefore, in sin, but he must not be given the occasion to act in accordance with his weakness, but instead he must be cared for and made whole. Otherwise, he would certainly sin in all his actions, because he would not act out of chastity and his weakness would become a mortal sin because he manifested it in action, even though by the grace of God this weakness is only a venial sin. Just so also the man of a weak faith, whom we spoke of before, would obey his weakness if he did something that would not be of faith.

In this passage, the word "faith" must therefore be understood in two ways: One way would be to take it to mean belief and conscience. This is how many interpret this passage. Another way would be, after the fashion of the apostle, simply to regard it as identical with faith in Christ.[43] And, with due respect for these other interpreters, I thus understand this passage. For just as one can act against his conscience in faith, one can also do so in every other virtue. One who is not sufficiently continent acts against his conscience if he fornicates, for it dictates to him to be chaste and not to fornicate. And yet because he is weak, he can be made to stumble and as he acts against the dictate of his conscience, he falls. Just so he that is weak in faith does and does not believe. He does the right because he believes, and he sins because he does not believe. As soon as he is inveigled not to believe, he sins.

[43] *Gl. ord.* and Lyra.

ROMANS, CHAPTER FIFTEEN

Now we that are stronger ought to bear the infirmities of the
weak and not to please ourselves. (Rom. 15:1.)
Thus love bears all and "all things," and thus Moses and the
prophets bore the people of Israel. This "bearing" means making
one's own the sins of all men and to suffer with them. It is love
that does this, and it speaks in this manner: "Who is weak, and I
am not weak? Who is scandalized, and I am not on fire?" (II Cor.
11:29). In the same spirit, he exhorts in Gal. 6:2: "Bear one another's burdens and thus fulfill the law of Christ." And in the
same passage, he says: "Brethren, if any man be overtaken by any
fault, you who are spiritual instruct such a one in the spirit of
meekness, considering yourself, lest you also be tempted." (Gal.
6:1.) And in I Cor. 10:12: "He that stands, let him take heed, lest
he fall," and "If any man think himself to be something, whereas
he is nothing, he deceives himself" (Gal. 6:3). And Phil. 2:5–7:
"Let this mind be in you which was also in Christ Jesus who, being
in the form of God, thought it not robbery to be equal with God,
but emptied himself, taking the form of a servant."
Just so it is also with the natural body: the bones support the
flesh and the weak members are not rejected by the strong ones
but get more care than the strong ones. And the comely parts
cover the uncomely ones, as it says in I Cor. 12:22–23: "Those
which seem to be the more feeble members of the body are more
necessary. And such as we think the less honorable members of
the body, about these we put more abundant honor; and those
which are our uncomely parts have more abundant comeliness."
Consider then, first, the individual social orders. God has not
forsaken any of them to such an extent that he has not ordained
some good and worthy people in them in order that they might

cover also the others with respectability. Thus one spares bad women for the sake of the good ones; and good priests cover the bad ones; and unworthy monks receive honor for the sake of the worthy ones.

But here senseless people rise in opposition against a whole order, as if they were clean and had no dirt on themselves, whereas before and behind and inwardly as well they are nothing but a meeting place and workshop of sows and pigs. Hence, no woman, no priest, no monk is exempt from their criticism! Here the following word of the apostle applies: "Why are you so pleased with yourself, you fool, that you think yourself to be something, whereas you are nothing?" (Gal. 6:3).

On the other hand, it is a fact that those who see that their honorableness serves as a cover for those who lack it try to avoid their fellow men to whom they lend respectability. They are the greatest fools of all, because they believe that they are what they are by their own power and they do not know that they are what they are for the sake of others. Hence, they loathe them and do not want to be in their company. Heretics act in this way and so do many others who are filled with pride. They would not behave in this manner if they were not self-satisfied.

It is as if a woman would not want to be with other women unless they were all clean. The apostle says to her: Listen to me, sister![1] Are you one that stands? Yes, but take heed, lest you fall. For no woman stands so that she cannot fall. And none lies down so that she cannot get up. Why? "God has power to make her stand." (Rom. 14:4.) He also has power to forsake her. Many have fallen who stood very firmly indeed; they stood more firmly than the towers of Babylon. And many have risen again who had fallen greatly. Those there fell because they were pleased with themselves, and these here rose because they were displeased with themselves.

We can say the same of the priests. If a priest does not want to be a priest because he cannot work together with bad colleagues, he is told: Domine John, you stand, and you are pleased with yourself, but take heed lest you fall and find yourself more displeased with yourself than with those other fellows who now displease you.

So it is also with those monks who go to pieces because they detest having to serve unprofitable fellows and to associate with them, for they yearn for nothing so much as to be governors, friends, and companions only of worthy, perfect, and sensible monks. Hence, they run from one place to another, but in vain,

---

[1] "Hoer, susterlein, hoer!" ("Höre, Schwesterlein, höre!")

for the order of things has been ordained to be this: *Every one of us must be willing to bear the shame of his fellows.*[2] (This applies, for example, to the burghers who must do this on behalf of the councilmen in this affair.)[3] It is hard to bear another's shame and to have a share in it, even though one is innocent, but, nevertheless, it is a very fine and meritorious thing to do. It will be easy to do if one deliberates upon the fact that though it was hard also for Christ to bear our shame, he bore it willingly.

"None, therefore, lives to himself alone." (Rom. 14:7.)

But the greatest of all fools are those who forget, as I said before, that they themselves are steeped in filth but inveigh against priests, monks, and women, and make all of them bear the brunt of the wrong that one of them has done. One must say to them: Did you never wet your mother's lap and make a stench? Or are you now clean all over? Is there no dirty or soiled spot on your entire body? If you are so clean, it is a wonder that a long time ago the apothecaries did not buy you instead of the balsam shrub, inasmuch as your whole person is nothing but sweet-smelling balsam. If your mother had treated you like this, you would have perished in your own filth.

This is why God gave Daniel and his friends to the people of Israel in the Babylonish captivity (Dan. 1:6 ff.) and this is why he brought Esther and Mordecai before Ahasuerus (Esth. 2:7 ff.).

So then, the word "to please oneself"[4] here means to be displeased with himself in everything. For it cannot be that others can please one at the same time that he is pleased with himself. People who try this do not want to bear the burden of another (Gal. 6:2) but they desire to share in his privileges. Indeed, they want to be borne by all, but they themselves do not want to bear anyone. Their one occupation is to revile, judge, defame, accuse, and despise others. They have no compassion on others, but they are filled with indignation against them. They alone are clean. Isaiah has them in mind when he says: "That say: Depart from me, come not near me, because you are unclean: these shall be smoke in my anger, a fire burning all the day" (Isa. 65:5). Such a fellow was also that Pharisee in the Gospel (Luke 18:10 ff.) who with so much vanity took delight in his own righteousness and could only revile, accuse, and condemn the publicans and all other men. All these people I am speaking of are like him.

---

[2] *"Eyner muss des anderen schanddeckel seyn."* (*"Einer muss des anderen Schanddeckel sein."*) Cf. Ficker, p. 515, n. 25.

[3] This remark, says Ficker (p. 515, n. 26), refers perhaps to a dispute between the bishop of Brandenburg and the city council of Wittenberg.

[4] *Hoc ... "placere sibi" est displicere sibi in omnibus.*

Blessed Augustine says about this same Pharisee in his exposition of Psalm 71:[5] "Ah, you are glad that you are good and that he is evil." But how does he go on? 'Unjust, extortioners, adulterers, as also is this publican.' This is no longer joy but scorn!" It is characteristic of these people that they are scornful in this way. They do not rejoice in their own righteousness so much as in the fact that others are unrighteous. If others were as righteous as they are, they would not rejoice at all. In fact this would greatly displease them.

Let every one of us please his neighbor unto good, to edification. (Rom. 15:2.)

"In this way," Blessed Gregory writes,[6] "love reaches out for the neighbor so that it can be love. One certainly cannot say that anyone has this kind of love for himself." And I stated in the Gloss[7] that love is not self-love but love of the neighbor. This is also what the apostle taught immediately upon his rejection of self-complacency; he affirmed that one must please one's neighbor. So then: "to please one's neighbor" does not mean "to please oneself."

But this statement of Gregory's and our own appear to be in conflict with a certain well-known definition of the different ways of loving and their order. For, referring to Blessed Augustine, the Master of the Sentences also adduces the following definition: "We must love first God, then our own soul, after that the soul of our neighbor, and finally our body."[7a] Ordered love, therefore, begins with itself.[8]

In answer to this we say: As long as we persist in not properly understanding the nature of love, we fail to realize it.[9] For as long as we are the first to lay claim to any good we are in no way concerned for our neighbor.

But true love of yourself is hatred of yourself. As our Lord says: "He that loves his soul shall lose it, and he that hates his soul shall find it" (John 12:25; Mark 8:35; Matt. 10:39; 16:35; Luke

---

[5] Augustine, *Enarr. in Ps.* 70, 4.

[6] Gregory, *Hom. in Ev.*, I, 17, 1.

[7] "*Charitas est amor non in seipsum, sed in alterum.*" In the interlinear gloss, Luther uses this same definition (*WA* 56, 136, 8).

[7a] Cf. Augustine, *De doctr. Christ.*, I, 23, 22; cf. *De civ. Dei*, XIX. 14; Peter Lombard, *Coll. in ep. Pauli (ad I Tim.,* 1, 1–5), PL 192, 329.

[8] "*Ergo charitas ordinata incipit a seipsa*" (cf. Lyra's statement in connection with his exposition of Rom. 5:12: "*Quia secundum ordinem charitatis magis debet diligere propriam salutem quam alterius*").

[9] "*Respondetur, quod hoc ipsum est unum illorum, quibus abducti sumus a charitate, dum male intelleximus.*"

9:24). And the apostle says in Phil. 2:4: "Each one not considering the things that are his own, but those that are other men's" and in I Cor. 13:5: "Love does not seek its own."

He, therefore, that hates himself and loves his neighbor loves himself truly. For then he loves himself outside himself and thus he has a pure love for himself as long as he loves himself in his neighbor.

Hence, with due respect for the judgment of others and with reverence for the fathers, I must state what is on my mind, and speaking like a fool, I say: It does not seem to me to be a solid understanding of the commandment "You shall love your neighbor," if one interprets it in terms of the notion that in view of the fact that the commandment itself says "as yourself," the one who loves is the model[10] according to which he loves his neighbor. For one derives the following conclusion from this: You must love yourself first and according to the pattern[11] of this self-love of yours you must also love your neighbor.[12] In support of this interpretation, one then quotes the following saying of the Man of Wisdom: "Have pity on your soul, pleasing God" (Ecclus. 30:21), and, of course, one puts the emphasis on the pronoun "your" as if he meant to say: Have pity first on your own soul and then on your neighbor's. I do not want to reject this interpretation entirely, but I believe that the emphasis is on the noun "soul." The meaning of the saying then would be: If you wish that your spirit shall be saved, do not spare your body. Be hardhearted toward the old man in you and thus you will be merciful toward the new man in you. For "better is the iniquity of a man than a woman doing a good turn" (Ecclus. 42:14), i.e., it is more salutary if the spirit inflicts evil and injury on the flesh than if the flesh pampers and caresses the spirit, or if it "does it a good turn" according to its standards of "good." It is better that man, i.e., the spirit, does what seems bad to the flesh than that he lets it do what it regards as good. The "prudence of the flesh" has an amazing sense for its own advantage; it is "more cunning than any beasts of the earth" (Gen. 3:1). The will of a superior, even if it causes loss, is better than that of a disobedient underling, even if it brings advantage.

I believe, therefore, that by this commandment "as yourself" man is not commanded to love himself but he is shown the wicked love with which in fact he loves himself; in other words, it says to

---

[10] *"Forma."*
[11] *"Exemplar."*
[12] Lyra writes in connection with his exposition of Lev. 19:18: *"Dilectio: qua diligitur . . . proximus sicut ipsemet diligens."*

him: You are wholly bent in on yourself and versed in self-love,[13] and you will not be straightened out and made upright unless you cease entirely to love yourself and, forgetting yourself, love only your neighbor. The evidence that we are crooked is[14] that we want to be loved by all and that we seek our own in everything. But what it means to be upright[15] consists in this, that if you do to everyone else what according to this crooked way of yours you want done to yourself, you do good as eagerly as you used to do evil.[16] This does not mean that we are commanded to do evil; not at all, but we are commanded to have the same eagerness for the love of others as for self-love. In the same way, Adam is "the figure of him who is to come" (Rom. 5:14), i.e., of Christ, the Second Adam. In the same way in which we are evil in Adam, we must be good in Christ. This is said in order to bring out a comparison but not in order to enjoin imitation. The same is true here: "You shall love your neighbor as yourself" does not mean at all: "You shall love your neighbor as you shall love yourself"; if it did, this would be specifically commanded. As a matter of fact, it is so specifically not commanded that what is commanded (namely, the love of the neighbor) is based on what is prohibited (namely, self-love).

Consequently, you do evil if you love yourself; you will be free from this evil only if you love your neighbor in the same way in which you love yourself, i.e., if you cease to love yourself. If you do this, also this law will cease, for then it will no longer be necessary for you to love your neighbor as yourself, inasmuch as you no longer love yourself. Nor will it be necessary for you to love yourself as the neighbor, inasmuch as by loving your neighbor you already love yourself most truly and all others in turn love you.

Notice also, how carefully the apostle chooses his words. He does not say: We should not please ourselves, but "we should please others."[17] For if they pleased us, it would no longer be necessary for us to bear their infirmities, i.e., that which displeases us in them—just the opposite ought to happen: we should please others. This is what the apostle enjoins also in I Cor. 10:32-33: "Be without offense to the Jews and to the Gentiles and to the

---

[13] "*Curvus es totus in te et versus in tui amorem.*" Cf. Luther's exposition of Rom. 5:4 and Rom. 6:6.

[14] "*Perversitas enim est.*"

[15] "*Rectitudo autem est.*"

[16] Luther writes: "You do evil as eagerly as you did good." But this is undoubtedly an error of writing.

[17] Here is another error of writing. Luther says, "But the others ought to please us" ("*alii debent nobis placere*"). This is obviously a mistake, for Paul writes, "Let every one of you please his neighbor."

church of God as I also in all things please all men." In his homily on the sayings of our Lord,[18] Blessed Augustine deals excellently and fully with the question, for what purpose one should do this, and he answers it, of course, in terms of what the apostle states in the same passage: "not seeking that which is profitable to myself, but to many, that they may be saved" (I Cor. 10:33).

He does not want to say anything against the proverb "You cannot please everybody." For he does please all men, i.e., as far as he can, he acts in such a way that he should deservedly please everybody. This is why he says here: **unto good,** i.e., in the direction of the good; in other words: so that one is moved toward a good with which one can be pleased, not toward the good as such, but **to edification,** i.e., toward a good that edifies, inasmuch as there are also goods that do not edify.

We must also note here that the apostle likes to contrast edification with giving offense, and conversely. He says, for example, above in ch. 14:19 of the letter before us: "Let us follow after the things that are of peace" (namely, so that others will not be offended) "and keep the things that are of edification" (namely, so that they do not give offense). Peace is the opposite of giving offense, and edification, of scandal, and taking care of the weak is the opposite of making them still weaker. In this sense, he spoke of these three above in v. 21: "It is good not to eat anything whereby your brother is offended" (i.e., disquieted; this is in contrast to peace) "or scandalized" (i.e., in contrast to being edified, he falls and is made worse), "or made weak" (in contrast to being cared for).

For Christ did not please himself, but as it is written: **The reproaches of them that reproached thee fall upon me.** (Rom. 15:3.)

We must not understand this only with respect to the reproaches of the Jews, for then it would not belong to the theme that is here being treated. The apostle means to point to Christ as an example, for he has borne all our infirmities, as Isaiah says: "Surely, he has borne our griefs and carried our sins" (Isa. 53:4). This is also what is meant by the word of Phil. 2:5: "Let this mind be in you which was also in Christ Jesus." As we glorify God whenever we do good —"that your good works," our Lord says in Matt. 5:16, "glorify your Father which is in heaven"—so we dishonor God by our evil works and inflict reproach and shame upon him, i.e., we cause him to be reviled, so the apostle says above in ch. 2:23–24 of the letter before us: "By the transgression of the law, you dishonor God, for as it is written: Through you the name of God is blasphemed

18 Cf. Augustine, *Sermo* 54.

among the Gentiles" (Isa. 52:5; Ezek. 36:20). This is also why we pray: "Hallowed be thy name" (Matt. 6:9), i.e., let it be honored and feared as holy.

Someone may perhaps want to understand this word to say that the "reproaches" that have fallen upon him are the penalties we owe for our sins. But this is not right, because it is not our penalties that reproach God but our guilt. Therefore, it is our guilt that has fallen upon him, i.e., he has suffered the penalty for it and done satisfaction for us. Had he wanted to please himself and had he loved himself, he certainly would not have done this. But now he has loved us and has hated himself and emptied himself and given all of himself totally for us.

This is the reason why love enables us not to be displeased with our neighbor but to have patience with him. It does not let us be self-complacent, inasmuch as it is patient itself. But everyone who is filled with the pride of righteousness is impatient and self-satisfied because he does not have love.

Hence, the apostle says that although all these things were written with respect to Christ, they were nevertheless "written for our learning," that "through patience" with our neighbors "and the comfort of the Scriptures we might have hope."

For what things soever were written were written for our learning: **that through patience and the comfort of the Scriptures we might have hope.**[19] (Rom. 15:4.)

What a beautiful combination of words this is! "Through patience and the comfort of the Scriptures we can have hope." But, to be sure, only if hope is nothing tangible. "For what a man sees, why does he hope for?" (Rom. 8:24.) Hope, therefore, takes away all tangible things. Hence, we need patience. However, he substitutes a word of comfort for these things so as to uphold us lest we grow weak in patience.

To give up all tangible reality for mere words and the Scripture—this is something great. Not everyone is able to do this, but only those who have died to all tangible things, at least in feeling, even though actually they do use them, but then because of necessity, not voluntarily. These are the Christians who have heard the

---

[19] Luther writes as follows in the marginal gloss (*WA* 56, 137, 18 ff.): "Here he meets an unoutspoken objection, namely: 'How does this concern us? This is literally said only of Christ.' His answer is this: Whatever is written about Christ is 'written for our learning' in order that we should imitate him. Hence we must not take it as something that is said of Christ only in a speculative way [*speculative*], but as something that is set before us as an example. Thus we can derive from this passage the remarkable lesson that every act of Christ's is meant to instruct us. In this sense he says here, 'What things soever were written, were written for our learning.'"

saying of their Master: "Every one of you that does not renounce all that he possesses cannot be my disciple" (Luke 14:33). "They use the world as if they used it not" (I Cor. 7:31) and they do good as if they did not. Everything they do is dedicated to God; they serve him in everything and seek nothing for themselves.

Now the God of patience and of comfort grant you to be of one mind one toward another, according to Jesus Christ, that with one mind and with one mouth you may glorify God and the Father of Jesus Christ. **Wherefore receive one another as Christ also received you unto the honor of God.** (Rom. 15:5–7.)
I.e., unto the glory of God, which means in order that God may be glorified thereby. How strange is the glory of God! He is glorified when sinners and the weak are received as friends. This is because it is his glory to be a benefactor to us. Hence, we glorify him, i.e., we give him the opportunity to show his beneficence, when we bring him those who can accept his benefit. We must, therefore, not bring the strong, the saints, and the wise. For God cannot be glorified in them, inasmuch as, since they do not feel that they need his beneficence, he cannot be beneficent toward them.

For I say that Jesus Christ was minister of the circumcision for the truth of God to confirm the promises made unto the fathers. But that the Gentiles are to glorify God for his mercy, it is written: Therefore will I confess to thee, O Lord, among the Gentiles, and will sing to thy name. And again he says: **Rejoice, ye Gentiles, with his people.** (Rom. 15:8–10.)
Lyra thinks that this word of Scripture is that of Isa. 35:1: "The land that was desolate and impassable shall be glad." Others point to Isa. 44:23: "Shout with joy, ye ends of the earth." But it seems to me, on the one hand, that the apostle has Isa. 66:10 in mind: "Rejoice with Jerusalem, and be glad with her, all you that love her." This call goes out from Jerusalem, i.e., from the Lord's people to others, and to no others but the Gentiles, for they are not Jerusalem. This is the reason why the apostle, in quoting this saying, adds the word "Gentiles" and why he explains "Jerusalem" by saying instead "his people."
On the other hand, if the apostle had only the prophetic meaning in mind, the oracle appears to be a combination of different passages of the psalms, as for example, Ps. 67:4: "Let the nations be glad and rejoice, for thou judgest the people with justice" and Ps. 97:1: "The Lord has reigned, let the earth rejoice: let many islands be glad," etc.
And again: "Praise the Lord, all ye Gentiles; and magnify him

all you people." And again Isaiah says: **There shall be the root of Jesse;** and he that shall rise up to rule the Gentiles, in him the Gentiles shall hope. (Rom. 15:11–12.)

As we stated in the Gloss,[20] "root" does not mean here Jesse himself, but Christ, according to Isa. 53:2. Or else the prophet should have said: "the rod of Jesse" or "the flower of Jesse" as it is written in Isa. 11:1: "There shall come forth a rod out of the root of Jesse, and a flower shall rise up out of this root" and likewise in Rev. 22:16: "I am the root of David." According to the flesh, therefore, Christ has his root in David and the patriarchs from whom he stemmed, but, according to the spirit, he himself is the root out of which the whole church has grown. In the context of the flesh, he is the flower of his fathers, but, in the spirit, they are his flower.

Furthermore, we must examine how the translations agree with one another. Blessed Jerome says: "who stands as an ensign of the peoples"; the Septuagint reads: "who shall arise in order that he be a prince of the nations." Paul says: **who shall rise up to rule the Gentiles.** But he that stands is certainly risen, and he that is an ensign for the peoples certainly directs the peoples. For he is an ensign in order that the nations should be led thereto. Herein the nature of Christ's Kingship is expressed, for it is the exercise of royal authority in faith, in a symbol, in what is not apparent, and not in tangible reality. But the princes of this world rule their peoples tangibly, namely, by their physical presence and by physical means. Moreover, the phrases "they shall beseech him" and "in him they shall hope" can easily be reconciled with each other. For he that beseeches is one who hopes.

And then there is the phrase: "And his resting place shall be honor," i.e., glory. Jerome thinks that his translation is clearer, namely: "And his grave shall be glorious." He says[21] that according

---

20 In the marginal gloss, Luther writes as follows (*WA* 56, 139, 14 ff.): " 'Root' does not mean here, as practically all painters imagine, the patriarch (as the ancestor of the race) who is the deepest root of the tree, but 'root' means here the stump that, so to speak, has remained after the tree died and has miraculously grown to be a huge tree, i.e., it is Christ spread out in a great church. Thus he describes himself as 'the grain of wheat that brings forth much fruit' (John 12:24–25) and as a grain of mustard seed that becomes a great tree (Matt. 13:31 f.). And Num. 24:17 says, 'A star shall arise out of Jacob, and a Scepter shall spring up from Israel.' 'Root' signifies, then, the death and the Passion of Christ, i.e., Christ as he was humiliated to the point of nothingness and as such raised again ['*humiliatum ad nihilum usque et sic exaltatum*'], as it is written in Isa. 53:2, 'He shall grow up before him as a tender plant, and as a root of a dry ground' (these metaphors signify the Passion and the resurrection)."
21 Cf. Jerome, *Comment, in Isaiam* (on Isa. 11:12).

to the Latin way of speaking *requies* (rest) is not commonly used to denote the "sleep of death."

But to my way of thinking, this seems to render the saying still more obscure. For some[22] are thereby led to think that the grave of Christ is glorious because it was cut from stone and because he himself was anointed with precious salves. Neither Blessed Jerome nor the Septuagint nor the Spirit wanted to say this. But Blessed Jerome wanted to express the glory of the content through that which serves as the container.

The meaning of the saying, then, is this: the death and the grave of Christ will be honored and celebrated throughout the world forever and ever. Yet this contradicts the nature of death, inasmuch as the death and the grave of other men ordinarily drag away their glory, fame, and honor, and put an end to them. "Their memory has perished with a noise." (Ps. 9:6.) But here the opposite took place: he was not only not swallowed up by death and the grave but he made his death glorious.

Now the God of hope fill you with all joy and peace in believing, that you may abound in hope and in the power of the Holy Spirit. (Rom. 15:13.)

It is strange to call God a "God of hope." But this is the sign by which the apostle distinguishes the false gods from the true God. The false gods are demons and as such they are the gods of tangible reality.[23] They possess them that do not know what it means to hope because they depend upon external things. But he that depends on the true God has laid all tangible things aside and lives by naked hope.[24] To call God "the God of hope" is therefore the same as to call him the God of hopers. He certainly is not the God but the enemy and judge of people who despair easily and are unable to trust anyone.

In short, he is the "God of hope" because he is the Giver of hope, and, even more, because only hope worships him. Just as he is called "the God of Abraham, Isaac, and Jacob" and "the God of Israel," so he is called the "God of hope," for where hope is, there one worships him.

Fill you with all joy and peace, i.e., with a trusting conscience and mutual concord. The apostle puts joy ahead of peace because joy makes man peaceful and composed in himself. When he is com-

---

[22] Lyra.

[23] *"Dii rei."*

[24] *"Nuda spe vivit."* Cf. Luther's sermon (of the same period of his life as these lectures) in which "hope" is defined as *"in nudum Deum confidere"* ("to trust in the naked God"), *WA* 1, 85, 2 f.

posed, it is easy for him to be at peace with others. But a man who is gloomy and upset becomes easily restless and excitable in his relations with others. Yet we can have all this only in believing, because our joy and peace are not based on anything tangible, but, beyond all external things, on hope. Otherwise, it would not be the God of hope, the giver of hidden goods, who gives them to us—joy in sorrow and personal affliction, and peace in external tumult and persecution. Where faith is lacking, one breaks down in sorrow and persecution, because then tangible realities are no longer available for him to rely on. But persecution makes hope abound, as the apostle says above in ch. 5:4 of this letter: "Trial works hope," and this by the power of the Holy Spirit. It is not because we rely on our own powers that "trial works hope," for then we should be weak and powerless in persecutions, but "the Spirit helps our infirmities" (Rom. 8:26) and thus we not only can hold out but will also be made perfect and finally triumph.

And I myself also, my brethren, am assured of you, that you *also are full of love, replenished with all knowledge, so that you are able to admonish one another.* (Rom. 15:14.)
Notice how skillfully and appropriately these words are arranged! First comes "full of love" and then replenished with all knowledge. For knowledge without a love that edifies inflates a man. Moreover, they would not be able to admonish one another if they were not full of love. For knowledge that is only knowledge stays confined to itself and swells up and does not deign to instruct someone else. It wants only to be seen and is full of contempt for others. But love imparts knowledge and edifies. Yet love that is without knowledge does not edify. To be sure, a holy simplicity that goes out from a rewarding and exemplary life is edifying. But a knowing love[25] is edifying in itself as well as by what it communicates,[26] while mere knowledge gives offense if it sets itself up as an example, and it is incommunicative as well. Therefore, love with knowledge and mere knowledge stand in sharp contrast to each other. Knowledge seeks its own, is self-satisfied and detests others; hence, it does not fear to scandalize people by its example, yet it refuses to render an account of itself by a communicative word. By contrast, love is communicative and it refrains from doing anything that causes offense, because this would not be communicative.

But I have written to you, brethren, more boldly in some sort, as it were putting you in mind, because of the grace given me from
25 *"Docta charitas."*
26 *"Verbo."*

God. That I should be the minister of Christ Jesus among the Gentiles, sanctifying the gospel of God, that the oblation of the Gentiles may be made acceptable and sanctified in the Holy Spirit. I have therefore glory in Christ Jesus toward God. For I dare not speak of any of those things which Christ works not by me, for the obedience of the Gentiles *by word and deed, by virtue of signs and wonders, in the power of the Holy Spirit, so that from Jerusalem round about as far as unto Illyricum, I have replenished the gospel of Christ.* (Rom. 15:15–19.)

The apostle wants to say that it is not he that speaks and acts in whatever he is speaking and doing for the obedience of the Gentiles, but Christ. As he writes in II Cor. 13:3: "Do you seek a proof of Christ that speaks in me?" Hence he says that he does not dare speak anything that Christ does not speak in him. Moreover, he "couples" this word "speak" with the word "he works," in order to make mention of both, the word as well as the work. It is as if he had said: I do not dare speak and work anything that Christ does not speak or work; inasmuch as he had said "speak" in the first part of the sentence, it was not necessary to add "work," and so he put this in the second part. There again it was not necessary to repeat "he speaks," inasmuch as he that works in one will all the more also speak in him, because it is easier to speak than to do. Furthermore, since "working" comprehends within itself both speaking and doing, he wanted to put a special emphasis on the phrase **the things which Christ works not in me** in order thereby to give expression to the fact that not only his speaking was Christ's but also all he was doing.

Now I know that others[27] are of the opinion that the apostle speaks in this way in order to exclude any arrogance. They suggest that he meant to say: I glory before God in Christ, but I do not dare glory in what the false apostles are glorifying in, namely, in something that God is not working in them, for they boast about that which they did not do or God did not do in them. But the first interpretation is much more plausible to me, namely, that the negative statement must be taken for an affirmation; and this is made evident by the phrase that follows: "for the obedience of the Gentiles." For Christ did not "work nothing" for the obedience of the Gentiles, but he worked everything in the apostle who now glories in this instead of in his own accomplishments. The meaning of the saying, then, is this: I glory in being a minister among the Gentiles, sanctifying the gospel. And I glory in this not because it is my doing but because Christ does it through me, and through him this glorying of mine will be valid even before God.

---

27 Erasmus.

And I have so preached this gospel, *not where Christ was named, lest I should build upon another man's foundation. But as it is written: They to whom he was not spoken of shall see, and* **they that have not heard shall understand.** (Rom. 15:20–21.)

The translator seems to have feared that what the apostle actually said would sound offensive. For in Greek the apostle says frankly:[28] "I have been ambitious so to preach the gospel." Now, to be sure, the word "ambitious" cannot be understood here in terms of its specific significance, as it is used, for example, by Pliny,[29] when he says about the Jordan: "As far as local sites permit, it is *ambitiosus.*" (One calls *ambitiosus* that which desires to encompass much and seeks to extend and enlarge itself in all directions just as a river overflows and spreads itself over many places.) But the word that is used in this passage is *"philotimou-menos"* i.e., desirous of glory and honor.

The Greek therefore has two versions of the phrase "I have preached," namely, either: "I have been ambitious to preach" or: "From the desire for honor, I have endeavored to preach." Now what shall we say to this? Was the apostle really ambitious? Does he here furnish the ambitious a means of defending themselves by his example? God forbid! He himself said in a previous sentence (Rom. 15:17): "I have glory in Christ." And, in I Cor. 9:15, he writes: "It is good for me to die rather than that any man should make my glory void." If he did seek this glory for his own sake, this glory of his is null and void. But he sought it only for the sake of others, namely, for the following reasons:

(1) The authority of his apostolate should not be diminished, for this would be a hindrance to the faith of the Gentiles to whom he was sent as the chosen apostle.

(2) It is from overflowing love that he speaks in this way: because he desired to save as many as possible, he did not want to preach where Christ was already known, lest meanwhile he might be delayed from preaching to those who did not know him yet. This is why he quotes the saying of Isaiah, ch. 52:15: **They that have not heard shall understand;** in other words: he must preach Christ where he is not known, lest by preaching where he is known time may be lost when he should have been preached to others. It is also not without significance that he did not say: "Where other apostles have preached, I did not preach," for this would have been arrogant and ambitious, as if he did not deign to preach where others had preached. But what he does say is: "Where Christ was named, there I have not preached." Thereby he wants to indicate that he

[28] Luther is here dependent on Faber and Erasmus.
[29] Pliny, *Nat. hist.,* V, 71.

abstained from preaching where it was not necessary, in order to be able to preach where it *was* necessary.

All this explains sufficiently why he acted as he did, but it does not yet clear up his use of the word *"philotimoumenos."* For one can do all these things without having to say that he yearns for honor. But he says expressly that he did what he did from a striving for glory and honor. The question which we must ask here is, therefore, not: Did he or did he not do this from a striving for glory? but: What kind of glory did he strive for? Therefore:

(3) We must note that preaching the gospel was a despised and dishonorable office, as it still is today. For it receives no honor and glory but is exposed to every kind of reproach, disgrace, persecution, etc., even to the extent of the saying of Christ: "For he that shall be ashamed of me before men, of him I shall be ashamed before the angels of God" (Luke 9:26). Also Jeremiah confesses that "the word of God was made a reproach" to him "and a derision all the day" (Jer. 20:8). And in Ps. 14:6, it is said: "You have confounded the counsel of the poor man, because God is his hope." And also Christ confesses everywhere in the psalms that he was despised and that "shame had covered his face" (Ps. 69:7). In the same way he says: "O God, thou knowest my foolishness" (Ps. 69:5) and the want of respect to which I am exposed. Now what befalls Christ, and this means truth—for Christ is the truth—befalls also the ministers of Christ, i.e., of the truth. For example, the apostle says in I Cor. 4:9–10: "I think that God has set forth us apostles as men appointed to death. For we are made a spectacle to the world, and to angels, and to men. We are fools for Christ's sake, but you are wise in Christ; we are weak, but you are strong." And then he goes on to say: "We are made as the refuse of the world, the offscouring of all, even until now" (I Cor. 4:13).

So then, inasmuch as preaching the gospel has nothing to do with honor, he regards the disgrace of it as his glory, and he does so out of a wonderful and truly apostolic love, only in order to help others thereby. For preaching where Christ is known is not disgraceful, because there the initial outburst of contempt for the gospel has been endured and overcome. But where Christ is not yet known, the disgrace that is heaped upon the gospel is still fresh and all the harder to bear.

This is what he means when he says in ch. 1:14 of this letter: "To the Greeks and the barbarians, to the wise and the unwise, I am a debtor." "For I am not ashamed of the gospel" (Rom. 1:16); in other words: I regard preaching the gospel as an office of honor and I am ambitious for it (i.e., I seek its honor), while others shrink back from it because of its shame. In this sense, it says in

Acts 5:41: "And the apostles went from the presence of the council, rejoicing that they were accounted worthy to suffer reproach
for the name of Jesus." Does "rejoicing" here mean anything else
than that they took this reproach as if it were a glory? In this
sense, he said before: "I have therefore glory in Christ before
God" (Rom. 15:17), i.e., even though because of this I am disgraced among men before the world. As it says in Ps. 119:46: "I
spoke of thy testimonies before kings and was not put to shame,"
i.e., I did not blush with shame but regarded it as an honor to
speak of thee. But, ordinarily, people who blush with shame are
scandalized, because they fear to be confounded. In the same
psalm, he often begs to be freed from this reproach. He says: "Remove from me reproach and contempt" (Ps. 119:22); and again:
"Turn away my reproach of which I am afraid" (Ps. 119:39); and
in another place, he says: "We are a reproach to the rich and contempt to the proud" (Ps. 123:4).

(4) He makes still another point which is only a little different
from the third one: it is to the effect that he means by "glory" the
glory of the conscience before God, i.e., he preaches the gospel in
order that he may have the testimony, not of an evil, but of a good
conscience. In this sense he says: "Our glory is this: the testimony
of a good conscience" (II Cor. 1:12). And so in order to have a
rich conscience before God that he had done his duty most faithfully, he hastened to preach Christ only where he was not yet
known. In this sense, he says in I Cor. 9:15, as we stated before,
that it would be better for him to die than that his glory should be
made void, i.e., than that his conscience should be hurt.

Our conscience either puts us to shame or robes us with honor
before God. To be sure, there is none who is not sometimes confounded in his conscience (otherwise, Christ died in vain), but
everyone must strive to violate or wound his conscience as little
as possible and to keep it as clear and honorable as he can, and he
must see to it that what is then left over or remains hidden is
covered and excused and forgiven by faith and hope in Christ.

In this sense, the apostle was ambitious to preach the gospel: he
strove to enrich his conscience. But one cannot enrich his conscience in a better way than by serving others from love, even if
this should lead to disgrace and a cross. Such a disgrace is glory to
him because of the glory he has in his conscience. Now this is what,
I think, the apostle had in mind: he sought the glory that was hidden in his open shame; he was outwardly disgraced but honored in
his conscience, despised before men but glorified before God.

Truth gives birth to hatred. But this hatred brings forth grace.
Hence, we must "ambitiously" seek to be hated, i.e., we must seek
grace even through hatred.

But lest we appear completely to reject the opinion of others, for example that of Erasmus and of those who agree with him, we concede that he also strove with a certain holy ambition to be the apostle of the Gentiles (strictly speaking, this is here out of place, because he does not say that he only refrained from preaching where other apostles had preached, but wherever Christ was named; but also to the Gentiles his name was already known, as, for example, in Rome). But let us concede that, because "he was separated to preach the gospel to the uncircumcised," he endeavored with pious ambition to fulfill his duty as if he alone had to bring light to the Gentiles. Therein he gave the strongest proof of his love. For the ambition of doing good is rare indeed; it is truly apostolic. To preach the gospel means to bestow the greatest of all benefits upon men, even if it is done under the greatest persecutions and over against the resistance of the whole world. Therefore, to strive, as it were, for the honor (and this is the strongest of all desires!) to bestow the greatest of all benefits upon men and to do this for nothing (for nothing, I say, but what a "for nothing"!) and to receive only all sorts of evil in return—is this not a superhuman, a thoroughly apostolic, indeed, a divine kind of ambition? Or does a man who is benevolent for nothing not deserve to be put on a pedestal? I am asking you! Think about this!

The gospel is an unspeakably wonderful gift that cannot be compared with any riches, honors, or pleasures.

Furthermore, if a man gives good gifts—even to his enemies and to those who render him evil—what good does he do in comparison with the benefit that an evangelist bestows upon men! Yet a man who gives good gifts only to his friends is less than he, though such a man is very rare indeed; and lesser still is a man who only lends his goods, and least of all is he that gives nothing, but the worst of all is he that steals the goods that belong to others either by thought[30] (and almost the whole human race is doing this) or by deed[31] (and most men are doing this).

In boasting of his office, therefore, the apostle does nothing else than that he sings the praises of the gospel. And what is more necessary for men who despise and impugn the gospel than that they hear it praised!

So then, he does seek glory, but this glory is nothing else than the salvation of those among whom he seeks it.[32]

---

[30] "*Vel affectu.*"
[31] "*Vel effectu.*"
[32] Luther did not write extensively on chapter 16, only comparatively brief interlinear and marginal glosses but no scholion. He had doubts whether Paul actually attached all these personal greetings to his letter to the Romans. (Cf. *WA* 56, 149, 11 ff.)

BIBLIOGRAPHY AND INDEXES

BIBLIOGRAPHY

I. List of Ancient and Medieval Works, Quoted by Luther or Referred to in the Explanatory Notes

CSEL—*Corpus Scriptorum Ecclesiasticorum Latinorum*
LCL —The Loeb Classical Library
PG —Migne, J. P., *Patrologiae cursus completus, series Graeca*
PL —Migne, J. P., *Patrologiae cursus completus, series Latina*

Aegidius Romanus, *Opus super primo libro sententiarum.* Venice, 1507.
Aegidius Romanus, *Super secundo libro sententiarum opus praeclarissimum.* Venice, 1482.
Aesop, *Fabulae.* (See J. Jacobs, *Fables of Jacob;* New York, 1889.)
Ailly, Pierre d', *Quaestiones super primum, tertium et quartum sententiarum.* Venice, 1500.
Ambrose, *De paradiso* (PL 14, 275–314).
Ambrose, *De sacramentis* (PL 16, 417–464; CSEL 73, 13–85).
Ambrosiaster, *Commentarium in epistulam ad Romanos* (PL 17, 47–191).
Aristotle, *Categoriae,* in *Works* (ed. by W. D. Ross), Vol. I. Oxford, 1928.
Aristotle, *De anima,* in *Works* (ed. by W. D. Ross), Vol. III. Oxford, 1931.
Aristotle, *Ethica Nichomachea,* in *Works* (ed. by W. D. Ross), Vol. IX. Oxford, 1925.
Aristotle, *Physics,* in *Works* (ed. by W. D. Ross), Vol. II. Oxford, 1930.
Augustine, *Confessiones* (PL 32, 659–868; CSEL 33).
Augustine, *Contra duas epistolas Pelagianorum* (PL 44, 549–640; CSEL 60, 423–570).

Augustine, *Contra Julianum* (PL 44, 641–880).

Augustine, *De beata vita* (PL 32, 959–976; CSEL 63, 89–116).

Augustine, *De civitate Dei* (PL 41, 13–804; CSEL 40, 1 and 2).

Augustine, *De doctrina Christiana* (PL 34, 15–120).

Augustine, *De gratia Christi et peccato originali* (PL 44, 359–412; CSEL 42, 125–206).

Augustine, *De nuptiis et concupiscentia ad Valerianum* (PL 44, 413–474; CSEL 42, 209–319).

Augustine, *De opere monachorum* (PL 40, 547–580; CSEL 41, 529–596).

Augustine, *De ordine* (PL 32, 976–1020; CSEL 63, 119–185).

Augustine, *De peccatorum meritis et remissione* (PL 44, 109–200; CSEL 60, 3–154).

Augustine, *De spiritu et littera* (PL 44, 199–246; CSEL 60, 155–232).

Augustine, *De Trinitate* (PL 42, 819–1098).

Augustine, *Enarratio in Ps. 70* (PL 36, 874–901).

Augustine, *Enchiridion ad Laurentium* (PL 40, 251–288).

Augustine, *Epistolae* (PL 33; CSEL 34; 44; 57; 58).

Augustine, *Expositio quarundam propositionum ex ep. ad Romanos* (PL 35, 2063–2104).

Augustine, *Opus imperfectum contra Julianum* (PL 45, 1049–1608).

Augustine, *Retractationes* (PL 32, 584–665; CSEL 36).

Augustine, *Sermones* (PL 38 and 39).

Augustine, *Tractatus in ep. ad Johannem* (PL 35, 1977–2062).

Augustine, *Tractatus in Joann.* (PL 35, 1379–1976).

Bernard of Clairvaux, *De consideratione* (PL 182, 727–806).

Bernard of Clairvaux, *Epistulae* (PL 182, 67–722).

Bernard of Clairvaux, *Sermones in cantica canticorum* (PL 183, 785–1198).

Bernard of Clairvaux, *Sermones in festo annunciationis Mariae virginis* (PL 183, 383–398).

Bernard of Clairvaux, *Sermones in vigilia nativitatis Domini* (PL 183, 87–115).

Biblia cum glosa ordinaria et expositione Lyre literali et morali mecnon additionibus (Pauli Burgensis) ac replicis (Matthiae Doering). Basel, 1498.

Biel, Gabriel, *Collectorium in quattuor libros sententiarum.* Lyons, 1514.

Biel, Gabriel, *Sacri canonis missae expositio.* Tübingen, 1499.

Biel, Gabriel, *Super quattuor libros sententiarum.* Tübingen, 1501.

Burgos, Paul of, *Scrutinium Scriptorum.* Mainz, 1478.

Cassian, John, *De institutis cenobiorum* (PL 49, 53–476).

Catullus, *Carmina* (LCL). New York, 1912.
Chrysostom, John, *Homilae in ep. ad Romanos* (PG 60, 391–682).
Cicero, *De oratore* (LCL), 2 vols. New York, 1939–1942.
Dionysius Areopagita, *Mystica theologica* (PG 3, 997–1064).
Duns Scotus, *Primus, secundus, tertius, quartus sententiarum. Opera* (ed. Wadding-Vivès). Paris, 1891–1895.
Erasmus, *Novum instrumentum omne cum annotationibus.* Basel, 1516.
Faber Stapulensis, *Epistolae Pauli Apostoli.* 1st ed., Paris, 1512; 2d ed., Paris, 1515.
Faber Stapulensis, *Quincuplex Psalterium.* Paris, 1509.
Garcia, *Lexicon scholasticum philosopho-theologicum.* Quarachi, 1910.
Gregory the Great, *Libri II Homiliarum in Evangelia* (PL 76, 1075–1310).
Gregory the Great, *Libri II Homiliarum in Ezechielem* (PL 76, 785–1074).
Hilary of Poitiers, *De Trinitate* (PL 10, 9–471).
Horace, *Epistolarum Liber* (LCL). New York, 1929.
Horace, *Satira* (LCL). New York, 1926.
Jerome, *Commentarius in ep. ad Titum* (PL 26, 555–598).
Jerome, *Commentarius in Esaiam* (PL 24, 17–678).
Juvenal, *Satira* (LCL). New York, 1918.
Lombard, Peter, *Collectanea in ep. ad Romanos* (PL 191, 1302–1534).
Lombard, Peter, *Collectanea in ep. Pauli* (PL 191, 1297–1696; 192, 9–520).
Lombard, Peter, *Libri quatuor sententiarum* (PL 192, 519–962; critical ed. in 2 vols., Quarachi, 1916).
Montanus, Baptista, *De patientia* (*Opera,* Paris, 1513).
Ockham, William of, *Adnotationes super quatuor libros sententiarum.* Lyons, 1495.
Ockham, William of, *Quodlibeta septem.* Paris, 1487.
Ockham, William of, *Summule in libros physicorum.* Rome, 1637.
Ovid, *Amores* (LCL). New York, 1914.
Ovid, *Tristia* (LCL). New York, 1914.
Paltz, John von, *Celifodina,* Leipzig, 1511.
Persius, *Satira* (LCL). New York, 1918.
Plautus, *Amphitrion* (LCL). New York, 1906.
Pliny, *Naturalis historia* (LCL), 10 vols. New York, 1938–1952.
Pürstinger, Berthold, *Onus ecclesiae.* Landshut, 1524.
Regula Augustini (PL 32, 1377–1383).
Reuchlin, John, *De Rudimentis hebraicis.* Pforzheim, 1906.

Reuchlin, John, *Septem psalmi poenitentiales hebraici cum grammatica translacione latina*. Tübingen, 1512.

Reuchlin, John, *Vocabularius breviloquus*. Strassburg, 1504.

Seneca, *Epistolae morales* (LCL), 3 vols. New York, 1917–1925.

Speculum exemplorum. Strassburg, 1487.

Staupitz, John von, *Von der nachfolgung des willigen sterbens Christi* (in *Opera*, ed. Knaake). Potsdam, 1867.

Suetonius, *De XII vitis Caesarum* (LCL). New York, 1914.

Tauler, John, *Die Predigten* (ed. F. Vetter). Berlin, 1910.

Terence, *Andria* (LCL). New York, 1918.

Terence, *Heautontimorumenos* (LCL). New York, 1918.

Terence, *Phormio* (LCL). New York, 1912.

Theologia deutsch (ed. Franz Pfeiffer, with commentary by Kurt F. Riedler). Thalwil, Zurich, 1947.

Thiele, Ernst, *Luthers Sprichwörtersammlung*. Weimar, 1900.

Thomas Aquinas, *Summa Theologica*. Turin, 1948–1950.

Trutvetter, Jodocus, *Summa in totam physicen*. Erfurt, 1514.

Trutvetter, Jodocus, *Summulae totius logice*. Erfurt, 1501.

Tungern, Arnold von, *Articuli sive propositiones de iudaico favore nimis suspecto ex libello theutonico domini Ioannis Reuchlin*. 1512.

Valerius Maximus, *Factorum dictorumque mirabilium libri IX*. Mainz, 1471.

Valla, Laurentius, *Adnotationes in latinam Novi Testamenti interpretationem* (ed. Erasmus). Paris, 1505.

Vergil, *Aeneid* (LCL), 2 vols. New York, 1916–1918.

Vergil, *Bucolica Eclogues* (LCL). New York, 1916.

Vitae Patrum (PL 73; 74).

Vitae Patrum, Verba Seniorum (PL 73, 851–1062).

Zerbolt, Gerard, *Tractatus de spiritualibus ascensionibus*. 1475.

II. Select Works on Luther's Lectures on Romans

Althaus, Paul, *Paulus und Luther über den Menschen*. Gütersloh. 1938.

Auer, Johannes, *Die Entwicklung der Gnadenlehre in der Hochscholastik*. 2 vols. Freiburg, 1942–1951.

Baudry, L., *Guillaume d' Occam*. Paris, 1949–1950.

Bendiscioli, M., "L'agostinismo dei reformatori protestanti" (*Rev. des études augustiniennes* [1955], 203–224).

Bizer, Ernst, *Fides ex auditu. Eine Untersuchung über die Entdeckung der Gerechtigkeit Gottes durch Martin Luther*. 2d ed. Neukirchen, 1961.

Boehmer, Heinrich, *Der junge Luther* (ed. H. Bornkamm). 7th ed. Leipzig, 1955.

Bonwetsch, Nathanil, "Röm. 1, 14 ff. in der Alten Kirche und in Luthers Vorlesung über den Römerbrief" (*Neue Kirchl. Zeitschrift* 30 [1919], 135–156).

Bornkamm, Heinrich, "Justitia Dei in der Scholastic und bei Luther" (*Archiv für Reformationsgeschichte* 39 [1942], 30–62).

Bornkamm, Heinrich, "Luthers Bericht über seine Entdeckung der iustitia Dei" (*Archiv für—Reformationsgeschichte* 37 [1940], 117–127).

Bornkamm, Heinrich, *Luther und das Alte Testament*. Tübingen, 1948.

Cristiani, L., "Luther et Saint Augustin" (in *Augustinus Magister* [Paris, 1955], Vol. II, 1029–1038).

Denifle, Heinrich, *Luther und Luthertum in der ersten Entwicklung, quellenmässig dargestellt*. 2 vols. Mainz, 1904.

Dobschütz, Ernst von, *Vom vierfachen Schriftsinn* (in *Harnack-Ehrung*, 1–13). Tübingen, 1921.

Dress, Walter, *Die Theologie Gersons*. Berlin, 1931.

Ebeling, Gerhard, "Die Anfänge von Luthers Hermeneutik" (*Zeitschrift für Theologie und Kirche* 48 [1951], 172–229).

Ebeling, Gerhard, *Luthers Evangelienauslegung*. München, 1942.

Ellwein, Eduard, "Schlatters Kritik an Luthers Römerbriefvorlesung" (*Zwischen den Zeiten* 5 [1927], 530 ff.).

Feckes, Carl, *Die Rechtfertigungslehre des Gabriel Biel*. Münster, 1925.

Frick, Robert, *Luthers Römerbriefvorlesung. Ein Beitrag zur Frage der pneumatischen Exegese* (in "*Dienst an Theologie und Kirche*" [= *Festgabe für A. Schlatter*], Berlin, 1927, 79–96).

Grane, Leif, "Gabriel Biels Lehre von der Allmacht Gottes" (*Zeitschrift für Theologie und Kirche* 53 [1956], 53–74).

Guelluy, R., *Philosophie et théologie chez Guillaume d'Ockham*. Paris, 1947.

Gyllenbrock, Axel, *Rechtfertigung und Heilgung in der frühen evangelischen Theologie Luthers*. Uppsala Universitets Arskrift, 1952.

Haar, Johann, *Initium creaturae Dei. Eine Untersuchung über Luthers Begriff der "neuen Kreatur."* Gütersloh, 1939.

Hägglund, Bengtt, *Theologie und Philosophie bei Luther und in der okhamistischen Tradition*. Lund, 1955.

Hahn, Fritz, "Faber Stapulensis und Luther" (*Zeitschrift für Kirchengeschichte* 57 [1938], 356–432).

Hahn, Fritz, "Luthers Auslegungsgrundsätze und ihre theologischen Voraussetzungen" (*Zeitschr. f. syst. Theologie* XII [1935], 165–218).

Hamel, Adolf, *Der junge Luther und Augustin.* 2 vols. Gütersloh, 1934–1935.

Hermann, Rudolf, *Gesammelte Studien zur Theologie Luthers und der Reformation.* Göttingen, 1960.

Hilburg, J., *Luthers Frömmigkeit in seiner Vorlesung über den Römerbrief.* Microfilm. Göttingen, 1951.

Hirsch, Emanuel, "Initium theologiae Lutheri" (in *Luther Studien,* Vol. II). Gütersloh, 1955.

Hirsch, Emanuel, *Luther Studien,* Vol. I (*Drei Kapitel zu Luthers Lehre vom Gewissen*). Gütersloh, 1954.

Hirsch, Emanuel, "Luther über die oratio mentalis" (*Zeitschr. f. syst. Theologie* VI [1928], 136–141).

Holl, Karl, *Gesammelte Aufsätze.* Vol. I: *Luther.* 2d ed. Tübingen, 1923: "Was verstand Luther unter Religion?" (1–110); "Die Rechtfertigungslehre in Luthers Vorlesung über den Römerbrief mit besonderer Rücksicht auf die Frage der Heilsgewissheit" (110–154); "Der Neubau der Sittlichkeit" (155–287); "Die Entstehung von Luthers Kirchenbegriff" (228–325); "Luthers Bedeutung für den Fortschrift der Auslegungskunst" (544–582).

Iserloh, Erwin, *Gnade und Eucharistie in der philosophischen Theologie des Wilhelm von Ockham.* Wiesbaden, 1956.

Iwand, Hans Joachim, *Glaubensgerechtigkeit nach Luthers Lehre,* 2d ed. München, 1952.

Iwand, Hans Joachim, *Rechtfertigungslehre und Christusglaube. Eine Untersuchung zur Systematik Luthers in ihren Anfängen.* Leipzig, 1930.

Jacob, Günther, *Das Bild vom "Weg in der Mitte" in der Theologie Luthers* (in *"Kosmos und Ecclesia"* [Kassel, 1953], 84–92).

Kattenbusch, Ferdinand, "Glauben und Denken" (*Zeitschrift für Theologie und Kirche* [1931], 373–399).

Lagrange, M. J., *Luther on the Eve of the Revolt,* tr. by W. J. Reilly. New York, Cathedral Library Ars., 1918. (Depends almost entirely on Denifle.)

Lindbeck, G., "Nominalism and the Problem of Meaning as Illustrated by Pierre d' Ailli on Predestination and Justification" (*Harvard Theological Review* 52 [1959], 43–60).

Link, Wilhelm, *Das Ringen Luthers um die Freiheit der Theologie von der Philosophie.* München, 1940.

Loewenich, Walter von, *Gebet und Kreuz. Zu Luthers Auslegung von Röm. 4, 26 (Luther* 9 [1927], 3–13).

Loewenich, Walter von, *Luther als Ausleger der Synoptiker.* München, 1954.

Loewenich, Walter von, *Zur Gnadenlehre bei Augustin und bei Luther (Archiv für Reformationsgeschichte* 44 [1953], 52–63).

Lohse, Bernhard, *Ratio und Fides. Eine Untersuchung über die ratio in der Theologie Luthers.* Göttingen, 1958.

Loofs, Friedrich, "Der 'articulus stantis et cadentis ecclesiae' " (*Theologische Studien und Kritiken* 90 [1917], 323–420).

Loofs, Friedrich, "Justitia Dei passiva" in *Luthers Anfängen* (*Theologische Studien und Kritiken* 84 [1911], 461–473).

Meissinger, K. A., *Der katholische Luther.* München, 1952.

Meissinger, K. A., *Luthers Exegese in der Frühzeit.* Leipzig, 1910.

Mueller, A. V., *Luther und Tauler.* Gotha, 1918.

Pelikan, Jaroslav, *Luther, the Expositor* (companion vol., *Works,* American ed.). St. Louis, 1959.

Pfeiffer, Gerhard, "Das Ringen des jungen Luther um die Gerechtigkeit Gottes" (*Luther-Jahrbuch* 26 [1959], 25–55).

Pinomaa, L., *Die profectio bei Luther* (in *Festschrift für W. Elert* [Berlin, 1955], 119–127).

Prenter, Regin, *Spiritus Creator.* München, 1954; Engl. tr., Philadelphia, 1953.

Quanbeck, Warren A., "Luther's Early Exegesis" (*Luther Today,* 37–107). Decorah, Iowa, 1957.

Renaudet, Auguste, *Préréforme et Humanisme à Paris (1494–1517).* 2d ed. Paris, 1953.

Roth, Erich, *Sakrament nach Luther.* Berlin, 1952.

Rupp, E. G., *Luther's Progress to the Diet of Worms.* Chicago, 1951.

Rupp, E. G., *The Righteousness of God. A Reconsideration of the Character and Work of Martin Luther.* London and New York, 1953.

Saarnivaara, Uuras, *Luther Discovers the Gospel.* St. Louis, 1951.

Saint-Blencat, Louis, "Luthers Verhältnis zu Lombardus" (*Zeitschr. f. syst. Theologie* XXII [1953], 300–311).

Scheel, Otto, *Die Entwicklung Luthers bis zum Abschluss der Vorlesung über den Römerbrief.* Leipzig, 1910.

Scheel, Otto, *Dokumente zu Luthers Entwicklung.* 2d ed. Tübingen, 1929.

Scheel, Otto, *Taulers Mystik und Luthers reformatorische Entdeckung* (*Festschrift für Julius Kaftan* [Tübingen, 1920], 298 ff.).

Schlatter, Adolf, *Luthers Deutung des Römerbriefes.* Gütersloh, 1917.

Schmidt, F. W., "Der Gottesgedanke in Luthers Römerbriefvorlesung" (*Theologische Studien und Kritiken* 93 [1920], 117–248).

Schubert, Hans von, *Luthers Vorlesung über den Galaterbrief 1516/17* (= *Abhandlungen der Heidelberger Akademie der Wissenschaften, Phil.-hist. Klasse*, No. 5, Heidelberg, 1918).

Schüler, M., *Luthers Gottesbegriff nach seiner Schrift "De servo arbitrio"* (*Zeitschr. f. Kirchengeschichte* 55 [1936]).

Schwarz, Werner, *Principles and Problems of Biblical Translation* (Reuchlin, Erasmus, Luther). Cambridge, England, 1955.

Seeberg, Erich, *Luthers Theologie*. Vol. I: *Luthers Gottesanschauung.* Göttingen, 1929.

Vol. II: *Christus, Wirklichkeit und Urbild.* Stuttgart, 1937.

Seeberg, Reinhold, *Die Lehre Luthers* (= *Lehrbuch der Dogmengeschichte*, Vol. IV, 4th ed.). Leipzig, 1933.

Seeberg, Reinhold, *Die religiösen Grundgedanken des jungen Luther und ihr Verhältnis zu dem Ockhamismus und der deutschen Mystik.* Berlin, 1931.

Strohl, Henri, *L'épanouissement de la pensée religieuse de Luther de 1515 à 1520.* Strasbourg, 1924.

Tarvainen, O., "Der Gedanke der Conformitas Christi in Luthers Theologie" (*Zeitschr. f. syst. Theologie* XX [1953], 26–43).

Thimme, Hans, *Christi Bedeutung für Luthers Glauben.* Gütersloh, 1933.

Vignaux, P., *Justification et Prédestination au XVIᵉ siècle.* Paris, 1934.

Vignaux, P., *Luther commentateur des Sentences.* Paris, 1939/40.

Vignaux, P., *Nominalisme* (*Dictionnaire de théologie catholique*, II, 717–784).

Vignaux, P., *Nominalisme au XIVᵉ siècle.* Paris, 1948.

Vignaux, P., *Occam* (*Dictionnaire de théologie catholique*, II, 864–904).

Vignaux, P., *Philosophy in the Middle Ages.* New York, 1959.

Vignaux, P., *Sur Luther et Ockham.* In *"Wilhelm Ockham"* (1349–1949). *Aufsätze zu seiner Philosophie und Theologie* (= *Franziskanische Studien* 32 [1950], 21–30.

Vogelsang, E., *Die Anfänge von Luthers Christologie.* Berlin, 1933.

Watson, Philip, *Let God Be God.* Philadelphia, 1949.

Wolf, E., *Peregrinatio. Studien zur reformatorischen Theologie und zum Kirchenproblem.* München, 1954.

Wood, A. Skevington, "The Theology of Luther's Lectures on Romans" (*Scottish Journ. of Theology* 3 [1950], 1–18; 113–126).

INDEXES

Proper Names*

*This and the following indexes were prepared by Mr. Albert Rabil, Jr., a graduate student at Union Theological Seminary, New York.

431

Subjects

437